BUILDING CON TRUC ION HANDBOOK

The *Building Co* THE authoritat rence for all construction students and professionals. Its detailed drawings clearly illustrate the construction of building elements, and have been an invaluable guide for builders since 1988. The principles and processes of construction are explained with the concepts of design included where appropriate. Extensive coverage of building construction practice, techniques, and regulations representing both traditional procedures and modern developments are included to provide the most comprehensive and easy to understand guide to building construction.

This new edition has been updated to reflect recent changes to the building regulations, as well as new material on the latest technologies used in domestic construction.

Building Construction Handbook is the essential, easy-to-use resource for undergraduate and vocational students on a wide range of courses including NVQ and BTEC National, through to Higher National Certificate and Diploma, to Foundation and three-year Degree level. It is also a useful practical reference for building designers, contractors and others engaged in the construction industry.

Roger Greeno is a well-known author of construction texts. He has extensive practical and consultancy experience in the industry, in addition to lecturing at several colleges of further and higher education, and the University of Portsmouth. He has also examined for City & Guilds, Edexcel, the Chartered Institute of Building and the University of Reading.

Roy Chudley, formerly Senior Lecturer in Building Technology at the Guildford College of Technology, U.K, is an established author of numerous respected construction texts.

BUILDING CONSTRUCTION HANDBOOK

Tenth edition

Roy Chudley

and

Roger Greeno

 Routledge
Taylor & Francis Group

LONDON AND NEW YORK

First edition published 1998
by Butterworth-Heinemann

This edition published 2014
by Routledge
2 Park Square, Milton Park, Abingdon, Oxon, OX14 4RN

Simultaneously published in the USA and Canada
by Routledge
711 Third Avenue, New York, NY 10017

Routledge is an imprint of the Taylor & Francis Group, an informa business

Knowledge and best practice in this field are constantly changing. As new research and experience broaden our understanding, changes in research methods, professional practices, or medical treatment may become necessary.

Practitioners and researchers must always rely on their own experience and knowledge in evaluating and using any information, methods, compounds, or experiments described herein. In using such information or methods they should be mindful of their own safety and the safety of others, including parties for whom they have a professional responsibility.

To the fullest extent of the law, neither the Publisher nor the authors, contributors or editors, assume any liability for any injury and/or damage to persons or property as a matter of products liability, negligence or otherwise, or form and use or operation of any methods, products, instructions, or ideas contained in the material herein.

British Library Cataloguing in Publication Data
A catalogue record for this book is available from the British Library

Library of Congress Cataloging-in-Publication Data
A catalog record has been requested for this book

ISBN13: 978-0-415-83638-8 (pbk)
ISBN13: 978-1-315-78032-0 (ebk)

Typeset in Chudley
by Taylor & Francis Books

MIX
Paper from
responsible sources
FSC
www.fsc.org   FSC® C013056

Printed and bound in Great Britain by
TJ International Ltd, Padstow, Cornwall

CONTENTS

Contents

Contents

PREFACE TO TENTH EDITION

The *Building Construction Handbook* originated in 1982 as a series of four "check-books" written and illustrated by Roy Chudley. In 1988 these successful study guides were consolidated into one volume under the present title. The format of comprehensive illustrations and support text has been maintained as revisions and updates are incorporated into new editions. This latest edition contains a fresh assessment of the practices, procedures, guidance and legislation appropriate to construction and maintenance of housing and other low-rise buildings. It also includes applications to medium and larger scale structures for commercial and industrial purposes.

Much of the work from earlier editions is retained as an important reference, acknowledging that the industry end product generally has a long life span representative of high capital investment. Product aftercare in the form of maintenance, repair, renovation, refurbishment, extensions and alterations can represent some 50% of the industry turnover, much more when bank lending is limited for new development. For this purpose, many established and traditional practices shown in earlier editions are retained. Existing practices also benchmark development as a basis from which contemporary design and technology evolve. This is in response to political, social and economic requirements through legislative directives for environmental issues, energy regulation, fuel conservation and the need for sustainability in construction.

The content of the book is extensive, although no textbook, not least this one, could ever incorporate all practices experienced in an industry so diverse as construction. The content is not exemplar and neither does it attempt to be prescriptive. It is a perspective of construction principles including guidance to processes and, where appropriate, associated design. Building is to some extent determined by availability of materials and skilled operatives; therefore local, regional and national factors will also be responsible for some variation.

Supplementary study material and detail can be obtained from professional journals, legislative papers, manufacturers' product literature, the many cross-references in the text and attending exhibits and seminars. The most valuable learning resource is observing and monitoring construction in progress.

RG 2014

1 GENERAL

BUILT ENVIRONMENT
THE STRUCTURE
PRIMARY AND SECONDARY ELEMENTS
COMPONENT PARTS AND FUNCTIONS
CONSTRUCTION ACTIVITIES
CONSTRUCTION DOCUMENTS
CONSTRUCTION DRAWINGS
BUILDING SURVEY
ENERGY PERFORMANCE CERTIFICATES
METHOD STATEMENT AND PROGRAMMING
WEIGHTS AND DENSITIES OF BUILDING MATERIALS
IMPOSED FLOOR LOADS
DRAWINGS – NOTATIONS
PLANNING APPLICATION
MODULAR COORDINATION
CONSTRUCTION REGULATIONS
CDM REGULATIONS
SAFETY SIGNS AND SYMBOLS
BUILDING REGULATIONS
ACCREDITED CONSTRUCTION DETAILS
CODE FOR SUSTAINABLE HOMES
BRITISH STANDARDS
EUROPEAN STANDARDS
PRODUCT AND PRACTICE ACCREDITATION
CI/SFB SYSTEM OF CODING
CPI SYSTEM OF CODING
UNICLASS SYSTEM OF CODING

Environment = surroundings which can be natural, man-made or a combination of these.

Built Environment = created by man with or without the aid of the natural environment.

grasses and wild flowers

deciduous and coniferous trees →

shrubs and bushes

rock outcrops

waterways and lakes

ELEMENTS of the NATURAL ENVIRONMENT

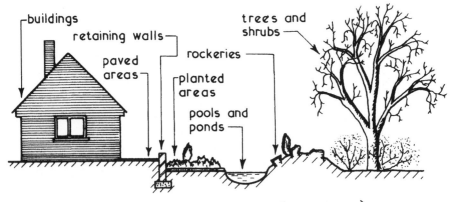

buildings

retaining walls

paved areas

rockeries

planted areas

pools and ponds

trees and shrubs

ELEMENTS of the BUILT ENVIRONMENT (EXTERNAL)

artificial light

texture and colour of internal finishes

daylight, ventilation and vision out

internal space heating

indoor plant cultivation

circulation space

furniture

ELEMENTS of the BUILT ENVIRONMENT (INTERNAL)

Environmental Considerations:
1. Planning requirements.
2. Building Regulations.
3. Land restrictions by vendor or lessor.
4. Availability of services.
5. Local amenities including transport.
6. Subsoil conditions.
7. Levels and topography of land.
8. Adjoining buildings or land.
9. Use of building.
10. Daylight and view aspects.

ORIENTATION ASPECTS

Examples ~

HOUSES

SCHOOLS

FACTORIES

HOSPITALS

Physical Considerations:

1. Natural contours of land.
2. Natural vegetation and trees.
3. Size of land and/or proposed building.
4. Shape of land and/or proposed building.
5. Approach and access roads and footpaths.
6. Services available.
7. Natural waterways, lakes and ponds.
8. Restrictions such as rights of way; tree preservation and ancient buildings.
9. Climatic conditions created by surrounding properties, land or activities.
10. Proposed future developments.

Examples ~

Split level construction to form economic shape.

Shape determined by existing trees.

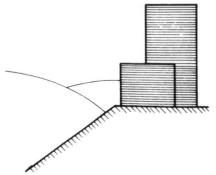

Plateau or high ground solution giving dry site conditions on sloping sites.

Stepped elevation or similar treatment to blend with the natural environment.

for design purposes ends are assumed to be free i.e. not fixed

beam

supporting wall

clear span

SIMPLY SUPPORTED BEAM

for design purposes ends assumed to have some degree of fixity

beam

supporting wall

effective span

BUILT-IN BEAM

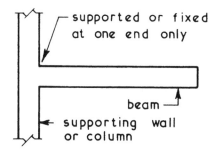

supported or fixed at one end only

beam

supporting wall or column

CANTILEVER BEAM

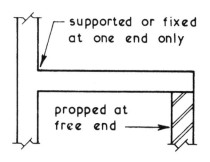

supported or fixed at one end only

propped at free end

PROPPED CANTILEVER

strut

STRUT

structural member which is subjected mainly to compression forces

column

VERTICAL STRUT

usually called a column stanchion or pier

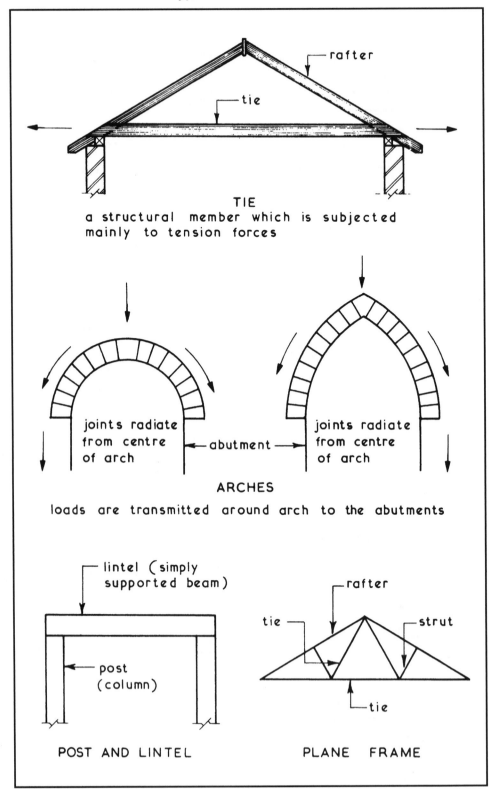

TIE
a structural member which is subjected
mainly to tension forces

joints radiate
from centre
of arch

←—abutment—→

joints radiate
from centre
of arch

ARCHES
loads are transmitted around arch to the abutments

lintel (simply
supported beam)

rafter

tie

strut

post
(column)

tie

POST AND LINTEL

PLANE FRAME

load-bearing
walls

SOLID CONSTRUCTION

structurally limited confined usually to buildings of
low height and short spans

main beams

secondary
beams

edge beams

columns

FRAMED OR SKELETAL CONSTRUCTION

structure consists of a series
of interconnected plates forming
structural walls and floors

PANEL OR BOX CONSTRUCTION

flat slab folded so that roof will
behave as a beam spanning along fold

diaphragms

columns
under
diaphragms

FOLDED PLATE CONSTRUCTION

Shell Roofs ~ these are formed by a structural curved skin covering a given plan shape and area.

Examples ~

double curvature shell formed by rotating a plain curved shape about a vertical axis

hemispherical rotational dome

vertical cut plane

pendentive

inscribed polygon

DOME OR ROTATIONAL SHELL

PENDENTIVE DOME

formed by a curved line moving over another curved line

cut cylinder giving a single curvature shell

diaphragm

TRANSLATIONAL DOME

BARREL VAULT

double curvature shells

double curvature saddle-shaped shell

diaphragm

CONOID SHELLS

HYPERBOLIC PARABOLOID

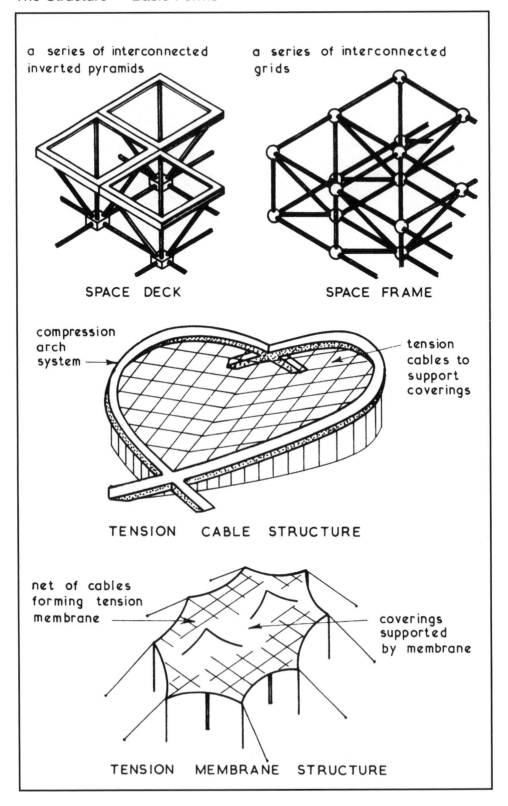

a series of interconnected inverted pyramids

a series of interconnected grids

SPACE DECK

SPACE FRAME

compression arch system

tension cables to support coverings

TENSION CABLE STRUCTURE

net of cables forming tension membrane

coverings supported by membrane

TENSION MEMBRANE STRUCTURE

Substructure ~ can be defined as all structure below the superstructure which in general terms is considered to include all structure below ground level but including the ground floor bed.

Typical Examples~

strip foundation

RC pad foundation

pile foundation

SERVICE DUCT

basement raft foundation

Superstructure ~ can be defined as all structure above substructure both internally and externally.

Primary Elements ~ basically components of the building carcass above the substructure excluding secondary elements, finishes, services and fittings.

Typical Examples~

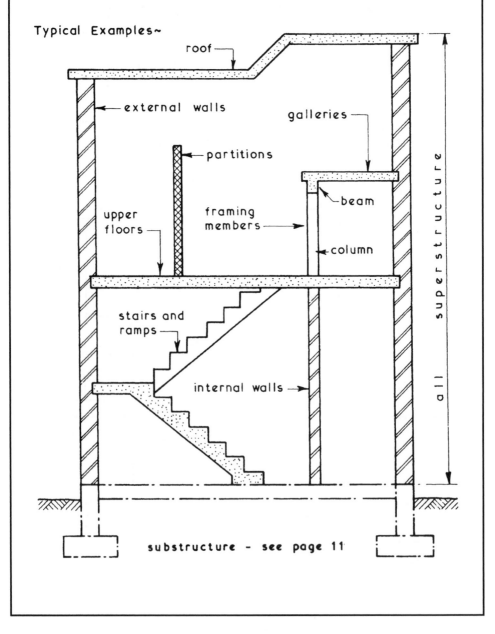

Secondary Elements ~ completion of the structure including completion around and within openings in primary elements.

Typical Examples~

borrowed lights and hatches →

windows

doors and door frames

doors and door linings →

EXTERNAL WALLS

INTERNAL WALLS

balustrade

stairs ~ primary element

BALUSTRADES

secondary element

primary element

FLOATING FLOORS

secondary element

primary element

CAVITY FLOORS

secondary element

primary element→

FLOOR TRAPS

FLOORS

floor or roof ~ primary element

SUSPENDED CEILINGS

roof ~ primary element

ROOFLIGHTS

13

Finish ~ the final surface which can be self-finished as with a trowelled concrete surface or an applied finish such as floor tiles.

Typical Examples~

EXTERNAL WALLS

- tile hanging
- weather boarding
- rendering

INTERNAL WALLS

- paint or wallpaper
- plaster
- wall ~ primary element
- dry lining
- trims

FLOORS

- tiles or carpet
- screed
- floor ~ primary element
- quarry tiles
- wood blocks
- floor~ primary element

STAIRS

- tread and riser finish such as tiles or carpet
- nosing trims
- stairs ~ primary element

ROOFS

- tiles or slates
- roof ~ primary element
- built-up roofing felts asphalt and metal coverings

CEILINGS

- plasterboard and plaster

Domestic Structures ~

load of roof coverings plus any snow and wind loads transferred to roof members

loads accepted by roof members transferred to walls

loads over openings transferred via a lintel to the jambs on either side

ceiling loads plus any loads in roof transferred to ceiling joists

total floor loads transferred to wall

dead and live loads of flooring transferred to floor joists

total floor loads transferred to internal load bearing wall

wall loads transferred to foundations

wall loads transferred to foundations

ground floor loads transferred direct to ground

total wall loads transferred via foundations to a suitable load bearing capacity subsoil

Framed Structures ~

roof loads accepted by beams transferred to columns

load of infill panel transferred to edge beam at base

load of roof coverings plus any snow and wind loads transferred to roof slab

loads accepted by roof slab transferred to beams

total roof loads transmitted down columns

edge beam acts as a main beam

live and loads of floor transferred to main and secondary beams

main and edge beam loads transferred to columns

total column loads transferred to foundation

secondary beam loads transferred to main beams

total on foundation transferred to subsoil

External Envelope ~ consists of the materials and components which form the external shell or enclosure of a building, i.e. walls, ground floor, roof, windows, doors and roof-lights. These may be load bearing or non-load bearing according to the structural form of the building.

Primary Functions ~

weather exclusion

thermal insulation

heat loss

heat

sound insulation

envelope to have acceptable appearance

provide ventilation

security and safety

envelope to have adequate strength, stability, durability and fire resistance

provide natural daylight to interior

provide visual contact with outside

provide access and egress

resist moisture penetration rising through the wall and floor from the ground

Internal Separation and Compartmentation

Dwelling Houses ~

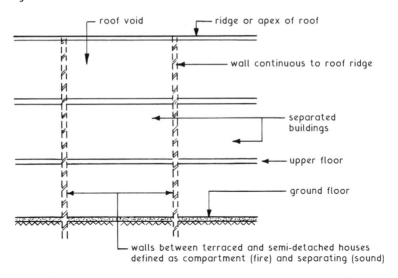

- roof void
- ridge or apex of roof
- wall continuous to roof ridge
- separated buildings
- upper floor
- ground floor
- walls between terraced and semi-detached houses defined as compartment (fire) and separating (sound)

Flats ~

- stairwell/protected shaft
- separated living units
- compartment walls (fire), separating walls (sound)
- compartment floor (fire), separating floor (sound)

Note: Floors within a maisonette are not required to be "compartment".

For non-residential buildings, compartment size is limited by floor area depending on the building function (purpose group) and height.

Compartment ~ a building or part of a building with walls and floors constructed to contain fire and to prevent it from spreading to another part of the same building or to an adjoining building.

Separating floor/wall ~ element of sound resisting construction between individual living units.

A Building or Construction Site can be considered as a temporary factory employing the necessary resources to successfully fulfil a contract.

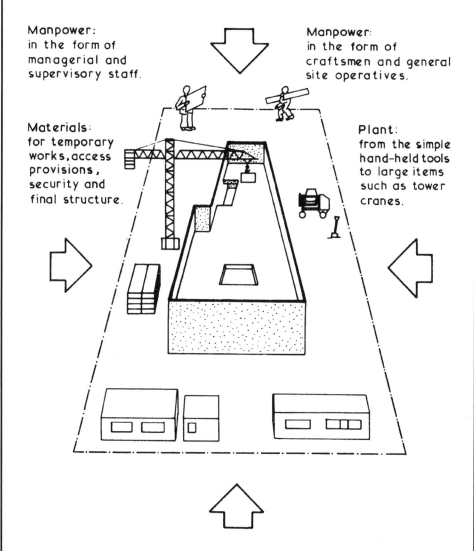

Manpower:
in the form of managerial and supervisory staff.

Manpower:
in the form of craftsmen and general site operatives.

Materials:
for temporary works, access provisions, security and final structure.

Plant:
from the simple hand-held tools to large items such as tower cranes.

Money:
in the form of capital investment from the building owner to pay for the land, design team fees and a building contractor who uses his money to buy materials, buy or hire plant and hire labour to enable the project to be realised.

SCHEDULES
1. Collation of similar standard items referenced to drawings.
2. Colour and decor schemes.

CONTRACT DOCUMENT
Usually a pro forma document but could be specially prepared. Sets out the precise conditions and terms of contract.

ENGINEERS' DRAWINGS
1. Small drawings giving general arrangements.
2. Drawings to larger scales giving specific details and data.

ARCHITECTS' DRAWINGS
1. Small scale plans and elevations showing general arrangement and layout.
2. Drawings to larger scales giving specific details and data.

BILL OF QUANTITIES or CONTRACT BILLS
Written document prepared in accordance with the Standard Method of Measurement. Enables estimator to prepare tender sum.

SPECIFICATION
Written document setting out in detail the specific requirements for materials and workmanship.

PRELIMINARY SKETCH

Location Drawings ~

Site Plans – used to locate site, buildings, define site levels, indicate services to buildings, identify parts of site such as roads, footpaths and boundaries and to give setting-out dimensions for the site and buildings as a whole. Suitable scale not less than 1:2500

Floor Plans – used to identify and set out parts of the building such as rooms, corridors, doors, windows, etc. Suitable scale not less than 1:100

Elevations – used to show external appearance of all faces and to identify doors and windows. Suitable scale not less than 1:100

Sections – used to provide vertical views through the building to show method of construction. Suitable scale not less than 1:50

Component Drawings – used to identify and supply data for components to be supplied by a manufacturer or for components not completely covered by assembly drawings. Suitable scale range 1:100 to 1:1

Assembly Drawings – used to show how items fit together or are assembled to form elements. Suitable scale range 1:20 to 1:5

All drawings should be fully annotated, fully dimensioned and cross-referenced.

Ref. BS EN ISO 7519: Technical drawings. Construction drawings. General principles of presentation for general arrangement and assembly drawings.

Sketch ~ this can be defined as a draft or rough outline of an idea; it can be a means of depicting a three-dimensional form in a two-dimensional guise. Sketches can be produced free-hand or using rules and set squares to give basic guidelines.

All sketches should be clear, show all the necessary detail and above all be in the correct proportions.

Sketches can be drawn by observing a solid object or they can be produced from conventional orthographic views but in all cases can usually be successfully drawn by starting with an outline 'box' format giving length, width and height proportions and then building up the sketch within the outline box.

Example~   Square-based Chimney Pot.

VERTICAL SECTION

PLAN

GIVEN   DATA

outline box

hatching to convey shape and shadows

FREE·HAND SKETCH

Orthographic Projection ~ a means of drawing independent views of a solid object on a plane surface.

NORTH ELEVATION

WEST ELEV.

SOUTH ELEVATION

EAST ELEV.

PLAN

N

Example ~ Small Garage and Workshop

The arrangement of the plan and elevations is known as First Angle Projection and is the recommended method of presenting drawings of building works.

NB. the usual annotation and dimensions found on general drawing have been omitted for clarity.

Isometric Projections ~ a pictorial projection of a solid object on a plane surface drawn so that all vertical lines remain vertical and of true scale length, all horizontal lines are drawn at an angle of 30° and are of true scale length; therefore scale measurements can be taken on the vertical and 30° lines but cannot be taken on any other inclined line.

A similar drawing can be produced using an angle of 45° for all horizontal lines and is called an Axonometric Projection.

this line is inclined and is therefore not of true scale length

hatching can be used to convey shape and form

30°   30°

ISOMETRIC PROJECTION SHOWING SOUTH AND WEST ELEVATIONS OF SMALL GARAGE AND WORKSHOP ILLUSTRATED ON PAGE 23

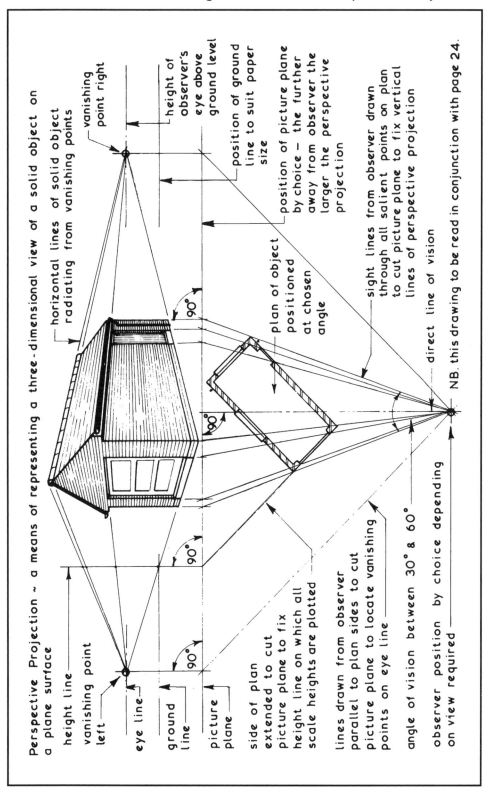

Perspective Projection ~ a means of representing a three-dimensional view of a solid object on a plane surface

height line

vanishing point left

eye line

ground line

picture plane

side of plan extended to cut picture plane to fix height line on which all scale heights are plotted

lines drawn from observer parallel to plan sides to cut picture plane to locate vanishing points on eye line

angle of vision between 30° & 60°

observer position by choice depending on view required

horizontal lines of solid object radiating from vanishing points

vanishing point right

height of observer's eye above ground level

position of ground line to suit paper size

position of picture plane by choice — the further away from observer the larger the perspective projection

plan of object positioned at chosen angle

sight lines from observer drawn through all salient points on plan to cut picture plane to fix vertical lines of perspective projection

direct line of vision

NB. this drawing to be read in conjunction with page 24.

90°
90°
90°
90°

25

SIDE ELEVATION (Right)

SIDE ELEVATION (Left)

REAR ELEVATION

FRONT ELEVATION

FIRST FLOOR PLAN

GROUND FLOOR PLAN

FOUR BEDROOMED HOUSE

Title

Scale   Date

Drawing Ref.   RG/HNC,D/'10

BEDROOM

BATH

A.C.

MASTER BEDROOM

BATH

GALLERY

BEDROOM

BEDROOM

2 No ROOFLIGHTS

LIVING ROOM

DINING ROOM

W.C.

STUDY

HALL

KITCHEN

GARAGE

UTILITY

GARAGE

BLOCK PLAN
Min. 1:500

SITE PLAN
Min. 1:2500

PARK ROAD

N

Construction Defects - correct application of materials produced to the recommendations of British, European and International Standards authorities, in accordance with local building regulations, bye-laws and the rules of building guarantee companies, i.e. National House Building Council (NHBC) and MD Insurance Services, should ensure a sound and functional structure. However, these controls can be seriously undermined if the human factor of quality workmanship is not fulfilled. The following guidance is designed to promote quality controls:

BS 8000: Workmanship on building sites.

Building Regulations, Approved Document to support Regulation 7 - materials and workmanship.

No matter how good the materials, the workmanship and supervision, the unforeseen may still affect a building. This may materialise several years after construction. Some examples of these latent defects include: woodworm emerging from untreated timber, electrolytic decomposition of dissimilar metals inadvertently in contact, and chemical decomposition of concrete. Generally, the older a building the more opportunity there is for its components and systems to have deteriorated and malfunctioned. Hence the need for regular inspection and maintenance. The profession of facilities management has evolved for this purpose and is represented by the British Institute of Facilities Management (BIFM).

Property values, repairs and replacements are of sufficient magnitude for potential purchasers to engage the professional services of a building surveyor. Surveyors are usually members of the Royal Institution of Chartered Surveyors (RICS). The extent of survey can vary, depending on a client's requirements. This may be no more than a market valuation to secure financial backing, to a full structural survey incorporating specialist reports on electrical installations, drains, heating systems, etc.

Further reading:

BRE Digest No. 268 - Common defects in low-rise traditional housing. Available from Building Research Establishment Bookshop - www.brebookshop.com.

Established Procedure — the interested purchaser engages a building surveyor.

UK Government Requirements — the seller to provide an energy performance certificate. This is a fuel use and efficiency appraisal on a numerical scale. See pages 32 and 33.

Survey document preliminaries:

* Title and address of property

* Client's name, address and contacts

* Survey date and time

* Property status — freehold, leasehold or commonhold

* Occupancy — occupied or vacant. If vacant, source of keys

* Extent of survey, e.g. full structural + services reports

* Specialists in attendance, e.g. electrician, heating engineer, etc.

* Age of property (approx. if very dated or no records)

* Disposition of rooms, i.e. number of bedrooms, etc.

* Floor plans and elevations if available

* Elevation (flooding potential) and orientation (solar effect)

* Estate/garden area and disposition if appropriate

* Means of access — roads, pedestrian only, rights of way

Survey tools and equipment:

* Drawings + estate agent's particulars if available

* Notebook and pencil/pen

* Binoculars and a camera with flash facility

* Tape measure, spirit level and plumb line

* Other useful tools, to include small hammer, torch, screwdriver and manhole lifting irons

* Moisture meter

* Ladders — eaves access and loft access

* Sealable bags for taking samples, e.g. wood rot, asbestos, etc.

Estate and garden:
* Location and establishment of boundaries
* Fences, gates and hedges – material, condition and suitability
* Trees – type and height, proximity to building
* Pathways and drives – material and condition
* Outbuildings – garages, sheds, greenhouses, barns, etc.
* Proximity of water courses

Roof:
* Tile type, treatment at ridge, hips, verge and valleys
* Age of covering, repairs, replacements, renewals, general condition, defects and growths
* Eaves finish, type and condition
* Gutters – material, size, condition, evidence of leakage
* Rainwater downpipes as above
* Chimney – dpcs, flashings, flaunching, pointing, signs of movement
* Flat roofs – materials, repairs, abutments, flashings and drainage

Walls:
* Materials – type of brick, rendering, cladding, etc., condition and evidence of repairs
* Solid or cavity construction, if cavity extent of insulation and type
* Pointing of masonry, painting of rendering and cladding
* Air brick location, function and suitability
* Dpc, material and condition, position relative to ground level
* Windows and doors, material, signs of rot or damage, original or replacement, frame seal
* Settlement – signs of cracking, distortion of window and door frames – specialist report

Drainage:
A building surveyor may provide a general report on the condition of the drainage and sanitation installation. However, a full test for leakage and determination of self-cleansing and flow conditions to include fibre-optic scope examination is undertaken as a specialist survey.

Roof space:
* Access to all parts, construction type – traditional or trussed
* Evidence of moisture due to condensation – ventilation at eaves, ridge, etc.
* Evidence of water penetration – chimney flashings, abutments and valleys
* Insulation – type and quantity
* Party wall in semi-detached and terraced dwellings – suitability as fire barrier
* Plumbing – adequacy of storage cistern, insulation, overflow function

Floors:
* Construction – timber, precast or cast in-situ concrete? Finish condition?
* Timber ground floor – evidence of dampness, rot, woodworm, ventilation, dpcs
* Timber upper floor stability, i.e. wall fixing, strutting, joist size, woodworm, span and loading

Stairs:
* Type of construction and method of fixing – built in-situ or preformed
* Soffit, re. fire protection (plasterboard?)
* Balustrading – suitability and stability
* Safety – adequate screening, balusters, handrail, pitch angle, open tread, tread wear

Finishes:
* General décor, i.e. paint and wallpaper condition – damaged, faded
* Woodwork/joinery – condition, defects, damage, paintwork
* Plaster – ceiling (plasterboard or lath and plaster?) – condition and stability
* Plaster – walls – render and plaster or plasterboard, damage and quality of finish
* Staining – plumbing leaks (ceiling), moisture penetration (wall openings), rising damp
* Fittings and ironmongery – adequacy and function, weather exclusion and security

Supplementary enquiries should determine the extent of additional building work, particularly since the planning threshold of 1948. Check for planning approvals, permitted development and Building Regulation approvals, exemptions and completion certificates.

Services – apart from a cursory inspection to ascertain location and suitability of system controls, these areas are highly specialised and should be surveyed by those appropriately qualified.

Energy Performance Certificate (EPC) applications include:

- Construction of new buildings.
- Extensions to existing buildings.
- Alterations to existing buildings to provide an increase or a reduction in the number of separate occupancies, e.g. a house conversion into flats or vice versa.
- Refurbishment or modification to include provision or extension of fixed energy consuming building services for hot water, heating, air conditioning or mechanical ventilation (applies to buildings with a floor area exceeding 1000 m^2 but can also be required for smaller buildings depending on specification of installation).
- Part of the marketing particulars when selling or letting a new or existing property.

The above applications relate quite simply to buildings that are roofed, have enclosing walls and use energy consuming appliances to condition the internal space. Some building types are exempted an EPC, these include the following:

- Buildings listed under the Planning (Listed Buildings and Conservation Areas) Act.*
- Buildings within a conservation area as determined under Section 69 of the Act.*
- Structures included in the monuments schedule under Section 1 of the Ancient Monuments and Archaeological Areas Act.*
- Churches and other buildings designated primarily for worship.
- Temporary buildings with less than two years' expected use.
- Industrial buildings, workshops and non-residential agricultural buildings/barns with low demands on energy.
- Detached buildings other than dwellings with usable floor area of less than 50 m^2.

* The objective is to preserve the character and appearance of specific buildings that would otherwise be altered or spoilt by applying contemporary energy efficiency requirements.

Ref. The Energy Performance of Buildings (Certificates and Inspections) (England and Wales) Regulations.

An Energy Performance Certificate (EPC) provides a rating for fuel use efficiency in a building. This rating relates to the amount of carbon dioxide (CO_2) emitted by the energy producing appliances.

Asset rating ~ an estimate of the fuel energy required to meet the needs of a building during normal occupancy. A performance rating based on a building's age, location/exposure, size, glazing system, materials, insulation, general condition, fuel use controls and fixed appliance efficiency, e.g. boiler (SEDBUK rating see page 562). Rating is alphabetical from A to G, A the highest grade for energy efficiency with lowest impact on environmental damage in terms of CO_2 emissions. An EU-type energy rating label is part of the certification documents. It is similar to the example shown on page 566 as applied to windows. The alphabetic rating relates directly to SAP numerical ratings (see page 559) as follows:

EPC asset rating (SAP rating) ~

A (92 – 100)	B (81 – 91)	C (69 – 80)	D (55 – 68)
E (39 – 54)	F (21 – 38)	G (1 – 20)	

Operational rating ~ an alternative to asset rating, using the numerical scale for energy consumed over a period of time. This could be presented monthly or seasonally to indicate varying demands.

CO_2 emission rate calculations for new-build and refurbishment work ~

Before work commences the local building control authority (LA) to be provided with the following for approval:
  Target CO_2 emission rate by calculation (TER).
  Dwelling CO_2 emission rate by calculation and design (DER).
  Building design specification relative to calculated CO_2 emissions.
After (within five days of completion), LA to be provided with certification confirming:
  Target CO_2 emissions.
  Calculated CO_2 emissions as constructed.
  Confirmation that the building design specification is adhered to. If not, details of variations to be provided.

Note: TER and DER energy performance requirements are expressed in mass of CO_2 in units of kg per m^2 floor area per year. See also pages 567 and 568.

EPC content:
Address and location of the building assessed.
Activity/function of the building, e.g. dwelling house.
Date of construction, approximate if very old.
Construction, e.g. solid walls, cavity walls, etc.
Materials of construction.
Heat energy source, system type and fuel used.
Electrical energy source, lighting and power provision.
Energy efficiency asset rating.
Environmental impact rating (CO_2 emissions).
Recommendations for improvements.
Date of issue (valid 10 years unless significant changes occur).
Reference/registration number.
Assessor's name, accreditation number and scheme number.

EPC assessor/surveyor ~ an appropriately qualified energy assessment member of an accredited scheme approved by the Secretary of State for the Department for Communities and Local Government (DCLG), as defined in the Energy Performance of Buildings (Certificates and Inspections) (England and Wales) Regulations. Within five days of work completion, the assessor must provide the building owner with an EPC and the local authority to be informed of the details of the EPC reference as entered in the register maintained under Regulation 31.

Recommendations for improvements ~ in addition to an energy assessment survey and rating, the assessor is required to provide a report identifying areas that could improve the energy performance of a building. Examples may include cost-effective recommendations for cavity wall insulation, increased insulation in the roof space, provision of a central-heating room temperature control thermostat, double/secondary glazing, etc. These recommendations to include a cost analysis of capital expenditure relative to potential savings over time and enhanced asset rating that the building could attain.

Related refs.:
Building Regulation 29 – Declaration of giving an EPC.
Building Regulations Approved Document L.
Standard Assessment Procedure.
Energy Performance of Buildings Directive – 2010/31/EU.

Dwelling type . . . .   Ref. No. . . . .
Assessment date . . . .   Type of assessment . . . .
Certificate date . . . .   Total floor area . . . .

This certificate can be used to:

· Compare the energy efficiency with other properties/dwellings.

· Determine the potential economies of energy saving installations.

Estimated energy costs over 3 years: £3,750
Energy saving potential over 3 years: £1,330

Estimated energy costs of this dwelling over 3 years:

	Current cost	Potential cost	Potential savings
Lighting	£380	£190	£190
Heating	£2,820	£1,980	£840
Hot water	£550	£250	£300
Totals	£3,750	£2,420	£1,330

Figures do not include costs of running subsidiary appliances such as TV, fridge, cooker, etc.

Energy Efficiency Rating:

Very energy efficient

92+	A
81-91	B
69-80	C
55-68	D
39-54	E
21-38	F
1-20	G

Energy inefficient

Current   Potential

83

56

Diagram shows current efficiency rating.

Higher the rating, the lower the fuel costs.

Potential rating includes recommendations indicated below.

Average rating for a dwelling in England and Wales is band D (60).

Recommended measures:

	Indicative capital cost	Typical savings over 3 years
Increase loft insulation	£150 - £350	£125
Solar photovoltaic panels	£9,000 - £14,000	£700
Low energy lighting throughout	£120	£150

A method statement precedes preparation of the project programme and contains the detail necessary for construction of each element of a building. It is prepared from information contained in the contract documents – see page 20. It also functions as a brief for site staff and operatives in sequencing activities, indicating resource requirements and determining the duration of each element of construction. It complements construction programming by providing a detailed analysis of each activity.

A typical example for foundation excavation could take the following format:

Activity	Quantity	Method	Output/hour	Labour	Plant	Days
Strip site for excavation	300 m²	Exc. to reduced level over construction area – JCB-4CX face shovel/loader. Topsoil retained on site.	50 m²/hr	Exc. driver +2 labourers	JCB-4CX backhoe/loader	0·75
Excavate for foundations	60 m³	Excavate foundation trench to required depth – JCB-4CX backhoe. Surplus spoil removed from site.	15 m³/hr	Exc. driver +2 labourers. Truck driver	JCB-4CX backhoe/loader. Tipper truck	0·50

PROJECT | TWO-STOREY OFFICE AND WORKSHOP | CONTRACT No. 1234

MONTH/YEAR

DATE: W/E

Week No.: 1 2 3 4 5 6 7 8 9 10 11 12 13 14 15 16 17 18 19 20 21 22 23 24 25 26 27 28 29 30 31 32 33 34 35 36 37

No.	Activity
1	Set up site
2	Level site and fill
3	Excavate founds
4	Conc. foundations
5	Brickwork < dpc
6	Ground floor
7	Drainage
8	Scaffold
9	Brickwork > dpc
10	1st. floor carcass
11	Roof framing
12	Roof tiling
13	1st. floor deck
14	Partitions
15	1st. fix joiner
16	1st. fix services
17	Glazing
18	Plaster & screed
19	2nd. fix joiner
20	2nd. fix services
21	Paint & dec.
22	Floor finishes
23	Fittings & fixtures
24	Clean & make good
25	Roads & landscape
26	Clear site
27	Commissioning

Annotations: pin — string line — activity duration — progress to date — planned completion

Typical Weights of Building Materials

Material	Weight (kg/m^2)
BRICKS, BLOCKS and PAVING –	
Clay brickwork – 102.5 mm	
low density	205
medium density	221
high density	238
Calcium silicate brickwork – 102.5 mm	205
Concrete blockwork, aerated	78
.... lightweight aggregate	129
Concrete flagstones (50 mm)	115
Glass blocks (100 mm thick) 150 × 150	98
...........................200 × 200	83
ROOFING –	
Slates – see page 518	
Thatching (300 mm thick)	40·00
Tiles – plain clay	63·50
.. – plain concrete	93·00
.. single lap, concrete	49·00
Tile battens (50 × 25) and felt underlay	7·70
Bituminous felt underlay	1·00
Bituminous felt, sanded topcoat	2·70
3 layers bituminous felt	4·80
HD/PE breather membrane underlay	0·20
SHEET MATERIALS –	
Aluminium (0·9 mm)	2·50
Copper (0·9 mm)	4·88
Cork board (standard) per 25 mm thickness	4·33
.... (compressed)	9·65
Hardboard (3·2 mm)	3·40
Glass (3 mm)	7·30
Lead (1·25 mm)	14·17
.. .. (3 mm)	34·02
Particle board/chipboard (12 mm)	9·26
.. .. (22 mm)	16·82
Planking, softwood strip flooring (ex 25 mm)	11·20
.... hardwood	16·10
Plasterboard (9·5 mm)	8·30
.... (12·5 mm)	11·00
.... (19 mm)	17·00
Plywood per 25 mm	15·00
PVC floor tiling (2·5 mm)	3·90
Strawboard (25 mm)	9·80

Material	Weight (kg/m²)
Weatherboarding (20 mm)	7·68
Woodwool (25 mm)	14·50
INSULATION	
Glass fibre thermal (100 mm)	2·00
.... acoustic	4·00
APPLIED MATERIALS -	
Asphalt (18 mm)	42
Plaster, 2 coat work	22
STRUCTURAL TIMBER:	
Rafters and joists (100 × 50 @ 400 c/c)	5·87
Floor joists (225 × 50 @ 400 c/c)	14·93

Densities:

Material	Approx. density (kg/m³)
Cement	1440
Concrete (aerated)	640
.... (broken brick)	2000
.... (natural aggregates)	2300
.... (no-fines)	1760
.... (reinforced)	2400
Metals:	
Aluminium	2710
Brass	8500
Copper	8930
Lead	11325
Steel	7860
Tin	7300
Zinc	7140
Timber (softwood/pine)	480 (average)
...... (hardwood, e.g. maple, teak, oak)	720 ......
Water	1000

Typical Imposed Floor Loads

Structural design of floors will be satisfied for most situations by using the minimum figures given for uniformly distributed loading (UDL). These figures provide for static loading and for the dynamics of occupancy. The minimum figures given for concentrated or point loading can be used where these produce greater stresses.

Application	UDL (kN/m^2)	Concentrated (kN)
Dwellings ~		
Communal areas	1.5	1.4
Bedrooms	1.5	1.8
Bathroom/WC	2.0	1.8
Balconies (use by one family)	1.5	1.4
Commercial/Industrial ~		
Hotel/motel bedrooms	2.0	1.8
Communal kitchen	3.0	4.5
Offices and general work areas	2.5	2.7
Kitchens/laundries/laboratories	3.0	4.5
Factories and workshops	5.0	4.5
Balconies – guest houses	3.0	1.5/m run at outer edge
Balconies – communal areas in flats	3.0	1.5/m run at outer edge
Balconies – hotels/motels	4.0	1.5/m run at outer edge
Warehousing/Storage ~		
General use for static items	2.0	1.8
Reading areas/libraries	4.0	4.5
General use, stacked items	2.4/m height	7.0
Filing areas	5.0	4.5
Paper storage	4.0/m height	9.0
Plant rooms	7.5	4.5
Book storage	2.4/m height (min. 6.5)	7.0

See also:

BS EN 1991-1-1: Densities, self-weight, imposed loads for buildings.

BS EN 1991-1-3: Snow loads.

BS EN 1991-1-4: Wind actions.

Drawings ~ these are the principal means of communication between the designer, the builder and other parties to a contract.

Drawings should therefore be clear, accurate, contain all the necessary information and be capable of being easily read.

Design practices have their own established symbols and notations for graphical communication. Some of these are shown on this and the next three pages. Other guidance can be found in BS EN ISOs 4157 and 7519.

Typical Examples~

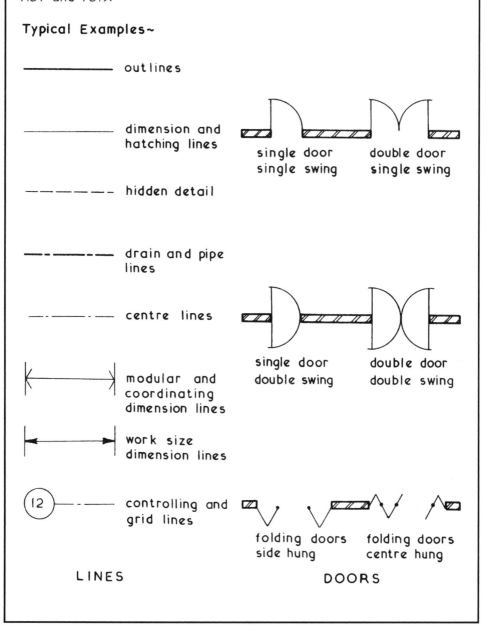

──────── outlines

──────── dimension and hatching lines

single door
single swing

double door
single swing

─ ─ ─ ─ ─ hidden detail

── ─ ── ─ drain and pipe lines

─ · ──── · centre lines

single door
double swing

double door
double swing

modular and coordinating dimension lines

work size dimension lines

(12) ─ · ── controlling and grid lines

folding doors
side hung

folding doors
centre hung

LINES   DOORS

41

Hatchings ~ the main objective is to differentiate between the materials being used thus enabling rapid recognition and location. Whichever hatchings are chosen they must be used consistently throughout the whole set of drawings. In large areas it is not always necessary to hatch the whole area.

Symbols ~ these are graphical representations and should wherever possible be drawn to scale but above all they must be consistent for the whole set of drawings and clearly drawn.

Typical Examples~

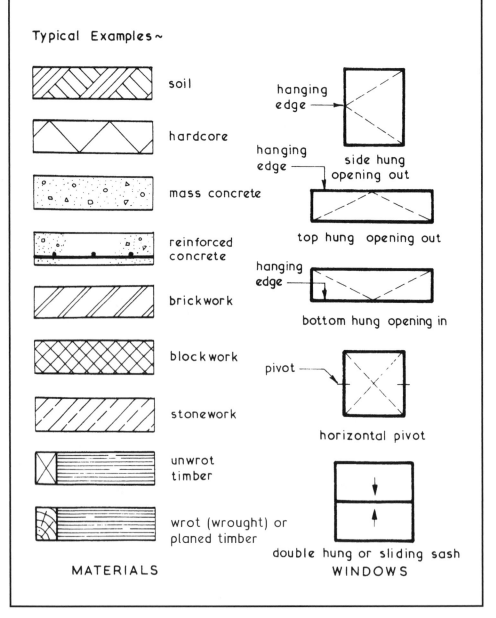

MATERIALS

WINDOWS

Name	Symbol	Name	Symbol
Rainwater pipe	◯ RWP	Distribution board	☐
Gully	☐ G	Electricity meter	⊙
Inspection chambers	IC ─▭─ soil or foul · IC ─◯─ surface water	Switched socket outlet	◗
Boiler	☐ B	Switch	●
Sink	☐ S ·	Two-way switch	●
Bath	▭ ·	Pendant switch	●
Wash basin	W·B	Filament lamp	◯
Shower unit	S	Fluorescent lamp	◯
Urinal	stall bowl	Bed	▱
Water closet	▭ ◯	Table and chairs	

TYPICAL COMPONENT, FITMENT AND ELECTRICAL SYMBOLS

NB dimensions and full annotation omitted for clarity

TYPICAL PLAN OF A TWO-BEDROOM BUNGALOW

Principal legislation ~

Town & Country Planning Act 1990 and Planning Act 2008 – Effect control over volume of development, appearance and layout of buildings.

Public Health Acts 1936 to 1961 – Limit development with regard to emission of noise, pollution and public nuisance.

Highways Act 1980 – Determines layout and construction of roads and pavements.

Building Act 1984 – Effects the Building Regulations 2010, which enforce minimum material and design standards.

Civic Amenities Act 1967 – Establishes conservation areas, providing local authorities with greater control of development.

Town and Country Amenities Act 1974 – Local authorities empowered to prevent demolition of buildings and tree felling.

Procedure ~

Outline Planning Application – This is necessary for permission to develop a proposed site. The application should contain:
An application form describing the work.
A site plan showing adjacent roads and buildings (1:2500).
A block plan showing the plot, access and siting (1:500).
A certificate of land ownership.

Detail or Full Planning Application – This follows outline permission and is also used for proposed alterations to existing buildings.

It should contain: details of the proposal, to include trees, materials, drainage and any demolition.

Site and block plans (as above). A certificate of land ownership. Building drawings showing elevations, sections, plans, material specifications, access, landscaping, boundaries and relationship with adjacent properties (1:100).

Permitted Developments – House extensions may be exempt from formal application. Conditions vary depending on house position relative to its plot and whether detached or attached. See next two pages.

Note: Most developments are subject to Building Regulation approval. Some exemptions are shown on page 69.

Certificates of ownership – Article 7 of the Town & Country Planning (General Development Procedure) Order 1995:
Cert. A – States the applicant is sole site freeholder (page 51).
Cert. B – States the applicant is part freeholder or prospective purchaser and all owners of the site know of the application (page 51).
Cert. C – As Cert. B, but the applicant is only able to ascertain some of the other landowners.
Cert. D – As Cert. B, but the applicant cannot ascertain any owners of the site other than him/herself.

Permitted development ~ on 1 October 2008 regulations were introduced to simplify the planning approval process for relatively small-scale construction work to existing houses. The approval, known as permitted development, to be undertaken without the cost and time-consuming process of formalising a detailed/full planning application to the local planning authority (LPA). Before October 2008 permitted development existed as a nominal volume percentage increase over the house size without much clarification beyond that. The new regulations, entitled The Town and Country Planning (General Permitted Development) (Amendment) (No.2) (England) Order 2008, will reduce the number of former planning applications by about a quarter. There are limitations for permitted development that relate to the position and size of a house as it stood on 1 July 1948 or when first built if later. Proposals for property enlargement beyond these constraints must be submitted for formal planning approval.

Application ~ permitted development applies specifically to extensions and alterations to houses, but not flats. This does not necessarily include all houses. Houses in conservation areas and those listed for historical interest may be excluded. The LPA should be consulted for clarification on all proposals, as planning departments will interpret the "Order" with regard to their locality. Exemption from the formal planning process does not include exemption from Building Regulation approval. Most extensions and some alterations will still require this (see pages 61 to 70).

Lawful Development Certificate (LDC) ~ this is an option that can be sought from the LPA. It is an alternative to submitting a full planning application where there is any doubt or ambiguity about work that would qualify for permitted development. It is not intended as a planning permit, but it is documented proof that the building created by extending or altering a house is lawful. Even if alterations are clearly defined by permitted development, the option of obtaining a LDC may be considered worthwhile to satisfy any queries if prospective future purchasers of the property require the work substantiated. As well as establishing the lawfulness of proposed work, an application for a LDC can be retrospective.

Ref. Town and Country Planning Act 1990, Sections 191 and 192.

Limits and conditions, subject to LPA interpretation:
- Maximum of half the area of land around the house taken up with extension or other buildings (as the house stood on 1 July 1948 or when first built if later).
- No extension beyond the principal elevation or a side elevation that fronts a highway.
- Single-storey extension:
    Attached house, max. 3m beyond the rear wall.
    Detached house, max. 4m beyond the rear wall.
- Additional storeys to a rear extension, max. 3m in depth.
- Two-storey extension not closer than 7m to the rear boundary.
- Over one storey high, roof pitch to match existing.
- Max. eaves height of 3m if the extension is within 2m of a boundary.
- Max. eaves and ridge height no higher than existing.
- Side elevation extension max. 4m height. Width not greater than half that of the original house (see above, re. 1948).
- Materials to match existing.
- No verandas, balconies or raised platforms (> 300mm high).
- No chimney, flue or discharge stack installation, alteration or replacement if it exceeds the highest part of the roof by 1 m.
- Upper floor extension with side-facing windows obscure glazed.
- Upper floor side-facing extension windows to be non-opening or if openable the opening parts at least 1.7 m above floor.
- In conservation areas, subject to LPA agreement, single-storey rear extension only. No exterior cladding and no side extensions.
- No enlargement, additions or alterations to a roof to extend beyond the plane of slope of the existing roof which forms the principal elevation of the house and fronts a highway. An exception of up to 150mm perpendicular to the plane may be permitted.
- Roof space extension:
    Terraced house, 40m^3 max. increase over the existing roof space.
    Semi-detached or detached house, 50m^3 max. increase over the existing roof space.
- Porch outside of an external door:
    External ground area not to exceed 3m^2.
    Height above the ground not to exceed 3m.
    Greater than 2m from a boundary with a highway.
- Driveway or paving exceeding 5m^2 to be of gravel, porous asphalt or any other material that will allow the drainage of water.

PLANNING APPLICATION

APPLICATION No

Use this form to apply for Planning Permission for:-
- an Extension
- a Loft Conversion
- a New or Altered Access
- a High Wall or Fence
- a Garage or Outbuilding
- a Satellite Dish

Please return:-
- 6 copies of the Form
- 6 copies of the Plans
- a Certificate under Article 7
- the correct fee

DATE RECEIVED

1. NAME AND ADDRESS OF APPLICANT

Post Code _____

Tel. No. _____

2. NAME AND ADDRESS OF AGENT (If Used)

Post Code _____

Tel. No. _____

3. ADDRESS OF PROPERTY TO BE ALTERED OR EXTENDED

4. OWNERSHIP

Please indicate applicants interest in the property and complete the appropriate Certificate under Article 7.

Freeholder ☐   Other ☐

Leaseholder ☐

Purchaser ☐

5. BRIEF DESCRIPTION OF WORKS (include any demolition work)

6. DESCRIPTION OF EXTERNAL MATERIALS

7. ACCESS AND PARKING

Will your proposal affect?   Please tick appropriate boxes

Vehicular Access   Yes ☐   No ☐

A Public Right of Way   Yes ☐   No ☐

Existing Parking   Yes ☐   No ☐

9. TREES

Does the proposal involve the felling of any trees?

Please tick box   Yes ☐   No ☐

If yes, please show details on plans

8. DRAINAGE

a. Please indicate method of Surface Water Disposal

b. Please indicate method of Foul Water Disposal
Please tick one box

Mains Sewer ☐   Septic Tank ☐

Cesspit ☐   Other ☐

10. PLEASE SIGN AND DATE THIS FORM BEFORE SUBMITTING

I/We hereby apply for Full Planning Permission for the development described above and shown on the accompanying plans.

Signed _____   Date _____

Date _____

On behalf of (if agent) _____

Use this form to apply for **Planning Permission for:-**
Outline Permission
Full Permission
Approval of Reserved Matters
Renewal of Temporary Permission
Change of Use

Please return:-
* 6 copies of the Form
* 6 copies of the Plans
* a Certificate under
 Article 7
* the correct fee

DATE RECEIVED

DATE VALID

1. NAME AND ADDRESS OF APPLICANT

_____
_____
_____
_____
_____

Post Code _____

Day Tel. No. _____ Fax No. _____

Email: _____

2. NAME AND ADDRESS OF AGENT (If Used)

_____
_____
_____
_____
_____

Post Code _____

Tel. No. _____ Fax No. _____

Email: _____

3. ADDRESS OR LOCATION OF LAND TO WHICH APPLICATION RELATES

_____
_____
_____

State Site Area _____ Hectares

This must be shown edged in Red on the site plan

4. OWNERSHIP

Please indicate applicants interest in the property and complete the appropriate Certificate under Article 7.

Freeholder ☐   Other ☐

Leaseholder ☐   Purchaser ☐

Any adjoining land owned or controlled and not part of application must be edged Blue on the site plan

5. WHAT ARE YOU APPLYING FOR?   Please tick one box and then answer relevant questions.

☐ **Outline Planning Permission** Which of the following are to be considered?

☐ Siting ☐ Design ☐ Appearance ☐ Access ☐ Landscaping

☐ **Full Planning Permission/Change of Use**

☐ **Approval of Reserved Matters following Outline Permission.**

O/P No. _____ Date_____ No. of Condition this application refers to: _____

☐ **Continuance of Use without complying with a condition of previous permission**

P/P No. _____ Date_____ No. of Condition this application relates to: _____

☐ **Permission for Retention of works.**

Date of use of land or when buildings or works were constructed: _____ Length of temporary permission: _____

Is the use temporary or permanent? _____ No. of previous temporary permission if applicable: _____

6. BRIEF DESCRIPTION OF PROPOSED DEVELOPMENT

Please indicate the purpose for which the land or buildings are to be used. _____
_____
_____

7. NEW RESIDENTIAL DEVELOPMENTS. Please answer the following if appropriate:

What type of building is proposed? _____

No. of dwellings: _____ No. of storeys: _____ No. of habitable rooms: _____

No. of garages: _____ No. of parking spaces: _____ Total grass area of all buildings: _____

How will surface water be disposed of? _____

How will foul sewage be dealt with? _____

8. ACCESS

Does the proposed development involve any of the following? Please tick the appropriate boxes.

New access to a highway ☐ Pedestrian ☐ Vehicular

Alteration of an existing highway ☐ Pedestrian ☐ Vehicular

The felling of any trees ☐ Yes ☐ No

If you answer Yes to any of the above, they should be clearly indicated on all plans submitted.

9. BUILDING DETAIL

Please give details of all external materials to be used, if you are submitting them at this stage for approval.

_____

_____

List any samples that are being submitted for consideration. _____

_____

10. LISTED BUILDINGS OR CONSERVATION AREA

Are any listed buildings to be demolished or altered? ☐ Yes ☐ No

If Yes, then Listed Building Consent will be required and a separate application should be submitted.

Are any non-listed buildings within a Conservation Area to be demoiished? ☐ Yes ☐ No

If Yes, then Conservation Area consent will be required to demolish. Again, a separate application should be submitted.

11. NOTES

A special Planning Application Form should be completed for all applications involving Industrial, Warehousing, Storage, or Shopping development.

An appropriate Certificate must accompany this application unless you are seeking approval to Reserved Matters.

A separate application for Building Regulation approval is also required.

Separate applications may also be required if the proposals relate to a listed building or non-listed building within a Conservation Area.

12. PLEASE SIGN AND DATE THIS FORM BEFORE SUBMITTING

I/We hereby apply for Planning Permission for the development described above and shown on the accompanying plans.

Signed _____

50

TOWN AND COUNTRY PLANNING ACT

TOWN AND COUNTRY PLANNING (General Development Procedure) ORDER
Certificates under Article 7 of the Order

CERTIFICATE A   **For Freehold Owner (or his/her Agent)**

I hereby certify that:-

1.   No person other than the applicant was an owner of any part of the land to which the application relates at the beginning of the period of 21 days before the date of the accompanying application.

2.   ***Either (i)** None of the land to which the application relates constitutes or forms part of an agricultural holding:

      *or (ii) *(I have) (the applicant has) given the requisite notice to every person other than *(myself) (himself) (herself) who, 21 days before the date of the application, was a tenant of any agricultural holding any part of which was comprised in the land to which the application relates, viz:-

Name and Address of Tenant..

....

.... Signed .... Date.........................

Date of Service of Notice....................................... *On Behalf of ....

CERTIFICATE B   **For Part Freehold Owner or Prospective Purchaser (or his/her Agent) able to ascertain all the owners of the land**

I hereby certify that:-

1.   *(I have) (the applicant has) given the requisite notice to all persons other than (myself) (the applicant) who, 21 days before the date of the accompanying application were owners of any part of the land to which the application relates, viz:-

Name and Address of Owner ....

....

.... Date of Service of Notice ....

2.   ***Either (i)** None of the land to which the application relates constitutes or forms part of an agricultural holding;

      *or (ii) *(I have) (the applicant has) given the requisite notice to every person other than *(myself) (himself) (herself) who, 21 days before the date of the application, was a tenant of any agricultural holding any part of which was comprised in the land to which the application relates, viz:-

Name and Address of Tenant..

....

.... Signed .... Date.........................

Modular Coordination ~ a module can be defined as a basic dimension which could, for example, form the basis of a planning grid in terms of multiples and submultiples of the standard module.

Typical Modular Coordinated Planning Grid ~

Let M = the standard module

Structural Grid ~ used to locate structural components such as beams and columns.

Planning Grid ~ based on any convenient modular multiple for regulating space requirements such as rooms.

Controlling Grid ~ based on any convenient modular multiple for location of internal walls, partitions, etc.

Basic Module Grid ~ used for detail location of components and fittings.

All the above grids, being based on a basic module, are contained one within the other and are therefore interrelated. These grids can be used in both the horizontal and vertical planes, thus forming a three-dimensional grid system. If a first preference numerical value is given to M dimensional coordination is established − see next page.

Ref. BS 6750: Specification for modular coordination in building.

Dimensional Coordination ~ the practical aims of this concept are to:

1. Size components so as to avoid the wasteful process of cutting and fitting on site.
2. Obtain maximum economy in the production of components.
3. Reduce the need for the manufacture of special sizes.
4. Increase the effective choice of components by the promotion of interchangeability.

BS 6750 specifies the increments of size for coordinating dimensions of building components thus:

Preference	1st	2nd	3rd	4th
Size (mm)	300	100	50	25

the 3rd and 4th preferences having a maximum of 300 mm

Dimensional Grids – the modular grid network as shown on page 52 defines the space into which dimensionally coordinated components must fit. An important factor is that the component must always be undersized to allow for the joint which is sized by the obtainable degree of tolerance and site assembly:

Controlling Lines, Zones and Controlling Dimensions – these terms can best be defined by example:

FACE GRID   AXIAL GRID

Construction Regulations ~ these are Statutory Instruments made under the Factories Acts of 1937 and 1961. They are now largely superseded by the Health and Safety at Work, etc. Act 1974, but still have relevance to aspects of hazardous work on construction sites. The requirements contained within these documents must therefore be taken into account when planning construction operations and during the actual construction period. Reference should be made to the relevant document for specific requirements but the broad areas covered can be shown thus:

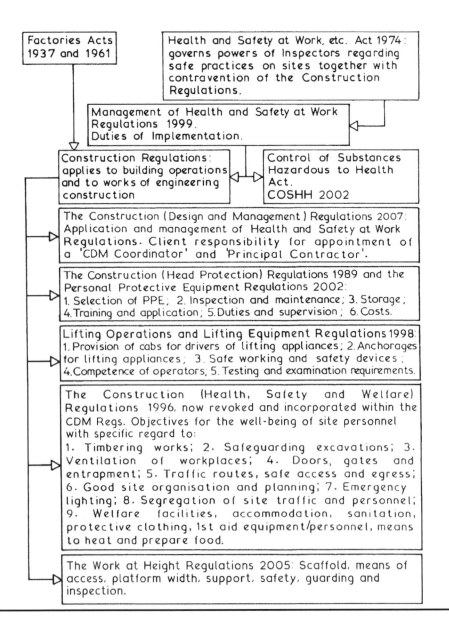

Objective – To create an all-party integrated and planned approach to health and safety throughout the duration of a construction project.

Administering Body – The Health and Safety Executive (HSE).

Scope – The CDM Regulations are intended to embrace all aspects of construction, with the exception of very minor works.

Responsibilities – The CDM Regulations apportion responsibility to everyone involved in a project to cooperate with others and for health and safety issues to all parties involved in the construction process, i.e. client, designer, CDM coordinator and principal contractor.

Client – Appoints a CDM coordinator and the principal contractor. Provides the CDM coordinator with information on health and safety matters and ensures that the principal contractor has prepared an acceptable construction phase plan for the conduct of work. Ensures adequate provision for welfare and that a health and safety file is available.

Designer – Establishes that the client is aware of their duties. Considers the design implications with regard to health and safety issues, including an assessment of any perceived risks. Coordinates the work of the CDM coordinator and other members of the design team.

CDM Coordinator – Ensures that:
• A pre-tender, construction phase plan is prepared.
• The HSE are informed of the work.
• Designers are liaising and conforming with their health and safety obligations.
• A health and safety file is prepared.
• Contractors are of adequate competence with regard to health and safety matters and advises the client and principal contractor accordingly.

Principal Contractor – Develops a construction phase plan, collates relevant information and maintains it as the work proceeds. Administers day-to-day health and safety issues. Cooperates with the CDM coordinator, designers and site operatives preparing risk assessments as required.

Note: Requirements defined under the withdrawn Construction (Health, Safety and Welfare) Regulations are incorporated into the CDM Regulations.

Health and Safety at Work, etc. Act 1974

The Health and Safety
(Safety Signs and Signals)
Regulations 1996

Management of Health and
Safety at Work Regulations
1999 (Management Regulations)

Under these regulations, employers are required to provide and maintain health and safety signs conforming to European Directive 92/58 EEC:

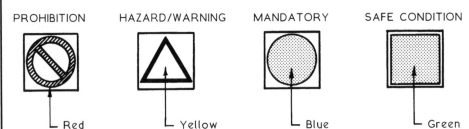

PROHIBITION — Red

HAZARD/WARNING — Yellow

MANDATORY — Blue

SAFE CONDITION — Green

In addition, employers' obligations include the need to provide:

Risk Assessment — provide and maintain safety signs where there is a risk to health and safety, e.g. obstacles. Train staff to comprehend safety signs.

Pictorial Symbols — pictograms alone are acceptable but supplementary text, e.g. FIRE EXIT, is recommended.

Fire/Emergency Escape Signs — A green square or rectangular symbol.

Positioning of signs — primarily for location of fire exits, fire equipment, alarms, assembly points, etc. Not to be located where they could be obscured.

Marking of Hazardous Areas — to identify designated areas for storing dangerous substances: Dangerous Substances (Notification and Marking of Sites) Regulations 1990. Yellow triangular symbol.

Pipeline Identification — pipes conveying dangerous substances to be labelled with a pictogram on a coloured background conforming to BS 1710: Specification for identity of pipelines and services and BS 4800: Schedule of paint colours for building purposes. Non-dangerous substances should also be labelled for easy identification.

Typical Examples on Building Sites ~

PROHIBITION (Red)

| Authorised personnel only | Children must not play on this site | Smoking prohibited | Access not permitted |

HAZARD/WARNING (Yellow)

| Dangerous substance | Flammable liquid | Danger of electric shock | Compressed gas |

MANDATORY (Blue)

| Safety helmets must be worn | Protective footwear must be worn | Use ear protectors | Protective clothing must be worn |

SAFE CONDITIONS (Green)

FIRE EXIT

| Emergency escapes | | Treatment area | Safe area |

Ref. BS ISO 3864-1: Graphical symbols. Safety colours and safety signs. Design principles for safety signs and safety markings.

Control over the way that buildings are constructed originated from attempts to regulate development density in response to demand for more living space as city populations increased. Although there is little surviving documentation to support effective building controls from the time, archived records of London dating from the 12th century do provide some indication that communal issues of convenience and privacy were monitored by the city administration. These included provisions for sanitation, dividing walls and control over encroachment.

Throughout the latter part of the Middle Ages (about 1200 to 1500), regulation in London was haphazard and spontaneous, usually effected on the basis of complaints about building nuisance, whereby the city mayor and aldermen presided over a court hearing. The outcome was determined on the complainant's evidence and expert reports from appointed surveyors. An exception was an overall ban on thatched roofs in London following a serious spread of fire in 1212.

Other densely populated cities established their own means for controlling building work. Fire hazard was the principle criteria and restrictions were applied to limit the ever rising timber framed houses where storeys were built upon existing storeys and extensive jetties of dubious construction overhung the streets below.

The bubonic plague (1665 to 1666) followed by the Great Fire of London (1666) provided an unplanned opportunity to significantly reconsider procedures for new building work. Redevelopment with regard to better living standards and the health and safety of building occupants resulted from the introduction of the London Building Act in 1667. This Act enabled city surveyors to enforce regulations which included:

- Non-combustible material for the main structure, i.e. brick or stone.
- Wall thickness of a minimum specification.
- Limited storey height.
- No projections or jetties over the streets below.
- Minimum street widths to function as fire breaks.

London Building Acts of 1707, 1709, 1764 and 1772 widened control of building development to suburban areas beyond the city boundary. Further provisions prohibited the use of timber for application to decorative cornices and established minimum heights for parapet walls.

London Building Act 1774 ~ known as the *Black Act,* consolidated previous Building Acts as well as determining acceptable construction methods for the whole of London's suburban areas. It remained effective well into the 19th. century, until the introduction of the Metropolitan Building Act of 1844. The main objective of the 1774 Act was to fire proof the exterior of buildings by prohibiting superfluous use of timber ornamentation and other wooden features. An exception was made for timber doors and window frames. These were permitted if recessed at least 4″ (100mm) behind the wall face. The London Building Acts were emulated throughout other provincial towns and cities in the UK. This was mainly in response to outbreaks of fire spreading between cheaply constructed and uncontrolled, overdeveloped timber housing.

Metropolitan Building Act 1844 ~ this extended the area around London covered by building controls. It empowered the appointment of district surveyors to visit building sites and inspect work in progress.

Public Health Act 1848 ~ created municipal *Boards of Health* through local authorities in England and Wales. Mandatory provisions included minumum standards for structural stability, sanitation, light and ventilation and for the prevention of dampness in buildings.

Local Government Act 1858 ~ extended the powers of local authorities to supervise and control building construction through bye-laws. The national government published guidelines known as the *Form of Bye-laws* which were adopted by most local authorities. These permitted LAs to demand deposit of plans and specifications for new building work and substantial alterations to existing buildings.

Public Health Act 1875 ~ consolidated existing building control legislation for England and Wales. Ireland and Scotland passed similar legislation in 1878 and 1897 respectively. The most notable provision was a requirement for installation of damp proof courses in walls.

Thereafter, LAs administered their own interpretation of building control through their bye-laws. This presented problems, as standards varied throughout the UK. It was not until the mid-20th century that some form of unification was introduced.

Public Health Act 1936 ~ this covered all buildings intended for human occupation and was primarily concerned with provisions for drainage and sanitation. Empowered LAs with responsibility for adoption and maintenance of public sewers and drains. Introduced new guidelines in the form of model bye-laws which LAs could enforce.

Model Bye-laws 1952 ~ produced as a means for unifying the standards of building throughout England and Wales. One model for all areas was designed to avoid urban and rural variations in performance standards. Introduced *deemed to satisfy* provisions with reference to established quality benchmarks such as British Standards.

Building (Scotland) Act 1959 ~ enabled Scotland to adopt national building standards which formed the first Building Regulations in the UK. These came into force in 1964.

Public Health Act 1961 ~ statutory unification of building standards that became the forerunner to the first Building Regulations. Proposed replacement of local bye-laws with nationally acceptable regulations. Central government responsibility for establishing minimum building standards administered through the LAs of England and Wales.

Building Regulations 1966 on ~ the first unified regulations made as a statutory instrument. Excluded inner London, Scotland and Ireland. In 1972 amendments and updates were issued as a second edition. In the same year the Building Regulations (Northern Ireland) Order was established as the first regulations for that region. These were modeled closely on the second edition for England and Wales. In 1976, further amendments were consolidated into the third edition, which incorporated Approved Documents as *deemed to satisfy* practice guidelines that could be used to satisfy the regulations.

Building Act 1984 ~ consolidated various other building legislation and redefined the Building Regulations. From 1985 the regulations were based on performance and presented in a simpler format. Previous editions were considered too prescriptive, confusing and inflexible. That year the Building (Inner London) Regulations incorporated most of the 1985 regulations for England and Wales with some limited exceptions. Bye-laws made under the previous London Acts no longer applied. In 2012 Wales determined its own building regulations.

The Building Regulations ~ this is a Statutory Instrument which sets out the minimum performance standards for the design and construction of buildings and where applicable to the extension and alteration of buildings. The regulations are supported by other documents which generally give guidance on how to achieve the required performance standards. The relationship of these and other documents is set out below:

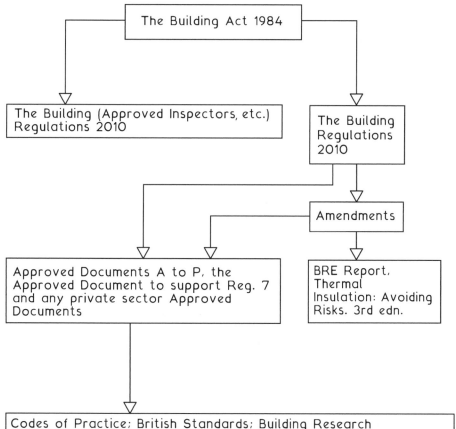

Building Regulations apply throughout the UK. Specific requirements for England, Wales, Scotland and Northen Ireland are administered by their regional governments.

Approved Documents ~ these publications support the Building Regulations. They are prepared by the Department for Communities and Local Government, approved by the Secretary of State and issued by The Stationery Office. The Approved Documents (ADs) have been compiled to give practical guidance to comply with the performance standards set out in the various Regulations. They are not mandatory but show compliance with the requirements of the Building Regulations. If other solutions are used to satisfy the requirements of the Regulations, proving compliance rests with the applicant or designer.

Approved Document A — STRUCTURE

Approved Document B — FIRE SAFETY
Volume 1 — Dwelling houses
Volume 2 — Buildings other than dwelling houses

Approved Document C — SITE PREPARATION AND RESISTANCE
TO CONTAMINANTS AND MOISTURE

Approved Document D — TOXIC SUBSTANCES

Approved Document E — RESISTANCE TO THE PASSAGE OF SOUND

Approved Document F — VENTILATION

Approved Document G — SANITATION, HOT WATER SAFETY
AND WATER EFFICIENCY

Approved Document H — DRAINAGE AND WASTE DISPOSAL

Approved Document J — COMBUSTION APPLIANCES AND FUEL
STORAGE SYSTEMS

Approved Document K — PROTECTION FROM FALLING, COLLISION
AND IMPACT

Approved Document L — CONSERVATION OF FUEL AND POWER
L1A — New dwellings
L1B — Existing dwellings
L2A — New buildings other than dwellings
L2B — Existing buildings other than dwellings

Approved Document M — ACCESS TO AND USE OF BUILDINGS

Approved Document P — ELECTRICAL SAFETY-DWELLINGS

Approved Document to support Regulation 7
MATERIALS AND WORKMANSHIP

Example in the Use of Approved Documents ~

Problem: the sizing of suspended upper floor joists to be spaced at 400mm centres with a clear span of 3·600m for use in a two-storey domestic dwelling.

Building Regulation A1: states that the building shall be constructed so that the combined dead, imposed and wind loads are sustained and transmitted by it to the ground –

(a) safely, and
(b) without causing such deflection or deformation of any part of the building, or such movement of the ground, as will impair the stability of any part of another building.

Approved Document A: guidance on sizing floor joists can be found in 'Span Tables for Solid Timber Members in Dwellings', published by the Timber Research And Development Association (TRADA), and BS EN 1995-1-1: Design of timber structures. General. Common rules and rules for building.

Solution :-

Dead load (kN/m^2) supported by joist excluding mass of joist:

Floor finish — carpet	– 0·03	⎫ weights of
Flooring — 20mm thick particle board	– 0·15	⎬ materials
Ceiling — 9·5mm thick plasterboard	0·08	from BS648
Ceiling finish — 3mm thick plaster	– 0·04	⎭
total dead load —	0·30kN/m^3	

Dead loading is therefore in the 0·25 to 0·50kN/m^2 band
From table on page 776 suitable joist sizes are:- 38 × 200, 50 × 175, 63 ×175 and 75 ×150.

Final choice of section to be used will depend upon cost; availability; practical considerations and/or personal preference.

Building Control ~ unless the applicant has opted for control by a private approved inspector under The Building (Approved Inspectors, etc.) Regulations 2010 the control of building works in the context of the Building Regulations is vested in the Local Authority. There are two systems of control: namely the Building Notice and the Deposit of Plans. The sequence of systems is shown below:

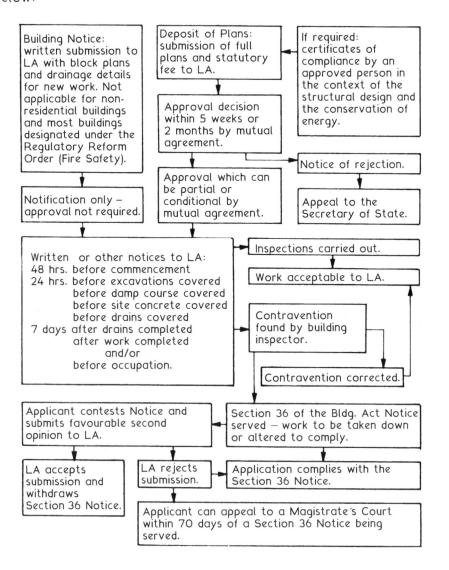

NB. In some stages of the above sequence statutory fees are payable as set out in The Building (Local Authority Charges) Regulations 2010.

Building Regulations Approval ~ required if ''Building Work'' as defined in Regulation 3 of the Building Regulations is proposed. This includes:

• Construction or extension of a building.
• Alterations to an existing building that would bring into effect any of the complying regulations.
• Installing replacement windows where the installer is not known to the local Building Control Authority as being a 'competent' registered installer, e.g. FENSA (**FEN**estration **S**elf-**A**ssessment) scheme.
• Alteration or installation of building services and fittings that bring into effect any of the complying regulations.
• Installation of cavity wall insulation.
• Underpinning of a building's foundations.
• Change of purpose or use of a building.

'Competent' persons are appropriately qualified and experienced to the satisfaction of a relevant scheme organiser. For example, Capita Group's 'Gas Safe Register' of engineers for gas installation and maintenance services. They can 'self-certify' that their work complies with Building Regulations, thereby removing the need for further inspection (see next page).

Local Authority Building Control ~ the established procedure as set out diagrammatically on the preceding page with an application form of the type shown on page 70 and accompanying documents as indicated on page 68.

Private Sector Building Control ~ an alternative, where suitably qualified and experienced inspectors approved by the Local Authority undertake the application approval and site inspections. An 'Initial Notice' from the client and their appointed inspector is lodged with the Local Authority.

Whichever building control procedure is adopted, the methodology is the same, i.e. Deposit of Plans or Building Notice (see page 68).

Refs.: The Building (Approved Inspectors, etc.) Regulations.
    The Association of Consultant Approved Inspectors.

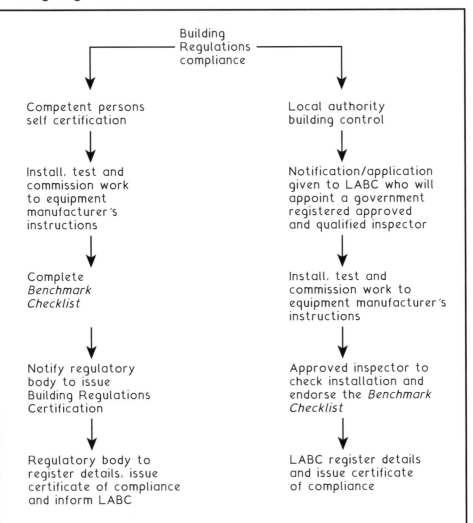

Benchmark Checklist ~ an initiative that places responsibilities on manufacturers and installers to provide equipment of an appropriate standard for the situation. Further requirements are that it is installed, commissioned and serviced to the manufacturer's requirements in accordance with the relevant Building Regulations.

Some Examples of Building Regulations Notification Work Acceptable by Registered Competent Persons ~ air pressure testing, cavity wall insulation, electrical and gas installation, micro-generation installation, renewable technologies and replacement windows.

Local Authority Building Control ~ as described in the previous two pages. A public service administered by borough and unitary councils through their building control departments.

Approved Inspectors ~ a private sector building control alternative as outlined on the preceding page. Approved inspectors may be suitably qualified individuals or corporate bodies employing suitably qualified people, e.g. National House Building Council (NHBC Ltd) and MD Insurance Services Ltd.

Borough councils can contract out the building control process to approved inspectors. Validation and site examinations follow the established format shown on page 64, with approved inspectors substituting for LA.

Both NHBC and MD Insurance publish their own construction rules and standards that supplement the Building Regulations. These form the basis for their own independent quality control procedures whereby their Inspectors will undertake stage and periodic examinations of work in progress to ensure that these standards are adhered to. The objective is to provide new home buyers with a quality assured product warranted against structural defects (10–15 years), provided the house builder has satisfied certain standards for registration. Therefore, the buyer should be provided with a completion certificate indicating Building Regulations approval and a warranty against defects.

Robust Details ~ Building Regulations A.D. E – Resistance to the passage of sound; requires that the separating walls, floors and stairs in new dwellings are sufficiently resistant to airborne and impact sound transmission. Sound measurement tests defined in the associated BSs specified in the Approved Document must be undertaken by an approved inspector/building control official before completion.

An alternative or a means for exemption of pre-completion testing is for the builder to notify the building inspector that sound insulation construction details are registered and specified to those approved by Robust Details Ltd. This is a not-for-profit company established by the house building industry to produce guidance manuals containing details of acceptable sound resistant construction practice.

Deposit of Plans or Full Plans Application ~

· Application form describing the proposed work.
· Location plan, scale not less than 1:2500.
· Block plan, scale not less than 1:1250 showing north point, lines of drains (existing and proposed) and size and species of trees within 30 m.
· Plans, sections and elevations, scale not less than 1:50 (1:100 may be acceptable for elevations).
· Materials specification.
· Structural calculations where appropriate, e.g. load-bearing beams.
· Fee depending on a valuation of work.

The appointed inspector examines the application and, subject to any necessary amendments, an approval is issued. This procedure ensures that work on site is conducted in accordance with the approved plans. Also, where the work is being financed by a loan, the lender will often insist the work is only to a Full Plans approval.

Building Notice ~

· A simplified application form.
· Block plan as described above.
· Construction details, materials specification and structural calculations if considered necessary by the inspector.
· Fee depending on a valuation of work.

This procedure is only really appropriate for minor work, for example, extensions to existing small buildings such as houses. Building control/inspection occurs as each element of the work proceeds. Any Building Regulation contravention will have to be removed or altered to attain an acceptable standard.

Regularisation ~

· Application form.
· Structural calculations if relevant.
· A proportionally higher fee.

Applies to unauthorised work undertaken since November 1985. In effect a retrospective application that will involve a detailed inspection of the work. Rectification may be necessary before approval is granted.

The guidance shown indicates the categories of buildings that do not normally require submission of a Building Notice or Deposit of Plans for approval by the Building Control Section of the Local Authority. However, they may still require planning permission – see page 45

Small detached buildings:-
1. floor area < 15m² not containing sleeping accommodation, or
2. floor area < 30m² not containing sleeping accommodation, and either:
  • constructed substantially from non-combustible materials, or
  • located in excess of 1m from the boundary

greenhouse, unless for commercial use, i.e. retailing, packing or exhibiting

carport*

conservatory*

open sides

porch*

boundary

see note 2 above

* Single storey ground level additions which are not open to the house and are < 30m² floor area, to include carport, covered yard, conservatory and porch.

Notes: 1. a carport must be open on at least two sides.
2. conservatories must have fully glazed laminated or toughened glass, or translucent plastic roofs.
3. glazed doors and windows in a porch or conservatory as defined in Buildings Regulations Approved Document K – see page 458
4. single storey additions should not impede escape from an upper floor window specified for emergency egress. Building Regulations. A.D.: B1 Section 2

BUILDING REGULATIONS APPLICATION

APPLICATION No

Use this form to give notice of intention to erect, extend, or alter a building, install fittings or make a material change of use of the building.	Unless specified differently overleaf, Please return:- • 2 copies of the Form • 4 copies of the Plans • the correct fee

DATE RECEIVED

1. NAME AND ADDRESS OF APPLICANT
Applicant will be invoiced on commencement of work.

_____
_____
_____
_____

Post Code _____

Tel. No. _____

2. NAME AND ADDRESS OF AGENT (If Used)

_____
_____
_____
_____

Post Code _____

Tel. No. _____

3. ADDRESS OR LOCATION OF PROPOSED WORK

_____
_____
_____
_____

4. DESCRIPTION OF PROPOSED WORKS

_____
_____
_____
_____

5. IF NEW BUILDING OR EXTENSION PLEASE STATE PROPOSED USE

_____
_____

6. IF EXISTING BUILDING PLEASE STATE PRESENT USE

_____
_____

7. DRAINAGE

Please state means of:-

Water Supply _____

Foul Water Disposal _____

Storm Water Disposal _____

8. CONDITIONS

Do you consent to the Plans being passed subject to conditions where appropriate?   Yes ☐   No ☐

Do you agree to an extension of time if this is required by the Council?   Yes ☐   No ☐

9. COMPLETION CERTIFICATE

Do you wish the Council to issue a Completion Certificate upon satisfactory completion of the work?

Yes ☐   No ☐

10. REGULATORY REFORM ORDER (Fire Safety) 2005

Is the building intended for any other purpose than occupation as a domestic living unit by one family group?

Yes ☐   No ☐

11. FEE

Please state estimated cost of the work (at current market value) £.......................... Amount of Fee submitted £......................

Has Planning Permission been sought?   Yes ☐   No ☐   If Yes, please give Application No _____

12. PLEASE SIGN AND DATE THIS FORM BEFORE SUBMITTING

I/We hereby give notice of intention to carry out the work set out above and deposit the attached drawings and documents in accordance with the requirements of Regulations 11 (1) (b). Also enclosed is the appropriate Plan Fee and I understand that a further Fee will be payable when the first inspection of work on site is made by the Local Authority.

Signed _____ Date _____ On behalf of (if agent) _____

Purpose ~ to provide a checklist that assists designers and builders to attain performance standards that will satisfy the energy efficiency requirements of Part L to the Building Regulations. Also, to provide a measure against which the building control inspectorate can ensure conformity.

Documentation ~ a UK Department for Communities and Local Government (DCLG) publication. This contains a series of construction details that are applied to five different building techniques. The fully detailed illustrations are for relatively light construction appropriate to dwellings. The details and supplementary support notes concentrate on continuity of thermal insulation with a regard for thermal (cold) bridging and on quality of construction to maintain airtightness.

Publication sections and details ~

Section 1: Introduction relating mainly to continuity of insulation and airtightness.

Section 2: Detailed drawings and checklists for constructing the external envelope.

The five types of construction are:
· Externally insulated masonry solid walls.
· Part and fully filled cavity insulated masonry walls.
· Internally insulated masonry walls.
· Timber framed walls.
· Lightweight steel framed walls.

Note: All five construction practice details include the critical areas of junctions and interfaces between wall and roof, ground and intermediate floors. Treatment at door and window openings is also included with specific applications where appropriate.

Refs.:
The Building Regulations 2010 and associated Approved Document L: Conservation of Fuel and Power.
Accredited Construction Details, Communities and Local Government publications.

Published ~ 2006 by the Department for Communities and Local Government (DCLG) in response to the damaging effects of climate change. The code promotes awareness and need for new energy conservation initiatives in the design of new dwellings.

Objective ~ to significantly reduce the 27% of UK CO_2 emissions that are produced by 25 million homes. This is to be a gradual process, with the target of reducing CO_2 and other greenhouse gas emissions from all UK sources by 80% by 2050 relative to 1990 levels. Interim objectives are 28% by 2017, 34% by 2022 and 50% by 2027.

Sustainability ~ measured in terms of a quality standard designed to provide new homes with a factor of environmental performance. This measure is applied primarily to categories of thermal energy, use of water, material resources, surface water run-off and management of waste.

Measurement ~ a 'green' star rating that indicates environmental performance ranging from one to six stars. Shown below is the star rating criteria applied specifically to use of thermal energy. A home with a six star rating is also regarded as a Zero Carbon Home.

Proposed Progression ~

Percentage Improvement compared with A.D. L 2006	Year	Code level star rating
10	-	1
18	-	2
25	2010	3
44	2013	4
100	2016	5 and 6

Zero Carbon Home ~ zero net emissions of CO_2 from all energy use in the home. This incorporates insulation of the building fabric, heating equipment, hot water systems, cooling, washing appliances, lighting and other electrical/electronic facilities. Net zero emissions can be measured by comparing the carbon emissions produced in consuming on- or off-site fossil fuel energy use in the home, with the amount of on-site renewable energy produced. Means for producing low or zero carbon energy include micro combined heat and power units, photovoltaic (solar) panels, wind generators and ground energy heat pumps (see Building Services Handbook).

British Standards ~ these are publications issued by the British Standards Institution which give recommended minimum standards for materials, components, design and construction practices. These recommendations are not legally enforceable but some of the Building Regulations refer directly to specific British Standards and accept them as deemed to satisfy provisions. All materials and components complying with a particular British Standard are marked with the British Standards kitemark thus: together with the appropriate BS number.

This symbol assures the user that the product so marked has been produced and tested in accordance with the recommendations set out in that specific standard. Full details of BS products and services can be obtained from Customer Services, BSI, 389 Chiswick High Road, London W4 4AL. Standards applicable to building may be purchased individually or in modules for General Construction, Materials, Health and Safety, Project and Design, Interior and Utility and Eurocodes. British Standards are constantly under review and are amended, revised and rewritten as necessary; therefore a check should always be made to ensure that any standard being used is the current issue. There are over 1500 British Standards which are directly related to the construction industry and these are prepared in five formats:

1. British Standards – these give recommendations for the minimum standard of quality and testing for materials and components. Each standard number is prefixed BS.

2. Codes of Practice – these give recommendations for good practice relative to design, manufacture, construction, installation and maintenance with the main objectives of safety, quality, economy and fitness for the intended purpose. Each code of practice number is prefixed CP or BS.

3. Draft for Development – these are issued instead of a British Standard or Code of Practice when there is insufficient data or information to make firm or positive recommendations. Each draft number is prefixed DD. Sometimes given a BS number and suffixed DC, i.e. Draft for public Comment.

4. Published Document – these are publications which cannot be placed into any one of the above categories. Each published document is numbered and prefixed PD.

5. Publicly Available Specification - client sponsored standards produced to BSI guidelines. Reviewed after two years to determine whether they should become established as a BS. Prefixed PAS.

European Standards – since joining the European Union (EU), trade and tariff barriers have been lifted. This has opened up the market for manufacturers of construction-related products, from all EU and European Economic Area (EEA) member states. Before 2004, the EU was composed of 15 countries: Austria, Belgium, Denmark, Finland, France, Germany, Greece, Ireland, Italy, Luxemburg, Netherlands, Portugal, Spain, Sweden and the United Kingdom. It now includes Bulgaria, Cyprus, the Czech Republic, Estonia, Hungary, Latvia, Lithuania, Malta, Poland, Romania, Slovakia, Slovenia, Iceland, Liechtenstein and Norway. Nevertheless, the wider market is not so easily satisfied, as regional variations exist. This can create difficulties where product dimensions and performance standards differ. For example, thermal insulation standards for masonry walls in Mediterranean regions need not be the same as those in the UK. Also, preferred dimensions differ across Europe in items such as bricks, timber, tiles and pipes.

European Standards are prepared under the auspices of Comité Européen de Normalisation (CEN), of which the BSI is a member. European Standards that the BSI have not recognised or adopted are prefixed EN. These are EuroNorms and will need revision for national acceptance.

For the time being, British Standards will continue and, where similarity with other countries' standards and ENs can be identified, they will run side by side until harmonisation is complete and approved by CEN.

e.g. BS EN 295 complements the previous national standard:
    BS 65 – Vitrefied clay pipes . . . for drains and sewers.

European Pre-standards are similar to BS Drafts for Development. These are known as ENVs.

Some products which satisfy the European requirements for safety, durability and energy efficiency carry the CE mark. This is not to be assumed as a mark of performance and is not intended to show equivalence to the BS kitemark. However, the BSI is recognised as a Notified Body by the EU and as such is authorised to provide testing and certification in support of the CE mark.

International Standards – these are prepared by the International Organisation for Standardisation and are prefixed ISO. Many are compatible with, complement and have superseded BSs, e.g. ISO 9001 Quality Management Systems and BS 5750: Quality Systems.

For manufacturers' products to be compatible and uniformly acceptable in the European market, there exists a process for harmonising technical specifications. These specifications are known as harmonised European product standards (hENs), produced and administered by the Comité Européen de Normalisation (CEN). European Technical Approvals (ETAs) are also acceptable where issued by the European Organisation for Technical Approvals (EOTA).

CPR harmonises the following compliance requirements:
· Energy economy and heat retention.
· Hygiene, health and environment.
· Mechanical resistance and stability.
· Protection against noise.
· Safety and accessibility in use.
· Safety in case of fire.
· Sustainable use of natural resources.

Member states of the European Economic Area (EEA) are legally required to ensure their construction products satisfy the above basic criteria.

UK attestation accredited bodies include: BBA, BRE and BSI.

CE mark – a marking or labelling for conforming products. A 'passport' permitting a product to be legally marketed in any EEA. It is not a quality mark, e.g. BS kitemark, but where appropriate this may appear with the CE marking.

CE marking – reproduced with kind permission of Rockwool Ltd.

Building Research Establishment ~ The BRE was founded as a UK Government agency in 1921. It was known initially as the Building Research Department and thereafter until the early 1970s as the Building Research Station.

In addition to UK Government funding, some financial support is now provided by the European Union. Additional funding is derived from a variety of sources, including commercial services for private industry and from publications. The latter includes the BRE's well-known regular issue of research information products, i.e. Digests, Information Papers, Good Building Guides and Good Repair Guides.

UK Government support is principally through the Department for Business Enterprise and Regulatory Reform (BERR) and the Department for Communities and Local Government (DCLG). The DCLG works with the BRE in formulating specific aspects of the Approved Documents to the Building Regulations. Commissioned research is funded by the BRE Trust.

The BRE incorporates and works with other specialised research and material testing organisations, e.g. see LPCB, below. It is accredited under the United Kingdom Accreditation Service (UKAS) as a testing laboratory authorised to issue approvals and certifications such as CE product marking (see pages 75 and 76). Certification of products, materials and applications is effected through BRE Certification Ltd.

Loss Prevention Certification Board (LPCB) ~ The origins of this organisation date back to the latter part of the 19th century, when it was established by a group of building insurers as the Fire Offices' Committee (FOC).

Through a subdivision known as the Loss Prevention Council (LPC), the FOC produced a number of technical papers and specifications relating to standards of building construction and fire control installations. These became the industry standards that were, and continue to be, frequently used by building insurers as supplementary to local bye-laws and latterly the Building Regulation Approved Documents.

In the late 1980s the LPC was renamed the LPCB as a result of reorganisation within the insurance profession. At this time the former LPC guidance documents became established in the current format of Loss Prevention Standards.

In 2000 the LCPB became part of the BRE and now publishes its Standards under BRE Certification Ltd.

British Board of Agrément (BBA) ~ an approvals authority established in 1966, known then as the Agrément Board. It was based on the French Government's system of product approval. In 1982 it was renamed. Accredited by UKAS and a UK representative in EOTA.

The BBA's UK premises are at the BRE in Garston, near Watford, a convenient location for access to the BRE's research and testing facilities. It is an independent organisation with the purpose of impartially assessing materials, systems, practices, new market products and existing products being used in a new or innovative way. The objective is to evaluate these where an existing British Standard, Eurostandard or similar quality benchmark does not exist. Agrément certification is a quality assurance standard for products and innovations not covered by a CE mark and/or a BS kitemark. Once established, an agrément certificate may be used to attain CE marking or for development into a new BS.

Agrément certificates are only issued after rigorous testing and critical analysis criteria are satisfied, relative to intended application and fitness for purpose. Where new materials, products, components, installation processes and installations are proposed, an agrément certificate may be regarded as sufficiently authoritative for proof of Building Regulations compliance.

The Construction Industry Research and Information Association (CIRIA) ~ established in 1960 as the Civil Engineering Research Council (CERC) with the objective of financing research with money raised from industry. In 1967 it was renamed, thereafter as a non-profit making company owned by other companies, universities, government departments and various other public sector organisations. All subscriptions and fee income is invested into seminars, training and research.

Main areas of activity:
- Research – industry wide covering construction and the environment.
- Publications – a catalogue of over 600 titles.
- Training – short courses, seminars and conferences.
- Networks – support processes at training events, seminars and workshops.
- Information services – newsletters, bulletins and a biannual magazine.

CI/SfB System ~ a coded filing system for the classification and storing of building information and data. It was created in Sweden under the title of Samarbetskommittën för Byggnadsfragor and was introduced into this country in 1961 by the RIBA. In 1968 the CI (Construction Index) was added to the system which is used nationally and recognised throughout the construction industry. The system consists of five sections called tables which are subdivided by a series of letters or numbers and these are listed in the CI/SfB index book to which reference should always be made in the first instance to enable an item to be correctly filed or retrieved.

Table 0 – Physical Environment

This table contains ten sections 0 to 9 and deals mainly with the end product (i.e. the type of building.) Each section can be further subdivided (e.g. 21, 22, etc.) as required.

Table 1 – Elements

This table contains ten sections numbered (--) to (9-) and covers all parts of the structure such as walls, floors and services. Each section can be further subdivided (e.g. 31, 32, etc.) as required.

Table 2 – Construction Form

This table contains 25 sections lettered A to Z (O being omitted) and covers construction forms such as excavation work, blockwork, cast in-situ work etc., and is not subdivided but used in conjunction with Table 3.

Table 3 – Materials

This table contains 25 sections lettered a to z (l being omitted) and covers the actual materials used in the construction form such as metal, timber, glass, etc., and can be subdivided (e.g. n1, n2, etc.) as required.

Table 4 – Activities and Requirements

This table contains 25 sections lettered (A) to (Z), (O being omitted) and covers anything which results from the building process such as shape, heat, sound, etc. Each section can be further subdivided ((M1), (M2) etc.) as required.

CPI System of Coding ~ the Coordinated Project Information initiative originated in the 1970s in response to the need to establish a common arrangement of document and language communication, across the varied trades and professions of the construction industry. From this evolved the Common Arrangement of Work Sections (CAWS) first published in 1987. Since then it has been effectively used with the publication of the Standard Method of Measurement 7th edition (SMM 7), the National Building Specification (NBS) and the Drawings Code. (Note: The NBS is also produced in CI/SfB format.) Later editions of CAWS are aligned with Uniclass.

The arrangement in all documents is a coordination of alphabetic sections, corresponding to elements of work, the purpose being to avoid mistakes, omissions and other errors which have in the past occurred between drawings, specification and bill of quantities descriptions.

The coding is a combination of letters and numbers, spanning three levels:

Level 1 has 24 headings from A to Z (omitting I and O). Each heading relates to part of the construction process, such as groundwork (D), Joinery (L), surface finishes (M), etc.

Level 2 is a subheading, which in turn is subgrouped numerically into different categories. So, for example, Surface Finishes is sub-headed; Plaster, Screeds, Painting, etc. These subheadings are then extended further, thus Plaster becomes; Plastered/Rendered Coatings, Insulated Finishes, Sprayed Coatings, etc.

Level 3 is the work section subgrouped from level 2, to include a summary of inclusions and omissions.

As an example, an item of work coded M21 signifies:

> M – Surface finishes
> 2 – Plastered coatings
> 1 – Insulation with rendered finish

The coding may be used to:
(a) simplify specification writing
(b) reduce annotation on drawings
(c) rationalise traditional taking-off methods

Uniclass ~ the Unified Classification for the Construction Industry was created in the 1990s by the Construction Project Information Committee (CPIC) [see below] and first published by the RIBA in 1997.

Purpose ~ to organise product literature and project information into a structured library format. It incorporates the Common Arrangement of Work Sections (CAWS) and the Electronic Product Information Cooperation (EPIC) system of structuring product literature and information.

Composition ~ comprises 15 tables (coded A to Q, I and O omitted), each table an independent classification of specific information that can be used solely or in combination with other table references where subject matter is complex or diverse.

EPIC ~ an established European coding system for technical product literature and information. Widely used across continental Europe but less so in the UK. Favoured by some product manufacturers in their presentation of data to architects and engineers.

Product literature label showing CI/SfB, Uniclass and EPIC notation ~

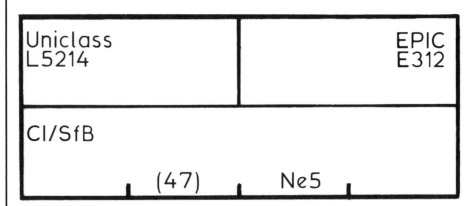

CPIC members ~
Construction Confederation (CC).
Royal Institute of British Architects (RIBA).
Chartered Institute of Architectural Technologists (CIAT).
Chartered Institution of Building Services Engineers (CIBSE).
Royal Institution of Chartered Surveyors (RICS).
Institution of Civil Engineers (ICE).

BIM ~ terminology specific to the construction industry as a summary description for collating, organising and managing technical information and project data.

Development and Background ~ information modelling is not new in concept. The practice of creating and maintaining libraries of readily accessible, searchable and transferable building information has produced several orderly and systematic arrangements. Not least the established coding systems outlined on the preceding three pages; namely, CI/SfB, CPI (incorporating CAWS, NBS and SMM7) and Uniclass. As independent systems these have their limitations. Certain parts are becoming oversubscribed as new technologies and processes evolve. The CI/SfB alpha-numeric mix of letters, numbers and brackets is not entirely compatible with digital formatting. Used in combination, there is cross correlation and common identification of some coded classifications, but there remains an element of variation and disparity. Unification of data formatting and presentation is an objective that BIM seeks to address to simplify information transfer between projects and more widely across the industry.

Structured data can be presented within three categories:

- Building Information Modelling ~ as outlined above, a business information process providing access for all involved with a construction project from client through design, assembly and after care.

- Building Information Model ~ digital representation of the business process that provides structured data management to include schedules and reports in spreadsheet format for the various stages of a project's development.

- Building Information Management ~ the organisation and administrative strategy for control of a project using data from the building information model. A communication process that applies from initial concept and inception of a building, throughout the construction process and with regard to the long term maintenance and intended life span of a completed asset.

Project information and data classification systems:

BPIC ~ Building Project Information Committee, formed in 1987. Produced the Common Arrangement of Work Sections (CAWS) as a simplified specification and referencing system. Renamed CPIC, Construction Project Information Committee in the mid 90s. In 1997 introduced Uniclass as a structured product literature and information classification.

BS ISO 12006-2: (Building construction. Organisation of information about construction works. Framework for classification of information) ~ guidance on information exchange, data organisation and classification systems.

CAWS ~ a letter and number (alpha-numeric) coded notation of work sections, groups and sub-groups produced primarily to coordinate entries in specifications and bills of quantities. Compatible with SMM7, NBS and NES. See page 79.

CI/SfB ~ introduced to the UK in 1961 with revisions in 1968 and 1976. The forerunner to subsequent indexing systems, it has gained wide acceptance across the construction industry. Now functions mainly as library referencing of product literature. Its bracketed combinations of letters and numbers limit its application to digital technology. See page 78.

COBie ~ Construction Operations Building information exchange. A shared data standard management system applied to the intended life span of a building. It provides a spreadsheet source of data based on reports and models relating to existing completed projects. From this data storage facility, structured information can be transferred and used for planning and managing subsequent similar building types.

EPIC ~ Electronic Product Information Cooperation. Popular across continental Europe as a coding system for manufacturers' product literature. Used by some UK architectural and engineering practices as a basis for data presentation. See page 80.

continued . . . . .

NBS ~ National Building Specification, the UK national standard specification for building work. Part of RIBA Enterprises Ltd. NBS also have other information resource products including the Construction Information Service (CIS) produced jointly with IHS, Information Handling Services.

NBS Create ~ a data standard for documenting and sharing structured information based on existing work schedules and manufacturers' product details. Links NBS to building information modelling.

NBS National BIM Library ~ an information resource covering all aspects of the building fabric and elements of construction. The content of the library is based on ". . . . . proprietory and pre-configured generic objects . . . . .".

NES ~ National Engineering Specification for building services projects. Standard, concise specifications endorsed by CIBSE, Chartered Institution of Building Services Engineers and BSRIA, Building Services Research and Information Association.

RIBA Plan of Work ~ established in 1964 by the Royal Institute of British Architects as a methodical procedure for the design team to apply to building projects. Its `work stages' and `key tasks' have become universally accepted by the other building professions as a planning model, as guidance for progressing projects and for processing contract procurement. Subsequent revisions, notably in 1998, 2007 and 2011 have retained its relevance.

SMM ~ Standard Method of Measurement, originated in 1922 with several revisions since then. It is used mainly by quantity surveyors as a model for producing bills of quantities for builders' estimators to price when tendering for work. The SMM's rules for measurement are used throughout the world. In current format it is written to comply with CPI guidance (see page 79). Maintained by the RICS, Royal Institution of Chartered Surveyors.

Uniclass ~ first produced in 1997 and subsequently revised, provides a tabulated system of classifications that represent project information and product literature. Incorporates CAWS and EPIC. See page 80.

Notes

2 SITE WORKS

PROPOSED FIVE-STOREY BLOCK   PROPOSED GARAGES

PAVED AREA

PAVED AREA

ROADWAY

ROADWAY

EXISTING   TREES

SITE MEASUREMENT
SITE INVESTIGATIONS
SOIL INVESTIGATION
SOIL ASSESSMENT AND TESTING
SITE LAYOUT CONSIDERATIONS
SITE SECURITY
SITE LIGHTING AND ELECTRICAL SUPPLY
SITE OFFICE ACCOMMODATION
SITE HEALTH AND WELFARE PROVISION
MATERIALS STORAGE
MATERIALS TESTING
TIMBER DECAY AND TREATMENT
PROTECTION ORDERS FOR TREES AND SHRUBS
LOCATING PUBLIC UTILITY SERVICES
SETTING OUT
LEVELS AND ANGLES
ROAD CONSTRUCTION
TUBULAR SCAFFOLDING AND SCAFFOLDING SYSTEMS
SHORING SYSTEMS
DEMOLITION

Site Analysis – prior to purchasing a building site it is essential to conduct a thorough survey to ascertain whether the site characteristics suit the development concept. The following guidance forms a basic checklist:

* Refer to Ordnance Survey maps to determine adjacent features, location, roads, facilities, footpaths and rights of way.

* Conduct a measurement survey to establish site dimensions and levels.

* Observe surface characteristics, i.e. trees, steep slopes, existing buildings, rock outcrops, wells.

* Inquire of local authority whether preservation orders affect the site and if it forms part of a conservation area.

* Investigate subsoil. Use trial holes and borings to determine soil quality and water table level.

* Consider flood potential, possibilities for drainage of water table, capping of springs, filling of ponds, diversion of streams and rivers.

* Consult local utilities providers for underground and overhead services, proximity to site and whether they cross the site.

* Note suspicious factors such as filled ground, cracks in the ground, subsidence due to mining and any cracks in existing buildings.

* Regard neighbourhood scale and character of buildings with respect to proposed new development.

* Decide on best location for building (if space permits) with regard to 'cut and fill', land slope, exposure to sun and prevailing conditions, practical use and access.

See also desk and field studies on page 91.

Irregular plan surface areas ~ these are typical of many building sites, with odd-shaped boundaries and directional changes.

Methods for measurement ~ modern instruments and computational techniques, including photogrammetry, can provide accurate calculation of site areas. Traverse data coordinates from theodolite readings can also be used. Fieldwork measurements and simple calculations are an adequate and economic means for obtaining reasonable area estimates for most modest size sites. These can be undertaken from scaled maps or preferably from a scaled drawing of the area following a measured survey.

Estimates based on scaled site drawings ~

· Gridded tracing paper superimposed over the plotted area and the number of squares counted.

E.g. If each square scaled is 10 m × 10 m (100 m²), the approximate site area is:

  8 full squares at 100 m² = 800 m²
  3.5 squares made up of proportional squares = 350 m²
  Total area is approximately 800 m² + 350 m² = 1150 m²

· Give and take for irregular boundaries.

Thomas Simpson (1710–1761) ~ a British mathematician who derived interpolation and numerical methods of integration for calculation of areas under curves.

Simpson's rule ~

$$A = w \left[(h_1 + h_7) + 4(h_2 + h_4 + h_6) + 2(h_3 + h_5)\right] \div 3$$

Where: A = estimate of site area (m²)
w = width or equal distances between ordinates (m)
h = height or length of parallel ordinates (m)

Note: requires an odd number of ordinates and an even number of areas.

E.g.

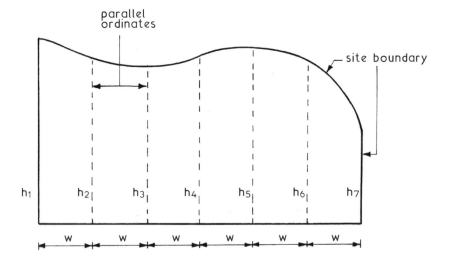

If, h_1 = 40 m, h_2 = 36 m, h_3 = 34 m, h_4 = 34 m, h_5 = 38 m, h_6 = 36 m, and h_7 = 20 m. w = 12 m.

A = 12 [(40 + 20) + 4(36 + 36 + 36) + 2(34 + 38)] ÷ 3
A = 12 [60 + 432 + 144] ÷ 3
A = 12 × 636 ÷ 3
A = 2544 m²

Note: An area 100 m × 100 m (10,000 m²) = 1 hectare (1ha).

In the above calculation, 2544 m² = 0.2544 ha.

In imperial measurement there are approximately 2.5 (2.471) acres to 1ha. Therefore 0.2544 ha = 0.6286 acres.

Method ~ a little less accurate than Simpson's rule as it does not assume a curved boundary, but it is adequate in most situations for providing a reasonable estimate of site area. As with Simpson's rule, the site plan area is divided into several parallel strips of equal width (w).

E.g.

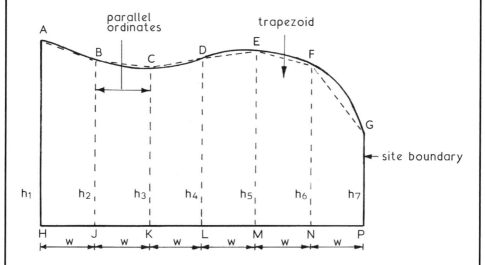

Area of trapezoid ABHJ = $[(h_1 + h_2) \div 2] \times w$
Area of trapezoid BCJK = $[(h_2 + h_3) \div 2] \times w$
   and so on until:
Area of trapezoid FGNP = $[(h_6 + h_7) \div 2] \times w$

Therefore the total plot area (A) will be the sum of the trapezoids expressed as:

$$A = w \{[(h_1 + h_7) \div 2] + h_2 + h_3 + h_4 + h_5 + h_6\}$$

E.g. Using the site dimensions from the previous page:

$$A = 12 \{[(40 + 20) \div 2] + 36 + 34 + 36 + 38 + 36\}$$
$$A = 12 \{30 + 36 + 34 + 36 + 38 + 36\}$$
$$A = 12 \times 210$$
$$A = 2520\,m^2$$

A fair comparison with the same area calculation of $2544\,m^2$ using Simpson's rule on the previous page. Greater accuracy can be achieved by reducing the ordinate widths (w).

Site Investigation For New Works ~ the basic objective of this form of site investigation is to collect systematically and record all the necessary data which will be needed or will help in the design and construction processes of the proposed work. The collected data should be presented in the form of fully annotated and dimensioned plans and sections. Anything on adjacent sites which may affect the proposed works or conversely anything appertaining to the proposed works which may affect an adjacent site should also be recorded.

Typical Data Required ~

boundary hedges and /or fencing

existing trees – type, girth, spread and height

orientation

property boundary lines and location of site

trees and buildings on adjacent site

existing buildings

details of above-ground obstructions such as transmisson lines

62·85
+
spot levels

contour lines

63·00

full data as to type, size, depth and location of all services such as gas, water, drains, electricity, telephone and relay services

planning or similar restrictions on proposed building or structure

subsoil investigation data of soil types and properties together with ground water conditions

62·57

Bench-marks and OS levels

existing sewers

to Oldtown   A 3214   to Newtown

Procedures ~

1. Desk study
2. Field study or walk-over survey
3. Laboratory analysis (see pages 100-101 and 106-111)

Desk Study ~ collection of known data, to include:

· Ordnance Survey maps - historical and modern, note grid reference.
· Geological maps - subsoil types, radon risk.
· Site history - green-field/brown-field.
· Previous planning applications/approvals.
· Current planning applications in the area.
· Development restrictions - conservation orders.
· Utilities - location of services on and near the site.
· Aerial photographs.
· Ecology factors - protected wildlife.
· Local knowledge - anecdotal information/rights of way.
· Proximity of local land-fill sites - methane risk.

Field Study ~ intrusive visual and physical activity to:

· Establish site characteristics from the desk study.
· Assess potential hazards to health and safety.
· Appraise surface conditions:
  * Trees - preservation orders.
  * Topography and geomorphological mapping.
· Appraise ground conditions:
  * Water table.
  * Flood potential - local water courses and springs.
  * Soil types.
  * Contamination - vegetation die-back.
  * Engineering risks - ground subsidence, mining, old fuel tanks.
  * Financial risks - potential for the unforeseen.
· Take subsoil samples and conduct in-situ tests.
· Consider the need for subsoil exploration, trial pits and boreholes.
· Appraise existing structures:
  * Potential for reuse/refurbishment.
  * Archaeological value/preservation orders.
  * Demolition - costs, health issues (e.g. asbestos).

Purpose ~ primarily to obtain subsoil samples for identification, classification and ascertaining the subsoil's characteristics and properties. Trial pits and augered holes may also be used to establish the presence of any geological faults and the upper or lower limits of the water table.

Typical Details ~

minimum plan size to provide access for operatives 1·200 x 1·200

maximum economic depth 4·000

formed by hand or mechanical means of excavation

TRIAL PITS

diameter range 50 to 150 mm

maximum economic depth 6·000

formed with hand operated post hole auger or bucket auger

HAND AUGER HOLES

General use ~

dry ground which requires little or no temporary support to sides of excavation.

Subsidiary use~
to expose and/or locate underground services.

Advantages ~
subsoil can be visually examined in-situ – both disturbed and undistrubed samples can be obtained.

General use ~

dry ground but liner tubes could be used if required to extract subsoil samples at a depth beyond the economic limit of trial holes.

Advantages ~
generally a cheaper and simpler method of obtaining subsoil samples than the trial pit method.

Trial pits and holes should be sited so that the subsoil samples will be representative but not interfering with works.

Site Investigation ~ this is an all-embracing term covering every aspect of the site under investigation.

Soil Investigation ~ specifically related to the subsoil beneath the site under investigation and could be part of or separate from the site investigation.

Purpose of Soil Investigation ~

1. Determine the suitability of the site for the proposed project.
2. Determine an adequate and economic foundation design.
3. Determine the difficulties which may arise during the construction process and period.
4. Determine the occurrence and/or cause of all changes in subsoil conditions.

The above purposes can usually be assessed by establishing the physical, chemical and general characteristics of the subsoil by obtaining subsoil samples which should be taken from positions on the site which are truly representative of the area but are not taken from the actual position of the proposed foundations. A series of samples extracted at the intersection points of a 20·000 square grid pattern should be adequate for most cases.

Soil Samples ~ these can be obtained as disturbed or as undisturbed samples.

Disturbed Soil Samples ~ these are soil samples obtained from boreholes and trial pits. The method of extraction disturbs the natural structure of the subsoil but such samples are suitable for visual grading, establishing the moisture content and some laboratory tests. Disturbed soil samples should be stored in labelled airtight jars.

Undisturbed Soil Samples ~ these are soil samples obtained using coring tools which preserve the natural structure and properties of the subsoil. The extracted undisturbed soil samples are labelled and laid in wooden boxes for dispatch to a laboratory for testing. This method of obtaining soil samples is suitable for rock and clay subsoils but difficulties can be experienced in trying to obtain undisturbed soil samples in other types of subsoil.

The test results of soil samples are usually shown on a drawing which gives the location of each sample and the test results in the form of a hatched legend or section.

Ref. BS EN 1997-2: Geotechnical design. Ground investigation and testing.

Soil Investigation

Depth of Soil Investigation ~ before determining the actual method of obtaining the required subsoil samples the depth to which the soil investigation should be carried out must be established. This is usually based on the following factors:

1. Proposed foundation type.
2. Pressure bulb of proposed foundation.
3. Relationship of proposed foundation to other foundations.

Typical Examples ~

Pressure bulbs of less than 20% of original loading at foundation level can be ignored – this applies to all foundation types.

NB. For further examples see next page.

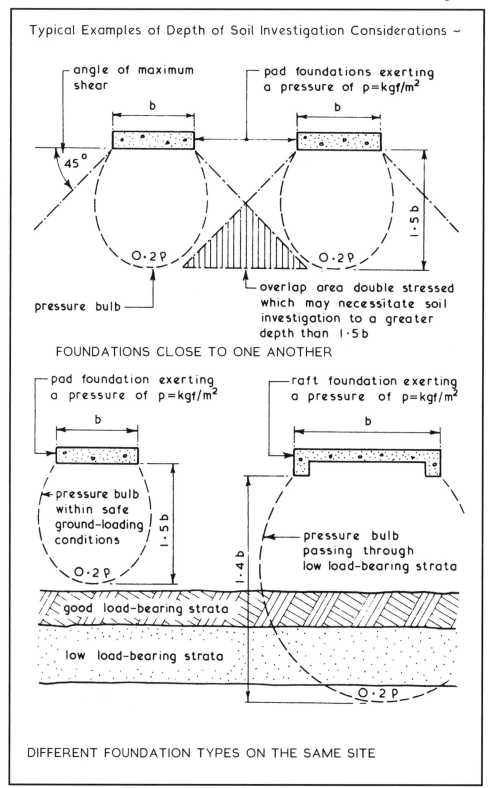

Typical Examples of Depth of Soil Investigation Considerations ~

angle of maximum shear

pad foundations exerting a pressure of $p=kgf/m^2$

b

$45°$

b

$1·5 b$

$0·2p$

$0·2p$

overlap area double stressed which may necessitate soil investigation to a greater depth than $1·5b$

pressure bulb

FOUNDATIONS CLOSE TO ONE ANOTHER

pad foundation exerting a pressure of $p=kgf/m^2$

raft foundation exerting a pressure of $p=kgf/m^2$

b

b

pressure bulb within safe ground-loading conditions

$1·5 b$

$1·4 b$

pressure bulb passing through low load-bearing strata

$0·2p$

good load-bearing strata

low load-bearing strata

$0·2p$

DIFFERENT FOUNDATION TYPES ON THE SAME SITE

Soil Investigation Methods ~ method chosen will depend on several factors:

1. Size of contract.
2. Type of proposed foundation.
3. Type of sample required.
4. Types of subsoils which may be encountered.

As a general guide the most suitable methods in terms of investigation depth are:

1. Foundations up to   3·000   deep – trial pits.
2. Foundations up to 30·000   deep – borings.
3. Foundations over 30·000   deep – deep   borings   and   in-situ examinations from tunnels and/or deep pits.

Typical Trial Pit Details ~

disturbed samples taken from spoil removed to form trial pit

trial pit excavated by hand or using small mechanical excavator

1·200   1·200

maximum economic depth   4·000

visual examination possible from within excavated trial pit

undisturbed soil samples can be taken from any position within excavated trial pit

NB. in wet subsoils the need for timbering to the sides of the trial pit and the need for a pump may outweigh any advantages.

NB. For details of other soil investigation methods see the next two pages.

Boring Methods to Obtain Disturbed Soil Samples:

1. Hand or Mechanical Auger – suitable for depths up to 3·000 using a 150 or 200 mm diameter flight auger.
2. Mechanical Auger – suitable for depths over 3·000 using a flight or Cheshire auger – a liner or casing is required for most granular soils and may be required for other types of subsoil.
3. Sampling Shells – suitable for shallow to medium depth borings in all subsoils except rock.

Typical Details ~

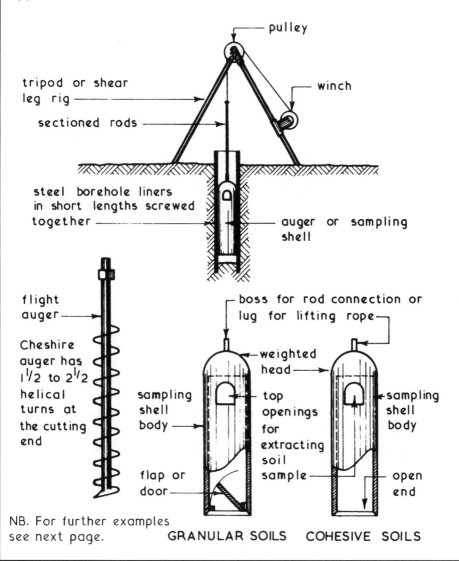

pulley

tripod or shear leg rig

sectioned rods

winch

steel borehole liners in short lengths screwed together

auger or sampling shell

flight auger

Cheshire auger has 1½ to 2½ helical turns at the cutting end

boss for rod connection or lug for lifting rope

weighted head

sampling shell body

top openings for extracting soil sample

sampling shell body

flap or door

open end

NB. For further examples see next page.

GRANULAR SOILS   COHESIVE SOILS

Wash Boring ~ this is a method of removing loosened soil from a borehole using a strong jet of water or bentonite which is a controlled mixture of fullers earth and water. The jetting tube is worked up and down inside the borehole, the jetting liquid disintegrates the subsoil which is carried in suspension up the annular space to a settling tank. The settled subsoil particles can be dried for testing and classification. This method has the advantage of producing subsoil samples which have not been disturbed by the impact of sampling shells; however, it is not suitable for large gravel subsoils or subsoils which contain boulders.

Typical Wash Boring Arrangement ~

Mud-rotary Drilling ~ this is a method which can be used for rock investigations where bentonite is pumped in a continuous flow down hollow drilling rods to a rotating bit. The cutting bit is kept in contact with the bore face and the debris is carried up the annular space by the circulating fluid. Core samples can be obtained using coring tools.

Core Drilling ~ water or compressed air is jetted down the borehole through a hollow tube and returns via the annular space. Coring tools extract continuous cores of rock samples which are sent in wooden boxes for laboratory testing.

Borehole Data ~ the information obtained from trial pits or boreholes can be recorded on a pro forma sheet or on a drawing showing the position and data from each trial pit or borehole thus:

LOCATION PLAN OF BOREHOLES

Boreholes can be taken on a 15·000 to 20·000 grid covering the whole site or in isolated positions relevant to the proposed foundation(s).

BOREHOLE DATA

As a general guide the cost of site and soil investigations should not exceed 1% of estimated project costs.

Soil Assessment ~ prior to designing the foundations for a building or structure the properties of the subsoil(s) must be assessed. These processes can also be carried out to confirm the suitability of the proposed foundations. Soil assessment can include classification, grading, tests to establish shear strength and consolidation. The full range of methods for testing soils is given in BS 1377: Methods of test for soils for civil engineering purposes.

Classification ~ soils may be classified in many ways such as geological origin, physical properties, chemical composition and particle size. It has been found that the particle size and physical properties of a soil are closely linked and are therefore of particular importance and interest to a designer.

Particle Size Distribution ~ this is the percentages of the various particle sizes present in a soil sample as determined by sieving or sedimentation. BS 1377 divides particle sizes into groups as follows:

Gravel particles – over 2mm
Sand particles – between 2mm and 0·06mm
Silt particles – between 0·06mm and 0·002mm
Clay particles – less than 0·002mm

The sand and silt classifications can be further divided thus:

CLAY	SILT			SAND			GRAVEL
	fine	medium	coarse	fine	medium	coarse	
0·002	0·006	0·02	0·06	0·2	0·6	2	>2

The results of a sieve analysis can be plotted as a grading curve thus:

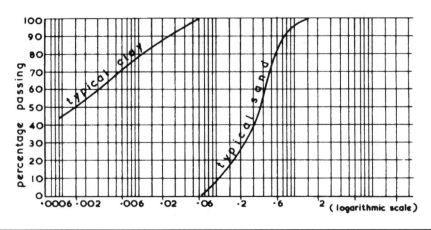

Triangular Chart ~ this provides a general classification of soils composed predominantly from clay, sand and silt. Each side of the triangle represents a percentage of material component. Following laboratory analysis, a sample's properties can be graphically plotted on the chart and classed accordingly.

E.g. Sand – 70%, Clay – 10% and Silt – 20% = Sandy Loam.

Note:

Silt is very fine particles of sand, easily suspended in water.
Loam is very fine particles of clay, easily dissolved in water.

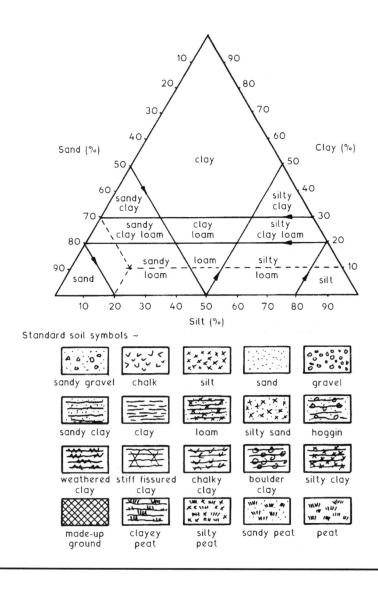

Standard soil symbols ~

sandy gravel	chalk	silt	sand	gravel
sandy clay	clay	loam	silty sand	hoggin
weathered clay	stiff fissured clay	chalky clay	boulder clay	silty clay
made-up ground	clayey peat	silty peat	sandy peat	peat

Plate Loading Test ~ otherwise known as the plate bearing test. By comparison with the more scientific testing procedures described on the next few pages, this test is rudimentary in simplicity. However, it is a cost effective application as a preliminary means for assessing the bearing capacity of unknown soil conditions.

Procedure ~ a trial hole is excavated to the anticipated depth of foundation bearing. Within the excavation is placed a steel test plate of proportionally smaller area than the finished foundation. This plate is then loaded with a proportionally smaller loading than the building load and settlement monitored to establish a building load/soil settlement relationship.

Traditionally, heavy weights of steel billets, concrete blocks, bricks or sandbags were mounted over the test plate gradually increasing the load as the relative settlement was recorded. This somewhat precarious material intensive procedure is superseded by using a hydraulic jack between test plate and a kentledge forming a platform for dense objects such as concrete blocks as shown below.

Typical test results shown on the next page.

Plate Loading Test Results ~

Load in kN/m² (1 tonne force equates to 9.81 kN)

Typical representation of settlement relative to load over time

Load increased 100 kN/m² at 12 hour intervals

Max. design load ⊁ ultimate load ÷3

Limitations ~ although useful for determining subsoil properties at shallow depths, this test is limited to a relatively small area of test plate. As shown on pages 94 and 95, the extent of pressure bulb under the test load will be less than the pressure bulb beneath the actual foundation. Therefore this test does not account for the underlying soil conditions beyond the pressure bulb sphere of the test plate.

Plate Loading Test Numerical Example ~

A steel column pad foundation with anticipated design dimensions of one square metre supporting a load of 30 tonnes. Using a proportionally reduced test plate of 25% foundation area (500 mm × 500 mm) this will be required to carry 30 ÷ 4 tonnes, i.e. 7.5 tonnes. The usual safety margin with these tests is a factor of 3, therefore 7.5 tonnes × 3 will be 22.5 tonnes or 225 kN ultimate loading to be applied.

Site Soil Tests ~ these tests are designed to evaluate the density or shear strength of soils and are very valuable since they do not disturb the soil under test. Three such tests are the standard penetration test, the vane test and the unconfined compression test, all of which are fully described in BS 1377; Methods of test for soils for civil engineering purposes.

Standard Penetration Test ~ this test measures the resistance of a soil to the penetration of a split spoon or split barrel sampler driven into the bottom of a borehole. The sampler is driven into the soil to a depth of 150mm by a falling standard weight of 65kg falling through a distance of 760mm. The sampler is then driven into the soil a further 300mm and the number of blows counted up to a maximum of 50 blows. This test establishes the relative density of the soil.

TYPICAL SPLIT BARREL SAMPLER

TYPICAL RESULTS

Non-cohesive soils:

No. of Blows	Relative Density
0 to 4	very loose
4 to 10	loose
10 to 30	medium
30 to 50	dense
50+	very dense

Cohesive soils:

No. of Blows	Relative Density
0 to 2	very soft
2 to 4	soft
4 to 8	medium
8 to 15	stiff
15 to 30	very stiff
30+	hard

The results of this test in terms of number of blows and amounts of penetration will need expert interpretation.

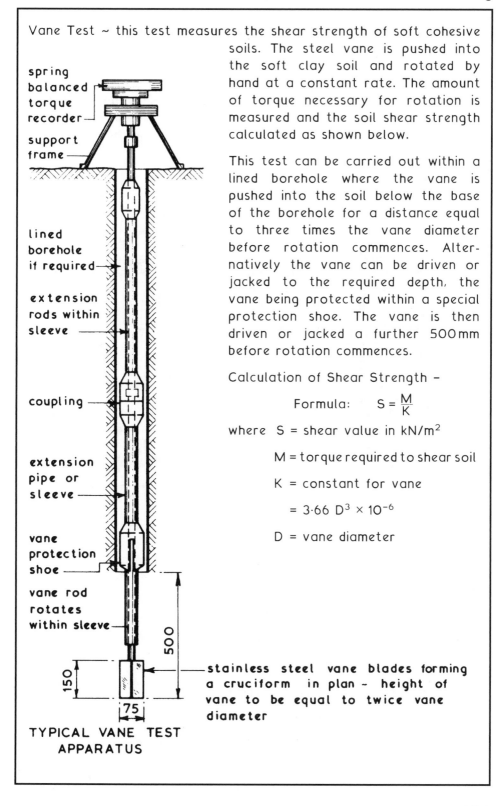

Vane Test ~ this test measures the shear strength of soft cohesive soils. The steel vane is pushed into the soft clay soil and rotated by hand at a constant rate. The amount of torque necessary for rotation is measured and the soil shear strength calculated as shown below.

This test can be carried out within a lined borehole where the vane is pushed into the soil below the base of the borehole for a distance equal to three times the vane diameter before rotation commences. Alternatively the vane can be driven or jacked to the required depth, the vane being protected within a special protection shoe. The vane is then driven or jacked a further 500mm before rotation commences.

Calculation of Shear Strength –

$$\text{Formula:} \quad S = \frac{M}{K}$$

where S = shear value in kN/m^2

M = torque required to shear soil

K = constant for vane

  = 3·66 D^3 × 10^{-6}

D = vane diameter

spring balanced torque recorder

support frame

lined borehole if required

extension rods within sleeve

coupling

extension pipe or sleeve

vane protection shoe

vane rod rotates within sleeve

500

150

75

stainless steel vane blades forming a cruciform in plan – height of vane to be equal to twice vane diameter

TYPICAL VANE TEST APPARATUS

Unconfined Compression Test ~ this test can be used to establish the shear strength of a non-fissured cohesive soil sample using portable apparatus either on site or in a laboratory. The 75mm long × 38mm diameter soil sample is placed in the apparatus and loaded in compression until failure occurs by shearing or lateral bulging. For accurate reading of the trace on the recording chart a transparent viewfoil is placed over the trace on the chart.

Typical Apparatus Details~

rotating handle to apply compression load

chart recording load to shear sample under test

upper moving plate

spring for measuring compressing load

autographic recording arm

fixed plate

soil sample

lower moving plate

SIDE ELEVATION   FRONT ELEVATION

Typical Results ~ showing compression strengths of clays:

Very soft clay	– less than 25 kN/m^2
Soft clay	– 25 to 50 kN/m^2
Medium clay	– 50 to 100 kN/m^2
Stiff clay	– 100 to 200 kN/m^2
Very stiff clay	– 200 to 400 kN/m^2
Hard clay	– more than 400 kN/m^2

NB. The shear strength of clay soils is only half of the compression strength values given above.

Laboratory Testing ~ tests for identifying and classifying soils with regard to moisture content, liquid limit, plastic limit, particle size distribution and bulk density are given in BS 1377.

Bulk Density ~ this is the mass per unit volume which includes mass of air or water in the voids and is essential information required for the design of retaining structures where the weight of the retained earth is an important factor.

Shear Strength ~ this soil property can be used to establish its bearing capacity and also the pressure being exerted on the supports in an excavation. The most popular method to establish the shear strength of cohesive soils is the Triaxial Compression Test. In principle this test consists of subjecting a cylindrical sample of undisturbed soil (75mm long × 38mm diameter) to a lateral hydraulic pressure in addition to a vertical load. Three tests are carried out on three samples (all cut from the same large sample), each being subjected to a higher hydraulic pressure before axial loading is applied. The results are plotted in the form of Mohr's circles.

Shear Strength ~ this can be defined as the resistance offered by a soil to the sliding of one particle over another. A simple method of establishing this property is the Shear Box Test in which the apparatus consists of two bottomless boxes which are filled with the soil sample to be tested. A horizontal shearing force (S) is applied against a vertical load (W), causing the soil sample to shear along a line between the two boxes.

Typical Results ~

Granular Soils - as load increases, friction between particles increases; therefore shear strength is increased.

Cohesive Soils - the very small particles develop no friction; therefore shear strength remains constant.

Mixture of Soils - small angle of internal friction is developed as load increases.

Consolidation of Soil ~ this property is very important in calculating the movement of a soil under a foundation. The laboratory testing apparatus is called an Oedometer.

75 mm dia. × 18 mm thick soil sample placed in a metal ring and capped with porous discs, then placed in water-filled tray and subjected to load

lever arm
weights – load increased every 24 hrs and time / settlement curve drawn

Shrinkable Soils ~ soils subject to volume changes due to variation in moisture content. Pages 245 to 248 show the causes and effects of soil swelling and shrinkage.

Shrinkable Soil Classification ~

- > 35% fine particles.
- Plasticity index (PI) ≥ 10%.

Fine Particles ~ minute portions of clay (loam) or silt having a nominal diameter of < 60 μm (0.06mm).

Plasticity Index (PI) ~ a numerical measure of the potential for a soil to change in volume. Can be determined by the Atterberg* limits test on fine particles < 425 μm (0.425mm). Particles greater than this are removed by sieving.

$$PI = Liquid\,limit\,(LL) - Plastic\,limit\,(PL)$$

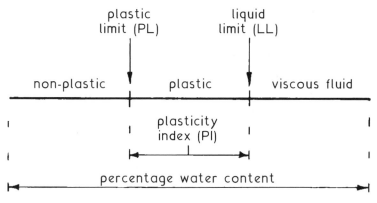

Note: See next page for PL and LL

Soils with a high PI tend to be mainly composed of clay, those with a low PI, of silt.

Plasticity index (PI)	Characteristic plastic quality
0	None
1 – 5	Slight
5 – 10	Low
10 – 20	Medium
20 – 40	High
> 40	Very high

*Albert Atterberg (1846 – 1916) Swedish chemist.

Modified Plasticity Index (MPI) ~ a variation of the plasticity index as shown by formula:

$$MPI = PI \times \% \text{ of soil particles} < 425 \,\mu m \div 100$$

MPI (%)	Soil volume change potential
≥ 40	High
20 – 40	Medium
10 – 20	Low

Atterberg Limits Test ~ (liquid limit and plastic limit) for fine grained soil. As shown on the previous page, determines the state of a soil in terms of non-plastic, plastic and viscous fluid.

Plastic Limit ~ a simple test established by hand rolling a sample of soil on a flat non-porous surface. Soil is defined as plastic when the sample retains its shape down to a very small diameter. The plastic limit occurs when the slender thread of soil breaks apart at a diameter of about 3mm. Considered non-plastic if the thread of soil cannot be rolled down to 3mm at any moisture content. A measure of the relatively low water content at which a soil changes from a plastic state to a solid state.

Liquid Limit ~ water or moisture content when a soil sample changes from plastic to liquid behavioural characteristics. Can also be regarded as the relatively high water content at which soil changes from a liquid to a plastic state.

Atterberg's Original Test Procedure ~ pat of clay soil placed in a porcelain bowl and a groove cut through the middle of the sample. By hand striking the bowl several times the relative characteristics of different clay soils could be measured by the number of blows required to close the groove. This arbitrary test process was later standardised following experimental research attributed to Arthur Casagrande. His procedure quantified and defined results for liquid limit, as outlined on the next page.

Casagrande's Modified Test ~ a refinement of Atterberg's test using a metal bowl of about 100 mm diameter known as a Casagrande* cup. Into this the soil sample is placed and a 13 mm standard groove cut through the middle. By rotating a cam, the cup drops 10 mm onto a rubber base. Liquid limit is determined by measuring the moisture content (MC) of samples when the groove closes at 25 drops of the cup.

$$MC = \frac{\text{Mass of moist sample} - \text{Mass of dried sample}}{\text{Mass of dried sample}} \times \frac{100}{1}$$

Eg. A soil sample of wet mass 200 grams having an oven dried mass of 168 grams.

$$MC = \frac{200 - 168}{168} \times \frac{100}{1} = 19\%$$

Casagrande Cup Test Apparatus ~

metal bowl or Casagrande cup

scroll cam

10 mm

handle

rubber base

13 mm groove

cohesive soil sample

*Arthur Casagrande (1902 – 1981) Australian born American geophysicist. Also associated with development of the oedometer, shear box and triaxial shear compression tests.

General Considerations ~ before any specific considerations and decisions can be made regarding site layout a general appreciation should be obtained by conducting a thorough site investigation at the pre-tender stage and examining in detail the drawings, specification and Bill of Quantities to formulate proposals of how the contract will be carried out if the tender is successful. This will involve a preliminary assessment of plant, materials and manpower requirements plotted against the proposed time scale in the form of a bar chart (see page 37).

Access Considerations ~ this must be considered for both on- and off-site access. Routes to and from the site must be checked as to the suitability for transporting all the requirements for the proposed works. Access on site for deliveries and general circulation must also be carefully considered.

Typical Site Access Considerations ~

site boundary

paved areas and roads forming part of the contract - can these be constructed or partially completed at an early stage and used for site access and general circulation?

temporary road(s) to ease site circulation and/or congestion - are these necessary or desirable? can the extra cost be justified?

sight lines

approach roads - are they suitable? if not what are the alternatives? are there any one way only systems? are right hand turns into the site allowed? what are the requirements for sight lines?

Storage Considerations ~ amount and types of material to be stored. Security and weather protection requirements. Allocation of adequate areas for storing materials and allocating adequate working space around storage areas. Siting of storage areas to reduce double handling to a minimum without impeding the general site circulation and/or works in progress.

Accommodation Considerations ~ number and type of site staff anticipated. Calculate size and select units of accommodation and check to ensure compliance with the minimum welfare requirements of the Construction (Design and Management) Regulations. Select siting for offices to give easy and quick access for visitors but at the same time giving a reasonable view of the site. Select siting for mess room and toilets to reduce walking time to a minimum without impeding the general site circulation and/or works in progress.

Temporary Services Considerations ~ what, when and where are they required? Possibility of having permanent services installed at an early stage and making temporary connections for site use during the construction period. Coordination with the various service undertakings is essential.

Plant Considerations ~ what plant, when and where is it required? Static or mobile plant? If static select the most appropriate position and provide any necessary hardstanding. If mobile check on circulation routes for optimum efficiency and suitability. Provision of space and hardstanding for on-site plant maintenance if required.

Fencing and Hoarding Considerations ~ what is mandatory and what is desirable? Local vandalism record, type or types of fence and/or hoarding required, possibility of using fencing which is part of the contract by erecting this at an early stage in the contract.

Safety and Health Considerations ~ check to ensure that outcome of the above considerations comply with the minimum requirements set out in the various Construction Regulations and in the Health and Safety at Work, etc. Act 1974.

NB. For a typical site layout example see next page.

Typical Site Layout Example ~

existing trees

garages built first
and used as a lock
up store

GARAGES

protective fencing

PAVED AREA

Toilets
(temporary
connection
to drain)

site boundary fencing

temporary fencing

General Storage Compound

ROADWAY

Mess and Drying Rooms

Site Staff Car Park

Bending

Reinforcement

Formwork

Timber Storage

Tower Crane

PAVED AREA

line of scaffold

PROPOSED 5 STOREY BLOCK

Cement Store

Fine Aggregate

Coarse Agg.

Mixer

temporary water supply

stand pipe

ROADWAY

Visitors Car Park

Site Offices

Timekeeper

Toilets
(temporary
connection
to drain)

Scaffold Storage

signboard

electricity

permanent water supply

telephone

close-boarded hoarding with lockable entrance gates

Site Security ~ the primary objectives of site security are:

1. Security against theft.
2. Security from vandals.
3. Protection from innocent trespassers.

The need for and type of security required will vary from site to site according to the neighbourhood, local vandalism record and the value of goods stored on site. Perimeter fencing, internal site protection and night security may all be necessary.

Typical Site Security Provisions ~

floodlighting – dual purpose – enables work to proceed in poor daylight levels and could be used as a measure of night security

lockable store for small and/or valuable items

perimeter fencing at least 1·800 high

internal fencing around storage compound

hut for gateman to check on validity of all persons entering the site

close-boarded hoarding adjacent to public highway and footpath-see details on the next two pages

strong and lockable site entrance gates

115

Hoardings ~ under the Highways Act 1980 a close-boarded fence hoarding must be erected prior to the commencement of building operations if such operations are adjacent to a public footpath or highway. The hoarding needs to be adequately constructed to provide protection for the public, resist impact damage, resist anticipated wind pressures and adequately lit at night. Before a hoarding can be erected a licence or permit must be obtained from the local authority who will usually require 10 to 20 days' notice. The licence will set out the minimum local authority requirements for hoardings and define the time limit period of the licence.

Typical Hoarding Details ~

200 × 75 softwood posts at 1·500 c/c

bulkhead night warning lights

2·400 high × 1·200 wide external quality plywood sheets fixed to timber rails – some local authorities require the facing to be painted a light colour

75 × 75 softwood sheeting rails fixed to posts

minimum working space 1·000

1·200 minimum

ground level

footpath

900 minimum

150 mm minimum mass concrete surround

Hoardings can be constructed using other materials such as a frame of scaffold tubing faced with corrugated sheeting.
Return ends and access by means of a lockable gate or door may also be required.

100 x 50 raking struts at 2·000°/c if required

75 x 75 sheeting rails fixed to posts

50 x 50 fixing stakes

All timber to be softwood G.S. grade

bulkhead night warning light

2·400 high x 1·200 wide external quality plywood or similar sheets fixed to timber rails

100 x 100 posts at 2·000°/c

guard rail

night warning lights

300 x 300 timber fender painted white

footway with ramps at each end out of sheet material decking on 125 x 50 joists at 450°/c

900 min.

1·200 min.

fixing straps

2·200

750

100 x 100 precast concrete spurs set in mass concrete to project 1·000

ground level

150mm minimum mass concrete surround

600 min.

Site Lighting ~ this can be used effectively to enable work to continue during periods of inadequate daylight. It can also be used as a deterrent to would-be trespassers. Site lighting can be employed externally to illuminate the storage and circulation areas and internally for general movement and for specific work tasks. The types of lamp available range from simple tungsten filament lamps to tungsten halogen and discharge lamps. The arrangement of site lighting can be static where the lamps are fixed to support poles or mounted on items of fixed plant such as scaffolding and tower cranes. Alternatively the lamps can be sited locally where the work is in progress by being mounted on a movable support or handheld with a trailing lead. Whenever the position of site lighting is such that it can be manhandled it should be run on a reduced voltage of 110 V single phase as opposed to the mains voltage of 230 V.

To plan an adequate system of site lighting the types of activity must be defined and given an illumination target value which is quoted in lux (lx). Recommended minimum target values for building activities are:

External lighting	–	general circulation ⎱ materials handling ⎰	10 lx
Internal lighting	–	general circulation	5 lx
		general working areas	15 lx
		concreting activities	50 lx
		carpentry and joinery ⎱ bricklaying ⎰ plastering	100 lx
		painting and decorating ⎱ site offices ⎰	200 lx
		drawing board positions	300 lx

Such target values do not take into account deterioration, dirt or abnormal conditions; therefore it is usual to plan for at least twice the recommended target values. Generally the manufacturers will provide guidance as to the best arrangement to use in any particular situation but lamp requirements can be calculated thus:

$$\text{Total lumens required} = \frac{\text{area to be illluminated (m}^2) \times \text{target value (lx)}}{\text{utilisation factor 0·23 [dispersive lights 0·27]}}$$

After choosing lamp type to be used:

$$\text{Number of lamps required} = \frac{\text{total lumens required}}{\text{lumen output of chosen lamp}}$$

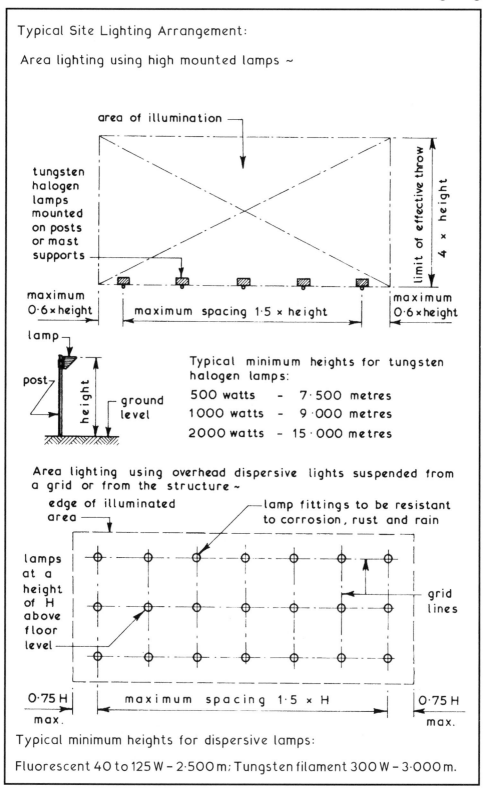

Typical Site Lighting Arrangement:

Area lighting using high mounted lamps ~

area of illumination

tungsten halogen lamps mounted on posts or mast supports

limit of effective throw 4 × height

maximum 0·6×height

maximum spacing 1·5 × height

maximum 0·6×height

lamp
post
height
ground level

Typical minimum heights for tungsten halogen lamps:

500 watts	–	7·500 metres
1000 watts	–	9·000 metres
2000 watts	–	15·000 metres

Area lighting using overhead dispersive lights suspended from a grid or from the structure ~

edge of illuminated area

lamp fittings to be resistant to corrosion, rust and rain

lamps at a height of H above floor level

grid lines

0·75 H max.

maximum spacing 1·5 × H

0·75 H max.

Typical minimum heights for dispersive lamps:

Fluorescent 40 to 125 W – 2·500 m; Tungsten filament 300 W – 3·000 m.

Walkway and Local Lighting ~ to illuminate the general circulation routes bulkhead and/or festoon lighting could be used either on a standard mains voltage of 230 V or on a reduced voltage of 110 V. For local lighting at the place of work hand lamps with trailing leads or lamp fittings on stands can be used and positioned to give the maximum amount of illumination without unacceptable shadow cast.

Typical Walkway and Local Lighting Fittings ~

die-cast aluminium alloy body

supply cable

water- and weatherproof front glass

vandal resistant translucent polycarbonate diffuser

white stove enamelled reflector

galvanised steel base

BULKHEAD LAMP
(300 mm × 8 W fluorescent)

LAMP AND STAND
(110V tungsten filament)

sealed end to cable

rainproof lampholders

60 W tungsten filament bulbs

weather resistant cable

weatherproof fitted plug

glass fibre shades or wire guards if required

FESTOON LIGHTING

weatherproof fitted plug

moulded rubber lampholder

fitted wire guard to 110V tungsten filament lamp

weather resistant cable

HANDHELD LAMP WITH TRAILING LEAD

Electrical Supply to Building Sites ~ a supply of electricity is usually required at an early stage in the contract to provide light and power to the units of accommodation. As the work progresses power could also be required for site lighting, handheld power tools and large items of plant. The supply of electricity to a building site is the subject of a contract between the contractor and the local area electricity company who will want to know the date when supply is required; site address together with a block plan of the site; final load demand of proposed building and an estimate of the maximum load demand in kilowatts for the construction period. The latter can be estimated by allowing 10 W/m^2 of the total floor area of the proposed building plus an allowance for high load equipment such as cranes. The installation should be undertaken by a competent electrical contractor to ensure that it complies with all the statutory rules and regulations for the supply of electricity to building sites.

Typical Supply and Distribution Equipment ~

ISA

230 V single-phase supply to area site lighting

400V 3-phase or 230V single-phase

—MDA

incoming supply
400V 3-phase

400V 3-phase supply to plant

mains supply

Earth Monitor Unit (EMU)—

single or 3-phase

Incoming Site Assembly (ISA) contains electricity authority's equipment to control, meter and protect supply circuit

Main Distribution Assembly (MDA) control and distribution of 400V 3-phase and 230V single-phase supply circuits

400V circuit single or 3-phase

110 V
16 & 20 amp outlets—
110V

16; 20; 32 & 60 amp outlets—
110 V circuit

400V circuit

Extension Outlet Assembly (EOA)

Socket Outlet Assembly (SOA)

Transformer Assembly (TA)

The units must be strong, durable and resistant to rain penetration with adequate weather seals to all access panels and doors. All plug and socket outlets should be colour coded: 400V – red; 230V – blue; 110V – yellow.

Office Accommodation ~ the arrangements for office accommodation to be provided on site is a matter of choice for each individual contractor. Generally, separate offices would be provided for site agent, clerk of works, administrative staff, site surveyors and sales staff.

The minimum requirements of such accommodation are governed by the Offices, Shops and Railway Premises Act 1963 unless they are:

1. Mobile units in use for not more then six months.
2. Fixed units in use for not more than six weeks.
3. Any type of unit in use for not more than 21 man hours per week.
4. Office for exclusive use of self-employed person.
5. Office used by family-only staff.

Sizing Example ~

Office for site agent and assistant plus an allowance for three visitors.
Assume an internal average height of 2·400.
Allow 3·7m^2 minimum per person and 11·5m^3 minimum per person.
Minimum area = 5 × 3·7 = 18·5m^2
Minimum volume = 5 × 11·5 = 57·5m^3

Assume office width of 3·000 then minimum length required is
$$= \frac{57·5}{3 \times 2·4} = \frac{57·5}{7·2} = 7·986 \text{ say } 8·000$$
Area check 3 × 8 = 24m^2 which is > 18·5m^2 ∴ satisfactory

Typical Example ~

Portable cabin with four adjustable steel legs with attachments for stacking. Panelling of galvanised steel sheet and rigid insulation core. Plasterboard inner lining to walls and ceiling. Pyro-shield windows with steel shutters and a high security steel door.

   Ref. Fire prevention on construction sites – the joint code of practice on protection from fire of construction sites and buildings undergoing renovation. Published by Construction Industry Publications and The Fire Protection Association.

Applicable where the work is notifiable to the HSE, i.e. work extends to more than 30 days or it involves more than 500 person days.

First aid:
- box readily accessible and distinctly marked.
- contents sufficient for the number of persons on site.
- person appointed with responsibility for first aid facilities and calls to emergency ambulance service (not necessarily a qualified first aider).
- information displayed confirming name of appointed person.
- person trained (first aider) in first aid at work holding an HSE recognised FAW qualification or an emergency first aid at work EFAW qualification.

No. of site personnel	Minimum requirements
< 5	One appointed person preferably trained in first aid
5 - 50	One trained in EFAW or FAW depending on assessment of possible injuries
> 50	One trained in FAW for every 50 persons or part thereof

Sanitary facilities ~
- toilets, separate male and female if possible.
- lockable doors.

Minimum where men and women are employed:

No. of persons on site	No. of WCs	No. of washbasins
≤ 5	1	1
6 - 25	2	2

Thereafter an additional WC and basin for every 25 persons.

Minimum where only men are employed:

No. of men on site	No. of WCs	No. of urinals
1 - 15	1	1
16 - 30	2	1
31 - 45	2	2
46 - 60	3	2
61 - 75	3	3
76 - 90	4	3
91 - 100	4	4

Portable toilets for use where there is no plumbing and drainage, at least one per seven persons, emptied at least once a week.

Washing facilities:
- next to toilets and changing areas.
- hot and cold water or mixed warm water.
- soap, towels or hot air dryer.
- adequate ventilation and lighting.
- washbasins large enough to wash face, hands and forearms.
- showers for particularly dirty work.

Drinking water:
- wholesome supply direct from the mains.
- bottled water acceptable if mains supply unavailable.
- cups or other drinking vessels at outlets or a drinking fountain.

Accommodation for rest, shelter, changing and eating:
- separate provisions if men and women are on site.
- located close to washing facilities.
- heated place for shelter from inclement weather.
- space for changing with security for personal clothing, etc.
- lockers and/or place to hang clothes.
- place for wet clothing to be dried.
- rest facilities with tables and raised-back chairs.
- ventilation and lighting.
- means for heating water and warming food unless a separate provision is made for providing meals.

Note: All facilities to be cleaned regularly and serviced with soap, paper, towels, etc.

Refs.: Health and Safety at Work, etc. Act 1974.
Construction (Design and Management) Regulations 2007 [incorporating the Construction (Health, Safety and Welfare) Regulations of 1996].
Health and Safety (First Aid) Regulations 1981.
Workplace (Health, Safety and Welfare) Regulations 1992.
Management of Health and Safety at Work Regulations 1999.

See also requirements and responsibilities for personal protective equipment and clothing summarised on the next page.

Definition ~ 'all equipment (including clothing affording protection against the weather) which is intended to be worn or held by a person at work which protects them against one or more risks to their health and safety.' Personal Protective Equipment Regulations.

Provision ~ by an employer at no cost to employees. Self-employed to provide their own, unless in an employer–employee relationship.

Types of PPE generally required ~
Face and eyes:
· disposable face masks.
· respirators/breathing apparatus (special training required).
· air-fed helmets (special training required).
· safety glasses, similar to ordinary glasses, may have side shields.
· shield, one-piece moulded lens worn over other glasses.
· goggles, flexible plastic frame with elastic headband.
· face guard, shield or visor to fully enclose the eyes from dust, etc.
Hearing:
· earmuffs – helmet mounted available.
· earplugs and ear inserts (canal caps).
Legs and feet:
· safety boots/shoes, steel toe cap and slip-resistant sole.
· Wellington boots, steel toe cap and studded soles available.
· anti-static electricity insulated footwear.
· knee pads, gaiters, leggings and spats.
Body:
· high visibility waistcoats.
· overalls, coveralls and boiler suits.
· aprons, chain mail or leather.
· life jackets.
· safety harnesses.
· insulated and waterproof clothing.
Hands:
· gloves, waterproof and/or insulating.
· gauntlets.
· armlets and wristcuffs.

Risk assessment ~
Hazard – any situation that has the potential to harm.
Risk – possibility of damage, injury or loss caused by a hazard.
Responsibility – all persons in and associated with the work place.

Site Storage ~ materials stored on site prior to being used or fixed may require protection for security reasons or against the adverse effects which can be caused by exposure to the elements.

Small and Valuable Items ~ these should be kept in a secure and lockable store. Similar items should be stored together in a rack or bin system and only issued against an authorised requisition.

Large or Bulk Storage Items ~ for security protection these items can be stored within a lockable fenced compound. The form of fencing chosen may give visual security by being of an open nature but these are generally easier to climb than the close-boarded type of fence which lacks the visual security property.

Typical Storage Compound Fencing ~

Close-boarded fences can be constructed on the same methods used for hoardings – see pages 116 & 117.

CHAIN LINK FENCING WITH PRECAST CONCRETE POSTS

Alternative Fence Types ~ woven wire fence, strained wire fence, cleft chestnut pale fence, wooden palisade fence, wooden post and rail fence and metal fences – see BS 1722: Fences, for details.

Storage of Materials ~ this can be defined as the provision of adequate space, protection and control for building materials and components held on site during the construction process. The actual requirements for specific items should be familiar to students who have completed studies in construction technology at an introductory level but the need for storage and control of materials held on site can be analysed further:

1. Physical Properties – size, shape, weight and mode of delivery will assist in determining the safe handling and stacking method(s) to be employed on site, which in turn will enable handling and storage costs to be estimated.
2. Organisation – this is the planning process of ensuring that all the materials required are delivered to site at the correct time, in sufficient quantity, of the right quality, the means of unloading is available and that adequate space for storage or stacking has been allocated.
3. Protection – building materials and components can be classified as durable or non-durable; the latter will usually require some form of weather protection to prevent deterioration whilst in store.
4. Security – many building materials have a high resale and/or usage value to persons other than those for whom they were ordered and unless site security is adequate material losses can become unacceptable.
5. Costs – to achieve an economic balance of how much expenditure can be allocated to site storage facilities the following should be taken into account:

   • storage areas, fencing, racks, bins, etc.
   • protection requirements.
   • handling, transporting and stacking requirements.
   • salaries and wages of staff involved in storage of materials and components.
   • heating and/or lighting if required.
   • allowance for losses due to wastage, deterioration, vandalism and theft.
   • facilities to be provided for subcontractors.

6. Control – checking quality and quantity of materials at delivery and during storage period, recording delivery and issue of materials and monitoring stock holdings.

Site Storage Space ~ the location and size(s) of space to be allocated for any particular material should be planned by calculating the area(s) required and by taking into account all the relevant factors before selecting the most appropriate position on site in terms of handling, storage and convenience. Failure to carry out this simple planning exercise can result in chaos on site or having on site more materials than there is storage space available.

Calculation of Storage Space Requirements ~ each site will present its own problems since a certain amount of site space must be allocated to the units of accommodation, car parking, circulation and working areas, therefore the amount of space available for materials storage may be limited. The size of the materials or component being ordered must be known together with the proposed method of storage and this may vary between different sites of similar building activities. There are therefore no standard solutions for allocating site storage space and each site must be considered separately to suit its own requirements.

Typical Examples ~

Bricks – quantity = 15,200 to be delivered in strapped packs of 380 bricks per pack each being 1100 mm wide × 670 mm long × 850 mm high. Unloading and stacking to be by forklift truck to form two rows two packs high.

Area required:- number of packs per row = $\dfrac{15,200}{380 \times 2}$ = 20

length of row = 10 × 670 = 6·700
width of row = 2 × 1100 = 2·200

allowance for forklift approach in front of stack = 5·000 ∴ minimum brick storage area = 6·700 long × 7·200 wide

Timber – to be stored in open-sided top covered racks constructed of standard scaffold tubes. Maximum length of timber ordered = 5·600. Allow for rack to accept at least 4 No. 300 mm-wide timbers placed side by side then minimum width required = 4 × 300 = 1·200
Minimum plan area for timber storage rack = 5·600 × 1·200
Allow for end loading of rack equal to length of rack
∴ minimum timber storage area = 11·200 long × 1·200 wide
Height of rack to be not more than 3 × width = 3·600

Areas for other materials stored on site can be calculated using the basic principles contained in the examples above.

Site Allocation for Materials Storage ~ the area and type of storage required can be determined as shown on pages 126 to 128, but the allocation of an actual position on site will depend on:

1. Space available after areas for units of accommodation have been allocated.
2. Access facilities on site for delivery, vehicles.
3. Relationship of storage area(s) to activity area(s) – the distance between them needs to be kept as short as possible to reduce transportation needs in terms of time and costs to the minimum. Alternatively storage areas and work areas need to be sited within the reach of any static transport plant such as a tower crane.
4. Security – needs to be considered in the context of site operations, vandalism and theft.
5. Stockholding policy – too little storage could result in delays awaiting materials to be delivered, too much storage can be expensive in terms of weather and security protection requirements apart from the capital used to purchase the materials stored on site.

Typical Example ~

NB. temporary site services omitted for clarity.

Bricks ~ may be supplied loose or strapped in unit loads and stored on timber pallets

bricks stacked on edge in rows

bricks in alternate directions to form end columns →

2·400 maximum

level, well-drained ground ⌐

polythene or similar cover weighted at bottom to protect bricks against atmospheric pollution and/or inclement weather

arris protection ⌐

plastic or metallic straps →

timber pallet →

500 brick unit load

holes for prongs of fork-lift unloader

typical unit loads of 76, 152, 228, 380 and 416 bricks

Blocks ~ may be supplied loose or in unit loads on timber pallets

Roofing Tiles ~ may be supplied loose, in plastic-wrapped packs or in unit loads on timber pallets

blocks stacked in 'columns' ⌐

protective cover ⌐

8 courses maximum

6 rows maximum

ridge tiles stored on ends ⌐

end laid flat and staggered ⌐

Drainage Pipes ~ supplied loose or strapped together on timber pallets

loose bricks forming end 'column'

pipes stacked horizontally with ends reversed in alternate rows →

driven-in timber stacks forming end restraint

pipes stacked horizontally

straight barrel pipes

socket ends project beyond spigot ends

timber batten under spigot

battered end maximum height 1·500

Gullies, etc. should be stored upside down and supported to remain level

Baths ~ stacked or nested vertically or horizontally on timber battens

Timber and Joinery Items ~ should be stored horizontally and covered but with provison for free air flow

protective cover to be used if required

lightweight roof covering

rack to have open ends

open sided rack →

timber sizes kept separate

framing out of scaffold tubes or timber

sole plate

Basins ~ stored similar to baths but not more than four high if nested one on top of another

Corrugated and Similar Sheet Materials ~ stored flat on a level surface and covered with a protective polythene or similar sheet material

Cement, Sand and Aggregates ~ for supply and storage details see pages 326 and 332.

Site Tests ~ the majority of materials and components arriving on site will conform to the minimum recommendations of the appropriate British Standard and therefore the only tests which need to be applied are those of checking quantity received against amount stated on the delivery note, ensuring quality is as ordered and a visual inspection to reject damaged or broken goods. The latter should be recorded on the delivery note and entered in the site records. Certain site tests can however be carried out on some materials to establish specific data such as the moisture content of timber which can be read direct from a moisture meter. Other simple site tests are given in the various British Standards to ascertain compliance with the recommendations, such as tests for dimensional tolerances and changes given in BS EN 771-1 and BS EN 772-16 which cover random sampling of clay bricks of up to 10 units. An alternative site test can be carried out by measuring a sample of 24 bricks taken at random from a delivered load thus:

5085 to 5235

215

65

TEST FOR LENGTH

24 bricks laid dry end to end

2415 to 2505

102·5

215

TEST FOR WIDTH

24 bricks laid dry side by side

1515 to 1605

65

102·5

TEST FOR DEPTH

24 bricks laid dry bed face to bed face

Refs.: BS EN 772-16: Methods of test for masonry units.
BS EN 771-1: Specification for masonry units.

Site Test ~ apart from the test outlined on page 132 site tests on materials which are to be combined to form another material such as concrete can also be tested to establish certain properties which if not known could affect the consistency and/or quality of the final material.

Typical Example ~ Testing Sand for Bulking

This data is required when batching concrete by volume – test made at commencement of mixing and if change in weather

1 — rule to measure depth of damp sand (say 150mm)

— straight-sided container

approx. 2/3 D — loosely placed damp sand sample

D

2 — sufficient clean water to half fill container

1/2 D

D — damp sand sample removed from container and set aside

3 — rule to measure depth of saturated sand (say 124mm)

— water

— saturated sand – sand placed in water 50% at a time and tamped with a rod to remove any air

4   Calculation:

$$\text{bulking} = \frac{\text{difference in height between damp and saturated sand}}{\text{depth of saturated sand}}$$

$$\% \text{ bulking} = \frac{150 - 124}{124} \times 100 = \frac{26}{124} \times 100 = 20 \cdot 96774\%$$

Therefore volume of sand should be increased by 21% over that quoted in the specification.

NB. a given weight of saturated sand will occupy the same space as when dry but more space when damp.

Silt Test for Sand ~ the object of this test is to ascertain the cleanliness of sand by establishing the percentage of silt present in a natural sand since too much silt will weaken the concrete

measuring cylinder marked in millilitres

1. make up salt water solution of 5 ml salt to 500 ml water

salt water solution up to 50 ml mark

2. add sand sample to salt water up to 50 ml mark

add more salt water solution up to 150 ml mark and shake cylinder well

3. allow mixture to stand for three hours and measure height of silt
- salt water
- silt
- sand

4. Height of silt layer should not be more than 6 ml or 6% of height of sand sample

Obtaining Samples for Laboratory Testing ~ these tests may be required for checking aggregate grading by means of a sieve test, checking quality or checking for organic impurities, but whatever the reason the sample must be truly representative of the whole:

1.
scoop
aggregate pile

samples extracted by means of a scoop from at least ten different positions in the pile

sample required:

fine aggregate – 50 kg
coarse aggregate – 200 kg

2.
well mixed sample divided into four equal parts – opposite quarters are discarded – remainder of sample remixed and quartered – whole process is repeated until required size of sample is left.

samples required:

fine aggregate ≯ 4 mm – 3 kg
coarse aggregate ≯ 10 mm – 6 kg
　　　　　　　 ≯ 20 mm – 25 kg
　　　　　　　 ≯ 40 mm – 50 kg

Ref. BS EN 12620: Aggregates for concrete.

The quality of site mixed concrete should be monitored, especially to ensure uniformity of mix components and consistency of batches. When constituents are known to be constant by design, the water/cement ratio of consecutive batches can be compared by using a slump test. Water for hydration is about one quarter of the cement weight, but if a w/c ratio of 0.25 were used the mix would be too stiff and unworkable. Therefore, a w/c ratio of 0.5 is more usual; the additional water providing a lubricant for the aggregates and cement. Increasing the w/c ratio above 0.5 will make the concrete easier to work, but it will be detrimental to the final compressive strength (see page 329) unless other measures are incorporated to counter this, e.g. steel or fabric reinforcement.

Slump Test Equipment ~ shown below, an open ended frustum of a cone, tamping rod and a rule. Dimensions in mm.

Procedure ~ the cone is one-quarter filled with concrete and tamped 25 times. Further filling and tamping is repeated three more times until the cone is full and the sample levelled off. The cone is removed and the concrete slump measured. The measurement should be consistent for all samples of concrete being used in the same situation.

Typical Slump Specification ~ generally between 50 and 100 mm depending on application. See page 331 for slump consistency classes applicable to standard prescribed site batched concrete mixes.

Ref. BS EN 12350-2: Testing fresh concrete. Slump test.

Procedure for Testing Batched Concrete from Source ~

· Wet concrete samples extracted from the mixer batch are placed into machine faced steel casting moulds in 50mm layers.
· Each layer compacted at least 35 times (150mm cube) or 25 times (100mm cube) with a tamping bar.
· Alternatively, each layer may be consolidated by external vibration from an electric or pneumatic hammer.
· Surplus concrete trowelled off and samples marked with time, date and job reference.
· Samples left for 24 hours ±30 minutes and covered with a damp cloth.
· After 24 hours, samples removed from moulds and submersed in water at 20°C ± 2°C.
· At 7 days, hydraulic compression test applied to sample cubes to determine stress failure strength.
· If strength specification not achieved, other samples from the same batch tested at 28 days.
· If 28 day samples fail compressive strength requirement, core samples may be taken from placed concrete for further laboratory analysis.

Equipment ~

25 x 25mm square end tamping bar

concrete sample with trowelled surface and identification

X 156
3/6

380 mm

test cube

150 x 150 x 150mm standard steel test cube mould thinly coated inside with oil, if aggregate ⩽ 20mm a 100mm cube mould may be used

pressure gauge

hydraulic pressure applied to the sides of sample as cast

smooth plane steel plates

sample before test

sample after stress failure

28 day characteristic crushing strength categories below which not more than 5% of test results are permitted to fail, are: 7.5, 10, 15, 20, 25, 30 and 35N/mm^2. 40, 45 and 50N/mm^2 are also specified, mainly for prestressed reinforced concrete.

Ref. BS EN 12390-1: Testing hardened concrete. Shape, dimensions and other requirements for specimens and moulds.

Non-destructive testing of concrete. Also known as in-place or in-situ tests.

Changes over time and in different exposures can be monitored.

References: BS 6089: Assessment of in-situ compressive strength in structures and precast concrete components.
BS 1881: Testing concrete.
BS EN 13791: Assessment of in-situ compressive strength in structures and precast concrete components.

Provides information on: strength in-situ, voids, flaws, cracks and deterioration.

Rebound hammer test — attributed to Ernst Schmidt after he devised the impact hammer in 1948. It works on the principle of an elastic mass rebounding off a hard surface. Varying surface densities will affect impact and propagation of stress waves. These can be recorded on a numerical scale known as rebound numbers. It has limited application to smooth surfaces of concrete only. False results may occur where there are local variations in the concrete, such as a large piece of aggregate immediately below the impact surface. Rebound numbers can be graphically plotted to correspond with compressive strength.

Ref. BS EN 12504-2: Testing concrete in structures. Non-destructive testing. Determination of rebound number.

SCHMIDT HAMMER

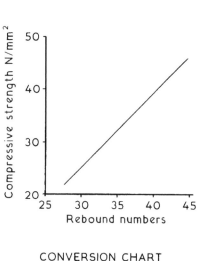

CONVERSION CHART
(illustration only)

Penetration or Windsor probe test ~ there are various interpretations of this test. It is a measure of the penetration of a steel alloy rod, fired by a predetermined amount of energy into concrete. In principle, the depth of penetration is inversely proportional to the concrete compressive strength. Several recordings are necessary to obtain a fair assessment and some can be discarded particularly where the probe cannot penetrate some dense aggregates. The advantage over the rebound hammer is provision of test results at a greater depth (up to 50 mm).

Pull-out test ~ this is not entirely non-destructive as there will be some surface damage, albeit easily repaired. A number of circular bars of steel with enlarged ends are cast into the concrete as work proceeds. This requires careful planning and location of bars with corresponding voids provided in the formwork. At the appropriate time, the bar and a piece of concrete are pulled out by tension jack. Although the concrete fails in tension and shear, the pull-out force can be correlated to the compressive strength of the concrete.

Ref. BS 1881-207: Testing concrete. Recommendations for the assessment of concrete strength by near-to-surface tests.

Vibration test ~ a number of electronic tests have been devised, which include measurement of ultrasonic pulse velocity through concrete. This applies the principle of recording a pulse at predetermined frequencies over a given distance. The apparatus includes transducers in contact with the concrete, pulse generator, amplifier, and time measurement to digital display circuit. For converting the data to concrete compressive strength, see BS EN 12504-4: Testing concrete. Determination of ultrasonic pulse velocity.

A variation, using resonant frequency, measures vibrations produced at one end of a concrete sample against a receiver or pick up at the other. The driving unit or exciter is activated by a variable frequency oscillator to generate vibrations varying in resonance, depending on the concrete quality. The calculation of compressive strength by conversion of amplified vibration data is by formulae found in BS 1881-209: Testing concrete. Recommendations for the measurement of dynamic modulus of elasticity.

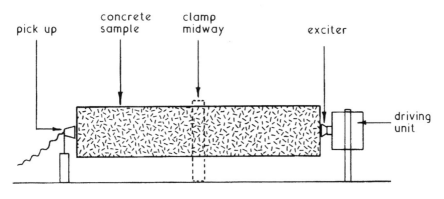

RESONANT FREQUENCY TEST

Other relevant standards:

BS 1881-122: Testing concrete. Method for determination of water absorption.
BS 1881-124: Testing concrete. Methods for analysis of hardened concrete.
BS EN 12390-7: Testing hardened concrete. Density of hardened concrete.

The quality of softwood timber for structural use depends very much on the environment in which it is grown and the species selected. Timber can be visually strength graded, but this is unlikely to occur at the construction site except for a general examination for obvious handling defects and damage during transit. Site inspection will be to determine that the grading authority's markings on the timber comply with that specified for the application.

Format of strength grade markings on softwood timber for structural uses ~

accredited certification authority (see below)*

grader or company licence number

British spruce

TRADA 1234 B/S

BS 4978 KD GS C14

kiln dried ⌐

grade – general structural (SS = special structural)

accredited certification authority (see below)*

grader or company licence number

European whitewood/redwood

C.A.T.G. 123/456 EW/ER

BS EN 14081 DRY mss C24

British Standard quality reference

alternative condition indicator

BS strength class

*Accredited certification authorities include BM TRADA Certification Ltd. and Certification And Timber Grading Ltd.

Refs.: BS 4978: Visual strength grading of softwood. Specification.
BS EN 14081: Timber structures. Strength graded structural timber with rectangular cross section (four parts).

Grading ~ either visually or by computerised machine. Individual rectangular timber sections are assessed against permissible defect limitations and grade marked accordingly.

UK grading standard ~ BS 4978.
European grading standard ~ BS EN 14081 (four parts).

The two principal grades apart from rejects are GS (general structural) and SS (special structural) preceded with an M if graded by machine.

Additional specification is to BS EN 338: Structural timber. Strength classes. This standard provides softwood strength classifications from C14 to C40 as well as a separate classification of hardwoods.

A guide to softwood grades with strength classes for timber from the UK, Europe and North America ~

Source/species	Strength class (BS EN 338)						
	C14	C16	C18	C22	C24	C27	C30
UK:							
British pine	GS			SS			
British spruce	GS		SS				
Douglas fir	GS		SS				
Larch	GS				SS		
Ireland:							
Sitka and Norway spruce	GS		SS				
Europe:							
Redwood or white-wood		GS			SS		
USA:							
Western whitewood	GS		SS				
Southern pine		GS			SS		
USA/Canada:							
Spruce/pine/fir or hemlock		GS			SS		
Douglas fir and larch		GS			SS		
Canada:							
Western red cedar	GS		SS				
Sitka spruce	GS		SS				

141

BS EN 338: Structural softwood classifications and typical strength properties ~

BS EN 338 strength class	Bending parallel to grain (N/mm²)	Tension parallel to grain (N/mm²)	Compression parallel to grain (N/mm²)	Compression perpendicular to grain (N/mm²)	Shear parallel to grain (N/mm²)	Modulus of elasticity Mean (N/mm²)	Modulus of elasticity Minimum (N/mm²)	Characteristic density (kg/m³)	Average density (kg/m³)
C14	4.1	2.5	5.2	2.1	0.60	6800	4600	290	350
C16	5.3	3.2	6.8	2.2	0.67	8800	5800	310	370
C18	5.8	3.5	7.1	2.2	0.67	9100	6000	320	380
C22	6.8	4.1	7.5	2.3	0.71	9700	6500	340	410
C24	7.5	4.5	7.9	2.4	0.71	10800	7200	350	420
TR26	10.0	6.0	8.2	2.5	1.10	11000	7400	370	450
C27	10.0	6.0	8.2	2.5	1.10	12300	8200	370	450
C30	11.0	6.6	8.6	2.7	1.20	12300	8200	380	460
C35	12.0	7.2	8.7	2.9	1.30	13400	9000	400	480
C40	13.0	7.8	8.7	3.0	1.40	14500	10000	420	500

Notes: 1. Strength class TR26 is specifically for the manufacture of trussed rafters.

2. Characteristic density values are given specifically for the design of joints. Average density is appropriate for calculation of dead load.

3. For a worked example of a softwood timber joist/beam design using data for strength classification C24 (e.g. SS graded European redwood) see pages 777 and 778.

Visual strength grading ~ 'process by which a piece of timber can be sorted, by means of visual inspection, into a grade to which characteristic values of strength, stiffness and density may be allocated.' Definition from BS EN 14081-1.

Characteristics:

Knots ~ branch growth from or through the main section of timber weakening the overall structural strength. Measured by comparing the sum of the projected cross sectional knot area with the cross-sectional area of the piece of timber. This is known as the knot area ratio (KAR). Knots close to the edge of section have greater structural significance; therefore this area is represented as a margin condition at the top and bottom quarter of a section. A margin condition exists when more than half the top or bottom quarter of a section is occupied by knots.
MKAR = Margin knot area ratio.
TKAR = Total knot area ratio.

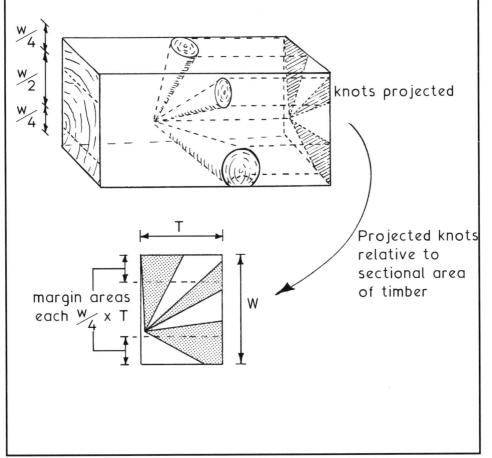

knots projected

Projected knots relative to sectional area of timber

margin areas each $^W/_4$ x T

Fissures and resin pockets ~ defects in growth. Fissures, also known as shakes, are usually caused by separation of annual growth rings. Fissures and resin pockets must be limited in structural timber as they reduce resistance to shear and bending parallel to the grain.

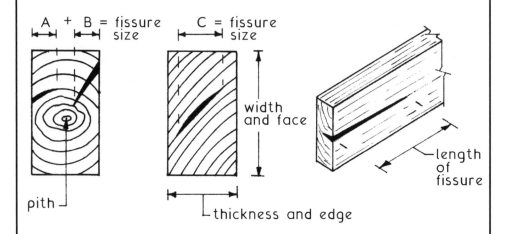

A + B = fissure size
C = fissure size
width and face
length of fissure
pith
thickness and edge

Slope of grain ~ an irregularity in growth or where the log is not cut parallel to the grain. If excessive this will produce a weakness in shear. Measurement is by scoring a line along the grain of the timber surface and comparing this with the parallel sides of the section.

grain reasonably parallel
X
1
slope of grain = 1 in X

Insect damage ~ no active allowed. Woodworm holes acceptable if only nominal. Wood wasp holes not permitted.

Sapstain ~ acceptable.

Wane or waney edge ~ occurs on timber cut close to the outer surface of the log producing incomplete corners. Measurement is parallel to the edge or face of section and it is expressed as a fraction of the surface dimension.

Growth rate ~ measurement is applied to the annual growth ring separation averaged over a line 75mm long. If pith is present the line should commence 25mm beyond and if 75mm is impractical to achieve, the longest possible line is taken.

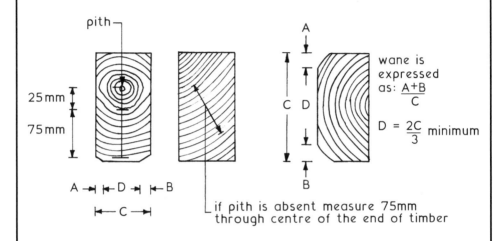

wane is expressed as: $\frac{A+B}{C}$

$D = \frac{2C}{3}$ minimum

if pith is absent measure 75mm through centre of the end of timber

Distortion ~ measurement over the length and width of section to determine the amount of bow, spring and twist.

Bow

Spring

Twist

Characteristics and tolerances of GS and SS graded timber ~

Criteria	GS	SS
KAR: No margin condition	MKAR≤1/2 TKAR≤1/2	MKAR≤1/2 TKAR≤1/3
	Or:	
KAR: Margin condition	MKAR>1/2 TKAR≤1/3	MKAR>1/2 TKAR≤1/5
Fissures and resin pockets: Not through thickness Through thickness	Defects≤1/2 timber thickness <1.5 m or 1/2 timber length take lesser <1.0 m or 1/4 timber length take lesser If at ends fissure length maximum 2 × timber width	Defects≤1/2 timber thickness <1.0 m or 1/4 timber length take lesser <0.5 m or 1/4 timber length take lesser If at ends fissure length < width of timber section
Slope of grain:	Maximum 1 in 6	Maximum 1 in 10
Wane:	Maximum 1/3 of the full edge and face of the section – length not limited	
Resin pockets: Not through thickness Through thickness	Unlimited if shorter than width of section otherwise as for fissures Unlimited if shorter than 1/2 width of section otherwise as for fissures	
Growth rate of annual rings:	Average width or growth <10mm	Average width or growth <6mm
Distortion: –bow –spring –twist	<20 mm over 2m <12 mm over 2m <2 mm per 25mm width over 2m	<10 mm over 2m <8 mm over 2m <1 mm per 25mm width over 2m

Structural softwood cross-sectional size has established terminology such as sawn, basic and unwrought as produced by conversion of the log into commercial dimensions, e.g. 100 × 50 mm and 225 × 75 mm (4″ × 2″ and 9″ × 3″ respectively, as the nearest imperial sizes).

Timber is converted in imperial and metric sizes depending on its source in the world. Thereafter, standardisation can be undertaken by machine planing the surfaces to produce uniformly compatible and practically convenient dimensions, i.e. 225 mm is not the same as 9″. Planed timber has been variously described as nominal, regularised and wrought, e.g. 100 × 50 mm sawn becomes 97 × 47 mm when planed and is otherwise known as ex. 100 × 50 mm, where ex means out of.

Guidance in BS EN 336 requires the sizes of timber from a supplier to be redefined as 'Target Sizes' within the following tolerances:

T1 ~ Thickness and width$\leq$100 mm, −1 to +3 mm.

Thickness and width>100 mm, −2 to +4 mm.

T2 ~ Thickness and width$\leq$100 mm, −1 to +1 mm.

Thickness and width>100 mm, −1.5 to +1.5 mm.

T1 applies to sawn timber, e.g. 100 × 75 mm.

T2 applies to planed timber, e.g. 97 × 72 mm.

Further example ~ a section of timber required to be 195 mm planed × 50 mm sawn is specified as: 195 (T2) × 50 (T1).

Target sizes for sawn softwood (T1) ~

50, 63, 75, 100, 125, 150, 175, 200, 225, 250 and 300 mm.

Target sizes for planed/machined softwood (T2) ~

47, 60, 72, 97, 120, 145, 170, 195, 220, 245 and 295 mm.

Ref. BS EN 336: Structural timber. Sizes, permitted deviations.

Conversion ~ after timber is sawn into commercially useable sections, it is seasoned (oven dried) to a moisture content of between 10% and 15% depending on species.

$$\text{Moisture content} = \frac{\text{Mass when wet} - \text{Mass when dried}}{\text{Mass when dried}} \times 100\%$$

Protection ~ the moisture content of seasoned timber is much less than timber in its natural state, therefore timber will readily absorb water if it is unprotected.

The effects of water absorption may be:

· Deformities and distortion (see page 145).
· Rot and decay (see pages 149 and 150).
· Swelling and shrinkage.

Swelling and shrinkage will be most noticeable after fixing, unless the seasoned moisture content is maintained by correct storage at the suppliers, on site and by adequate protection in use.

Movement ~ shrinkage occurs as wood dries below its fibre saturation point. It will also expand if water is allowed to penetrate the open fibres. Volume change is not the same or even proportionally the same, as potential for movement varies directionally:

· Longitudinally – minimal, i.e. 0.1% to 0.3%.
· Transversely/radially – 2% to 6%.
· Tangentially – 5% to 10%.

tangential movement
e.g. 8% in 25mm = 2mm

transverse or radial movement
e.g. 4% in 200 mm = 8mm

movement longitudinally is relatively small, e.g. 0.1% in 2 m = 2mm

Damp conditions can be the source of many different types of wood-decaying fungi. The principal agencies of decay are:

* Dry rot (Serpula lacrymans or merulius lacrymans), and
* Wet rot (Coniophora cerabella)

Dry rot – this is the most difficult to control as its root system can penetrate damp and porous plaster, brickwork and concrete. It can also remain dormant until damp conditions encourage its growth, even though the original source of dampness is removed.

   Appearance – white fungal threads which attract dampness from the air or adjacent materials. The threads develop strands bearing spores or seeds which drift with air movements to settle and germinate on timber having a moisture content exceeding about 25%. Fruiting bodies of a grey or red flat profile may also identify dry rot.

Typical surface appearance of dry rot –

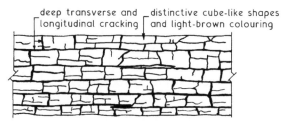

deep transverse and longitudinal cracking — distinctive cube-like shapes and light-brown colouring

Wet rot – this is limited in its development and must have moisture continually present, e.g. a permanently leaking pipe or a faulty dpc. Growth pattern is similar to dry rot, but spores will not germinate in dry timber.

   Appearance – fungal threads of black or dark-brown colour. Fruiting bodies may be olive-green or dark brown and these are often the first sign of decay.

Typical surface appearance of wet rot –

reddish-brown colouring — large longitudinal cracking with minor lateral cracks

Causes:
* Defective construction, e.g. broken roof tiles; no damp-proof course.
* Installation of wet timber during construction, e.g. framing sealed behind plasterboard linings; wet joists under floor decking.
* Lack of ventilation, e.g. blocked air-bricks to suspended timber ground floor; condensation in unventilated roof spaces.
* Defective water services, e.g. undetected leaks on internal pipework; blocked or broken rainwater pipes and guttering.

General treatment:
* Remove source of dampness.
* Allow affected area to dry.
* Remove and burn all affected timber and sound timber within 500 mm of fungal attack.
* Remove contaminated plaster and rake out adjacent mortar joints to masonry.

Note: This is normally sufficient treatment where wet rot is identified. However, where dry rot is apparent the following additional treatment is necessary:
* Sterilise surface of concrete and masonry.
  Heat with a blow torch until the surface is too hot to touch. Apply a proprietary fungicide† generously to warm surface. Irrigate badly affected masonry and floors, i.e. provide 12 mm diameter boreholes at about 500 mm spacing and flood or pressure inject with fungicide.

† 20:1 dilution of water and sodium pentachlorophenate, sodium orthophenylphate or mercuric chloride. Product manufacturers' safety in handling and use measures must be observed when applying these chemicals.

Replacement work should ensure that new timbers are pressure impregnated with a preservative. Cement and sand mixes for rendering, plastering and screeds should contain a zinc oxychloride fungicide.

Further reading –
BRE: Timber pack (ref. AP 265) – various Digests, Information Papers, Good Repair Guides and Good Building Guides.
In-situ timber treatment using timber preservatives – HSE Books.

Ref. Bldg. Regs. Approved Document C, Site preparation and resistance to contaminants and moisture.

Trees are part of our national heritage and are also the source of timber. To maintain this source a control over tree felling has been established under the Forestry Act which places the control responsibility on the Forestry Commission. Local planning authorities also have powers under the Town and Country Planning Act and the Town and Country Amenities Act to protect trees by making tree preservation orders. A TPO may be applied if the LPA consider that it is "expedient in the interests of amenity to make provision for the preservation of trees or woodlands in their area" (Section 198[1] of the Town and Country Planning Act). Before cutting down, uprooting, severing roots, topping off, lopping, damaging or destroying a tree, a formal application must be submitted to the LPA for consent. Contravention of such an order can lead to a substantial fine and a compulsion to replace any protected tree which has been removed or destroyed. Trees on building sites which are covered by a tree preservation order should be protected by a suitable fence.

tree covered by a tree preservation order

cleft chestnut or similar fencing at least 1·200 high erected to the full spread and completely encircling the tree

Definition and interpretation of what constitutes a tree (e.g. trunk diameter, overall height, etc.) will vary and may be considered subjective. Therefore, appeals will be considered. If upheld, an agreement for replacement trees is usual, in at least the same quantity of the same species within the proposed development site. Trees, shrubs, bushes and tree roots which are to be removed from site can usually be grubbed out using handheld tools such as saws, picks and spades. Where whole trees are to be removed for relocation special labour and equipment is required to ensure that the roots, root earth ball and bark are not damaged.

Ref. BS 5837: Trees in relation to design, demolition and construction. Recommendations.

Buildings of special historic or architectural interest are protected by provisions in the Planning (Listed Buildings and Conservation Areas) Act. English Heritage, funded by the Department for Culture, Media and Sport and from donations and commercial activities, is responsible for safeguarding and protecting the character of buildings that could otherwise be lost through demolition or unsympathetic alterations, extensions, modifications, refurbishment or inadequate maintenance.

Buildings considered to be a national asset and worthy of preservation are listed. Statutory listing applies to about half-a-million buildings. This status places responsibility on their owners to keep them in good order. These buildings are legally protected, therefore proposals for development on the site that they occupy as well as proposals for both internal and external alterations are subject to a listed building consent being obtained from the local planning authority.

Examples of the type of work may include the following:
· Extensions and any demolition.
· Removal of internal walls and floors.
· Changes to room layout.
· Window and door replacement.
· Painting of unpainted surfaces.
· Exposed plumbing and electrical installations.
· Alterations to internal features, e.g. doors, panelling, fireplaces.
· Changes to existing materials/colour specifications.
· Removal of finishes to expose brickwork and structural timber.
The LPA should be consulted about all proposed work. It is a fineable offence to alter the character of listed buildings without the necessary consent and an order can be imposed on the building owner to rectify matters at their expense.

Categories of listing ~
Grade I: Buildings of exceptional interest.
Grade II*: Particularly important buildings of more than special interest.
Grade II: Buildings of special interest, warranting preservation; 90% of listed buildings are in this category.
The grading applies in England and Wales. Similar provisions exist for Northern Ireland and Scotland.
See also the Royal Commission on Historical Monuments.

Services which may be encountered on construction sites and the authority responsible are:

Water – Local Water Company

Electricity – transmission ~ RWE npower, EDF Energy and E-on.
　　　　　　　distribution ~ In Britain there are 14 separate regional grids managed by licensed independent network operators, e.g. Electricity North West.

Gas – Local gas or energy service providers, e.g. British Gas.

Telephones – National Telecommunications Companies, e.g. BT, and Vodaphone.

Drainage – Local Authority unless a private drain when owner(s) is (are) responsible.

All the above authorities must be notified of any proposed new services and alterations or terminations to existing services before any work is carried out.

Locating Existing Services on Site ~

Method 1 – By reference to maps and plans prepared and issued by the respective responsible authority.

Method 2 – Using visual indicators ~

Method 3 – Detection specialist contractor employed to trace all forms of underground services using electronic subsurface survey equipment.

Once located, position and type of service can be plotted on a map or plan, marked with special paint on hard surfaces and marked with wood pegs with indentification data on earth surfaces.

Setting Out the Building Outline ~ this task is usually undertaken once the site has been cleared of any debris or obstructions and any reduced-level excavation work is finished. It is usually the responsibility of the contractor to set out the building(s) using the information provided by the designer or architect. Accurate setting out is of paramount importance and should therefore only be carried out by competent persons and all their work thoroughly checked, preferably by different personnel and by a different method.

The first task in setting out the building is to establish a baseline to which all the setting out can be related. The baseline very often coincides with the building line which is a line, whose position on site is given by the local authority in front of which no development is permitted.

Typical Setting Out Example ~

outline of building marked by cord fixed to corner posts

alternative method for corners

diagonal checks

site boundary→

90° to all corners

▽← temporary bench mark or site datum post

corner posts

base- and/or building line

90° angles obtained using site square, theodolite or builders square

footpath   road kerb

* setting dimensions measured with a tape, ranging rods may be required to establish straight line between corner posts

nail in centre of post

50 × 50 corner post driven firmly into the ground

cord marking outline of building

outline marked on ground with dry lime or similar powder

Temporary Bench mark: this is a fixed point on site to which all levels are related and should be established at an early stage in the contract. Where possible it should relate to an ordnance bench mark. On site it can be any permanent feature such as a drain cover or a firmly driven post.

Setting Out Trenches ~ the objective of this task is twofold. First, it must establish the excavation size, shape and direction; and second, it must establish the width and position of the walls. The outline of building will have been set out and using this outline profile boards can be set up to control the position, width and possibly the depth of the proposed trenches. Profile boards should be set up at least 2·000 clear of trench positions so that they do not obstruct the excavation work. The level of the profile crossboard should be related to the site datum and fixed at a convenient height above ground level if a traveller is to be used to control the depth of the trench. Alternatively the trench depth can be controlled using a level and staff related to site datum. The trench width can be marked on the profile with either nails or saw cuts and with a painted band if required for identification.

Typical Details ~

foundation and trench

wall

profile boards

TYPICAL LAYOUT (profiles not to scale)

trench

wall

saw cuts

painted band

600 to 1·000

50 × 50 posts

150 × 38 crossboard

posts driven into the ground at least 600 mm

TYPICAL PROFILE BOARD

profile boards

traveller sighted between two profiles

profile boards

cords between profiles

trench width marked with a line or dots of dry lime powder for hand excavation

centre line of trench marked with dry lime powder for machine excavation using trench width bucket

cord between profiles

concrete strip foundation

peg marking top of concrete

pegs marking top of concrete

concrete trench fill foundation

NB. Corners of walls transferred from intersecting cord lines to mortar spots on concrete foundations using a spirit level.

Setting Out a Framed Building ~ framed buildings are usually related to a grid, the intersections of the grid lines being the centre point of an isolated or pad foundation. The grid is usually set out from a baseline which does not always form part of the grid. Setting out dimensions for locating the grid can either be given on a drawing or they will have to be accurately scaled off a general layout plan. The grid is established using a theodolite and marking the grid line intersections with stout pegs. Once the grid has been set out offset pegs or profiles can be fixed clear of any subsequent excavation work. Control of excavation depth can be by means of a traveller sighted between sight rails or by level and staff related to site datum.

Typical Details ~

2nd position of theodolite - sighted onto A4 turned 90° and points B1 to F1 fixed and marked

1st position of theodolite - sighted onto F4 and points B4 to E4 fixed and marked theodolite turned 90° and points A3 to A1 fixed and marked

3rd theodolite position to fix points F2 and F3

▽ TBM or site datum

internal grid points fixed by setting up theodolite over any of the perimeter points

grid lines

boundary

base line

* setting out dimensions to establish grid line A4 to F4

sight rail fixed at known level

fenced peg - alternative to profile

profile board

cords

profile board

pad template

excavation

grid setting out peg

traveller sighted between sight rails to control depth

1. Pad template positioned with cords between profiles and pad outline marked with dry lime or similar powder.

2. Pad pits excavated using traveller sighted between sight rails fixed at a level related to site datum.

Setting Out Reduced Level Excavations ~ the overall outline of the reduced level area can be set out using a theodolite, ranging rods, tape and pegs working from a baseline. To control the depth of excavation, sight rails are set up at a convenient height and at positions which will enable a traveller to be used.

Typical Details ~

1. Setting up sight rails:

staff reading gives height of collimation of level

necessary staff reading calculated to give level at desired height

level

sight line

temporary bench mark or site datum post

sight rail fixed here

ground level

sight rail posts

2. Controlling excavation depth:

site datum post set in concrete

corner posts to fix outline of excavation area

sight rails fixed at desired level

outline of excavation area marked with dry sand or similar material

corner post

formation level

free standing traveller

edge of excavation area

sight rails - face painted black and white

height of traveller = desired level of sight rail - formation level

Datum ~ altitude zero taken at mean sea level. This varies between different countries, but for UK purposes it was established at Newlyn in Cornwall from tide data recorded between May 1915 and April 1921. Relative levels defined by bench marks are located throughout the country. The most common are identified as carved arrows cut into walls of permanent structures. Reference to Ordnance Survey maps of an area will indicate bench mark positions and their height above sea level, hence the name Ordnance Datum (OD).

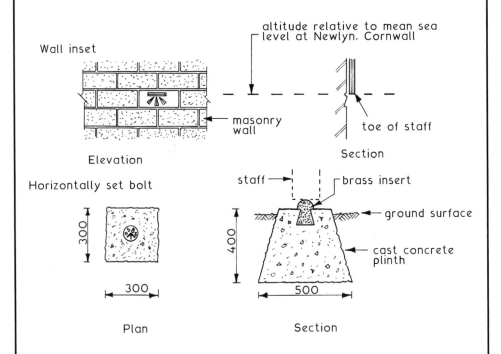

Taking site levels ~ the nearest OD bench mark may be impractical to access. The alternative is to establish a datum or temporary bench mark (TBM) from a fixture such as a manhole cover. Otherwise, a fixed position for a TBM could be a robust post set in concrete or a cast concrete plinth set in the ground to one side of ongoing work.

Instruments consist of a level (tilting or automatic) and a staff. A tilting level is basically a telescope mounted on a tripod for stability. Correcting screws establish accuracy in the horizontal plane by air bubble in a vial and focus is by adjustable lens. Cross hairs of horizontal and vertical lines indicate image sharpness on an extending staff of 3, 4 or 5m length. Staff graduations are in 10mm intervals on an "E" pattern as shown on the next page. Estimates are taken to the nearest millimetre. An automatic level is much simpler to use, eliminating the need for manual adjustment. It is approximately levelled by centre bulb bubble. A compensator within the telescope effects fine adjustment.

TILTING LEVEL

Taking levels ~ an Ordnance Datum bench mark or a temporary bench mark is located. The levelling instrument and tripod are positioned on firm ground and sighted to the bench mark. Further staff height readings are taken at established positions around the site or at measured intervals corresponding to a grid pattern at convenient intervals, typically 10m. Each intersection of the grid lines represents a staff position, otherwise known as a station. Levels taken from the staff readings (4 No. from the grid corners) are computed with the plan area calculations (100m^2 for a 10m grid). From this the volume of site excavation or cut and fill required to level the site can be calculated.

Application ~ methods to determine differences in ground levels for calculation of site excavation volumes and costs.

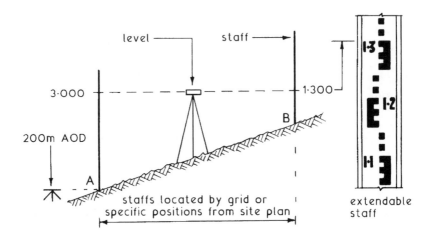

level ——— staff ———

3·000

200m AOD

A

B

1·300

staffs located by grid or specific positions from site plan

extendable staff

Rise and fall:

Staff reading at A = 3·00m, B = 1·30m
Ground level at A = 200m above ordnance datum (AOD)
Therefore level at B = 200m + rise (– fall if declining)
So level at B = 200 + (3·00 – 1·30) = 201·7m

Height of collimation (HC):

HC at A = Reduced level (RL) + staff reading
= 200 m + 3·00m = 203m AOD
Level at B = HC at A – staff reading at B
= 203 – 1·30 = 201·7m

height above mean sea level at Newlyn

carved bench mark

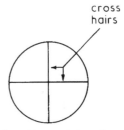

cross hairs

view through level

Theodolite — a tripod mounted instrument designed to measure angles in the horizontal or vertical plane.

The theodolite in principle

Measurement — a telescope provides for focal location between instrument and subject. Position of the scope is defined by an index of angles. The scale and presentation of angles varies from traditional micrometer readings to computer-compatible crystal displays. Angles are measured in degrees, minutes and seconds, e.g. 165° 53' 30".

vertical	horizontal
87° 07' 00"	165° 53' 30"

Direct reading micrometer scale

Application — at least two sightings are taken and the readings averaged. After the first sighting, the horizontal plate is rotated through 180° and the scope is also rotated 180° through the vertical to return the instrument to its original alignment for the second reading. This process will move the vertical circle from right face to left face, or vice versa. It is important to note the readings against the facing — see below.

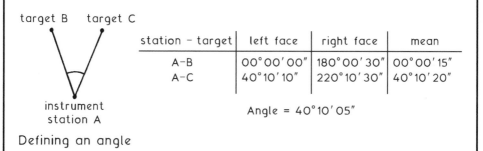

station – target	left face	right face	mean
A–B	00°00'00"	180°00'30"	00°00'15"
A–C	40°10'10"	220°10'30"	40°10'20"

Angle = 40°10'05"

Defining an angle

Road Construction ~ within the context of building operations roadworks usually consist of the construction of small estate roads, access roads and driveways together with temporary roads laid to define site circulation routes and/or provide a suitable surface for plant movements. The construction of roads can be considered under three headings:

1. Setting out (this and next two pages).
2. Earthworks (see page 165).
3. Paving Construction (see pages 165–167).

Setting Out Roads ~ this activity is usually carried out after the topsoil has been removed using the dimensions given on the layout drawing(s). The layout could include straight lengths junctions, hammer heads, turning bays and intersecting curves.

Straight Road Lengths – these are usually set out from centre lines which have been established by traditional means

NB. curve road lengths set out in a similar manner

Junctions and Hammer Heads –

Centre lines fixed by traditional methods. Tape hooked over pin at chainage zero and passed around chainage point pin at 8.750 then returned to chainage zero via the radius pin with a tape length of 29.875. Radius pin held tape length 17.500 and tape is moved until tight between all pins. Radius pin is driven and a 6.000 tape length is swung from the pin to trace out curve which is marked with pegs or pins

Tape length $= 17.50 + \sqrt{2} \times 8.75$
$= 29.875$

Lane Width ~ established by assessment of the amount of traffic flow and speed restriction. For convenience of road users, the minimum width can be based on a vehicle width not exceeding 2.500 m plus an allowance for clearance of at least 0.500 m between vehicles. This will provide an overall dimension of 5.500 m for two-way traffic. One-way traffic will require a lane width of at least 3.000 m.

Road Junctions ~ drivers of vehicles approaching a junction from any direction should have a clear view of other road users. Unobstructed visibility is required within vertical sight lines, triangular on plan. These provide a distance and area within which other vehicles and pedestrians can be seen at specific heights above the carriageway. No street furniture, trees or other obstructions are permitted within these zones, as indicated in the diagram below and on the next page.

Vertical Sight Lines ~ vertical in height and horizontal or near horizontal for driver and pedestrian visibility. These clear sight lines are established between a driver's eye height of between 1.050 m and 2.000 m to allow for varying vehicle heights, to an object height of between 0.600 m and 2.000 m over the horizontal plane.

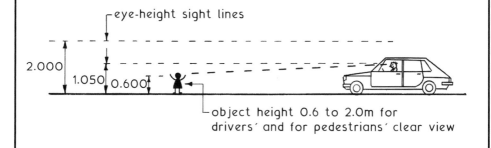

eye-height sight lines

2.000
1.050 0.600

object height 0.6 to 2.0m for drivers' and for pedestrians' clear view

Horizontal Sight Lines ~ these should be provided and maintained thereafter with a clear view, to prevent the possibility of danger from vehicle drivers having obstructed outlook when approaching junctions. The recommended dimensions vary relative to the category of road classification and the speed restriction.

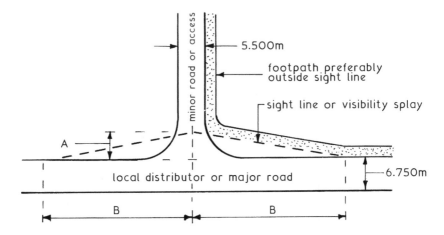

Guidance for dimensions A and B ~

Type of road	Min. dimension A (m)
Access to a single dwelling or a small development of about half-a-dozen units	2.0
Minor road junctions within developed areas	2.4
Minor road junctions at local distributor roads	4.5
Busy minor road junctions, access roads, district or local distributor roads and other major junctions	9.0

Speed restriction mph (kph)	Min. major road dimension B (m)
20 (32)	45
30 (48)	90
40 (64)	120
50 (80)	160
60 (90)	215
70 (112)	295

Refs.: Planning Policy Guidance (PPG) 13, DCLG.
Manual for Streets, DfT and DCLG. Manual for Streets 2, The Chartered Institution of Highways and Transport.

Earthworks ~ this will involve the removal of topsoil together with any vegetation, scraping and grading the required area down to formation level plus the formation of any cuttings or embankments. Suitable plant for these operations would be tractor shovels fitted with a 4 in 1 bucket (page 208); graders (page 207) and bulldozers (page 205). The soil immediately below the formation level is called the subgrade whose strength will generally decrease as its moisture content rises; therefore if it is to be left exposed for any length of time protection may be required. Subgrade protection may take the form of a covering of medium-gauge plastic sheeting with generous overlaps. To preserve the strength and durability of the subgrade it may be necessary to install cut off subsoil drains alongside the proposed road (see Road Drainage on page 876).

Paving Construction ~ once the subgrade has been prepared and any drainage or other buried services installed the construction of the paving can be undertaken. Paved surfaces can be either flexible or rigid in format. Flexible or bound surfaces are formed of materials applied in layers directly over the subgrade whereas rigid pavings consist of a concrete slab resting on a granular base (see pages 166 and 167).

Typical Flexible Paving Details ~

surfacing = base layer + wearing course

60mm thick base course of dense bitumen macadam or asphalt laid to form the crossfalls and/or gradients

wearing course of coated macadam or asphalt having good non-skid properties; reasonable resistance to glare and an acceptable life — should be laid within three days of base layer

sub-base of crushed stone or dry lean mix concrete (1:15) laid in 100 to 150mm thick compacted layers - total thickness related to loading and subgrade strength

subgrade

NB. no road joints required

Rigid Pavings ~ these consist of a reinforced or unreinforced in-situ concrete slab laid over a base course of crushed stone or similar material which has been blinded to receive a polythene sheet slip membrane. The primary objective of this membrane is to prevent grout loss from the in-situ slab.

Typical Rigid Paving Details ~

40 to 80 mm end cover

welded fabric

asphalt or similar topping if required

50 to 60mm cover

in-situ concrete paving slab - depth to design

polythene sheet slip membrane

80 mm-thick crushed stone blinded base layer

subgrade

The paving can be laid between metal road forms or timber edge formwork. Alternatively the kerb stones could be laid first to act as permanent formwork.

25mm diameter x 600mm long steel fixing stake

housing for sliding plate

5 or 6 mm thick pressed steel standard road form

stake housings welded to web of road form

sliding plate housing

stop for sliding plate

sliding plate connector

standard road form length 3·000

50

3 No. fixing stakes

5 No. fixing stakes

100 to 250

fixing stake housing

100 to 250

STANDARD ROAD FORM

FLEXIBLE ROAD FORM

166

Joints in Rigid Pavings ~ longitudinal and transverse joints are required in rigid pavings to:

1. Limit size of slab.
2. Limit stresses due to subgrade restraint.
3. Provide for expansion and contraction movements.

The main joints used are classified as expansion, contraction or longitudinal, the latter being the same in detail as the contraction joint differing only in direction. The spacing of road joints is determined by:

1. Slab thickness.
2. Whether slab is reinforced or unreinforced.
3. Anticipated traffic load and flow rate.
4. Temperature at which concrete is laid.

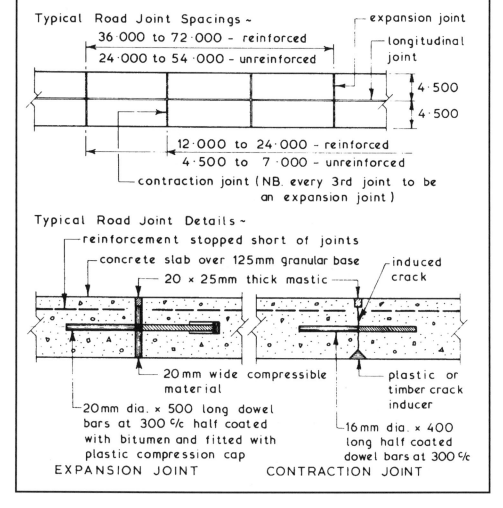

Typical Road Joint Spacings ~

36·000 to 72·000 – reinforced
24·000 to 54·000 – unreinforced

expansion joint
longitudinal joint

4·500
4·500

12·000 to 24·000 – reinforced
4·500 to 7·000 – unreinforced

contraction joint (NB. every 3rd joint to be an expansion joint)

Typical Road Joint Details ~

reinforcement stopped short of joints
concrete slab over 125mm granular base
20 × 25mm thick mastic
induced crack

20mm wide compressible material

20mm dia. × 500 long dowel bars at 300 c/c half coated with bitumen and fitted with plastic compression cap

EXPANSION JOINT

plastic or timber crack inducer

16mm dia. × 400 long half coated dowel bars at 300 c/c

CONTRACTION JOINT

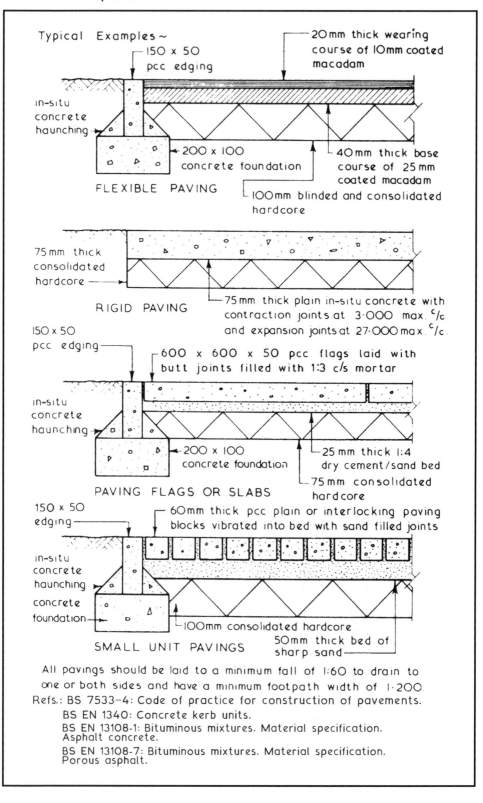

Typical Examples ~

150 x 50 pcc edging

20mm thick wearing course of 10mm coated macadam

in-situ concrete haunching

200 x 100 concrete foundation

40mm thick base course of 25mm coated macadam

100mm blinded and consolidated hardcore

FLEXIBLE PAVING

75mm thick consolidated hardcore

75mm thick plain in-situ concrete with contraction joints at 3·000 max. ^{c}/c and expansion joints at 27·000 max. ^{c}/c.

RIGID PAVING

150 x 50 pcc edging

600 x 600 x 50 pcc flags laid with butt joints filled with 1:3 c/s mortar

in-situ concrete haunching

200 x 100 concrete foundation

25mm thick 1:4 dry cement/sand bed

75mm consolidated hardcore

PAVING FLAGS OR SLABS

150 x 50 edging

60mm thick pcc plain or interlocking paving blocks vibrated into bed with sand filled joints

in-situ concrete haunching

concrete foundation

100mm consolidated hardcore

50mm thick bed of sharp sand

SMALL UNIT PAVINGS

All pavings should be laid to a minimum fall of 1:60 to drain to one or both sides and have a minimum footpath width of 1·200.
Refs.: BS 7533-4: Code of practice for construction of pavements.
   BS EN 1340: Concrete kerb units.
   BS EN 13108-1: Bituminous mixtures. Material specification. Asphalt concrete.
   BS EN 13108-7: Bituminous mixtures. Material specification. Porous asphalt.

Available sections ~ manufactured in 915 mm lengths from silver/grey aggregate concrete.

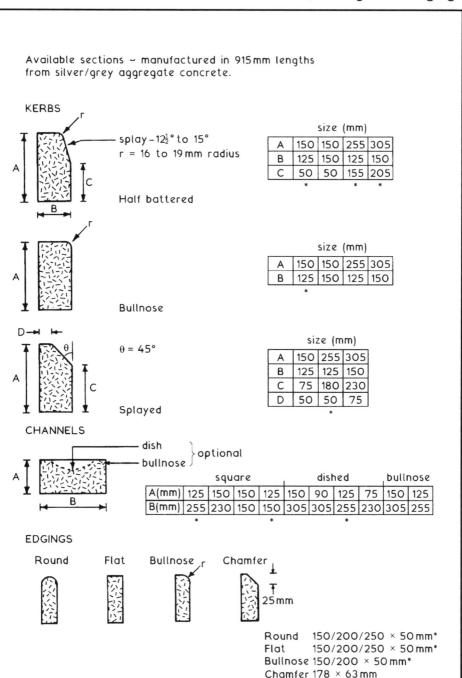

KERBS

splay – 12½° to 15°
r = 16 to 19 mm radius

Half battered

	size (mm)			
A	150	150	255	305
B	125	150	125	150
C	50	50	155	205

Bullnose

	size (mm)			
A	150	150	255	305
B	125	150	125	150

θ = 45°

Splayed

	size (mm)		
A	150	255	305
B	125	125	150
C	75	180	230
D	50	50	75

CHANNELS

dish ⎫
bullnose ⎬ optional

	square				dished				bullnose	
A(mm)	125	150	150	125	150	90	125	75	150	125
B(mm)	255	230	150	150	305	305	255	230	305	255

EDGINGS

Round   Flat   Bullnose   Chamfer

25 mm

Round   150/200/250 × 50 mm*
Flat   150/200/250 × 50 mm*
Bullnose 150/200 × 50 mm*
Chamfer 178 × 63 mm

*denotes BS sections

NB. Further components such as drop/tapered kerbs are available for vehicle accesses. Quadrants and angles provide for directional change.

Concrete paving flags - BS dimensions:

Type	Size (nominal)	Size (work)	Thickness (T)
A – plain	600 × 450	598 × 448	50 or 63
B – plain	600 × 600	598 × 598	50 or 63
C – plain	600 × 750	598 × 748	50 or 63
D – plain	600 × 900	598 × 898	50 or 63
E – plain	450 × 450	448 × 448	50 or 70
TA/E – tactile	450 × 450	448 × 448	50 or 70
TA/F – tactile	400 × 400	398 × 398	50 or 65
TA/G – tactile	300 × 300	298 × 298	50 or 60

Note: All dimensions in millimetres.

Tactile flags – manufactured with a blistered (shown) or ribbed surface. Used in walkways to provide warning of hazards or to enable recognition of locations for people whose visibility is impaired. See also Department of Transport Disability Circular DU 1/86[1], for uses and applications.

Type	A (mm)	B (mm)
E	64	33
F	66·8	33
G	75	37·5

(+ or −2 mm)

Ref. BS EN 1339: Concrete paving flags. Requirements and test methods.

Landscaping ~ in the context of building works this would involve reinstatement of the site as a preparation to the landscaping in the form of lawns, paths, pavings, flower and shrub beds and tree planting. The actual planning, lawn laying and planting activities are normally undertaken by a landscape subcontractor. The main contractor's work would involve clearing away all waste and unwanted materials, breaking up and levelling surface areas, removing all unwanted vegetation, preparing the subsoil for and spreading topsoil to a depth of at least 150mm.

Services ~ the actual position and laying of services is the responsibility of the various service boards and undertakings. The best method is to use the common trench approach; avoid as far as practicable laying services under the highway.

Typical Common Trench Details ~

Road Signs ~ these can range from markings painted on roads to define traffic lanes, rights of way and warnings of hazards to signs mounted above the road level to give information, warning or directives, the latter being obligatory. See also, pages 56 and 57.

Typical Examples ~

INFORMATION   WARNING - ROAD-WORKS   DIRECTIVE - NO LEFT TURN

Tubular Scaffolding

Scaffolds ~ temporary platforms to provide a safe working place at a convenient height. Usually required when the working height is 1·500 or more above ground level.

Component Parts of a Tubular Scaffold ~

all tubes to comply with BS EN 39 or BS 1139-1.2

standard

transoms or putlogs

longitudinal horizontal member called a ledger — fixed to standards with double couplers

transom or putlog

ledger

vertical member usually called a standard spaced at 1·800 to 2·400 centres depending on load to be carried

blade end   standard

transverse horizontal member called a putlog — fixed to ledger with a putlog coupler

transom or putlog

putlog coupler   standard   ledger

double coupler

ledger

base plate with locating spigot plan size 150 × 150

transverse horizontal member called a transom fixed to ledgers

HORIZONTAL COMPONENTS

timber sole plate under base plates on soft or uneven ground

façade brace

cross-brace

all bracing fixed with swivel couplers

VERTICAL COMPONENT   SLOPING COMPONENTS

Refs.: BS EN 39: Loose steel tubes for tube and coupler scaffolds.

BS 1139-1.2: Metal scaffolding. Tubes. Specification for aluminium tube.

BS EN 12811-1: Temporary equipment. Scaffolds. Performance requirements and general design.

Work at Height Regulations.

Occupational Health and Safety Act. Scaffold regulations.

Putlog Scaffolds ~ these are scaffolds which have an outer row of standards joined together by ledgers which in turn support the transverse putlogs which are built into the bed joints or perpends as the work proceeds; they are therefore only suitable for new work in bricks or blocks.

Typical Details ~

guard rail

wire mesh brick guard

intermediate guard rail

wall under construction

toe board clip

toe board

boarded working platform - see page 175

putlog

ledger

blade end built into wall

100mm wide gap for plumb rule

ladder secured top and bottom to terminate at least 1·050 above working platform

1·350 to 1·500

putlog coupler

double coupler

putlog

ledger

1·350 to 1·500

standards at 2·000 centres

pitch 75° or '4 up 1 out'

base plate

sole plate

1·400 maximum

for tying-in details see page 176

173

Independent Scaffolds ~ these are scaffolds which have two rows of standards, each row joined together with ledgers which in turn support the transverse transoms. The scaffold is erected clear of the existing or proposed building but is tied to the building or structure at suitable intervals – see page 176.

Typical Details ~

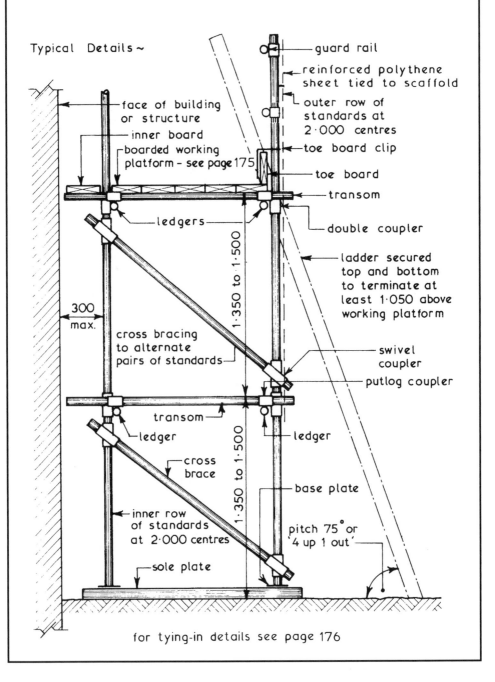

- guard rail
- reinforced polythene sheet tied to scaffold
- outer row of standards at 2·000 centres
- toe board clip
- toe board
- transom
- double coupler
- ladder secured top and bottom to terminate at least 1·050 above working platform
- swivel coupler
- putlog coupler
- base plate
- pitch 75° or '4 up 1 out'

- face of building or structure
- inner board
- boarded working platform – see page 175

ledgers

300 max.

cross bracing to alternate pairs of standards

1·350 to 1·500

transom

ledger

cross brace

inner row of standards at 2·000 centres

1·350 to 1·500

sole plate

ledger

for tying-in details see page 176

Working Platforms ~ these are close-boarded or plated level surfaces at a height at which work is being carried out and they must provide a safe working place of sufficient strength to support the imposed loads of operatives and/or materials. All working platforms above ground level must be fitted with a toe board and a guard rail.

Typical Details ~

boards to be free of defects to BS 2482: Specification for timber scaffold boards

150 mm minimum

225 mm wide × 38 mm thick × 3·900 long softwood standard scaffold board

25mm wide × 0·9mm thick galvanised hoop iron binding to both ends to prevent splitting

maximum overhang 4 × board thickness

38

bevelled piece at board overlap

1·500 max.   1·500 max.

transom or putlog

boards to be evenly supported on at least three supports per board length

SCAFFOLD BOARDS FOR WORKING PLATFORMS

inner row of standards

guard rail

300 max.

800 minimum

outer row of standards

600 min.

470 max.

950 minimum

deposited material

toe board clips

150 min.

toe board

transom

ledger

working platform

NB. intermediate guard rail will also satisfy 470mm max. gap

NB. above dimensions also apply to putlog scaffolds

Any height at or below ground level

175

Tubular Scaffolding

Tying-in ~ all putlog and independent scaffolds should be tied securely to the building or structure at alternate lift heights vertically and at not more than 6·000 centres horizontally. Putlogs should not be classified as ties.

Suitable tying-in methods include connecting to tubes fitted between sides of window openings or to internal tubes fitted across window openings; the former method should not be used for more than 50% of the total number of ties. If there is an insufficient number of window openings for the required number of ties external rakers should be used.

Typical Details ~

Mobile Scaffolds ~ otherwise known as mobile tower scaffolds. They can be assembled from preformed framing components or from standard scaffold tube and fittings. Used mainly for property maintenance. Must not be moved whilst occupied by persons or equipment.

Typical detail ~

4 No. corner standards

guard rails

close-boarded working platform, min. plan size 1.200 x 1.200

toe board

transom

ledger

cross bracing

transom

ledger

cross bracing

125mm min. diameter castor wheels with integral brake and locking device fixed to corner standards

double coupler

swivel coupler

470 max.

150 min.

950 min.

not less than least lateral dimension

max. free standing height 8.000 (external), 12.000 (internal)
external towers not more than 2.5 times least lateral dimension
internal towers not more than 3.0 times least lateral dimension

Ladder Access:
Inclined within the tower to hinged access door in platform.
Secured to tower so as not to foul the ground.
Lowest rung max. 400mm above the ground.

177

Some basic fittings ~

Swivel coupler

swing-over bolt

swivel joint

swing-over bolt

scaffold tube

tube clamp

Double coupler

swing-over bolt

tube clamp

scaffold tube

Wrapover putlog coupler

swing-over bolt

tube clamp

Putlog end

swing-over bolt

putlog tube

blade

Split joint pin

bolt

scaffold tube

split sections

Reveal pin

scaffold tube

circular nut with "podger" recess

face plate

Base plate

scaffold tube over circular spigot welded to 150mm square plate

Patent Scaffolding ~ these are systems based on an independent scaffold format in which the members are connected together using an integral locking device instead of conventional clips and couplers used with traditional tubular scaffolding. They have the advantages of being easy to assemble and take down using semi-skilled labour and should automatically comply with the requirements set out in the Work at Height Regulations 2005. Generally cross bracing is not required with these systems but façade bracing can be fitted if necessary. Although simple in concept patent systems of scaffolding can lack the flexibility of traditional tubular scaffolds in complex layout situations.

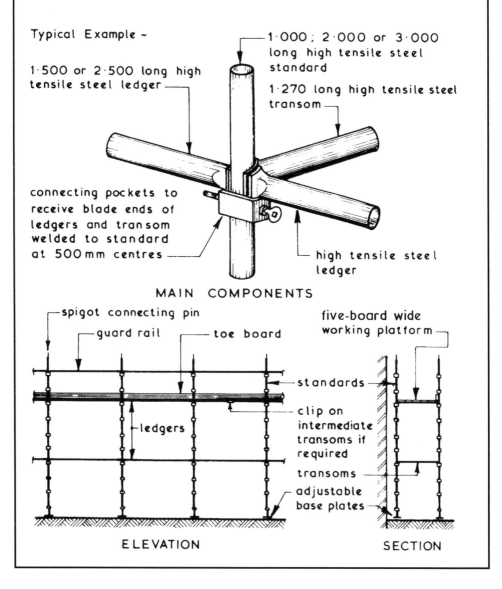

Typical Example ~

1·500 or 2·500 long high tensile steel ledger

1·000 ; 2·000 or 3·000 long high tensile steel standard

1·270 long high tensile steel transom

connecting pockets to receive blade ends of ledgers and transom welded to standard at 500 mm centres

high tensile steel ledger

MAIN COMPONENTS

spigot connecting pin
guard rail
toe board
ledgers

five-board wide working platform

standards
clip on intermediate transoms if required
transoms
adjustable base plates

ELEVATION

SECTION

179

Scaffolding Systems ~ these are temporary stagings to provide safe access to and egress from a working platform. The traditional putlog and independent scaffolds have been covered on pages 172 to 176 inclusive. The minimum design, safety, inspection and performance requirements applicable to traditional scaffolds apply equally to special scaffolds. Special scaffolds are designed to fulfil a specific function or to provide access to areas where it is not possible and/or economic to use traditional formats. They can be constructed from standard tubes or patent systems; the latter complying with most regulation requirements are easy and quick to assemble but lack the complete flexibility of the traditional tubular scaffolds.

Birdcage Scaffolds ~ these are a form of independent scaffold normally used for internal work in large buildings such as public halls and churches to provide access to ceilings and soffits for light maintenance work like painting and cleaning. They consist of parallel rows of standards connected by leaders in both directions, the whole arrangement being firmly braced in all directions. The whole birdcage scaffold assembly is designed to support a single working platform which should be double planked or underlined with polythene or similar sheeting as a means of restricting the amount of dust reaching the floor level.

Slung Scaffolds ~ these are a form of scaffold which is suspended from the main structure by means of wire ropes or steel chains and is not provided with a means of being raised or lowered. Each working platform of a slung scaffold consists of a supporting framework of ledgers and transoms which should not create a plan size in excess of 2·500 × 2·500 and be held in position by not less than six evenly spaced wire ropes or steel chains securely anchored at both ends. The working platform should be double planked or underlined with polythene or similar sheeting to restrict the amount of dust reaching the floor level. Slung scaffolds are an alternative to birdcage scaffolds and although more difficult to erect have the advantage of leaving a clear space beneath the working platform which makes them suitable for cinemas, theatres and high-ceilinged banking halls.

Suspended Scaffolds ~ these consist of a working platform in the form of a cradle which is suspended from cantilever beams or outriggers from the roof of a tall building to give access to the façade for carrying out light maintenance work and cleaning activities. The cradles can have manual or power control and be in single units or grouped together to form a continuous working platform. If grouped together they are connected to one another at their abutment ends with hinges to form a gap of not more than 25mm wide. Many high-rise buildings have a permanent cradle system installed at roof level and this is recommended for all buildings over 30·000 high.

Typical Example ~

balance is achieved when kentledge × tail length = cradle load × cantilever but for safety kentledge × tail length = at least 3(cradle load × cantilever) unless outriggers are securely bolted to roof structure to prevent overturning

900mm wide × 2·400 long power operated cradle

Cantilever Scaffolds ~ these are a form of independent tied scaffold erected on cantilever beams and used where it is impracticable, undesirable or uneconomic to use a traditional scaffold raised from ground level. The assembly of a cantilever scaffold requires special skills and should therefore always be carried out by trained and experienced personnel.

Typical Example ~

façade bracing to be used as required

Truss-out Scaffold ~ this is a form of independent tied scaffold used where it is impracticable, undesirable or uneconomic to build a scaffold from ground level. The supporting scaffold structure is known as the truss-out. The assembly of this form of scaffold requires special skills and should therefore be carried out by trained and experienced personnel.

Typical Example ~

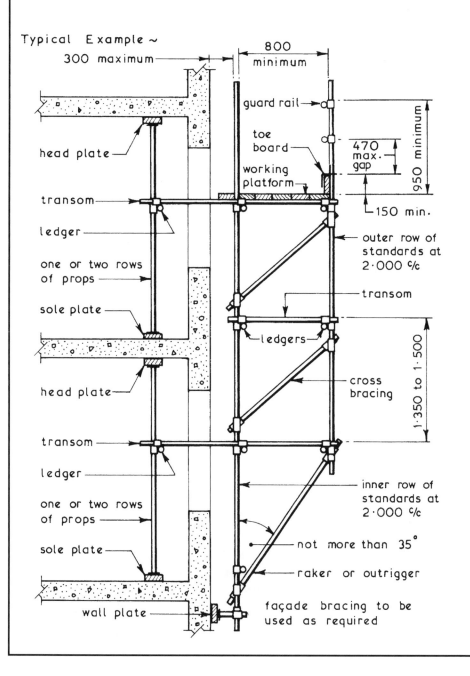

300 maximum

800 minimum

head plate

transom

ledger

one or two rows of props

sole plate

head plate

transom

ledger

one or two rows of props

sole plate

wall plate

guard rail

toe board

working platform

470 max. gap

150 min.

950 minimum

outer row of standards at 2·000 c/c

transom

ledgers

1·350 to 1·500

cross bracing

inner row of standards at 2·000 c/c

not more than 35°

raker or outrigger

façade bracing to be used as required

Gantries ~ these are elevated platforms used when the building being maintained or under construction is adjacent to a public footpath. A gantry over a footpath can be used for storage of materials, housing units of accommodation and supporting an independent scaffold. Local authority permission will be required before a gantry can be erected and they have the power to set out the conditions regarding minimum sizes to be used for public walkways and lighting requirements. It may also be necessary to comply with police restrictions regarding the loading and unloading of vehicles at the gantry position. A gantry can be constructed of any suitable structural material and may need to be structurally designed to meet all the necessary safety requirements.

Typical Example ~

independent tubular or patent scaffold

timber-boarded working platform underlined with polythene or similar sheeting supported on timber joists - spacing and size to design

close-boarded guard rail or fence to all open sides of gantry

night warning lights to suit local authority requirements

structural steel support columns - spacing and size to design

structural steel cross and longitudinal beams to design

support cleats

bulkhead lights

close-boarded hoarding

clear working space 1·000 min.

guard rail

public walkway usual minimum 1·200

boarded walkway on joists with approach ramps

warning lights road

existing building or building under construction

public footpath

kerb

300 × 300 timber fender painted white and fixed with straps to columns

Principle Considerations ~

• Structural stability and integrity.
• Safety of personnel using a scaffold and for those in the vicinity.

Relevant Factors ~

• Simple configurations of putlog and independent scaffold, otherwise known as *basic systems* (see National Access and Scaffolding Confederation [NASC] technical guidance) do not require specific design calculations. Structural calculations are to be prepared by an appropriately qualified person for other applications.
• Assembly, alterations and dismantling to be undertaken in accordance with NASC technical guidance or system scaffolding manufacturer's instructions.
• Scaffold erectors to be competence qualified, e.g. having attended a Construction Industry Scaffolders Registration Scheme (CISRS) course and be in possession of a *scaffolder's card*. Trainees to be supervised by a competent qualified person, e.g. foreman scaffolder.
• Non-basic scaffolds should have a sequence and methodology for assembly and dismantling, plus further guidance for any anticipated alterations included with the design information. Any unforeseen alterations should receive specific design consideration.
• On completion, the scaffold supplier should provide a 'handover certificate' endorsed with references to design drawings and calculations. Any limitations of use, with particular mention of platform safe working loads, to be documented.
• Completed scaffolds to be inspected by a competent person, i.e. suitably qualified by experience and training. The latter assessed by the CISRS or by certificated attendance on a system scaffold manufacturer's course. This does not apply to basic systems mentioned in the first bullet point. These can be approved by a person of sufficient site experience such as a site manager.
• Inspection reports to be undertaken daily before work commences, after adverse weather and when alterations, modifications or additions are made. Any defects noted and corrective action taken.
• Incomplete scaffolds should be suitably signed for non-access. Physical barriers to be in place during assembly and dismantling.
• Inspection records to be documented and filed. These to include location and description of the scaffold, time and date of inspection, result of inspection and any actions taken. The report to be authorised by signature and endorsed with the inspector's job title.

Shoring ~ this is a form of temporary support which can be given to existing buildings with the primary function of providing the necessary precautions to avoid damage to any person or property from collapse of the supported structure.

Shoring Systems ~ there are three basic systems of shoring which can be used separately or in combination with one another to provide the support(s), namely:

1. Dead Shoring – used primarily to carry vertical loadings.
2. Raking Shoring – used to support a combination of vertical and horizontal loadings.
3. Flying Shoring – an alternative to raking shoring to give a clear working space at ground level.

Typical Shoring Situations ~

DEAD SHORE (page 187)   RAKING SHORE (page 188)

FLYING SHORE (pages 189 to 191)

Dead Shores ~ these shores should be placed at approximately 2·000 c/c and positioned under the piers between the windows, any windows in the vicinity of the shores being strutted to prevent distortion of the openings. A survey should be carried out to establish the location of any underground services so that they can be protected as necessary. The sizes shown in the detail below are typical; actual sizes should be obtained from tables or calculated from first principles. Any suitable structural material such as steel can be substituted for the timber members shown.

Typical Detail ~

300 x 300 needle

dry mortar packing

floor and ceiling finishes removed locally around shore legs

w.i. dogs to both sides

bracing as required

300 x 300 shore legs

100 x 100 ceiling struts at 2·000 c/c

hoarding if required can be attached or free standing

1·000 minimum working space

225 x 75 head plate

300 x 300 shore legs taken down to a solid bed

folding wedges

w.i. dogs

folding wedges

w.i. dogs

300 x 300 sleeper

225 x 75 sole plate

300 x 300 sleeper

Raking Shoring ~ these are placed at 3·000 to 4·500 c/c and can be of single, double, triple or multiple raker format. Suitable materials are timber, structural steel and framed tubular scaffolding.

Typical Multiple Raking Shore Detail ~

250 x 75 wall plate secured with w.i. wall hooks

100 x 100 x 200 cleat

100 x 150 x 400 needle

250 x 250 rider

225 x 50 binding to both sides

halving joint in running length

100

250 x 250 top raking shore

250 x 250 middle raking shore

225 x 50 binding to both sides

folding wedges

250 x 250 bottom raking shore

225 x 50 binding to both sides

250 x 250 back shore

250 x 100 sole plate

distance piece

grillage or platform out of 200 x 100 timbers

minimum angle for rakers 40°
maximum angle for rakers 70°
angle between top shore and sole plate 89°

needle

cleat

wall hook

wall plate

raker

DETAIL AT HEAD OF RAKER

Flying Shores ~ these are placed at 3.000 to 4.500 c/c and can be of a single or double format. They are designed, detailed and constructed to the same basic principles as that shown for raking shores on page 188. Unsymmetrical arrangements are possible providing the basic principles for flying shores are applied – see page 191.

Typical Single Flying Shore Detail ~

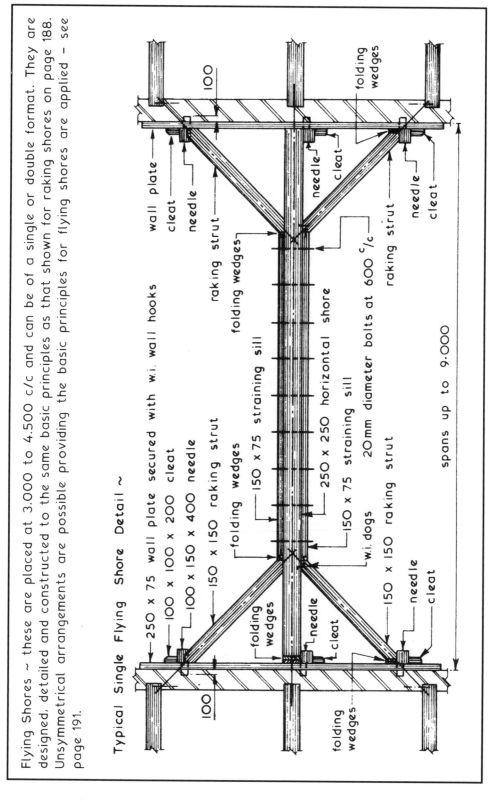

wall plate
cleat
needle
folding wedges
raking strut
needle
cleat
folding wedges
needle
cleat
raking strut
100
250 x 250 horizontal shore
20mm diameter bolts at 600 c/c
150 x 75 straining sill
150 x 75 straining sill
w.i. dogs
150 x 150 raking strut
needle
cleat
folding wedges
spans up to 9.000
250 x 75 wall plate secured with w.i. wall hooks
100 x 100 x 200 cleat
100 x 150 x 400 needle
150 x 150 raking strut
folding wedges
folding wedges
150 x 75 straining sill
needle
cleat
100

Typical Double Flying Shore Detail ~

250 x 75 wall plate secured with w.i. wall hooks
100 x 100 x 200 cleat
100 x 150 x 400 needle
150 x 150 raking strut
folding wedges
150 x 75 straining sill

wall plate
cleat
needle
raking strut
folding wedges
250 x 250 horizontal shore

20mm diameter bolts at 600°/c

brace
w.i. dogs
stud

150 x 150 brace
150 x 150 stud or post

250 x 250 horizontal shore
150 x 75 straining sill
20mm diameter bolts at 600°/c

needle
cleat
needle
cleat

raking strut

folding wedges

stud

150 x 150 raking strut

folding wedges

needle
cleat

folding wedges

brace

needle
cleat

folding wedges

spans up to 12.000

100

100

Unsymmetrical Flying Shores ~ arrangements of flying shores for unsymmetrical situations can be devised if the basic principles for symmetrical shores is applied (see page 189). In some cases the arrangement will consist of a combination of both raking and flying shore principles.

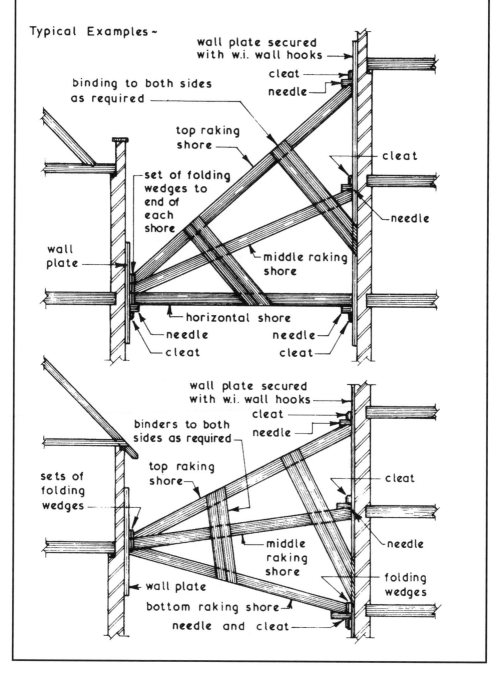

Typical Examples ~

wall plate secured with w.i. wall hooks

cleat

needle

binding to both sides as required

top raking shore

cleat

set of folding wedges to end of each shore

needle

wall plate

middle raking shore

horizontal shore

needle

cleat

needle

cleat

wall plate secured with w.i. wall hooks

cleat

needle

binders to both sides as required

top raking shore

cleat

sets of folding wedges

middle raking shore

needle

wall plate

folding wedges

bottom raking shore

needle and cleat

Temporary Support Determination ~ the basic sizing of most temporary supports follows the principles of elementary structural design. Readers with this basic knowledge should be able to calculate such support members which are required, particularly those used in the context of the maintenance and adaptation of buildings such as a dead shoring system.

Typical Example ~

Rafter length: $\cos 35° = \dfrac{3\cdot7}{X}$

$\therefore X = \dfrac{3\cdot7}{\cos 35°} = \dfrac{3\cdot7}{0\cdot8192} = 4\cdot520$

3·700

one-brick solid wall

3·000

dead shores at 2·000 c/c

props to carry floor load

4·500

3·000

(see Note 2)

Loadings:

Roof ~	kg/m²
tiles	71·0
battens	3·4
felt	2·0
rafters	7·5
	83·9

say 84·0 kg/m²

Ceiling ~	kg/m²
joists	7·5
finishes	15·0
	22·5

say 23·0 kg/m²

Wall ~	kg/m²
brickwork	490·0
plaster finish	6·8
	496·8

say 500·0 kg/m²

Weight of roof per metre run of wall = 84 × 4·52 = 379·68
Weight of ceiling per metre run of wall = 23 × 3·70 = 85·10
Weight of wall per metre run of wall = 500 × 3·00 = 1500·00

Total weight of wall per metre run = 1964·78

Total weight supported by needle = 1964·78 × shore centres
= 1964·78 × 2·000
= 3929·56 kg
say 3930 kg

For design calculations see pages 193 to 194.
Note 1: Typical weights of building materials, pages 38 to 39.
Note 2: Effective span (3.000 c/c) is often preferred to clear span for design of flexural members.

Design calculations reference previous page.

Timber strength class C22, See page 142 for data.

Needle Design:

$W = 3930$ kg
hence force
$= 3930 \times 9 \cdot 81 \doteq 39300$ N

$R_A = R_B = \dfrac{W}{2}$

$= \dfrac{39300}{2}$

$L = 3 \cdot 000$

$R_A \qquad R_B$

$= 19650$ N

$BM = \dfrac{WL}{4} = \dfrac{39300 \times 3000}{4} = 29475000$ Nmm

MR = stress $\times$ section modulus $= fZ = f\dfrac{bd^2}{6}$

assume $b = 300$ mm and $f = 6.8$ N/mm²

then $29475000 = \dfrac{6 \cdot 8 \times 300 \times d^2}{6}$

$d = \sqrt{\dfrac{29475000 \times 6}{6 \cdot 8 \times 300}} = 294$ mm

use 300 × 300 timber section or 2 No. 150 × 300 sections bolted together with timber connectors.

Props to Needle Design:

$$\text{area} = \dfrac{\text{load}}{\text{stress}} = \dfrac{19650}{7 \cdot 5} = 2620 \text{ mm}^2$$

∴ minimum timber size $= \sqrt{2620} = 52 \times 52$ mm

check slenderness ratio:

slenderness ratio $= \dfrac{\text{effective length}}{\text{breadth}} = \dfrac{4500}{52} = 86 \cdot 5$

the 52 × 52mm section is impractically small with a very high slenderness ratio, therefore a more stable section of say 300 × 225mm would be selected giving a slenderness ratio of 4500/225 = 20 (stability check, next page)

Check crushing at point of loading on needle:

wall loading on needle $= 3930$ kg $= 39300$ N $= 39 \cdot 3$ kN

area of contact = width of wall × width of needle

$= 215 \times 300 = 64500$ mm²

safe compressive stress perpendicular to grain $= 2 \cdot 3$ N/mm²

∴ safe load $= \dfrac{64500 \times 2 \cdot 3}{1000} = 148 \cdot 3$ kN which is $> 39 \cdot 3$ kN

Stability check using the example from previous page ~

Timber of strength classification C22 (see page 142):

Modulus of elasticity, 6500N/mm^2 minimum.

Grade stress in compression parallel to the grain, 7.5N/mm^2.

Grade stress ratio = 6500 ÷ 7.5 = 867

The grade stress and slenderness ratios are used to provide a modification factor for the compression parallel to the grain. The following table shows some of these factors:

| Grade stress ratio | Effective length/breadth of section (slenderness ratio) | | | | | | | | |
	3	6	12	18	24	30	36	42	48
400	0.95	0.90	0.74	0.51	0.34	0.23	0.17	0.11	0.10
600	0.95	0.90	0.77	0.58	0.41	0.29	0.21	0.16	0.13
800	0.95	0.90	0.78	0.63	0.48	0.36	0.26	0.21	0.16
1000	0.95	0.90	0.79	0.66	0.52	0.41	0.30	0.24	0.19
1200	0.95	0.90	0.80	0.68	0.56	0.44	0.34	0.27	0.22
1400	0.95	0.90	0.80	0.69	0.58	0.47	0.37	0.30	0.24
1600	0.95	0.90	0.81	0.70	0.60	0.49	0.40	0.32	0.27
1800	0.95	0.90	0.81	0.71	0.61	0.51	0.42	0.34	0.29
2000	0.95	0.90	0.81	0.71	0.62	0.52	0.44	0.36	0.31

By interpolation, a grade stress of 867 and a slenderness ratio of 20 indicates that 7.5N/mm^2 is multiplied by 0.57.

Applied stress should be ≤7.5 × 0.57 = 4.275 N/mm^2.

Applied stress = axial load ÷ prop section area
= 19650N ÷ (300 × 225mm) = 0.291 N/mm^2

0.291N/mm^2 is well within the allowable stress of 4.275 N/mm^2, therefore 300 × 225mm props are satisfactory.

Ref. BS EN 1995-1-1: Design of timber structures. General. Common rules and rules for buildings.

Town and Country Planning Act ~ demolition is generally not regarded as development, but planning permission will be required if the site is to have a change of use. Attitudes to demolition can vary between local planning authorities and consultation should be sought.

Planning (Listed Buildings and Conservation Areas) Act ~ listed buildings and those in conservation areas will require local authority approval for any alterations. Consent for change may be limited to partial demolition, particularly where it is necessary to preserve a building frontage for historic reasons. See the arrangements for temporary shoring on the preceding pages.

Building Act ~ intention to demolish a building requires six weeks' written notice of intent. The next page shows the typical outline of a standard form for submission to the building control department of the local authority, along with location plans. Notice must also be given to utilities providers and adjoining/adjacent building owners, particularly where party walls are involved. Small buildings of volumes less than 50 m^3 are generally exempt. Within six weeks of the notice being submitted, the local authority will specify their requirements for shoring, protection of adjacent buildings, debris disposal and general safety requirements under the HSE.

Public Health Act ~ the local authority can issue a demolition enforcement order to a building owner, where a building is considered to be insecure, a danger to the general public and detrimental to amenities.

Highways Act ~ concerns the protection of the general public using a thoroughfare in or near to an area affected by demolition work. The building owner and demolition contractor are required to ensure that debris and other materials are not deposited in the street unless in a suitable receptacle (skip) and the local authority highways department and police are in agreement with its location. Temporary road-works require protective fencing and site hoardings must be robust and secure. All supplementary provisions such as hoardings and skips may also require adequate illumination. Provision must be made for immediate removal of poisonous and hazardous waste.

Anytown Borough Council
Building Control Section
Anytown
UK

Tel: . . . .
Fax: . . . .
Email: . . . .

NOTICE TO LOCAL AUTHORITY TO CARRY OUT DEMOLITION WORKS

THE BUILDING ACT 1984 – SECTION 80

It is my intention to commence demolition of:

. . . .

. . . .

. . . .

As shown on the attached site plan, on the . . . . (date)

This date is at least six weeks from the date of this notice. Under section 81 of the Building Act, I anticipate your notification within six weeks.

Copies of this notice have been sent to:

• The occupants/owners of any/all buildings adjacent to the proposed demolition.
• The public services/utilities supply companies.

Signed . . . .   Date . . . .

Company name and address . . . .

. . . .

. . . .

Demolition ~ skilled and potentially dangerous work that should only be undertaken by experienced contractors.

Types of demolition ~ partial or complete removal. Partial is less dynamic than complete removal, requiring temporary support to the remaining structure. This may involve window strutting, floor props and shoring. The execution of work is likely to be limited to manual handling with minimal use of powered equipment.

Preliminaries ~ a detailed survey should include:

* an assessment of condition of the structure and the impact of removing parts on the remainder.
* the effect demolition will have on adjacent properties.
* photographic records, particularly of any noticeable defects on adjacent buildings.
* neighbourhood impact, i.e. disruption, disturbance, protection.
* the need for hoardings, see pages 113 to 117.
* potential for salvaging/recycling/reuse of materials.
* extent of basements and tunnels.
* services – need to terminate and protect for future reconnections.
* means for selective removal of hazardous materials.

Insurance ~ general builders are unlikely to find demolition cover in their standard policies. All risks indemnity should be considered to cover claims from site personnel and others accessing the site. Additional third party cover will be required for claims for loss or damage to other property, occupied areas, business, utilities, private and public roads.

Salvage ~ salvaged materials and components can be valuable: bricks, tiles, slates, steel sections and timber are all marketable. Architectural features such as fireplaces and stairs will command a good price. Reclamation costs will be balanced against the financial gain.

Asbestos ~ this banned material has been used in a variety of applications including pipe insulation, fire protection, sheet claddings, linings and roofing. Samples should be taken for laboratory analysis and if necessary, specialist contractors engaged to remove material before demolition commences.

Generally ~ the reverse order of construction to gradually reduce the height. Where space is not confined, overturning or explosives may be considered.

Piecemeal ~ use of handheld equipment such as pneumatic breakers, oxy-acetylene cutters, picks and hammers. Care should be taken when salvaging materials and other reusable components. Chutes should be used to direct debris to a suitable place of collection (see page 220).

Pusher Arm ~ usually attached to a long reach articulated boom fitted to a tracked chassis. Hydraulic movement is controlled from a robust cab structure mounted above the tracks.

Wrecking Ball ~ largely confined to history, as even with safety features such as anti-spin devices, limited control over a heavy weight swinging and slewing from a crane jib will be considered unsafe in many situations.

Impact Hammer ~ otherwise known as a 'pecker'. Basically a large chisel operated by pneumatic power and fitted to the end of an articulated boom on a tracked chassis.

Nibbler ~ a hydraulically operated grip fitted as above that can be rotated to break brittle materials such as concrete.

Overturning ~ steel wire ropes of at least 38 mm diameter attached at high level and to an anchored winch or heavy vehicle. May be considered where controlled collapse is encouraged by initial removal of key elements of structure, typical of steel framed buildings. Alternative methods should be given preference.

Explosives ~ demolition is specialised work and the use of explosives in demolition is a further specialised practice limited to very few licensed operators. Charges are set to fire in a sequence that weakens the building to a controlled internal collapse.

Some additional references ~

BS 6187: Code of practice for full and partial demolition.

The Construction (Design and Management) Regulations.

The Management of Health and Safety at Work Regulations.

Concept ~ to reduce waste by designing for deconstruction.

Linear (wasteful, non-sustainable) process ~

```
┌──────────────┐      ┌──────────────┐        ┌──────────────┐
│ Production and│ ◄─── │ Material     │        │ Disposal/    │
│ component     │      │ resource     │        │ landfill     │
│ manufacture   │      │ extraction   │        │ of residual  │
│               │      │              │        │ material     │
└──────────────┘      └──────────────┘        └──────────────┘
      │                                               ▲
      │                                               │
      ▼                                               │
┌──────────────┐      ┌──────────────┐                │      Limited
│ Building      │ ───► │ Decommission │ ───────────────┘      under
│ assembly      │      │ and          │                       EU Landfill
│ and occupancy │      │ demolition   │                       Directive
│ over design   │      │              │                       (Defra)
│ life          │      │              │
└──────────────┘      └──────────────┘
```

Closed-loop (near zero waste, sustainable) process ~

```
┌──────────────┐      ┌──────────────┐        ┌──────────────┐
│ Material     │ ───► │ Production and│ ───►  │ Building      │
│ resource     │      │ component     │        │ assembly      │
│ extraction   │      │ manufacture   │        │ and occupancy │
│              │      │               │        │ over design   │
└──────────────┘      └──────────────┘        │ life          │
      ▲                      ▲                 └──────────────┘
      │                      │                         │
┌──────────────┐      ┌──────────────┐                │
│ Reconditioning│ ◄── │ Decommissioning│ ◄────────────┘
│ and recycling │      │ and           │
│ of components │      │ deconstruction│
│              │      │ of components │
└──────────────┘      └──────────────┘
      ┆                      ┆
      ▼                      ▼
```

Reusable examples may include:

•Recycled concrete aggregate (RCA) and broken
masonry for hardcore, backfill, landscaping, etc.
•Recovered: structural timber joists and joinery.
           architectural components/features.
           slates and tiles.
           structural steel standard sections.

Notes

3 BULDERS PLANT

GENERAL CONSIDERATIONS
BULLDOZERS
SCRAPERS
GRADERS
TRACTOR SHOVELS
EXCAVATORS
TRANSPORT VEHICLES
HOISTS
RUBBLE CHUTES AND SKIPS
CRANES
CONCRETING PLANT

General Considerations ~ items of builders plant ranging from small handheld power tools to larger pieces of plant such as mechanical excavators and tower cranes can be considered for use for one or more of the following reasons:

1. Increased production.
2. Reduction in overall construction costs.
3. Carry out activities which cannot be carried out by the traditional manual methods in the context of economics.
4. Eliminate heavy manual work, thus reducing fatigue and as a consequence increasing productivity.
5. Replacing labour where there is a shortage of personnel with the necessary skills.
6. Maintain the high standards required, particularly in the context of structural engineering works.

Economic Considerations ~ the introduction of plant does not always result in economic savings since extra temporary site works such as road-works, hardstandings, foundations and anchorages may have to be provided at a cost which is in excess of the savings made by using the plant. The site layout and circulation may have to be planned around plant positions and movements rather than around personnel and material movements and accommodation. To be economic plant must be fully utilised and not left standing idle, since plant, whether hired or owned, will have to be paid for even if it is non-productive. Full utilisation of plant is usually considered to be in the region of 85% of on-site time, thus making an allowance for routine, daily and planned maintenance which needs to be carried out to avoid as far as practicable plant breakdowns which could disrupt the construction programme. Many pieces of plant work in conjunction with other items of plant such as excavators and their attendant haulage vehicles; therefore a correct balance of such plant items must be obtained to achieve an economic result.

Maintenance Considerations ~ on large contracts where a number of plant items are to be used it may be advantageous to employ a skilled mechanic to be on site to carry out all the necessary daily, preventive and planned maintenance tasks together with any running repairs which could be carried out on site.

Plant Costing ~ with the exception of small pieces of plant, which are usually purchased, items of plant can be bought or hired or where there are a number of similar items a combination of buying and hiring could be considered. The choice will be governed by economic factors and the possibility of using the plant on future sites, thus enabling the costs to be apportioned over several contracts.

Advantages of Hiring Plant:

1. Plant can be hired for short periods.
2. Repairs and replacements are usually the responsibility of the hire company.
3. Plant is returned to the hire company after use, thus relieving the building contractor of the problem of disposal or finding more work for the plant to justify its purchase or retention.
4. Plant can be hired with the operator, fuel and oil included in the hire rate.

Advantages of Buying Plant:

1. Plant availability is totally within the control of the contractor.
2. Hourly cost of plant is generally less than hired plant.
3. Owner has choice of costing method used.

Typical Costing Methods ~

1. Straight Line — simple method

Capital Cost = £ 100 000
Anticipated life = 5 years
Year's working = 1500 hrs
Resale or scrap value = £ 9000
Annual depreciation ~

$$= \frac{100\,000 - 9000}{5} = £\,18\,200$$

Hourly depreciation ~

$$= \frac{18200}{1500} = 12 \cdot 13$$

Add 2% insurance = 0·27
10% maintenance = 1·33
Hourly rate = £13·73

2. Interest on Capital Outlay – widely used more accurate method

Capital Cost	= £ 100 000
C.I. on capital (8% for 5 yrs) =	46 930
	146 930
Deduct resale value	9 000
	137 930
+ Insurance at 2% =	2 000
+ Maintenance at 10% =	10 000
	149 930

Hourly rate ~

$$= \frac{149\,930}{5 \times 1500} = £\,20 \cdot 00$$

NB. add to hourly rate running costs.

Output and Cycle Times ~ all items of plant have optimum output and cycle times which can be used as a basis for estimating anticipated productivity taking into account the task involved, task efficiency of the machine, operator's efficiency and in the case of excavators the type of soil. Data for the factors to be taken into consideration can be obtained from timed observations, feedback information or published tables contained in manufacturer's literature or reliable textbooks.

Typical Example ~

Backacter with $1m^3$ capacity bucket engaged in normal trench excavation in a clayey soil and discharging directly into an attendant haulage vehicle.

Optimum output	= 60 bucket loads per hour
Task efficiency factor	= 0.8 (from tables)
Operator efficiency factor	= 75% (typical figure)
∴ Anticipated output	= 60 x 0.8 x 0.75
	= 36 bucket loads per hour
	= 36 x 1 = 36 m^3 per hour

An allowance should be made for the bulking or swell of the solid material due to the introduction of air or voids during the excavation process

∴ Net output allowing for a 30% swell = 36 − (36 x 0.3)

$$= \text{say } 25m^3 \text{ per hr.}$$

If the Bill of Quantities gives a total net excavation of $950\,m^3$

time required = $\dfrac{950}{25}$ = <u>38 hours</u>

or assuming an 8-hour day–1/2 hour maintenance time in

days = $\dfrac{38}{7.5}$ = say <u>5 days</u>

Haulage vehicles required = $1 + \dfrac{\text{round trip time of vehicle}}{\text{loading time of vehicle}}$

If round trip time = 30 min. and loading time = 10 min.

number of haulage vehicles required = $1 + \dfrac{30}{10} = 4$

This gives a vehicle waiting overlap ensuring excavator is fully utilised which is economically desirable.

Bulldozers ~ these machines consist of a track or wheel mounted power unit with a mould blade at the front which is controlled by hydraulic rams. Many bulldozers have the capacity to adjust the mould blade to form an angledozer and the capacity to tilt the mould blade about a central swivel point. Some bulldozers can also be fitted with rear attachments such as rollers and scarifiers.

The main functions of a bulldozer are:

1. Shallow excavations up to 300 m deep either on level ground or sidehill cutting.
2. Clearance of shrubs and small trees.
3. Clearance of trees by using raised mould blade as a pusher arm.
4. Acting as a towing tractor.
5. Acting as a pusher to scraper machines (see next page).

NB. Bulldozers push earth in front of the mould blade with some side spillage whereas angledozers push and cast the spoil to one side of the mould blade.

Typical Bulldozer Details ~

protective cab and roll bar

exhaust pipe

4 cylinder diesel engine

typical maximum speeds in km/h:
forward gears - 11
reverse gear - 7

fuel tank

towing hook

mould blade with tilt and angle capacity - maximum digging depth 300 mm

steel track shoes

NB. Protective cab/roll bar to be fitted before use.

Scrapers ~ these machines consist of a scraper bowl which is lowered to cut and collect soil where site stripping and levelling operations are required involving large volume of earth. When the scraper bowl is full the apron at the cutting edge is closed to retain the earth and the bowl is raised for travelling to the disposal area. On arrival the bowl is lowered, the apron opened and the spoil pushed out by the tailgate as the machine moves forward. Scrapers are available in three basic formats:

1. Towed Scrapers – these consist of a four-wheeled scraper bowl which is towed behind a power unit such as a crawler tractor. They tend to be slower than other forms of scraper but are useful for small capacities with haul distances up to 300·00.
2. Two axle Scrapers – these have a two-wheeled scraper bowl with an attached two-wheeled power unit. They are very manoeuvrable with a low rolling resistance and very good traction.
3. Three axle Scrapers – these consist of a two-wheeled scraper bowl which may have a rear engine to assist the four-wheeled traction engine which makes up the complement. Generally these machines have a greater capacity potential than their counterparts, are easier to control and have a faster cycle time.

To obtain maximum efficiency scrapers should operate downhill if possible, have smooth haul roads, hard surfaces broken up before scraping and be assisted over the last few metres by a pushing vehicle such as a bulldozer.

Typical Scraper Details ~

scraper bowl
struck capacity 14m^3
heaped capacity 20m^3
width of cut 3·000
depth of cut 450mm max.

8-cylinder diesel engine attached power unit with a top forward speed of 45 km/h

pusher block for bulldozer

tailgate

apron

NB. Protective cab/roll bar to be fitted before use.

Graders ~ these machines are similar in concept to bulldozers in that they have a long, slender, adjustable mould blade, which is usually slung under the centre of the machine. A grader's main function is to finish or grade the upper surface of a large area usually as a follow up operation to scraping or bulldozing. They can produce a fine and accurate finish but do not have the power of a bulldozer; therefore they are not suitable for over-site excavation work. The mould blade can be adjusted in both the horizontal and vertical planes through an angle of 300° the latter enabling it to be used for grading sloping banks.

Two basic formats of grader are available:

1. Four Wheeled – all wheels are driven and steered which gives the machine the ability to offset and crab along its direction of travel.
2. Six Wheeled – this machine has four wheels in tandem drive at the rear and two front-tilting idler wheels, giving it the ability to counteract side thrust.

Typical Grader Details ~

CUTTING, SHAPING AND GRADING BANKS

maximum speeds:
finishing - 10 km/h
banking - 6 km/h

4·000 wide × 600mm high mould board with a finishing tolerance capacity of ± 5mm

Tractor Shovels ~ these machines are sometimes called loaders or loader shovels and their primary function is to scoop up loose materials in the front-mounted bucket, elevate the bucket and manoeuvre into a position to deposit the loose material into an attendant transport vehicle. Tractor shovels are driven towards the pile of loose material with the bucket lowered; the speed and power of the machine will enable the bucket to be filled. Both tracked and wheeled versions are available, the tracked format being more suitable for wet and uneven ground conditions than the wheeled tractor shovel which has greater speed and manoeuvring capabilities. To increase their versatility tractor shovels can be fitted with a four-in-one bucket, enabling them to carry out bulldozing, excavating, clam lifting and loading activities.

Typical Tractor Shovel Details ~

Excavating Machines ~ these are one of the major items of builders plant and are used primarily to excavate and load most types of soil. Excavating machines come in a wide variety of designs and sizes but all of them can be placed within one of three categories:

1. Universal Excavators - this category covers most forms of excavators all of which have a common factor: the power unit. The universal power unit is a tracked based machine with a slewing capacity of 360° and by altering the boom arrangement and bucket type different excavating functions can be obtained. These machines are selected for high output requirements and are rope controlled.
2. Purpose Designed Excavators - these are machines which have been designed specifically to carry out one mode of excavation and they usually have smaller bucket capacities than universal excavators; they are hydraulically controlled with a shorter cycle time.
3. Multi-purpose Excavators - these machines can perform several excavating functions having both front and rear attachments. They are designed to carry out small excavation operations of low output quickly and efficiently. Multi-purpose excavators can be obtained with a wheeled or tracked base and are ideally suited for a small building firm with low excavation plant utilisation requirements.

Skimmers ~ these excavators are rigged using a universal power unit for surface stripping and shallow excavation work up to 300 mm deep where a high degree of accuracy is required. They usually require attendant haulage vehicles to remove the spoil and need to be transported between sites on a low-loader. Because of their limitations and the alternative machines available they are seldom used today.

bucket discharge position

boom suspension ropes

diesel engine universal tracked power unit

straight boom hinged from front of power unit

bucket rope

machine moves forward when skimming

sliding bucket

Face Shovels ~ the primary function of this piece of plant is to excavate above its own track or wheel level. They are available as a universal power unit-based machine or as a hydraulic purpose-designed unit. These machines can usually excavate any type of soil except rock which needs to be loosened, usually by blasting, prior to excavation. Face shovels generally require attendant haulage vehicles for the removal of spoil and a low-loader transport lorry for travel between sites. Most of these machines have a limited capacity of between 300 and 400 mm for excavation below their own track or wheel level.

Typical Face Shovel Details ~

Backacters ~ these machines are suitable for trench, foundation and basement excavations and are available as a universal power unit-based machine or as a purpose-designed hydraulic unit. They can be used with or without attendant haulage vehicles since the spoil can be placed alongside the excavation for use in backfilling. These machines will require a low-loader transport vehicle for travel between sites. Backacters used in trenching operations with a bucket width equal to the trench width can be very accurate with a high output rating.

Typical Backacter Details ~

bucket discharge position

bucket raised in tucked position

jib hoist rope

bucket arm

front discharge bucket

bucket rope

diesel engine universal tracked power unit

machine moves backwards during excavation

bucket in discharge position

bucket raised in tucked position

two-piece boom

track mounted diesel engine power unit

hydraulic rams

hydraulic ram

front discharge bucket

dipper arm

Draglines ~ these machines are based on the universal power unit with basic crane rigging to which is attached a drag bucket. The machine is primarily designed for bulk excavation in loose soils up to 3·000 below its own track level by swinging the bucket out to the excavation position and hauling or dragging it back towards the power unit. Dragline machines can also be fitted with a grab or clamshell bucket for excavating in very loose soils.

Typical Dragline Details ~

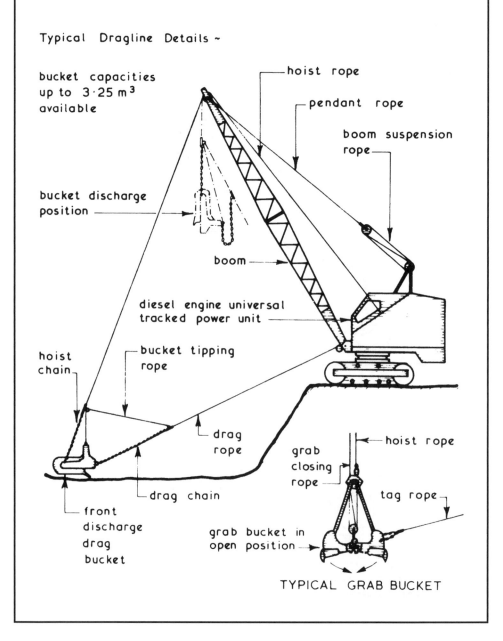

bucket capacities up to 3·25 m³ available

hoist rope

pendant rope

boom suspension rope

bucket discharge position

boom

diesel engine universal tracked power unit

hoist chain

bucket tipping rope

drag rope

hoist rope

grab closing rope

tag rope

front discharge drag bucket

drag chain

grab bucket in open position

TYPICAL GRAB BUCKET

Multi-purpose Excavators ~ these machines are usually based on the agricultural tractor with two- or four-wheel drive and are intended mainly for use in conjunction with small excavation works such as those encountered by the small to medium sized building contractor. Most multi-purpose excavators are fitted with a loading/excavating front bucket and a rear backacter bucket both being hydraulically controlled. When in operation using the backacter bucket the machine is raised off its axles by rear-mounted hydraulic outriggers or jacks and in some models by placing the front bucket on the ground. Most machines can be fitted with a variety of bucket widths and various attachments such as bulldozer blades, scarifiers, grab buckets and post hole auger borers.

Typical Multi-purpose Excavator Details ~

bucket in raised position

bucket in discharge position

enclosed glazed cab with all round vision

bucket raised in tucked position

bucket in discharge position

pivot connection giving 180° arc of operation

boom

four-cylinder diesel engine tractor

hydraulic outriggers

dipper arm

ram

loading/excavating bucket - capacities up to 1m³ - widths up to 2·000

backacter or backhoe bucket - capacities up to 0·28 m³ — widths up to 900 mm

typical maximum road speed 30 km/h

Transport Vehicles ~ these can be defined as vehicles whose primary function is to convey passengers and/or materials between and around building sites. The types available range from the conventional saloon car to the large low-loader lorries designed to transport other items of builders plant between construction sites and the plant yard or depot.

Vans – these transport vehicles range from the small two-person plus a limited amount of materials to the large vans with purpose-designed bodies such as those built to carry large sheets of glass. Most small vans are usually fitted with a petrol engine and are based on the manufacturer's standard car range whereas the larger vans are purpose designed with either petrol or diesel engines. These basic designs can usually be supplied with an uncovered tipping or non-tipping container mounted behind the passenger cab for use as a `pick-up´ truck.

Passenger Vehicles – these can range from a simple framed cabin which can be placed in the container of a small lorry or `pick-up´ truck to a conventional bus or coach. Vans can also be designed to carry a limited number of seated passengers by having fixed or removable seating together with windows fitted in the van sides, thus giving the vehicle a dual function. The number of passengers carried can be limited so that the driver does not have to hold a PSV (public service vehicle) licence.

Lorries – these are sometimes referred to as haul vehicles and are available as road- or site-only vehicles. Road haulage vehicles have to comply with all the requirements of the Road Traffic Acts which among other requirements limit size and axle loads. The off-highway or site-only lorries are not so restricted and can be designed to carry two to three times the axle load allowed on the public highway. Site-only lorries are usually specially designed to traverse and withstand the rough terrain encountered on many construction sites. Lorries are available as non-tipping, tipping and special-purpose carriers such as those with removable skips and those equipped with self-loading and unloading devices. Lorries specifically designed for the transportation of large items of plant are called low-loaders and are usually fitted with integral or removable ramps to facilitate loading and some have a winching system to haul the plant onto the carrier platform.

Dumpers ~ these are used for the horizontal transportation of materials on and off construction sites generally by means of an integral tipping skip. Highway dumpers are of a similar but larger design and can be used to carry materials such as excavated spoil along the roads. A wide range of dumpers are available of various carrying capacities and options for gravity or hydraulic discharge control with front tipping, side tipping or elevated tipping facilities. Special format dumpers fitted with flat platforms, rigs to carry materials skips and rigs for concrete skips for crane hoisting are also obtainable. These machines are designed to traverse rough terrain but they are not designed to carry passengers, and this misuse is the cause of many accidents involving dumpers.

Typical Dumper Details ~

diesel engine giving a maximum forward speed of 16 km/h

sprung steel seat

roll bar

gravity tipping skip with heaped capacity of $0.62 \, m^3$

steering wheels

STANDARD DUMPER

diesel engine giving a maximum forward speed of 16 km/h

hydraulic tipping skip mounted on 180° slewing turntable with five set positions

driving wheels

SWIVEL SKIP DUMPER

hydraulically operated rear tipping skip with a heaped capacity of $10 \, m^3$

driving cab

diesel engine giving a maximum forward speed of 50 km/h

two- or four-wheel drive versions available

HIGHWAY DUMPER

Fork Lift Trucks ~ these are used for the horizontal and limited vertical transportation of materials positioned on pallets or banded together such as brick packs. They are generally suitable for construction sites where the building height does not exceed three storeys. Although designed to negotiate rough terrain site fork lift trucks have a higher productivity on firm and level soils. Three basic fork lift truck formats are available, namely straight mast, overhead and telescopic boom with various height, reach and lifting capacities. Scaffolds onto which the load(s) are to be placed should be strengthened locally or a specially constructed loading tower could be built as an attachment to or as an integral part of the main scaffold.

Typical Fork Lift Truck Details ~

telescopic straight mast
forward tilt 3° max.
backward tilt 10° max.
maximum lift height –
5·700
maximum load – 1·5
tonnes

diesel
engine

twin
lifting
forks

STRAIGHT MAST FORK LIFT

telescopic boom
maximum forward
reach – 3·350
maximum lift
height – 8·500
maximum load –
2 tonnes

twin
lifting
forks

cab

diesel engine

TELESCOPIC BOOM FORK LIFT

hydraulically controlled
overhead lifting arm
maximum forward reach –
2·350
maximum lift height –
6·500
maximum load –
1·5 tonnes

diesel
engine

twin lifting
fork

NB. loads must be placed
correctly on forks and
the fork lift truck must not
be overloaded

OVERHEAD FORK LIFT

Hoists ~ these are designed for the vertical transportation of materials, passengers, or materials and passengers (see page 218). Materials hoists are designed for one specific use (i.e. the vertical transportation of materials) and under no circumstances should they be used to transport passengers. Most material hoists are of a mobile format which can be dismantled, folded onto the chassis and moved to another position or site under their own power or towed by a haulage vehicle. When in use material hoists need to be stabilised and/or tied to the structure and enclosed with a protective screen.

Typical Materials Hoist Details ~

top bracket with automatic overrun control

protective screen out of scaffolding placed around mast to form a hoistway fitted gates at least 2·000 high at all landing levels to be supplied and erected by main contractor

lattice hoist mast 7·320 high which can be extended by adding further hoist mast sections to 32·000 high providing tie support is given every 2·750 above the initial 7·320 mast height

hoist rope

control rope operated from outside protective screen

tubular mast support struts

1·500 wide × 1·200 deep two barrow hardwood timber hoist platform with a maximum load capacity of 500kg

diesel or electric power unit

2·000

anti-walk-through screen around power unit

timber buffer plate

stabilising jacks or outriggers

Passenger Hoists ~ these are designed to carry passengers, although most are capable of transporting a combined load of materials and passengers within the lifting capacity of the hoist. A wide selection of hoists are available ranging from a single cage with rope suspension to twin cages with rack and pinion operation mounted on two sides of a static tower.

Typical Passenger Hoist Details ~

face of structure

standards

ties to structure at 12·000 centres

2·700-high cage to carry 12 persons or a total payload of 1000 kg at speeds of 40 to 100 metres per minute

landings as required

NB. operation of hoist is from within the cage and the hoist must be fitted to prevent any overrun

passenger hoist tower assembled from 1·500-long sections to a maximum tied height of 240·000

climbing rack

working platform on top of cage for scaffold-type crane used to extend hoist tower

electric motor and pinion housed behind cage

1·680-long x 1·370-wide enclosed passenger cage

access gate hoist

2·600-high wire mesh screen enclosure to lowest hoist position

reinforced concrete base

Summary:

- Enclosures and gates at least two metres high to protect people at ground level from the moving platform and counterweight.

- Except when loading or unloading, access gates to be closed.

- Platform to have a fail-safe mechanism capable of supporting a full load in event of hoisting equipment failure.

- Automatic overrun prevention devices to be fitted at the top and bottom.

- Micro-switch feature on the gates to prevent platform being operated until the gates are properly closed and to prevent the gates being opened in between landings.

- Control from one point only if not controlled from within the cage.

- Operator to have an unobstructed view throughout the hoist's travel, or a banksman/signaller to be appointed to cover all landings.

- Additional safety features to include an automatic braking system, multiple roping and back-up cylinder for hydraulic hoists. Equipment specification to have a high factor of safety.

- Safe working load (SWL), otherwise expressed as *rated capacity* or *working load limit* for materials and passengers to be clearly displayed on the platform.

- Assembly and completion to be approved by an appropriately experienced and trained person. Pre-checks required at the start of each working day and after alterations and repairs. Periodic examinations to be undertaken as determined by use and exposure. All inspections to be documented, dated and filed.

* Passenger hoists to have the cage designed to retain occupants without becoming trapped or to be struck by debris falling down the hoist shaft.

* Material loads to be restrained or contained to prevent tipping or spillage.

Ref. The Lifting Operations and Lifting Equipment Regulations 1998 (known by the acronym LOLER).

NB. LOLER regulations are made under the Health and Safety at Work, etc. Act. They also apply to cranes, fork lift trucks and mobile elevating work platforms.

Rubble Chutes and Skips

Rubble Chutes ~ these apply to contracts involving demolition, repair, maintenance and refurbishment. The simple concept of connecting several perforated dustbins is reputed to have been conceived by an ingenious site operative for the expedient and safe conveyance of materials.

In purpose-designed format, the tapered cylinders are produced from reinforced rubber with chain linkage for continuity. Overall unit lengths are generally 1100mm, providing an effective length of 1m. Hoppers and side entry units are made for special applications.

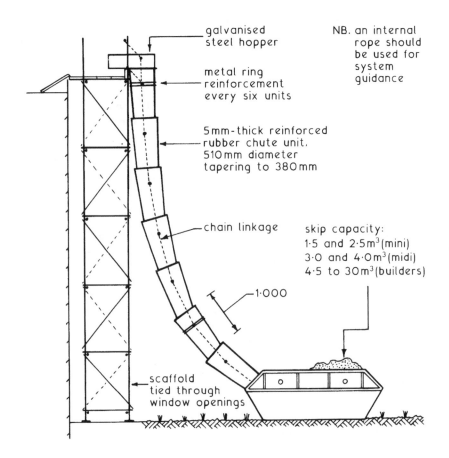

galvanised steel hopper

NB. an internal rope should be used for system guidance

metal ring reinforcement every six units

5mm-thick reinforced rubber chute unit, 510mm diameter tapering to 380mm

chain linkage

skip capacity:
1·5 and 2·5m³(mini)
3·0 and 4·0m³(midi)
4·5 to 30m³(builders)

1·000

scaffold tied through window openings

Ref. Highways Act – written permit (licence) must be obtained from the local authority highways department for use of a skip on a public thoroughfare. It will have to be illuminated at night and may require a temporary traffic light system to regulate vehicles.

Cranes ~ these are lifting devices designed to raise materials by means of rope operation and move the load horizontally within the limitations of any particular machine. The range of cranes available is very wide and therefore choice must be based on the loads to be lifted, height and horizontal distance to be covered, time period(s) of lifting operations, utilisation factors and degree of mobility required. Crane types can range from a simple rope and pulley or gin wheel to a complex tower crane but most can be placed within one of three groups, namely mobile, static and tower cranes.

Typical Crane Classifications ~

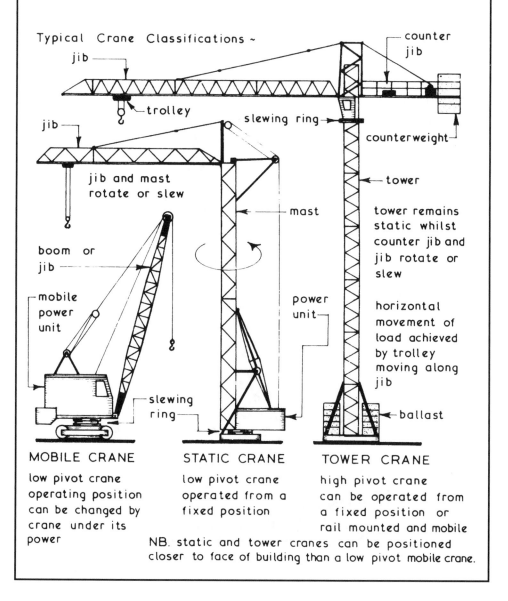

MOBILE CRANE
low pivot crane operating position can be changed by crane under its power

STATIC CRANE
low pivot crane operated from a fixed position

TOWER CRANE
high pivot crane can be operated from a fixed position or rail mounted and mobile

NB. static and tower cranes can be positioned closer to face of building than a low pivot mobile crane.

Self Propelled Cranes ~ these are mobile cranes mounted on a wheeled chassis and have only one operator position from which the crane is controlled and the vehicle driven. The road speed of this type of crane is generally low, usually not exceeding 30km p.h. A variety of self propelled crane formats are available ranging from short height lifting strut booms of fixed length to variable length lattice booms with a fly jib attachment.

Typical Self Propelled Crane Details ~

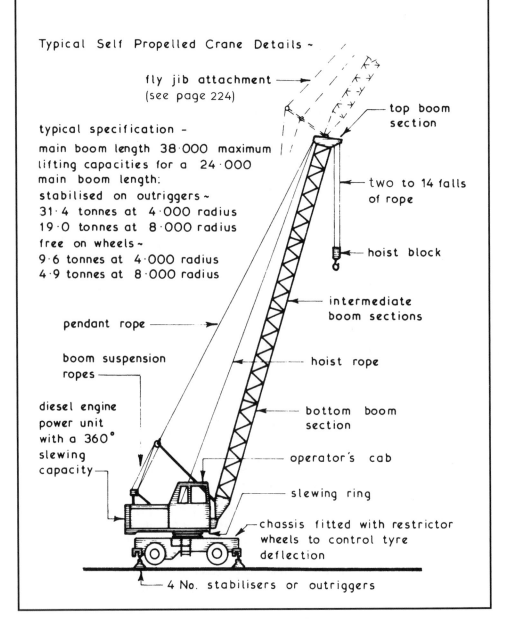

fly jib attachment ——
(see page 224)

top boom section

typical specification -

main boom length 38·000 maximum
lifting capacities for a 24·000
main boom length:
stabilised on outriggers ~
31·4 tonnes at 4·000 radius
19·0 tonnes at 8·000 radius
free on wheels ~
9·6 tonnes at 4·000 radius
4·9 tonnes at 8·000 radius

two to 14 falls of rope

hoist block

intermediate boom sections

pendant rope ——

boom suspension ropes ——

hoist rope

diesel engine power unit with a 360° slewing capacity

bottom boom section

operator's cab

slewing ring

chassis fitted with restrictor wheels to control tyre deflection

4 No. stabilisers or outriggers

Lorry Mounted Cranes ~ these mobile cranes consist of a lattice or telescopic boom mounted on a specially adapted truck or lorry. They have two operating positions: the lorry being driven from a conventional front cab and the crane being controlled from a different location. The lifting capacity of these cranes can be increased by using outrigger stabilising jacks and the approach distance to the face of the building decreased by using a fly jib. Lorry mounted telescopic cranes require a firm surface from which to operate and because of their short site preparation time they are ideally suited for short hire periods.

Typical Lorry Mounted Telescopic Crane Details ~

typical specification –

boom length 18·000
lifting capacities:
stabilised on outriggers ~
11·8 tonnes at 5·000 radius
4·3 tonnes at 11·000 radius
free on wheels ~
2·4 tonnes at 5·000 radius
0·5 tonnes at 11·000 radius
maximum road speed 65km/h

single or multiple falls of rope

hoist block

hoist rope

telescoping double-acting hydraulic ram housed within boom sections

telescopic boom sections

all-round vision cab housing road driving and crane operation controls

twin double-acting hydraulic luffing rams

diesel powered lorry

slewing ring

duplicate crane controls at rear

4 No. outrigger stabilising jacks

Lorry Mounted Lattice Jib Cranes ~ these cranes follow the same basic principles as the lorry mounted telescopic cranes but they have a lattice boom and are designed as heavy duty cranes with lifting capacities in excess of 100 tonnes. These cranes will require a firm, level surface from which to operate and can have a folding or sectional jib which will require the crane to be rigged on site before use.

Typical Lorry Mounted Lattice Jib Crane Details ~

fly jib strut

fly jib hoist block

fly jib

fly jib stay rope

multiple falls of rope

jib hoist block

sectionalised lattice jib

gantry mast

diesel engine power unit with 360° slewing capacity mounted on slewing ring

auxiliary hoist rope

main hoist rope

pendant or luffing rope

jib suspension ropes

diesel engine lorry

4 No. outrigger stabilising jacks

typical specification –
maximum jib length 54·860
fly jib length 15·000
maximum load 55 tonnes
using jib length of 7·600
and an operating radius of
3·600 with outriggers or
15·000 tonnes free on wheels
lifting capacity of fly jib
approximately half that of
jib for defined radii
maximum road speed 45 km/h

Track Mounted Cranes ~ these machines can be a universal power unit rigged as a crane (see page 210) or a purpose-designed track mounted crane with or without a fly jib attachment. The latter type are usually more powerful with lifting capacities of up to 45 tonnes. Track mounted cranes can travel and carry out lifting operations on most sites without the need for special road and hardstand provisions but they have to be rigged on arrival after being transported to site on a low-loader lorry.

Typical Track Mounted or Crawler Crane Details ~

maximum jib length 30·000 which can be extended by a fly jib attachment 9·000 or 12·000 long giving a load capacity of 5·5 tonnes at 7·000 radius or outreach for the combination

fly jib attachment (see page 222)

multiple falls of rope

hoist block

pendant or luffing rope

hoist rope

gantry mast

jib suspension ropes

typical specification – using a boom length of 30·000 maximum loads are: 15·8 tonnes at 4·000 radius 5·4 tonnes at 12·000 radius 2·2 tonnes at 24·000 radius maximum travelling speed 1·6km/h

sectionalised lattice jib

diesel powered crawler unit with 360° slewing capacity

Gantry Cranes ~ these are sometimes called portal cranes and consist basically of two 'A' frames joined together with a cross-member on which transverses the lifting appliance. In small gantry cranes (up to 10 tonnes lifting capacity) the 'A' frames are usually wheel mounted and manually propelled whereas in the large gantry cranes (up to 100 tonnes lifting capacity) the 'A' frames are mounted on powered bogies running on rail tracks with the driving cab and lifting gear mounted on the cross-beam or gantry. Small gantry cranes are used primarily for loading and unloading activities in stock yards whereas the medium and large gantry cranes are used to straddle the work area such as in power station construction or in repetitive low- to medium-rise developments. All gantry cranes have the advantage of three-direction movement:

1. Transverse by moving along the cross-beam.
2. Vertical by raising and lowering the hoist block.
3. Horizontal by forward and reverse movements of the whole gantry crane.

Typical Gantry Crane Details ~

lattice cross-beam or gantry

driving cab

hoist block

lattice 'A' frames

span between frames 20·000
maximum height under hook 25·000
maximum lifting capacity 20 tonnes
maximum travel speed along rails 100 metres per minute

powered bogies

lattice 'A' frame

counterweight or ballast

FRONT ELEVATION   END ELEVATION

Mast Cranes ~ these are similar in appearance to the familiar tower cranes but they have one major difference in that the mast or tower is mounted on the slewing ring and thus rotates, whereas a tower crane has the slewing ring at the top of the tower and therefore only the jib portion rotates. Mast cranes are often mobile, self-erecting, of relatively low lifting capacity and are usually fitted with a luffing jib. A wide variety of models are available and have the advantage over most mobile low pivot cranes of a closer approach to the face of the building.

Typical Mast Crane Details ~

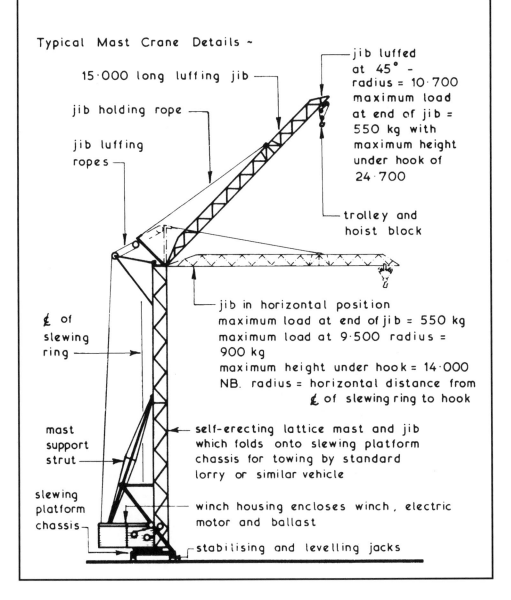

15·000 long luffing jib

jib holding rope

jib luffing ropes

jib luffed at 45° - radius = 10·700 maximum load at end of jib = 550 kg with maximum height under hook of 24·700

trolley and hoist block

jib in horizontal position
maximum load at end of jib = 550 kg
maximum load at 9·500 radius = 900 kg
maximum height under hook = 14·000
NB. radius = horizontal distance from ₵ of slewing ring to hook

₵ of slewing ring

mast support strut

slewing platform chassis

self-erecting lattice mast and jib which folds onto slewing platform chassis for towing by standard lorry or similar vehicle

winch housing encloses winch, electric motor and ballast

stabilising and levelling jacks

Tower Cranes ~ most tower cranes have to be assembled and erected on site prior to use and can be equipped with a horizontal or luffing jib. The wide range of models available often makes it difficult to choose a crane suitable for any particular site but most tower cranes can be classified into one of four basic groups thus:

1. Self-supporting Static Tower Cranes – high lifting capacity with the mast or tower fixed to a foundation base – they are suitable for confined and open sites (see page 229).

2. Supported Static Tower Cranes – similar in concept to self-supporting cranes and are used where high lifts are required, the mast or tower being tied at suitable intervals to the structure to give extra stability (see page 230).

3. Travelling Tower Cranes – these are tower cranes mounted on power bogies running on a wide gauge railway track to give greater site coverage – only slight gradients can be accommodated, therefore a reasonably level site or specially constructed railway support trestle is required (see page 231).

4. Climbing Cranes – these are used in conjunction with tall buildings and structures. The climbing mast or tower is housed within the structure and raised as the height of the structure is increased. Upon completion the crane is dismantled into small sections and lowered down the face of the building (see page 232).

All tower cranes should be left in an 'out of service' condition when unattended and in high wind conditions, the latter varying with different models but generally wind speeds in excess of 60 km p.h. would require the crane to be placed in an out of service condition thus:

cab left unattended

jib left on free slew and pointed in direction of the wind on the leeward side

jib

fuel and power supplies turned off

rail-mounted crane wheels to be clamped or chocked

load removed, hook raised to highest position and the trolley parked as close as possible to the tower

tower

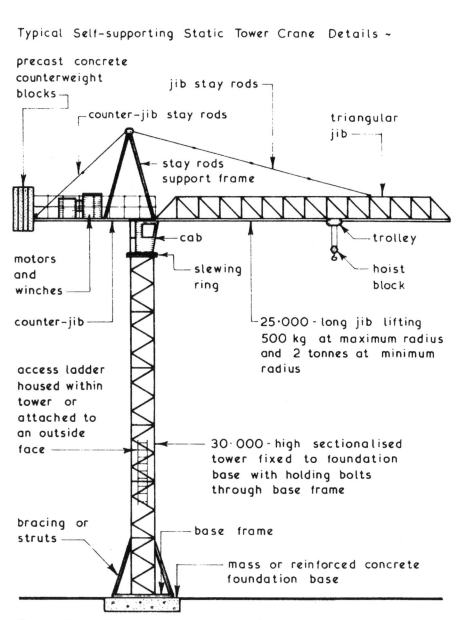

Typical Self-supporting Static Tower Crane Details ~

precast concrete counterweight blocks

counter-jib stay rods

jib stay rods

triangular jib

stay rods support frame

cab

motors and winches

slewing ring

trolley

hoist block

counter-jib

25·000 - long jib lifting 500 kg at maximum radius and 2 tonnes at minimum radius

access ladder housed within tower or attached to an outside face

30·000 - high sectionalised tower fixed to foundation base with holding bolts through base frame

bracing or struts

base frame

mass or reinforced concrete foundation base

Tower Crane Operation ~ two methods are in general use:

1. Cab Control - the crane operator has a good view of most of the lifting operations from the cab mounted at the top of the tower but a second person or banksman is required to give clear signals to the crane operator and to load the crane.

2. Remote Control - the crane operator carries a control box linked by a wandering lead to the crane controls.

Typical Supported Static Tower Crane Details ~

counter-jib stay rods

jib stay rods

triangular jib

motors and winches

slewing tower

counter-jib

cab

trolley

precast concrete counterweight blocks

slewing ring

hoist block

height above last tie not more than 75% of free-standing height

3rd tie

anchorages to building

spacing of all further ties not more than 20% of free-standing height

2nd tie

access ladder with safety hoops fixed to external face of tower

not more than 30% of free-standing height

1st tie

sectionalised tower fixed to foundation base with holding bolts through base frame

2·000 min.

building under construction

not more than 50% of free-standing height

bracing or struts

reinforced concrete foundation

base frame

NB. the above tie spacings are typical for specific cranes: see supplier's data.

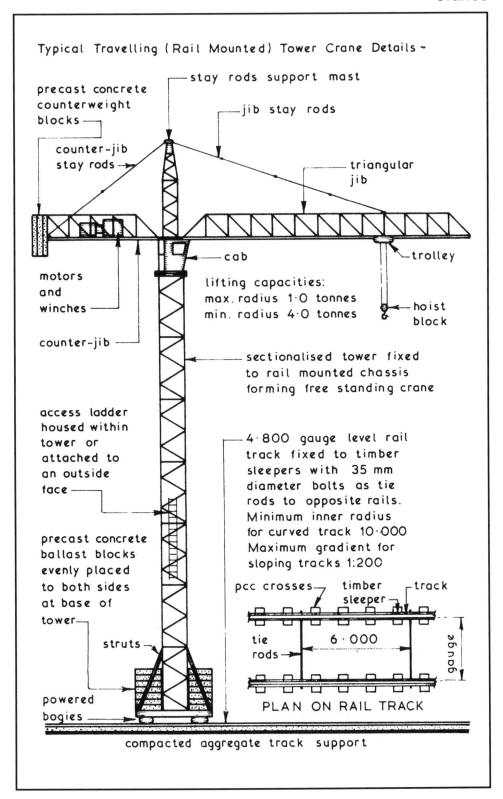

Typical Travelling (Rail Mounted) Tower Crane Details ~

stay rods support mast

precast concrete counterweight blocks

jib stay rods

counter-jib stay rods

triangular jib

cab

trolley

motors and winches

lifting capacities:
max. radius 1·0 tonnes
min. radius 4·0 tonnes

hoist block

counter-jib

sectionalised tower fixed to rail mounted chassis forming free standing crane

access ladder housed within tower or attached to an outside face

4·800 gauge level rail track fixed to timber sleepers with 35 mm diameter bolts as tie rods to opposite rails. Minimum inner radius for curved track 10·000 Maximum gradient for sloping tracks 1:200

precast concrete ballast blocks evenly placed to both sides at base of tower

pcc crosses

timber sleeper

track

struts

tie rods

6·000

gauge

powered bogies

PLAN ON RAIL TRACK

compacted aggregate track support

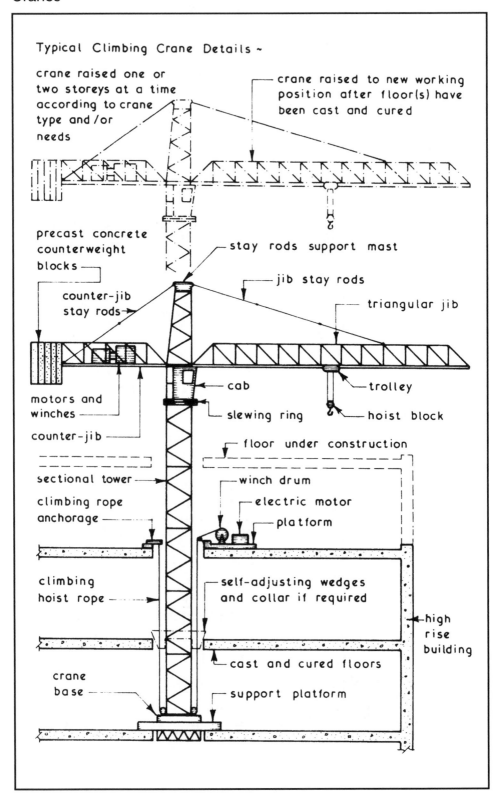

Typical Climbing Crane Details ~

crane raised one or two storeys at a time according to crane type and / or needs

crane raised to new working position after floor(s) have been cast and cured

precast concrete counterweight blocks

stay rods support mast

jib stay rods

counter-jib stay rods

triangular jib

motors and winches

cab

trolley

slewing ring

hoist block

counter-jib

floor under construction

sectional tower

winch drum

climbing rope anchorage

electric motor

platform

climbing hoist rope

self-adjusting wedges and collar if required

high rise building

crane base

cast and cured floors

support platform

Concreting ~ this site activity consists of four basic procedures:

1. Material Supply and Storage – this is the receiving on site of the basic materials namely cement, fine aggregate and coarse aggregate and storing them under satisfactory conditions (see Concrete Production – Materials on pages 325 and 326).
2. Mixing – carried out in small batches this requires only simple handheld tools whereas when demand for increased output is required mixers or ready mixed supplies could be used (see Concrete Production on pages 327 to 332 and Concreting Plant on pages 234 to 239).
3. Transporting – this can range from a simple bucket to barrows and dumpers for small amounts. For larger loads, especially those required at high level, crane skips could be used:

crane hook bar

skip loaded whilst lying on its back giving low loading height

four-leg chain sling

discharge handle

pressed steel container

pressed steel container

roll over frame

standing frame

discharge handle

discharge chute

bottom discharge

ROLL OVER SKIP
capacities - 0·4 to 2·3 m^3

STANDING SKIP
capacities - 0·4 to 6·0 m^3

For the transportation of large volumes of concrete over a limited distance concrete pumps could be used (see page 237).
4. Placing Concrete – this activity involves placing the wet concrete in the excavation, formwork or mould; working the concrete between and around any reinforcement; vibrating and/or tamping and curing (see Concreting Plant on page 238 and Formwork on page 600).

Further refs. BS 8000-2.1 and 2.2: Workmanship on building sites. Codes of practice for concrete work. Also, BS EN 1992-1-1 and -2: Design of concrete structures.

Concrete Mixers ~ apart from the very large output mixers most concrete mixers in general use have a rotating drum designed to produce a concrete without segregation of the mix.

Concreting Plant ~ the selection of concreting plant can be considered under three activity headings:
1. Mixing. 2. Transporting. 3. Placing.

Choice of Mixer ~ the factors to be taken into consideration when selecting the type of concrete mixer required are:

1. Maximum output required (m^3/hour).
2. Total output required (m^3).
3. Type or method of transporting the mixed concrete.
4. Discharge height of mixer (compatibility with transporting method).

Concrete mixer types are generally related to their designed output performance, therefore when the answer to the question 'How much concrete can be placed in a given time period?' or alternatively 'What mixing and placing methods are to be employed to mix and place a certain amount of concrete in a given time period?' has been found the actual mixer can be selected. Generally a batch mixing time of 5 minutes per cycle or 12 batches per hour can be assumed as a reasonable basis for assessing mixer output.

Small Batch Mixers ~ these mixers have outputs of up to 200 litres per batch with wheelbarrow transportation an hourly placing rate of 2 to 3 m^3 can be achieved. Most small batch mixers are of the tilting drum type. Generally these mixers are hand loaded which makes the quality control of successive mixes difficult to regulate.

Typical Example ~

hand wheel to control drum

petrol or diesel engine

towing bar

steel or tyred wheels

SIDE ELEVATION

steel mixing drum – discharges either side

drum capacity 100 litres mixed

940

600

END ELEVATION

Medium Batch Mixers ~ outputs of these mixers range from 200 to 750 litres and can be obtained at the lower end of the range as a tilting drum mixer or over the complete range as a non-tilting drum mixer with either reversing drum or chute discharge. The latter usually has a lower discharge height. These mixers usually have integral weight batching loading hoppers, scraper shovels and water tanks, thus giving better quality control than the small batch mixers. Generally they are unsuitable for wheelbarrow transportation because of their high output.

Typical Examples ~

electric cable to scraper shovel control

loading hopper in loading position – hopper raised by double acting hydraulic ram

55 litre water tank

steel mixing drum with rear discharge – 200 litre mixed capacity

NB. the volume output of all concrete mixers is approx. 30% less than the dry input volume due to the consolidation which takes place during mixing.

to loading or scraper shovel

weigh gauge

diesel engine

1060

TILTING DRUM MIXER

loading hopper in loading position

55 litre water tank

280 litre reversing mixing drum

shovel control switch

shovel dragline

loading or scraper shovel

diesel engine

weigh gauge

pressed steel wheels

1140

REVERSING DRUM MIXER

Transporting Concrete ~ the usual means of transporting mixed concrete produced in a small capacity mixer is by wheelbarrow. The run between the mixing and placing positions should be kept to a minimum and as smooth as possible by using planks or similar materials to prevent segregation of the mix within the wheelbarrow.

Dumpers ~ these can be used for transporting mixed concrete from mixers up to 600 litre capacity when fitted with an integral skip and for lower capacities when designed to take a crane skip.

STANDARD TYPE DUMPER   **CRANE SKIP DUMPER**

Ready Mixed Concrete Trucks ~ these are used to transport mixed concrete from a mixing plant or depot to the site. Usual capacity range of ready mixed concrete trucks is 4 to 6 m³. Discharge can be direct into placing position via a chute or into some form of site transport such as a dumper, crane skip or concrete pump.

Concrete Pumps ~ these are used to transport large volumes of concrete in a short time period (up to 100 m³ per hour) in both the vertical and horizontal directions from the pump position to the point of placing. Concrete pumps can be trailer or lorry mounted and are usually of a twin cylinder hydraulically driven format with a small bore pipeline (100 mm diameter) with pumping ranges of up to 85·000 vertically and 200·000 horizontally depending on the pump model and the combination of vertical and horizontal distances. It generally requires about 45 minutes to set up a concrete pump on site including coating the bore of the pipeline with a cement grout prior to pumping the special concrete mix. The pump is supplied with pumpable concrete by means of a constant flow of ready mixed concrete lorries throughout the pumping period after which the pipeline is cleared and cleaned. Usually a concrete pump and its operator(s) are hired for the period required.

Typical Concrete Pump Details ~

maximum height placing boom position

intermediate placing boom position

steel placing boom hydraulically raised into required placing position and lowered onto lorry for transporting

100 mm diameter flexible delivery pipe

alternative intermediate placing boom position

lorry mounted concrete pump controlled from lorry or by remote control with a wandering lead

angled placing boom position

horizontal placing boom position

rear mounted feed hopper

diesel powered lorry supported on jacked outriggers whilst pumping

Placing Concrete ~ this activity is usually carried out by hand with the objectives of filling the mould, formwork or excavated area to the correct depth, working the concrete around any inserts or reinforcement and finally compacting the concrete to the required consolidation. The compaction of concrete can be carried out using simple tamping rods or boards, or alternatively it can be carried out with the aid of plant such as vibrators.

Poker Vibrators ~ these consist of a hollow steel tube casing containing a rotating impeller which generates vibrations as its head comes into contact with the casing –

Poker vibrators should be inserted vertically and allowed to penetrate 75mm into any previously vibrated concrete.

Clamp or Tamping Board Vibrators ~ clamp vibrators are powered either by compressed air or electricity whereas tamping board vibrators are usually petrol driven –

CLAMP VIBRATOR   TAMPING BOARD VIBRATOR

Power Float – a hand-operated electric motor or petrol engine, surmounted over a mechanical surface skimmer. Machines are provided with an interchangeable revolving disc and a set of blades. These are used in combination to produce a smooth, dense and level surface finish to in-situ concrete beds.

The advantages offset against the cost of plant hire are:

* Eliminates the time and materials needed to apply a finishing screed.
* A quicker process and less labour-intensive than hand trowelling.

Application – after transverse tamping, the concrete is left to partially set for a few hours. Amount of setting time will depend on a number of variables, including air temperature and humidity, mix specification and machine weight. As a rough guide, walking on the concrete will leave indentations of about 3–4 mm. A surfacing disc is used initially to remove high tamping lines, before two passes with blades to finish and polish the surface.

petrol engine

3·5 litre fuel tank

motor (on/off), rotation speed and blade height controls

handle arm extendible to operator's waist height

four case-hardened steel reversible blades rotating at up to 150 rpm

900mm diameter guard ring and close mesh safety cover (part shown)

Power or mechanical float

Definition ~ curing of concrete can be explained as a series of chemical reactions that occur between cement in a concrete mix and the water, a process known as hydration. For concrete to achieve its correct design strength, hydration must be carefully controlled. In effect, it is the process of initial setting of concrete into a solid mass and subsequent hardening.

Adhesion ~ cement combining with water forms an adhesive paste. It sets slowly, gaining strength and hardening over time. In a thoroughly mixed batch of concrete the paste functions as a glue, adhering to the aggregates and binding them into a solid mass. Hydration continues indefinitely as the concrete gets harder. The critical period is within the first few hours as the concrete changes state from a liquid to a solid. Under controlled curing conditions concrete attains design strength after about 28 days.

Temperature ~ the hydration of cement generates a rise in temperature, possibly up to 20° C, therefore it is very important to regulate the cement content (see w/c ratio on page 329). Too much cement will cause excessive thermal expansion followed by contraction on cooling and setting, introducing potential for thermal stress cracking. The ideal ambient temperature during concreting is between 10° C and 24° C. This should be maintained throughout curing.

Water Retention ~ initial setting time is the most crucial for concrete to gain its design strength, therefore water must be retained and prevented from evaporating. Conversely, the addition of water from exposure to rain during the initial setting must also be prevented. Once set (24 hours after pouring) surface water can be a useful means of hydration control. Ideally, fresh concrete should be kept moist for at least 7 days when using OPC, otherwise shrinkage will induce tensile stresses manifesting in surface cracks. With other cements such as the rapid setting and hardening types, the manufacturer should be consulted to establish optimum curing time.

Curing Methods ~ the longer the time during which fresh concrete is kept moist, the more efficient will be the hardening process. Concrete should be protected from exposure to sunshine and high air temperatures in summer, drying winds, potentially freezing low air temperatures in winter and low relative humidy.

Setting ~ concrete will normally set within the working day. This can vary somewhat with air temperatures as indicated below.

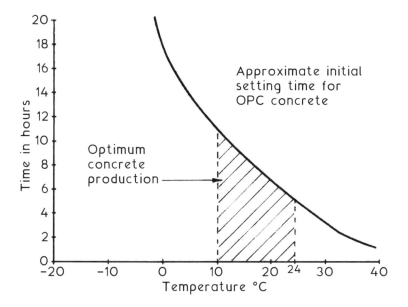

Methods for Retaining Water Content in Set Concrete ~

• Sealing by leaving the formwork/shuttering in place.
• Covering with an impervious membrane, e.g. plastic sheeting.
• Spraying with water.
• Spraying with a purpose made curing agent. A solvent based acrylic resin will also function as a surface sealant (polyurethane acrylic).
• Ponding by covering the concrete with a layer of water creating a temporary reservoir.
• For winter use, an insulating cover or blanket possibly with an electric element to prevent water content freezing.
• Steaming – appropriate in factory controlled situations. A sealed compartment contains circulation of a vapour of warm moist air.

Note: Period of curing should be as long as is practicable, maintained above 5°C for a minimum of 7 days. Demand for progress may limit these ideal measures hence the availability of mix additives and special cements with rapid setting and hardening properties. These should only be used with strict application of the manufacturer's instructions and/or to the structural engineer's specification.

Notes

242

4 SUBSTRUCTURE

FOUNDATIONS – FUNCTION, MATERIALS AND SIZING
FOUNDATION BEDS
SHORT BORED PILE FOUNDATIONS
FOUNDATION TYPES AND SELECTION
PILED FOUNDATIONS
RETAINING WALLS
GABIONS AND MATTRESSES
BASEMENT CONSTRUCTION
WATERPROOFING BASEMENTS
EXCAVATIONS
CONCRETE PRODUCTION
COFFERDAMS
STEEL SHEET PILING
CAISSONS
UNDERPINNING
GROUND WATER CONTROL
SOIL STABILISATION AND IMPROVEMENT
RECLAMATION OF WASTE LAND
TREATMENT OF CONTAMINATED SUBSOIL

Foundations ~ the function of any foundation is to safely sustain and transmit to the ground on which it rests the combined dead, imposed and wind loads in such a manner as not to cause any settlement or other movement which would impair the stability or cause damage to any part of the building.

Example ~

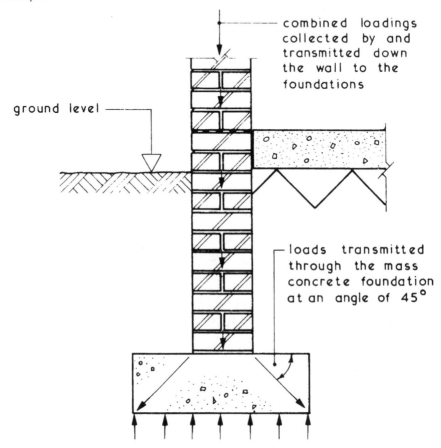

combined loadings collected by and transmitted down the wall to the foundations

ground level

loads transmitted through the mass concrete foundation at an angle of 45°

Subsoil beneath foundation is compressed and reacts by exerting an upward pressure to resist foundation loading. If foundation load exceeds maximum passive pressure of ground (i.e. bearing capacity) a downward movement of the foundation could occur. Remedy is to increase plan size of foundation to reduce the load per unit area or alternatively reduce the loadings being carried by the foundations.

Subsoil Movements ~ these are due primarily to changes in volume when the subsoil becomes wet or dry and occurs near the upper surface of the soil. Compact granular soils such as gravel suffer very little movement whereas cohesive soils such as clay do suffer volume changes near the upper surface. Similar volume changes can occur due to water held in the subsoil freezing and expanding – this is called Frost Heave.

Typical Examples ~

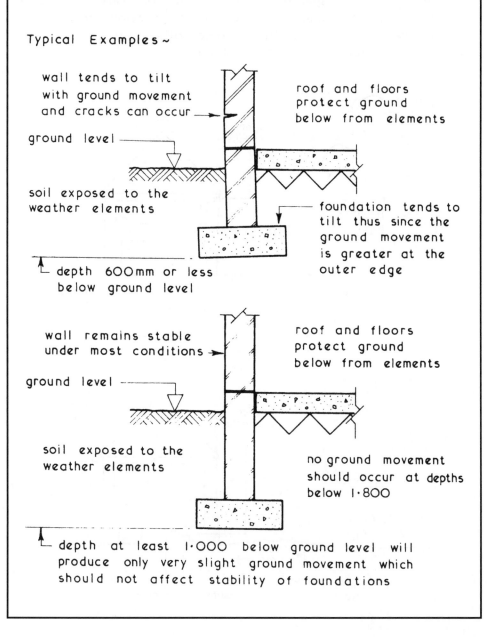

wall tends to tilt with ground movement and cracks can occur

roof and floors protect ground below from elements

ground level

soil exposed to the weather elements

foundation tends to tilt thus since the ground movement is greater at the outer edge

depth 600mm or less below ground level

wall remains stable under most conditions

roof and floors protect ground below from elements

ground level

soil exposed to the weather elements

no ground movement should occur at depths below 1·800

depth at least 1·000 below ground level will produce only very slight ground movement which should not affect stability of foundations

Trees ~ damage to foundations. Substructural damage to buildings can occur with direct physical contact by tree roots. More common is the indirect effect of moisture shrinkage or heave, particularly apparent in clay subsoils.

Shrinkage is most evident in long periods of dry weather, compounded by moisture abstraction from vegetation. Notably broad-leaved trees such as oak, elm and poplar in addition to the thirsty willow species. Heave is the opposite. It occurs during wet weather and is compounded by previous removal of moisture-dependent trees that would otherwise effect some drainage and balance to subsoil conditions.

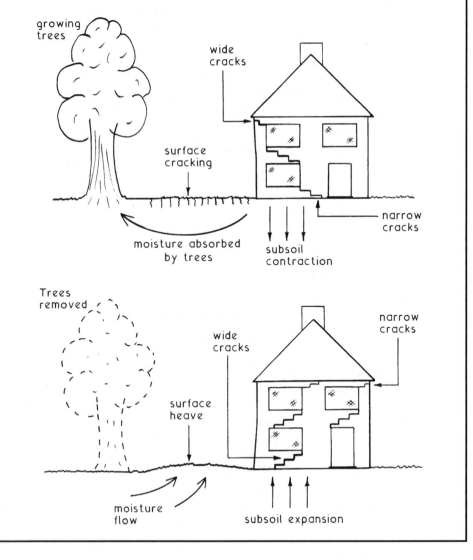

Trees ~ effect on foundations. Trees up to 30 m distance may have an effect on foundations, therefore reference to local authority building control policy should be undertaken before specifying construction techniques.

Traditional strip foundations are practically unsuited, but at excavation depths up to 2·5 or 3·0m, deep strip or trench fill (preferably reinforced) may be appropriate. Short bored pile foundations are likely to be more economical and particularly suited to depths exceeding 3·0m.

For guidance only, the illustration and table provide an indication of foundation depths in shrinkable subsoils.

H = Mature height of tree
D = Distance to centre of tree

D/H – Distance from tree/Height of tree

Tree species	0·10	0·25	0·33	0·50	0·66	0·75	1·00
Oak, elm, poplar and willow	3·00	2·80	2·60	2·30	2·10	1·90	1·50
All others	2·80	2·40	2·10	1·80	1·50	1·20	1·00

Minimum foundation depth (m)

Trees ~ preservation orders (see page 151) may be waived by the local planning authority. Permission for tree felling is by formal application and will be considered if the proposed development is in the economic and business interests of the community. However, tree removal is only likely to be acceptable if there is an agreement for replacement stock being provided elsewhere on the site.

In these circumstances there is potential for ground heave within the 'footprint' of felled trees. To resist this movement, foundations must incorporate an absorbing layer or compressible filler with ground floor suspended above the soil.

DEEP STRIP OR
TRENCH FILL FOUNDATION

raised concrete floor slab

150 mm min. void

external compressible material if justified

compressible material 'clayboard' on inside of foundation

polythene slip membrane

500 mm

SHORT BORED PILE FOUNDATION

floor structure as above (see also page 416)

additional compressible material on beam face if required

compressible material to inside and underside of perimeter beam

reinforced concrete piles, spaced according to subsoil condition

Cracking in Walls ~ cracks are caused by applied forces which exceed those that the building can withstand. Most cracking is superficial, occurring as materials dry out and subsequently shrink to reveal minor surface fractures of < 2 mm. These insignificant cracks can be made good with proprietary fillers.

Severe cracking in walls may result from foundation failure, due to inadequate design or physical damage. Further problems could include:

* Structural instability
* Rain penetration
* Air infiltration
* Heat loss
* Sound insulation reduction
* Visual depreciation

A survey should be undertaken to determine:
1. The cause of cracking, i.e.
    * Loads applied externally (tree roots, subsoil movement).
    * Climate/temperature changes (thermal movement).
    * Moisture content change (faulty dpc, building leakage).
    * Vibration (adjacent work, traffic).
    * Changes in physical composition (salt or ice formation).
    * Chemical change (corrosion, sulphate attack).
    * Biological change (timber decay).
2. The effect on a building's performance (structural and environmental).
3. The nature of movement – completed, ongoing or intermittent (seasonal).

Observations over a period of several months, preferably over a full year, will determine whether the cracking is new or established and whether it is progressing.

Simple method for monitoring cracks –

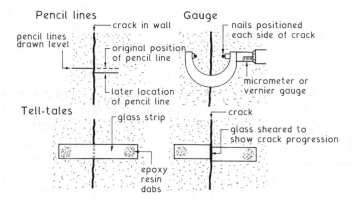

Further reading – BRE Digest 251: Assessment of damage in low rise buildings.

Foundation Materials ~ from page 244 one of the functions of a foundation can be seen to be the ability to spread its load evenly over the ground on which it rests. It must of course be constructed of a durable material of adequate strength. Experience has shown that the most suitable material is concrete.

Concrete is a mixture of cement + aggregates + water in controlled proportions.

CEMENT

Manufactured from clay and chalk and is the matrix or binder of the concrete mix. Cement powder can be supplied in bags or bulk –

Bags ~

25 kg

airtight sealed bags requiring a dry, damp-free store.

Bulk ~

12 to 50 tonnes

delivered by tanker and pumped into storage silo.

AGGREGATES

Coarse aggregate is generally defined as a material which is retained on a 4mm sieve.

coarse aggregate

4mm sieve

fine aggregate

Fine aggregate is generally defined as a material which passes a 4mm sieve. Aggregates can be either natural rock which has disintegrated or crushed stone or gravel.

WATER

Must be of a quality fit for drinking.

MIXES

These are expressed as a ratio thus:
1:3:6/20mm
which means –
1 part cement.
3 parts of fine aggregate.
6 parts of coarse aggregate.
20mm – maximum size of coarse aggregate for the mix.

Water is added to start the chemical reaction and to give the mix workability ~ the amount used is called the Water/Cement Ratio and is usually about 0·4 to 0·5.

Too much water will produce a weak concrete of low strength whereas too little water will produce a concrete mix of low and inadequate work-ability.

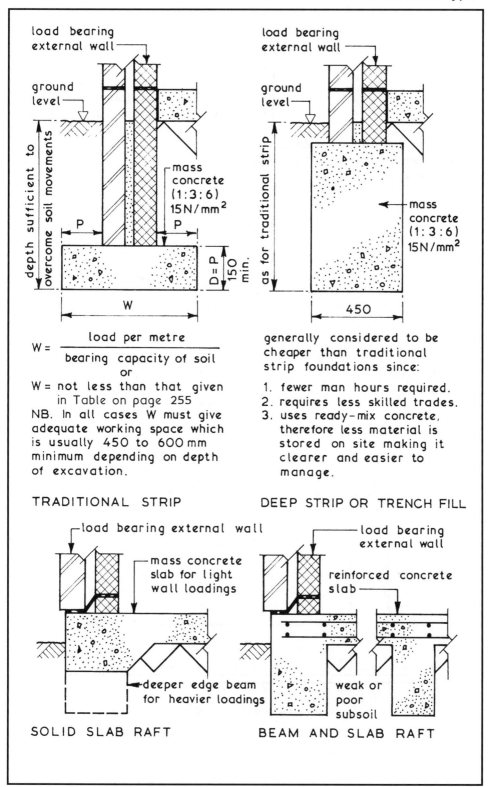

load bearing external wall

ground level

depth sufficient to overcome soil movements

mass concrete (1:3:6) 15N/mm²

P ← → P

D=P 150 min.

W

$$W = \frac{\text{load per metre}}{\text{bearing capacity of soil}}$$

or

W = not less than that given in Table on page 255

NB. In all cases W must give adequate working space which is usually 450 to 600 mm minimum depending on depth of excavation.

TRADITIONAL STRIP

load bearing external wall

ground level

as for traditional strip

mass concrete (1:3:6) 15N/mm²

450

generally considered to be cheaper than traditional strip foundations since:

1. fewer man hours required.
2. requires less skilled trades.
3. uses ready-mix concrete, therefore less material is stored on site making it clearer and easier to manage.

DEEP STRIP OR TRENCH FILL

load bearing external wall

mass concrete slab for light wall loadings

deeper edge beam for heavier loadings

SOLID SLAB RAFT

load bearing external wall

reinforced concrete slab

weak or poor subsoil

BEAM AND SLAB RAFT

251

centrally placed
reinforced concrete
column or isolated
brick pier

50 to 75 mm thick
blinding layer of ash,
coarse sand or a
lean mix concrete

reinforced
concrete
base

NB. ideal plan shape
for the base is
a square

area of base to be such
that the unit load per m²
does not exceed bearing
capacity of the subsoil

ISOLATED PAD

columns or piers placed
so that their centre of
gravity coincides with
that of the base

reinforced concrete
base

blinding

COMBINED PAD

Bed ~ a concrete slab resting on and supported by the subsoil, usually forming the ground floor surface. Beds (sometimes called over-site concrete) are usually cast on a layer of hardcore which is used to make up the reduced level excavation and thus raise the level of the concrete bed to a position above ground level.

Typical Example ~

mass concrete bed (1:3:6 / 20 mm mix 15 N / mm^2). Thickness for domestic work is usually 100 to 150 mm and the bed is constructed so as to prevent the passage of moisture from the ground to the upper surface of the floor - this is usually achieved by incorporating into the design a damp-proof membrane ~ for details see page 759

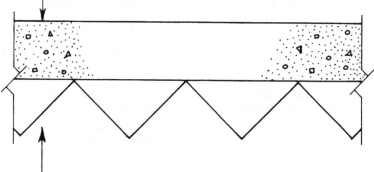

100 to 150mm-thick layer of hardcore ~ material used should be inert and not affected by water. Suitable materials are gravel; crushed rock; quarry waste; concrete rubble; brick or tile rubble; blast furnace slag and pulverised fuel ash (fly ash). The hardcore material should be laid evenly and well compacted with the upper surface blinded with fine grade material such as sand. Sand blinding fills the gaps in the hardcore to prevent concrete wastage and to provide a relatively smooth and level surface for a 0.3mm LDPE (1200 gauge polythene) dpm where required.

Basic Sizing ~ the size of a foundation is basically dependent on two factors:

1. Load being transmitted, max 70 kN/m (dwellings up to three storeys).
2. Bearing capacity of subsoil under proposed foundation.

For guidance on bearing capacities for different types of subsoil see BS EN 1997-1: Geotechnical design. General rules and BS 8103-1: Structural design of low rise buildings. Also, directly from soil investigation results.

Typical Examples ~

safe bearing capacity of compact gravel subsoil = 100 kN/m²

$$W = \frac{load}{bearing\ capacity} = \frac{50}{100}$$

= 500 mm minimum

safe bearing capacity of clay subsoil = 80 kN/m²

$$W = \frac{load}{bearing\ capacity} = \frac{50}{80}$$

= 625 mm minimum

The above widths may not provide adequate working space within the excavation and can be increased to give required space. Guidance on the minimum width for a limited range of applications can be taken from the table on the next page.

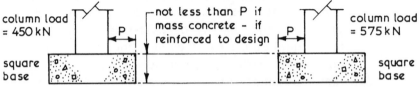

column load = 450 kN

square base

bearing capacity of subsoil 150 kN/m²

$$area\ of\ base = \frac{load}{bc} = \frac{450}{150}$$

$$= 3\ m^2 \therefore side = \sqrt{3}$$

= 1·732 min.

column load = 575 kN

square base

bearing capacity of subsoil 85 kN/m²

$$area\ of\ base = \frac{load}{bc} = \frac{575}{85}$$

$$= 6·765\ m^2 \therefore side = \sqrt{6·765}$$

= 2·6 min.

Ground type	Ground condition	Field test	Max. total load on load-bearing wall (kN/m)					
			20	30	40	50	60	70
			Minimum width (mm)					
Rock	Not inferior to sandstone, limestone or firm chalk	Requires a mechanical device to excavate.	At least equal to the width of the wall					
Gravel Sand	Medium density Compact	Pick required to excavate. 50 mm square peg hard to drive beyond 150 mm.	250	300	400	500	600	650
Clay Sandy clay	Stiff Stiff	Requires pick or mechanical device to aid removal. Can be indented slightly with thumb.	250	300	400	500	600	650
Clay Sandy clay	Firm Firm	Can be moulded under substantial pressure by fingers.	300	350	450	600	750	850
Sand Silty sand Clayey sand	Loose Loose Loose	Can be excavated by spade. 50 mm square peg easily driven.	400	600	Conventional strip foundations unsuitable for a total load exceeding 30 kN/m			
Silt Clay Sandy clay Silty clay	Soft Soft Soft Soft	Finger pushed in up to 10 mm. Easily moulded with fingers.	450	650				
Silt Clay Sandy clay Silty clay	Very soft Very soft Very soft Very soft	Finger easily pushed in up to 25 mm. Wet sample exudes between fingers when squeezed.	Conventional strip inappropriate. Steel-reinforced wide strip, deep strip or piled foundation selected subject to specialist advice					

Adapted from Table 10 in the Bldg. Regs., A.D: A – Structure.

Typical Procedure (for guidance only) –

Dead load per m run (see pages 38 and 39)

Substructure brickwork, 1 m × 1 m × 476 kg/m²	=	476 kg
... ... cavity conc. (50 mm), 1 m × 1 m × 2300 kg/m³	=	115 kg
Foundation concrete, 0·15 m × 1 m × 0·5 m × 2300 kg/m³	=	173 kg
Superstructure brickwork, 5 m × 1 m × 221 kg/m²	=	1105 kg
... ... blockwork & ins., 5 m × 1 m × 79 kg/m²	=	395 kg
... ... 2 coat plasterwork, 5 m × 1 m × 22 kg/m²	=	110 kg
Floor joists/boards/plstrbrd., 2·5 m × 1 m × 42·75 kg/m²	=	107 kg
Ceiling joists/plstrbrd/ins., 2·5 m × 1 m × 19·87 kg/m²	=	50 kg
Rafters, battens & felt, 2·9 m × 1 m × 12·10 kg/m²	=	35 kg
Single lap tiling, 2·9 m × 1 m × 49 kg/m²	=	142 kg
		2708 kg

Note: kg × 9·81 = Newtons

Therefore: 2708 kg × 9·81 = 26565 N or 26·56 kN

Imposed load per m run (see BS EN 1991-1-1: Densities, self-weight, imposed loads for buildings) –

Floor, 2·5 m × 1 m × 1·5 kN/m² = 3·75 kN

Roof, 2·9 m × 1 m × 1·5 kN/m² (snow) = 4·05 kN

7·80 kN

Note: For roof pitch >30°, snow load = 0·75 kN/m²

Dead + imposed load is 26·56 kN + 7·80 kN = 34·36 kN

Given that the subsoil has a safe bearing capacity of 75 kN/m²,

W = load ÷ bearing capacity = 34·36 ÷ 75 = 0·458 m or 458 mm

   Therefore a foundation width of 500 mm is adequate.

Note: This example assumes the site is sheltered. If it is necessary to make allowance for wind loading, reference should be made to BS EN 1991-1-4: Wind actions.

Stepped Foundations ~ these are usually considered in the context of strip foundations and are used mainly on sloping sites to reduce the amount of excavation and materials required to produce an adequate foundation.

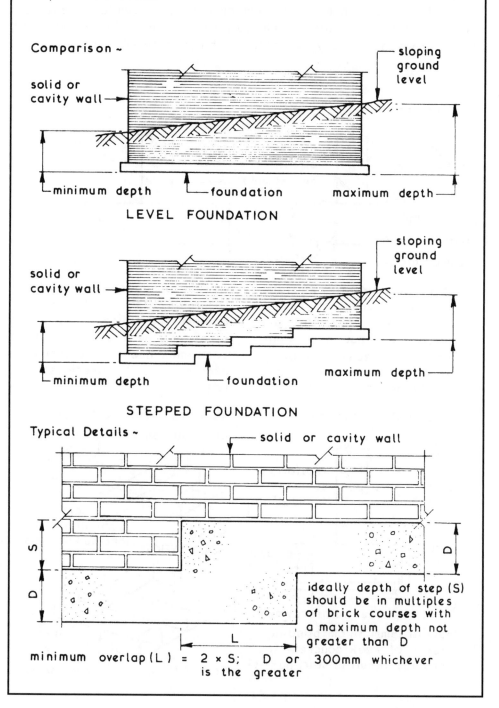

Comparison ~

solid or cavity wall →

sloping ground level

minimum depth   foundation   maximum depth

LEVEL FOUNDATION

solid or cavity wall →

sloping ground level

minimum depth   foundation   maximum depth

STEPPED FOUNDATION

Typical Details ~   solid or cavity wall

S

D

D

L

ideally depth of step (S) should be in multiples of brick courses with a maximum depth not greater than D

minimum overlap (L) = 2 × S; D or 300mm whichever is the greater

Concrete Foundations ~ concrete is a material which is strong in compression but weak in tension. If its tensile strength is exceeded cracks will occur, resulting in a weak and unsuitable foundation. One method of providing tensile resistance is to include in the concrete foundation bars of steel as a form of reinforcement to resist all the tensile forces induced into the foundation. Steel is a material which is readily available and has high tensile strength.

Comparisons ~

foundation tends to bend, the upper fibres being compressed and the lower fibres being stretched and put in tension - remedies: increase size of base or design as a reinforced concrete foundation

size of foundation increased to provide the resistance against the induced tensile stresses - generally not economic due to the extra excavation and materials required

Typical RC Foundation

Reinforcement Patterns

STRIP FOUNDATION

SQUARE BASE

Short Bored Piles ~ these are a form of foundation which are suitable for domestic loadings and clay subsoils where ground movements can occur below the 1·000 depth associated with traditional strip and trench fill foundations. They can be used where trees are planted close to a new building since the trees may eventually cause damaging ground movements due to extracting water from the subsoil and root growth. Conversely where trees have been removed this may lead to ground swelling.

Typical Details ~

cavity insulation
floor screed
external wall
50 mm rigid insulation
damp-proof membrane
damp-proof course
ground level
mass concrete ground floor
cavity filling
compacted hardcore

reinforced concrete ground beam cast in trench over short bored pile heads – size of beam and reinforcement to design or from tables

40 mm thick sand or lean concrete blinding

depth of pile governed by level of suitable bearing capacity ground and/or stability of clay subsoil – economic maximum depth 4·500

250 to 300 mm diameter according to design

Typical spacing of piles 1·800 to 2·500

bored and cast in-situ piles of mass concrete maximum spacing to design

Typical loading 40 to 125 kN per pile

Piles formed by lorry or tractor mounted auger capable of drilling 80 piles per day

Simple RC Raft Foundations

Simple Raft Foundations ~ these can be used for lightly loaded buildings on poor soils or where the top 450 to 600 mm of soil is overlaying a poor-quality substrata.

Typical Details ~

REINFORCED CONCRETE RAFT WITH EDGE THICKENING

REINFORCED CONCRETE RAFT WITH EDGE BEAM

Foundation Design Principles ~ the main objectives of foundation design are to ensure that the structural loads are transmitted to the subsoil(s) safely, economically and without any unacceptable movement during the construction period and throughout the anticipated life of the building or structure.

Basic Design Procedure ~ this can be considered as a series of steps or stages:

1. Assessment of site conditions in the context of the site and soil investigation report.

2. Calculation of anticipated structural loading(s).

3. Choosing the foundation type taking into consideration:

    • Soil conditions;
    • Type of structure;
    • Structural loading(s);
    • Economic factors;
    • Time factors relative to the proposed contract period;
    • Construction problems.

4. Sizing the chosen foundation in the context of loading(s), ground bearing capacity and any likely future movements of the building or structure.

Foundation Types ~ apart from simple domestic foundations most foundation types are constructed in reinforced concrete and may be considered as being shallow or deep. Most shallow types of foundation are constructed within 2·000 of the ground level but in some circumstances it may be necessary to take the whole or part of the foundations down to a depth of 2·000 to 5·000 as in the case of a deep basement where the structural elements of the basement are to carry the superstructure loads. Generally foundations which need to be taken below 5·000 deep are cheaper when designed and constructed as piled foundations and such foundations are classified as deep foundations. (For piled foundation details see pages 266 to 286.)

Foundations are usually classified by their type such as strips, pads, rafts and piles. It is also possible to combine foundation types such as strip foundations connected by beams to and working in conjunction with pad foundations.

Strip Foundations ~ these are suitable for most subsoils and light structural loadings such as those encountered in low to medium rise domestic dwellings where mass concrete can be used. Reinforced concrete is usually required for all other situations.

Typical Strip Foundation Types ~

TRADITIONAL STRIP
low rise domestic dwellings or similar buildings

DEEP STRIP or TRENCH FILL
alternative to traditional strip

$$W \text{ (minimum)} = \frac{\text{load per metre}}{\text{bearing capacity of soil}}$$

REINFORCED CONCRETE STRIP
used where induced tension exceeds concrete's own tensile resistance

CONTINUOUS COLUMN
used for closely spaced or close to boundary columns

Pad Foundations ~ suitable for most subsoils except loose sands, loose gravels and filled areas. Pad foundations are usually constructed of reinforced concrete and where possible are square in plan.

Typical Pad Foundation Types ~

ISOLATED or PAD FOUNDATION
designed to span in two directions therefore main bars are placed in the bottom both ways

STEEL GRILLAGE
used for heavy concentrated loads - seldom employed today

RECTANGULAR PAD
used where width of base is restricted

plan shape can be a rectangle or where length is restricted a trapezium

COMBINED COLUMN FOUNDATIONS - outer column close to boundary or existing wall

Raft Foundations ~ these are used to spread the load of the superstructure over a large base to reduce the load per unit area being imposed on the ground and this is particularly useful where low bearing capacity soils are encountered and where individual column loads are heavy.

Typical Raft Foundation Types ~

RC column

75mm high kicker

binders

main bars

reinforced concrete raft of uniform thickness over whole area - simple to design and construct but can be wasteful in amount of concrete used

column starter bars

75mm thick blinding   main bars   distribution bars

SOLID SLAB RAFT

reinforced concrete or steel columns positioned on beam intersections

ground beams

reinforced concrete raft spanning over ground beams

used on poor soils where the beams are employed to spread the column loads over the raft

blinding

reinforced concrete ground beam

NB. Ground beams can be designed as upstand beams with a precast concrete suspended floor at ground level thus creating a void space between raft and ground floor.

BEAM AND SLAB RAFT

Cantilever Foundations ~ these can be used where it is necessary to avoid imposing any pressure on an adjacent foundation or underground service.

Typical Cantilever Foundation Types ~

Cantilever foundations designed and constructed in reinforced concrete

Piled Foundations ~ these can be defined as a series of columns constructed or inserted into the ground to transmit the load(s) of a structure to a lower level of subsoil. Piled foundations can be used when suitable foundation conditions are not present at or near ground level making the use of deep traditional foundations uneconomic. The lack of suitable foundation conditions may be caused by:

1. Natural low bearing capacity of subsoil.
2. High water table – giving rise to high permanent dewatering costs.
3. Presence of layers of highly compressible subsoils such as peat and recently placed filling materials which have not sufficiently consolidated.
4. Subsoils which may be subject to moisture movement or plastic failure.

Classification of Piles ~ piles may be classified by their basic design function or by their method of construction:

END BEARING PILES

pile transmits load direct to firm strata – it also receives lateral restraint from subsoil

FRICTION OR FLOATING PILES

pile transmits load to surrounding soil via friction between surface of pile and soil which in effect lowers bulb of pressure

NB. Piles can work in a combination of the above design functions

REPLACEMENT PILES

hole for pile shaft bored in the ground and the resultant void filled with reinforced or plain in-situ concrete

DISPLACEMENT PILES

preform pile driven into ground displacing the subsoil through which it passes

Replacement Piles ~ these are often called bored piles since the removal of the spoil to form the hole for the pile is always carried out by a boring technique. They are used primarily in cohesive subsoils for the formation of friction piles and when forming pile foundations close to existing buildings where the allowable amount of noise and/or vibration is limited.

Replacement Pile Types ~

PERCUSSION BORED

small or medium-size contracts with up to 300 piles

load range - 300 to 1300 kN

length range - up to 24·000

diameter range - 300 to 900

may have to be formed as a pressure pile in waterlogged subsoils

(see page 268)

FLUSH BORED

large projects - these are basically a rotary bored pile using bentonite as a drilling fluid

load range - 1000 to 5000 kN

length range - up to 30·000

diameter range - 600 to 1500

(see page 269)

ROTARY BORED

Small Diameter - <600 mm

light loadings - can also be used in groups or clusters with a common pile cap to receive heavy loads

load range - 50 to 400 kN

length range - up to 15·000

diameter range - 240 to 600

(see pages 270 and 272)

Large Diameter - >600 mm

heavy concentrated loadings - may have an underreamed or belled toe

load range - 800 to 15000 kN

length range - up to 60·000

diameter range - 600 to 2400

(see page 271)

NB. The above given data depicts typical economic ranges. More than one pile type can be used on a single contract.

Percussion Bored Piles

Typical Details ~

power winch

pulley

tripod or shear leg rig

limited headroom of 1·800 possible

hoist rope

weighted head

cruciform plan shaped steel body

cutting ring

short lengths (1·000 to 1·400) of steel lining tube screwed together

clay cutter

steel lining tubes sink under own weight

BORING IN COHESIVE SOIL

hoist rope

weighted head

granular soil shell

flap

top holes for soil extraction

cutting edge

BORING IN GRANULAR SOIL

shear leg rig

collar with lugs

hydraulic jacks

reinforcement cage

internal drop hammer

concrete tamped by drop hammer

steel lining tubes jacked out of bore hole as concrete is placed and tamped

FORMING PILE USING DROP HAMMER

shear leg rig

loading hopper and air lock

valve

compressed air supply

reinforcement cage

concrete consolidated by air pressure

steel lining tubes pulled out of bore hole by winch as concrete is placed and consolidated

FORMING PILE USING AIR PRESSURE

Flush Bored Piles

Typical Details ~

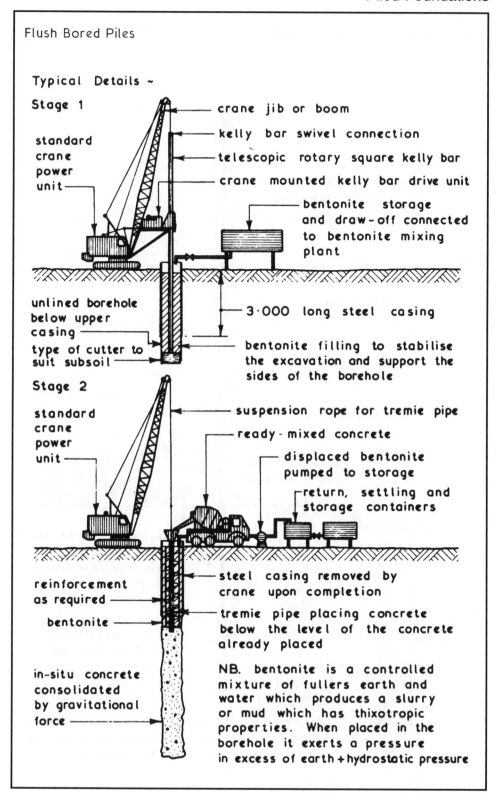

Stage 1

standard crane power unit

crane jib or boom

kelly bar swivel connection

telescopic rotary square kelly bar

crane mounted kelly bar drive unit

bentonite storage and draw-off connected to bentonite mixing plant

unlined borehole below upper casing

3·000 long steel casing

type of cutter to suit subsoil

bentonite filling to stabilise the excavation and support the sides of the borehole

Stage 2

standard crane power unit

suspension rope for tremie pipe

ready-mixed concrete

displaced bentonite pumped to storage

return, settling and storage containers

reinforcement as required

steel casing removed by crane upon completion

bentonite

tremie pipe placing concrete below the level of the concrete already placed

in-situ concrete consolidated by gravitational force

NB. bentonite is a controlled mixture of fullers earth and water which produces a slurry or mud which has thixotropic properties. When placed in the borehole it exerts a pressure in excess of earth + hydrostatic pressure

Small Diameter Rotary Bored Piles

Typical Details ~

derrick or mast housing lifting ropes and single or telescopic kelly bar

drilling rig can be lorry mounted as shown or crane mounted as shown on pages 269 and 271

kelly bar

hydraulic derrick rams

winch

power unit

pile cap - see page 286

reasonably level ground surface

outrigger jacks to stabilise and level vehicle when drilling

reinforcement to design

pile shaft

borehole fully lined, partially lined or unlined according to type(s) of subsoil

auger type or drilling bucket to suit conditions

completed pile - in-situ concrete consolidated by gravitational force and placed by tremie pipe if water is present in borehole

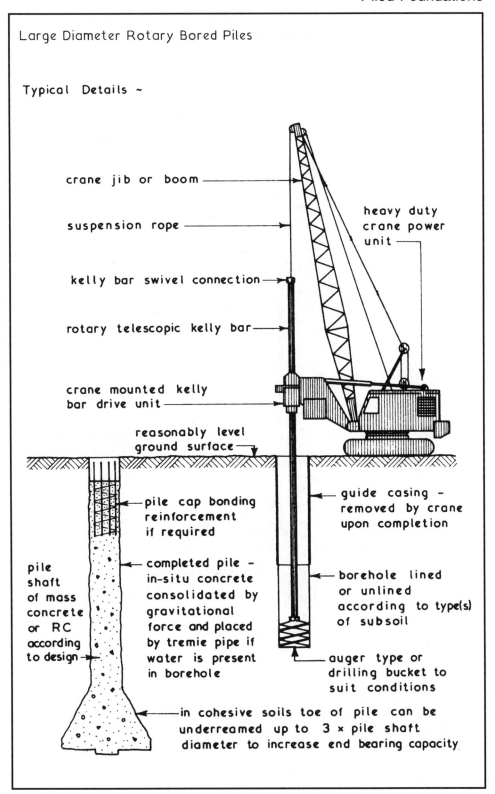

Large Diameter Rotary Bored Piles

Typical Details ~

crane jib or boom

suspension rope

kelly bar swivel connection

rotary telescopic kelly bar

crane mounted kelly bar drive unit

reasonably level ground surface

heavy duty crane power unit

pile cap bonding reinforcement if required

pile shaft of mass concrete or RC according to design

completed pile - in-situ concrete consolidated by gravitational force and placed by tremie pipe if water is present in borehole

guide casing - removed by crane upon completion

borehole lined or unlined according to type(s) of subsoil

auger type or drilling bucket to suit conditions

in cohesive soils toe of pile can be underreamed up to 3 × pile shaft diameter to increase end bearing capacity

Continuous Flight Auger Bored Piles

Typical Details ~

kelly bar

pulleys suspension arm

mobile kelly bar drive

Completed pile shaft as shown on page 270

kelly bar drive guide

flight auger

hydraulic ram

tracked power unit

auger guide collar

stabiliser

Standard pile diameters are 300, 450 and 600 mm. Depth of borehole to about 15 m.

Grout Injection Piling ~

A variation of continuous flight auger bored piling that uses an open ended hollow core to the flight. After boring to the required depth, high slump concrete is pumped through the hollow stem as the auger is retracted. Spoil is displaced at the surface and removed manually. In most applications there is no need to line the boreholes, as the subsoil has little time to be disturbed. A preformed reinforcement cage is pushed into the wet concrete.

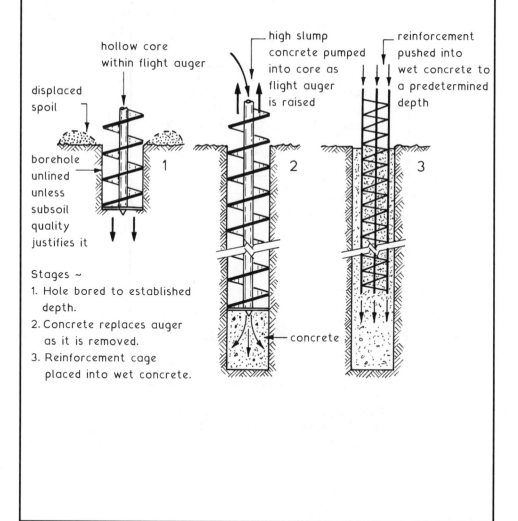

hollow core within flight auger

high slump concrete pumped into core as flight auger is raised

reinforcement pushed into wet concrete to a predetermined depth

displaced spoil

borehole unlined unless subsoil quality justifies it

1

2

3

concrete

Stages ~
1. Hole bored to established depth.
2. Concrete replaces auger as it is removed.
3. Reinforcement cage placed into wet concrete.

Displacement Piles ~ these are often called driven piles since they are usually driven into the ground, displacing the earth around the pile shaft. These piles can be either preformed or partially preformed if they are not cast in-situ and are available in a wide variety of types and materials. The pile or forming tube is driven into the required position to a predetermined depth or to the required 'set' which is a measure of the subsoil's resistance to the penetration of the pile and hence its bearing capacity by noting the amount of penetration obtained by a fixed number of hammer blows.

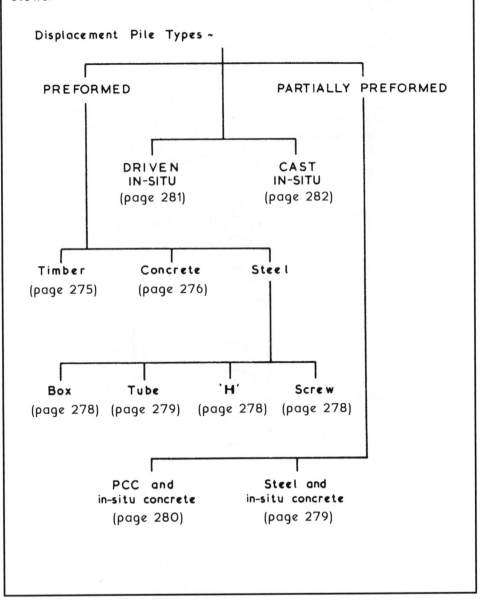

Displacement Pile Types ~

PREFORMED   PARTIALLY PREFORMED

DRIVEN   CAST
IN-SITU   IN-SITU
(page 281)   (page 282)

Timber   Concrete   Steel
(page 275)   (page 276)

Box   Tube   'H'   Screw
(page 278)   (page 279)   (page 278)   (page 278)

PCC and   Steel and
in-situ concrete   in-situ concrete
(page 280)   (page 279)

Timber Piles ~ these are usually square sawn and can be used for small contracts on sites with shallow alluvial deposits overlaying a suitable bearing strata (e.g. river banks and estuaries). Timber piles are percussion driven.

Typical Example ~

mild steel band

timber body

Typical Data:

load range - 50 to 350kN

length range - up to 12·000
without splicing

size range - 225 × 225
300 × 300 *
350 × 350 *
400 × 400 *
450 × 450
600 × 600

* common sizes

mild steel fixing straps

mild steel shoe

NB. timber piles are not easy to splice and are liable to attack by marine borers when set in waters; therefore such piles should always be treated with a suitable preservative before being driven.

Preformed Concrete Piles ~ variety of types available which are generally used on medium to large contracts of not less than one hundred piles where soft soil deposits overlie a firmer strata. These piles are percussion driven using a drop or single-acting hammer.

Typical Example [West's Hardrive Precast Modular Pile] ~

cable for hoisting pile lengths

piling rig

leader

drop hammer ~ see page 283

braces

helmet

power unit

reasonably level ground surface

splicing collar

reinforced precast concrete pile lengths from 2·500 to 10·000

precast concrete or steel shoe unit

Typical Data:
load range – 200 to 1000 kN
length range – 7·000 to 18·000
size range – 250 × 250 up to 450 × 450

Splicing of pile lengths is difficult unless particular pile type has a special splicing joint collar

Preformed Concrete Piles – jointing with a peripheral steel splicing collar as shown on the preceding page is adequate for most concentrically or directly loaded situations. Where very long piles are to be used and/or high stresses due to compression, tension and bending from the superstructure or the ground conditions are anticipated, the four or eight lock pile joint [AARSLEFF PILING] may be considered.

hardwood or dense plastic driving plate removed

steel dowel with void for pin

treated steel shutter and pile lock bonded to pile reinforcement

high tensile steel locking pin

lower preformed concrete pile section*

*upper section as lower section but inverted and dowels located over holes

Pile dimensions (mm)	Possible no. of locks per joint
250 × 250, 300 × 300, 350 × 350 and 400 × 400	4
350 × 350, 400 × 400 and 450 × 450	8

Steel Box and 'H' Sections ~ standard steel sheet pile sections can be used to form box section piles whereas the 'H' section piles are cut from standard rolled sections. These piles are percussion driven and are used mainly in connection with marine structures.

Typical Examples ~

FRODINGHAM
BOX PILE

RENDHEX
BOX PILE

UNIVERSAL
BEARING PILE

Typical Data:

load range - box piles 300 to 1500 kN
bearing piles 300 to 1700 kN

length range - all types up to 36·000

size range - various sizes and profiles available

Steel Screw Piles ~ rotary driven and used for dock and jetty works where support at shallow depths in soft silts and sands is required.

Typical Example ~

steel shaft ⟶

cast iron
helix ⟶

Typical Data:

load range - 400 to 3000 kN

length range - up to 24·000

size range -   shafts 150 to
350 mm dia.
overall blades
600 to 1200

Steel Tube Piles ~ used on small to medium-size contracts for marine structures and foundations in soft subsoils over a suitable bearing strata. Tube piles are usually bottom driven with an internal drop hammer. The loading can be carried by the tube alone but it is usual to fill the tube with mass concrete to form a composite pile. Reinforcement, except for pile cap bonding bars, is not normally required.

Typical Example [BSP Cased Pile] ~

standard crane power unit and rigging

timber trestle as tube support and guide frame

reasonably level ground surface

steel tube out of strip with butt welded helix

drop hammer acting on concrete plug

D

plug of very low water content earth dry concrete

2·5 D

steel base plate welded to end of tube

Typical Data :-

load range - 300 to 1500 kN

length range - up to 24·000 but can be extended by welding on extra lengths

diameter range - 250 to 750

Partially Preformed Piles ~ these are composite piles of precast concrete and in-situ concrete or steel and in-situ concrete (see page 279). These percussion-driven piles are used on medium to large contracts where bored piles would not be suitable owing to running water or very loose soils.

Typical Example [West's Shell Pile] ~

piling rig

cable for hoisting pile shells

power unit

drop hammer

helmet connected to steel mandrel

access platform on leader tube

reasonably level ground surface

pile located between pair of steel leader tubes

Typical Pile Details ~

pile shells located on mandrel while being driven

polypropylene reinforced concrete shells

steel jointing band

reinforcement to design

in-situ concrete filling to core

steel jointing band

900

900

steel mandrel inside shell pile core

Typical Data:

load range - 300 to 1200 kN

length range - up to 30·000

diameter range - 380 to 500 mm

precast concrete driving shoe

Driven In-situ Piles ~ used on medium to large contracts as an alternative to preformed piles particularly where final length of pile is a variable to be determined on site.

Typical Example [Franki Driven In-situ Pile] ~

winch rope

tube holding ropes

reasonably level ground

drawn steel tube

2 to 3 tonne internal drop hammer

600 to 900 compacted gravel to form plug

whilst tube is held the drop hammer forces the gravel plug out of the tube to form an enlarged toe

as gravel plug is hammered friction between plug and tube drags the tube into the ground

1. DRIVING TUBE

drawn steel tube

internal drop hammer

enlarged toe

stiff concrete

2. FORMING ENLARGED TOE

tube is withdrawn as hammer compacts concrete

drop hammer operates inside of reinforcement cage

charges of semi-dry concrete

reinforcement to design

enlarged toe

pile shaft

3. FORMING PILE SHAFT

The drawn steel tube is supported in the leaders of a piling rig or frame during the formation of the pile

Typical Data:
load range - 300 to 1 300 kN
length range - up to 18·000
diameter range - 300 to 600 mm

Cast In-situ Piles ~ an alternative to the driven in-situ piles (see page 281)

Typical Example [Vibro Cast In-situ Pile] ~

reasonably level ground

steel tube supported in the leaders of a piling rig or frame during pile formation

steel tube top driven to required depth or set

tube is raised by reverse action of hammer as concrete is placed

reinforcement to design

cast iron driving shoe

concrete is tamped by means of rapid up and down blows from hammer as the steel tube is withdrawn

1. DRIVING TUBE

downward blow

in-situ concrete forced into weak pockets in the soil by tamping action of tube

upward blow

Typical Data:

load range - 300 to 1300 kN

length range - up to 18·000

diameter range - 300 to 600 mm

driving shoe left in

2. FORMING PILE SHAFT

282

Piling Hammers ~ these are designed to deliver an impact blow to the top of the pile to be driven. The hammer weight and drop height is chosen to suit the pile type and nature of subsoil(s) through which it will be driven. The head of the pile being driven is protected against damage with a steel helmet which is padded with a sand bed or similar material and is cushioned with a plastic or hardwood block called a dolly.

Drop Hammers ~ these are blocks of iron with a rear lug(s) which locate in the piling rig guides or leaders and have a top eye for attachment of the winch rope. The number of blows which can be delivered with a free fall of 1·200 to 1·500 ranges from 10 to 20 per minute. The weight of the hammer should be not less than 50% of the concrete or steel pile weight and 1 to 1·5 times the weight of a timber pile.

Single Acting Hammers ~ these consist of a heavy falling cylinder raised by steam or compressed air sliding up and down a fixed piston. Guide lugs or rollers are located in the piling frame leaders to maintain the hammer position relative to the pile head. The number of blows delivered ranges from 36 to 75 per minute with a total hammer weight range of 2 to 15 tonnes.

283

Double Acting Hammers ~ these consist of a cast iron cylinder which remains stationary on the pile head whilst a ram powered by steam or compressed air for both up and down strokes delivers a series of rapid blows which tends to keep the pile on the move during driving. The blow delivered is a smaller force than that from a drop or single acting hammer. The number of blows delivered ranges from 95 to 300 per minute with a total hammer weight range of 0·7 to 6·5 tonnes. Diesel powered double acting hammers are also available.

Diesel Hammers ~ these are self-contained hammers which are located in the leaders of a piling rig and rest on the head of the pile. The driving action is started by raising the ram within the cylinder which activates the injection of a measured amount of fuel. The free-falling ram compresses the fuel above the anvil causing the fuel to explode and expand resulting in a downward force on the anvil and upward force which raises the ram to recommence the cycle which is repeated until the fuel is cut off. The number of blows delivered ranges from 40 to 60 per minute with a total hammer weight range of 1·0 to 4·5 tonnes.

Vibrating Hammer ~ used with preformed displacement piles driven into clay, sand or gravel subsoils.

Application ~ unit suspended by cable from a crane, positioned and secured to the top of the pile. Steel pipe, H section and sheet pile profiles are most suited to this procedure.

Function ~ two electric motors are used to propel eccentric rotors in opposing directions. The vibrations generated combine with the weight of the unit to transmit through the pile. This breaks down the subsoils resistance to shear and enables the pile to penetrate. Resistance can be reduced by water jetting at the toe of the pile.

Advantages ~ relatively silent in operation, a considerable benefit in built-up areas. Use of electricity is non-polluting in the immediate site area. No impact, therefore pile cap is unlikely to be damaged.

Disadvantage ~ electricity is not always available during preliminary ground works.

Pile Caps ~ piles can be used singly to support the load but often it is more economical to use piles in groups or clusters linked together with a reinforced concrete cap. The pile caps can also be linked together with reinforced concrete ground beams.

The usual minimum spacing for piles is:

1. Friction Piles – 1·100 or not less than 3 × pile diameter, whichever is the greater.
2. Bearing Piles – 750 mm or not less than 2 × pile diameter, whichever is the greater.

Typical Examples ~

TWO PILE CAP   THREE PILE CAP   FIVE PILE CAP

ELEVATION OF PILE CAP AND BEAM

Typical Pile Cap Depths

pile size	depth (D)
300	700
350	800
400	900
450	1 000
500	1 100
550	1 200
600	1 400

Pile Testing ~ it is advisable to test load at least one pile per scheme. The test pile should be overloaded by at least 50% of its working load and this load should be held for 24 hours. The test pile should not form part of the actual foundations. Suitable testing methods are:

1. Jacking against kentledge placed over test pile.
2. Jacking against a beam fixed to anchor piles driven in on two sides of the test pile.

Retaining Walls ~ the major function of any retaining wall is to act as an earth-retaining structure for the whole or part of its height on one face, the other being exposed to the elements. Most small height retaining walls are built entirely of brickwork or a combination of brick facing and blockwork or mass concrete backing. To reduce hydrostatic pressure on the wall from ground water an adequate drainage system in the form of weep holes should be used. Alternatively subsoil drainage behind the wall could be employed.

Typical Example of Combination Retaining Wall ~

Small Height Retaining Walls ~ retaining walls must be stable and the usual rule of thumb for small height brick retaining walls is for the height to lie between two and four times the wall thickness. Stability can be checked by applying the middle third rule –

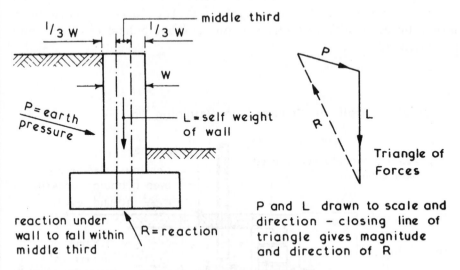

reaction under wall to fall within middle third

R = reaction

Triangle of Forces

P and L drawn to scale and direction – closing line of triangle gives magnitude and direction of R

Typical Example of Brick Retaining Wall ~

pcc weathered coping stone

pervious membrane over granular backfill

ground level

200mm wide 25mm nominal diameter 'no-fines' granular backfill

75mm diameter PVC sleeved weep holes at 2·000 c/c

mass concrete 1:2:4 / 20mm agg. foundation

20mm wide flexcell or similar expansion joints at 30·000 c/c

free standing height

retaining height not greater than 1·000

retaining wall of dense clay engineering bricks laid to english bond in cm.mt 1:3

drainage channel

50

75

225

225

900

Retaining Walls up to 6·000 high ~ these can be classified as medium height retaining walls and have the primary function of retaining soils at an angle in excess of the soil's natural angle of repose. Walls within this height range are designed to provide the necessary resistance by either their own mass or by the principles of leverage.

Design ~ the actual design calculations are usually carried out by a structural engineer who endeavours to ensure that:

1. Overturning of the wall does not occur.
2. Forward sliding of the wall does not occur.
3. Materials used are suitable and not overstressed.
4. The subsoil is not overloaded.
5. In clay subsoils slip circle failure does not occur.

The factors which the designer will have to take into account:

1. Nature and characteristics of the subsoil(s).
2. Height of water table – the presence of water can create hydrostatic pressure on the rear face of the wall, it can also affect the bearing capacity of the subsoil together with its shear strength, reduce the frictional resistance between the underside of the foundation and the subsoil and reduce the passive pressure in front of the toe of the wall.
3. Type of wall.
4. Material(s) to be used in the construction of the wall.

Retaining Wall Terminology ~

Earth Pressures ~ these can take one of two forms, namely:

1. Active Earth Pressures – these are those pressures which tend to move the wall at all times and consist of the wedge of earth retained plus any hydrostatic pressure. The latter can be reduced by including a subsoil drainage system behind and/or through the wall.

2. Passive Earth Pressures ~ these are a reaction of an equal and opposite force to any imposed pressure thus giving stability by resisting movement.

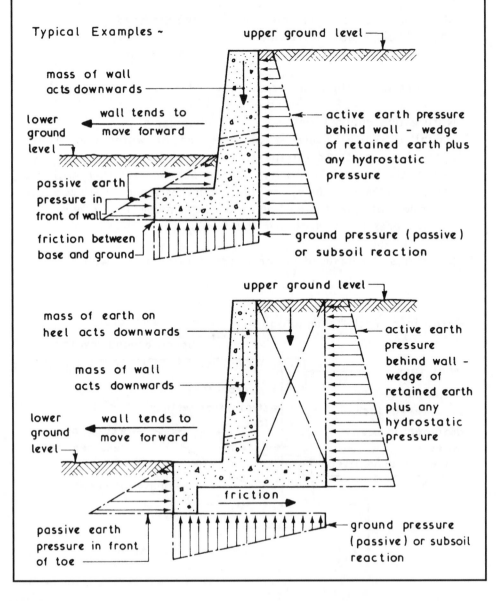

Typical Examples ~

Mass Retaining Walls ~ these walls rely mainly on their own mass to overcome the tendency to slide forward. Mass retaining walls are not generally considered to be economic over a height of 1·800 when constructed of brick or concrete and 1·000 high in the case of natural stonework. Any mass retaining wall can be faced with another material but generally any applied facing will not increase the strength of the wall and is therefore only used for aesthetic reasons.

Typical Brick Mass Retaining Wall Details ~

precast concrete
weathered coping
stone

dpc

ground level

bricks to have a
crushing strength
of not less than
20·5 MN/m² and
to be laid with a
mortar mix of
1:¼:3 (cement :
lime : sand) –
vertical movement
joints should be
provided at not
more than 15·000
centres

back of wall to be coated
with bituminous paint or
lined with heavy duty
polythene sheet

COHESIVE
SUBSOIL

900

1·800 maximum

40

rubble filling
behind wall
and weep holes

525

75 mm diameter
weep holes at
1·800 c/c

PVC or similar pipe
lining to weep holes

ground level

225   225

300

mass concrete
foundation

450

225

890

Typical Brick Faced Mass Concrete Retaining Wall Detail ~

precast concrete
weathered coping

ground level

previous membrane
over backfill

12 mm gap filled
with mortar as
work proceeds

nominal
25 mm
'no fines'
granular
backfill

900

450

dense engineering
quality facing bricks
laid in stretcher
bond and tied to
concrete wall with
galvanised butterfly
wall ties at 1·000 %
horizontally and
600 mm % vertically
in a staggered
pattern

200

mass
concrete
wall – mix
as given
for base

75 mm diameter
PVC sleeved
weep holes at
1·800 %

650

ground
level

40

1·250

weak
concrete
backfill
up to weep
hole invert

100

75

250

mass concrete
base (1:2:4/
20 mm agg.)
characteristic
strength of
21 N/mm² at
28 days

20 mm dia.
mild steel
dowel rods
at 450 %

600

1·300

NB. Expansion
joints at 30 m %.

Cantilever Retaining Walls ~ these are constructed of reinforced concrete with an economic height range of 1·200 to 6·000. They work on the principles of leverage where the stem is designed as a cantilever fixed at the base and base is designed as a cantilever fixed at the stem. Several formats are possible and in most cases a beam is placed below the base to increase the total passive resistance to sliding. Facing materials can be used in a similar manner to that shown on page 292.

Typical Formats ~

Typical Details ~

concrete to be 1:2:4/ 20 mm aggregate with minimum cube crushing strength of 21 N/mm² at 28 days

welded fabric to control shrinkage cracks

75 mm diameter weep holes at 1·800 ℅

previous membrane over nominal 25mm 'no fines' granular backfill

main bars at 300 ℅

nominal diameter distribution bars

main bars at 150 ℅

distribution bars

450mm wide beam

75mm blinding

welded fabric

Formwork ~ concrete retaining walls can be cast in one of three ways – full height; climbing (page 295) or against earth face (page 296).

Full Height Casting ~ this can be carried out if the wall is to be cast as a free-standing wall and allowed to cure and gain strength before the earth to be retained is backfilled behind the wall. Considerations are the height of the wall, anticipated pressure of wet concrete, any strutting requirements and the availability of suitable materials to fabricate the formwork. As with all types of formwork a traditional timber format or a patent system using steel forms could be used.

Typical Details ~

recoverable bolt and plate washer

struts – timber or adjustable steel as required

softwood walings in pairs

framed plywood formwork panels

alternative wall tie – greased spacer tube with through bolt

reinforcement omitted for clarity

wall thickness

plastic or hardwood cones – length equal to concrete cover over reinforcement

high tensile steel coil wall tie (left in)

Procedure:

1. Erect one form side, align, plumb and check.

2. Insert and position reinforcement cage.

3. Erect other form side, align, plumb and check.

4. Cast wall.

75mm high kicker

formation level

base cast and cured

75mm thick blinding

Climbing Formwork or Lift Casting ~ this method can be employed on long walls, high walls or where the amount of concrete which can be placed in a shift is limited.

Typical Details ~

spacer if required

raking struts to be used as required

100 × 50 softwood studs in pairs fixed to back of wall forms at 900 c/c

1·125

wall thickness

1·200 high × 2·400 long plywood faced framed wall forms

1·125

bolts and spacer tubes or steel coil wall ties

formation level

75mm high kicker

base cast and cured

reinforcement omitted for clarity

75mm thick blinding

STAGE ONE OR FIRST LIFT

bolts and spacer tubes or steel coil wall ties

first lift forms reversed

1·200

raking struts not required after first lift

bolt holes from first lift no longer required to be made good

75

first lift of wall cast and cured sufficiently to support second lift formwork

hardwood folding wedges

1·125

through bolt fixings

NB. All subsequent lifts as for second lift.

wall can be constructed using climbing shoes instead of studs

STAGE TWO OR SECOND LIFT

Casting Against Earth Face ~ this method can be an adaptation of the full height or climbing formwork systems. The latter uses a steel wire loop tie fixing to provide the support for the second and subsequent lifts.

Typical Details ~

100 × 50 × 2·325 long studs in pairs fixed to back of wall forms at 900 c/c

recoverable bolt and washer

1·200 high × 2·400 long plywood faced framed wall forms

struts as required

sole plate fixed to base

earth face

plastic or hardwood cones

high tensile steel wire loop tie

75 mm high kicker

base cast and cured

STAGE ONE OR FIRST LIFT

first lift wall form reversed

bolt holes from first lift no longer required to be made good

hardwood folding wedges

formation level

NB. All subsequent lifts as shown for second lift.

steel wire loop tie if more than two lifts required

first lift of wall cast and cured to support second lift formwork

steel wire loop ties cast in

STAGE TWO OR SECOND LIFT

Masonry units — these are an option where it is impractical or cost-ineffective to use temporary formwork to in-situ concrete. Exposed brick or blockwork may also be a preferred finish. In addition to being a structural component, masonry units provide permanent formwork to reinforced concrete poured into the voids created by:

* Quetta bonded standard brick units, OR
* Stretcher bonded standard hollow dense concrete blocks.

Reinforced quetta bonded brickwork

vertical reinforcement bars

Elevation, as Flemish bond

$1\frac{1}{2}$ B or 327 mm

Plan

void filled with steel reinforced concrete from foundation

Reinforced hollow concrete blocks

steel bar reinforcement

Elevation

250 mm

Plan

concrete filling in voids

Standard hollow concrete block to BS 6073-2

215 mm

440 mm

60-250 mm

Purpose-made hollow block for use with additional horizontal reinforcement

Construction – a reinforced concrete base is cast with projecting steel bars accurately located for vertical continuity. The wall may be built solid, e.g. Quetta bond, with voids left around the bars for subsequent grouting. Alternatively, the wall may be of wide cavity construction, where the exposed reinforcement is wrapped in 'denso' grease tape for protection against corrosion. Steel bars are threaded at the top to take a tensioning nut over a bearing plate.

Typical post-tensioned masonry retaining wall

Staged post-tensioning to high masonry retaining walls

Refs. BS EN 1996-1-1: Design of masonry structures. General rules for reinforced and unreinforced masonry structures.

PD 6697: Recommendations to BS EN 1996-1-1.

Crib Retaining Walls — a system of precast concrete or treated timber components comprising headers and stretchers which interlock to form a three-dimensional framework. During assembly the framework is filled with graded stone to create sufficient mass to withstand ground pressures.

Principle —

batter
1:4 timber
1:6—8 concrete

upper ground

headers

stretchers with joints staggered

graded granular fill within cribs and up to 1 m behind wall

lower ground
concrete foundation with surface of incline finished rough

subsoil drain

NB. height limited to 10 m with timber.

Components —

stretcher 100 × 50 mm up to 2.2 m long

Timber preserved with copper/chrome/arsenic

header 100 × 50 mm, 0.6—1.4 m long spaced at 550 mm

stretcher   header

Reinforced concrete, sulphate resisting 50 N/mm²

stretcher

header

stretcher 1.2 or 1.5 m

header 300 × 125 mm, 0.65, 1.2 or 1.6 m long

Soil Nailing ~ a cost effective geotechnic process used for retaining large soil slopes, notably highway and railway embankments.

Function ~ after excavating and removing the natural slope support, the remaining wedge of exposed unstable soil is pinned or nailed back with tendons into stable soil behind the potential slip plane.

Types of Soil Nails or Tendons:

• Solid deformed steel rods up to 50 mm in diameter, located in boreholes up to 100 mm in diameter. Cement grout is pressurised into the void around the rods.
• Hollow steel, typically 100 mm diameter tubes with an expendable auger attached. Cement grout is injected into the tube during boring to be ejected through purpose-made holes in the auger.
• Solid glass reinforced plastic (GRP) with resin grouts.

Embankment Treatment ~ the exposed surface is faced with a plastic coated wire mesh to fit over the ends of the tendons. A steel head plate is fitted over and centrally bolted to each projecting tendon, followed by spray concreting to the whole face.

Typical Application ~

soil nails at 10° incline, 1.5 to 2.5 m spacing and at up to 20 m depth

tendon

unstable soil

plant-mounted drilling rig

potential slip plane

70° cut

natural support angle of soil

Gabion ~ a type of retaining wall produced from individual rectangular boxes made from panels of wire mesh, divided internally and filled with stones. These units are stacked and overlapped (like stretcher bonded masonry) and applied in several layers or courses to retained earth situations. Typical sizes, 1·0m long x 0·5m wide x 0·5m high, up to 4·0m long x 1·0m wide x 1·0m high.

Mattress ~ unit fabrication is similar to a gabion but of less thickness, smaller mesh and stone size to provide some flexibility and shaping potential. Application is at a much lower incline. Generally used next to waterways for protection against land erosion where tidal movement and/or water level differentials could scour embankments. Typical sizes, 3·0m long x 2·0m wide x 0·15m thick, up to 6·0m long x 2·0m wide x 0·3m thick.

Design of Retaining Walls ~ this should allow for the effect of hydrostatics or water pressure behind the wall and the pressure created by the retained earth (see page 290). Calculations are based on a 1m unit length of wall, from which it is possible to ascertain:

1. The resultant thrust

2. The overturning or bending moment

pressure diagram

P = resultant thrust
w = density of material
h = height of wall
θ = soil angle of repose (see page 322)

$$P(liquid) = \frac{wh^2}{2}$$

$$P(earth) = \frac{wh^2}{2} \times \frac{1-\sin\theta}{1+\sin\theta} \quad \begin{bmatrix} \text{Rankine's} \\ \text{formula} \end{bmatrix}$$

pressure at base (water) = wh kg/m²

pressure at base (earth) = wh $\left(\frac{1-\sin\theta}{1+\sin\theta}\right)$ kg/m²

P, the resultant thrust, will act through the centre of gravity of the pressure diagram, i.e. at h/3.

The overturning moment due to water is therefore:

$$\frac{wh^2}{2} \times \frac{h}{3} \text{ or } \frac{wh^3}{6}$$

and for earth:

$$\frac{wh^2}{2} \times \frac{1-\sin\theta}{1+\sin\theta} \times \frac{h}{3} \text{ or } \frac{wh^3}{6} \times \frac{1-\sin\theta}{1+\sin\theta}$$

Typical example ~

density of water = 1000 kg/m³
density of soil = 1500 kg/m³
soil angle of repose = 30° (sand)

For water:

$$P = \frac{wh^2}{2} = \frac{1000 \times (3.3)^2}{2} = 5445 \text{ kg}$$

NB. kg × gravity = Newtons

Therefore, 5445 kg × 9·81 = 53·42 kN

The overturning or bending moment will be:

P × h/3 = 53·42 kN x 1.1 m = 58·8 kNm

For earth:

$$P = \frac{wh^2}{2} \times \frac{1-\sin\theta}{1+\sin\theta}$$

$$P = \frac{1500 \times (3.3)^2}{2} \times \frac{1-\sin 30°}{1+\sin 30°} = 2723 \text{ kg} \text{ or } 26.7 \text{ kN}$$

The overturning or bending moment will be:
P × h/3 = 26·7 kN × 1·1m = 29·4 kNm

A graphical design solution, to determine the earth thrust (P) behind a retaining wall. Data from previous page:

h = 3·300 m

θ = 30°

w = 1500 kg/m³

Wall height is drawn to scale and plane of repose plotted. The wedge section is obtained by drawing the plane of rupture through an angle bisecting the plane of repose and vertical back of the wall. Dimension 'y' can be scaled or calculated:

Tangent $x = \dfrac{y}{3 \cdot 3}$ x = 30°, and tan 30° = 0·5774

therefore, y = 3·3 × 0·5774 = 1·905 m

Area of wedge section = $\dfrac{3 \cdot 3}{2}$ × 1·905 m = 3·143 m²

Volume of wedge per metre run of wall = 3·143 x 1 = 3·143 m³

Weight .. .. = 3·143 × 1500 = 4715 kg

Vector line A – B is drawn to a scale through centre of gravity of wedge section, line of thrust and plane of rupture to represent 4715 kg.

Vector line B – C is drawn at the angle of earth friction (usually same as angle of repose, i.e. 30° in this case), to the normal to the plane of rupture until it meets the horizontal line C – A.

Triangle ABC represents the triangle of forces for the wedge section of earth, so C – A can be scaled at 2723 kg to represent (P), the earth thrust behind the retaining wall.

Open Excavations ~ one of the main problems which can be encountered with basement excavations is the need to provide temporary support or timbering to the sides of the excavation. This can be intrusive when the actual construction of the basement floor and walls is being carried out. One method is to use battered excavation sides cut back to a safe angle of repose thus eliminating the need for temporary support works to the sides of the excavation.

Typical Example of Open Basement Excavations ~

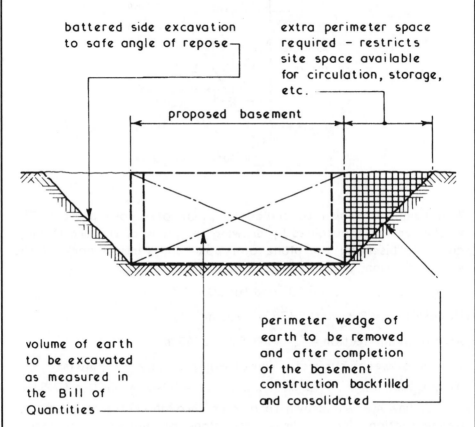

battered side excavation to safe angle of repose

extra perimeter space required - restricts site space available for circulation, storage, etc.

proposed basement

volume of earth to be excavated as measured in the Bill of Quantities

perimeter wedge of earth to be removed and after completion of the basement construction backfilled and consolidated

In economic terms the costs of plant and manpower to cover the extra excavation, backfilling and consolidating must be offset by the savings made by omitting the temporary support works to the sides of the excavation. The main disadvantage of this method is the large amount of free site space required.

Perimeter Trench Excavations ~ in this method a trench wide enough for the basement walls to be constructed is excavated and supported with timbering as required. It may be necessary for runners or steel sheet piling to be driven ahead of the excavation work. This method can be used where weak subsoils are encountered so that the basement walls act as permanent timbering whilst the mound or dumpling is excavated and the base slab cast. Perimeter trench excavations can also be employed in firm subsoils when the mechanical plant required for excavating the dumpling is not available at the right time.

Typical Details ~

STAGE 1 - EXCAVATION OF PERIMETER TRENCH

STAGE 2 - CONSTRUCTION OF BASEMENT WALLS

STAGE 3 - CONSTRUCTION OF BASEMENT SLAB

Complete Excavation ~ this method can be used in firm subsoils where the centre of the proposed basement can be excavated first to enable the basement slab to be cast thus giving protection to the subsoil at formation level. The sides of excavation to the perimeter of the basement can be supported from the formation level using raking struts or by using raking struts pitched from the edge of the basement slab.

Typical Details ~

face timbering left projecting as safety barrier

150 x 150 raking struts at 2·000 ^{c}/c

150 x 150 puncheons at 2·000 ^{c}/c

150 x 150 walings

225 x 38 binders to both sides

150 x 75 sole piece

formation level

ground level

FIRM SUBSOIL

225 x 75 sole piece

RAKING STRUTS FROM FORMATION LEVEL

face timbering left projecting as safety barrier

150 x 150 raking struts at 2·000 ^{c}/c

150 x 150 puncheons at 2·000 ^{c}/c

150 x 150 walings

225 x 38 binders to both sides

225 x 75 sole piece bolted to slab

RC basement slab

ground level

FIRM SUBSOIL

225 x 75 sole pieces

RAKING STRUTS FROM BASEMENT SLAB

306

Excavating Plant ~ the choice of actual pieces of plant to be used in any construction activity is a complex matter taking into account many factors. Specific details of various types of excavators are given on pages 209 to 213. At this stage it is only necessary to consider basic types for particular operations. In the context of basement excavation two forms of excavator could be considered.

1. Backactors – these machines are available as cable rigged or hydraulic excavators suitable for trench and bulk excavating. Cable rigged backactors are usually available with larger bucket sizes and deeper digging capacities than the hydraulic machines but these have a more positive control and digging operation and are also easier to operate.

2. Face Shovels – these are robust machines designed to excavate above their own wheel or track level and are suitable for bulk excavation work. In basement work they will require a ramp approach unless they are to be lifted out of the excavation area by means of a crane. Like backactors face shovels are available as cable rigged or hydraulic machines.

Basement Construction ~ in the general context of buildings a basement can be defined as a storey which is below the ground storey and is therefore constructed below ground level. Most basements can be classified into one of three groups:

1. Retaining Wall and Raft Basements - this is the general format for basement construction and consists of a slab raft foundation which forms the basement floor and helps to distribute the structural loads transmitted down the retaining walls.

suspended slab and beams - provide lateral restraint to top of retaining wall

BASEMENT

retaining wall - resists earth and hydrostatic pressures, transmits superstructure loads to slab raft

slab raft - distributes loads and resists upward hydrostatic pressure

edge thickening

2. Box and Cellular Raft Basements - similar method to above except that internal walls are used to transmit and spread loads over raft as well as dividing basement into cells.

suspended ground floor slab

basement retaining wall

solid slab raft

CELLULAR   BASEMENT

openings in walls as required

internal walls in one or two directions

3. Piled Basements - the main superstructure loads are carried to the basement floor level by columns where they are finally transmitted to the ground via pile caps and bearing piles. This method can be used where low bearing capacity soils are found at basement floor level.

suspended ground floor slab

basement retaining wall

solid slab raft

BASEMENT

columns carrying superstructure loads to pile caps and piles

pile caps

bearing piles

Deep Basement Construction ~ basements can be constructed within a cofferdam or other temporary supported excavation (see Basement Excavations on pages 304 to 306) up to the point when these methods become uneconomic, unacceptable or both due to the amount of necessary temporary support work. Deep basements can be constructed by installing diaphragm walls within a trench and providing permanent support with ground anchors or by using the permanent lateral support given by the internal floor during the excavation period (see next page). Temporary lateral support during the excavation period can be provided by lattice beams spanning between the diaphragm walls (see next page).

Typical Ground Anchor Support Details ~

NB. vertical ground anchors installed through the lowest floor can be used to overcome any tendency to flotation during the construction period.

Top down construction ~
Basement Construction with Permanent Lateral Support

ground floor slab and beams cast
against earth and in trenches prior
to excavation work for basement to
provide permanent lateral support
at top edge of walls

ground
level

cast in-situ
diaphragm
basement
wall

access hole for
men and materials

intermediate slab and beams cast
before next stage of excavation

access hole

excavation in progress

formation
level

cast in-situ
diaphragm
basement
wall

Basement Construction with Temporary Lateral Support

steel lattice beams in one or two
directions fixed to top edge of
diaphragm walls to provide temporary
lateral support

ground
level

cast in-situ
diaphragm
basement
wall

future floor slabs and beams
provide permanent lateral
support

excavation in progress

formation
level

cast in-situ
diaphragm
basement
wall

Top Down Construction with Superstructure ~ an extension of the principles outlined on the previous page where basement floors are constructed as excavation proceeds. Applied to construction of tall buildings, particularly in congested areas where existing buildings are in close proximity. Suited to deep basements where construction above ground can be conducted simultaneously with construction below ground, thereby optimising progress. Also suitable for underground car parks and railway stations.

Sequence Guidance (illustrated next page) ~

- Ground water controls/dewatering installed and activated (subject to sub-surface composition and water table height).

- Cast in-situ concrete diaphragm perimeter walls installed, possibly using contiguous or secant piling methods.

- Holes bored for piled foundations.

- Steel reinforcement cage positioned in boreholes.

- Load-bearing plunge columns (standard steel UC sections) lowered inside reinforcement cage.

- Boreholes concreted to ground level.

- In-situ reinforced concrete slab cast at ground level with shuttering to create suitable size opening(s) for excavation plant access. This and subsequent sub-floors act as lateral bracing to perimeter walls.

- Superstructure commences.

- Subsoil extracted through slab opening. Possible use of crane and bucket or long arm excavator. After initial soil removal, small backacters may be able to operate below ground floor slab.

- First basement formation level established and in-situ concrete floor slab cast with suitable size opening to access the next level down.

- Excavation procedure repeated to formation level of second basement floor and slab cast with access void if further sub-floors required.

- Continue until design depth and number of sub-floors is reached.

- Basement construction completed with waterproofing (tanking) and finishes.

- Continue with superstructural construction.

Top Down Construction Principles Illustrated ~

Diaphragm walls and plunge column piled foundation

standard steel
column with steel
plate attachment

diaphragm wall of
reinforced concrete
contiguous or
secant piling
around periphery

in-situ concrete
bored pile foundation

steel
reinforced
cage

UC section

Reinforced ground floor slab cast with access for excavation and commencement of superstructure

cast in-situ
reinforced concrete slab

void in slab
for access

UC secured
to top of
plunge column

ground level

continuity steel
reinforcement

subsoil excavated
down to first
basement floor
formation level

Sub-floors concreted whilst superstructure proceeds

access for excavation and
concreting, through floor void
and between cast in-situ piles

ground floor slab

UC

first basement
floor completed

diaphragm
wall

second/lowest
basement floor
completed

interior bored pile
foundations

Waterproofing Basements ~ basements can be waterproofed by one of three basic methods, namely:

1. Use of dense monolithic concrete walls and floor.
2. Tanking techniques (see pages 315 and 316).
3. Drained cavity system (see page 317).

Dense Monolithic Concrete – the main objective is to form a watertight basement using dense high quality reinforced or prestressed concrete by a combination of good materials, good workmanship, attention to design detail and on-site construction methods. If strict control of all aspects is employed a sound, watertight structure can be produced but it should be noted that such structures are not always water vapourproof. If the latter is desirable some waterproof coating, lining or tanking should be used. The watertightness of dense concrete mixes depends primarily upon two factors:

1. Water/cement ratio.
2. Degree of compaction.

The hydration of cement during the hardening process produces heat; therefore to prevent early stage cracking the temperature changes within the hardening concrete should be kept to a minimum. The greater the cement content the more is the evolution of heat; therefore the mix should contain no more cement than is necessary to fulfil design requirements. Concrete with a free water/cement ratio of 0.5 is watertight and although the permeability is three times more at a ratio of 0.6 it is for practical purposes still watertight but above this ratio the concrete becomes progressively less watertight. For lower water/cement ratios the workability of the mix would have to be increased, usually by adding more cement, to enable the concrete to be fully compacted.

Admixtures – if the ingredients of good design, materials and workmanship are present watertight concrete can be produced without the use of admixtures. If admixtures are used they should be carefully chosen and used to obtain a specific objective:

1. Water-reducing admixtures – used to improve workability.
2. Retarding admixtures – slow down rate of hardening.
3. Accelerating admixtures – increase rate of hardening – useful for low temperatures – calcium chloride not suitable for reinforced concrete.
4. Water-repelling admixtures – effective only with low water head, will not improve poor-quality or porous mixes.
5. Air-entraining admixtures – increase workability – lower water content.

Joints ~ in general these are formed in basement constructions to provide for movement accommodation (expansion joints) or to create a convenient stopping point in the construction process (construction joints). Joints are lines of weakness which will leak unless carefully designed and constructed; therefore they should be simple in concept and easy to construct.

Basement slabs ~ these are usually designed to span in two directions and as a consequence have relatively heavy top and bottom reinforcement. To enable them to fulfil their basic functions they usually have a depth in excess of 250mm. The joints, preferably of the construction type, should be kept to a minimum and if waterbars are specified they must be placed to ensure that complete compaction of the concrete is achieved.

Typical Basement Slab Joint Details ~

construction joint ——————————————— structural slab

NB. face of joint to be prepared by exposing the aggregate before casting adjoining bay or section.

reinforcement continuous through joint

blinding

PVC water bar laid on blinding

Basement Walls ~ joints can be horizontal and/or vertical according to design requirements. A suitable waterbar should be incorporated in the joint to prevent the ingress of water. The top surface of a kicker used in conjunction with single-lift pouring if adequately prepared by exposing the aggregate should not require a waterbar but if one is specified it should be either placed on the rear face or consist of a centrally placed mild steel strip inserted into the kicker whilst the concrete is still in a plastic state.

Typical Basement Wall Joint Details ~

150 mm wide mild steel strip

150 mm kicker

filler

water bar

mastic seal

20 mm wide joint

PVC or rubber water bar

EXPANSION JOINT   CONSTRUCTION JOINT

Mastic Asphalt Tanking ~ the objective of tanking is to provide a continuous waterproof membrane which is applied to the base slab and walls with complete continuity between the two applications. The tanking can be applied externally or internally according to the circumstances prevailing on site. Alternatives to mastic asphalt are polythene sheeting; bituminous compounds; epoxy resin compounds and bitumen laminates.

External Mastic Asphalt Tanking ~ this is the preferred method since it not only prevents the ingress of water but it also protects the main structure of the basement from aggressive sulphates which may be present in the surrounding soil or ground water.

Typical External Tanking Details ~

25 × 25 splayed chase

half brick or 100 mm block protective walling in cm.mt. (1:3)

30 mm thick cement/sand grout if required to ensure good interface contact

20 mm thick vertical asphalt applied in three coats to rough concrete face

50 × 50 two coat angle fillet

150 mm 'pickup'

reinforced concrete floor slab

distribution bars

main bars

reinforced concrete basement wall

main bars

distribution bars

reinforced concrete basement slab

50 mm thick cement/sand (1:3) protective screed

30 mm thick horizontal asphalt applied in three coats over concrete base

100 mm thick mass concrete base

Waterproofing Basements

Internal Mastic Asphalt Tanking ~ this method should only be adopted if external tanking is not possible since it will not give protection to the main structure and unless adequately loaded may be forced away from the walls and/or floor by hydrostatic pressure. To be effective the horizontal and vertical coats of mastic asphalt must be continuous.

Typical Internal Tanking Details ~

25 × 25 splayed chase

reinforced concrete floor slab

reinforced concrete basement wall

distribution bars

main bars

20 mm thick vertical asphalt applied in three coats to rough concrete face

three coat asphalt collar applied over bitumen primer to extend at least 75 mm on both sides of tanking

sleeve, duct or pipe through wall

50 × 50 two coat angle fillet

30 mm thick cement/sand grout if required to ensure good interface contact

brick or block loading wall

reinforced concrete loading slab

main bars

distribution bars

water bar to kicker

50 mm thick protective screed

reinforced concrete basement slab

75 mm thick blinding

30 mm thick horizontal asphalt applied in three coats over concrete base

NB. Brick basement walls can be built of keyed bricks or the joints can be raked out to a depth of 20mm to provide key for asphalt tanking.

316

Drained Cavity System ~ this method of waterproofing basements can be used for both new and refurbishment work. The basic concept is very simple in that it accepts that a small amount of water seepage is possible through a monolithic concrete wall and the best method of dealing with such moisture is to collect it and drain it away. This is achieved by building an inner non-load-bearing wall to form a cavity which is joined to a floor composed of special triangular tiles laid to falls which enables the moisture to drain away to a sump from which it is either discharged direct or pumped into the surface water drainage system. The inner wall should be relatively vapour tight or alternatively the cavity should be ventilated.

Typical Details ~

TOP VIEW - HALF TILE   BOTTOM VIEW - STANDARD TILE

reinforced concrete basement wall

50 mm wide cavity

brick or block non-load bearing inner wall

wall finish   damp-proof membrane

skirting   precast concrete 'Dryangle' floor tiles

floor finish

65 mm thick screed   reinforced concrete floor slab - upper laid to fall to sump

75 mm thick blinding

Basements benefit considerably from the insulating properties of the surrounding soil. However, that alone is insufficient to satisfy the typical requirements for wall and floor U-values of 0·35 and 0·25 W/m²K, respectively.

Refurbishment of existing basements may include insulation within dry lined walls and under-the-floor screed or particle board overlay. This should incorporate an integral vapour control layer to minimise risk of condensation.

External insulation of closed cell rigid polystyrene slabs is generally applied to new construction. These slabs combine low thermal conductivity with low water absorption and high compressive strength. The external face of insulation is grooved to encourage moisture run-off. It is also filter faced to prevent clogging of the grooves. Backfill is granular.

Typical application~

Note: reinforcement in concrete omitted, see details on previous pages.

Tables and calculation methods to determine heat energy transfer for basements are provided in BS EN ISO 13370: Thermal performance of buildings. Heat transfer via the ground. Calculation methods.

Excavation ~ to hollow out – in building terms to remove earth to form a cavity in the ground.

Types of Excavation ~

Oversite – the removal of topsoil (Building Regulations requirement).

depth varies from site to site but is usually in a 150 to 300 mm range. Topsoil contains plant life, animal life and decaying matter which makes the soil compressible and therefore unsuitable for supporting buildings.

s u b s o i l

Reduce Level – carried out below over-site level to form a level surface on which to build and can consist of both cutting and filling operations. The level to which the ground is reduced is called the formation level.

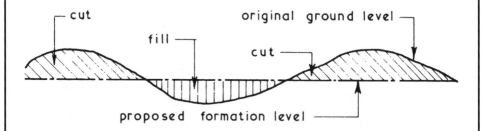

NB. Water in Excavations – this should be removed since it can:

1. Undermine sides of excavation.
2. Make it impossible to adequately compact bottom of excavation to receive foundations.
3. Cause puddling which can reduce the bearing capacity of the subsoil.

Trench Excavations ~ narrow excavations primarily for strip foundations and buried services – excavation can be carried out by hand or machine.

Typical Examples ~

battered faces

width required

vertical or straight faces

natural angle of repose or rest

Disadvantage ~ extra cost of over-excavating and extra backfilling.

Advantage ~ no temporary support required to sides of excavation.

Disadvantage ~ sides of excavation may require some degree of temporary support.

Advantage ~ minimum amount of soil removed and therefore minimum amount of backfilling.

Pier Holes ~ isolated pits primarily used for foundation pads for columns and piers or for the construction of soakaways.

sides of excavation can be battered or straight as described above – deep pier holes may have to be over-excavated in plan to provide good access to and good egress from the working area for both men and materials.

NB. Legislation affecting safety in excavation is contained in the Construction (Design and Management) Regulations.

Site Clearance and Removal of Topsoil ~

On small sites this could be carried out by manual means using handheld tools such as picks, shovels and wheelbarrows.

On all sites mechanical methods could be used, the actual plant employed being dependent on factors such as volume of soil involved, nature of site and time elements.

topsoil - upper level of earth usually not exceeding 300mm deep

excavation - mechanical shovel or bulldozer

roll bar

dumper to move spoil

Reduced Level Excavations ~
On small sites — hand processes as given above.
On all sites mechanical methods could be used dependent on factors given above.

bulldozer for cut-and-fill operations

mechanical shovel and attendant lorries for cut-only operations

proposed formation level

Trench and Pit Excavations ~
On small sites — hand processes as given above but if depth of excavation exceeds 1·200 some method of removing spoil from the excavation will have to be employed.

On all sites mechanical methods could be used dependent on factors given above.

on large sites a trenching machine could be used

formation level

backactor - spoil placed alongside excavation or into attendant lorry

All subsoils have different abilities in remaining stable during excavation works. Most will assume a natural angle of repose or rest unless given temporary support. The presence of ground water apart from creating difficult working conditions can have an adverse effect on the subsoil's natural angle of repose.

Typical Angles of Repose ~
Excavations cut to a natural angle of repose are called battered.

| DRAINED CLAY 45° | WET CLAY 16° | GRAVEL & DRY SAND 40° | WET SAND 22° |

Factors for Temporary Support of Excavations ~

Time factors such as period during which excavation will remain open and the time of year when work is carried out.

The need for an assessment of risk with regard to the support of excavations and protection of people within is a legal responsibility under the Health and Safety at Work, etc. Act and the Construction (Design and Management) Regulations.

Temporary Support ~ in the context of excavations this is called timbering irrespective of the actual materials used. If the sides of the excavation are completely covered with timbering it is known as close timbering whereas any form of partial covering is called open timbering.

An adequate supply of timber or other suitable material must be available and used to prevent danger to any person employed in an excavation from a fall or dislodgement of materials forming the sides of an excavation.

A suitable barrier or fence must be provided to the sides of all excavations or alternatively they must be securely covered.

Materials must not be placed near to the edge of any excavation, nor must plant be placed or moved near to any excavation so that persons employed in the excavation are endangered.

Typical Example ~

wedges or pages as required

100 x 100 walings

folding wedges

225 x 50 poling boards as open timbering

100 x 100 struts at 1·800 $^c/_c$

100 x 100 puncheons at 1·800 $^c/_c$

225 x 75 sole piece

450 minimum

spoil heap barrier at least 600 mm high

FIRM SUBSOIL

adjustable metal struts to BS 4074 could be used if distance between walings is not more than 1·670

for further details and data see next page

Poling Board ~ a form of temporary support which is placed in position against the sides of excavation after the excavation work has been carried out. Poling boards are placed at centres according to the stability of the subsoils encountered.

Runner ~ a form of temporary support which is driven into position ahead of the excavation work either to the full depth or by a drive-and-dig technique where the depth of the runner is always lower than that of the excavation.

Trench Sheeting ~ form of runner made from sheet steel with a trough profile — can be obtained with a lapped joint or an interlocking joint.

Water ~ if present or enters an excavation, a pit or sump should be excavated below the formation level to act as a collection point from which the water can be pumped away.

Typical Example ~

225 x 50 runners as close timbering left projecting to form the barrier

folding wedges

barrier out of tubes

100 x 100 walings

all timbering sizes shown are typical - actual sizes should be selected from design charts or calculated from first principles

100 x 100 struts at 1·800 ᶜ/c

LOOSE OR WET SUBSOIL

100 x 100 puncheons at 1·800 ᶜ/c

formation level

225 x 75 sole piece

300 mm minimum

Concrete ~ a mixture of cement + fine aggregate + coarse aggregate + water in controlled proportions and of a suitable quality.

Cement ~ powder produced from clay and chalk or limestone. In general most concrete is made with ordinary or rapid hardening Portland cement, both types being manufactured to the recommendations of BS EN 197-1. Ordinary Portland cement is adequate for most purposes but has a low resistance to attack by acids and sulphates. Rapid hardening Portland cement does not set faster than ordinary Portland cement but it does develop its working strength at a faster rate. For a concrete which must have an acceptable degree of resistance to sulphate attack, the quantity of tricalcium aluminate is reduced during the manufacture of Portland cement (4% instead of 10% in OPC). BS EN 15743 contains reference to this type of sulphate-resisting cement.

25 kg

BAGS

12t to 50t

SILOS

Aggregates ~ shape, surface texture and grading (distribution of particle sizes) are factors which influence the workability and strength of a concrete mix. Fine aggregates are generally regarded as those materials which pass through a 4mm sieve whereas coarse aggregates are retained on a 4mm sieve. Dense aggregates have a density of more than 1200kg/m^3 for coarse aggregates and more than 1250kg/m^3 for fine aggregates. These are detailed in BS EN 12620: Aggregates for concrete. Lightweight aggregates include clinker; foamed or expanded blastfurance slag and exfoliated and expanded materials such as vermiculite, perlite, clay and sintered pulverised fuel ash to BS EN 13055-1.

coarse aggregate

4mm sieve

fine aggregate

Water ~ must be clean and free from impurities which are likely to affect the quality or strength of the resultant concrete. Pond, river, canal and sea water should not be used and only water which is fit for drinking should be specified.

drinking water quality

Cement ~ whichever type of cement is being used it must be properly stored on site to keep it in good condition. The cement must be kept dry since contact with any moisture whether direct or airborne could cause it to set. A rotational use system should be introduced to ensure that the first batch of cement delivered is the first to be used.

Typical Storage Methods ~

polythene or similar waterproof cover

stored cement bags - total height not more than 1·000

watertight and fireproof "shed"

well fitted lockable doors

raised dry platform

cover weighted down around edges

timber bearers or sleepers

galv. steel sides

adjustable legs and bearing plate

SMALL CONTRACTS   MEDIUM SIZE CONTRACTS

LARGE CONTRACTS — for bagged cement watertight container as above. For bulk delivery loose cement, a cement storage silo.

Aggregates ~ essentials of storage are to keep different aggregate types and/or sizes separate, store on a clean, hard, free draining surface and to keep the stored aggregates clean and free of leaves and rubbish.

keep constant check on moisture content of stored materials

retaining and separating walls of bulk timbers or similar materials

fine aggregate

coarse aggregate

hard, clean surface which drains away from stored aggregates

Concrete Batching ~ a batch is one mixing of concrete and can be carried out by measuring the quantities of materials required by volume or weight. The main aim of both methods is to ensure that all consecutive batches are of the same standard and quality.

Volume Batching ~ concrete mixes are often quoted by ratio such as 1:2:4 (cement : fine aggregate or sand : coarse aggregate). Cement weighing 50 kg has a volume of 0·033 m³; therefore for the above mix 2 × 0·033 (0·066 m³) of sand and 4 × 0·033 (0·132 m³) of coarse aggregate is required. To ensure accurate amounts of materials are used for each batch a gauge box should be employed, its size being based on convenient handling. Ideally a batch of concrete should be equated to using 50 kg of cement per batch. Assuming a gauge box 300 mm deep and 300 mm wide with a volume of half the required sand the gauge box size would be – volume = length × width × depth = length × 300 × 300.

$$length = \frac{volume}{width \times depth} = \frac{0·033}{0·3 \times 0·3} = 0·366 \text{ m}$$

lifting handles

contents struck off level

bottomless gauge box

levelling rod

mixing board or banker of adequate size for batch being mixed

internal dimensions of gauge box as calculated

For the above given mix fill gauge box once with cement, twice with sand and four times with coarse aggregate.

An allowance must be made for the bulking of damp sand which can be as much as 33⅓%. General rule of thumb unless using dry sand: allow for 25% bulking.

Materials should be well mixed dry before adding water.

Weight or Weigh Batching ~ this is a more accurate method of measuring materials for concrete than volume batching since it reduces considerably the risk of variation between different batches. The weight of sand is affected very little by its dampness which in turn leads to greater accuracy in proportioning materials. When loading a weighing hopper the materials should be loaded in a specific order:

1. Coarse aggregates – tend to push other materials out and leave the hopper clean.
2. Cement – this is sandwiched between the other materials since some of the fine cement particles could be blown away if cement is put in last.
3. Sand or fine aggregates – put in last to stabilise the fine lightweight particles of cement powder.

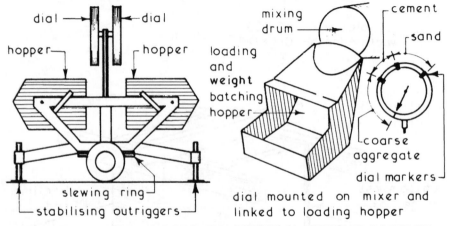

INDEPENDENT WEIGHT BATCHER INTEGRAL WEIGHT BATCHER

Typical Densities ~ cement – 1440 kg/m³ sand – 1600 kg/m³ coarse aggregate – 1440 kg/m³

Water/Cement Ratio ~ water in concrete has two functions:

1. Starts the chemical reaction which causes the mixture to set into a solid mass.
2. Gives the mix workability so that it can be placed, tamped or vibrated into the required position.

Very little water is required to set concrete (approximately 0·2 w/c ratio) and the surplus evaporates leaving minute voids; therefore the more water added to the mix to increase its workability the weaker is the resultant concrete. Generally w/c ratios of 0·4 to 0·5 are adequate for most purposes. See next page.

Free Water ~ water on the surface of aggregates where stored in stock piles plus water added during the mixing process. Does not include any water that is absorbed by the aggregate.

Free Water/Cement Ratio ~ a high w/c ratio increases the workability of concrete. This may be convenient for placing but it should be controlled in order to regulate the final concrete strength.

Note: The w/c ratio is found by dividing the weight of water in a batch by the weight of cement. E.g. If a batch contains 50 kg of water and 100 kg of cement, the w/c ratio is 0.5.

Concrete ~ a composite with many variables, represented by numerous gradings which indicate components, quality and manufacturing control.

Grade mixes: C7.5, C10, C15, C20, C25, C30, C35, C40, C45, C50, C55 and C60; F3, F4 and F5; IT2, IT2.5, and IT3.

C = Characteristic compressive

F = Flexural $\Big\}$ strengths at 28 days (N/mm^2)

IT = Indirect tensile

NB. If the grade is followed by a 'P', e.g. C30P, this indicates a prescribed mix (see below).

Grades C7.5 and C10 — Unreinforced plain concrete.

Grades C15 and C20 — Plain concrete or if reinforced containing lightweight aggregate.

Grades C25 — Reinforced concrete containing dense aggregate.

Grades C30 and C35 — Post-tensioned reinforced concrete.

Grades C40 to C60 — Pre-tensioned reinforced concrete.

Categories of mix:

1. Prescribed Mix — components are predetermined (to a recipe) to ensure strength requirements. Variations exist to allow the purchaser to specify particular aggregates, admixtures and colours. All grades permitted.

2. Standard Prescribed Mix — applicable to minor works such as house construction, particularly where weight or volume batching is used for small quantities. See next page for standard (ST) mixes with C30 strength class concrete.

3. Designed Mix — concrete is specified to an expected performance. Criteria can include characteristic strength, durability and workability, to which a concrete manufacturer will design and supply an appropriate mix. All grades permitted.

4. Designated Mix — selected for specific applications. General (GEN) graded 0-4, 7.5-25 N/mm^2 for foundations, floors and external works. Foundations (FND) graded 2, 3, 4A and 4B, 35N/mm^2 mainly for sulphate resisting foundations.

Paving (PAV) graded 1 or 2, 35 or 45 N/mm^2 for roads and drives.

Reinforced (RC) graded 30, 35, 40, 45 and 50 N/mm^2 mainly for pre-stressing.

See also BS EN 206-1: Concrete. Specification, performance, production and conformity, and BS's 8500-1 and -2: Concrete.

Standard prescribed mixes for site batching are graded for concrete with a characteristic compressive strength of 30 N/mm² at 28 days. Compressive strength is achieved by laboratory testing sample cubes as detailed on page 136.

Weight Batched Proportions ~

Standard prescribed mix	Consistence class (slump)	Cement bag (kg)	Fine agg. (kg)	Coarse agg. (kg) max. 20 mm	Mix ratio
ST1	S1	25	84	126	1:3.35:5.02
ST2	S2	25	72	107	1:2.87:4.28
ST2	S3	25	65	97	1:2.58:3.88
ST2	S4	25	68	83	1:2.72:3.30
ST3	S2	25	63	95	1:2.52:3.80
ST4	S2	25	56	83	1:2.23:3.33
ST5	S2	25	48	72	1:1.92:2.88

Volume Batched Proportions~

Standard prescribed mix	Consistency class (slump)	Cement bag (kg)	Fine agg. (litres)	Coarse agg. (litres)
ST1	S1	25	60	85
ST2	S2	25	50	75
ST2	S3	25	45	70
ST2	S4	25	50	60
ST3	S2	25	45	65

Consistency Class ~ this refers to the amount of water in the mix, affecting workability and final strength. See page 135.

Consistency class	Slump (mm)
S1	10 - 40
S2	50 - 90
S3	100 - 150
S4	160 – 210

Concrete Supply ~ this is usually geared to the demand or the rate at which the mixed concrete can be placed. Fresh concrete should always be used or placed within 30 minutes of mixing to prevent any undue drying out. Under no circumstances should more water be added after the initial mixing.

Small Batches ~ small, easily transported mixers with

 output capacities of up to 100 litres can be used for small and intermittent batches. These mixers are versatile and robust machines which can be used for mixing mortars and plasters as well as concrete.

Medium to Large Batches ~ mixers with output capacities

 from 100 litres to 10m^3 with either diesel or electric motors. Many models are available with tilting or reversing drum discharge, integral weigh batching and loading hopper and a controlled water supply.

Ready Mixed Concrete ~ used mainly for large concrete batches of up to 6 m^3. This method of concrete supply has the advantages of eliminating the need for site space to accommodate storage of materials, mixing plant and the need to employ adequately trained site staff who can constantly produce reliable and consistent concrete

 mixes. Ready mixed concrete supply depots also have better facilities and arrangements for producing and supplying mixed concrete in winter or inclement weather conditions. In many situations it is possible to place the ready mixed concrete into the required position direct from the delivery lorry via the delivery chute or by feeding it into a concrete pump. The site must be capable of accepting the 20 tonnes laden weight of a typical ready mixed concrete lorry with a turning circle of about 15·000. The supplier will want full details of mix required and the proposed delivery schedule.

Ref. BS EN 206-1: Concrete. Specification, performance, production and conformity.

Cofferdams ~ these are temporary enclosures installed in soil or water to prevent the ingress of soil and/or water into the working area with the cofferdam. They are usually constructed from interlocking steel sheet piles which are suitably braced or tied back with ground anchors. Alternatively a cofferdam can be installed using any structural material which will fulfil the required function.

Typical Cofferdam Details ~

steel kicking plate welded to waling

UB end waling bolted to side UB walings through welded-on end plates

single skin of interlocking steel sheet piles

corner piece

corner piece

UB side waling

UB side waling

ground level

upper struts and walings

kicking plate

ground level

UB main strut bolted to side waling

UB secondary struts fixed to end walings main struts

end fixing plate welded to strut

lower struts and walings

NB. puncheons and wedges to be used as required.

formation level

'cut off length' to suit soil and sheet pile type

for details of sheet pile sections and installation see next page.

Steel Sheet Piling ~ apart from cofferdam work, steel sheeting can be used in excavations and to form permanent retaining walls. Three common formats of steel sheet piles with interlocking joints are available with a range of section sizes and strengths up to a maximum length of 30 m.

FRODINGHAM SHEET PILES (general use)

STRAIGHT WEB
(circular work)

LARSSEN SHEET PILES (general use)

all piles supplied with lifting or slinging holes positioned in top end of pile

Installing Steel Sheet Piles ~ to ensure that the sheet piles are pitched and installed vertically a driving trestle or guide frame is used. These are usually purpose built to accommodate a panel of 10 to 12 pairs of piles. The piles are lifted into position by a crane and driven by means of a percussion piling hammer or alternatively they can be pushed into the ground by hydraulic rams acting against the weight of the power pack which is positioned over the heads of the pitched piles.

Typical Installation Details ~

last pair of piles to be part driven as anchor piles to next panel of piles →

spacer blocks

timber trestle

pitched panel of steel sheet piles

first pair of piles part driven to act as anchor piles

metal strap or bridle

puncheon

leg

bearer

guide waling

SIDE ELEVATION

END ELEVATION

Note: Rot-proof PVC sheet piling is also available.

Alternative guide rail support system to that shown on the preceding page. This uses standard steel sections with components bolted together for simple assembly and dismantling. Tack welding is an option instead of bolting, with welds removed by angle grinder for dismantling on completion of pile driving.

UC guide rail/waling (same other side)

intermediate steel sheet piles suspended and lowered by crane into adjacent interlocking joint, then driven/vibrated into the ground

channel cross head

RSJ or channel brace (same other side)

1.5 m to 2.0m

channels

two steel sheet piles located in ground approximately 15 m apart, with bracing framework of steel channels and joists

Steel trench sheeting is available in various profiles, including the following ~

B = 330mm, D = 35mm, T = 3.5mm

B = 400mm, D = 50mm, T = 6.0mm

Applications ~

- Cofferdams

- Ground water control/diversion

- Barrier for ground water treatment systems

- Retaining walls

- Containment walls

- Flood protection

- Coastal protection, bulkheads and sea walls

- Tunnelling, cut and cover

- River weir walls

- Slope stabilisation

- Baffle walls

Compound Profiles ~

Larssen Box

Frodingham Plated Box

Note: Tack welding is jointing adjacent pieces of steel discontinuously.

Ref. BS EN 12063: Execution of special geotechnical work. Sheet pile walls.

Caissons ~ these are box-like structures which are similar in concept to cofferdams but they usually form an integral part of the finished structure. They can be economically constructed and installed in water or soil where the depth exceeds 18·000. There are four basic types of caisson, namely:

1. Box Caissons
2. Open Caissons
3. Monolithic Caissons
4. Pneumatic Caissons – used in water – see next page.

usually of precast concrete and used in water being towed or floated into position and sunk – land caissons are of the open type and constructed in-situ.

Typical Caissons Details ~

precast concrete caisson sunk by flooding or adding weight

water level

diaphragm cross walls as required

void

integral base slab

prepared bed

void filled with in-situ concrete after installation

BOX CAISSON

in-situ or precast concrete suspended cover slab

precast concrete wall unit(s) – often circular in plan

in-situ concrete plug or base

void filled as required

OPEN CAISSON

climbing formwork

cast-in bentonite feed pipes

excavation carried out inside caisson which sinks under own weight as walls are extended

excavation level

ground level

bentonite slurry in 75mm wide annular space

LAND CAISSON

precast concrete caisson

excavation wells

water level

MONOLITHIC CAISSON

Pneumatic Caissons ~ these are sometimes called compressed air caissons and are similar in concept to open caissons. They can be used in difficult subsoil conditions below water level and have a pressurised lower working chamber to provide a safe, dry working area. Pneumatic caissons can be made of concrete whereby they sink under their own weight or they can be constructed from steel with hollow walls which can be filled with water to act as ballast. These caissons are usually designed to form part of the finished structure.

Typical Pneumatic Caisson Details ~

air lock to operatives' access shaft

air lock to materials supply shaft

upper platform and storage area

water level

operatives' access ladder shaft

materials supply shaft

concrete caisson walls

roof to working chamber

bed level

pressurised working chamber (maximum safe working pressure 310 kN/m²)

2·000 - 3·000

excavation level

excavation carried out within working chamber and caisson sinks under own weight

When required depth is reached a concrete slab or plug is cast over the formation level and chamber sealed with mass concrete

Culvert ~ construction for subways and underground passageways. Often used below elevated roads and railways as access for pedestrians, animals (badger crossings), sewers, tidal outfalls and as voids for the general location of pipes and cables.

Types ~ box, conduit or pipe, manufactured from reinforced concrete for placing in large excavations before backfilling; a technique known as cut and cover. Excavations may require temporary support from sheet steel piling. Ground dewatering may also be necessary.

In-situ concrete

Precast concrete crown on in-situ concrete base

Precast concrete sections in standard lengths of 1.000, 1.500 or 2.000 m and up to 4.000 m width or diameter

Principles of Procedure ~ after excavating to the appropriate depth, the base is levelled (slightly inclined for drainage) and finished with well compacted selected stone granules. Granular material is used to consolidate the soil and to ease movement of the precast concrete sections as they are pulled into place. After crane lowering several sections into approximate locations, the first is positioned, levelled and restrained for attachment of anchor tension units. The remaining sections are pulled into place as shown below. Spigot and socket joints are sealed with a synthetic rubber gasket or mastic sealant. Thereafter, further sections are added, similarly positioned and jointed. Subsequently, the complete installation is backfilled for ground reinstatement.

Assembly of precast concrete sections

bolted down tensioner

precast concrete section

chain tensioned

bolted down anchor

tensioner handle

A

first section restrained

recesses cut at joint positions

threads for handling loops and for securing tensioner and anchor

gl

Joint detail at A

joint surfaces primed

spigot

socket

synthetic rubber sealing ring or mastic sealant in spigot recess

75 mm

5 to 10 mm

Underpinning ~ the main objective of most underpinning work is to transfer the load carried by a foundation from its existing bearing level to a new level at a lower depth. Underpinning techniques can also be used to replace an existing weak foundation. An underpinning operation may be necessary for one or more of the following reasons:

1. Uneven Settlement – this could be caused by uneven loading of the building, unequal resistance of the soil action of tree roots or cohesive soil settlement.

2. Increase in Loading – this could be due to the addition of an extra storey or an increase in imposed loadings such as that which may occur with a change of use.

3. Lowering of Adjacent Ground – usually required when constructing a basement adjacent to existing foundations.

General Precautions ~ before any form of underpinning work is commenced the following precautions should be taken:

1. Notify adjoining owners of proposed works giving full details and temporary shoring or tying.

2. Carry out a detailed survey of the site, the building to be underpinned and of any other adjoining or adjacent building or structures. A careful record of any defects found should be made and where possible agreed with the adjoining owner(s) before being lodged in a safe place.

3. Indicators or 'tell-tales' should be fixed over existing cracks so that any subsequent movements can be noted and monitored.

4. If settlement is the reason for the underpinning works a thorough investigation should be carried out to establish the cause and any necessary remedial work put in hand before any underpinning works are started.

5. Before any underpinning work is started the loads on the building to be underpinned should be reduced as much as possible by removing the imposed loads from the floors and installing any props and/or shoring which is required.

6. Any services which are in the vicinity of the proposed underpinning works should be identified, traced, carefully exposed, supported and protected as necessary.

Underpinning to Walls ~ to prevent fracture, damage or settlement of the wall(s) being underpinned the work should always be carried out in short lengths called legs or bays. The length of these bays will depend upon the following factors:

1. Total length of wall to be underpinned.

2. Wall loading.

3. General state of repair and stability of wall and foundation to be underpinned.

4. Nature of subsoil beneath existing foundation.

5. Estimated spanning ability of existing foundation.

Generally suitable bay lengths are:

1·000 to 1·500 for mass concrete strip foundations supporting walls of traditional construction.

1·500 to 3·000 for reinforced concrete strip foundations supporting walls of moderate loading.

In all cases the total sum of the unsupported lengths of wall should not exceed 25% of the total wall length.

The sequence of bays should be arranged so that working in adjoining bays is avoided until one leg of underpinning has been completed, pinned and cured sufficiently to support the wall above.

Typical   Underpinning   Schedule ~

schedule shows two-bay working - once all the underpinning legs have been completed the working bays will have combined to form a trench enabling a complete and final check to be made before backfilling

— bay width to give adequate working space - minimum 1·000

—wall and foundation to be underpinned

| 1 | 3 | 5 | 2 | 4 | 6 | 4 | 2 | 5 | 3 | 1 |

1·500 long working bays

Typical Traditional Underpinning Details~

datum board and plumb line

timbering as required

existing wall

projection to existing foundation removed

existing foundation

final pinning

consolidated backfill placed in trench after completion and inspection of all the underpinning work

hand placed and compacted 1:12 concrete filling

underpinning wall

dowel bars

new foundation

UNDERPINNING BAY ~ TYPICAL SECTION

existing wall

existing foundation with projection removed

underside of foundation cleaned to receive final pinning

25mm thick rich 'dry' well rammed cement mortar (1:2 or 3) - allow 12 hours for wall to settle before final pinning

tooted ends to underpinning wall

25 mm dia. x 400 mm long dowel bars

new mass concrete foundation

UNDERPINNING BAY ~ TYPICAL ELEVATION

Jack Pile Underpinning ~ this method can be used when the depth of a suitable bearing capacity subsoil is too deep to make traditional underpinning uneconomic. Jack pile underpinning is quiet, vibration free and flexible since the pile depth can be adjusted to suit subsoil conditions encountered. The existing foundations must be in a good condition since they will have to span over the heads of the pile caps which are cast onto the jack pile heads after the hydraulic jacks have been removed.

Typical Details ~

wall to be underpinned

timbering to underpinning bay excavation as required

to pump

existing foundation

underpinning bay

pressure pipe

short lengths of steel beam and plate sections joined together and used to spread pressure on foundation

hydraulic jack

steel dowel bars grouted in at each joint

300 x 300 precast concrete jack pile sections added to pile length one at a time until depth of pile provides sufficient resistance to further penetration

axial steel lined hole for dowel bars

750

leading section with pointed steel toe cast in during manufacture

600

Needle and Pile Underpinning ~ this method of underpinning can be used where the condition of the existing foundation is unsuitable for traditional or jack pile underpinning techniques. The brickwork above the existing foundation must be in a sound condition since this method relies on the `arching effect' of the brick bonding to transmit the wall loads onto the needles and ultimately to the piles. The piles used with this method are usually small diameter bored piles – see page 268.

Typical Details ~

wall to be underpinned

reinforced concrete needle or beam

wall to be underpinned

reinforced concrete cantilever needle or beam

final pinning

final pinning

existing foundation

blinding

existing foundation

small diameter bored piles

small diameter bored piles

Alternative Layouts ~

wall to be underpinned

needle or beam

existing foundation

pile

TRADITIONAL - simple

ZIG ZAG - uses less piles

'Pynford' Stool Method of Underpinning ~ this method can be used where the existing foundations are in a poor condition and it enables the wall to be underpinned in a continuous run without the need for needles or shoring. The reinforced concrete beam formed by this method may well be adequate to spread the load of the existing wall or it may be used in conjunction with other forms of underpinning such as traditional and jack pile.

Typical Details ~

Stage 1 - holes formed in wall to receive steel or precast concrete stools

Stage 2 - stools inserted and pinned to soffit of brickwork over opening

Stage 3 - brickwork between pinned stools removed to leave wall supported on pinned stools

1·000   precast concrete spreader pads

Stage 4 - reinforcement fabricated and placed around pinned stools

Stage 5 - formwork erected and beam cast

Stage 6 - formwork removed, beam allowed to cure before being pinned to underside of wall

reinforcement cage

formwork to beam side

finish beam - stools left in

Root Pile or Angle Piling ~ this is a much simpler alternative to traditional underpinning techniques, applying modern concrete drilling equipment to achieve cost benefits through time saving. The process is also considerably less disruptive, as large volumes of excavation are avoided. Where sound bearing strata can be located within a few metres of the surface, wall stability is achieved through lined reinforced concrete piles installed in pairs, at opposing angles. The existing floor, wall and foundation are pre-drilled with air-flushed percussion auger, giving access for a steel lining to be driven through the low grade/clay subsoil until it impacts with firm strata. The lining is cut to terminate at the underside of the foundation and the void steel reinforced prior to concreting.

interior

wall to be underpinned

existing foundation

low grade subsoil or made up ground

double angled reinforced concrete piling at opposing angles-spaced according to extent of damage and soil condition

steel lining

firm strata

In many situations it is impractical to apply angle piling to both sides of a wall. Subject to subsoil conditions being adequate, it may be acceptable to apply remedial treatment from one side only. The piles will need to be relatively close spaced.

Underpinning Columns ~ columns can be underpinned in the some manner as walls using traditional or jack pile methods after the columns have been relieved of their loadings. The beam loads can usually be transferred from the columns by means of dead shores and the actual load of the column can be transferred by means of a pair of beams acting against a collar attached to the base of the column shaft.

Typical Details ~

pair of precast concrete short beams bolted together to form collar

25mm deep chase

pair of precast concrete or steel beams bolted together

hydraulic jack

reinforced concrete column

bored or jack pile

concrete bearing pad as alternative to pile

foundation to be underpinned

kentledge of precast concrete blocks or similar to act as counterweight

steel column

pair of steel channels with web plates welded to steel column

hydraulic jack

pile cap

pair of steel or precast concrete beams bolted together

pair of bored or jack piles

foundation to be underpinned

Classification of Water ~ water can be classified by its relative position to or within the ground thus –

surface water — run off from an earth surface ≈10 % of water falling onto surface but on hard paved areas run off is usually 75 to 90 %

ground water - water held in the subsoil and is usually percolating down towards the water table

water table - upper level of water held in the soil which varies with wet and dry periods

subsoil water - water held in the ground below the water table

Problems of Water in the Subsoil:

1. A high water table could cause flooding during wet periods.
2. Subsoil water can cause problems during excavation works by its natural tendency to flow into the voids created by the excavation activities.
3. It can cause an unacceptable humidity level around finished buildings and structures.

Control of Ground Water ~ this can take one of two forms which are usually referred to as temporary and permanent exclusion –

TEMPORARY EXCLUSION

PERMANENT EXCLUSION

Permanent Exclusion ~ this can be defined as the insertion of an impermeable barrier to stop the flow of water within the ground.

Temporary Exclusion ~ this can be defined as the lowering of the water table and within the economic depth range of 1·500 can be achieved by subsoil drainage methods; for deeper treatment a pump or pumps are usually involved.

Simple Sump Pumping ~ suitable for trench work and/or where small volumes of water are involved.

Sizing Pumps ~

allow for friction loss due to fittings in terms of pipe length – added to actual pipe length

allowances for friction and head loss available from manufacturers' charts or tables

calculate or estimate water flow

allow for loss of head due to friction in pipe length – i.e. pipe length including an allowance for bends.

total head = suction lift + delivery head + loss of head

Jetted Sumps ~ this method achieves the same objectives as the simple sump methods of dewatering (previous page) but it will prevent the soil movement associated with this and other open sump methods. A borehole is formed in the subsoil by jetting a metal tube into the ground by means of pressurised water, to a depth within the maximum suction lift of the extract pump. The metal tube is withdrawn to leave a void for placing a disposable wellpoint and plastic suction pipe. The area surrounding the pipe is filled with coarse sand to function as a filtering media.

Typical Example ~

Wellpoint Systems ~ method of lowering the water table to a position below the formation level to give a dry working area. The basic principle is to jet into the subsoil a series of wellpoints which are connected to a common header pipe which is connected to a vacuum pump. Wellpoint systems are suitable for most subsoils and can encircle an excavation or be laid progressively alongside as in the case of a trench excavation. If the proposed formation level is below the suction lift capacity of the pump a multi-stage system can be employed — see next page.

Typical Details ~

38mm dia. jetting and riser pipe

150mm dia. lightweight header pipe

stop valve

flexible connection pipe

retaining collar

75mm diameter slotted strainer cover

perforated inner tube

water flows through strainer cover and perforated tube into riser pipe

jetting shoe

riser pipe and wellpoint under suction from pump

1·300

up to 1·000

jetting pipe connected to high pressure jetting pump and the water jet emitted from the jetting shoe moves soil particles away, enabling wellpoint to sink

rubber ball valve

JETTING

DEWATERING

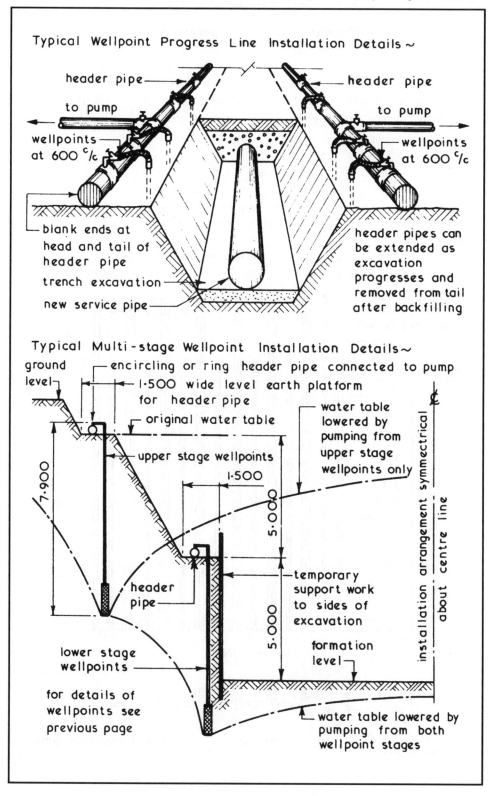

Typical Wellpoint Progress Line Installation Details ~

header pipe
to pump
wellpoints at 600 c/c

header pipe
to pump
wellpoints at 600 c/c

blank ends at head and tail of header pipe
trench excavation
new service pipe

header pipes can be extended as excavation progresses and removed from tail after backfilling

Typical Multi-stage Wellpoint Installation Details ~

ground level
encircling or ring header pipe connected to pump
1·500 wide level earth platform for header pipe
original water table
upper stage wellpoints
1·500
7·900
header pipe
lower stage wellpoints
for details of wellpoints see previous page

water table lowered by pumping from upper stage wellpoints only
5·000
temporary support work to sides of excavation
5·000
formation level
water table lowered by pumping from both wellpoint stages

installation arrangement symmetrical about centre line

353

Thin Grouted Membranes ~ these are permanent curtain or cut-off non-structural walls or barriers inserted in the ground to enclose the proposed excavation area. They are suitable for silts and sands and can be installed rapidly but they must be adequately supported by earth on both sides. The only limitation is the depth to which the formers can be driven and extracted.

Typical Details ~

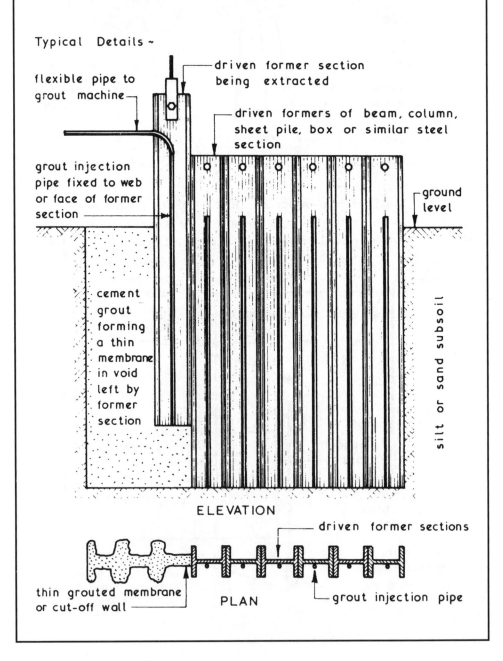

flexible pipe to grout machine

driven former section being extracted

driven formers of beam, column, sheet pile, box or similar steel section

grout injection pipe fixed to web or face of former section

ground level

cement grout forming a thin membrane in void left by former section

silt or sand subsoil

ELEVATION

driven former sections

thin grouted membrane or cut-off wall

PLAN

grout injection pipe

Contiguous or Secant Piling ~ this forms a permanent structural wall of interlocking bored piles. Alternate piles are bored and cast by traditional methods and before the concrete has fully hardened the interlocking piles are bored using a toothed flight auger. This system is suitable for most types of subsoil and has the main advantages of being economical on small and confined sites; capable of being formed close to existing foundations and can be installed with the minimum of vibration and noise. Ensuring a complete interlock of all piles over the entire length may be difficult to achieve in practice; therefore the exposed face of the piles is usually covered with a mesh or similar fabric and face with rendering or sprayed concrete. Alternatively a reinforced concrete wall could be cast in front of the contiguous piling. This method of ground water control is suitable for structures such as basements, road underpasses and underground car parks.

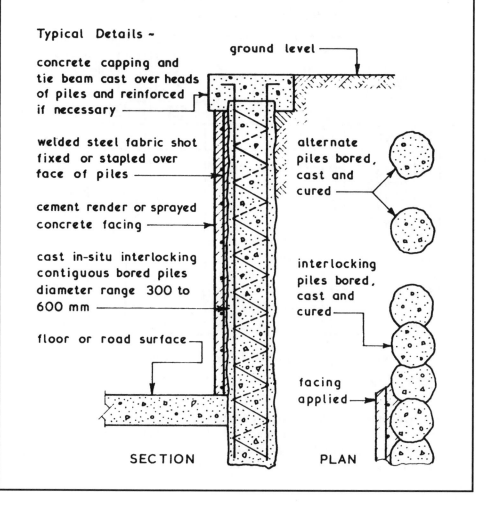

Typical Details ~

concrete capping and tie beam cast over heads of piles and reinforced if necessary

welded steel fabric shot fixed or stapled over face of piles

cement render or sprayed concrete facing

cast in-situ interlocking contiguous bored piles diameter range 300 to 600 mm

floor or road surface

ground level

alternate piles bored, cast and cured

interlocking piles bored, cast and cured

facing applied

SECTION

PLAN

Diaphragm Walls ~ these are structural concrete walls which can be cast in-situ (usually by the bentonite slurry method) or constructed using precast concrete components (see next page). They are suitable for most subsoils and their installation generates only a small amount of vibration and noise, making them suitable for works close to existing buildings. The high cost of these walls makes them uneconomic unless they can be incorporated into the finished structure. Diaphragm walls are suitable for basements, underground car parks and similar structures.

Typical Cast In-situ Concrete Diaphragm Wall Details ~

length of panel = 3 × hydraulic grab width

NB. Bentonite is a controlled mixture of fullers earth and water which produces a mud or slurry which has thixotropic properties and exerts a pressure in excess of earth + hydrostatic pressure present on sides of excavation.

Precast Concrete Diaphragm Walls ~ these walls have the some applications as their in-situ counterparts and have the advantages of factory-produced components but lack the design flexibility of cast in-situ walls. The panel or post and panel units are installed in a trench filled with a special mixture of bentonite and cement with a retarder to control the setting time. This mixture ensures that the joints between the wall components are effectively sealed. To provide stability the panels or posts are tied to the retained earth with ground anchors.

Typical Precast Concrete Diaphragm Wall Details ~

lifting lugs

pcc trench guide walls to hold units in place whilst slurry sets

bentonite sealed tongue and groove joint

ground anchor

pocket for ground anchor anchorage

trench filled with special bentonite slurry as excavation proceeds

face of wall units coated with special compound to reduce the adhesion of bentonite

formation level

PCC PANEL DIAPHRAGM WALL

bentonite remains in place

ground anchors

pcc post

pcc panel

pcc post

PCC POST AND PANEL DIAPHRAGM WALL

357

Grouting Methods ~ these techniques are used to form a curtain or cut off wall in high permeability soils where pumping methods could be uneconomic. The curtain walls formed by grouting methods are non-structural; therefore adequate earth support will be required and in some cases this will be a distance of at least 4·000 from the face of the proposed excavation. Grout mixtures are injected into the soil by pumping the grout at high pressure through special injection pipes inserted in the ground. The pattern and spacing of the injection pipes will depend on the grout type and soil conditions.

Grout Types ~

1. Cement Grouts – mixture of neat cement and water cement sand up to 1:4 or PFA (pulverised fuel ash) cement to a 1:1 ratio. Suitable for coarse-grained soils and fissured and jointed rock strata.

2. Chemical Grouts – one shot (premixed) or two shot (first chemical is injected followed immediately by second chemical resulting in an immediate reaction) methods can be employed to form a permanent gel in the soil to reduce its permeability and at the same time increase the soil's strength. Suitable for medium to coarse sands and gravels.

3. Resin Grouts – these are similar in application to chemical grouts but have a low viscosity and can therefore penetrate into silty fine sands.

Typical Cement Grouting Details ~

Ground Freezing Techniques ~ this method is suitable for all types of saturated soils and rock and for soils with a moisture content in excess of 8% of the voids. The basic principle is to insert into the ground a series of freezing tubes to form an ice wall thus creating an impermeable barrier. The treatment takes time to develop and the initial costs are high; therefore it is only suitable for large contracts of reasonable duration. The freezing tubes can be installed vertically for conventional excavations and horizontally for tunnelling works. The usual circulating brines employed are magnesium chloride and calcium chloride with a temperature of $-15°$ to $-25°C$ which would take 10 to 17 days to form an ice wall 1·000 thick. Liquid nitrogen could be used as the freezing medium to reduce the initial freezing period if the extra cost can be justified.

Typical Ground Freezing Details ~

brine return pipe

all pipes above ground level insulated with foamed polyurethane

brine supply pipe from freezing plant

white reflective polyethylene film lining to prevent thawing by radiant heat to excavation faces as required

100 to 150 mm diameter outer tube

steel freezing tubes at 1·000 c/c

circulating brine at -15° to -25°C

38 to 75 mm diameter inner tube

inner tube with open end

all excavation work takes place inside ice walls

outer tube with closed end

1·000 thick ice wall

Soil Stabilisation and Improvement

Soil Investigation ~ before a decision is made as to the type of foundation which should be used on any particular site a soil investigation should be carried out to establish existing ground conditions and soil properties. The methods which can be employed together with other sources of information such as local knowledge, ordnance survey and geological maps, mining records and aerial photography should be familiar to students at this level. If such an investigation reveals a naturally poor subsoil or extensive filling the designer has several options:

1. Not to Build – unless a new and suitable site can be found building is only possible if the poor ground is localised and the proposed foundations can be designed around these areas with the remainder of the structure bridging over these positions.

2. Remove and Replace – the poor ground can be excavated, removed and replaced by compacted fills. Using this method there is a risk of differential settlement and generally for depths over 4·000 it is uneconomic.

3. Surcharging – this involves preloading the poor ground with a surcharge of aggregate or similar material to speed up settlement and thereby improve the soil's bearing capacity. Generally this method is uneconomic due to the time delay before actual building operations can commence which can vary from a few weeks to two or more years.

4. Vibration – this is a method of strengthening ground by vibrating a granular soil into compacted stone columns either by using the natural coarse granular soil or by replacement – see pages 361 and 362.

5. Dynamic Compaction – this is a method of soil improvement which consists of dropping a heavy weight through a considerable vertical distance to compact the soil and thus improve its bearing capacity and is especially suitable for granular soils – see page 363.

6. Jet Grouting – this method of consolidating ground can be used in all types of subsoil and consists of lowering a monitor probe into a 150 mm diameter prebored guide hole. The probe has two jets the upper of which blasts water, concentrated by compressed air to force any loose material up the guide to ground level. The lower jet fills the void with a cement slurry which sets into a solid mass – see page 364.

Ground Vibration ~ the objective of this method is to strengthen the existing soil by rearranging and compacting coarse granular particles to form stone columns with the ground. This is carried out by means of a large poker vibrator which has an effective compacting radius of 1·500 to 2·700. On large sites the vibrator is inserted on a regular triangulated grid pattern with centres ranging from 1·500 to 3·000. In coarse-grained soils extra coarse aggregate is tipped into the insertion positions to make up levels as required whereas in clay and other fine particle soils the vibrator is surged up and down enabling the water jetting action to remove the surrounding soft material thus forming a borehole which is backfilled with a coarse granular material compacted in-situ by the vibrator. The backfill material is usually of 20 to 70 mm size of uniform grading within the chosen range. Ground vibration is not a piling system but a means of strengthening ground to increase the bearing capacity within a range of 200 to 500 kN/m².

Typical Details ~

lifting pulley

manifold section

follower section(s)

top jets to assist in removal

vibration isolator

vibrator section containing hydraulic motor with rotating eccentric

compacted stone column

water and hydraulic hoses

side fins to prevent vibrator from twisting

nose cone housing lower jetting nozzle

Typical Vibrator Data:
length - 5·000
weight - 2 tonnes
vibration - 30 to 60 hz.

standard track mounted crane

361

Sand Compaction – applied to non-cohesive subsoils where the granular particles are rearranged into a denser condition by poker vibration.

The crane-suspended vibrating poker is water-jetted into the ground using a combination of self-weight and water displacement of the finer soil particles to penetrate the ground. Under this pressure, the soil granules compact to increase in density as the poker descends. At the appropriate depth, which may be determined by building load calculations or the practical limit of plant (generally 30 m max.), jetting ceases and fine aggregates or sand are infilled around the poker. The poker is then gradually withdrawn compacting the granular fill in the process. Compaction continues until sand fill reaches ground level. Spacing of compaction boreholes is relatively close to ensure continuity and an integral ground condition.

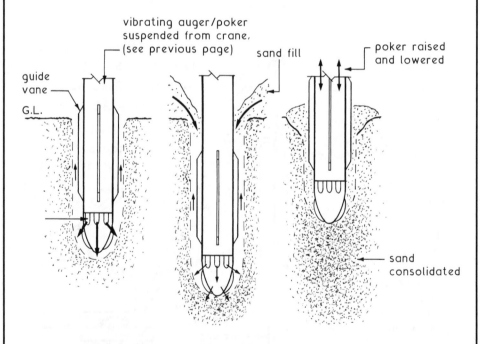

1. Vibrating poker penetrates ground under full water jet pressure.

2. At design depth, water pressure is reduced and sand fill introduced and compacted.

3. With resistance to compaction, poker is raised and lowered to consolidate further sand.

Sand compaction procedure

Dynamic Compaction ~ this method of ground improvement consists of dropping a heavy weight from a considerable height and is particularly effective in granular soils. Where water is present in the subsoil, trenches should be excavated to allow the water to escape and not collect in the craters formed by the dropped weight. The drop pattern, size of weight and height of drop are selected to suit each individual site but generally three or four drops are made in each position forming a crater up to 2·500 deep and 5·000 in diameter. Vibration through the subsoil can be a problem with dynamic compaction operations; therefore the proximity and condition of nearby buildings must be considered together with the depth position and condition of existing services on site.

Typical Details ~

NB. Final ground level after compaction treatment and final levelling could be up to 1·500 lower than original ground level.

heavy duty track mounted crane

weight range 10 to 20 tonnes

depth up to 2·500 after 4 blows

crater up to 5·000 in diameter

free-fall distance range 15·000 to 25·000

compacted soil

20° to 40° spread

Jet Grouting ~ this is a means of consolidating ground by lowering a monitor probe into preformed boreholes. The probe is rotated and the sides of the borehole are subjected to a jet of pressurised water and air from a single outlet which enlarges and compacts the borehole sides. At the same time a cement grout is being introduced under pressure to fill the void being created. The water used by the probe and any combined earth is forced up to the surface in the form of a sludge. If the monitor probe is not rotated grouted panels can be formed. The spacing, depth and layout of the boreholes is subject to specialist design.

Typical Details ~

crawler mounted power unit →

motor - raises, lowers and rotates probe

guide frame

rotating monitor probe

150mm diameter borehole →

150mm diameter borehole

up to 40.000

water/air jet

cement grout jet

grouted column up to 2.000 diameter

crawler mounted power unit →

motor - raises and lowers probe

guide frame

sludge

preformed boreholes

150mm diameter borehole →

static monitor probe

up to 40.000

water/air jet

cement grout jet

panel lengths up to 2.400 →

Green-field – land not previously built upon. Usually part of the 'green-belt' surrounding urban areas, designated inappropriate for development in order to preserve the countryside. Limited development for agricultural purposes only may be permitted on 'green-belt' land.

Brown-field – derelict land formerly a developed site and usually associated with previous construction of industrial buildings. The UK government has an objective to build 60% of new homes on these sites.

Site Survey – land previously used for industrial bulidings could be contaminated with hazardous waste or pollutants. Therefore it is essential that a geo-technical survey is undertaken to determine whether contaminants are in the soil and ground water. Of particular concern are: acids, salts, heavy metals, cyanides and coal tars, in addition to organic materials which decompose to form the highly explosive gas methane. Analysis of the soil will determine a 'trigger threshold value', above which it will be declared sensitive to the end user. For example, a domestic garden or children's play area will have a low value relative to land designated for a commercial car park.

Site Preparation – when building on sites previously infilled with uncontaminated material, a reinforced raft-type foundation may be adequate for light structures. Larger buildings will justify soil consolidation and compaction processes to improve the bearing capacity. Remedial measures for subsoils containing chemicals or other contaminants are varied.

Legislation – the Environment Protection Act of 1990 attempted to enforce responsibility on local authorities to compile a register of all potentially contaminated land. This proved unrealistic and too costly due to inherent complexities. Since then, requirements under the Environment Act 1995, the Pollution Prevention and Control Act 1999, the PPC Regulations 2000 and the subsequent DCLG Planning Policy Statement (PPS 23, 2004): Planning and Pollution Control (Annex 2: Development on land affected by contamination) have made this more of a planning issue. It has become the responsibility of developers to conduct site investigations and to present details of proposed remedial measures as part of their planning application.

The traditional low-technology method for dealing with contaminated sites has been to excavate the soil and remove it to places licensed for depositing. However, with the increase in building work on brown-field sites, suitable dumps are becoming scarce. Added to this is the reluctance of ground operators to handle large volumes of this type of waste. Also, where excavations exceed depths of about 5m, it becomes less practical and too expensive. Alternative physical, biological or chemical methods of soil treatment may be considered.

Encapsulation – in-situ enclosure of the contaminated soil. A perimeter trench is taken down to rock or other sound strata and filled with an impervious agent such as bentonite clay. An impermeable horizontal capping is also required to link with the trenches. A high-specification barrier is necessary where liquid or gas contaminants are present as these can migrate quite easily. A system of monitoring soil condition is essential as the barrier may decay in time. Suitable for all types of contaminant.

Soil washing – involves extraction of the soil, sifting to remove large objects and placing it in a scrubbing unit resembling a huge concrete mixer. Within this unit water and detergents are added for a basic wash process, before pressure spraying to dissolve pollutants and to separate clay from silt. Eliminates fuels, metals and chemicals.

Vapour extraction – used to remove fuels or industrial solvents and other organic deposits. At variable depths, small diameter boreholes are located at frequent intervals. Attached to these are vacuum pipes to draw air through the contaminated soil. The contaminants are collected at a vapour treatment processing plant on the surface, treated and evaporated into the atmosphere. This is a slow process and it may take several months to cleanse a site.

Electrolysis – use of low voltage d.c. in the presence of metals. Electricity flows between an anode and cathode, where metal ions in water accumulate in a sump before pumping to the surface for treatment.

BIOLOGICAL

Phytoremediation – the removal of contaminants by plants which will absorb harmful chemicals from the ground. The plants are subsequently harvested and destroyed. A variant uses fungal degradation of the contaminants.

Bioremediation – stimulating the growth of naturally occurring microbes. Microbes consume petrochemicals and oils, converting them to water and carbon dioxide. Conditions must be right, i.e. a temperature of at least 10°C with an adequate supply of nutrients and oxygen. Untreated soil can be excavated and placed over perforated piping, through which air is pumped to enhance the process prior to the soil being replaced.

CHEMICAL

Oxidation – subsoil boreholes are used for the pumped distribution of liquid hydrogen peroxide or potassium permanganate. Chemicals and fuel deposits convert to water and carbon dioxide.

Solvent extraction – the subsoil is excavated and mixed with a solvent to break down oils, grease and chemicals that do not dissolve in water.

THERMAL

Thermal treatment (off site) – an incineration process involving the use of a large heating container/oven. Soil is excavated, dried and crushed prior to heating to 2500°C, where harmful chemicals are removed by evaporation or fusion.

Thermal treatment (in-situ) – steam, hot water or hot air is pressure-injected through the soil. Variations include electric currents and radio waves to heat water in the ground to become steam. Evaporates chemicals.

Ref. Building Regulations, Approved Document, C1: Site preparation and resistance to contaminants. Section 1: Clearance or treatment of unsuitable material. Section 2: Resistance to contaminants.

5 SUPERSTRUCTURE – 1

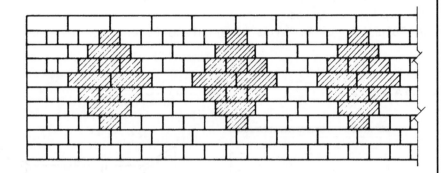

CHOICE OF MATERIALS

BRICK AND BLOCK WALLS

CAVITY WALLS

DAMP-PROOF COURSES AND MEMBRANES

GAS-RESISTANT MEMBRANES

CALCULATED BRICKWORK MORTARS

ARCHES AND OPENINGS

WINDOWS, GLASS AND GLAZING

DOMESTIC AND INDUSTRIAL DOORS

CROSSWALL CONSTRUCTION

FRAMED CONSTRUCTION

RENDERING AND CLADDING EXTERNAL WALLS

TIMBER PITCHED AND FLAT ROOFS

GREEN ROOFS

THERMAL INSULATION

U-VALUE CALCULATION

THERMAL BRIDGING

ACCESS FOR THE DISABLED

STAGE 1

Consideration to be given to the following:

1. Building type and usage.
2. Building owner's requirements and preferences.
3. Local planning restrictions.
4. Legal restrictions and requirements.
5. Site restrictions.
6. Capital resources.
7. Future policy in terms of maintenance and adaptation.

STAGE 2

Decide on positions, sizes and shapes of openings

STAGE 3

Decide on style, character and materials for openings

STAGE 4

brick

timber

stone

Decide on basic materials for fabric of roof and walls

STAGE 5

Review all decisions and make changes if required

Formation ~ millions of years ago planet earth originated as a ball of hot gases. Millions of years later the gases began to cool, solidify and liquefy to form large areas of land and seas. Today, a molten mass remains at the core, some 200 km below the surface, occasionally materialising in volcanic eruptions. The effect of cooling also created an atmospheric condition about the earth. As the gases solidified they formed into deposits of stone, varying in composition depending on their relative levels below the earth's crust and rate of cooling. Many of these stone deposits are materially suitable for building work and can be categorised under the following geological classifications:

- Igneous $2560 - 3200 \, kg/m^3$
- Sedimentary $1950 - 2750$ ..
- Metamorphic $2630 - 3040$ ..

Igneous ~ originated from volcanic activity, formed by the crystallisation of molten rock. Can be sub-divided into:

Plutonic – solidified very slowly, deep into the lower part of the earth's surface, e.g. granite.
Hypabyssal – solidified less slowly, near to the earth's upper surface, e.g. porphyry.
Volcanic – solidified rapidly at the earth's outer surface, e.g. pumice.

Sedimentary ~ composed of particles of older rocks broken down by erosion due to the receding water levels that at one time covered much of the earth's surface. Fierce winds and ice also had a disintegrating effect on exposed stone deposits. Sedimentary deposits tend to lie in roughly horizontal stratified formations. These are sometimes loose as in sand and shingle, otherwise may be consolidated by superimposed loads with particles cemented together by minerals carried in water. In this dense form, sandstone and limestone can be shaped as building blocks. Chalk and shale are other examples.

Metamorphic ~ originally igneous or sedimentary, but changed structurally by geological processes involving heat, pressure and chemical reaction due to the presence of fluids. Examples include marble a form of metamorphic limestone, and slate a metamorphic clay.

Sources ~ stones of various types occur worldwide. Some are mined, but most are reasonably accessible from surface workings at quarries. Removal is by blasting and then wedge cutting into slabs, blocks and thin sections of workable sizes. Thereafter it is sawn and split into commercial sizes, dressed and/or polished for final purpose. The UK and Ireland have many sources of stone to include the following:

Type	Location	Colour
Granite	Cornwall	Light grey
	Highlands and Western Isles	Bright grey to black
	Leicestershire	Various, light to dark
	Westmorland, Cumbria	Reddish brown
	Down, Ireland	Greenish grey
Limestone	Portland, Dorset	White to light brown
	Bath, West Country	White to cream
	Lincolnshire	Cream to buff
	Wiltshire	Light brown
	Somerset	Yellowish grey
	Kent	Blue grey
	Leicestershire	Cream to yellow
	Nottinghamshire	Yellowish brown
	Oxfordshire	Buff
Sandstone	Yorkshire	Grey and light brown
	Forest of Dean, Gloucs.	Grey/blue, grey/pink
	Gloucestershire	Dull blue
	Glamorganshire	Dull blue
	Derbyshire	Buff and light grey
	Sussex	Buff, brown specs
Marble	Dorset	Green/blue or grey
	Derbyshire	Light grey
	Argyllshire	Pale green/white
	Galway, Ireland	Green

Stonework is often a preferred alternative to brickwork, particularly where local planning requirements stipulate that vernacular characteristics are maintained.

Naturally Quarried Stones ~ these vary marginally in appearance, even when extracted in the same location from one quarry. Texture and slight colour variation adds to the character and visual attractiveness, along with the presence of veins, crystals, fossils and other visible features that manifest with wear and exposure.

Artificial Stones ~ otherwise known as reconstituted, reconstructed or cast stone. These are factory manufactured by casting natural stone aggregates of 15 mm maximum size with white or coloured cement into moulds of a specific dimensions. The usual ratio is 3 to 4 parts of aggregate to 1 part cement. These defect free blocks produced under quality controlled conditions are an economical substitute for natural stone. Block sizes can vary to suit specific applications, but colour and texture are uniform. A variation is a 20 to 25 mm facing of natural stone aggregate, fine sand aggregate and cement (possibly colour pigmented) set over a base of wet concrete.

Further working of cast stone can produce a high quality surface finish to very accurate overall dimensions. In this precise form, blocks can be used as an artificial type of ashlar facing over brickwork or standard blockwork backgrounds, (see below for a definition of ashlar and next page for a summary of ashlar walling).

The long term weathering qualities of cast stone differ from that of natural stone. Natural stone weathers slowly with a gradual and fairly consistent colour change. Artificial stone has the characteristics of concrete. With time it may crack, become dull and attract dirt staining at joints, corners and projecting features such as copings and sills.

Ashlar ~ hewn and dressed stone facing block.
Ashlaring ~ stonework comprising blocks of stone finely squared and dressed to a precise finish and dimensions, laid to courses of not less than 300 mm in height.

Refs.: BS 1217: Cast stone. Specification.
      BS EN 771-5: Specification for masonry units. Manufactured stone masonry units.

Ashlaring ~ as defined on the preceding page, a wall facing of high quality stone laid with very thin joints. It is a classic façade treatment to many existing prestigious buildings, but now rarely used due to the cost of manufacturing the stone to fine tolerances and the time consuming craftsmanship required for construction. Examples are included here not just for historical reference; many buildings constructed with ashlar walling are the subject of ongoing refurbishment, conversion, modification, adaptation and repair. Limestone is popular for ashlar, produced in thicknesses between 100 and 300 mm and bedded in a mortar known as mason's putty. The traditional mix for this mortar comprises stone dust, lime putty and portland cement in the ratio of 7:5:2.

Channelled   Vee and   Vee
                    channel

Examples of joint profiles to ashlar walling units (dimensions in mm)

coping

baluster

plinth

in-situ reinforced concrete flat roof or floor

cornice

bituminous paint

ashlar facing max. length 2.5 x height

brick backing

328

113   215

300

450

300

450

300

render and plaster finish

dpc

mass concrete foundation

solid concrete floor

Example of existing ashlar stonework
(dimensions in mm)

Construction shown here is a reference to existing practice. In established towns and cities there are often many examples of ashlar stonework faced buildings. Not all are smooth faced as the stone sometimes features surface patterning.

A contemporary variation of the ashlar effect is achieved with cavity wall construction, where artificial or cast stone is deployed over the whole façade (similar to the detail on page 378). This effect can be used on a limited scale using the cast stone as an isolated feature, e.g. at quoins, sills and around openings for doors and windows. The ashlar effect can also be replicated in medium and high rise buildings by using cast stone (concrete) cladding. The principles of this are shown in Part 6.

Rubble Walls ~ walls constructed of stones used either in a random rough or uneven form as extracted from the quarry, or roughly dressed to a square or rectangular shape. Walls of this type are common in rural areas, particularly those close to quarry locations. Many walls are dry bonded as estate and farm boundaries. Otherwise, stones are laid with a relatively deep bed joint of mortar to accommodate irregularities, often as garden features and external walls to dwellings. Lime based mortar is preferred with long runs of stone walling as it is less prone to thermal movement cracking than cement mortar.

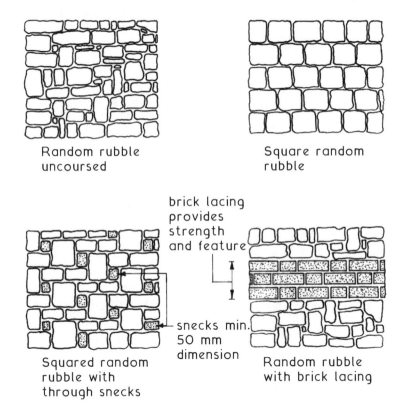

Random rubble
uncoursed

Square random
rubble

brick lacing
provides
strength
and feature

snecks min.
50 mm
dimension

Squared random
rubble with
through snecks

Random rubble
with brick lacing

Common Treatment at Dressed Stone Arch Openings ~ examples
show rubble walling to the left and ashlar to the right.

coursed random
rubble wall

centre-line of
semi-circular arch

ashlar wall

keystone

extrados

intrados

curved voussoirs

quoin stones

coursed random
rubble wall

ashlar wall

keystone

stepped
voussoirs

crossetted
voussoirs

intrados

quoin stones

377

In many areas where locally quarried stone is the established building material, traditions are maintained and specified as part of planning compliance requirements. Dressed stone is an example of an established external feature and can be used as an alternative to brickwork as the outer leaf of cavity walls. Stone widths of 150 to 225 mm are usual, although as little as 100 mm is possible with mechanically cut and finished stone. However, this type of precise finishing produces an effect resembling ashlar rather than rubble. A lightweight concrete block inner leaf provides lateral support and stability with wall ties positioned at the maximum spacings shown on page 400.

300 mm random rubble outer leaf

dpc min. 150 mm above ground

150 mm lightweight concrete block inner leaf

50 mm min. cavity insulated as required

wall ties spaced as shown on page 400

cavity filled with concrete at least 225 mm below dpc

mass concrete strip foundation

Note: Solid walls of stone need to be at least 300 mm wide to ensure stability; in excess of 400 mm (depending on quality) to resist penetration of rainfall.

Shaping and Moulding ~ bricks were originally made by hand kneading clay into an open wooden box. The box dimensions typically 250 mm × 125 mm × 75 mm (10″ × 5″ × 3″) with a protrusion in the bottom if a *frog* or indent was required as a mortar key. Oversized dimensions allowed for shrinkage.

Drying and Burning ~ after surplus clay was struck off, the *green* brick was turned out of the mould and stacked with others in a drying shed for 3 to 6 weeks. The bricks were then burnt in open *clamps*. This involved stacking in open flue formations to a height of 3 to 4 metres with layers of fine coal laid between the bricks. Fine particles of coal could also be mixed with the clay during the moulding process. On setting the *clamp*, fires were placed and ignited leaving the bricks to burn for several days. Bricks were produced in this way by the Romans and more so during the Middle Ages. There is evidence that the Babylonians used this procedure over 6000 years ago.

Hardwood hand mould or frame for standard size clay bricks

Outline examples of moulds for hand made purpose made specials

Notes:
- *Clamp* burning is still used by some of the smaller brick companies, but most producers now use controlled kiln burning as described on the next page.
- Bricks made with fine coal deposits have characteristic purple/blue markings. They have become known as *stocks*.
- Small batch orders for purpose made bricks as shown on page 396, are still made by hand in specially shaped moulds.

Machine Manufacture ~ during the industrial revolution (mid 18th. to 19th. centuries) greater demand for bricks led to brick production on an industrial scale. Machinery was introduced to mass produce pressed bricks in moulds and for wire cutting extruded clay. Both techniques are the basis of production today. Wire cutting to size is used where clay is mechanically forced through a brick sized opening. Circular bars in the central area of the opening leave two or three perforations to provide for a mortar key when laid.

Kiln Drying and Firing ~ in 1858 the German, Friedrich Hoffmann devised the circular or oval kiln system containing several chambers. The chambers have loading doors, fire holes and flues connecting to a common chimney. Each chamber represents a different stage of drying, pre-heating, firing* (1100 °C) and cooling, all of which are undertaken on a large scale without transportation. A later development is the straight tunnel kiln with a central firing zone. With this, bricks stacked on trolleys run on a narrow railway line through slowly increasing and decreasing heat zones. Both types of kiln are used today, although the tunnel is generally preferred as this is easier to control.

* Fired using natural gas, fuel oil or solid fuel.

History ~ originated during the 19th. century as a form of cast artificial stone. Caustic lime and sand were mixed with water into a workable consistency and left until the lime was completely hydrated. It was then pressed into moulds for steam curing and initial hardening. After dry stacking for several weeks the bricks matured to a usable strength.

Development ~ by the end of the 19th. century, processing was considerably improved. Steam at 200°C was pressurised in an *autoclave* (a sealed vessel used to create a chemical reaction between the lime and sand under high pressure; approximately 15 bar or 1.5 MN/m^2). The reaction formed hydrosilicates (hydrated calcium silicates) resulting in an extremely durable and strong building brick. This principle is the basis for calcium silicate brick production today.

Typical Composition ~ Silica (sand) 84%
    Lime (quicklime or hydrated lime) 7%
    Alumina and oxide of lime 2%
    Water, manganese and alkalis 7%

Properties ~ Similar production costs to clay brick manufacture
    High crushing strength (see below)
    Dimensionally accurate, ie. edges straight, even and without defects, warping or twisting
    Uniformity of dull white colour and of texture (perceived as uninteresting by some)

Variations ~ Flint-lime, produced by adding powdered flint
    Colouring agents; options for buffs, blues, mauves, etc.

Typical Brick Compressive Strength Comparisons ~
    Hand made clay – 6 to 14 MN/m^2
    Machine made clay – 15 to 20 MN/m^2
    Stock (clay) – 10 to 20 MN/m^2
    Engineering brick (clay) – 50 to 70 MN/m^2
    Sand-lime – 20 to 50 MN/m^2 (see BS EN 771-2)

Environmental Impact ~ due to less energy fuel use in production and without generating the air pollutants that occur with clay brick manufacture, considered to have a relative low environmental impact.

Solid Brick Walls

Bricks ~ these are walling units within a length of 337·5 mm, a width of 225 mm and a height of 112·5 mm. The usual size of bricks in common use is length 215 mm, width 102·5 mm and height 65 mm and like blocks they must be laid in a definite pattern or bond if they are to form a structural wall. Bricks are usually made from clay (BS EN 771-1) or from sand and lime (BS EN 771-2) and are available in a wide variety of strengths, types, textures, colours and special shaped bricks to BS 4729.

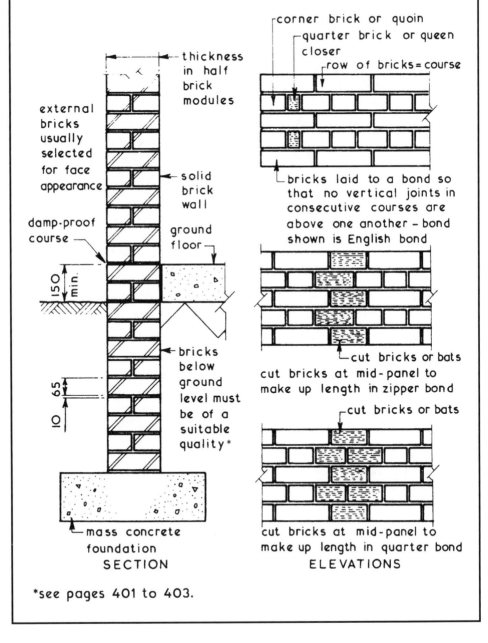

thickness in half brick modules

external bricks usually selected for face appearance

solid brick wall

damp-proof course

ground floor

150 min.

65

10

bricks below ground level must be of a suitable quality*

mass concrete foundation
SECTION

corner brick or quoin

quarter brick or queen closer

row of bricks = course

bricks laid to a bond so that no vertical joints in consecutive courses are above one another – bond shown is English bond

cut bricks or bats

cut bricks at mid-panel to make up length in zipper bond

cut bricks or bats

cut bricks at mid-panel to make up length in quarter bond
ELEVATIONS

*see pages 401 to 403.

382

Typical Details ~

Bonding ~ an arrangement of bricks in a wall, column or pier laid to a set pattern to maintain an adequate lap.

Purposes of Brick Bonding:

1. Obtain maximum strength whilst distributing the loads to be carried throughout the wall, column or pier.
2. Ensure lateral stability and resistance to side thrusts.
3. Create an acceptable appearance.

Lap Forms ~

HALF BONDING
used in half brick thick walls built in stretcher bond

QUARTER BONDING
used in most bonds built with standard bricks

THIRD BONDING
used in bonds built with metric bricks

Simple Bonding Rules:

1. Bond is set out along length of wall working from each end to ensure that no vertical joints are above one another in consecutive courses.

NB all odd numbered courses set out as course 1 and all even numbered courses set out as course 2

2. Walls which are not in exact bond length can be set out thus –

BROKEN BOND   REVERSED BOND

3. Transverse or cross joints continue unbroken across the width of wall unless stopped by a face stretcher.

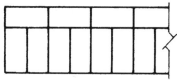

English Bond ~ formed by laying alternate courses of stretchers and headers it is one of the strongest bonds but it will require more facing bricks than other bonds (89 facing bricks per m^2).

Typical Example ~

stopped end

attached pier or pilaster - for alternative bonding arrangement see next page

return wall

attached pier or pilaster

queen closer

queen closer

PLAN ON ODD NUMBERED COURSES

stopped end

queen closer

attached pier

$^3/_4$ bats

return wall

attached pier

queen closer

queen closer

PLAN ON EVEN NUMBERED COURSES

ELEVATION

Flemish Bond ~ formed by laying headers and stretchers alternately in each course. Not as strong as English bond but is considered to be aesthetically superior and uses less facing bricks (79 facing bricks per m²).

Typical Example ~

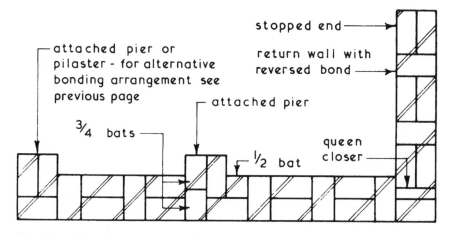

PLAN ON ODD NUMBERED COURSES

PLAN ON EVEN NUMBERED COURSES

ELEVATION

┌ I course of headers to
3 courses of stretchers

┌ I header to 3 stretchers
in each course

ENGLISH GARDEN WALL
BOND - gives quick lateral
spread of load - uses less
facings than English bond.

FLEMISH GARDEN WALL
BOND - enables a fair face
to be kept on both sides
of a one brick thick wall.

ENGLISH CROSS BOND - header placed next to end
stretcher in every other stretcher course which thus
staggers stretchers enabling patterns or diapers to be
picked out in different texture or coloured bricks.

PLAN ON ODD COURSES

┌ 2/3 bats   ┌ voids

PLAN ON EVEN COURSES

RAT TRAP BOND - uses brick on edge courses - hollow
pockets or voids reduce total weight of wall and by
the bricks on edge there is an overall saving of materials.

RAKING STRETCHER BOND

A variation of stretcher bond with less symmetry of load distribution. Each brick overlaps the brick below by a quarter.

DUTCH BOND

Similar to English cross bond using bricks of colour or texture variation to create a pattern. Three quarter bricks are used at ends instead of queen closers.

MONK BOND

Two stretcher faces to one header each course. Headers stagger and may be picked out in colour or texture differing to the stretchers. Many variations of monk bond exist.

FLEMISH CROSS BOND

Similar to Flemish bond. Two headers replace a stretcher every seventh course. Coloured or textured bricks pick out diamond shapes.

Stack Bonding – the quickest, easiest and most economical bond to lay, as there is no need to cut bricks or to provide special sizes. Visually the wall appears unbonded as continuity of vertical joints is structurally unsound, unless wire bed-joint reinforcement is placed in every horizontal course, or alternate courses where loading is moderate. In cavity walls, wall ties should be closer than normal at 600 mm max. spacing horizontally and 225 mm max. spacing vertically and staggered.

Horizontal stack bond

Vertical stack bond

Application – this distinctive uniform pattern is popular as non-structural infill panelling to framed buildings and for non-load bearing exposed brickwork partitions.

cavity wall ties at 600 mm max. horizontal spacing and 3 courses max. vertically

bed joints reinforced with high tensile mesh woven stainless steel wire in 25 or 75 m standard rolls

Reinforced stack bond

Attached Piers ~ the main function of an attached pier is to give lateral support to the wall of which it forms part from the base to the top of the wall. It also has the subsidiary function of dividing a wall into distinct lengths whereby each length can be considered as a wall. Generally walls must be tied at end to an attached pier, buttressing or return wall.

Typical Examples ~

roof giving lateral support to wall

attached pier from foundation to roof

wall

foundation

wall with no lateral support at top of wall

attached pier from foundation to top of wall

foundation

Requirements for the external wall of a small single storey non-residential building or annex exceeding 2.5 m in length or height and of floor area not exceeding 36 m²:

- Minimum thickness, 90 mm, i.e. 102.5 mm brick or 100 mm block.
- Built solid of bonded brick or block masonry and bedded in cement mortar.
- Surface mass of masonry, minimum 130 kg/m² where floor area exceeds 10 m².
- No lateral loading permitted excepting wind loads.
- Maximum length or width not greater than 9 m.
- Maximum height as shown on page 391.
- Lateral restraint provided by direct bearing of roof and as shown on page 543.
- Maximum of two major openings in one wall of the building. Height maximum 2.1 m, width maximum 5 m (if two openings, total width maximum 5 m).
- Other small openings permitted, as shown on next page.
- Bonded or connected to piers of minimum size 390 × 190 mm at maximum 3 m centres for the full wall height as shown above. Pier connections are with pairs of wall ties of 20 × 3 mm flat stainless steel type at 300 mm vertical spacing.

Attached piers as applied to half brick (90mm min.) thick walls ~

- Major openings A and B are permitted in one wall only. Aggregate width is 5m maximum. Height not greater than 2.1m. No other openings within 2m.
- Other walls not containing a major opening can have smaller openings of maximum aggregate area 2.4 m².
- Maximum of only one opening between piers.
- Distance from external corner of a wall to an opening at least 390mm unless the corner contains a pier.
- The minimum pier dimension of 390 × 190 mm can be varied to 327 × 215 mm to suit brick sizes.

Construction of half brick and 100 mm thick solid concrete block walls (90 mm min.) with attached piers, has height limitations to maintain stability. The height of these buildings will vary depending on the roof profile; it should not exceed the lesser value in the following examples ~

Detached non-residential garages and workshops

Flat roof garage attachment   Lean-to garage attachment

Pitched roof garage attachment

door and window opening limitations as previous page

NB. All dimensions are maximum.

Height is measured from top of foundation to top of wall except where shown at an intermediate position. Where the underside of the floor slab provides an effective lateral restraint, measurements may be taken from here.

Movement ~ caused by building settlement, moisture absorption and drying out and thermal expansion and contraction.

Effects ~ provided the mortar is weaker than the bricks, the effects of movement within normal expectations will be accommodated without unsightly cracking and damage. See page 423 for guidance on mortar composition and strengths.

Limitations ~ moisture and thermal movement is reversible up to a limit. Clay brick walls can move about 1mm in every 1m of wall, so for a visually and practically acceptable movement joint width of 12 mm, the spacing should not exceed 12 m. For calcium silicate (sand-lime) bricks the maximum spacing is 9 m as they have greater movement characteristics.

Applications ~
    Plan Views

Note: Joint at A in blockwork at 6 m max. spcing may be staggered, i.e. not directly opposite joint in brickwork to promote integrity and to reduce differential movement.

See page 734 for lightweight concrete block walls.

The appearance of a building can be significantly influenced by the mortar finishing treatment to masonry. Finishing may be achieved by jointing or pointing.

Jointing — the finish applied to mortar joints as the work proceeds.

Pointing — the process of removing semi-set mortar to a depth of about 20mm and replacing it with fresh mortar. Pointing may contain a colouring pigment to further enhance the masonry.

Finish Profiles, Typical Examples Shown Pointed ~

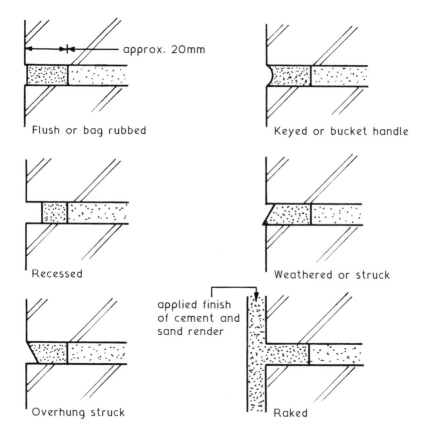

Flush or bag rubbed

Keyed or bucket handle

Recessed

Weathered or struck

Overhung struck

Raked

applied finish of cement and sand render

Examples of pointing to masonry

NB. Recessed and overhung finishes should not be used in exposed situations, as rainwater can be detained. This could encourage damage by frost action and growth of lichens.

Brickwork should be reasonably uniform in colour, texture and finish. The natural composition of clay source material is variable, even where closely extracted. Combined with kiln baking to about 1100° C, no two bricks will be identical in dimensions and shape. Therefore, some allowance for characteristic irregularities of individual units is acceptable, see page 132. When assessing acceptable thickness and tolerance of brickwork joints, overall areas are considered and not the joints between individual units.

Note: Sand lime (calcium silicate) bricks are an exception. These are produced to relatively precise dimensional tolerances with a uniformity of colour and texture, see page 381.

Bed Joints, Deviation From the Horizontal ~

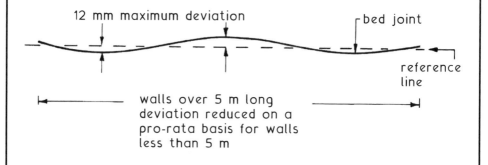

12 mm maximum deviation

bed joint

reference line

walls over 5 m long deviation reduced on a pro-rata basis for walls less than 5 m

Bed Joints, Thickness ~

8 successive joints*

individual bed joint max. 5 mm variation from the average*

perpends should not deviate significantly from the vertical

Specials – these are required for feature work and application to various bonds, as shown on the preceding pages. Bonding is not solely for aesthetic enhancement. In many applications, e.g. English bonded manhole walls, the disposition of bricks is to maximise wall strength and integrity. In a masonry wall the amount of overlap should not be less than one quarter of a brick length. Specials may be machine or hand cut from standard bricks, or they may be purchased as purpose-made. These purpose-made bricks are relatively expensive as they are individually manufactured in hardwood moulds.

Standard bricks and cut specials

Ref. BS 4729: Clay and calcium silicate bricks of special shapes and sizes. Recommendations.

Purpose-made Special Bricks

Brickwork can be repetitive and monotonous, but with a little imagination and skilled application it can be a highly decorative art form. Artistic potential is made possible by the variety of naturally occurring brick colours, textures and finishes, the latter often applied as a sanding to soft clay prior to baking. Furthermore, the range of pointing techniques, mortar colourings, brick shapes and profiles can combine to create countless possibilities for architectural expression.

Bricks are manufactured from baked clay, autoclaved sand/lime or concrete. Clay is ideally suited to hand making special shapes in hardwood moulds. Some popular formats are shown below, but there is no limit to creative possibilities.

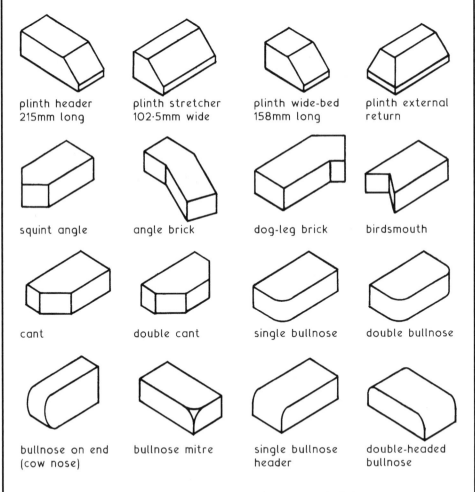

plinth header 215mm long	plinth stretcher 102·5mm wide	plinth wide-bed 158mm long	plinth external return
squint angle	angle brick	dog-leg brick	birdsmouth
cant	double cant	single bullnose	double bullnose
bullnose on end (cow nose)	bullnose mitre	single bullnose header	double-headed bullnose

Purpose-made and special shape bricks

Plinths — used as a projecting feature to enhance external wall appearance at its base. The exposed projection determines that only frost-proof quality bricks are suitable and that recessed or raked-out joints which could retain water must be avoided.

Typical External Wall Base —

Alternatives

Corbel — a projecting feature at higher levels of a building. This may be created by using plinth bricks laid upside-down with header and stretcher formats maintaining bond. For structural integrity, the amount of projection (P) must not exceed one-third of the overall wall thickness (T). Some other types of corbel are shown on the next page.

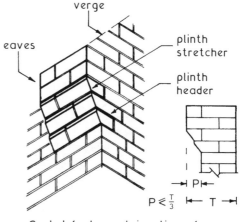

$$P \leqslant \tfrac{T}{3}$$

Corbel feature at junction of eaves and verge

397

Corbel – a type of inverted plinth, generally located at the higher levels of a building to create a feature. A typical example is quarter bonded headers as a detail below window openings.

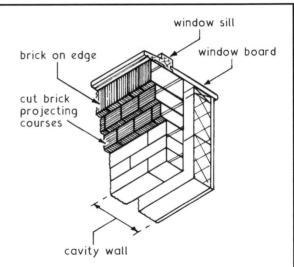

Corbelled sill

Dentil Coursing – a variation on continuous corbelling where alternative headers project. This is sometimes referred to as table corbelling.

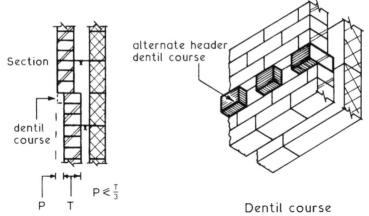

Dentil course

Dog Toothing – a variation on a dentil course created by setting the feature bricks at 45°.

Dog toothing

NB. Cavity insulated as required.

Blocks ~ these are walling units exceeding in length, width or height the dimensions specified for bricks in BS EN 772-16. Precast concrete blocks should comply with the recommendations set out in BS 6073-2 and BS EN 771-3. Blocks suitable for external solid walls are classified as load bearing and are required to have a minimum declared compressive strength of not less than 2.9 N/mm^2.

Typical Details ~

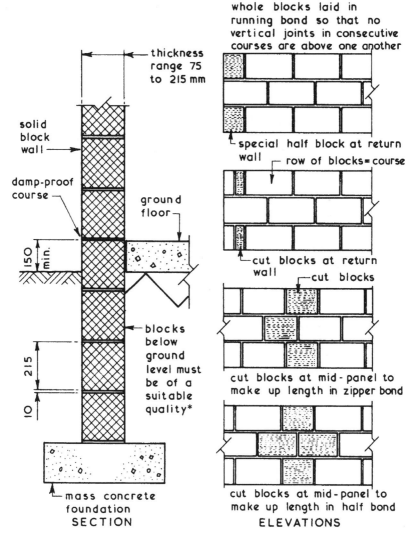

*See pages 401 to 403.

Refs.: BS 6073-2: Precast concrete masonry units.
BS EN 772-16: Methods of test for masonry units.
BS EN 771-3: Specification for (concrete) masonry units.

Cavity Walls ~ these consist of an outer brick or block leaf or skin separated from an inner brick or block leaf or skin by an air space called a cavity. These walls have better thermal insulation and weather-resistance properties than a comparable solid brick or block wall and therefore are in general use for the enclosing walls of domestic buildings. The two leaves of a cavity wall are tied together with wall ties located at $2.5/m^2$, or at equivalent spacings shown below and as given in Section 2C of Approved Document A – Building Regulations.

With butterfly-type ties the width of the cavity should be between 50 and 75 mm. Where vertical twist-type ties are used the cavity width can be between 75 and 300 mm. Cavities are not normally ventilated and are closed by roof insulation at eaves level.

WALL TIE SPACINGS

200 to 425 x 20 x 3 to 4.8mm galvanised* vertical twist-type wall tie embedded at least 50mm

200 x 3.15mm diameter galvanised* butterfly-type wall tie

TYPICAL METAL WALL TIES

Ref: BS EN 845-1: Specification for ancillary components for masonry. Wall ties, tension straps, hangers and brackets.

* Stainless steel or non-ferrous ties are now preferred.

Minimum requirements ~

Thickness of each leaf, 90 mm.

Width of cavity, 50 mm.

Wall ties at 2.5/m² (see previous page).

Compressive strength of bricks, 6 N/mm² up to two storeys.*

Compressive strength of blocks, 2.9 N/mm² up to two storeys.*

* For work between the foundation and the surface a 6 N/mm² minimum brick strength is normally specified or 2.9 N/mm² minimum concrete block strength (see next page for variations).

Combined thickness of each leaf + 10 mm whether used as an external wall, a separating wall or a compartment wall, should be not less than 1/16 of the storey height** which contains the wall.

** Generally measured between the undersides of lateral supports, e.g. undersides of floor or ceiling joists, or from the underside of upper floor joists to half-way up a laterally restrained gable wall. See Approved Document A, Section 2C for variations and next page.

Wall dimensions for minimum combined leaf thicknesses of 90 mm + 90 mm + 10 mm (190 mm min. actual thickness) ~

Height	Length
3.5 m max.	12.0 m max.
3.5 m – 9.0 m	9.0 m max.

Wall dimensions for minimum combined leaf thickness of 280 mm + 10 mm (290 mm actual thickness), e.g. 190 mm + 100 mm for one storey height and a minimum 180 mm combined leaf thickness + 10 mm (i.e. 90 mm + 100 mm) for the remainder of its height ~

Height	Length
3.5 – 9.0 m	9.0 – 12.0 m
9.0 m – 12.0 m	9.0 m max.

Wall dimensions for minimum combined leaf thickness of 280 mm + 10 mm (290 mm actual thickness) for two-storey height and a minimum 180 mm combined leaf thickness + 10 mm (190 mm actual thickness) for the remainder of its height ~

Height	Length
9.0 m – 12.0 m	9.0 m – 12.0 m

Wall length is measured from centre to centre of restraints by buttress walls, piers or chimneys.

For other wall applications, see the reference to calculated brickwork on page 419.

Cavity Walls

Single storey

Two storeys

timber roof construction

H

← A   → A

H
→ A   ← A
A   A

↑ A   ↑ A

upper level of floor

upper level of floor

A if < 1 m   140 mm min.
B if > 1 m   concrete block
              or 215 mm
              brick if > 1 m

Three storeys

timber roof construction

H
→ A   ← A
← B

H
→ A   ← A
← B

H
← C   → B
← B

← C   B →
← B

upper level of floor

140 mm min.
concrete block
or 215 mm brick

Key for H ≤ 2.7 m (N/mm²
min. compressive strength) ~

	Conc.blocks	Bricks
A	2.9	6.0
B	7.3	9.0
C	7.3	18.0

Note 1: If H > 2.7 m, A should be at least 7.3 N/mm² for concrete blocks and 9 N/mm² for brickwork, or as indicated in the diagrams (take greater value).

Note 2: The above applies to standard format bricks of 215 mm × 102.5 mm × 65 mm with < 25% formed voids (20% for bricks with frogs). For bricks with voids > 25% (max. 55%) see Table 6 in Approved Document A, Section 2C.

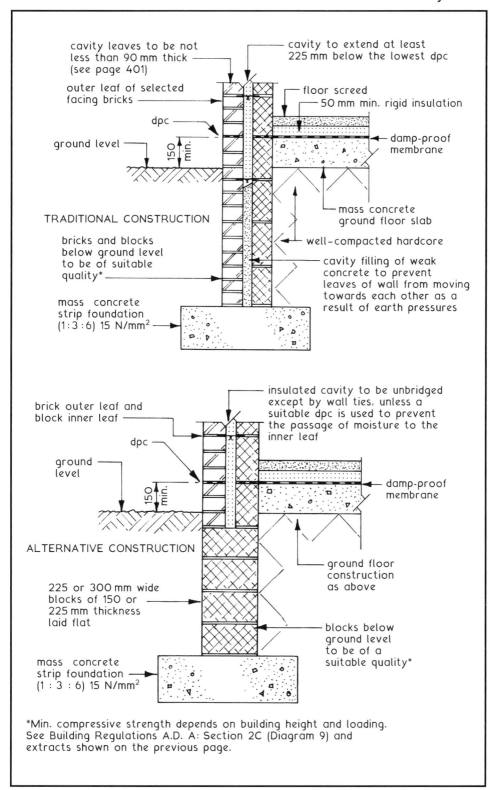

cavity leaves to be not less than 90 mm thick (see page 401)

cavity to extend at least 225 mm below the lowest dpc

outer leaf of selected facing bricks

floor screed

50 mm min. rigid insulation

dpc

ground level

150 min.

damp-proof membrane

TRADITIONAL CONSTRUCTION

mass concrete ground floor slab

bricks and blocks below ground level to be of suitable quality*

well-compacted hardcore

cavity filling of weak concrete to prevent leaves of wall from moving towards each other as a result of earth pressures

mass concrete strip foundation (1:3:6) 15 N/mm²

insulated cavity to be unbridged except by wall ties, unless a suitable dpc is used to prevent the passage of moisture to the inner leaf

brick outer leaf and block inner leaf

dpc

ground level

150 min.

damp-proof membrane

ALTERNATIVE CONSTRUCTION

ground floor construction as above

225 or 300 mm wide blocks of 150 or 225 mm thickness laid flat

blocks below ground level to be of a suitable quality*

mass concrete strip foundation (1 : 3 : 6) 15 N/mm²

*Min. compressive strength depends on building height and loading. See Building Regulations A.D. A: Section 2C (Diagram 9) and extracts shown on the previous page.

Parapet ~ a low wall projecting above the level of a roof, bridge or balcony forming a guard or barrier at the edge. Parapets are exposed to the elements, justifying careful design and construction for durability.

Typical Details ~

precast concrete weathered coping

40mm min.

dpc

brickwork of "moderate" exposure specification*

thickness of wall as given in Diagram 4 in AD 'A'

roof slab, vapour control layer, screed and covering

T (1 bk. solid and 1/2 bk. cavity wall). H ⩾860mm.

SOLID WALL- HIGH LEVEL

precast concrete weathered coping

rigid dpc over cavity

flexible non-ferrous metal flashing & dpc

weep holes at 900 c/c

150 min.

roof slab, vapour control layer, screed and finish

CAVITY WALL- HIGH LEVEL

350mm max. if above adopt high level detail

roof as above

SOLID WALL- LOW LEVEL

350mm max. if above adopt high level detail

roof as above

CAVITY WALL- LOW LEVEL

Ref. BS EN 771-1: Specification for (clay) masonry units.

*'severe' exposure specification in the absence of a protective coping.

Historically, finned or buttressed walls have been used to provide lateral support to tall, single storey masonry structures such as churches and cathedrals. Modern applications are similar in principle and include theatres, gymnasiums, warehouses, etc. Where space permits, they are an economic alternative to masonry cladding of steel or reinforced concrete framed buildings. The fin or pier is preferably brick bonded to the main wall. It may also be connected with horizontally bedded wall ties, sufficient to resist vertical shear stresses between fin and wall.

BONDED FIN WALL   TIED FIN WALL

Structurally, the fins are deep piers which reinforce solid or cavity masonry walls. For design purposes the wall may be considered as a series of 'T' sections composed of a flange and a pier. If the wall is of cavity construction, the inner leaf is not considered for bending moment calculations, although it does provide stiffening to the outer leaf or flange.

FIN WALL AS A STRUCTURAL 'T' SECTION

405

Masonry diaphragm walls are an alternative means of constructing tall, single storey buildings such as warehouses, sports centres, churches, assembly halls, etc. They can also be used as retaining and boundary walls with planting potential within the voids. These voids may also be steel reinforced and concrete filled to resist the lateral stresses in high retaining walls.

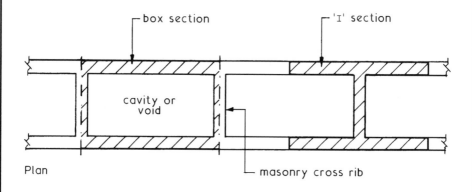

box section   'I' section

cavity or void

Plan   masonry cross rib

A diaphragm wall is effectively a cavity wall where the two leaves of masonry are bonded together with cross ribs and not wall ties. It is stronger than a conventionally tied cavity wall and for structural purposes may be considered as a series of bonded 'I' sections or box sections. The voids may be useful for housing services, but any access holes in the construction must not disturb the integrity of the wall. The voids may also be filled with insulation to reduce heat energy losses from the building, and to prevent air circulatory heat losses within the voids. Where thermal insulation standards apply, this type of wall will have limitations as the cross ribs will provide a route for cold bridging. U-values will increase by about 10% compared with conventional cavity wall construction of the same materials.

Ref. BS EN 1996: Design of masonry structures.
      PD 6697: Recommendations for the design of masonry structures.

Individual masonry units may not be uniform in dimensions and shape. This characteristic is particularly applicable to natural stone masonry and to kiln manufactured clay bricks. Dimensional variations and other irregularities must be accommodated within an area of walling. The following is acceptable:

Vertical Alignment and Straightness ~

*Walls > 5m height, max. 12mm out of plumb. Limited to 8mm/storey height. E.g. typical storey height of 2.5m = 3.2mm/m.

Horizontal Alignment ~

Damp-proof Courses and Membranes

Function – the primary function of any damp-proof course (dpc) or damp-proof membrane (dpm) is to provide an impermeable barrier to the passage of moisture. The three basic ways in which damp-proof courses are used is to:

1. Resist moisture penetration from below (rising damp).
2. Resist moisture penetration from above.
3. Resist moisture penetration from horizontal entry.

Typical Examples ~

PENETRATION FROM BELOW
(Ground Floor/External Wall)

PENETRATION FROM ABOVE
(Window/Door Head)

HORIZONTAL ENTRY (Window/Door Jamb)

See also: BSs 743, 6398, 6515, 8102 and 8215.

408

Building Regulations, Approved Document C2, Section 5:
A wall may be built with a 'damp-proof course of bituminous material,
polyethylene, engineering bricks or slates in cement mortar, or any
other material that will prevent the passage of moisture.'

Material	Remarks
Lead BS EN 12588 Code 4 (1·8 mm)	May corrode in the presence of mortar. Both surfaces to be coated with bituminous paint. Workable for application to cavity trays, etc.
Copper BS EN 1172 0·25 mm	Can cause staining to adjacent masonry. Resistant to corrosion.

Bitumen   BS 6398 in various bases:
  Hessian   3·8 kg/m²
  Fibre   3·3 ·· ··
  Asbestos   3·8 ·· ··
  Hessian & lead   4·4 ·· ··
  Fibre & lead   4·4 ·· ··
	Hessian or fibre may decay with age, but this will not affect efficiency. Tearable if not protected. Lead bases are suited where there may be a high degree of movement in the wall. Asbestos is now prohibited.

LDPE BS 6515 0·46 mm (polyethylene)	No deterioration likely, but may be difficult to bond, hence the profiled surface finish. Not suited under light loads.
Bitumen polymer and pitch polymer 1·10 mm	Absorbs movement well. Joints and angles made with product manufacturer's adhesive tape.
Polypropylene BS 5139 1.5 to 2.0 mm	Preformed dpc for cavity trays, cloaks, direction changes and over lintels.

NB. All the above dpcs to be lapped at least 100 mm at joints and
adhesive sealed. Dpcs should be continuous with any dpm in the floor.

Material			Remarks
Mastic asphalt	BS 6925	$12\,kg/m^2$	Does not deteriorate. Requires surface treatment with sand or scoring to effect a mortar key.
Engineering bricks	BS EN 771-1 BS EN 772-7	<4·5% absorption	Min. two courses laid breaking joint in cement mortar 1:3. No deterioration, but may not blend with adjacent facings.
Slate	BS EN 12326-1	4 mm	Min. two courses laid as above. Will not deteriorate, but brittle so may fracture if building settles.

Refs.:

BS 743: Specification for materials for damp-proof courses.

BS 8102: Code of practice for protection of structures against water from the ground.

BS 8215: Code of practice for design and installation of damp-proof courses in masonry construction.

BRE Digest 380: Damp-proof courses.

Note: It was not until the Public Health Act of 1875, that it became mandatory to install damp-proof courses in new buildings. Structures constructed before that time, and those since, which have suffered dpc failure due to deterioration or incorrect installation, will require remedial treatment. This could involve cutting out the mortar bed-joint two brick courses above ground level in stages of about 1m in length. A new dpc can then be inserted with mortar packing, before proceeding to the next length. No two adjacent sections should be worked consecutively. This process is very time consuming and may lead to some structural settlement. Therefore, the measures explained on the following two pages are usually preferred.

Materials – Silicone solutions in organic solvent.
      Aluminium stearate solutions.
      Water-soluble silicone formulations (siliconates).

Methods – High pressure injection (0·70–0·90 MPa) solvent based.
      Low pressure injection (0·15–0·30 MPa) water based.
      Gravity feed, water based.
      Insertion/injection, mortar based.

Pressure injection – 12mm diameter holes are bored to about two-thirds the depth of masonry, at approximately 150mm horizontal intervals at the appropriate depth above ground (normally two to three brick courses). These holes can incline slightly downwards. With high (low) pressure injection, walls in excess of 120mm (460 mm) thickness should be drilled from both sides. The chemical solution is injected by pressure pump until it exudes from the masonry. Cavity walls are treated as each leaf being a solid wall.

Gravity feed – 25mm diameter holes are bored as above. Dilute chemical is transfused from containers which feed tubes inserted in the holes. This process can take from a few hours to several days to effect. An alternative application is insertion of frozen pellets placed in the boreholes. On melting, the solution disperses into the masonry to be replaced with further pellets until the wall is saturated.

water-soluble silicon

reservoirs attached to tubes in boreholes at max. 175mm spacing

$\dfrac{2T}{3}$

T

25mm diameter inclined borehole into bed-joint

Gravity infusion of silicon in solution

Injection mortars – 19 mm diameter holes are bored from both sides of a wall, at the appropriate level and no more than 230 mm apart horizontally, to a depth equating to three-fifths of the wall thickness. They should be inclined downwards at an angle of 20 to 30°. The drill holes are flushed out with water, before injecting mortar from the base of the hole and outwards. This can be undertaken with a hand operated caulking gun. Special cement mortars contain styrene butadiene resin (SDR) or epoxy resin and must be mixed in accordance with the manufacturer's guidance.

Notes relating to all applications of chemical dpcs:

* Before commencing work, old plasterwork and rendered undercoats are removed to expose the masonry. This should be to a height of at least 300 mm above the last detectable (moisture meter reading) signs of rising dampness (1 metre min.).

* If the wall is only accessible from one side and both sides need treatment, a second deeper series of holes may be bored from one side, to penetrate the inaccessible side.

* On completion of work, all boreholes are made good with cement mortar. Where dilute chemicals are used for the dpc, the mortar is rammed the full length of the hole with a piece of timber dowelling.

* The chemicals are effective by bonding to, and lining the masonry pores by curing and solvent evaporation.

* The process is intended to provide an acceptable measure of control over rising dampness. A limited amount of water vapour may still rise, but this should be dispersed by evaporation in a heated building.

Refs.:

BS 6576: Code of practice for diagnosis of rising damp in walls of buildings and installation of chemical damp-proof courses.
BRE Digest 245: Rising damp in walls: diagnosis and treatment.
BRE Digest 380: Damp-proof courses.
BRE Good Repair Guide 6: Treating rising damp in houses.

In addition to damp-proof courses failing due to deterioration or damage, they may be bridged as a result of:

* Faults occurring during construction.
* Work undertaken after construction, with disregard for the damp-proof course.

Typical Examples ~

Solid walls

paving or earth stacked against wall — dpc — original ground level

external rendering over the dpc — dpm

bridging through repointing — screed

Cavity walls

surface dpm — dpc — poor quality concrete and screed

dpm — misalignment of dpc and dpm

mortar droppings in cavity — poor workmanship

Thermal insulation regulations may require insulating dpcs to prevent cold bridging around window and door openings in cavity wall construction (see pages 580 and 581). By locating a vertical dpc with a bonded insulant at the cavity closure, the dpc prevents penetration of dampness from the outside, and the insulation retains the structural temperature of the internal reveal. This will reduce heat losses by maintaining the temperature above dewpoint, preventing condensation, wall staining and mould growth.

Application ~

width to suit application

polyethylene dpc bonded to expanded polystyrene (insulation only) or 25 mm compressible mineral wool (insulation and fire resistance)

facing brick outer leaf

cavity insulated as required

lightweight insulating block inner leaf

Isometric perspective

plastic ties clipped into cavity closer recess

cut block cavity closer

Plan

Alternative ~ uPVC full cavity closer/cavity barrier with non-combustible rock mineral wool core.
Note: products with EPS core can be used where fire integrity is not critical.

wall tie with insulation retainer

Refs.: Building Regulations, Approved Document L: Conservation of fuel and power.
BRE Report – Thermal Insulation: avoiding risks (3rd. ed.).
Building Regulations, Approved Document B3 (Vol. 1), Section 6: Concealed spaces (cavities).

Penetrating Gases ~ Methane and Radon

Methane – methane is produced by deposited organic material decaying in the ground. It often occurs with carbon dioxide and traces of other gases to form a cocktail known as landfill gas. It has become an acute problem in recent years, as planning restrictions on 'green-field' sites have forced development of derelict and reclaimed 'brown-field' land.

The gas would normally escape into the atmosphere, but under a building it pressurises until percolating through cracks, cavities and junctions with services. Being odourless, it is not easily detected until contacting a naked flame, then the result is devastating!

Radon ~ a naturally occurring colour/odourless gas produced by radioactive decay of radium. It originates in uranium deposits of granite subsoils as far apart as the south-west and north of England and the Grampian region of Scotland. Concentrations of radon are considerably increased if the building is constructed of granite masonry. The combination of radon gas and the tiny radioactive particles known as radon daughters are inhaled. In some people with several years' exposure, research indicates a high correlation with cancer related illness and death.

Protection of buildings and the occupants from subterranean gases can be achieved by passive or active measures incorporated within the structure:

1. Passive protection consists of a complete airtight seal integrated within the ground floor and walls. A standard LDPE damp-proof membrane of 0.3mm thickness should be adequate if carefully sealed at joints, but thicknesses of up to 1mm are preferred, combined with foil and/or wire reinforcement.

2. Active protection requires installation of a permanently running extract fan connected to a gas sump below the ground floor. It is an integral part of the building services system and will incur operating and maintenance costs throughout the building's life.

NB. See next page for construction details.

Gas-resistant Construction

Suspended concrete floor   PASSIVE

cavity wall insulated as required

stepped cavity tray/dpc

screed

insulation

LDPE membrane min. 1200 gauge (0.3 mm)

weep hole

air brick

dpc

sealed joint

precast reinforced concrete floor

min. 150mm

Solid floor (2 possibilities)

reinforced concrete slab

LDPE membrane   finished slab level

damp- and gas-proof membrane

vent outlet above eaves

vent riser if trench paved over

granular trench

min. 200 mm granular layer

subfloor vent pipe

EPS profiled matting heights — 80, 100, 150 & 200 mm

reinforced concrete slab

LDPE membrane   paving slab

ACTIVE

fan

110 mm uPVC extract duct

void

perforated bricks

granular fill

sump centrally located

Calculated Brickwork ~ for small and residential buildings up to three storeys high the sizing of load bearing brick walls can be taken from data given in Section 2C of Approved Document A. The alternative methods for these and other load bearing brick walls are given in:

BS EN 1996: Design of masonry structures.
BS 8103-2: Structural design of low rise buildings. Code of practice for masonry walls for housing.

The main factors governing the load bearing capacity of brick walls and columns are:

1. Thickness of Wall.
2. Strength of bricks used.
3. Type of mortar used.
4. Slenderness ratio of wall or column.
5. Eccentricity of applied load.

Thickness of Wall ~ this must always be sufficient throughout its entire body to carry the design loads and induced stresses. Other design requirements such as thermal and sound insulation properties must also be taken into account when determining the actual wall thickness to be used.

Effective Thickness ~ this is the assumed thickness of the wall or column used for the purpose of calculating its slenderness ratio – see page 419.

Typical Examples ~

COLUMN OR ISOLATED PIER
effective thickness = t_P

SOLID WALL
eff. th. = t

CAVITY WALL
eff. th. = $\frac{2}{3}(t_1 + t_2)$
or t_1 or t_2 (take greater)

CAVITY WALL STIFFENED BY PIER

effective thickness
= $\frac{2}{3}(t_1 +$ effective thickness $t_2)$
effective thickness of t_2 can be ascertained by multiplying t_2 by a stiffening coefficient (see page 420)

Strength of Bricks ~ due to the wide variation of the raw materials and methods of manufacture bricks can vary greatly in their compressive strength. The compressive strength of a particular type of brick or batch of bricks is taken as the arithmetic mean of a sample of ten bricks tested in accordance with the appropriate British Standard. A typical range for clay bricks would be from 20 to 170 MN/m² the majority of which would be in the 20 to 90 MN/m² band. Calcium silicate bricks have a compressive strength between 20 and 50 MN/m².

Strength of Mortars ~ mortars consist of an aggregate (sand) and a binder which is usually cement; cement plus additives to improve workability; or cement and lime. The factors controlling the strength of any particular mix are the ratio of binder to aggregate plus the water:cement ratio. The strength of any particular mix can be ascertained by taking the arithmetic mean of a series of test cubes or prisms – see page 423.

Wall Design Strength ~ the basic stress of any brickwork depends on the crushing strength of the bricks and the type of mortar used to form the wall unit. This relationship can be plotted on a graph as shown below:

NB. 1 MN/m² equates to 1 N/mm².

Slenderness Ratio ~ this is the relationship of the effective height to the effective thickness thus:

$$\text{Slenderness ratio} = \frac{\text{effective height}}{\text{effective thickness}} = \frac{h}{t} \not> 27$$

Effective Height ~ this is the dimension taken to calculate the slenderness ratio as opposed to the actual height.

Typical Examples – actual height = H   effective height = h

NO LATERAL SUPPORT
AT TOP

CONCRETE FLOOR
BEARING ON WALL

FLOOR EFFECTIVELY
TIED TO WALL
(see pages 771 & 773)

Effective Thickness ~ this is the dimension taken to calculate the slenderness ratio as opposed to the actual thickness.

Typical Examples – actual thickness = T effective thickness = t

SOLID WALLS

CAVITY WALLS

WALLS STIFFENED BY PIERS

$t = T$

$t = 0.66(T_1 + T_2)$
or T_1 or T_2
(take greater)

stiffening pier or wall

$t = T \times$ stiffening coefficient
(see next page)

Stress Reduction ~ the permissible stress for a wall is based on the basic stress multiplied by a reduction factor related to the slenderness factor and the eccentricity of the load:

$\frac{T}{6}$ eccentricity is expressed as a fraction of wall's thickness

Piers, Effective Thickness ~

Effective Thickness = tK

Effective Thickness = 0.66 (t_1+t_2K) or t_1 or t_2K (take greater)

Key: t = actual wall thickness
t_1 = actual thickness of cavity leaf without attached pier
t_2 = actual thickness of leaf with attached pier
tp = pier thickness
K = stiffening coefficient
Sp = pier spacing
Wp = pier width

Stiffening Coefficient K ~

$Sp \div Wp$	$tp \div t$ = 1	2	3
≤ 6	K = 1.0	1.4	2.0
10	1.0	1.2	1.4
≥ 20	1.0	1.0	1.0

Linear interpolation may be applied

E.g.

$Sp \div Wp = 2150 \div 215 = 10$
$tp \div t = 328 \div 215 = 1.523$
By interpolation, K = 1.104
Effective thickness, tK = 215 × 1.104 = 237.4 mm

Piers and Columns, Effective Height Calculations ~

tp ≤ 1.5t design
as a pier

tp > 1.5t design as a column
effective thickness = tp or b
depending on direction of bending

E.g. A one-and-a-half brick column of 4.000m effective height/ length. See page 645 for factors affecting the effective length of a column.

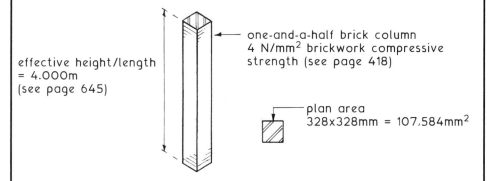

effective height/length
= 4.000m
(see page 645)

one-and-a-half brick column
4 N/mm² brickwork compressive
strength (see page 418)

plan area
328x328mm = 107,584mm²

It is usual to incorporate a factor of safety into these calculations. Using a figure of 2, the brickwork safe bearing strength will be:

$$4\,\text{N/mm}^2 \div 2 = 2\,\text{N/mm}^2$$

Permissible load will be:

$$2\,\text{N/mm}^2 \times 107{,}584 = 215{,}168\,\text{Newtons}$$

$$\text{Newtons} \div \text{gravity}\ (9.81\,\text{m/s}^2) = \text{kilograms}$$

$$215{,}168 \div 9.81 = 21{,}933\,\text{kg}\ (22\,\text{tonnes approx.})$$

Note: This example is a very simple application that has assumed that there is no axial loading with bending or eccentric forces such as lateral loading from the structure or from wind loading. It also has a low slenderness ratio (effective height/length to least lateral dimension), i.e. 4000 mm ÷ 328 mm = 12.2. See pages 602 and 603 for the effect of buckling factors where greater slenderness ratios apply.

Lime ~ traditional mortars are a combination of lime, sand and water. These mixes are very workable and have sufficient flexibility to accommodate a limited amount of wall movement due to settlement, expansion and contraction. The long term durability of lime mortars is poor as they can break down in the presence of atmospheric contaminants and surface growths. Nevertheless, lime is frequently specified as a supplementary binder with cement, to increase mix workability and to reduce the possibility of joint shrinkage and cracking, a characteristic of stronger cement mortars.

Cement ~ the history of cement-type mortar products is extensive. Examples dating back to the Mesopotamians and the Egyptians are not unusual; one of the earliest examples from over 10,000 years ago has been found in Galilee, Israel. Modern mortars are made with Portland cement, the name attributed to a bricklayer named Joseph Aspdin. In 1824 he patented his improved hydraulic lime product as Portland cement, as it resembled Portland stone in appearance. It was not until the 1920s that Portland cement, as we now know it, was first produced commercially by mixing a slurry of clay (silica, alumina and iron-oxides) with limestone (calcium carbonate). The mix is burnt in a furnace (calcinated) and the resulting clinker crushed and bagged.

Mortar ~ mixes for masonry should have the following properties:

* Adequate strength
* Workability
* Water retention during laying
* Plasticity during application
* Adhesion or bond
* Durability
* Good appearance ~ texture and colour

Modern mortars are a combination of cement, lime and sand plus water. Liquid plasticisers exist as a substitute for lime, to improve workability and to provide some resistance to frost when used during winter.

Masonry cement ~ these proprietary cements generally contain about 75% Portland cement and about 25% of fine limestone filler with an air entraining plasticiser. Allowance must be made when specifying the mortar constituents to allow for the reduced cement content. These cements are not suitable for concrete.

Refs.: BS 6463-101, 102 and 103: Quicklime, hydrated lime and natural calcium carbonate.
BS EN 197-1: Cement. Composition, specifications and conformity criteria for common cements.

Ready mixed mortar ~ this is delivered dry for storage in purpose-made silos with integral mixers as an alternative to site blending and mixing. This ensures:

* Guaranteed factory quality controlled product
* Convenience
* Mix consistency between batches
* Convenient facility for satisfying variable demand
* Limited wastage
* Optimum use of site space

Mortar and cement strength ~ see also page 418. Test samples are made in prisms of 40×40 mm cross section, 160mm long. At 28 days samples are broken in half to test for flexural strength. The broken pieces are subject to a compression test across the 40 mm width. An approximate comparison between mortar strength $(MN/m^2$ or $N/mm^2)$, mortar designations (i to v) and proportional mix ratios is shown in the classification table below. Included is guidance on application.

Proportional mixing of mortar constituents by volume is otherwise known as a prescribed mix or simply a recipe.

Mortar classification ~

Traditional designation	BS EN 998-2 Strength	Proportions by volume cement/lime/sand	cement/sand	Application
i	12	1:0.25:3	1:3	Exposed external
ii	6	1:0.5:4–4.5	1:3–4	General external
iii	4	1:1:5–6	1:5–6	Sheltered internal
iv	2	1:2:8–9	1:7–8	General internal
v	–	1:3:10–12	1:9–10	Internal, grouting

Relevant standards;

BS EN 1996: Design of masonry structures.
BS EN 196: Methods of testing cement.
BS EN 998-2: Specification for mortar for masonry. Masonry mortar.
PD 6678: Guide to the specification of masonry mortar.
BS EN 1015: Methods of test for mortar for masonry.

Supports Over Openings ~ the primary function of any support over an opening is to carry the loads above the opening and transmit them safely to the abutments, jambs or piers on both sides. A support over an opening is usually required since the opening infilling such as a door or window frame will not have sufficient strength to carry the load through its own members.

Type of Support ~

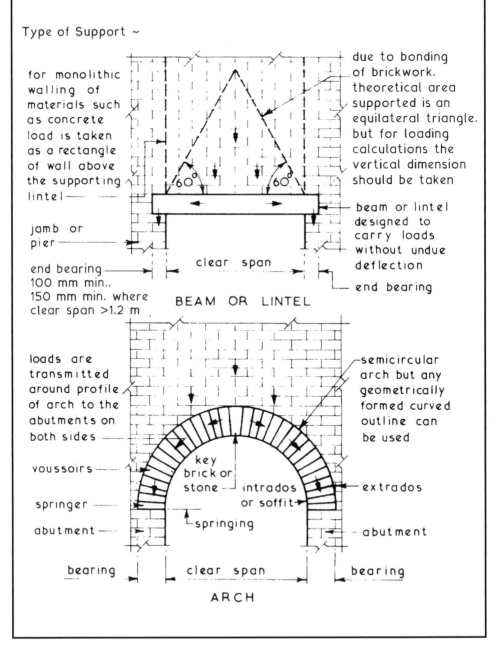

for monolithic walling of materials such as concrete load is taken as a rectangle of wall above the supporting lintel

due to bonding of brickwork, theoretical area supported is an equilateral triangle, but for loading calculations the vertical dimension should be taken

60°   60°

jamb or pier

beam or lintel designed to carry loads without undue deflection

end bearing 100 mm min., 150 mm min. where clear span >1.2 m

clear span

end bearing

BEAM OR LINTEL

loads are transmitted around profile of arch to the abutments on both sides

semicircular arch but any geometrically formed curved outline can be used

voussoirs

key brick or stone   intrados or soffit

springing

extrados

springer

abutment

abutment

bearing

clear span

bearing

ARCH

Arch Construction ~ by the arrangement of the bricks or stones in an arch over an opening it will be self-supporting once the jointing material has set and gained adequate strength. The arch must therefore be constructed over a temporary support until the arch becomes self-supporting. The traditional method is to use a framed timber support called a centre. Permanent arch centres are also available for small spans and simple formats.

Typical Arch Formats ~

CAMBER ARCH

SEGMENTAL ARCH

DROP ARCH

3 CENTRE ARCH

ELEVATION

SECTION

TIMBER FRAMED CENTRE FOR SPANS UP TO 1·500

The profile of an arch does not lend itself to simple positioning of a damp-proof course. At best, it can be located horizontally at upper extrados level. This leaves the depth of the arch and masonry below the dpc vulnerable to dampness. Proprietary galvanised or stainless steel cavity trays resolve this problem by providing:

* Continuity of dpc around the extrados.

* Arch support/centring during construction.

* Arch and wall support after construction.

stainless or galvanised steel cavity tray and arch support

feature stone or brick voussoirs

concrete block inner leaf

brick outer leaf

tray follows profile of arch opening

expanded metal key for plaster

Section

Standard profiles are made to the traditional outlines shown on the previous two pages, in spans up to 2 m. Other options may also be available from some manufacturers. Irregular shapes and spans can be made to order.

Note: Arches in semicircular, segmental or parabolic form up to 2 m span can be proportioned empirically. For integrity of structure it is important to ensure sufficient provision of masonry over and around any arch.

The example in steel shown on the preceding page combines structural support with a damp-proof course, without the need for temporary support from a centre. Where traditional centring is retained, a lightweight preformed polypropylene cavity tray/dpc can be used. These factory-made plastic trays are produced in various thicknesses of 1.5 to 3 mm relative to spans up to about 2 m. Arch centres are made to match the tray profile and with care can be reused several times.

An alternative material is code 4 lead sheet.* Lead is an adaptable material but relatively heavy. Therefore, its suitability is limited to small spans particularly with non-standard profiles.

*BS EN 12588: Lead and lead alloys. Rolled lead sheet for building purposes. Lead sheet is coded numerically from 3 to 8 (1.25 to 3.50 mm – see page 531), which closely relates to the traditional specification in lbs./sq. ft.

lightweight concrete block inner leaf

polypropylene cavity tray/dpc

brick or cut stone arch

facing brick outer leaf

Ref. BS EN 1996: Design of masonry structures.

427

Openings ~ these consist of a head, jambs and sill. Different methods can be used in their formation, all with the primary objective of adequate support around the void. Details relate to older/existing construction and where thermal insulation is not critical. Application limited – see pages 580 and 581.

Typical Head Details ~

dpc to extend 150 mm beyond ends of lintel

precast concrete lintel BS EN 845-2

prestressed plank lintel with 2 courses of bricks over

EXPOSED LINTEL   PRESTRESSED LINTEL

dpc

pressed steel outer lintel

precast concrete lintel

weep holes at 900 ᶜ/c for exposed walls and lintels over 1·350 long

BOOT LINTEL   COMPOSITE LINTEL

dpc

pressed steel lintel

precast concrete lintel

galvanised mild steel angle outer lintel

mastic seal

PRESSED STEEL LINTEL   COMPOSITE LINTEL

Ref. BS EN 845-2: Specification for ancillary components for masonry. Lintels.

Jambs ~ these may be bonded as in solid walls or unbonded as in cavity walls. The latter must have some means of preventing the ingress of moisture from the outer leaf to the inner leaf and hence the interior of the building. Details as preceding page.

Application limited — see pages 580 and 581.

Typical Jamb Details ~

*Ref. BS 1245: Pedestrian doorsets and door frames made from sheet steel. Sepcification.

Sills ~ the primary function of any sill is to collect the rainwater which has run down the face of the window or door and shed it clear of the wall below.

Timber Sill 1, Cast Stone Subsill and Slate Sill have limited applications – see pages 580 and 581.
Typical Sill details ~

TIMBER SILL 1

TIMBER SILL 2

softwood window frame with hardwood sill

softwood casement window

quarry tile internal sill

softwood or mdf window board

solid wall

cavity wall

cavity insulation

38

dpc

CAST STONE SUBSILL

SLATE SILL

softwood casement window

softwood window board

combined slate sill and window board

galvanised metal water bar bedded in mastic

cast stone or concrete sill as subsill

38

dpc

Ref. BS 5642-1: Sills and copings. Specification for window sills of precast concrete, cast stone, clayware, slate and natural stone.

430

Traditional Construction – checked rebates or recesses in masonry solid walls were often provided at openings to accommodate door and window frames. This detail was used as a means to complement frame retention and prevent weather intrusion.

Typical checked masonry (pre-1940s)

Exposure Zones – checked reveal treatment is now required mainly where wind-driven rain will have most impact. This is primarily in the south-west and west coast areas of the British Isles, plus some isolated inland parts that will be identified by their respective local authorities.

Typical Checked Opening Details –

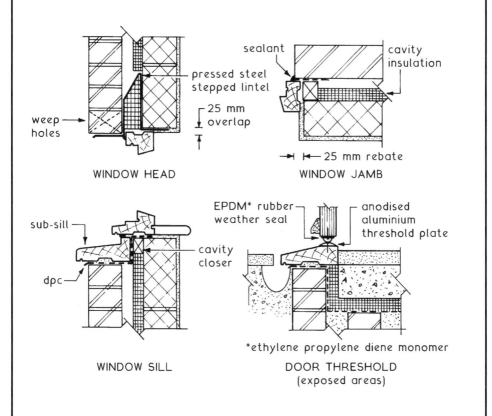

WINDOW HEAD

WINDOW JAMB

WINDOW SILL

DOOR THRESHOLD
(exposed areas)

*ethylene propylene diene monomer

Ref. Building Regulations, Approved Document C. Section 5: Walls. Driving rain exposure zones 3 and 4.

431

A window must be aesthetically acceptable in the context of building design and the surrounding environment.

glass and glazing to be suitable for window position and type

suitable and durable materials required for framing

thermal and sound insulation properties to be acceptable to client and within Building Regs.

sizing of openings to meet requirements of Building Regulations for limiting heat losses and fire escape

windows should be weather tight when opening lights are closed

perimeter joint to be adequately sealed

Windows should be selected or designed to resist wind loadings, be easy to clean and provide for safety and security. They should be sited to provide visual contact with the outside.

Habitable upper floor rooms should have a window for emergency escape. Min. opening area, $0.330m^2$. Min. height and width, $0.450m$. Max height of opening, $1.100m$ above floor.

sash side hung
opening out —

sash top hung
opening out —

FIXED LIGHT
usually used in
conjunction with
other types

SIDE HUNG
CASEMENT
simplest and
cheapest type
of opening window

TOP HUNG
CASEMENT
usually of small
size for controlled
ventilation

sash bottom
hung opening
in —

sash hung on centre
pivots —

BOTTOM HUNG
CASEMENT
use as for top
hung casement

VERTICAL
PIVOT

HORIZONTAL
PIVOT

high performance windows - dearer
than casement types - can be obtained
as reversible for easy cleaning

sashes hung on spring
balances or weights —

sashes run on
guide rails —

louvres hung on
centre pivots —

DOUBLE HUNG
SLIDING SASH

HORIZONTAL
SLIDING SASH

LOUVRE

gives good controlled ventilation
without any forward or backward
projection of sash

good ventilation
with only small
projections of
louvres

433

horn for
building in

frame head

top hung
ventilator

frame
jamb

side
hung
sash

mullion

frame sill

70 × 45
head

45 × 40
sash
framing

transom

glass

plastic
draught
sealer

TRADITIONAL

framed
fixed
light

horn

top hung ventilator

95 × 57 head

transom

side
hung
sash

transom

mullion

frame sill

direct glazed fixed sublight

frame
jamb

direct
glazed
fixed
light

putty

plastic
draught
sealer

glass

plastic
draught
sealer

41 × 46
sash
framing

134 × 70
sill

TYPICAL ELEVATIONS

TYPICAL VERTICAL SECTION
OF MODIFIED BS WINDOW

The standard range of casement windows used in the UK was derived from the English Joinery Manufacturer's Association (EJMA) designs of some 50 years ago. These became adopted in BS 644: Timber windows and doorsets. Fully finished factory assembled windows of various types. Specification. A modified type is shown on the preceding page. Contemporary building standards require higher levels of performance in terms of thermal and sound insulation (Bldg. Regs. Pt. L and E), air permeability, watertightness and wind resistance (BS ENs 1026, 1027 and 12211, respectively). This has been achieved by adapting Scandinavian designs with double and triple glazing to attain U-values as low as 1·2 W/m²K and a sound reduction of 50 dB.

ex. 100 × 75 mm head
ventilator void
ex. 75 × 63 mm sash
silicon sealed planted bead
hollow spacer with desiccant filling
28 mm factory sealed double glazing unit (20 mm air gap)
weather strip
pvc gasket/ setting block
lower glazing bead
sash
sash
ex. 150 × 75 mm sill
void to accommodate reversible hinge for easy cleaning
frame jamb

Horizontal section

Vertical section

Further refs.:
BS 6375 series: Performance of windows and doors.
BS 6375-1: Classification for weather tightness.
BS 6375-2: Classification for operation and strength characteristics.
PAS 24: Enhanced security performance requirements for doorsets and windows in the UK

HORIZONTAL SECTION B-B   VERTICAL SECTION A-A

Details show EJMA (see previous page) standardised designs for casements with double glazed factory produced hermetically sealed units. In the early 1960s EJMA evolved into the British Woodworking Manufacturers Association (BWMA) and subsequently the British Woodworking Federation (bWf). Although dated, the principles of these designs remain current.

436

Metal Windows ~ these can be obtained in steel (BS 6510) or in aluminium alloy (BS 4873). Steel windows are cheaper in initial cost than aluminium alloy but have higher maintenance costs over their anticipated life, both can be obtained fitted into timber subframes. Generally they give a larger glass area for any given opening size than similar timber windows but they can give rise to condensation on the metal components. Page 454 shows an example of an energy efficient improvement.

TYPICAL ELEVATION

1500

1500

top hung ventlight

fixed light

side hung casement sash

fixed sub-light

70 x 44 timber subframe head

head

top hung vent.

4mm glass factory glazed fixed light

25 x 33 o/a metal framing

70 x 57 transom

mastic seal

BS 6510 metal windows

putty

glass

25 x 33 o/a metal sash framing

aluminium alloy framing in mill, anodised or acrylic finishes

projecting or flush sills available

121 x 70 timber subframe sill

STEEL FRAME SECTIONS

TYPICAL VERTICAL SECTIONS

Refs.:
BS 4873: Aluminium alloy windows and doorsets. Specification.
BS 6510: Steel-framed windows and glazed doors. Specification.

437

Timber Windows ~ wide range of ironmongery available which can be factory fitted or supplied and fixed on site.

Metal Windows ~ ironmongery usually supplied with and factory fitted to the windows.

Typical Examples ~

malleable iron, curly tail pattern

pins

mortice plate

CASEMENT STAY — malleable iron, leaf pattern, half-round section with two pins
Sizes: 200; 250 and 300 mm

CASEMENT FASTENER

hot pressed aluminium, plain end pattern

CASEMENT STAY — cast aluminium, plain end pattern with one pin
Sizes: 250 and 300 mm

wedge plate

CASEMENT FASTENER

box staple

hot pressed brass

CASEMENT STAY — steel and brass, sliding screw-down pattern
Sizes: 250 and 300 mm

VENTLIGHT CATCH
used with bottom hung ventlights

CASEMENT STAY — steel, stayput pattern
Arm Sizes: 100; 140 and 175 mm

malleable iron or brass
Sizes: 150; 175 and 200mm

QUADRANT STAY

Sliding Sash Windows ~ these are an alternative format to the conventional side hung casement windows and can be constructed as a vertical or double hung sash window or as a horizontal sliding window in timber, metal, plastic or in any combination of these materials. The performance and design functions of providing daylight, ventilation, vision out, etc. are the same as those given for traditional windows in Windows – Performance Requirements on page 432.

Typical Double Hung Weight Balanced Window Details ~

ELEVATION

21mm thick pulley head
50mm long angle blocks
upper sash
92 x 21 head outside lining
48 x 41 sash framing
lower sash
glass

plywood parting slip suspended from pulley head
70 x 14 head inside lining
19 x 14 removable staff bead
41 x 22 glazing bar

plywood back lining
70 x 14 jamb inside lining
staff bead
sash cord
21 x 8 parting bead
glass
48 x 41 sash framing
21mm thick pulley stile
92 x 21 jamb outside lining
sash weights - access through pocket piece in pulley stile

21 x 8 parting bead
horn
57 x 41 bottom rail

sash cord
49 x 32 splayed and rebated meeting rails
41 x 22 glazing bar
33 x 19 draught stop
135 x 60 flush sill

JAMB DETAIL

VERTICAL SECTION

Sliding Sash Windows – Weight Balanced Details

plywood parting slip suspended from pulley head

70 x 14 jamb inside lining

70 x 14 head inside lining

HEAD

angle glue block

92 X 21 head outside lining

19 x 14 staff bead

pulley wheel

21mm pulley head

21 x 8 parting bead

48 x 41 sash frame

parting slip

sash cord

sash cord

21mm pulley stile

INTERMEDIATE

19 x 14 staff bead

92 X 21 outside lining

49 x 32 splayed and rebated meeting rails

horn

upper sash counter weight

plywood backing

48 x 41 sash frame

57 x 41 bottom rail

SILL

33 x 19 draught stop

135 x 60 flush sill

21 x 8 parting bead

Double Hung Sash Windows ~ these vertical sliding sash windows come in two formats when constructed in timber. The weight balanced format is shown on the preceding two pages. The alternative spring balanced type is illustrated below and overleaf. Various formats for sliding windows are specified in BS 644: Timber windows and doorsets.

Typical Double Hung Spring Balanced Window Details ~

ELEVATION

21 x 8 parting bead

114 x 33 solid head

48 x 21 head outside lining

48 x 41 sash framing

19 x 14 removable staff bead

upper sash

glass

spiral spring balance

lower sash

41 x 22 glazing bar

114 x 33 solid stile

staff bead

spring balance

horn

49 x 38 splayed and rebated meeting rails

21 x 8 parting bead

glass

glass

41 x 22 glazing bar

48 x 41 sash framing

48 x 21 jamb outside lining

57 x 41 bottom rail

33 x 19 draught stop

NB. if 114 x 60 solid stiles are used spring balances can be housed within grooves in the solid stile thickness.

135 x 60 flush sill

JAMB DETAIL

VERTICAL SECTION

441

HEAD

40 mm projecting horn

dowelled mortice and tenon joint

114 x 33 head

19 x 14 bead

21 x 8 parting bead

48 x 41 upper sash frame

48 x 21 head outer lining

INTERMEDIATE

21 x 8 parting bead

114 x 33 stile

19 x 14 bead

spring counter-balance

49 x 38 splayed and rebated meeting rails

48 x 21 outer lining

top fixing

tube housing coil spring

nylon bush

twisted rod

base fixing

SPIRAL BALANCE

48 x 41 lower sash frame

33 x 19 draught stop

SILL

135 x 60 flush sill

57 x 41 bottom rail

NB. The spring balance can be housed within the stile. Stile thickness will need to be at least 60 mm to accommodate the grooved recess.

Horizontally Sliding Sash Windows ~ these are an alternative format to the vertically sliding or double hung sash windows shown on pages 439 to 442 and can be constructed in timber, metal, plastic or combinations of these materials with single or double glazing. A wide range of arrangements are available with two or more sliding sashes which can have a ventlight incorporated into the outer sliding sash.

Typical Horizontally Sliding Sash Window Details ~

timber subframe

window frame bedded in sealant

nylon slipper shoes and polypropylene pile seals

outer sash — inner sash

ELEVATION

head of timber subframe

anodised aluminium framing

integral pull handle

inner sash

factory-glazed anodised aluminium horizontal sliding sash

outer sash

integral pull handle

window frame sealant bedded

inner sliding sash

weather-sealed meeting stiles

outer sliding sash

timber subframe

bushed nylon rollers

sill of timber subframe

VERTICAL SECTION

weather seal

HORIZONTAL SECTION

Pivot Windows ~ like other windows these are available in timber, metal, plastic or in combinations of these materials.

They can be constructed with centre jamb pivots enabling the sash to pivot or rotate in the horizontal plane or alternatively the pivots can be fixed in the head and sill of the frame so that the sash rotates in the vertical plane.

Typical Example ~

adjustable ventilator fitted in top rail of sash

100 x 75 frame head

65 x 65 sash framing

75 x 75 frame jamb

factory-sealed double glazing unit to pivot sash

heavy duty friction hinge with safety catches to window opening to lock it when reversed for window cleaning

locking handle connected to espagnolette giving two locking points and night ventilation position

65 x 65 sash framing

weather seal to all rebates

groove for 32 mm thick window board

150 x 75 hardwood sill

Bay Windows ~ these can be defined as any window with sidelights which projects in front of the external wall and is supported by a sill height wall. Bay windows not supported by a sill height wall are called oriel windows. They can be of any window type, constructed from any of the usual window materials and are available in three plan formats, namely square, splay and circular or segmental. Timber corner posts can be boxed, solid or jointed, the latter being the common method.

Typical Examples ~

side frame

head – mitred and jointed at corners

ventlights

transom

90°

jamb

corner post

fixed or opening sidelight

corner post

projecting and weathered sill

fixed or opening front lights

mullion

TYPICAL SQUARE BAY WINDOW (665mm projection)

width

jamb

corner post

mullion

554

60°

width

jamb

corner post

mullion

450

45°

60° SPLAY BAY WINDOW AND 45° SPLAY BAY WINDOW

width

jamb

jamb

mitred and jointed corner posts

22½°

990

22½°

TYPICAL 6 LIGHT CIRCULAR OR SEGMENTAL BAY WINDOW

Schedules ~ the main function of a schedule is to collect together all the necessary information for a particular group of components such as windows, doors and drainage inspection chambers. There is no standard format for schedules but they should be easy to read, accurate and contain all the necessary information for their purpose. Schedules are usually presented in a tabulated format which can be related to and read in conjunction with the working drawings.

Typical Example ~

WINDOW SCHEDULE – Sheet 1 of 1			Drawn By: RC	Date: 14/4/01		Rev.	
Contract Title & Number: Lane End Farm – H 341/80					Drg. Nos. C(31) 450–7		
Number	Type or catalogue ref.	Material	Overall size w x h	Glass	Ironmongery	Sill External	Internal
2	213 CV	hardwood	1200 x 1350	sealed units as supplied with frames	supplied with casements	2 cos. plain tiles subsill	150×150×15 quarry tiles
4	309 CVC	ditto	1770 x 900	ditto	ditto	ditto	25 mm thick softwood
4	313 CVC	ditto	1770 x 1350	ditto	ditto	sill of frame	ditto

Window manufacturers identify their products with a notation that combines figures with numbers. The objective is to simplify catalogue entries, specification clauses and schedules. For example:

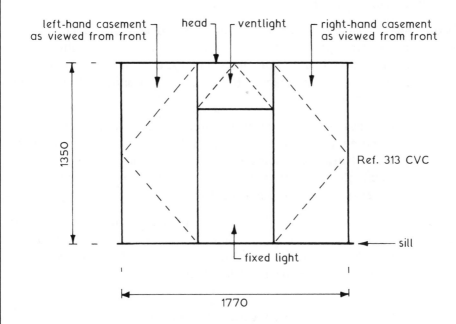

Notation will vary to some extent between the different joinery producers. The example of 313 CVC translates to:

3 = width divided into three units.
13 = first two dimensions of standard height, i.e. 1350mm.
C = casement.
V = ventlight.

Other common notations include:

N = narrow light.
P = plain (picture type window, i.e. no transom or mullion).
T = through transom.
S = sub-light, fixed.
VS = ventlight and sub-light.
F = fixed light.
B = bottom casement opening inwards.
RH/LH = right or lefthand as viewed from the outside.

Glass ~ this material is produced by fusing together soda, lime and silica with other minor ingredients such as magnesia and alumina. A number of glass types are available for domestic work and these include:

Clear Float ~ used where clear, undistorted vision is required. Available thicknesses range from 3mm to 25mm.

Clear Sheet ~ suitable for all clear glass areas but because the two faces of the glass are never perfectly flat or parallel some distortion of vision usually occurs. This type of glass is gradually being superseded by the clear float glass. Available thicknesses range from 3 mm to 6 mm.

Translucent Glass ~ these are patterned glasses, most having one patterned surface and one relatively flat surface. The amount of obscurity and diffusion obtained depends on the type and nature of pattern. Available thicknesses range from 4mm to 6mm for patterned glasses and from 5 mm to 10 mm for rough cast glasses.

Wired Glass ~ obtainable as a clear polished wired glass or as a rough cast wired glass with a nominal thickness of 7mm. Generally used where a degree of fire resistance is required. Georgian wired glass has a 12mm square mesh whereas the hexagonally wired glass has a 20mm mesh.

Choice of Glass ~ the main factors to be considered are:
1. Resistance to wind loadings. 2. Clear vision required.
3. Privacy. 4. Security. 5. Fire resistance. 6. Aesthetics.

Glazing Terminology ~

Glazing ~ the act of fixing glass into a frame or surround. In domestic work this is usually achieved by locating the glass in a rebate and securing it with putty or beading and should be carried out in accordance with the recommendations contained in the BS 6262 series: Glazing for buildings.

Timber Surrounds ~ linseed oil putty is the traditional material for sealing and retaining glass in wooden frames. It is a composite of crushed chalk and linseed oil (whiting). Rebate to be clean, dry and primed before glazing is carried out. Putty should be protected with paint within two weeks of application.

Metal Surrounds ~ metal casement putty if metal surround is to be painted – if surround is not to be painted a non-setting compound should be used.

A general purpose putty is also available. This combines the properties of the two types.

Double Glazing

Double Glazing ~ as its name implies this is where two layers of glass are used instead of the traditional single layer. Double glazing can be used to reduce the rate of heat loss through windows and glazed doors or it can be employed to reduce the sound transmission through windows. In the context of thermal insulation this is achieved by having a small air or argon gas-filled space within the range of 6 to 20 mm between the two layers of glass. The sealed double glazing unit will also prevent internal misting by condensation. If metal frames are used these should have a thermal break incorporated into their design. All opening sashes in a double glazing system should be fitted with adequate weather seals to reduce the rate of heat loss through the opening clearance gap.

In the context of sound insulation three factors affect the performance of double glazing. First, good installation to ensure airtightness, second, the weight of glass used and third, the size of air space between the layers of glass. The heavier the glass used the better the sound insulation and the air space needs to be within the range of 50 to 300 mm. Absorbent lining to the reveals within the air space will also improve the sound insulation properties of the system.

Typical Examples ~

approximate 'U' values
single glazing – 4.3 W/m²K
double glazing – 2.5 W/m²K

approximate sound reduction
6 mm single glazing – 27 dB
double glazing as shown – 42 dB

Secondary glazing of existing windows is an acceptable method for reducing heat energy losses at wall openings. Providing the existing windows are in a good state of repair, this is a cost-effective, simple method for upgrading windows to current energy efficiency standards. In addition to avoiding the disruption of removing existing windows, further advantages of secondary glazing include retention of the original window features, reduction in sound transmission and elimination of draughts. Applications are manufactured for all types of window, with sliding or hinged variations. The following details are typical of horizontal sliding sashes –

Elevation of frame

Detail B - Head and jamb

Detail A - Sill

Detail C - Meeting rails

Double hung weight balanced vertical sliding timber sash windows ~ a feature of many listed buildings, particularly those representing our architectural heritage. Preservation of original design is important and must be maintained, but there should also be a regard for current standards of insulation. Replacement with modern double glazed frames and casements is out of character and in many situations may be prohibited under the Planning (Listed Buildings and Conservation Areas) Act.

Application ~ secondary glazing fitted internally will not impact visually on the external elevation. If required it can be reversed, i.e. it can be removed with minimal inconvenience. Accessibility to the original window remains unimpeded. The illustration shows the simplicity of application to the window type detailed on page 439. Some minor changes may be necessary to replace the staff bead with a larger section to accommodate the casement frame and to modify the inner lining accordingly. External traditional appearance is preserved with the benefit of improved sound and thermal insulation, better security and elimination of draughts.

Modified traditional sliding sash window ~

parting bead

lower sash

sash weight

parting slip

extruded aluminium
side hung hinged
casement and frame

staff bead and inner
lining modified if required
to receive casement frame

Low emissivity or 'Low E' glass is specially manufactured with a surface coating to significantly improve its thermal performance. The surface coating has a dual function:

1. Allows solar short wave light radiation to penetrate a building.
2. Reflects long wave heat radiation losses back into a building.

short wave radiation

air or argon in sealed void

one surface coated 'E' pane to inside unit

short wave radiation penetrates

long wave radiation reflected

Exterior   Interior

double glazed unit   Typical Low E Glazing

Manufacturing processes:

1. Pyrolitic hard coat, applied on-line as the glass is made. Emissivity range, 0.15–0.20, e.g. Pilkington 'K'.
2. A sputtered soft coat applied after glass manufacture. Emissivity range, 0.05–0.10, e.g. Pilkington 'Kappafloat' and 'Suncool High Performance'.

Note: In relative terms, uncoated glass has a normal emissivity of about 0.90.

Indicative U-values for multi-glazed windows of 4 mm glass with a 16mm void width:

Glazing type	uPVC or wood frame	metal frame
Double, air filled	2.7	3.3
Double, argon filled	2.6	3.2
Double, air filled Low E (0.20)	2.1	2.6
Double, argon filled Low E (0.20)	2.0	2.5
Double, air filled Low E (0.05)	2.0	2.3
Double, argon filled Low E (0.05)	1.7	2.1
Triple, air filled	2.0	2.5
Triple, argon filled	1.9	2.4
Triple, air filled Low E (0.20)	1.6	2.0
Triple, argon filled Low E (0.20)	1.5	1.9
Triple, air filled Low E (0.05)	1.4	1.8
Triple, argon filled Low E (0.05)	1.3	1.7

Notes:

1. A larger void and thicker glass will reduce the U-value, and vice versa.

2. Data for metal frames assumes a thermal break of 4 mm (see next page).

3. Hollow metal framing units can be filled with a closed cell insulant foam to considerably reduce U-values.

Extruded aluminium profiled sections are designed and manufactured to create lightweight hollow window (and door) framing members.

Finish – untreated aluminium is prone to surface oxidisation. This can be controlled by paint application, but most manufacturers provide a variable colour range of polyester coatings finished in gloss, satin or matt.

Thermal insulation – poor insulation and high conductivity are characteristics of solid profile metal windows. This is much less apparent with hollow profile outer members, as they can be considerably enhanced by a thermal infilling of closed cell foam.

Condensation – a high strength two-part polyurethane resin thermal break between internal and external profiles inhibits cold bridging. This reduces the opportunity for condensation to form on the surface. The indicative U-values given on the preceding page are based on a thermal break of 4mm. If this is increased to 16mm, the values can be reduced by up to 0.2 W/m^2 K.

double glazed unit

synthetic rubber sealing gasket

hollow core may be filled with closed cell foam

standard profile outer frame for head, jamb and sill

sub-sill

polyurethane-resin thermal breaks

Hollow Core Aluminium Profiled Window Section

Inert gas fills ~ argon or krypton. Argon is generally used as it is the least expensive and more readily available. Where krypton is used, the air gap need only be half that with argon to achieve a similar effect. Both gases have a higher insulating value than air due to their greater density.

Densities (kg/m³):
     Air = 1.20
     Argon = 1.66
     Krypton = 3.49

Argon and krypton also have a lower thermal conductivity than air.

Spacers ~ generally hollow aluminium with a desiccant or drying agent fill. The filling absorbs the initial moisture present in between the glass layers. Non-metallic spacers are preferred as aluminium is an effective heat conductor.

Approximate solar gains with ordinary float glass ~

Single glazing   Double glazing   Triple glazing

'Low E' invisible coatings reduce the solar gain by up to one-third. Depending on the glass quality and cleanliness, about 10 to 15% of visible light reduction applies for each pane of glass.

Typical application ~

vertical section

synthetic rubber sealing strip

standard head and jamb profile*

'L' shaped glazing bead/clip and seal/gasket

synthetic rubber compression seal

glazed units of 3 mm glass and 12 mm gap or 4 mm glass and 16 mm gap

33 or 44 mm overall depth

middle and inner pane 'E' coated

air, argon or krypton filled gaps

synthetic rubber seal/gasket

casement frame*

window board, material optional

sill

hollow profile 'plastic' sections*, typically uPVC or glass fibres with polyester resin bonding

* Hollow profiles manufactured with a closed cell insulant foam/expanded polystyrene core.

Further considerations:
* U-value potential, less than 1.0 W/m²K.
* 'Low E' invisible metallic layer on one pane of double glazing gives a similar insulating value to standard triple glazing (see page 453).
* Performance enhanced with blinds between wide gap panes.
* High quality ironmongery required due to weight of glazed frames.
* Improved sound insulation, particularly with heavier than air gap fill.

There are many manufacturers of triple glazed units, each with their own design profile. Some feature a wide gap between two of the glass panes to incorporate Venetian blinds. This type of curtaining is used to control solar radiation and heat gain. Glass specification and thickness may also vary depending on thermal and sound insulation requirements. Blinds can be actuated automatically in response to pre-set thermostatic control or over-ridden manually.

Typical Profile ~

hermetically sealed inner double glazed panes

glazing bead

outer pane

Venetian blind between outer and middle pane

hollow profile aluminium glazing frame

EPDM composite weather and air tightness seal

polyester powder coated or colour anodised aluminium profile

closed-cell insulant

Potential for Sound Insulation Effectiveness ~

Glazing system	Max. sound reduction (dB)
Single glazed opening sash	20
Single glazed fixed light with weather strips	25
Double glazed, hermetically sealed with weather strips	35
Triple glazed, hermetically sealed, weather strips and blinds	45

Note: These units are considerably heavier than other window types, therefore they will need care in handling during site transportation. The manufacturer's purpose made jamb fixings should be used.

Door and vestibule frames   Windows

In these critical locations, glazing must satisfy one of the following:

1. Breakage to leave only a small opening with small detachable particles without sharp edges.

2. Disintegrating glass must leave only small detached pieces.

3. Inherent robustness, e.g. polycarbonate composition. Annealed glass acceptable but with the following limitations:

Thickness of annealed glass (mm)	Max. glazed area Height (m)	Width (m)
8	1·100	1·100
10	2·250	2·250
12	3·000	4·500
15	no limit	

4. Panes in small areas, <250mm wide and <0.5 m² area. e.g. leaded lights (4 mm annealed glass) and Georgian pattern (6 mm annealed glass).

5. Protective screening as shown with lower bar of screen <75 mm above finished floor level.

Ref. Building Regulations, A.D. K4: Protection against impact with glazing.

Manifestation or Marking of Glass ~ another aspect of the critical location concept which frequently occurs with contemporary glazed features in a building. Commercial premises such as open plan offices, shops and showrooms often incorporate large walled areas of uninterrupted glass to promote visual depth, whilst dividing space or forming part of the exterior envelope. To prevent collision, glazed doors and walls must have prominent framing or intermediate transoms and mullions. An alternative is to position obvious markings at two levels, as shown below. Glass doors could have large pull/push handles and/or IN and OUT signs in bold lettering. Other areas may be adorned with company logos, stripes, geometric shapes, etc.

Critical Locations ~ The Building Regulations, Approved Document – K, determines positions where potential personal impact and injury with glazed doors and windows are most critical. In these situations the glazing specification must incorporate a degree of safety such that any breakage would be relatively harmless. Additional measures in British Standard 6206 complement the Building Regulations and provide test requirements and specifications for impact performance for different classes of glazing material. See also BS 6262.

Refs.: Building Regulations, A.D. K5.2: Manifestation of glazing.
BS 6206: Specification for impact performance requirements for flat safety glass and safety plastics for use in buildings.
BS 6262 series: Glazing for buildings. Codes of practice.

Glass blocks have been used for some time as internal feature partitioning. They now include a variety of applications in external walls, where they combine the benefits of a walling unit with a natural source of light. They have also been used in paving to allow natural light penetration into basements.

sealed unit with integral cavity

80 or 100 mm standard thickness

clear, frosted or ribbed finish

Depending on joint thickness (3, 6 or 10 mm), face sizes are nominally: 150 x 150 mm,
200 x 200 mm,
300 x 300 mm,
100 x 200 mm or
150 x 200 mm.

Typical U-values: 100 mm block = 2.9 W/m^{2}K
80 mm block = 3.24 W/m^{2}K

Fire resistance, BS 476-22 - one hour integrity (load bearing capacity and fire containment).
Maximum panel size is 9m^2. Maximum panel dimension is 3 m.

Laying – glass blocks can be bonded like conventional brickwork, but for aesthetic reasons are usually laid with continuous vertical and horizontal joints.

Jointing – blocks are bedded in mortar with reinforcement from two nine-gauge galvanised steel wires in horizontal joints. Every third course for 150 mm units, every second course for 200 mm units and every course for 300 mm units. First and last course to be reinforced.

Ref.: BS 476-22: Fire tests on building materials and structures. Methods for determination of the fire resistance of non-load-bearing elements of construction.

Mortar – dryer than for bricklaying as the blocks are non-absorbent. The general specification will include: White Portland Cement (BS EN 197-1), High Calcium Lime (BS EN 459-1) and Sand. The sand should be white quartzite or silica type. Fine silver sand is acceptable. An integral waterproofing agent should also be provided. Recommended mix ratios – 1 part cement: 0.5 part lime: 4 parts sand.

structural surround

max. 3 m in any direction

* Perforated metal strap anchors fixed to head and jamb at same spacing as joint reinforcement. 600 mm long, bent to penetrate 1½ blocks.

Joint reinforcement in 9-gauge wire, 50 or 42 mm wide to suit block width. Terminated 50 mm short of jamb to allow for movement.

A

silicon sealant

glass block

joint reinforcement

anchor

expansion material

Detail 'A' - Section through jamb
NB. Same detail for head, except omit reinforcement.

B

glass block

mortar

bituminous emulsion

sill

Detail 'B' - Section through sill

Ref. BS EN 1051-1: Glass in building. Glass blocks and glass pavers. Definitions and description.

Doors — Performance Requirements

Doors ~ can be classed as external or internal. External doors are usually thicker and more robust in design than internal doors since they have more functions to fulfil.

Typical Functions ~

suitable finish and construction to withstand natural elements

good fit to exclude wind and rain

adequate locks and bolts for security

design to give required thermal and sound insulation

weathered at bottom to shed surface water

main function ~ to provide access and egress through enclosing fabric of building

glazed area to provide natural daylight to the interior

when closed door should act in conjunction with surrounding fabric as an enclosing element

design to give required fire resistance

dpc

EXTERNAL DOOR

when closed, door should act in conjunction with surrounding fabric as an internal dividing element

good fit to provide thermal comfort and privacy

adequate lock for security

colour and design to blend with internal decor

main function ~ to provide access and egress through internal wall or partition

design to give required thermal insulation, sound insulation and fire resistance

architrave

skirting

INTERNAL DOOR

462

External Doors ~ these are available in a wide variety of types and styles in timber, aluminium alloy or steel. The majority of external doors are however made from timber, the metal doors being mainly confined to fully glazed doors such as 'patio doors'.

Typical Examples of External Doors ~

610, 686 & 762

1829 & 1981

ledge

brace

ledge

matchboard panel

hanging edge

LEDGED AND BRACED DOOR

686, 762 & 838

1981

top rail

brace

stile

middle rail

hanging edge

bottom rail

FRAMED LEDGED AND BRACED DOOR

762 & 838

1981

top rail

plywood or glazed panels

stile

intermediate rails

plywood facing

bottom rail

1, 2, 3 OR 4 PANELLED DOORS

762 & 838

1981

skeleton framing

lightweight core filling

edge lipping

FLUSH DOORS

463

Typical examples of purpose made and non-standard external doors ~

PURPOSE MADE

TUDOR STYLE

GEORGIAN STYLE

PURPOSE MADE

Door Frames ~ these are available for all standard external doors and can be obtained with a fixed solid or glazed panel above a door height transom. Door frames are available for doors opening inwards or outwards. Most door frames are made to the recommendations set out in BS 4787: Internal and external wood doorsets, door leaves and frames. Specification for dimensional requirements.

Typical Example ~

pinned mortice and tenon joint

horn

83 × 57 softwood head

rebate for inward opening door

door frame built into external wall as work proceeds and secured with metal cramps at 450°/c

83 × 57 softwood jambs

25 × 6 galvanised mild steel water bar bedded in mastic

121 × 44 hardwood weathered sill

horn

83

57

12

9° splay

plastic draught sealer

HEAD AND JAMB SECTION

44

outward opening door

plastic draught sealer

9° splay

57

121

brush draught sealer

inward opening door

water bar

9° splay

44

121

TYPICAL DOOR FRAME

SILL SECTIONS

Door Ironmongery ~ available in a wide variety of materials, styles and finishers but will consist of essentially the same components:

Hinges or Butts – these are used to fix the door to its frame or lining and to enable it to pivot about its hanging edge.

Locks, Latches and Bolts ~ the means of keeping the door in its closed position and providing the required degree of security. The handles and cover plates used in conjunction with locks and latches are collectively called door furniture.

Letter Plates – fitted in external doors to enable letters, etc. to be deposited through the door.

Other items include Finger and Kicking Plates which are used to protect the door fabric where there is high usage,

Draught Excluders to seal the clearance gap around the edges of the door and Security Chains to enable the door to be partially opened and thus retain some security.

Typical Examples ~

BUTT HINGE available in steel, brass, nylon and aluminium

RIM NIGHT LATCH fitted on internal face

LETTER PLATE can be obtained with an integral knocker

RIM LOCK fitted on internal face

BARREL BOLT available in steel, brass and aluminium

MORTICE LOCK fitted within body of door

SECURITY DOOR CHAIN extruded brass with welded brassed steel chain

Industrial Doors ~ these doors are usually classified by their method of operation and construction. There is a very wide range of doors available and the choice should be based on the following considerations:

1. Movement – vertical or horizontal.
2. Size of opening.
3. Position and purpose of door(s).
4. Frequency of opening and closing door(s).
5. Manual or mechanical operation.
6. Thermal and/or sound insulation requirements.
7. Fire resistance requirements.

Typical Industrial Door Types ~

1. **Straight Sliding** -

SINGLE LEAF   DOUBLE LEAF   MULTI LEAF

These types can be top hung with a bottom guide roller or hung with bottom rollers and top guides – see page 468

2. Sliding / Folding -

MULTI LEAF END FOLDING   MULTI LEAF END FOLDING
HUNG BETWEEN REVEALS   HUNG BEHIND OPENING

These types can be top hung with a bottom guide roller or hung with bottom rollers and top guides – see page 469

3. Shutters -

HORIZONTAL FOLDING SHUTTER   ROLLER SHUTTER

Shutters can be installed between, behind or in front of the reveals – see page 470

Straight Sliding Doors ~ these doors are easy to operate, economic to maintain and present no problems for the inclusion of a wicket gate. They do however take up wall space to enable the leaves to be parked in the open position. The floor guide channel associated with top hung doors can become blocked with dirt, causing a malfunction of the sliding movement, whereas the rollers in bottom track doors can seize up unless regularly lubricated and kept clean. Straight sliding doors are available with either manual or mechanical operation.

Typical Example ~

ELEVATION

Sliding/Folding Doors ~ these doors are an alternative format to the straight sliding door types and have the same advantages and disadvantages except that the parking space required for the opened door is less than that for straight sliding doors. Sliding/folding are usually manually operated and can be arranged in groups of two to eight leaves.

Typical Example ~

469

Shutters ~ horizontal folding shutters are similar in operation to sliding/folding doors but are composed of smaller leaves and present the same problems. Roller shutters however do not occupy any wall space but usually have to be fully opened for access. They can be manually operated by means of a pole when the shutters are self-coiling, operated by means of an endless chain winding gear or mechanically raised and lowered by an electric motor but in all cases they are slow to open and close. Vision panels cannot be incorporated into the roller shutter but it is possible to include a small wicket gate or door in the design.

Typical Details ~

ELEVATION OF ROLLER

ELEVATION OF SHUTTER

PLAN ABOVE ROLLER

PLAN BELOW ROLLER

TYPICAL SECTION

Crosswall Construction ~ this is a form of construction where load bearing walls are placed at right angles to the lateral axis of the building, the front and rear walls being essentially non-load bearing cladding. Crosswall construction is suitable for buildings of up to five storeys high where the floors are similar and where internal separating or party walls are required such as in blocks of flats or maisonettes. The intermediate floors span longitudinally between the crosswalls providing the necessary lateral restraint and if both walls and floors are of cast in-situ reinforced concrete the series of 'boxes' so formed is sometimes called box frame construction. Great care must be taken in both design and construction to ensure that the junctions between the non-load bearing claddings and the crosswalls are weather tight. If a pitched roof is to be employed with the ridge parallel to the lateral axis an edge beam will be required to provide a seating for the trussed or common rafters and to transmit the roof loads to the crosswalls.

Typical Crosswall Arrangement Details ~

471

Typical Details ~

cladding

inner leaf not less than 120 kg/m²

bonded or tied crosswall

mastic seal

650 minimum

460 minimum

exposed faces to be treated to prevent the ingress of moisture with rendering, applied finishes such as mosaic or built with dense bricks

cladding

RC crosswall

mastic seal

cladding

460 minimum

exposed faces to be treated to prevent the ingress of moisture if necessary

460 minimum

Advantages of Crosswall Construction:

1. Load bearing and non-load bearing components can be standardised and in same cases prefabricated giving faster construction times.
2. Fenestration between crosswalls unrestricted structurally.
3. Crosswalls although load bearing need not be weather resistant as is the case with external walls.

Disadvantages of Crosswall Construction:

1. Limitations of possible plans.
2. Need for adequate lateral ties between crosswalls.
3. Need to weather adequately projecting crosswalls.

Floors:

An in-situ solid reinforced concrete floor will provide the greatest rigidity, all other forms must be adequately tied to walls.

System ~ comprises quality controlled factory produced components of plain reinforced concrete walls and prestressed concrete hollow or solid core plank floors.

Site Assembly ~ components are crane lifted and stacked manually with the floor panel edges bearing on surrounding walls. Temporary support will be necessary until the units are 'stitched' together with horizontal and vertical steel reinforcing ties located through reinforcement loops projecting from adjacent panels. In-situ concrete completes the structural connection to provide full transfer of all forces and loads through the joint. Precast concrete stair flights and landings are located and connected to support panels by steel angle bracketing and in-situ concrete joints.

Typical 'stitched' joint between precast concrete crosswall components ~

Concept ~ a cost-effective simple and fast site assembly system using load-bearing partitions and external walls to transfer vertical loads from floor panels. The floor provides lateral stability by diaphragm action between the walls.

Application ~ precast reinforced concrete crosswall construction systems may be used to construct multi-storey buildings, particularly where the diaphragm floor load distribution is transferred to lift or stair well cores. Typical applications include schools, hotels, hostels, apartment blocks and hospitals. External appearance can be enhanced by a variety of cladding possibilities, including the traditional look of face brickwork secured to the structure by in-built ties. Internal finishing may be with paint or plaster, but it is usually dry lined with plasterboard.

Location of 'stitched' in-situ reinforced concrete ties ~

precast, prestressed upper floor panel

precast reinforced concrete crosswall

precast, prestressed first floor panel

precast reinforced concrete crosswall

floor panels and walls stacked and 'stitched'

precast reinforced concrete external wall

Fire resistance and sound insulation are achieved by density and quality of concrete. The thermal mass of concrete can be enhanced by applying insulation in between the external precast panel and the masonry or other cladding.

Framing ~ an industry-based prefabricated house manufacturing process permitting rapid site construction, with considerably fewer site operatives than traditional construction. This technique has a long history of conventional practice in Scandinavia and North America, but has only gained credibility in the UK since the 1960s. Factory-made panels are based on a stud framework of timber, normally ex. 100 × 50 mm, an outer sheathing of plywood, particle-board or similar sheet material, insulation between the framing members and an internal lining of plasterboard. An outer cladding of brickwork weatherproofs the building and provides a traditional appearance.

Assembly techniques are derived from two systems:

1. Balloon frame

2. Platform frame

gable panel

intermediate floor

2-storey height panels

BALLOON FRAME

single-storey height panels

PLATFORM FRAME

A balloon frame consists of two-storey height panels with an intermediate floor suspended from the framework. In the UK, the platform frame is preferred with intermediate floor support directly on the lower panel. It is also easier to transport, easier to handle on site and has fewer shrinkage and movement problems.

Typical Details ~

trussed rafters at 600mm spacing

head binder

floor joist

upper panel sole plate

floor panel

joist

header

head binder

cavity closer/ barrier (see note 1)

trussed rafter

head binder

insulation

brick cladding

galv. steel ties every 5th course

dpc

galvanised steel angle

window head

tiled sub-sill

window-sill

dpc

ex.100 × 50 mm s/w framing (see note 2)

breather membrane over plywood sheathing

12·5mm vapour control lined plasterboard

sill plate bolted to foundation

screed

dpm

deep strip foundation

Notes:

1. Cavity barriers prevent fire spread. The principal locations are between elements and compartments of construction (see B. Regs. A.D. B3).

2. Thermal bridging through solid framing may be reduced by using rigid EPS insulation and lighter 'I' section members of plywood or oriented strand board (OSB).

Framing ~ comprising inner leaf wall panels of standard cold-formed galvanised steel channel sections as structural support, with a lined inner face of vapour check layer under plasterboard. These panels can be site assembled, but it is more realistic to order them factory made. Panels are usually produced in 600 mm wide modules and bolted together on site. Roof trusses are made up from steel channel or sigma sections. See page 628 for examples of standard steel sections and BS EN 10162: Cold rolled steel sections.

Standard channel and panel.

Background/history ~ the concept of steel framing for house construction evolved in the early 1920s, but development of the lightweight concrete 'breeze' block soon took preference. Due to a shortage of traditional building materials, a resurgence of interest occurred again during the early post-war building boom of the late 1940s. Thereafter, steel became relatively costly and uncompetitive as a viable alternative to concrete block or timber frame construction techniques. Since the 1990s more efficient factory production processes, use of semi-skilled site labour and availability of economic cold-formed sections have revived an interest in this alternative means of house construction.

Steel Frame Construction (2)

Typical Details ~

Eaves

bolted channel section truss

insulated cavity closer barrier (see Building Regs. A. D.: B3, Section 6 [Vol. 1] and 9 [Vol. 2]) and plywood bracket

storey height modular frame

channel section truss members

channel section floor joists

brickwork outer leaf

ground floor slab

header binder or wall plate

stud framing

50mm cavity

fire-retardant insulation

wall tie

breather membrane

Intermediate floor   Ground floor

insulation between studding and into cavity

plaster-board

plywood deck

dpc

channel section floor joists

insulated cavity barrier/fire stop if a compartment floor

12.5 mm vapour check plasterboard screwed to stud framework

anchor bolt

screed

insulation

dpm

concrete slab or beam and block floor

Advantages:
- Factory made, therefore produced to quality controlled standards and tolerances.
- Relatively simple to assemble on site – bolted connections in preformed holes.
- Dimensionally stable, consistent composition, insignificant movement.
- Unaffected by moisture, therefore will not rot.
- Does not burn.
- Inedible by insects.
- Roof spans potentially long relative to weight.

Disadvantages:
- Possibility of corrosion if galvanised protective layer is damaged.
- Deforms at high temperature, therefore unpredictable in fire.
- Electricity conductor – must be earthed.

Render ~ a mix of binder (cement) and fine aggregate (sand) with the addition of water and lime or a plasticiser to make the mix workable. Applied to walls as a decorative and/or waterproofing treatment.

Mix ratios ~ for general use, mix ratios are between 1:0.5:4–4.5 and 1:1:5–6 of cement, lime and sand. Equivalent using masonry cement and sand is 1:2.5–3.5 and 1:4–5. Unless a fine finish is required, coarse textured sharp sand is preferred for stability.

Background ~

Masonry — brick and block-work joints raked out 12 to 15 mm to provide a key for the first bonding coat. Metal mesh can be nailed to the surface as supplementary support and reinforcing.

Wood or similar sheeting — metal lathing, wire mesh or expanded metal of galvanised (zinc coated) or stainless steel secured every 300 mm. A purpose-made lathing is produced for timber-framed walls.

Concrete — and other smooth, dense surfaces can be hacked to provide a key or spatter-dashed. Spatter-dash is a strong mix of cement and sand (1:2) mixed into a slurry, trowelled roughly or thrown on to leave an irregular surface as a key to subsequent applications.

Three coat application to a masonry background

brickwork mortar joints raked out

galvanised wire mesh stapled every 300 mm

finish 6–8 mm

surface scratched

undercoat 8–10 mm

bonding coat 10–12 mm

Number of coats (layers) and composition ~ in sheltered locations, one 10 mm layer is adequate for regular backgrounds. Elsewhere, two or possibly three separate applications are required to adequately weatherproof the wall and to prevent the brick or block-work joints from 'grinning' through. Render mixes should become slightly weaker towards the outer layer to allow for greater flexure at the surface, i.e. less opportunity for movement and shrinkage cracking.

Finishes ~ smooth, textured, rough-cast and pebble-dashed.

Smooth – fine sand and cement finished with a steel trowel (6 to 8 mm).

Textured – final layer finished with a coarse brush, toothed implement or a fabric roller (10 to 12 mm with 3 mm surface treated).

Rough-cast – irregular finish resulting from throwing the final coat onto the wall (6 to 10 mm).

Pebble or dry dash – small stones thrown onto a strong mortar finishing coat (10 to 12 mm).

Render application to a timber framed background

timber framing

plywood sheathing

timber batten

breather membrane

rendered finish
in two coats min.

st/st wire reinforced lath
or expanded metal over breather
paper nailed to battens

Ref. BS EN 13914 – 1: Design, preparation and application of external rendering and internal plastering. External rendering.

Traditional renders ~ a site-mixed sand base with a cement and/or lime binder combined with water to produce a workable mix. Mostly used to cover poor quality or inexpensive backgrounds, producing a reasonably waterproof outer surface for decorative treatment. Can also be a design choice.

Polymer modified renders ~ delivered to site in factory-premixed 20 or 25kg bags for the addition of water prior to application. Recipes vary, but in principle manufacturers combine polymeric additives with the base materials of sand and cement. These may include latexes or emulsions, water soluble polymer powders and resins. Polyvinyl acetate (PVA) is the synthetic adhesive generally used. PVA is more commonly known as a wood glue, but in modified renders it functions as an emulsion in water to partially replace cement. Some products also include anti-crack fibres as a reinforcement.

Background ~ existing or newly constructed substrate of render, masonry, concrete, timber or insulation slab (see page 576). Must be sound, reasonably level, free of friable material, algae, litchens and any other surface growths. A fungicidal wash and stabilising solution/primer can be applied to control surface suction.

Application ~ two-coat work for irregular surfaces and refurbishment, 8–10mm base coat reinforced with galvanised or stainless steel mesh secured to the wall. Woven glass-fibre mesh can also be used, generally embedded in the base coat over existing cracks or damaged areas.

Finish ~ 6–8mm over scratched base coat. Surface treatments as described for traditional renders.

Properties ~

> Enhanced weatherproofing.
> Vapour permeable.
> Good resistance to impact.
> Inherent adhesion.
> Consistent mix produced in quality controlled factory conditions.
> Suitable for a variety of backgrounds.

Claddings to External Walls ~ external walls of block or timber frame construction can be clad with tiles, timber boards or plastic board sections. The tiles used are plain roofing tiles with either a straight or patterned bottom edge. They are applied to the vertical surface in the same manner as tiles laid on a sloping surface (see pages 504 and 507) except that the gauge can be wider and each tile is twice nailed. External and internal angles can be formed using special tiles or they can be mitred. Timber boards such as matchboarding and shiplap can be fixed vertically to horizontal battens or horizontally to vertical battens. Plastic moulded board claddings can be applied in a similar manner. The battens to which the claddings are fixed should be treated with a preservative against fungi and beetle attack and should be fixed with corrosion resistant nails.

Typical Details ~

breather membrane

38 × 25 battens at 600 c/c

265 × 165 plain or patterned tiles

gauge 100 to 115 mm

150 × 20 shiplap boarding

margin = gauge

38 × 25 battens

lap

190 × 165 bottom course tiles

75 × 65 tilting fillet

closing batten to bottom edge

block or timber framed external wall

block or timber framed external wall

VERTICAL TILE HANGING

TIMBER WEATHERBOARDING

Shrinkage ~ timber is subject to natural movement (page 148). With slender cladding sections allowance must be made to accommodate this by drying to an appropriate moisture content before fixing, otherwise gaps will open between adjacent boards.

Fixing ~ round head galvanised or stainless steel nails will avoid corrosion and metal staining. Lost head nails should be avoided as these can pull through. Annular ring shank nails provide extra grip. Pneumatic gun fixing to be applied with care to ensure no surface damage from impact. Nail length to penetrate the support battens by at least 22 mm. Two and a half times board thickness is usually specified. Dense timbers such as Siberian larch, Douglas fir and hardwoods should be pre-drilled 2 mm over nail diameter. Double nailing may be required in very exposed situations.

Various Timber Cladding Profiles ~

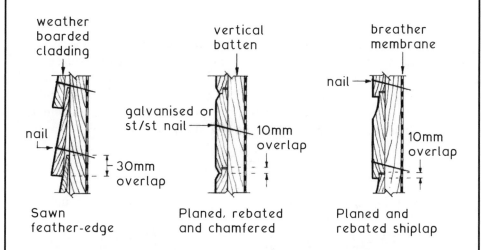

Ref. BS 1186-3: Timber for and workmanship in joinery. Specification for wood trim and its fixing.

External corner tiles are made to order as special fittings to standard plain tiles. In effect they are tile and a halfs turned through 90° (other angles can be made) and handed left or right, fixed alternately to suit the overlapping pattern.

special one-piece external corner tile

38 × 25 battens

vertical external 90° corner tile

265

165

80

plain tiles

An alternative is to accurately mitre cut the meeting sides of tiles. This requires pairs of tile and a halfs in alternate courses to maintain the bond. Lead soakers (1.75 mm) of at least 225 × 200 mm are applied to every course to weather the mitred cut edges. The top of each soaker is turned over the tiles and the bottom finished flush or slightly above the lower edge of tiles.

1.75 mm lead soaker

25 mm return

200

100

mitre cut plain tiles and tile and a halfs

plain tile

Internal corners are treated similarly to external corners by using special tiles of approximately tile and a half overall dimensions, turned through 90° (or other specified angle) in the opposing direction to external specials. These tiles are left and right handed and fixed alternately to vertical courses to maintain the overlapping bond.

165   80

vertical internal
90° corner tile

265

38 × 25 batten

plain tile

Internal angles can also be formed with mitre cut tiles, with tile and a half tiles in alternate courses. Lead soakers (1.75 mm) of 175 × 175 mm minimum dimensions are placed under each pair of corner tiles to weather the cut edges. As with external soakers, the lead is discretely hidden by accurate mitre cutting and shaping of tiles.

1.75mm lead soakers under
every course of corner tiles

100

25

150

38 × 25 batten

plain tile

mitre cut plain tiles
and tile and a halfs

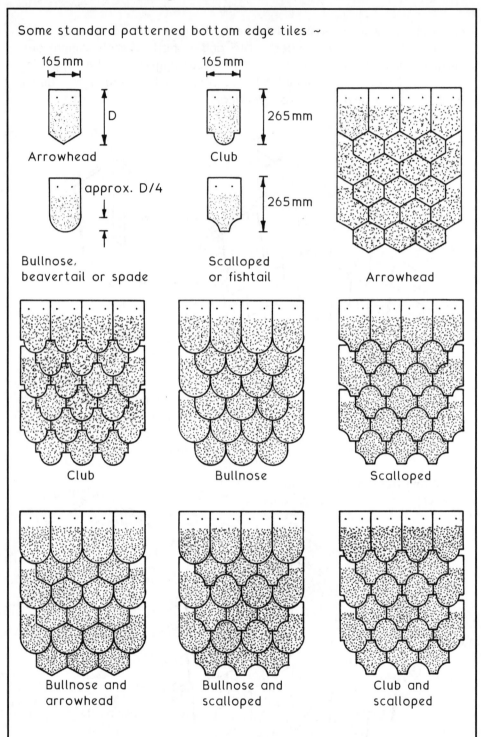

Some standard patterned bottom edge tiles ~

165mm

Arrowhead — D

165mm

Club — 265mm

Bullnose, beavertail or spade — approx. D/4

Scalloped or fishtail — 265mm

Arrowhead

Club

Bullnose

Scalloped

Bullnose and arrowhead

Bullnose and scalloped

Club and scalloped

NB. May also be used as a roof-tiling feature, generally in two to three courses at 1.5 to 2.0 m intervals to relieve plain tiling.

Ordinary splay cutting to roof verge ~

Tile and a half tiles at the end of each course, cut to the undercloak course of roof tiling. A second nail hole can be drilled at the head of each cut tile for secure fixing to the parallel batten.

Winchester cutting to roof verge ~

More attractive than ordinary splay cutting. Two cut tiles are required at the end of each course, varying in size depending on the roof pitch. Tile and half tiles should be used for these to avoid narrow cuts.

A variation that also has two cut tiles at the end of each course, has the square (90°) edge of the first course of tiles next to the roof tiling undercloak course.

Mathematical Tile Cladding

Appearance and concept ~ a type of fake brickwork made up of clay tiles side and head lapped over each other to create the impression of brickwork, but without the expense. Joints/pointing can be in lime mortar or left dry.

History ~ originated during the eighteenth century, when they were used quite frequently on timber framed buildings notably in Kent and Sussex. Possibly this was to update and improve deteriorated weatherboarding or to avoid the brick tax of 1784. This tax was repealed in 1835.

Application ~ restoration to mathematically tiled older structures and as a lightweight cladding to modern timber-framed construction where the appearance of a brickwork façade is required.

Application shown in a Flemish bond ~

counter battens at 600 c/c if required

38 × 25 mm battens spaced at tile length-lap

st/st screw

65 mm

breather membrane underlay

102.5 mm

215 mm

102.5 mm

Brick slips ~ thin bricks resembling tiles of 15 to 20mm thickness with face dimensions the same as standard bricks (see page 395) and a finish or texture to match. Other terminology includes brick tiles, brick cladding units, slip bricks and briquettes.

Standard brick slip

Pistol brick slip
(corners and reveals)

Application ~ used to maintain continuity of appearance where brickwork infill panels are supported by a reinforced concrete frame, as shown on page 699. Originally slips were cut from whole bricks, a time consuming and wasteful process no longer necessary, as most brick manufacturers make slips to complement their stock items. Other uses are as a cost effective dressing to inexpensive or repaired backgrounds and for use where it is too difficult to build with standard bricks.

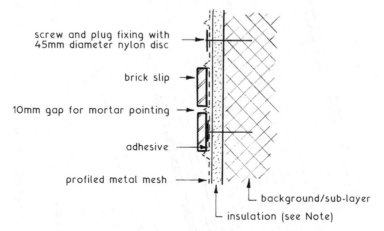

Support system ~ profiled galvanised or stainless steel mesh secured with screws and nylon discs 300mm horizontally and 150mm vertically apart into a sound background. Slips are stuck to the mesh with a structural adhesive of epoxy mortar, a two-part mix of resin and hardener combined with a sand filler.

Note: Extruded polystyrene closed cell foam insulating panel 25 to 50mm in thickness, adhesive secured to the background.

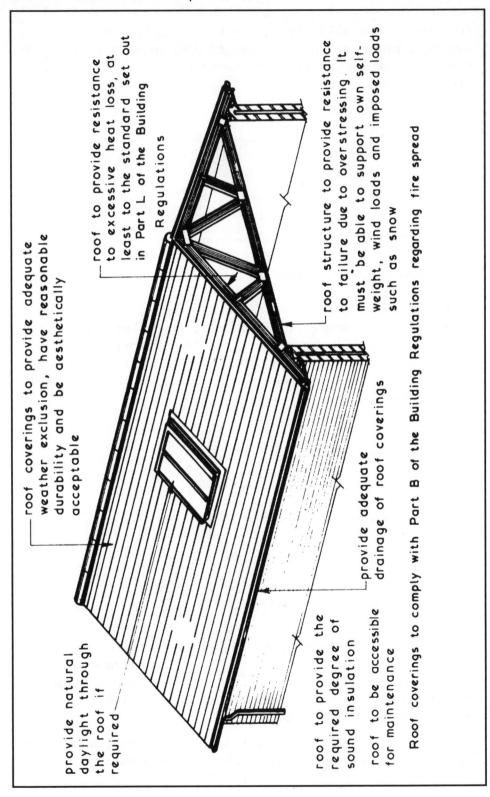

roof coverings to provide adequate weather exclusion, have reasonable durability and be aesthetically acceptable

roof to provide resistance to excessive heat loss, at least to the standard set out in Part L of the Building Regulations

roof structure to provide resistance to failure due to overstressing. It must be able to support own self-weight, wind loads and imposed loads such as snow

provide natural daylight through the roof if required

provide adequate drainage of roof coverings

roof to provide the required degree of sound insulation

roof to be accessible for maintenance

Roof coverings to comply with Part B of the Building Regulations regarding fire spread

Roofs ~ these can be classified as either:
        Flat – pitch from 0° to 10°
        Pitched – pitch over 10°

It is worth noting that for design purposes roof pitches over 70° are classified as walls.

Roofs can be designed in many different forms and in combinations of these forms, some of which would not be suitable and/or economic for domestic properties.

flashing to weather joint between roof and parapet

support wall projecting above roof level~ the projection is called a parapet

parapet

skirting

coping

small splayed kerb or water check to verge

roof slopes towards drainage edge or eaves-angle of slope governed by type of roof covering

fall

fascia

gutter to collect discharged rainwater from roof and convey it to the rainwater pipe(s)

verge ~ the non-drained edge of a roof

closing member of roof construction is called a fascia

rainwater pipe conveys discharged rainwater to the drains

FLAT ROOFS

491

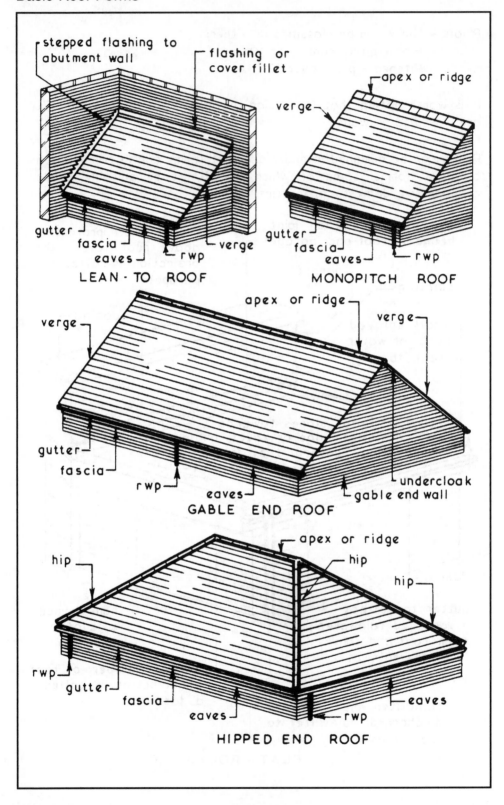

LEAN · TO ROOF

MONOPITCH ROOF

GABLE END ROOF

HIPPED END ROOF

THE MANSARD OR GAMBREL ROOF

A COMBINATION OF BASIC FORMS

Pitched Roofs ~ the primary functions of any domestic roof are to:

1. Provide an adequate barrier to the penetration of the elements.
2. Maintain the internal environment by providing an adequate resistance to heat loss.

A roof is in a very exposed situation and must therefore be designed and constructed in such a manner as to:

1. Safely resist all imposed loadings such as snow and wind.
2. Be capable of accommodating thermal and moisture movements.
3. Be durable so as to give a satisfactory performance and reduce maintenance to a minimum.

Component Parts of a Pitched Roof ~

valley – internal angle of a roof

hip – external angle of a roof

roof covering – provides resistance to penetration of elements and conveys surface water to gutter at eaves

ridge

ridge tile – capping to roof covering

ridge board – spine of roof carcass

rafter

hip tiles

gable end

eaves fascia

hip or jack rafters

verge – termination at a gable directs surface water back onto main roof area

purlin – reduces rafter span

battens – fixing medium for roof coverings and underlay which acts as secondary barrier to elements

rafters – support members for roof coverings

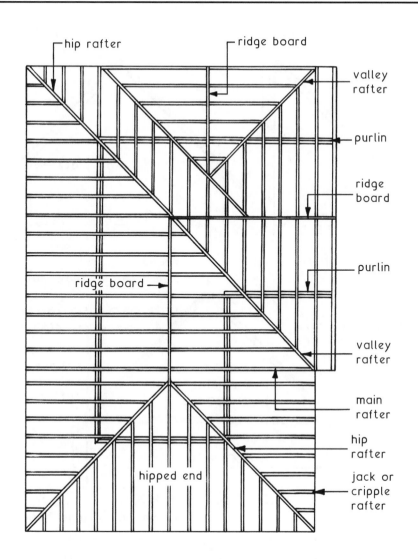

Purlins ~ guide to minimum size (mm) relative to span and spacing:

Span (m)	Spacing (m)		
	1.75	2.25	2.75
2.0	125 × 75	150 × 75	150 × 100
2.5	150 × 75	175 × 75	175 × 100
3.0	175 × 100	200 × 100	200 × 125
3.5	225 × 100	225 × 100	225 × 125
4.0	225 × 125	250 × 125	250 × 125

32mm thick pitching plate fixed to wall

100 x 50 rafters at 400 ᶜ/c

100 x 50 wall plate

2·400 max.

LEAN-TO ROOF

32mm thick ridge board

100 x 50 rafters at 400 ᶜ/c

rafters in pairs

100 x 50 wall plate

3·600 max.

COUPLE ROOF

pitches of roofs to suit type of roof covering

32mm thick ridge board

150 x 50 rafters in pairs at 400 ᶜ/c

200 x 50 collars or ceiling joists at 400 ᶜ/c

collars fixed to sides of rafters

100 x 50 wall plate

4·800 max.

CLOSED COUPLE ROOF

minimum sizes for members of domestic type roofs can be obtained from 'Span Tables for Solid Timber Members' published by TRADA Technology Ltd.

32mm thick ridge board

100 x 50 rafters in pairs at 400 ᶜ/c

150 x 50 collars at 400 ᶜ/c

dovetail halving joint

$\frac{1}{3}$ H max.

H

100 x 50 wall plate

5·500 max.

COLLAR ROOF

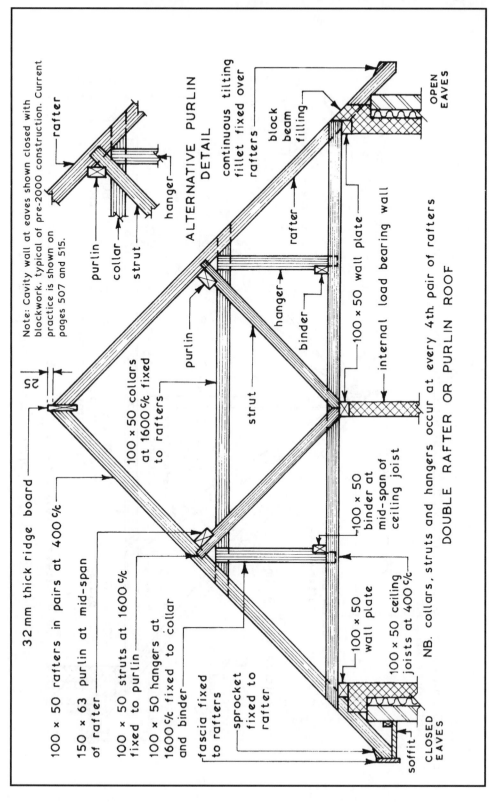

32 mm thick ridge board

100 × 50 rafters in pairs at 400 %c

150 × 63 purlin at mid-span of rafter

100 × 50 struts at 1600 %c fixed to purlin

100 × 50 hangers at 1600 %c fixed to collar and binder

fascia fixed to rafters

sprocket fixed to rafter

soffit

CLOSED EAVES

100 × 50 wall plate

100 × 50 binder at mid-span of ceiling joist

100 × 50 ceiling joists at 400 %c

NB. collars, struts and hangers occur at every 4th. pair of rafters

DOUBLE RAFTER OR PURLIN ROOF

100 × 50 collars at 1600 %c fixed to rafters

purlin

strut

hanger

binder

100 × 50 wall plate

internal load bearing wall

Note: Cavity wall at eaves shown closed with blockwork, typical of pre-2000 construction. Current practice is shown on pages 507 and 515.

ALTERNATIVE PURLIN DETAIL

purlin

collar

strut

hanger

rafter

continuous tilting fillet fixed over rafters

block beam filling

OPEN EAVES

rafter

25

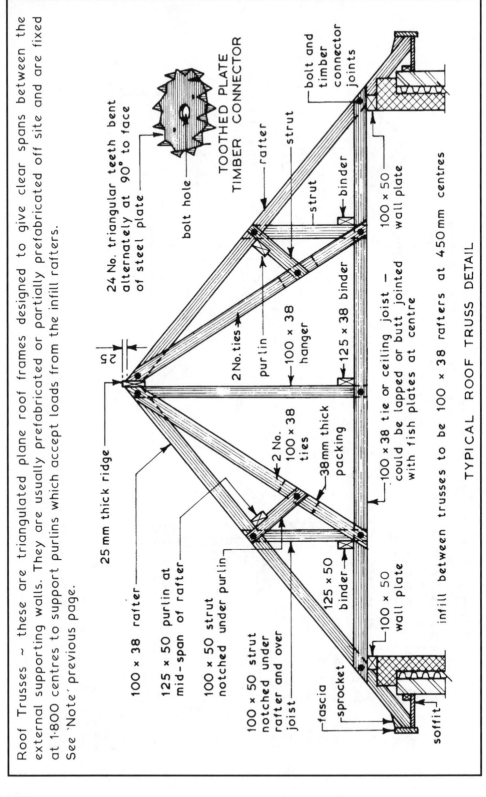

Roof Trusses ~ these are triangulated plane roof frames designed to give clear spans between the external supporting walls. They are usually prefabricated or partially prefabricated off site and are fixed at 1·800 centres to support purlins which accept loads from the infill rafters. See 'Note' previous page.

24 No. triangular teeth bent alternately at 90° to face of steel plate

bolt hole

TOOTHED PLATE
TIMBER CONNECTOR

rafter

strut

strut

binder

bolt and timber connector joints

100 × 50 wall plate

25 mm thick ridge

100 × 38 rafter

125 × 50 purlin at mid-span of rafter

100 × 50 strut notched under purlin

2 No. ties

purlin

100 × 38 hanger

125 × 38 binder

100 × 38 tie or ceiling joist – could be lapped or butt jointed with fish plates at centre

100 × 50 strut notched under rafter and over joist

2 No. 100 × 38 ties

38mm thick packing

125 × 50 binder

100 × 50 wall plate

fascia

sprocket

soffit

infill between trusses to be 100 × 38 rafters at 450mm centres

TYPICAL ROOF TRUSS DETAIL

Trussed Rafters ~ these are triangulated plane roof frames designed to give clear spans between the external supporting walls. They are delivered to site as a prefabricated component where they are fixed to the wall plates at 600 mm centres. Trussed rafters do not require any ridge boards or purlins since they receive their lateral stability by using larger tiling battens (50 × 25 mm) than those used on traditional roofs. See 'Note' on page 497.

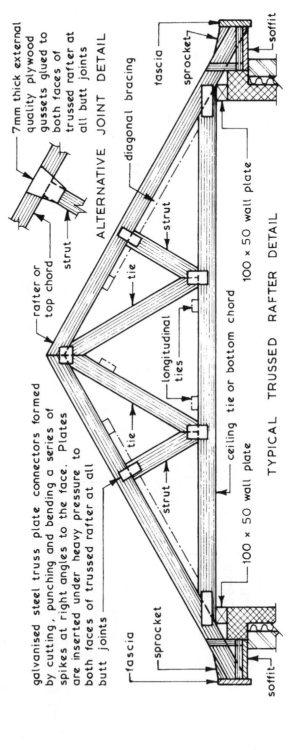

7mm thick external quality plywood gussets glued to both faces of trussed rafter at all butt joints

ALTERNATIVE JOINT DETAIL

rafter or top chord

strut

diagonal bracing

fascia

sprocket

soffit

strut

tie

longitudinal ties

100 × 50 wall plate

tie

strut

100 × 50 wall plate

ceiling tie or bottom chord

100 × 50 wall plate

TYPICAL TRUSSED RAFTER DETAIL

fascia

sprocket

soffit

galvanised steel truss plate connectors formed by cutting, punching and bending a series of spikes at right angles to the face. Plates are inserted under heavy pressure to both faces of trussed rafter at all butt joints

Longitudinal ties (75 × 38) fixed over ceiling ties and under internal ties near to roof apex and rafter diagonal bracing (75 × 38) fixed under rafters at gable ends from eaves to apex may be required to provide stability bracing – actual requirements specified by manufacturer. Lateral restraint to gable walls at top and bottom chord levels in the form of mild steel straps at 2·000 maximum centres over 2 No. trussed rafters may also be required.

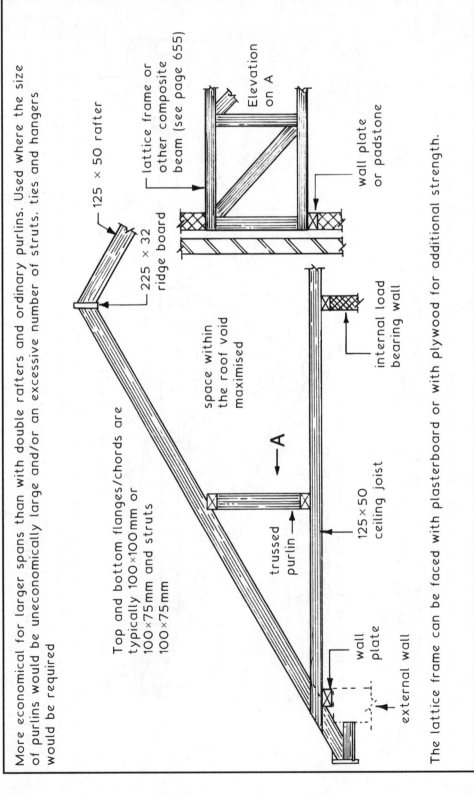

More economical for larger spans than with double rafters and ordinary purlins. Used where the size of purlins would be uneconomically large and/or an excessive number of struts, ties and hangers would be required

Top and bottom flanges/chords are typically 100×100 mm or 100×75 mm and struts 100×75 mm

125 × 50 rafter

225 × 32 ridge board

lattice frame or other composite beam (see page 655)

Elevation on A

wall plate or padstone

space within the roof void maximised

internal load bearing wall

A

trussed purlin

125×50 ceiling joist

wall plate

external wall

The lattice frame can be faced with plasterboard or with plywood for additional strength.

Gambrel roofs are double pitched with a break in the roof slope. The pitch angle above the break is less than 45° relative to the horizontal, whilst the pitch angle below the break is greater. Generally, these angles are 30° and 60°.

Gambrels are useful in providing more attic headroom and frequently incorporate dormers and rooflights. They have a variety of constructional forms.

Typically —

low pitch rafter

ridge board

alternative purlin support

birds mouth notching of rafters to partition head plate

30°

collar

high pitch rafter

rafter

partition stud framing

struts notched to brace and rafter

binder and sole plate

60°

ceiling tie and/or floor joist

wall plate

2 No. braces, one each side of rafters

Alternative for clear span and headroom

Note: size of timbers to suit spans and roof and internal loadings. See guidance in Building Regulations, Approved Document A.

Intermediate support can be provided in various ways as shown above. To create headroom for accommodation in what would otherwise be attic space, a double head plate and partition studding is usual. The collar beam and rafters can conveniently locate on the head plates or prefabricated trusses can span between partitions.

Valley construction and associated pitched roofing is used:

• to visually enhance an otherwise plain roof structure.
• where the roof plan turns through an angle (usually 90°) to follow the building layout or a later extension.
• at the intersection of main and projecting roofs above a bay window or a dormer window.

Construction may be by forming a framework of cut rafters trimmed to valley rafters as shown in the roof plan on page 495. Alternatively, and as favoured with building extensions, by locating a valley or lay board over the main rafters to provide a fixing for each of the jack rafters.

valley or lay board

jack rafter

common or main rafters

wall plate

ridge board

ceiling joist

Sprockets may be provided at the eaves to reduce the slope of a pitched roof. Sprockets are generally most suitable for use on wide, steeply pitched roofs to:

• enhance the roof profile by creating a feature.
• to slow down the velocity of rainwater running off the roof and prevent it from overshooting the gutter.

Where the rafters overhang the external wall, taper cut timber sprockets can be attached to the top of the rafters. Alternatively, the ends of rafters can be birds mouthed onto the wall plate and short lengths of timber the same size as the rafters secured to the rafter feet. In reducing the pitch angle, albeit for only a short distance, it should not be less than the minimum angle recommended for specific roof coverings.

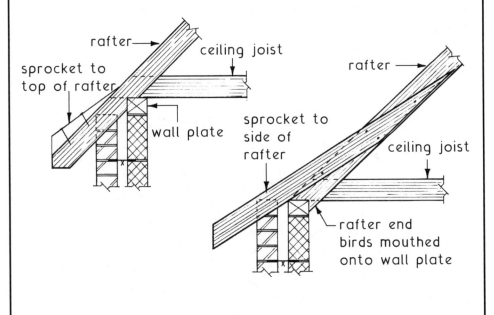

Types of sprocketed eaves

Roof Underlays ~ sometimes called sarking or roofing felt provides the barrier to the entry of snow, wind and rain blown between the tiles or slates. It also prevents the entry of water from capillary action.

Suitable Materials ~

Bitumen fibre-based felts – supplied in rolls 1 m wide and up to 25 m long. Traditionally used in house construction with a cold ventilated roof.

Breather or vapour permeable underlay – typically produced from HDPE fibre or extruded polypropylene fibre, bonded by heat and pressure. Materials permeable to water vapour are preferred as these do not need to be perforated to ventilate the roof space. Also, subject to manufacturer's guidelines, traditional eaves ventilation may not be necessary. Underlay of this type should be installed taut across the rafters with counter battens support to the tile battens. Where counter battens are not used, underlay should sag slightly between rafters to allow rain penetration to flow under tile battens.

counter batten
tile batten
tiling
vapour permeable underlay
rain blown under tiles deflected to gutter
100mm min. head and side laps to be adhesive or tape sealed
rafter

Underlays are fixed initially with galvanised clout nails or st/st staples but are finally secured with the tiling or slating batten fixings

Double Lap Tiles ~ these are the traditional tile covering for pitched roofs and are available made from clay and concrete and are usually called plain tiles. Plain tiles have a slight camber in their length to ensure that the tail of the tile will bed and not ride on the tile below. There are always at least two layers of tiles covering any part of the roof. Each tile has at least two nibs on the underside of its head so that it can be hung on support battens nailed over the rafters. Two nail holes provide the means of fixing the tile to the batten; in practice only every fourth course of tiles is nailed unless the roof exposure is high. Double lap tiles are laid to a bond so that the edge joints between the tiles are in the centre of the tiles immediately below and above the course under consideration.

Minimum pitch 35° machine-made, 45° hand-made.

Typical Plain Tile Details ~

STANDARD PLAIN TILE

EAVES OR TOP COURSE TILE

TILE AND A HALF TILE

HALF ROUND RIDGE TILE

CURVED VALLEY TILE

BONNET HIP TILE

For other types, shapes and sections see BS EN 1304: Clay roofing tiles and fittings. Product definitions and specifications.

Hand-made from extracted clay substrata. Sources of suitable clay in the UK are the brick making areas of Kent, Sussex and Leicestershire.

Tiles are shaped in a timber frame or clamp before being kiln fired at about 1000°C. Early examples of these tiles have been attributed to the Romans, but after they left the UK manufacture all but ceased until about the twelfth century. Historically and today, tile dimensions vary quite significantly, especially those from different regions and makers. In 1477 a Royal Charter attempted to standardise tiles to $10\frac{1}{2}'' \times 6\frac{1}{2}'' \times \frac{1}{2}''$ thick (265 × 165 × 12 mm) and this remains as the BS dimensions shown on the previous page. However, peg tile makers were set in their ways and retained their established local dimensions. This means that replacements have to be specifically produced to match existing tiles.

Peg tile showing general range of dimensions

225 to 255 mm

camber

150 to 160 mm

camber

tapered oak peg located behind batten

12 mm

square or round hole

Typical regional sizes ~

Sussex	$9\frac{1}{2}'' \times 6\frac{1}{4}''$	(240 × 160 mm)
Kent	$10'' \times 6''$	(255 × 150 mm)
Leicestershire	$11'' \times 7''$	(280 × 180 mm)

Typical details (cold roof) ~

purpose-made in-line tile ventilators spaced to provide equivalent of 5mm continuous gap postitioned at high level

half round ridge tiles bedded in cm. mt. (1:3) butt jointed in length with ends of ridge tiles filled with mortar and tile slip inserts

under ridge top course tile 38 x 25 timber battens (see Note 2)

plain tiles

margin

lap

ridge

airflow

rafters

gauge

underlay, see page 504

RIDGE DETAIL

margin = gauge

$$= \frac{\text{tile length} - \text{lap}}{2}$$

$$= \frac{265 - 65}{2}$$

$$= 100\text{mm}$$

plain tiles nailed to battens every 4th course

underlay

timber battens

rafters

ceiling joists

ventilation spacer

insulation between and over joists

eaves tile

vapour-check plasterboard ceiling (see Note 1)

gutter

50mm deep wall plate

soffit board

external wall with insulated cavity

fascia

cavity insulation

10mm wide continuous ventilation gap

EAVES DETAIL

Note 1: Through ventilation is necessary to prevent condensation from occurring in the roof space. A vapour check can also help limit the amount of moisture entering the roof void.

Note 2: 50 × 25 where rafter spacing is 600mm.

ventilation spacer

tile underlay

perforated polypropylene fascia ventilator grille

blocking piece permits truss overhang, preventing compressed insulation below ventilation spacer

PVC gutter skirt

VENTILATED EAVES FASCIA

insulation between and over joists

mineral wool with polyethylene cover (see Note 1)

thin board, e.g. calcium silicate cavity closer

insulated wide cavity wall

Alternative cavity closer

polypropylene seal to ridge tiles

PVC ventilation filler piece

st/st nail with neoprene seal

under ridge tile

breather membrane with polyester coated aluminium flashing over tiles

50mm wide ridge batten secured to roof structure with galv. steel straps

MECHANICALLY FIXED, VENTILATED RIDGE

tile batten

breather membrane (see Note 2)

Note 1: If a cavity closer is also required to function as a cavity barrier to prevent fire spread, it should provide at least 30 minutes' fire resistance (B. Reg. A.D. B3 Section 6 [Vol. 1] and 9 [Vol. 2]).

Note 2: A breather membrane is an alternative to conventional bituminous felt as an under-tiling layer. It has the benefit of restricting liquid water penetration whilst allowing water vapour transfer from within the roof space. This permits air circulation without perforating the under-tiling layer.

Typical detail (warm roof) ~

50 × 38mm counter battens over rafters

rigid insulation board

breather membrane underlay

rafter

tile battens, size and spacing to suit tile

vapour check plasterboard lining

floorboards

ceiling/floor joist

stop batten

insulated cavity wall, with insulation extended to meet roof insulation

Where a roof space is used for habitable space, insulation must be provided within the roof slope. Insulation above the rafters (as shown) creates a 'warm roof', eliminating the need for continuous ventilation. Insulation placed between the rafters creates a 'cold roof', where a continuous 50mm ventilation void above the insulation will assist in the control of condensation (see next page).

Suitable rigid insulants include; low density polyisocyanurate (PIR) foam, reinforced with long strand glass fibres, both faces bonded to aluminium foil with joints aluminium foil taped on the upper surface; high density mineral wool slabs over rafters with less dense mineral wool between rafters.

An alternative location for the breather membrane is under the counter battens. This is often preferred as the insulation board will provide uniform support for the underlay. Otherwise, extra insulation could be provided between the counter battens, retaining sufficient space for the underlay to sag between rafter positions to permit any rainwater penetration to drain to eaves.

Insulation in between rafters is an alternative to placing it above (see page 570). The following details show two possibilities, where if required supplementary insulation can be secured to the underside of rafters.

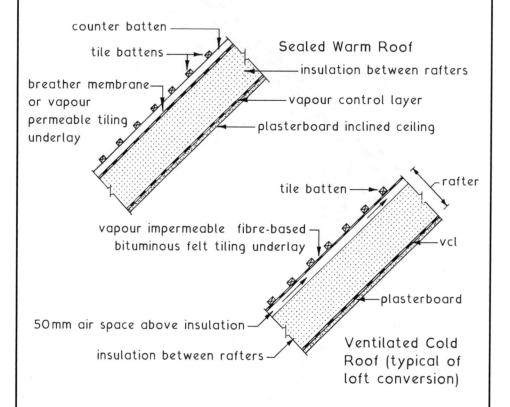

counter batten

tile battens

Sealed Warm Roof

insulation between rafters

breather membrane or vapour permeable tiling underlay

vapour control layer

plasterboard inclined ceiling

tile batten

rafter

vapour impermeable fibre-based bituminous felt tiling underlay

vcl

plasterboard

50 mm air space above insulation

insulation between rafters

Ventilated Cold Roof (typical of loft conversion)

Vapour control layer ~ condensation occurs where warm moist air contacts a cold layer. This could be in the roof space above inhabited rooms, where permeable insulation will not prevent movement of moisture in air and vapour from condensing on the underside of traditional tile underlay (sarking felt) and bituminous felt flat roof coverings. Venting of the roof space (see pages 540 to 541) will control condensation.

Alternatively it can be controlled with a well sealed vapour control layer (for instance, foil [metallised polyester] backed plasterboard) incorporated in the ceiling lining and used with a vapour permeable (breather membrane) underlay to the tiling. Joints and openings in the vcl ceiling (e.g. cable or pipe penetrations) should be sealed, but if this is impractical ventilation should be provided to the underside of the tile underlay.

SIPs are prefabricated 'sandwich' panels that can be used as an alternative to traditional rafters or trusses for roof construction. They can also be used for structural wall panels. Surface layers of plywood or OSB are separated by a core of insulation. The outer face can be provided with counter battens for securing tile battens.

Properties ~
High strength to weight ratio.
Good thermal insulation.
Continuity of insulation, no cold bridges.
Good sound insulation.
Fire-retardant core with improved resistance to fire by lining the inner face with plasterboard.
Dimensionally coordinated.
Factory cut to specification, including mitres and angles for ridge, valleys, hips, etc.
Rapid and simple site assembly.

Panel size ~ typically 1.2m wide in lengths up to 8.0m.

EPS, PIR or PUR foam insulating core adhesive bonded to facings
30x30mm tiling counter batten
airtight side abutments
45 x 18mm structural ribs
CROSS-SECTION
1200mm
12-18mm OSB top and bottom face panels
PART PERSPECTIVE

Typical thermal insulation values ~

Depth/thickness, exc. battens (mm)	U-value (W/m²K)
100	0.35
150	0.25
200	0.20
250	0.15

Key: EPS – Expanded polystyrene. PIR – Polyisocyanurate, rigid foam.

PUR – Rigid polyurethane. OSB – Oriented strand board.

Typical Details ~

38 x 25 timber batténs fixed to 100mm gauge

underlay

half round ridge tile

bonnet hip tiles nailed and bedded in cm.mt (1:3) to hip

tile slip bedded in cement mortar

eaves tile course

plain tiles bonded with hip tiles

HIP DETAIL USING BONNET HIP TILES

roofing felt or underlay

half round ridge tile

38 x 25 timber battens fixed to 100mm gauge

half round hip capping bedded in cm.mt (1:3)

galvanised hip iron screwed to top of hip rafter

eaves tile course

plain tiles mitred under hip capping

HIP DETAIL USING HALF ROUND TILES

curved valley tiles

38 x 25 timber battens fixed to 100mm gauge

underlay

plain tiles

eaves tile course

VALLEY DETAIL USING CURVED VALLEY TILES

Typical Details ~

70° angle turned 25mm into brick joint

2mm lead

STEPPED FLASHING

soaker

abutment wall

75

100

TYPICAL SOAKER

gauge + lap

plain tiles

38 x 25 s/w timber battens fixed to 100mm gauge

underlay

1.25 mm lead soakers

tile and a half tiles in alternate courses

stepped flashing dressed over upstand of soakers and wedged and pointed into brick joints

ABUTMENT DETAIL

underlay

plain tiles

single layer undercloak of plain tiles used sideways with surface tiles edge bedded over in cm. mt. (1:3) to give a neat finish with a slight tilt to direct rainwater back onto roof

gable end wall with 50mm verge overhang

38 x 25 s/w timber battens at 100mm gauge

eaves course

boxed end to fascia

tile and a half tiles in alternate courses

VERGE DETAIL

513

Single Lap Tiling ~ so called because the single lap of one tile over another provides the weather tightness as opposed to the two layers of tiles used in double lap tiling. Most of the single lap tiles produced in clay and concrete have a tongue and groove joint along their side edges and in some patterns on all four edges which forms a series of interlocking joints and therefore these tiles are called single lap interlocking tiles. Generally there will be an overall reduction in the weight of the roof covering when compared with double lap tiling but the batten size is larger than that used for plain tiles and as a minimum every tile in alternate courses should be twice nailed, although a good specification will require every tile to be twice nailed. The gauge or batten spacing for single lap tiling is found by subtracting the end lap from the length of the tile.

Typical Single Lap Tiles ~

ROLL TYPE TILE

minimum pitch 30°

head lap 75mm

side lap 30mm

gauge 343mm

linear coverage 300mm

TROUGH TYPE TILE

minimum pitch 15°

head lap 75mm

side lap 38mm

gauge 338mm

linear coverage 292mm

Typical Details ~

half round ridge tile

plain tile slip or dentils
bedded in cm. mt. in
troughs of profiled tiles

interlocking single lap
tiles each nailed or
clipped to battens

50 x 25
timber
batten

ridge

rafters

gauge

underlay

RIDGE DETAIL

lap

underside of deep profiles
filled with filler piece or
bedded in cm.mt. on eaves
course of plain tiles

margin

rafters

ventilation spacer

margin = gauge
= tile length – lap

ceiling joists

insulation

vapour check
plasterboard
(see Note 1, p. 507)

100 × 50 wall plate

fascia

soffit
board

external wall with thermal
blockwork inner leaf

ventilation
gap

cavity insulation

EAVES DETAIL

Hips – can be finished with a half round tile as a capping as shown
   for double lap tiling on page 512.

Valleys – these can be finished by using special valley trough tiles
   or with a lead lined gutter – see manufacturer's data.

Slates ~ slate is a natural dense material which can be split into thin sheets and cut to form a small unit covering suitable for pitched roofs in excess of 25° pitch. Slates are graded according to thickness and texture, the thinnest being known as 'Bests'. These are of 4 mm nominal thickness. Slates are laid to the same double lap principles as plain tiles. Ridges and hips are normally covered with half round or angular tiles whereas valley junctions are usually of mitred slates over soakers. Unlike plain tiles every course is fixed to the battens by head or centre nailing, the latter being used on long slates and on pitches below 35° to overcome the problem of vibration caused by the wind which can break head nailed long slates.

Typical Details ~

clay angular ridge tile

top course slate

head nailed slates

underlay

battens

rafters

margin

75mm head lap

ridge

RIDGE DETAIL

$$\text{gauge in mm} = \frac{\text{slate length} - (\text{lap} + 25)}{2}$$

underlay

rafters

battens

ventilation spacer

ceiling joists

gauge

eaves course slate

head nailed slates

margin

gutter

insulation

12.5mm plasterboard ceiling

100 x 50 wall plate

insulated cavity with thermal block and brick external wall

fascia

soffit

ventilation gap

EAVES DETAIL

NB. Gauge for centre nailed slates = (slate length − lap) ÷ 2.

The UK has been supplied with its own slate resources from quarries in Wales, Cornwall and Westermorland. Imported slate is also available from Spain, Argentina and parts of the Far East.

e.g. Countess slate, 510 × 255 mm laid to a 30° pitch with 75 mm head lap.

Batten gauge = (slate length − lap) ÷ 2
= (510 − 75) ÷ 2 = 218 mm.

Holing gauge = batten gauge + head lap + 8 to 15 mm,
= 218 + 75 + (8 to 15 mm) = 301 to 308 mm.

Side lap = 255 ÷ 2 = 127 mm.

Margin = batten gauge of 218 mm.

Eaves course length = head lap + margin = 293 mm.

Traditional slate names and sizes (mm) –

Empress	650 × 400	Wide Viscountess	460 × 255
Princess	610 × 355	Viscountess	460 × 230
Duchess	610 × 305	Wide Ladies	405 × 255
Small Duchess	560 × 305	Broad Ladies	405 × 230
Marchioness	560 × 280	Ladies	405 × 205
Wide Countess	510 × 305	Wide Headers	355 × 305
Countess	510 × 255	Headers	355 × 255
.. ..	510 × 230	Small Ladies	355 × 203
.. ..	460 × 305	Narrow Ladies	355 × 180

Sizes can also be cut to special order.

Generally, the larger the slate, the lower the roof may be pitched. Also, the lower the roof pitch, the greater the head lap.

Slate quality	Thickness (mm)	Weight at 75mm head lap (kg/m^2)
Best	4	26
Medium strong	5	Thereafter in proportion
Heavy	6	to thickness
Extra heavy	9	

Roof pitch (degrees)	Min. head lap (mm)
20	115
25	85
35	75
45	65

See also:

1. BS EN 12326-1: Slate and stone products for discontinuous roofing and cladding. Product specification.
2. Slate producers' catalogues.
3. BS 5534: Code of practice for slating and tiling.

Roof hip examples –

Close mitred hip, roof pitch > 30°

hip rafter

jack rafter

underlay in two layers, overlapping at least 300mm each side of hip

50 × 25mm batten

1.25mm lead soaker under each pair of mitred slates

opposing pairs of mitre cut slates

eaves course

standard slate

Mitred hip with clay or concrete hip tiles

hip rafter

batten

jack rafter

double layer of underlay at hip, at least 300mm overlap each side of hip

mitred slates

concrete or clay hip tile mortar bedded over mitred slates

hip iron at eaves

Roof valley examples –

50 × 25mm batten

1.25 mm lead soakers, min. 150 mm wide at head and at least half slate width at bottom

underlay in two layers at valley, min. 300mm each side of valley rafter

mitre cut slates in opposing pairs

standard slate

eaves course

Mitre cut valley
Limitations:
1. Roof pitch >45°
2. Valley angle <90°
3. Valley length <6m

Alternatives

valley rafter

wide lay boards in valley to support taper cut slates

two supplementary layers of underlay over lay boards to overlap normal underlay

two layers of underlay at valley

valley rafter

valley slates tapered to a smooth curve

Swept valley

225mm min. lay board on valley rafter, usually with additional board either side

jack rafter

Laced valley

NB. In swept valleys, cut and tapered slates are interleaved with 1.25 mm lead soakers.

Materials – water reed (Norfolk reed), wheat straw (Spring or Winter), Winter being the most suitable. Wheat for thatch is often known as wheat reed, long straw or Devon reed. Other thatches include rye and oat straws, and sedge. Sedge is harvested every fourth year to provide long growth, making it most suitable as a ridging material.

There are various patterns and styles of thatching, relating to the skill of the thatcher and local traditions.

Typical details –

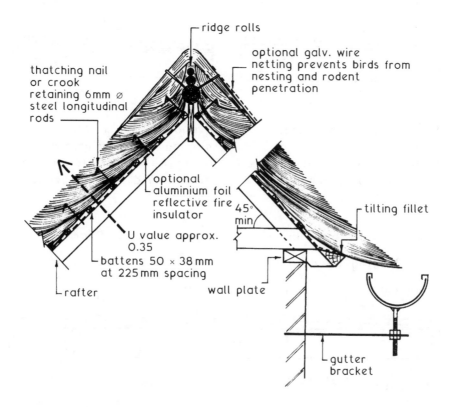

The material composition of thatch with its natural voids and surface irregularities provides excellent insulation when dry and compact. However, when worn with possible accumulation of moss and rainwater, the U-value is less reliable. Thatch is also very vulnerable to fire. Therefore, in addition to imposing a premium, insurers may require application of a surface fire retardant and a fire insulant underlay.

Flat Roofs ~ these roofs are very seldom flat with a pitch of 0° but are considered to be flat if the pitch does not exceed 10°. The actual pitch chosen can be governed by the roof covering selected and/or by the required rate of rainwater discharge off the roof. As a general rule the minimum pitch for smooth surfaces such as asphalt should be 1:80 or 0°-43' and for sheet coverings with laps 1:60 or 0°-57'.

Methods of Obtaining Falls ~

1. Joists cut to falls

Simple to fix but could be wasteful in terms of timber unless two joists are cut from one piece of timber

2. Joists laid to falls

Economic and simple but sloping soffit may not be acceptable, but this could be hidden by a flat suspended ceiling

3. Firrings with joist run

Simple and effective but does not provide a means of natural cross ventilation. Usual method employed.

4. Firrings against joist run

Simple and effective but uses more timber than 3 but does provide a means of natural cross ventilation

Wherever possible joists should span the shortest distance of the roof plan.

Timber Roof Joists ~ the spacing and sizes of joists is related to the loadings and span, actual dimensions for domestic loadings can be taken direct from recommendations in Approved Document A or they can be calculated as shown for timber beam designs. Strutting between joists should be used if the span exceeds 2·400 to restrict joist movements and twisting.

Typical Eaves Details ~

Ref. BS EN 13707: Flexible sheets for waterproofing. Reinforced bitumen sheets for roof waterproofing. Definitions and characteristics.

water check

stone chippings and 3-layer built-up roofing felt

insulation board

vcl

decking

softwood noggins at 400 c/c

firring

joist

fascia board

plasterboard

external wall with insulated cavity

strutting if required

mineral wool insulation between top of wall and decking

TYPICAL VERGE DETAILS – WARM DECK

abutment wall

1.75 mm lead flashing

insulation strip

chippings and felt

angle fillet

insulation board

vcl over decking

firring and joist

joist hanger

plasterboard

TYPICAL ABUTMENT DETAILS – WARM DECK

Ref. BS 8217: Reinforced bitumen membranes for roofing. Code of practice.

Further details ~

COLD DECK

- stone chippings
- 3-layer built-up roofing felt
- decking
- firring
- joist
- insulation quilt between joists
- vcl
- plasterboard
- cement particle board cavity seal
- fascia
- eaves ventilation

WARM DECK

- insulating roof board
- 1.75mm lead apron
- stepped dpc cavity tray
- vcl
- joist
- angle fillet

INVERTED WARM DECK

- inverted insulating roof board
- ceramic paving or pebbles/stone chippings
- waterproof membrane

Note: Insulation type and thickness varies with application and situation.

Timber Flat Roofs — Joist Sizes

Typical spans and loading for flat roof joists of general structural (GS) grade ~

Sawn size (mm x mm)	Dead weight of decking and ceiling, excluding the self-weight of the joists (kg/m²)								
	< 50			50–75			75–100		
	Spacing of joists (mm c/c)								
	400	450	600	400	450	600	400	450	600
	Maximum clear span (m)								
38 x 125	1.80	1.79	1.74	1.74	1.71	1.65	1.68	1.65	1.57
38 x 150	2.35	2.33	2.27	2.27	2.25	2.18	2.21	2.18	2.09
38 x 175	2.88	2.85	2.77	2.77	2.74	2.64	2.68	2.64	2.53
38 x 200	3.47	3.43	3.29	3.33	3.28	3.16	3.21	3.16	3.02
38 x 225	4.08	4.03	3.71	3.90	3.84	3.56	3.75	3.66	3.43
50 x 125	2.06	2.05	2.00	2.00	1.98	1.93	1.95	1.93	1.86
50 x 150	2.68	2.65	2.59	2.59	2.58	2.47	2.51	2.47	2.38
50 x 175	3.27	3.25	3.14	3.14	3.10	2.99	3.04	2.99	2.86
50 x 200	3.93	3.86	3.61	3.76	3.70	3.47	3.62	3.56	3.35
50 x 225	4.60	4.47	4.07	4.38	4.30	3.91	4.21	4.13	3.78
63 x 100	1.67	1.66	1.63	1.63	1.61	1.57	1.59	1.93	1.86
63 x 125	2.31	2.29	2.24	2.24	2.21	2.15	2.17	2.15	2.07
63 x 150	2.98	2.95	2.87	2.87	2.84	2.74	2.78	2.74	2.63
63 x 175	3.62	3.59	3.41	3.48	3.43	3.28	3.36	3.30	3.16
63 x 200	4.34	4.29	3.90	4.15	4.08	3.75	3.99	3.92	3.62
63 x 225	5.00	4.82	4.39	4.82	4.64	4.22	4.62	4.48	4.08
75 x 125	2.50	2.48	2.42	2.42	2.40	2.32	2.35	2.32	2.24
75 x 150	3.23	3.19	3.11	3.11	3.07	2.96	3.00	2.96	2.84
75 x 175	3.91	3.87	3.61	3.75	3.69	3.47	3.61	3.55	3.35
75 x 200	4.66	4.53	4.13	4.45	4.36	3.97	4.28	4.20	3.84
75 x 225	5.28	5.09	4.65	5.09	4.90	4.47	4.92	4.74	4.32

Notes:

1. See pages 38 and 39 for material dead weights.
2. See pages 141 and 142 for softwood classification and grades.

Timber Boards ~ traditional decking, rarely used now as manufactured composite boards are less expensive in materal cost and installation time. Softwood boards should be at least 19mm finished thickness on joists spaced at up to 450mm centres. Tongued and grooved boards are preferred to plain edge boards as butt jointed plain edge boards may tend to warp and deform. Boards should be tightly clamped, securely nailed with nail heads punched below the surface. Countersunk screw fixings are an alternative.

Plywood ~ exterior grade boarding often specified as WBP (water boiled proof), a reference to the bonding quality of the adhesive securing the ply veneers. Fixed on all four edges, requiring noggins/ struts between the joists. BS EN 636.

Particle Boards ~ general term for a variety of board materials derived from wood shavings and parings. Fixed with nails or screws as appropriate, as indicated for plywood.

Wood chipboard – Susceptible to movement and possibly decay if exposed to dampness. Therefore should be specified as moisture resistant to BS EN 312 types C3, C4 or C5. Usually identified by a dull green colour. Available pre-felted, i.e. with a factory-applied bituminous felt layer.

Oriented strand board (OSB) – a favoured alternative to chipboard as it is more stable in moist conditions. BS EN 300 types 3 and 4.

Cement bonded particle board – another alternative that has a high density and greater moisture resistance than other particle boards. BS EN 634-2.

Woodwool Slabs ~ composed of wood fibre shreds bonded together with cement. Produced in a variety of thicknesses, but for roof decking the minimum thickness is 50mm to satisfy strength requirements when accessed. Widths of 600mm are produced in lengths up to 4m. BS EN 13168.

Further information on composite board materials is on pages 860 and 861.

Conservation of Energy ~ this can be achieved in two ways:

1. Cold Deck – insulation is placed on the ceiling lining, between joists. See pages 523 and 525 for details. A metallised polyester lined plasterboard ceiling functions as a vapour control layer, with a minimum 50 mm air circulation space between insulation and decking. The air space corresponds with eaves vents and both provisions will prevent moisture buildup, condensation and possible decay of timber.

2. (a) Warm Deck – rigid* insulation is placed below the waterproof covering and above the roof decking. The insulation must be sufficient to maintain the vapour control layer and roof members at a temperature above dewpoint, as this type of roof does not require ventilation.

    (b) Inverted Warm Deck – rigid* insulation is positioned above the waterproof covering. The insulation must be unaffected by water and capable of receiving a stone dressing or ceramic pavings.

* Resin bonded mineral fibre roof boards, expanded polystyrene or polyurethane slabs.

Typical Warm Deck Details ~

Material ~ bitumen is found naturally in ground deposits on its own or as a component of asphalt. It is also produced during distillation of crude oil.

Composition ~ originally based on rag fibres as reinforcement to hot bitumen impregnated during manufacture. Modern bituminous felts have a matrix of glass fibre or polyester matting as reinforcement to a stabilising bitumen coating on both sides. These materials provide an effective binding and have superseded rags as a more robust base. The upper surface is lightly coated with sand or fine mineral granules to prevent the sheet from sticking to itself when rolled. Standard dimensions are rolls of 1m width in lengths of 8 to 10 m. Thickness varies depending on specification, but is usually about 3 to 4 mm. During manufacture some polymer modification is included with the bitumen. This is to reduce rigidity, making the material more flexible, workable and durable. Additives can be elastomers of atactic-polypropylene (APP) or styrene-butadiene-styrene (SBS).

Application ~ multi-layers, usually three, preferably in material specified to BS EN 13707 and laid to the recommendations of BS 8217. The first layer is laid at right angles to the fall commencing at the eaves. If the decking is timber, plywood or a wood composite, the first layer can be secured with large flat head nails, subsequent layers bonded together with hot molten bitumen. Side laps are at least 50 mm with 75 mm minimum laps at upper and lower ends. A variation known as torch-on is for use with specially made sheet. This is heated to the underside to produce a wave of molten bitumen as the sheet is unrolled. Timber product decking is not suitable for torch-on applications due to the fire risk, unless the surface is pre-felted and taped.

Finish ~ limestone, light-coloured shingle or granite chippings of 10 to 12 mm are suitable as weatherproofing, protection from solar radiation and resistance to fire. These are bonded to the surface with a cold or hot molten bitumen solution.

Composition ~ a natural fine-grained material from sedimentary deposits in parts of Derbyshire, Leicestershire and Shropshire. A variation mined mainly in France known as rock asphalt is extracted from bitumen impregnated sandstone and limestone. The base material is often modified to create a composite material. Additives include limestone to improve stability and oil to reduce hardness and brittleness. Synthetic or natural fibres can be added for reinforcement. For transportation and storage, asphalt is cast into blocks. On site the blocks are heated in a cauldron to about 200°C. Molten asphalt is transferred by bucket and spread manually with a wooden trowel.

Application ~ this consists of two layers of mastic asphalt laid breaking joints and built up to a minimum thickness of 20 mm and should be laid to the recommendations of BS 8218. The mastic asphalt is laid over an isolating membrane of black sheathing felt which should be laid loose with 50 mm minimum overlaps.

Typical Details ~

ABUTMENT DETAIL – COLD DECK

EAVES DETAIL – COLD DECK

Ref. BS 8218: Code of practice for mastic asphalt roofing.

Milled Lead Sheet ~ produced from refined lead to an initial thickness of about 125 mm. Thereafter it is rolled and cut to 12.000 m lengths, 2.400 m wide into the following thicknesses and categories:

BS 1178* Code No.	BS EN 12588/standard milled thickness (mm)	Weight (kg/m²) BS EN/milled	Colour marking
3	1.25/1.32	14.17/14.97	Green
-	1.50/1.59	17.00/18.03	Yellow
4	1.75/1.80	19.84/20.41	Blue
5	2.00/2.24	22.67/25.40	Red
6	2.50/2.65	28.34/30.05	Black
7	3.00/3.15	34.02/35.72	White
8	3.50/3.55	39.69/40.26	Orange

*BS 1178: Specification for milled sheet lead and strip for building purposes. This BS has been superseded by BS EN 12588: Lead and lead alloys. Rolled lead sheet for building purposes. The former BS codes are replaced with lead sheet thicknesses between 1.25 and 3.50 millimetres. They are included here, as these codes remain common industry reference. Codes originated before metrication as the approximate weight of lead sheet in pounds per square foot (lb/ft²), e.g. 3 lb/ft² became Code 3.

Other dimensions ~ cut widths between 75 mm and 600 mm in coils.

Density ~ approximately 11.325 kg/m³.

Application (colour marking) ~

Green and yellow – soakers.

Blue, red and black – flat roof covering in small, medium and large areas respectively (see table on page 534).

White and orange – lead lining to walls as protection from X-rays or for sound insulation, but can be used for relatively large areas of roof covering.

Timber Flat Roof Coverings – Lead Sheet

Thermal Movement ~ the coefficient of linear expansion for lead is 0.0000297 (2.97×10^{-6}) for every degree Kelvin.

E.g. If the exposure temperature range throughout a year is from –10°C to 35°C (45K), then a 2.000 m length of sheet lead could increase by: $0.0000297 \times 45 \times 2 = 0.00267$ m, or 2.67 mm.

Over time this movement will cause fatigue stress, manifesting in cracking. To prevent fracture, a smooth surface underlay should be used and the areas of lead sheet limited with provision of joints designed to accommodate movement.

Underlay ~ placed over plywood or similar smooth surface decking, or over rigid insulation boards. Bitumen impregnated felt or waterproof building paper have been the established underlay, but for new work a non-woven, needle punched polyester textile is now generally preferred.

Fixings ~ clips, screws and nails of copper, brass or stainless steel.

Jointing ~ for small areas such as door canopies and dormers where there is little opportunity for thermal movement, a simply formed welt can be used if the depth of rainwater is unlikely to exceed the welt depth.

Welted joint

25 mm

copper clips at 500 mm spacing, nailed to decking and folded within welt

underlay

decking

Jointing to absorb movement:

• Wood cored rolls in the direction of the roof slope (see next page).

• Drips at right angles to and across the roof slope (see next page).

Typical provision of wood cored rolls
and drips - detail at junction

drip 55mm min.

2mm lead sheet

50mm high
wood cored
roll, 25mm
wide at base

40mm splashlap

undercloak nailed
every 150mm to top
of roll

45

25mm rebate
for lead nailed
every 100mm

40mm splashlap
overcloak

anti-capillary groove

smooth surface decking
or decking plus underlay

Lead is a soft and malleable material. A skilled craftsman (traditionally a plumber) can manipulate lead sheet with hand tools originally made from dense timber such as boxwood, but now produced from high-density polythene. This practice is known as `bossing´ the lead to the profiles shown. Alternatively, the lead sheet can be cut and welded to shape.

Selection of lead working tools ~

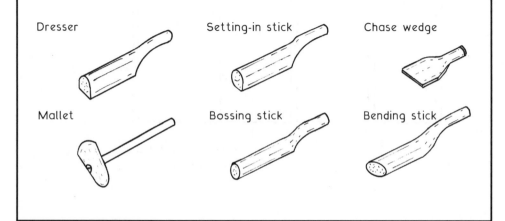

Dresser

Setting-in stick

Chase wedge

Mallet

Bossing stick

Bending stick

Spacing of wood cored rolls and drips varies with the thickness specification of lead sheet. The following is a guide ~

BS EN 12588 thickness (mm)	Maximum distance between drips (mm) [A]	Maximum distance between rolls (mm) [B]
1.25 and 1.50	Use for soakers only	
1.75	1500	500
2.00	2000	600
2.50	2250	675
3.00	2500	675
3.50	3000	750

Typical flat roof plan (page 491)

Single Ply Membranes ~ durable, resilient, flexible and lightweight sheet materials composed mainly of synthetic polymers. Some are reinforced with glass fibres depending on application and coverage area. A backing of glass fibre or polyester matting is often provided as a bonding interface.

Thickness ~ generally between 1 and 2 mm.

Fixing ~ product manufacturer's recommended adhesive applied to the sub-surface. Purpose made mechanical fixing devices are an alternative in situations that may be exposed to wind lift.

Materials ~ Polyvinyl chloride (PVC).
    Thermoplastics: Thermoplastic polyolefin (TPO).
           Chlorinated polyethylene (CPE).
           Ethylene interpolymer (EIP).
           Copolymer alloy (CPA).
           Acrylonitrile butadiene polymer (NBP).

Other Considerations ~
• PVC membranes can be solvent adhesive bonded at overlaps or hot air welded.
• Thermoplastics are hot air welded at seams and overlaps (homogenous jointing at about 400 to 500°C).
• Ethylene propylene diene monomer (EPDM) is a thermoset synthetic rubber that can only be adhesive sealed. Application of heat would physically break it down.

Typical Detail ~

single ply membrane
adhesive
rigid batt insulation
vapour control layer
boarded decking

Note: 'Warm deck' shown. 'Cold deck' construction details on pages 523 and 525.

Application

hand held low voltage
electric element welder
(see note below)

pressure applied
by hand roller

PVC single ply
membrane

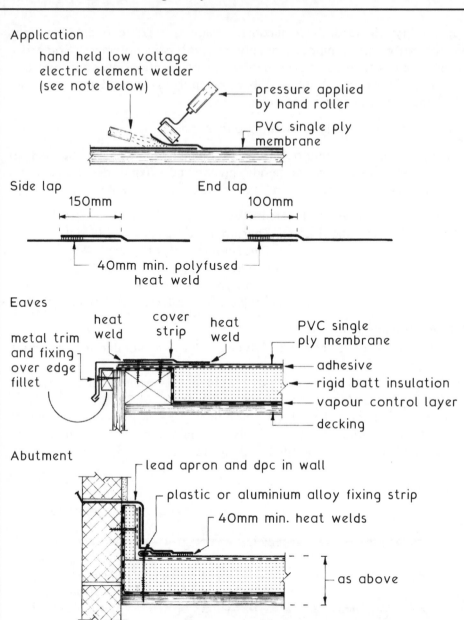

Side lap

150mm

End lap

100mm

40mm min. polyfused
heat weld

Eaves

heat
weld

cover
strip

heat
weld

PVC single
ply membrane

metal trim
and fixing
over edge
fillet

adhesive

rigid batt insulation

vapour control layer

decking

Abutment

lead apron and dpc in wall

plastic or aluminium alloy fixing strip

40mm min. heat welds

as above

Notes:

• Hand held welder and roller used mainly for small detail areas.
  Automatic (manually directed) welder/roller more effective for
  continuous seaming.

• See *Note* re. warm and cold deck construction on preceding
  page.

A dormer is the framework for a vertical window constructed from the roof slope. It may be used as a feature, but is more likely as an economical and practical means for accessing light and ventilation to an attic room. Dormers are normally external with the option of a flat or pitched roof. Frame construction is typical of the following illustrations, with connections made by traditional housed and tenoned joints or simpler galvanised steel brackets and hangers.

Dormer Window Types

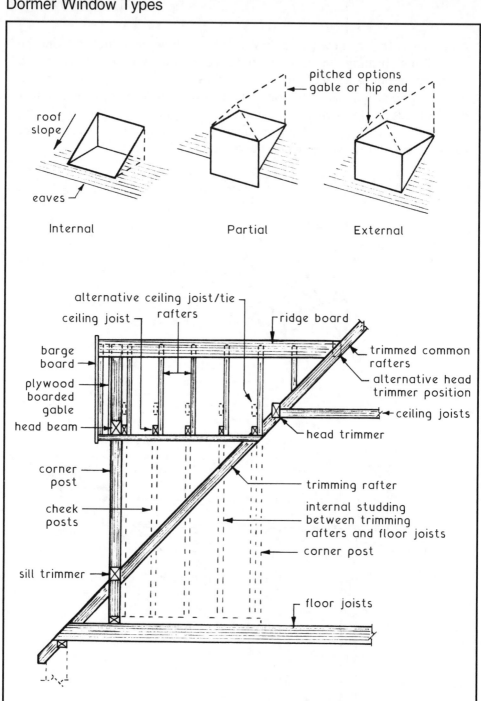

roof slope

eaves

Internal

pitched options
gable or hip end

Partial

External

alternative ceiling joist/tie

ceiling joist — rafters

ridge board

barge board

plywood boarded gable

head beam

corner post

cheek posts

sill trimmer

trimmed common rafters

alternative head trimmer position

ceiling joists

head trimmer

trimming rafter

internal studding between trimming rafters and floor joists

corner post

floor joists

Section through gable ended external dormer

A graceful interruption to the routine of a pitched roof, derived from thatched roofs where the thatch is swept over window openings. Other suitable coverings are timber shingles, plain tiles and small slates.

Main roof pitch $\geq$ 50°. Eyebrow pitch $\geq$ 35°.

Transition curve should be smooth with span to height ratio > 8:1. Less is possible, but may prove impractical and disproportionate.

Possible profile ~

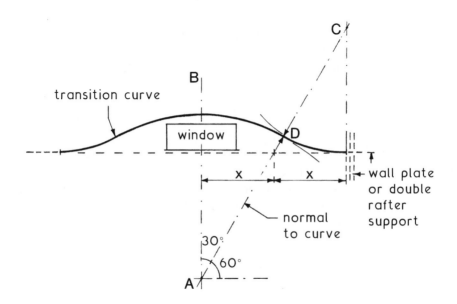

A–B is a line through the centre of the window opening.

A–D radius is positioned to clear the window head.

C–D radius is established near window base in continuity to A–D.

A purpose-made gluelam beam can be used to create the transition curve, effectively extending the wall plate to receive the eyebrow rafters. The curved beam for an intermediate eyebrow may be supported on joist hangers to double trimming rafters each side.

Air carries water vapour, the amount increasing proportionally with the air temperature. As the water vapour increases so does the pressure and this causes the vapour to migrate from warmer to cooler parts of a building. As the air temperature reduces, so does its ability to hold water and this manifests as condensation on cold surfaces. Insulation between living areas and roof spaces increases the temperature differential and potential for condensation in the roof void.

Condensation can be prevented by either of the following:

* Providing a vapour control layer on the warm side of any insulation.
* Removing the damp air by ventilating the colder area.

The most convenient form of vapour layer is vapour check plasterboard which has a moisture resistant lining bonded to the back of the board. A typical patented product is a foil or metallised polyester backed plasterboard in 9·5 and 12·5 mm standard thicknesses. This is most suitable where there are rooms in roofs and for cold deck flat roofs. Ventilation is appropriate to larger roof spaces.

cross flow of air — potential for moist air to accumulate

Partial roof void
ventilation through the eaves

ridge vents, see page 507

insulated ceiling

Total roof void ventilation through eaves and high level vents

Roof Ventilation – provision of eaves ventilation alone should allow adequate air circulation in most situations. However, in some climatic conditions and where the air movement is not directly at right angles to the building, moist air can be trapped in the roof apex. Therefore, supplementary ridge ventilation is recommended.

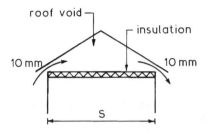

Insulation at ceiling level (1)
S = span <10m for
roof pitches 15°–35°

Insulation at ceiling level (2)
S = span >10m for
roof pitches 15°–35°
Any span for roof
pitches >35°

Insulation at ceiling level and central dividing wall
Roof pitches >15°
for any span

NB. Ventilation dimensions shown relate to a continuous strip (or equivalent) of at least the given gap.

5 mm

Mono-pitch or lean-to roof
Roof pitch >15°, any span

10 mm

insulation

5 mm   5 mm

50 mm clear
passage

Room within roof void
All pitches and spans

25 mm   25 mm

5 mm   5 mm

10 mm   10 mm

rooflight

5 mm   5 mm

Room within roof void with
obstructions
All pitches, all spans

25 mm   25 mm

50 mm clear
passage

25 mm   25 mm

Flat roof

Refs.: Building Regulations, Approved Document C – Site
preparation and resistance to contaminants and moisture.
Section 6 – Roofs.
BS 5250: Code of practice for control of condensation in
buildings.

BRE report – Thermal Insulation: avoiding risks (3rd. edn).

Lateral Restraint – stability of gable walls and construction at the eaves, plus integrity of the roof structure during excessive wind forces, requires complementary restraint and continuity through 30 × 5 mm cross-sectional area galvanised steel straps.

Exceptions may occur if the roof:

1. exceeds 15° pitch, and
2. is tiled or slated, and
3. has the type of construction known locally to resist gusts, and
4. has ceiling joists and rafters bearing onto support walls at not more than 1·2 m centres.

Application ~

543

Preservation ~ ref. Building Regulations: Materials and Workmanship. Approved Document to support Regulation 7.

Woodworm infestation of untreated structural timbers is common. However, the smaller woodborers such as the abundant Furniture beetle are controllable. It is the threat of considerable damage potential from the House Longhorn beetle that has forced many local authorities in Surrey and the fringe areas of adjacent counties to seek timber preservation listing in the Building Regulations (see Table 1 in the above reference). Prior to the introduction of pretreated timber (c. 1960s), the House Longhorn beetle was once prolific in housing in the south of England, establishing a reputation for destroying structural roof timbers, particularly in the Camberley area.

House Longhorn beetle data:

Latin name – Hylotrupes bajulus

Life cycle – Mature beetle lays up to 200 eggs on rough surface of untreated timber.

        After two to three weeks, larvae emerge and bore into wood, preferring sapwood to denser growth areas. Up to 10 years in the damaging larval stage. In three weeks, larvae change to chrysalides to emerge as mature beetles in summer to reproduce.

Timber appearance – powdery deposits (frass) on the surface and the obvious mature beetle flight holes.

Beetle appearance –

head and adjacent body segment characterised by grey hair and two distinct black spots — dark-brown or black back — approx. 25 mm

Other woodborers:

Furniture beetle – dark brown, 6–8 mm long, lays 20–50 eggs on soft or hardwoods. Boreholes only 1–2 mm diameter.

Lyctus powder post beetle – reddish brown, 10–15 mm long, lays 70–200 eggs on sapwood of new hardwood. Boreholes only 1–2 mm in diameter.

Death-watch beetle – dark brown, sometimes speckled in lighter shades. Lays 40–80 eggs on hardwood. Known for preferring the oak timbers used in old churches and similar buildings.

Boreholes about 3 mm diameter.

Preservation ~ treatment of timber to prevent damage from House Longhorn beetle.

In the areas specified (see previous page), all softwood used in roof structures including ceiling joists and any other softwood fixings should be treated with insecticide prior to installation. Specific chemicals and processes have not been listed in the Building Regulations since the 1976 issue. Timber treatment then was either:

- Vacuum/pressure impregnation with a blend of copper, chromium and arsenic (CCA), known commercially as 'tanalising'.
- Diffusion with sodium borate (boron salts).
- Steeping (min. 10 mins.) in organic solvent wood preservative.
- Steeping or soaking in tar oil (creosote). This has limitations due to staining of adjacent surfaces.

The current edition of Approved Document A (Structure) to the Building Regulations refers to guidance on preservative treatments in the British Wood Preserving and Damp-Proofing Association's Manual. Other guidance is provided in:

BS 5707: Specification for preparation for wood preservatives in organic solvents.

BS 8417: Preservation of wood. Code of practice.

BS EN 117: Wood preservatives.

Insect treatment adds about 10% to the cost of timber and also enhances its resistance to moisture. Other parts of the structure (e.g. floors and partitions) are less exposed to woodworm damage as they are enclosed. Also, there is a suggestion that if these areas received treated timber, the toxic fumes could be harmful to the health of building occupants. Current requirements for through ventilation in roofs have the added benefit of discouraging wood boring insects, as they prefer draught-free damp areas.

Note: EU directive CEN/TC 38 prohibits the use of CCA preservative for domestic applications and in places where the public may be in contact with it.

Green roof ~ green with reference to the general appearance of plant growths and for being environmentally acceptable. Part of the measures for constructing sustainable and ecologically friendly buildings.

Categories:
- Extensive ~ a relatively shallow soil base (typically 50 mm) and lightweight construction. Maximum roof pitch is 40° and slopes greater than 20° will require a system of baffles to prevent the soil moving. Plant life is limited by the shallow soil base to grasses, mosses, herbs and sedum (succulents, generally with fleshy leaves producing pink or white flowers).
- Intensive ~ otherwise known as a roof garden. This category has a deeper soil base (typically 400 mm) that will provide for landscaping features, small ponds, occasional shrubs and small trees. A substantial building structure is required for support and it is only feasible to use a flat roof.

Advantages:
- Absorbs and controls water run-off.
- Integral thermal insulation.
- Integral sound insulation.
- Absorbs air pollutants, dust and CO_2.
- Passive heat storage potential.

Disadvantages:
- Weight.
- Maintenance.

Construction ~ the following buildup will be necessary to fulfil the objectives and to create stability:
- Vapour control layer above the roof structure.
- Rigid slab insulation.
- Root resilient waterproof under-layer.
- Drainage layer.
- Filter.
- Growing medium (soil).
- Vegetation (grass, etc.)

NB. Examples of both extensive and intensive green roof construction are shown on the next page.

Typical extensive roof buildup ~

grass/sedum
soil
filter layer or fleece
drainage layer*
waterproof membrane
insulation
vapour control layer
reinforced concrete roof structure

* typically, expanded polystyrene with slots

Component	Weight (kg/m²)	Thickness (mm)
vcl	3	3
insulation	3	50
membrane	5	5
drainage layer	3	50
filter	3	3
soil	90	50
turf	40	20
	-------------	---------
	147 kg/m²	181 mm

147 kg/m² saturated weight x 9.81 = 1442 N/m² or 1.44 kN/m²

Typical intensive roof buildup ~

plants, shrubs and grasses
soil substrate up to 450 mm
filter layer or fleece
drainage layer
water retention fleece over waterproof membrane
insulation
vapour control layer
reinforced concrete roof structure

Depth to vcl, approximately 560 mm at about 750 kg/m² saturated weight. 750 kg/m² × 9.81 = 7358 N/m² or 7.36 kN/m².

Thermal insulation of external elements of construction is measured in terms of thermal transmittance rate, otherwise known as the U-value. It is the amount of heat energy in watts transmitted through one square metre of construction for every one degree Kelvin between external and internal air temperature, i.e. W/m^2K.

U-values are unlikely to be entirely accurate, due to:

* the varying effects of solar radiation, atmospheric dampness and prevailing winds.

* inconsistencies in construction, even with the best of supervision.

* 'bridging' where different structural components meet, e.g. dense mortar in lightweight blockwork.

Nevertheless, calculation of the U-value for a particular element of construction will provide guidance as to whether the structure is thermally acceptable. The Building Regulations, Approved Document L, Conservation of fuel and power, determines acceptable energy efficiency standards for modern buildings, with the objective of limiting the emission of carbon dioxide and other burnt gases into the atmosphere.

The U-value is calculated by taking the reciprocal of the summed thermal resistances (R) of the component parts of an element of construction:

$$U = \frac{1}{\Sigma R} = W/m^2K$$

R is expressed in m^2K/W. The higher the value, the better a component's insulation. Conversely, the lower the value of U, the better the insulative properties of the structure.

Building Regulations, Approved Document references:
L1A, Work in new dwellings.
L1B, Work in existing dwellings.
L2A, Work in new buildings other than dwellings.
L2B, Work in existing buildings other than dwellings.

Thermal resistances (R) are a combination of the different structural, surface and air space components which make up an element of construction. Typically:

$$U = \frac{1}{R_{so} + R_1 + R_2 + R_a + R_3 + R_4 \, etc \cdots + R_{si}} (m^2K/W)$$

Where: R_{so} = Outside or external surface resistance.
R_1, R_2, etc. = Thermal resistance of structural components.
R_a = Air space resistance, e.g. wall cavity.
R_{si} = Internal surface resistance.

The thermal resistance of a structural component (R_1, R_2, etc.) is calculated by dividing its thickness (L) by its thermal conductivity (λ), i.e.

$$R(m^2K/W) = \frac{L(m)}{\lambda (W/mK)}$$

E.g. 1. A 102 mm brick with a conductivity of 0·84 W/mK has a thermal resistance (R) of: 0·102 ÷ 0·84 = 0·121 m²K/W.

E.g. 2.

R₁ - 215 mm brickwork
λ = 0·84 W/mK

R_{so} = 0·055 m²K/W

R₂ -13 mm render and dense plaster
λ = 0·50 W/mK

R_{si} = 0·123 m²K/W

NB. the effect of mortar joints in the brickwork can be ignored, as both components have similar density and insulative properties.

$$U = \frac{1}{R_{so} + R_1 + R_2 + R_{si}}$$

$R_1 = 0·215 \div 0·84 = 0·256$
$R_2 = 0·013 \div 0·50 = 0·026$

$$U = \frac{1}{0·055 + 0·256 + 0·026 + 0·123} = 2·17 W/m^2K$$

Typical values in: m^2K/W

Internal surface resistances (R_{si}):

Walls – 0·123
Floors or ceilings for upward heat flow – 0·104
Floors or ceilings for downward heat flow – 0·148
Roofs (flat or pitched) – 0·104

External surface resistances (R_{so}):

Surface	Exposure		
	Sheltered	Normal	Severe
Wall – high emissivity	0·080	0·055	0·030
Wall – low emissivity	0·110	0·070	0·030
Roof – high emissivity	0·070	0·045	0·020
Roof – low emissivity	0·090	0·050	0·020
Floor – high emissivity	0·070	0·040	0·020

Sheltered – town buildings to 3 storeys.
Normal – town buildings 4 to 8 storeys and most suburban premises.

Severe – > 9 storeys in towns.
> 5 storeys elsewhere and any buildings on exposed coasts and hills.

Air space resistances (R_a):

Pitched or flat roof space – 0·180
Behind vertical tile hanging – 0·120
Cavity wall void – 0·180
Between high and low emissivity surfaces – 0·300
Unventilated/sealed – 0·180

Emissivity relates to the heat transfer across and from surfaces by radiant heat emission and absorption effects. The amount will depend on the surface texture, the quantity and temperature of air movement across it, the surface position or orientation and the temperature of adjacent bodies or materials. High surface emissivity is appropriate for most building materials. An example of low emissivity would be bright aluminium foil on one or both sides of an air space.

Typical values –

Material	Density (kg/m³)	Conductivity (λ) (W/mK)
WALLS:		
Boarding (hardwood)	700	0·18
...... (softwood)	500	0·13
Brick outer leaf	1700	0·84
... inner leaf	1700	0·62
Calcium silicate board	875	0·17
Ceramic tiles	2300	1·30
Concrete	2400	1·93
....	2200	1·59
....	2000	1·33
....	1800	1·13
.... (lightweight)	1200	0·38
.... (reinforced)	2400	2·50
Concrete block (lightweight)	600	0·18
.... (mediumweight)	1400	0·53
Cement mortar (protected)	1750	0·88
.... (exposed)	1750	0·94
Fibreboard	350	0·08
Gypsum plaster (dense)	1300	0·57
Gypsum plaster (lightweight)	600	0·16
Plasterboard	950	0·16
Tile hanging	1900	0·84
Rendering	1300	0·57
Sandstone	2600	2·30
Wall ties (st/st)	7900	17·00
ROOFS:		
Aerated concrete slab	500	0·16
Asphalt	1900	0·60
Bituminous felt in 3 layers	1700	0·50
Sarking felt	1700	0·50
Stone chippings	1800	0·96
Tiles (clay)	2000	1·00
...... (concrete)	2100	1·50
Wood wool slab	500	0·10

Typical values –

Material	Density (kg/m^3)	Conductivity (λ) (W/mK)
FLOORS:		
Cast concrete	2000	1·33
Hardwood block/strip	700	0·18
Plywood/particle board	650	0·14
Screed	1200	0·41
Softwood board	500	0·13
Steel tray	7800	50·00
INSULATION:		
Expanded polystyrene board	20	0·035
Mineral wool batt/slab	25	0·038
Mineral wool quilt	12	0·042
Phenolic foam board	30	0·025
Polyurethane board	30	0·025
Urea formaldehyde foam	10	0·040
GROUND:		
Clay/silt	1250	1·50
Sand/gravel	1500	2·00
Homogeneous rock	3000	3·50

Notes:

1. For purposes of calculating U-values, the effect of mortar in external brickwork is usually ignored as the density and thermal properties of bricks and mortar are similar.

2. Where butterfly wall ties are used at normal spacing in an insulated cavity $\leq$ 75 mm, no adjustment is required to calculations. If vertical twist ties are used in insulated cavities >75 mm, 0·020 W/m^{2}K should be added to the U-value.

3. Thermal conductivity (λ) is a measure of the rate that heat is conducted through a material under specific conditions (W/mK).

* Tables and charts - Insulation manufacturers' design guides and technical papers (walls, roofs and ground floors).
* Calculation using the Proportional Area Method (walls and roofs).
* Calculation using the Combined Method - BS EN ISO 6946 (walls and roofs).
* Calculation using BS EN ISO 13370 (ground floors and basements).

Tables and charts - these apply where specific U-values are required and standard forms of construction are adopted. The values contain appropriate allowances for variable heat transfer due to different components in the construction, e.g. twisted pattern wall ties and non-uniformity of insulation with the interruption by ceiling joists. The example below shows the tabulated data for a solid ground floor with embedded insulation of λ = 0.03 W/mK:

Perimeter (P) = 18 m
Floor area (A) = 20 m^2
P/A = 0·9
λ = 0·03 W/mK

Table shows values
for U = 0·25 W/m^{2}K

5·000

Solid concrete
ground floor

4·000

Typical table for floor insulation:

P/A	0·020	0·025	0·030*	0·035	0·040	0·045	W/mK
1·0	61	76	91	107	122	137	mm ins.
0·9*	60	75	<u>90</u>	105	120	135	.. ..
0·8	58	73	88	102	117	132	.. ..
0·7	57	71	85	99	113	128	.. ..
0·6	54	68	82	95	109	122	.. ..
0·5	51	64	77	90	103	115	.. ..

90 mm of insulation required.

Refs.: BS EN ISO 6946: Building components and building elements. Thermal resistance and thermal transmittance. Calculation method.
BS EN ISO 13370: Thermal performance of buildings. Heat transfer via the ground. Calculation methods.

Various applications to different ground floor situations are considered in BS EN ISO 13370. The following is an example of a solid concrete slab in direct contact with the ground. The data used is from the previous page.

Floor section

Perimeter = 18 m (exposed)
Floor area = 20 m²
λ for 90 mm insulation = 0.03 W/mK
Characteristic floor dimension = B^1
B^1 = Floor area ÷ (1/2 exp. perimeter)
B^1 = 20 ÷ 9 = 2.222 m

Formula to calculate total equivalent floor thickness for uninsulated and insulated all over floor:

$$dt = w + \lambda (R_{si} + R_f + R_{so})$$

where: dt = total equivalent floor thickness (m)
w = wall thickness (m)
λ = thermal conductivity of soil (W/mK) [see page 552]
R_{si} = internal surface resistance (m²K/W) [see page 550]
R_f = insulation resistance (0.09 ÷ 0.03 = 3 m²K/W)
R_{so} = external surface resistance (m²K/W) [see page 550]

Uninsulated: $dt = 0.3 + 1.5 (0.148 + 0 + 0.04) = 0.582$ m
Insulated: $dt = 0.3 + 1.5 (0.148 + 3 + 0.04) = 5.082$ m

Formulae to calculate U-values ~
Uninsulated or poorly insulated floor, $dt < B^1$:

$$U = (2\lambda) \div [(\pi B^1) + dt] \times \ln [(\pi B^1 \div dt) + 1]$$

Well insulated floor, $dt \geq B^1$:

$$U = \lambda \div [(0.457 \times B^1) + dt]$$

where: U = thermal transmittance coefficient (W/m²/K)
λ = thermal conductivity of soil (W/mK)
B^1 = characteristic floor dimension (m)
dt = total equivalent floor thickness (m)
ln = natural logarithm

Uninsulated floor ~
U = (2 × 1.5) ÷ [(3.142 × 2.222) + 0.582] × ln [(3.142 × 2.222) ÷ 0.582 + 1]
U = 0.397 × ln 12.996 = 1.02 W/m²K

Insulated floor ~
U = 1.5 ÷ [(0.457 × 2.222) + 5.082] = 1.5 ÷ 6.097 = 0.246 W/m²K

NB. Compares with the tabulated figure of 0.250 W/m²K on the previous page.

Proportional Area Method (Wall)

Fully insulated cavity wall

A standard block with mortar is 450 × 225 mm = 101250 mm²

A standard block format of 440 × 215 mm = 94600 mm²

The area of mortar per block = 6650 mm²

Proportional area of mortar = $\dfrac{6650}{101250} \times \dfrac{100}{1}$ = 6·57%(0·066)

Therefore the proportional area of blocks = 93·43%(0·934)

Thermal resistances (R):

Outer leaf + insulation (unbridged)
R_{so} = 0·055
brickwork = 0·122
insulation = 2·631
2·808
× 100% = 2·808

Inner leaf (unbridged)
blocks = 0·555
plaster = 0·081
R_{si} = 0·123
0·759
× 93·43% = 0·709

Inner leaf (bridged)
mortar = 0·114
plaster = 0·081
R_{si} = 0·123
= 0·318
× 6·57% = 0·021

$$U = \frac{1}{\Sigma R} = \frac{1}{2\cdot808 + 0\cdot709 + 0\cdot021} = 0\cdot283\,W/m^2K$$

Combined Method (Wall)

This method considers the upper and lower thermal resistance (R) limits of an element of structure. The average of these is reciprocated to provide the U-value.

Formula for upper and lower resistances = $\dfrac{1}{\Sigma(F_x \div R_x)}$

Where: F_x = Fractional area of a section

R_x = Total thermal resistance of a section

Using the wall example from the previous page:

Upper limit of resistance (R) through section containing blocks – (R_{so}, 0·055) + (brkwk, 0·122) + (ins, 2·631) + (blocks, 0·555) + (plstr, 0·081) + (R_{si}, 0·123) = 3·567 m²K/W

Fractional area of section (F) = 93·43% or 0·934

Upper limit of resistance (R) through section containing mortar – (R_{so} 0·055) + (brkwk, 0·122) + (ins, 2·631) + (mortar, 0·114) + (plstr, 0·081) + (R_{si}, 0·123) = 3·126 m²K/W

Fractional area of section (F) = 6·57% or 0·066

The upper limit of resistance =

$$\frac{1}{\Sigma(0{\cdot}943 \div 3{\cdot}567) + (0{\cdot}066 \div 3{\cdot}126)} = 3{\cdot}533 \, m^2K/W$$

Lower limit of resistance (R) is obtained by summating the resistance of all the layers –
(R_{so}, 0·055) + (brkwk, 0·122) + (ins, 2·631) + (bridged layer, 1 ÷ [0·934 ÷ 0·555] + [0·066 ÷ 0·114] = 0·442) + (plstr, 0·081) + (R_{si}, 0·123) = 3·454 m²K/W

Total resistance (R) of wall is the average of upper and lower limits = (3·533 + 3·454) ÷ 2 = 3·493 m²K/W

U-value = $\dfrac{1}{R}$ = $\dfrac{1}{3{\cdot}493}$ = 0·286 W/m²K

NB. Both proportional area and combined method calculations require an addition of 0·020 W/m²K to the calculated U-value. This is for vertical twist type wall ties in the wide cavity. See page 400 and note 2 on page 552.

Proportional Area Method (Roof)

$R_{so} = 0.045$

air space between tiles and felt, $R_1 = 0.120$

2 mm felt, $\lambda = 0.500$, $R_2 = 0.004$

100×50 mm rafters at 400 mm c/c, $\lambda = 0.140$, $R_3 = 0.714$

roof space, $R_a = 0.180$

200 mm insulation (100 mm between joists), $\lambda = 0.040$, $R_4 = 5$ (200 mm) & 2.5 (100 mm)

100×50 mm joists at 400 mm c/c, $\lambda = 0.140$, $R_5 = 0.714$

13 mm plaster board, $\lambda = 0.160$, $R_6 = 0.081$

$R_{si} = 0.104$

$35°$

Notes:
1. The air space in the loft area is divided between pitched and ceiling components, i.e. $R_a = 0.180 \div 2 = 0.090 \, m^2K/W$.
2. The U-value is calculated perpendicular to the insulation, therefore the pitched component resistance is adjusted by multiplying by the cosine of the pitch angle, i.e. 0.819.
3. Proportional area of bridging parts (rafters and joists) is $50 \div 400 = 0.125$ or 12.5%.
4. With an air space resistance value (R1) of $0.120 \, m^2K/W$ between tiles and felt, the resistance of the tiling may be ignored.

Thermal resistance (R) of the pitched component:

Raftered part
$R_{so} = 0.045$
$R_1 = 0.120$
$R_2 = 0.004$
$R_3 = 0.714$
$R_a = \underline{0.090}$
　　$0.973 \times 12.5\% = 0.122$

Non-raftered part
$R_{so} = 0.045$
$R_1 = 0.120$
$R_2 = 0.004$
$R_a = \underline{0.090}$
　　$0.259 \times 87.5\%$
　　$= 0.227$

Total resistance of pitched components =
$$(0.122 + 0.227) \times 0.819 = 0.286 \, m^2K/W$$

Thermal resistance (R) of the ceiling component:

Joisted part
$R_{si} = 0.104$
$R_6 = 0.081$
$R_5 = 0.714$
$R_4 = 2.500$ (100 mm)
$R_a = \underline{0.090}$
　　$3.489 \times 12.5\% = 0.436$

Fully insulated part
$R_{si} = 0.104$
$R_6 = 0.081$
$R_4 = 5.000$ (200 mm)
$R_a = \underline{0.090}$
　　$5.275 \times 87.5\%$
　　$= 4.615$

Total resistance of ceiling components = $0.436 + 4.615$
$$= 5.051 \, m^2K/W.$$

$$U = \frac{1}{\Sigma R} = \frac{1}{0.286 + 5.051} = 0.187 \, W/m^2K$$

Area weighted application ~ an allowance for a variation occurring in the construction of an external element.

E.g. Taking the roof U-value calculation shown on the previous page and including an uninsulated plywood loft hatch within the ceiling. The loft hatch occupies 10% of the overall ceiling area.

Ceiling/loft hatch section

ceiling joist

$R_a = 0.180 \div 2$
$= 0.090$

25 mm (0.025 m) plywood loft hatch door uninsulated, thermal conductivity (λ) of 0.140 W/mK

Rsi = 0.104

Resistance (R) of hatch material = 0.025 m ÷ 0.140 W/mK

$$= 0.178 \text{ m}^2\text{K/W}$$

Resistance of hatch = $R_{si} + R + R_a$

$$= 0.104 + 0.178 + 0.090$$

$$= 0.372 \text{ m}^2\text{K/W}$$

Proportional area resistance of hatch = 0.372 x 10% = 0.037 m²K/W

Resistance of ceiling = 5.051 m²K/W (see previous page)

Proportional area resistance of ceiling = 5.051 x 90% = 4.546 m²K/W

Resistance of pitched component = 0.286 m²K/W (see previous page)

$$U = \frac{1}{0.286 + 0.037 + 4.546} = \frac{1}{4.869} = 0.205 \text{ W/m}^2\text{K}$$

An area weighted higher U-value than the 0.187 W/m²K calculated on the previous page for a fully insulated ceiling.

NB. Proprietary loft hatches are manufactured to incorporate a substantial layer of insulating material.

Standard Assessment Procedure ~ the Approved Document to Part L of the Building Regulations emphasises the importance of quantifying the energy costs of running homes. For this purpose it uses the Government's Standard Assessment Procedure (SAP). SAP has a numerical scale of 1 to 100, although it can exceed 100 if a dwelling is a net energy exporter. It takes into account the effectiveness of a building's fabric relative to insulation and standard of construction. It also appraises the energy efficiency of fuel consuming installations such as ventilation, hot water, heating and lighting. Incidentals like solar gain also feature in the calculations.

As part of the Building Regulations approval procedure, energy rating (SAP) calculations are submitted to the local building control authority. SAP ratings are also required to provide prospective home purchasers or tenants with an indication of the expected fuel costs for hot water and heating. This information is documented and included with the property conveyance. The SAP calculation involves combining data from tables, work sheets and formulae. Guidance is found in Approved Document L, or by application of certified SAP computer software programs.

SAP rating average for all homes is about 50. A modernised 1930s house is about 70, that built to 1995 energy standards about 80 and a 2002 house about 90. Current quality construction standards should rate dwellings close to 100.

Ref. Standard Assessment Procedure for Energy Rating of Dwellings. The Stationery Office.

Air Permeability ~ airtightness in the construction of dwellings is an important quality control objective. Compliance is achieved by attention to detail at construction interfaces, e.g. by silicone sealing built-in joists to blockwork inner leafs and door and window frames to masonry surrounds; draft proofing sashes, doors and loft hatches. Guidance for compliance is provided in Limiting thermal bridging and air leakage: Robust construction details for dwellings and similar buildings, published by The Stationery Office. Dwellings failing to comply with these measures are penalised in SAP calculations. Alternatively, a certificate must be obtained to show pre-completion testing satisfying air permeability of less than 10 m^3/h per m^2 envelope area at 50 Pascals (Pa or N/m^2) pressure.

Thermal Insulation, Elements of Construction (1)

Dwellings in England and Wales ~ the worst acceptable, or the limiting heat energy loss through the enclosing fabric as an area weighted average U-value:

Element of construction	Area weighted average U-value (W/m²K)
External wall	0.30
Roof	0.20
Floor	0.25
Party wall	0.20
Windows, roof windows, glazed rooflights and pedestrian doors	2.00 (adjusted for slope)*

Note: Air permeability through the external envelope, not to exceed 10 m³/hour per m² at 50 Pascals (Pa) pressure.

Area weighted average U-value ~ for an element of construction this depends on the individual U-values of the components and the area they occupy within that element. Some examples with higher thermal transmittance than the adjacent construction to include the part of an external wall containing a meter cupboard and the part of a roof structure containing a loft hatch and/or a rooflight. Also, a window or door U-value is measured with the combined performance of the principal unit and its frame.

Objective U-values ~

Notwithstanding the limiting thermal transmittance values stated above, an objective target for U-values could be better than:

Element of construction	Area weighted average U-value (W/m²K)
External wall	0.18
Roof	0.13
Floor	0.13
Party wall	0.00
Windows, roof windows, glazed rooflights and glazed doors	1.40 (adjusted for slope)*
Doors opaque	1.00
Doors semi-glazed	1.20

NB. Air permeability objective not greater than 5 m³/hour per m² at 50 Pa.

* See next page.

Typical party wall U-values:

Construction type	U-value (W/m²K)
Solid	0.00
Cavity, unfilled without edge sealing	0.50
Cavity, unfilled with edge sealing	0.20
Cavity, filled with edge sealing	0.00

U-values for windows and rooflights ~ these are shown for the unit mounted in a vertical position. Where a window is inclined to the vertical, U-values should be modified relative to the angle of installation. The following table is a guide:

Inclination to the horizontal	U-value (W/m²K) increase	
	Double glazed	Triple glazed
< 20°	0.50	0.30
20° – 40°	0.40	0.20
40° – 60°	0.30	0.20
60° – 70°	0.20	0.10
>70°	0.00	0.00

E.g. A triple glazed rooflight with an area weighted average U-value of 1.50 W/m²K in a 45° pitched roof.
Revised U-value = 1.50 + 0.20 = 1.70 W/m²K.

Total window area and other measures for glazing provision and energy rating are considered on the next page.

References and further reading:

BRE Digest 443: Conventions for U-value calculations.

Building Regulations, Approved Documents:

L1A: Conservation of fuel and power in new dwellings.

L1B: Conservation of fuel and power in existing dwellings.

Domestic Building Services Compliance Guide – NBS for DCLG.

Windows, doors, rooflights and roof windows:

- New dwellings ~ a maximum area is not critical to Approved Document guidance to Building Regulation compliance, except that openable parts should not exceed one quarter of the total floor area. The contribution that window and door openings make to the overall energy efficiency of a dwelling, with particular regard to their U-values is included in SAP calculations. A measure of compliance can be achieved using the BFRC window energy rating and efficiency design guide shown on page 566.
- Existing dwellings ~ extensions and alterations. Approved Document guidance to Building Regulation compliance includes a reasonable provision to limit the total area to the equivalent of 25% of an extension floor area. The BFRC window energy rating of new installations is at least band C, i.e. higher than minus 20 (see page 566) or a U-value of not greater than 1.6 W/m²K (area weighted combining glazing and frame). Doors to have an area weighted U-value of not greater than 1.8 W/m²K.

Ref. BFRC ~ British Fenestration Registration Council.

Energy source:

A gas or oil fired central heating boiler with a SEDBUK efficiency rating of 90% (band rating A) is standard installation for new dwellings. There are transitional and exceptional circumstances that may permit lower band rated boilers. Where this occurs, the construction of the building envelope should compensate with very low U-values. An energy recovery system or an alternative/renewable energy system may also be considered as a trade-off. Acceptable standards for solid fuel boilers are provided to HETAS certification (see page 565).

SEDBUK band ratings ~ these are defined in the UK Government's publication, Standard Assessment Procedure for Energy Rating of Dwellings (SAP)

Note: SEDBUK band A = >90% efficiency
        .. B = 86–90%   ..
        .. C = 82–86%   ..
        .. D = 78–82%   ..
        .. E = 74–82%   ..
        .. F = 70–74%   ..
        .. G = <70%   ..

Ref. SEDBUK ~ Seasonal Efficiency of a Domestic Boiler in the UK.

New-build dwellings, limiting or worst acceptable and (objective target) heat energy loss values ~

unheated space
(resistance values can
apply depending on size
of space and exposed areas,
see SAP section 3)

0.25 (0.13)

* A WER (page 566)
above –30 may be an
acceptable alternative
subject to other SAP
objectives being satisfied
** See page 560

Extensions or alterations to existing dwellings, reasonable/ acceptable heat energy loss objectives ~

unheated space
(as above)

0.22

NB. Figures indicate the thermal transmittance coefficient through the fabric of construction. Otherwise known as the U-value, expressed in units of watts per square metre for every one degree Kelvin temperature difference (W/m²K).

There are many situations in the enclosing envelope of a building where the U-value of the principal construction is interrupted by necessary change. In these instances, U-values are averaged over the material components. Some examples include meter cupboard/cavity wall (illustrated), door/door frame, loft hatch/ceiling and rooflight/roof structure.

Formula ~

$$\text{Area weighted average} = \frac{(U_1 \times A_1) + (U_2 \times A_2) + (U_3 \times A_3), \text{etc.}}{A_1 + A_2 + A_3, \text{etc.}}$$

E.g. A 12.00m² cavity wall containing gas and electricity meter cupboards, each 0.410m wide x 0.610m high. Thermal transmittance factors 0.25 W/m²K and 0.45 W/m²K respectively.

Meter cupboard area = 0.41m x 0.61m x 2 = 0.50m²

Effective wall area = 12.00 m² less 0.50 m² = 11.50m²

meter cupboard area 0.25 m²

2 N°. (gas and electricity) A₂ = 0.50m²

U₁ = 0.25 W/m²K

effective wall area A₁ = 11.50 m²

U₂ = 0.45 W/m²K

Area weighted U-value ~

$$\frac{(0.25 \times 11.50) + (0.45 \times 0.50)}{11.50 + 0.50} = \frac{2.875 + 0.225}{12.00} = 0.258 \; W/m^2K$$

NB. See also page 558.

Further quality procedures (structure):

- Provision of insulation to be continuous. Gaps are unacceptable and if allowed to occur will invalidate the insulation value by thermal bridging.
- Junctions at elements of construction (wall/floor, wall/roof) to receive particular attention with regard to continuity of insulation.
- Openings in walls for windows and doors to be adequately treated with insulating cavity closers.

Further quality procedures (energy consumption):

- Hot water and heating systems to be fully commissioned on completion and controls set with regard for comfort, health and economical use of fuel.
- As part of the commissioning process for new wet heating system installations, they should be filled and drained (flushed out) and on refilling, the water should be blended with an anti-corrosion additive diluted to the manufacturer's instructions. This additive also functions as a pump lubricant, an anti-freeze and protection against scaling.
- A certificate confirming heating system commissioning and water treatment should be provided for the new installation user. This document to be accompanied by component manufacturer's operating and maintenance instructions.
Note: Commissioning of heating installations and the issue of certificates is by a qualified 'competent person' as recognised by the appropriate body: CAPITA GROUP, OFTEC or HETAS.
CAPITA GROUP ~ 'Gas Safe Register' of installers (has replaced CORGI).
OFTEC ~ Oil Firing Technical Association for the Petroleum Industry.
HETAS ~ Solid Fuel Heating Equipment Testing and Approval Scheme.

Further quality procedures (existing dwellings) ~

Where an existing dwelling is subject to alterations/extensions and improvements such as refurbishment, it is expected that reasonable provision be made to enhance the thermal properties of the external envelope of the existing structure.

European Window Energy Rating Scheme (EWERS) ~ an alternative to U-values for measuring the thermal efficiency of windows. U-values form part of the assessment, in addition to factors for solar heat gain and air leakage. In the UK, testing and labelling of window manufacturers' products is promoted by the British Fenestration Rating Council (BFRC). The scheme uses a computer to simulate energy movement over a year through a standard window of 1.480 × 1.230 m containing a central mullion and opening sash to one side.

Data is expressed on a scale from A–G in units of $kWh/m^2/year$.

    A > zero
    B −10 to 0
    C −20 to −10
    D −30 to −20
    E −50 to −30
    F −70 to −50
    G < −70

By formula, rating = (218.6 × g value) − 68.5 (U-value × L-value) where: g value = factor measuring effectiveness of solar heat block expressed between 0 and 1. For comparison:

        0.48 (no curtains)
        0.43 (curtains open)
        0.17 (curtains closed)

    U-value = weighted average transmittance coefficient
    L-value = air leakage factor

From the label shown opposite:
Rating = (218·6 × 0·5)
        − 68·5 (1·8 + 0·10)
        = 109·3 − 130·15
        = −20·85 i.e. −21

Typical format of a window energy rating label ~

ABC Joinery Ltd.
Window ref. XYZ 123

Energy index	−21
Climate zone	UK
Thermal trans. (U-value)	1.8 W/m^2K
Solar factor (g-value)	0.50
Air leakage (L-value)	$0.10 m^3/h/m^2$ at 50 Pa

Carbon Index ~ the Standard Assessment Procedure (SAP) for energy rating dwellings includes a facility to calculate annual emission of carbon dioxide (CO_2). This is measured in kilogrammes and can be related to floor area using the following established calculation method for determining a carbon factor (CF) and carbon index (CI):

CF = CO_2 ÷ (total floor area + 45)

CI = 17.7 – (9 log. CF)   Note: log. = logarithm to the base 10.

E.g. A dwelling of floor area 125 m^2 with CO_2 emissions of 2000 kg/yr.

CF = 2000 ÷ (125 + 45) = 11.76

CI = 17.7 – (9 log. 11.76) = 8.06

The carbon index ranges from zero to 10. Objective values for new dwellings should be at least 9.

DER and TER ~ A.D. L refers to the Dwelling Carbon Emissions Rate (DER) as another means for assessing carbon discharge. The DER is compared by calculation to a Target Carbon Emissions Rate (TER) based on data for type of lighting, floor area, building shape and fuel category. The DER is derived by appraising the potential CO_2 emission relative to the consumption of fuel in hot water, heating, lighting, cooling (if fitted), fans and pumps.

DER ≤ TER (units of kg/m^2 floor area/year)

Note: DER applies to dwellings. A similar Building Carbon Emissions Rate (BER) is used to assess CO_2 emissions for other building types.

TFEE ~ Target Fabric Energy Efficiency is a supplementary performance standard, introduced to A.D. L from 2014 for new buildings. The objective of TFEE is to reduce carbon emissions by 6% for dwellings and 9% for non-domestic buildings compared with 2010 requirements. Calculations incorporate factors for U-values, thermal bridging, air permeability, thermal mass, lighting and solar gains. FEE is measured in CO_2 emissions of kWh/m^2/yr.

Fuel type	CO_2 (kg per kWh) conversion factor
Gas	0.206
Electricity	0.527
Fuel oil	0.215

- Basis for improvement ~ total annual CO_2 emissions from building are around 150 million tonnes (MtC).
- CO_2 represents about 85% of all greenhouse gases produced by burning fossil fuels (methane 6%, nitrous oxide 5%, industrial trace gases the remainder).
- 25 million homes produce about 15% (74 MtC) of carbon emissions, representing a significant target for improvement (non-domestic buildings about 17%, 79 MtC).
- The table below shows the main sources of CO_2 emissions in MtC.

Source	1990	1995	2000	2005	2010	2012*
Residential/domestic	79	81	87	84	87	74
Business/non-domestic	113	107	107	97	79	79
Energy supply	241	210	203	216	195	192
Transport	120	120	125	129	119	116
Other	39	36	31	27	18	18
Total	592	554	553	553	498	479

Note: CO_2 emissions have declined significantly by about 19% since 1990, corresponding to about 3% less consumption of fuel energy. These figures are affected by higher energy efficiency of new buildings, climate/temperature change, improved efficiency of power generation and lower usage of carbon intensive coal. Allowing for these variables, in real terms there has been about a 6% reduction in energy use.
* Provisional figures.
Ref. DECC National statistics.

The energy efficiency of new homes is about 70% higher than those built in 1990. However, many older homes have been improved to include some of the following provisions:

Application	Potential reduction, CO_2 per annum (kg)
Loft insulation	1000
Double glazing	700
Draft proofing (doors, windows, floors)	300
Wall cavity insulation	750
Condensing boiler	875
Insulated hot water storage cylinder	160
Energy saving light bulb	45 (each)

Thermal Insulation ~ this is required within the roof of all dwellings in the UK. It is necessary to create a comfortable internal environment, to reduce the risk of condensation and to economise in fuel consumption costs.

To satisfy these objectives, insulation may be placed between and over the ceiling joists as shown below to produce a *cold roof* void. Alternatively, the insulation can be located above the rafters as shown on page 509. Insulation above the rafters creates a *warm roof* void and space within the roof structure that may be useful for habitable accommodation.

roof covering

timber battens

tile underlay

plastic or similar eaves ventilation strip to provide continuous air gap over insulation

gutter

roof structure

vcl

insulation between and over joists

plasterboard ceiling

wall plate

low density block inner leaf

cavity insulation

wall finish

ventilation holes or slot equivalent to continuous 10mm gap fitted with insect mesh

NB. All pipework in roof space should be insulated to prevent frost attack. The sides and top of cold water storage cisterns should be insulated to prevent freezing.

Application of Insulation with Typical U-values ~

Cold roof

Insulation (mm) between/over joists		U-value W/m²K
100	80	0.22
100	100	0.20
100	150	0.16
100	200	0.13
100	250	0.11
100	300	0.10

Note: 200, 250 and 300 mm over joist insulation in two layers.

Warm roof

Insulation (mm) underlay/overlay		U-value W/m²K
100	50	0.25
100	80	0.21
100	100	0.19
150	50	0.20
150	80	0.17
100	100	0.16

NB. Underlay insulation in between and fully filling the rafter depth. Overlay insulation board under counter battens secured to the top of rafters with helical skewers.

Various Applications with Typical Thermal Transmittance Values ~

Timber

waterproof covering — insulation board
vcl over decking
joist
12.5mm plasterboard

Insulation thickness (mm)	U-value W/m^{2}K
130	0.25
165	0.22
190	0.18
220	0.16
270	0.13

Concrete

waterproof covering — insulation board
vcl over 50mm screed
150mm dense concrete
12.5mm plasterboard on battens

Insulation thickness (mm)	U-value W/m^{2}K
130	0.25
165	0.22
190	0.18
220	0.16
270	0.13

Troughed or profiled steel decking

waterproof covering — insulation board
vcl
purlin

unsupported span (S). min. thickness insulation $\ngtr {}^S\!/_3$

Insulation thickness (mm)	U-value W/m^{2}K
145	0.25
165	0.22
210	0.18
230	0.16
280	0.13

NB. Insulation of mineral wool roofing board, with a thermal conductivity (λ) of 0.038 W/mK.

Thermal Insulation to Walls ~ the minimum performance standards for exposed walls set out in Approved Document L to meet the requirements of Part L of the Building Regulations can be achieved in several ways (see pages 560 and 563). The usual methods require careful specification, detail and construction of the wall fabric, insulating material(s) and/or applied finishes.

Typical examples of existing construction that would require upgrading to satisfy contemporary UK standards ~

20mm thick external cement and sand rendering

250mm thick aerated concrete blocks – density 475 kg/m^3

19mm thick plasterboard with vapour control layer on 20 mm thick battens

SOLID BLOCK WALL (U = 0·45 W/m^{2}K)

50mm wide cavity

50mm thick mineral wool/fibre cavity batts

102.5mm external brick outer leaf

100mm thick lightweight concrete block inner leaf – density 600kg/m^3

13mm thick lightweight plaster

CAVITY WALL WITH CAVITY INSULATING BATTS (U = 0·39W/m^{2}K)

Semi-exposed

50mm wide cavity

102.5mm external brick outer leaf

150mm thick lightweight concrete block inner leaf – density 475 kg/m^3

13mm thick lightweight plaster

TRADITIONAL CAVITY WALL (U = 0·58 W/m^{2}K)

Typical examples of contemporary construction practice that achieve a thermal transmittance or U-value below 0·30 W/m²K ~

120 mm mineral wool cavity batts

100 mm lightweight concrete block inner leaf

102.5 mm external brick outer leaf

13 mm lightweight plaster

FULL FILL CAVITY WALL, Block density 750 kg/m³   U = 0.25 W/m²K
Block density 600 kg/m³   U = 0.24 W/m²K
Block density 475 kg/m³   U = 0.23 W/m²K

75 mm mineral wool cavity batts

lightweight concrete blocks, density 460 kg/m³

102.5 mm external brick outer leaf

9.5 mm plasterboard on dabs

FULL FILL CAVITY WALL, T = 125 mm U = 0.28 W/m²K
T = 150 mm U = 0.26 W/m²K
T = 200 mm U = 0.24 W/m²K

50 mm wide cavity

breather membrane and sheathing board

40 mm mineral wool cavity batts

VCL and 12.5 mm plasterboard

102.5 mm external brick outer leaf

mineral wool batts

TIMBER FRAME PART CAVITY FILL, T = 100 mm U = 0.26 W/m²K
T = 120 mm U = 0.24 W/m²K
T = 140 mm U = 0.21 W/m²K

NB. Mineral wool insulating batts have a typical thermal conductivity (λ) value of 0·038 W/mK.

Improvements to various forms of existing construction with typical thermal transmittance U-values (W/m²K) ~

Masonry with external insulation

Insulation	U-value
0mm	2.17
80 ..	0.36
100 ..	0.30
120 ..	0.26
150 ..	0.21

215mm brick wall

13mm render and plaster

reinforcement mesh and 10mm render

mineral fibre slab insulation mechanically and adhesive fixed

215mm concrete block plastered internally

reinforcement mesh and 10mm render
mineral fibre slab insulation mechanically and adhesive fixed

OUTSIDE

Insulation	U-values	
	Med. dens blk. $\lambda = 0.5$	Ltwt. dens blk. $\lambda = 0.2$
80mm	0.36	0.29
100 ..	0.30	0.25
120 ..	0.26	0.22
150 ..	0.21	0.19

Masonry with internal insulation

mineral fibre slab insulation mechanically fixed and secured with adhesive to existing plastered wall, or supported between treated timber battens secured to the wall

brick or concrete block wall

optional external surface treatment will increase resistance to heat loss

12.5mm vapour control lined plasterboard

Insulation thickness and U-values as shown for external insulation.

NB. Expanded polystyrene board (EPS) is an alternative insulation material that will provide similar insulation values.

Cavity filling may be by:

• injected urea-formaldehyde (UF) foam, or
• blown in granulated fibres of mineral wool or perlite.

UF foam ~ a resin and a hardener mixed in solution. Placement into the wall cavity is from the ground upward, by compressed air injection through 12mm holes. After placement the foam hardens. An alternative material is an adhesive polyurethane (PUR) foam. This has an added benefit of bonding the two leaves of masonry, a remedial treatment where wall ties have corroded.

Granulated materials ~ a dry system, pressure injected from ground level upward through 20mm holes.

Typical thermal transmittance U-values (W/m²K) ~

Cavity (mm)	Med. dens. block $\lambda=0.5$	Ltwt. dens. block $\lambda=0.2$
50	0.54	0.47
75	0.40	0.36
100	0.32	0.29
125	0.27	0.25

Refs.: BS 5617: Specification for urea-formaldehyde foam systems suitable for thermal insulation of cavity walls with masonry or concrete inner and outer leaves.

BS 5618: Code of practice for thermal insulation of cavity walls (with masonry or concrete inner and outer leaves) by filling with urea-formaldehyde foam systems.

Approved Document D – Toxic substances, D1: Cavity insulation.

Surface treatment may be:

• External if space and access permits, or
• Internal with some loss of room volume, and possibly disturbance to existing surface attachments, e.g. shelves, radiators, electrical sockets and light fittings.

External

6mm thin coat polymer render (see Note 1)

mineral fibre slab insulation

half brick and 100mm concrete block wall with 50mm cavity, rendered and plastered internally

Typical U-values

Ins. (mm)	Med. dens. blk. $\lambda = 0.5$	Low dens. blk. $\lambda = 0.3$
50	0.51	0.48
75	0.38	0.36
100	0.30	0.29

Internal

half brick and 100mm concrete block wall with 50mm cavity, rendered and plastered internally

thermal wallboard or mineral fibre slab insulation with vapour control lined plasterboard, fixed to existing wall with multi-purpose adhesive dabs (see Note 2)

Typical U-values

Ins. (mm)	Med. dens. blk. $\lambda = 0.5$	Low dens. blk. $\lambda = 0.3$
50	0.44	0.42
75	0.34	0.33
100	0.28	0.27

Notes:

1. A modified alternative to conventional cement and sand render with a polymer, silicone or acrylic additive. Vapour permeable with good weatherproofing qualities.

2. Vapour control layer is an impervious lining of polythene or metal foil placed to the warm side of insulation. Prevents warm moisture from the interior of a house condensing on the cold parts of construction.

RSC ~ rainscreen cladding to existing solid masonry walls.

Upgrading existing structures by overcladding has the following benefits:

* Enhanced appearance.
* Protection to the substructural wall.
* Weather exclusion.
* Improved thermal insulation.
* Improved sound insulation.
* No loss or disruption to habitable internal space.

Solid masonry one brick walls typical of many pre-1950s houses have a U-value of about 2.20 W/m²K (see page 549). Surface insulation and overcladding can considerably reduce this figure to less than 0.50 W/m²K

rigid batt insulation*

aluminium alloy framing

insulation*
215 mm
brick wall

215 mm brick
solid wall

air space or
ventilation void

air space

screw
fixing and
bracket

cladding

Isometric

insulation
retainer

rainscreen
cladding panel

self drill/tap screw fixing

Vertical section

breather membrane

*Typically expanded polystyrene (EPS), polyurethane (PUR) or glass/mineral wool.

Additional details are shown on pages 705 to 707.

RSC ~ rainscreen cladding to existing and new build cavity walls.

The benefits for solid walls listed on the preceding page apply equally to existing and new cavity wall construction.

Cavity masonry walls for housing have varied materially over a period exceeding 100 years. Some comprise a brick outer and inner leaf, others brick outer leaf and concrete block inner leaf. The composition of concrete blocks has varied considerably over time. Aggregates have included breeze, pumice and wood shavings to name just a few examples. Most brick and block cavity walls have a U-value of around 1.50 W/m²K. Overcladding and insulation can reduce this figure to less than 0.4 W/m²K.

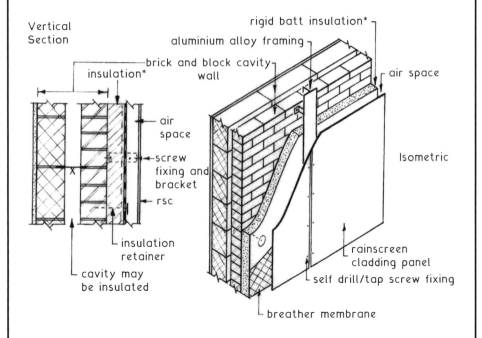

See page 552 for insulation types and comparable conductivity values.

*See previous page

The U-value (W/m²K) varies with floor shape and size. This is represented as the ratio of perimeter (P) to area (A). Page 553 has a worked example using insulation manufacturers' data for the P/A ratio.

Ground-bearing concrete

P/A ratio	Typical insulation thickness (mm)		
1.0	105	140	175
0.8	100	135	170
0.6	90	130	160
0.4	75	110	130
0.2	30	60	80
U	0.25	0.20	0.18

Suspended beam and block

P/A ratio	Typical insulation thickness (mm)		
1.0	110	145	175
0.8	105	140	165
0.6	100	130	155
0.4	90	120	145
0.2	60	95	125
U	0.25	0.20	0.18

Note: Figures apply to mineral wool insulation board, λ = 0.038 W/mK. Closed cell extruded polystyrene can also be used, λ = 0.029 W/mK.

Suspended timber

P/A ratio	Typical insulation thickness (mm)		
1.0	140	150	180
0.8	140	140	180
0.6	120	140	180
0.4	120	140	150
0.2	75	90	120
U	0.25	0.22	0.20

Thermal or Cold Bridging ~ this is heat loss and possible condensation, occurring mainly around window and door openings and at the junction between ground floor and wall. Other opportunities for thermal bridging occur where uniform construction is interrupted by unspecified components, e.g. occasional use of bricks and/or tile slips to make good gaps in thermal block inner leaf construction.

NB. This practice was quite common, but is no longer acceptable by current legislative standards in the UK.

Prime areas for concern ~

WINDOW SILL   WINDOW/DOOR JAMB

incomplete cavity insulation

heat loss through uninsulated wall

GROUND FLOOR AND WALL   WINDOW/DOOR HEAD

dpc

hollow steel lintel and incomplete cavity insulation

cavity insulation incomplete, possibly caused by mortar droppings building up and bridging the lower part of the cavity*

*Cavity should extend down at least 225mm below the level of the lowest dpc (A.D. C: Section 5).

As shown on the preceding page, continuity of insulated construction in the external envelope is necessary to prevent thermal bridging. Nevertheless, some discontinuity is unavoidable where the pattern of construction has to change. For example, windows and doors have significantly higher U-values than elsewhere. Heat loss and condensation risk in these situations is regulated by limiting areas, effectively providing a trade-off against very low U-values elsewhere.

The following details should be observed around openings and at ground floor ~

WINDOW SILL

cavity insulation to underside of window board

WINDOW/DOOR JAMB

proprietary cavity closer and insulated dpc (page 414)

lightweight insulation blocks

full or part full cavity insulation

GROUND FLOOR AND WALL

dpc

insulation batts installed at least 150mm below top of floor insulation

WINDOW/DOOR HEAD

cavity insulation cut to fit

open perpends

lintel filled with insulation

The possibility of a thermal or cold bridge occurring in a specific location can be appraised by calculation. Alternatively, the calculations can be used to determine how much insulation will be required to prevent a cold bridge. The composite lintel of concrete and steel shown below will serve as an example ~

Wall components, less insulation (steel in lintel is insignificant):

102.5 mm brickwork outer leaf,	$\lambda = 0.84$ W/mK
100 mm dense concrete lintel,	$\lambda = 1.93$ ..
13 mm lightweight plaster,	$\lambda = 0.16$ ..

Resistances of above components:

Brickwork,	$0.1025 \div 0.84 = 0.122$ m²K/W
Concrete lintel,	$0.100 \div 1.93 = 0.052$ ..
Lightweight plaster,	$0.013 \div 0.16 = 0.081$ ..

Resistances of surfaces:

$$\text{Internal } (R_{si}) = 0.123 \ ..$$
$$\text{Cavity } (R_a) = 0.180 \ ..$$
$$\text{External } (R_{so}) = 0.055 \ ..$$
$$\text{Summary of resistances} = 0.613 \ ..$$

To achieve a U-value of say 0·27 W/m²K,
total resistance required = $1 \div 0.27 = 3.703$ m²K/W

The insulation in the cavity at the lintel position is required to have a resistance of 3·703 − 0·613 = 3·09 m²K/W

Using a urethane insulation with a thermal conductivity (λ) of 0·025 W/mK, 0·025 × 3·09 = 0·077 m or 77 mm minimum thickness.

If the cavity closer has the same thermal conductivity, then:
Summary of resistance = 0·613 − 0·180 (Ra) = 0·433 m²K/W
Total resistance required = 3·703 m²K/W, therefore the cavity closer is required to have a resistance of: 3·703 − 0·433 = 3·270 m²K/W
Min. cavity closer width = 0·025 W/mK × 3·270 m²K/W = 0·082 m or 82 mm.

In practice, the cavity width and the lintel insulation would exceed 82 mm.

NB. data for resistances and λ values taken from pages 550 to 552.

Air Infiltration ~ heating costs will increase if cold air is allowed to penetrate peripheral gaps and breaks in the continuity of construction. Furthermore, heat energy will escape through structural breaks and the following are prime situations for treatment:

1. Loft hatch
2. Services penetrating the structure
3. Opening components in windows, doors and rooflights
4. Gaps between dry lining and masonry walls

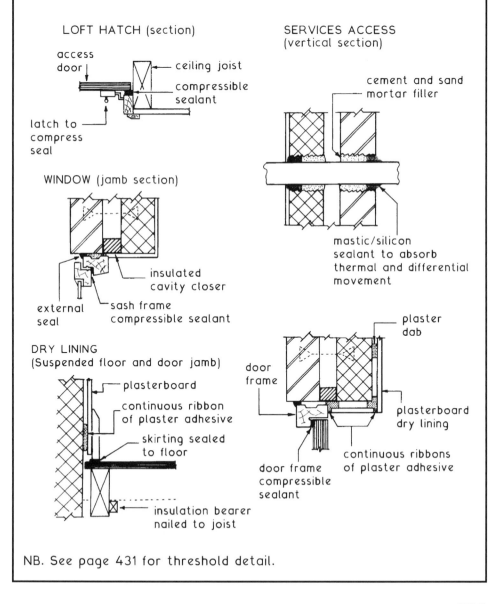

NB. See page 431 for threshold detail.

With new buildings and those subject to alterations, the objective is to optimise the use of fuel and power to minimise emission of carbon dioxide and other burnt fuel gases into the atmosphere. This applies principally to the installation of hot water, heating, lighting, ventilation and air conditioning systems.

Guidance to satisfy the Building Regulations is provided in Approved Document L2, but this is not prescriptive. It sets out a series of objectives relating to achievement of a satisfactory carbon emission standard. Other technical references and approvals are cross referenced in the Approved Document and these provide a significant degree of design flexibility in achieving its objectives.

Energy efficiency assessment in terms of limiting CO_2 emissions for a proposed building is determined by applying a series of procedures modelled on the specification of a building the same size and shape as the proposal. The performance standards are given in the 2013 National Calculation Methodology (NCM) modelling guide published by the DCLG. The proposed or actual building must be seen to have the same as or less carbon emissions by calculation. Improvements can be achieved in many ways, including the following:

- Limit the area or number of rooflights, windows and other openings.
- Improve the U-values of the external envelope. The limiting or worst acceptable are shown on the following page.
- Improve the building airtightness from the poorest acceptable air permeability of 10 m^3 per hour per m^2 of external envelope at 50 Pa.
- Improve the heating system efficiency by installing thermostatic, zone and optimum time controls. Fully insulate pipes, ducting, storage vessels and other energy consuming plant.
- Use high efficacy lighting fittings, automated controls and low voltage equipment.
- Apply heat recovery systems to ventilation and air conditioning systems.
- Install a building energy management system to monitor and regulate heating and air conditioning plant.
- Limit overheating with solar controls and purpose-made glazing.
- Provide continuity of insulation about the external envelope.
- Establish a commissioning and plant maintenance procedure, with a log book to record all repairs, replacements and inspections.

Further guidance: Non-domestic Building Services Compliance Guide. A DCLG (Dept. for Communities and Local Government) publication.

Buildings other than dwellings (England and Wales), worst acceptable or limiting heat energy loss through the enclosing fabric ~

Element of construction	Area weighted average U-value (W/m²K)
External wall	0.35
Roof	0.25
Floor	0.25
Windows, pedestrian doors, rooflights, roof windows and curtain walling	2.20
High use entrances and roof vents	3.50
Large vehicle access doors	1.50

Notes:
- For display windows and for building types that may be exempted, see Section 3 in A.D. L2A.
- U-values for inclined windows modified as shown on page 561.
- The worst acceptable thermal transmittance values allow for some design flexibility by permitting a trade-off against other fuel-saving features such as energy recovery systems.
- The U-value standard is set with regard to minimising the risk of condensation.
- Elements of construction will normally be expected to provide much better insulation than the limiting U-values. Objective or target design values could be better than:

External wall	0.23 W/m²K
Roof	0.15 ..
Floor	0.20 ..
Windows, etc.	1.50 ..

Building airtightness $\leq$ 5m³ per hour per m² at 50 Pa pressure.

Continuity of insulation ~ conformity can be shown in the form of a report produced for the local authority building control department by an accredited surveyor. The report can contain confirmation of:

* an approved design specification and construction practice to an acceptable standard, or
* a thermographic survey showing continuity of insulation over the external envelope. This is essential where it is impractical to fully inspect the work in progress.

Airtightness ~ tested by using portable fans of a capacity to suit the building volume. Smoke capsules in conjunction with fan pressurisation provide a visual indication of air leakage paths.

585

Main features of Approved Document (A.D.) M: Access to and use of buildings, and other associated guidance:

* Site entrance or car parking space to building entrance to be firm and level. Building approach width 900 mm min. A gentle slope is acceptable with a gradient up to 1 in 20 and up to 1 in 40 in cross-falls. A slightly steeper ramped access or easy steps should satisfy A.D. Sections 6.14 and 6.15, and 6.16 and 6.17 respectively.
* An accessible threshold for wheelchairs is required at the principal entrance – see illustration.
* Entrance door – minimum clear opening width of 775 mm.
* Corridors, passageways and internal doors of adequate width for wheelchair circulation. Minimum 750 mm – see also table 4 in A.D. Section 7.
* Stair minimum clear width of 900 mm, with provision of handrails both sides. Other requirements as A.D. K for private stairs.
* Accessible light switches, power, telephone and aerial sockets between 450 and 1200 mm above floor level.
* WC provision in the entrance storey or first habitable storey. Door to open outward. Clear wheelchair space of at least 750 mm in front of WC and a preferred dimension of 500 mm either side of the WC as measured from its centre.
* Special provisions are required for passenger lifts and stairs in blocks of flats, to enable disabled people to access other storeys. See A.D. Section 9 for details.

Refs.: Accessible thresholds in new housing – Guidance for house builders and designers. The Stationery Office.
BS 8300: Design of buildings and their approaches to meet the needs of disabled people. Code of practice.

Objective ~ car parking should be provided for visitors, customers and employees requiring access to a building. The main entrance to a building and any other entrances used by employees should be reasonably accessible on foot or by wheelchair from any of the allocated car parking spaces. Parking for the disabled should be prioritised, specifically designated and given larger bay areas to allow people with restricted mobility to access their vehicles unimpeded.

Provisions for designated parking spaces:

• Location to be clearly signed at the car park entrance.
• Specific bays to be clearly identified.
• Surfaces to be firm, durable and slip resistant on level ground with no undulations greater than 5 mm.
• No further distance than 50 m from the main entrance to a building.
• Bay width to be sufficient to allow car doors to fully open for wheelchair space and passenger transfer.
• Dropped kerb access of at least 1.20 m width for wheelchair access.
• Parking ticket machines to be in close proximity, with controls between 0.75 m and 1.20 m above the adjacent ground.

Designated parking bays ~

Main features:

* Site entrance, or car parking space to building entrance to be firm and level, i.e. maximum gradient 1 in 20 with a minimum car access zone of 1200 mm. Ramped and easy stepped approaches are also acceptable.

* Access to include tactile warnings, i.e. profiled (blistered or ribbed) pavings over a width of at least 1200 mm, for the benefit of people with impaired vision. Dropped kerbs are required to ease wheelchair use.

* Special provision for handrails is necessary for those who may have difficulty in negotiating changes in level.

* Guarding and warning to be provided where projections or obstructions occur, e.g. tactile paving could be used around window opening areas.

* Sufficient space for wheelchair manoeuvrability in entrances.

Minimum entrance width of 800 mm. Unobstructed space of at least 300 mm to the leading (opening) edge of door. Glazed panel in the door to provide visibility from 500 to 1500 mm above floor level. Entrance lobby space should be sufficient for a wheelchair user to clear one door before opening another.

* Width of door opening measured as the effective clear dimension at right angles to the wall containing a door, to include the door frame/lining and stop and any other projection.

continued......

* Main access and internal fire doors that self-close should have a maximum operating force of 20 Newtons at the leading edge. If this is not possible, a power operated door opening and closing system is required.

* Corridors and passageways, minimum unobstructed width 1200 mm. Internal lobbies as described on the previous page for external lobbies.

* Lift dimensions and capacities to suit the building size. Ref. BS EN 81 series: Safety rules for the construction and installation of lifts. Alternative vertical access may be by wheelchair stairlift, see BS EN 81-40 (special lifts and lifting platforms) and BS 6440: Powered vertical lifting platforms having non-enclosed or partially enclosed liftways intended for use by persons with impaired mobility.

* Stair minimum width 1200 mm, with step nosings brightly distinguished. Rise maximum 12 risers external, 16 risers internal between landings. Landings to have 1200 mm of clear space from any door swings. Step rise, maximum 170 mm and uniform throughout. Step going, minimum 250 mm (internal), 280 mm (external) and uniform throughout. No open risers. Handrail to each side of the stair.

* Number and location of WCs to reflect ease of access for wheelchair users. In no case should a wheelchair user have to travel more than one storey. Provision may be 'unisex' which is generally more suitable, or 'integral' with specific sex conveniences. Particular provision is outlined in Section 5 of the Approved Document.

* Section 4 of the Approved Document should be consulted for special provisions in restaurants, bars and hotel bedrooms, and for special provisions for spectator seating in theatres, stadia and conference facilities.

Refs.: Building Regulations, Approved Document M: Access to and use of buildings.
Disability Discrimination Act.
BS 9999: Code of practice for fire safety in the design, management and use of buildings.
BS 8300: Design of buildings and their approaches to meet the needs of disabled people. Code of practice.

Notes

6 SUPERSTRUCTURE – 2

REINFORCED CONCRETE SLABS

REINFORCED CONCRETE FRAMED STRUCTURES

STRUCTURAL CONCRETE, FIRE PROTECTION

FORMWORK

PRECAST CONCRETE FRAMES

PRESTRESSED CONCRETE

STRUCTURAL STEELWORK ASSEMBLY

STRUCTURAL STEELWORK CONNECTIONS

STRUCTURAL FIRE PROTECTION

PORTAL FRAMES

COMPOSITE TIMBER BEAMS

ROOF SHEET COVERINGS

LONG SPAN ROOFS

SHELL ROOF CONSTRUCTION

MEMBRANE ROOFS

ROOFLIGHTS

PANEL WALLS, RAINSCREEN CLADDING AND CURTAIN WALLING

CONCRETE CLADDINGS

CONCRETE SURFACE FINISHES AND DEFECTS

Simply Supported Slabs ~ these are slabs which rest on a bearing and for design purposes are not considered to be fixed to the support and are therefore, in theory, free to lift. In practice however they are restrained from unacceptable lifting by their own self-weight plus any loadings.

Concrete Slabs ~ concrete is a material which is strong in compression and weak in tension, and if the member is overloaded its tensile resistance may be exceeded leading to structural failure.

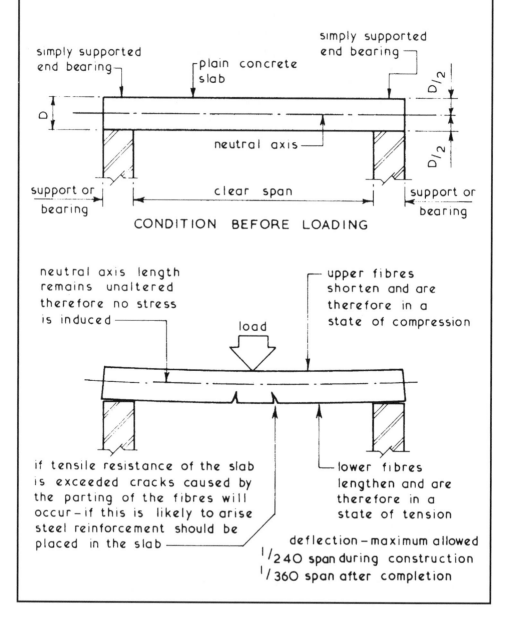

simply supported end bearing

simply supported end bearing

plain concrete slab

D

D/2

D/2

neutral axis

support or bearing

clear span

support or bearing

CONDITION BEFORE LOADING

neutral axis length remains unaltered therefore no stress is induced

upper fibres shorten and are therefore in a state of compression

load

if tensile resistance of the slab is exceeded cracks caused by the parting of the fibres will occur—if this is likely to arise steel reinforcement should be placed in the slab

lower fibres lengthen and are therefore in a state of tension

deflection — maximum allowed
$^{1}/240$ span during construction
$^{1}/360$ span after completion

Reinforcement ~ generally in the form of steel bars which are used to provide the tensile strength which plain concrete lacks. The number, diameter, spacing, shape and type of bars to be used have to be designed; a basic guide is shown on pages 597 and 598. Reinforcement is placed as near to the outside as practicable, with sufficient cover of concrete over the reinforcement to protect the steel bars from corrosion and to provide a degree of fire resistance. Slabs which are square in plan are considered to be spanning in two directions and therefore main reinforcing bars are used both ways, whereas slabs which are rectangular in plan are considered to span across the shortest distance and main bars are used in this direction only with smaller diameter distribution bars placed at right angles forming a mat or grid.

Typical Details ~

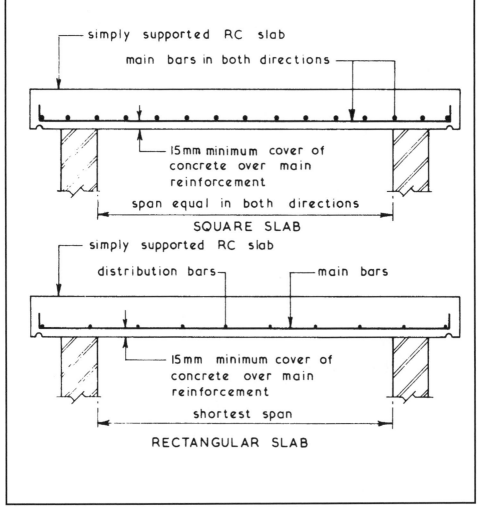

Construction ~ whatever method of construction is used the construction sequence will follow the same pattern:

1. Assemble and erect formwork.
2. Prepare and place reinforcement.
3. Pour and compact or vibrate concrete.
4. Strike and remove formwork in stages as curing proceeds.

Typical Example ~

edge formwork

main reinforcement - cover maintained by plastic or similar spacers - see Detail 'A'

distribution bars - position maintained by wire binding or clips - see Detail 'A'

concrete poured and compacted or vibrated around reinforcement

decking of suitable material such as plywood with all joints sealed or taped to prevent grout loss

surface finish as specified

adjustable steel or timber props at centres to suit spanning ability of joists

joists supporting decking spaced at centres to suit spanning ability of decking

tying wire or clip

plastic spacer

distribution bar

main bars

DETAIL 'A'

telescopic steel floor centres with sheet steel decking giving clear spans between support walls

ALTERNATIVE DECKING SUPPORT

Profiled galvanised steel decking is a permanent formwork system for construction of composite floor slabs. The steel sheet has surface indentations and deformities to effect a bond with the concrete topping. The concrete will still require reinforcing with steel rods or mesh, even though the metal section will contribute considerably to the tensile strength of the finished slab.

Typical Detail –

* For slab depth and span potential, see BS EN1994-1-1: Design of composite steel and concrete structures. General rules and rules for buildings.

Where structural support framing is located at the ends of a section and at intermediate points, studs are through-deck welded to provide resistance to shear –

There are considerable savings in concrete volume compared with standard in-situ reinforced concrete floor slabs. This reduction in concrete also reduces structural load on foundations.

Beams ~ these are horizontal load bearing members which are classified as either main beams which transmit floor and secondary beam loads to the columns or secondary beams which transmit floor loads to the main beams.

Concrete being a material which has little tensile strength needs to be reinforced to resist the induced tensile stresses which can be in the form of ordinary tension or diagonal tension (shear). The calculation of the area, diameter, type, position and number of reinforcing bars required is one of the functions of a structural engineer.

Typical RC Beam Details ~

Mild Steel Reinforcement – located in areas where tension occurs in a beam or slab. Concrete specification is normally 25 or 30 N/mm² in this situation.

Simple beam or slab

end support

main reinforcement:
100mm slab/beam = 10mm dia. at 112mm spacing or pitch
125 and 150mm slab/beam = 12mm dia. at 112mm spacing

Continuous beam or slab

end support   interim support

L = span

NB. Distribution or cross bars function as lateral reinforcement and supplement the unit's strength in tensile areas. They also provide resistance to cracking in the concrete as the unit contracts during setting and drying.

Pitch of main bars ≤ 3 × effective depth.

Pitch of distribution bars ≤ 5 × effective depth.

Guidance – simply supported slabs are capable of the following loading relative to their thickness:

Thickness (mm)	Self-weight (kg/m²)	Imposed load* (kg/m²)	Total load (kg/m²)	Total load (kN/m²)	Span (m)
100	240	500	740	7·26	2·4
125	300	500	800	7·85	3·0
150	360	500	860	8·44	3·6

NB. As a *rule of thumb*, it is easy to remember that for general use (as above), thickness of slab equates to 1/24 span.

* Imposed loading varies with application from 1·5 kN/m² (153 kg/m²) for domestic buildings, to over 10 kN/m² (1020 kg/m²) for heavy industrial storage areas. 500 kg/m² is typical for office filing and storage space. See BS EN 1991-1-1: Actions on structures. General actions. Densities, self-weight, imposed loads for buildings.

For larger spans – thickness can be increased proportionally to the span, e.g. 6 m span will require a 250 mm thickness.

For greater loading – slab thickness is increased proportionally to the square root of the load, e.g. for a total load of 1500 kg/m² over a 3m span:

$$\sqrt{\frac{1500}{800}} \times 125 = 171·2 \quad \text{i.e. } 175 \text{ mm}$$

Continuous beams and slabs have several supports, therefore they are stronger than simple beams and slabs. The spans given in the above table may be increased by 20% for interior spans and 10% for end spans.

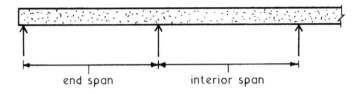

end span   interior span

Deflection limit on reinforced concrete beams and slabs is 1/250 span. Ref.:

BS EN 1992-1-1: Design of concrete structures. General rules and rules for buildings.

NB. See pages 642 and 643 for deflection formulae.

Bond Between Concrete and Steel – permissible stress for the bond between concrete and steel can be taken as one-tenth of the compressive concrete stress, plus $0.175 \, N/mm^2$*. Given the stresses in concrete and steel, it is possible to calculate sufficient grip length.

E.g. concrete working stress of $5 \, N/mm^2$
    steel working stress of $125 \, N/mm^2$
    sectional area of reinf. bar $= 3.142 \, r^2$ or $0.7854 \, d^2$
    tensile strength of bar $= 125 \times 0.7854 \, d^2$
    circumference of bar $= 3.142 \, d$
    area of bar in contact $= 3.142 \times d \times L$

Key: r = radius of steel bar
    d = diameter of steel bar
    L = Length of bar in contact

*   Conc. bond stress $= (0.10 \times 5 \, N/mm^2) + 0.175 = 0.675 \, N/mm^2$

   Total bond stress $= 3.142 \, d \times L \times 0.675 \, N/mm^2$

Thus, developing the tensile strength of the bar:

$$125 \times 0.7854 \, d^2 = 3.142 \, d \times L \times 0.675$$

$$98.175 \, d = 2.120 \, L$$

$$L = 46 \, d$$

As a guide to good practice, a margin of $14 \, d$ should be added to L. Therefore the bar bond or grip length in this example is equivalent to 60 times the bar diameter.

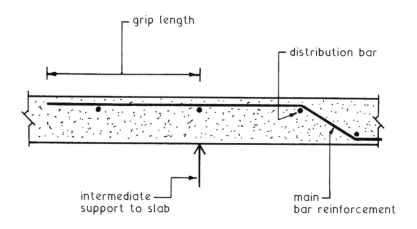

grip length

distribution bar

intermediate support to slab

main bar reinforcement

In-situ RC Framed Structures – Columns

Columns ~ these are the vertical load bearing members of the structural frame which transmits the beam loads down to the foundations. They are usually constructed in storey heights and therefore the reinforcement must be lapped to provide structural continuity.

600

With the exception of where bars are spliced ~

BEAMS

The distance between any two parallel bars in the horizontal should be not less than the greater of:

* 25mm
* the bar diameter where they are equal
* the diameter of the larger bar if they are unequal
* 6mm greater than the largest size of aggregate in the concrete

The distance between successive layers of bars should be not less than the greater of:

* 15mm (25mm if bars > 25mm dia.)
* the maximum aggregate size

An exception is where the bars transverse each other, e.g. mesh reinforcement.

COLUMNS

Established design guides allow for reinforcement of between 0·8% and 8% of column gross cross sectional area. A lesser figure of 0·6% may be acceptable. A relatively high percentage of steel may save on concrete volume, but consideration must be given to the practicalities of placing and compacting wet concrete. If the design justifies a large proportion of steel, it may be preferable to consider using a concrete clad rolled steel I section.

Transverse reinforcement ~ otherwise known as binders or links. These have the purpose of retaining the main longitudinal reinforcement during construction and restraining each reinforcing bar against buckling. Diameter, take the greater of:

* 6mm
* 0·25 × main longitudinal reinforcement

Spacing or pitch, not more than the lesser of:

* least lateral column dimension
* 12 × diameter of smallest longitudinal reinforcement
* 300mm

Helical binding ~ normally, spacing or pitch as above, unless the binding has the additional function of restraining the concrete core from lateral expansion, thereby increasing its load carrying potential. This increased load must be allowed for with a pitch:

* not greater than 75mm
* not greater than 0.166 × core diameter of the column
* not less than 25mm
* not less than 3 × diameter of the binding steel

NB. Core diameter is measured across the area of concrete enclosed within the centre line of the binding.

Simple Reinforced Concrete Column Design (1)

Typical RC Column Details ~

Steel Reinforced Concrete – a modular ratio represents the amount of load that a square unit of steel can safely transmit relative to that of concrete. A figure of 18 is normal, with some variation depending on materials specification and quality.

e.g.

Column on plan

Area of concrete = 88,743 mm²

Equivalent area of steel = 18 × 1257 mm² = 22626 mm²

Equivalent combined area of concrete and steel:

$$
\begin{array}{r}
88743 \\
+22626 \\
\hline
111369\text{mm}^2
\end{array}
$$

Using concrete with a safe or working stress of 5 N/mm², derived from a factor of safety of 5, i.e.

$$
\text{Factory of safety} = \frac{\text{Ultimate stress}}{\text{Working stress}} = \frac{25\,\text{N/mm}^2}{5\,\text{N/mm}^2} = 5\,\text{N/mm}^2
$$

5 N/mm² × 111369 mm² = 556845 Newtons
kg × 9·81 (gravity) = Newtons

Therefore: $\frac{556845}{9\cdot81}$ = 56763kg or 56·76 tonnes permissible load

NB. This is the safe load calculation for a reinforced concrete column where the load is axial and bending is minimal or non-existent, due to a very low slenderness ratio (effective length to least lateral dimension). In reality this is unusual and the next example shows how factors for buckling can be incorporated into the calculation.

Buckling or Bending Effect – the previous example assumed total rigidity and made no allowance for column length and attachments such as floor beams.

The working stress unit for concrete may be taken as 0.8 times the maximum working stress of concrete where the effective length of column (see page 645) is less than 15 times its least lateral dimension. Where this exceeds 15, a further factor for buckling can be obtained from the following:

Effective length ÷ Least lateral dimension	Buckling factor
15	1·0
18	0·9
21	0·8
24	0·7
27	0·6
30	0·5
33	0·4
36	0·3
39	0·2
42	0·1
45	0

Using the example from the previous page, with a column effective length of 9 metres and a modular ratio of 18:

Effective length ÷ Least lateral dimension = 9000 ÷ 300 = 30

From above table the buckling factor = 0·5

Concrete working stress = $5 \, N/mm^2$

Equivalent combined area of concrete and steel = $111369 \, mm^2$

Therefore: $5 \times 0·8 \times 0·5 \times 111369 = 222738$ Newtons

$$\frac{222738}{9·81} = 22705 kg \text{ or } 22·7 \text{ tonnes permissible load}$$

Bar Coding ~ a convenient method for specifying and coordinating the prefabrication of steel reinforcement in the assembly area. It is also useful on site, for checking deliveries and locating materials relative to project requirements. BS EN ISO 3766 provides guidance for a simplified coding system, such that bars can be manufactured and labelled without ambiguity for easy recognition and application on site.

A typical example is the beam shown on page 596, where the lower longitudinal reinforcement (mk·1) could be coded:

$$2T20\text{-}1\text{-}200B \text{ or, } \textcircled{1}2T\emptyset20\text{-}200\text{-}B\text{-}21$$

2 = number of bars
T = deformed high yield steel (460 N/mm², 8–40 mm dia.)
20 or, ∅20 = diameter of bar (mm)
1 or ① = bar mark or ref. no.
200 = spacing (mm)
B = located in bottom of member
21 = shape code

Other common notation:

R = plain round mild steel (250 N/mm², 8–16 mm dia.)
S = stainless steel
W = wire reinforcement (4–12 mm dia.)
T (at the end) = located in top of member
abr = alternate bars reversed (useful for offsets)

Thus, bar mk.2 = 2R10-2-200T or, ②R∅10-200-T-00
and mk.3 = 10R8-3-270 or, ③10R∅8-270-54

All but the most obscure reinforcement shapes are illustrated in the British Standard. For the beam referred to on page 596, the standard listing is:

BS code	Shape	Total bar length on centre line (mm)
OO	A	A
21		A + B + C − r − 2d (d = bar diameter)
54		2(A + B) + 12d

Ref. BS EN ISO 3766: Construction drawings. Simplified representation of concrete reinforcement.

Bar Schedule ~ this can be derived from the coding explained on the previous page. Assuming 10 No. beams are required:-

Site ref ....   Schedule ref ....

Prepared by ....   Date ....

Member	Bar mark	Type and size	No. of members	No. of bars in each	Total no.	Bar length (mm)	Shape code	A	B	C	D	E/r
Beam	1	T20	10	2	20	3080	21	200	2700	200		
	2	R10	10	2	20	2700	00	2700				
	3	R8	10	10	100	1336	54	400	220			

Note: r = 2 × d for mild steel
3 × d for high yield steel

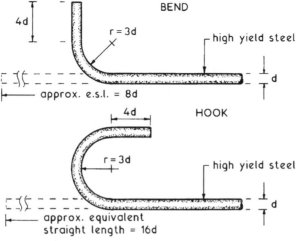

Bar coding ~

1st character	2nd character
0 No bends	0 Straight bars
1 1 bend	1 90° bends, standard radius, all bends towards same direction
2 2 bends	2 90° bends, non-standard radius, all bends towards same direction
3 3 bends	3 180° bends, non-standard radius, all bends towards same direction
4 4 bends	4 90° bends, standard radius, not all bends towards same direction
5 5 bends	5 Bends <90°, standard radius, all bends towards same direction
6 Arcs of circles	6 Bends <90°, standard radius, not all bends towards same direction
7 Complete helices	7 Arcs or helices

NB. 9 is used for special or non-standard shapes.

Material ~ Mild steel or high yield steel. Both contain about 99% iron, the remaining constituents are manganese, carbon, sulphur and phosphorus. The proportion of carbon determines the quality and grade of steel; mild steel has 0·25% carbon, high yield steel 0·40%. High yield steel may also be produced by cold working or deforming mild steel until it is strain hardened. Mild steel has the letter R preceding the bar diameter in mm, e.g. R20, and high yield steel the letter T or Y.

Standard bar diameters ~ 6, 8, 10, 12, 16, 20, 25, 32 and 40 mm.

Grade notation:

- Mild steel – grade 250 or 250 N/mm^2 characteristic tensile strength (0·25% carbon, 0·06% sulphur and 0·06% phosphorus).
- High yield steel – grade 460/425 (0·40% carbon, 0·05% sulphur and 0·05% phosphorus).

  460 N/mm^2 characteristic tensile strength: 6, 8, 10, 12 and 16 mm diameter.

  425 N/mm^2 characteristic tensile strength: 20, 25, 32 and 40 mm diameter.

Examples of steel reinforcement ~

Round   Square twisted   Ribbed   Stretched, twisted and ribbed   Ribbed and twisted

Elevations

Sections

Ref. BS 4449: Steel for the reinforcement of concrete, weldable reinforcing steel. Bar, coil and decoiled product. Specification.

Steel reinforcement mesh or fabric is produced in four different formats for different applications:

Format	Type	Typical application
A	Square mesh	Floor slabs
B	Rectangular mesh	Floor slabs
C	Long mesh	Roads and pavements
D	Wrapping mesh	Binding wire with concrete fire protection to structural steelwork

Standard sheet size ~ 4·8 m long × 2·4 m wide.
Standard roll size ~ 48 and 72 m long × 2·4 m wide.

Specification ~ format letter plus a reference number. This number equates to the cross sectional area in mm² of the main bars per metre width of mesh.
E.g. B385 is rectangular mesh with 7 mm dia. main bars, i.e. 10 bars of 7 mm dia. @ 100 mm spacing = 385 mm².

A

200   200

weld

cross bars
10, 8, 7, 6 & 5 mm

main bars 10, 8, 7, 6 & 5 mm

B

200   100

cross bars
8 & 7 mm

main bars 12, 10, 8, 7, 6 & 5 mm

C

400   100

cross bars
6 & 5 mm

main bars 10, 8, 7 & 6 mm

D

100   100

2.5 mm interwoven
main and cross wires

Refs.: BS 4483: Steel fabric for the reinforcement of concrete. Specification.

BS 4482: Steel wire for the reinforcement of concrete products. Specification.

607

Cover to reinforcement in columns, beams, foundations, etc. is required for the following reasons:

- To protect the steel against corrosion.
- To provide sufficient bond or adhesion between steel and concrete.
- To ensure sufficient protection of the steel in a fire (see Note).

If the cover is insufficient, concrete will spall away from the steel.

Minimum cover ~ never less than the maximum size of aggregate in the concrete, or the largest reinforcement bar size (take greater value). Guidance on minimum cover for particular locations ~

Below ground:

- Foundations, retaining walls, basements, etc., 40 mm, binders 25 mm.
- Marine structures, 65 mm, binders 50 mm.
- Uneven earth and fill 75 mm, blinding 40 mm.

Above ground:

- Ends of reinforcing bars, not less than 25 mm nor less than 2 × bar diameter.
- Column longitudinal reinforcement 40 mm, binders 20 mm.
- Columns <190 mm min. dimension with bars <12 mm dia., 25 mm.
- Beams 25 mm, binders 20 mm.
- Slabs 20 mm (15 mm where max. aggregate size is <15 mm).

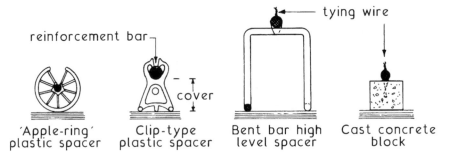

'Apple-ring' plastic spacer | Clip-type plastic spacer | Bent bar high level spacer | Cast concrete block

Note: Minimum cover for corrosion protection and bond may not be sufficient for fire protection and severe exposure situations.

For details of fire protection see Refs.:

Building Regulations, Approved Document B: Fire safety.
BS EN 1992-1-1: Design of concrete structures. General rules and rules for buildings.
BS EN 1992-1-2: Design of concrete structures. General rules. Structural fire design.

For general applications, including exposure situations, see next page.

Typical examples using dense concrete of calcareous aggregates (excluding limestone) or siliceous aggregates, e.g. flints, quartzites and granites ~

Column fully exposed ~

35 mm min. concrete cover to reinforcement

300 mm min. each face, 120 minutes' fire resistance
450 mm min. each face, 240 minutes' fire resistance

Column, maximum 50% exposed ~

concrete cover to reinforcement

240-minute fire resistant compartment wall

200 mm min., 120 minutes' fire resistance, 25 mm cover
350 mm min., 240 minutes' fire resistance, 35 mm cover

Column, one face only exposed ~

240-minute fire resistant compartment wall

160 mm min., 120 minutes' fire resistance
240 mm min., 240 minutes' fire resistance

25 mm min. cover

Beam and floor slab ~

125 mm min. thickness reinforced concrete compartment floor, 120 minutes' fire resistance, 35 mm cover

cover

150 mm min., 120 minutes' fire resistance, 50 mm cover
240 mm min., 240 minutes' fire resistance, 70 mm cover

Formwork ~ concrete when first mixed is a fluid and therefore to form any concrete member the wet concrete must be placed in a suitable mould to retain its shape, size and position as it sets. It is possible with some forms of concrete foundations to use the sides of the excavation as the mould but in most cases when casting concrete members a mould will have to be constructed on site. These moulds are usually called formwork. It is important to appreciate that the actual formwork is the reverse shape of the concrete member which is to be cast.

Falsework ~ the temporary structure which supports the formwork.

Principles ~

formwork sides can be designed to offer all the necessary resistance to the imposed pressures as a single member or alternatively they can be designed to use a thinner material which is adequately strutted — for economic reasons the latter method is usually employed

grout tight joints

formwork soffits can be designed to offer all the necessary resistance to the imposed loads as a single member or alternatively they can be designed to a thinner material which is adequately propped — for economic reasons the latter method is usually employed

wet concrete — density is greater than that of the resultant set and dry concrete

formwork sides — limits width and shape of wet concrete and has to resist the hydrostatic pressure of the wet concrete which will diminish to zero within a matter of hours depending on setting and curing rate

formwork base or soffit — limits depth and shape of wet concrete and has to resist the initial dead load of the wet concrete and later the dead load of the dry set concrete until it has gained sufficient strength to support its own dead weight which is usually several days after casting depending on curing rate.

Typical Simple Beam Formwork Details ~

25 x 50 ties at 600 c/c

75 x 25 cleats at 600 c/c

15mm thick plywood sides

75 x 32 struts

75 x 25 cleats at 600 c/c

cleat

21mm thick plywood soffit

100 x 50 crosshead or headtree

inner tube

w.i dogs to both sides

100 x 75 crosshead or headtree

collar

pin

75 x 32 braces

security chain for pin

150 x 75 props at 1·200 c/c

adjustable steel props in pairs at 1·200 c/c

outer tube

150 x 150 base plate

folding wedges

225 x 75 sole piece

SINGLE PROP SUPPORT

DOUBLE PROP SUPPORT

Erecting Formwork

1. Props positioned and levelled through.
2. Soffit placed, levelled and position checked.
3. Side forms placed, their position checked before being fixed.
4. Strutting position and fixed.
5. Final check before casting.

Suitable Formwork Materials ~ timber, steel and special plastics.

Striking or Removing Formwork

1. Side forms as soon as practicable usually within hours of casting this allows drying air movements to take place around the setting concrete.
2. Soffit formwork as soon as practicable usually within days but as a precaution some props are left in position until concrete member is self-supporting.

Beam Formwork ~ this is basically a three-sided box supported and propped in the correct position and to the desired level. The beam formwork sides have to retain the wet concrete in the required shape and be able to withstand the initial hydrostatic pressure of the wet concrete whereas the formwork soffit apart from retaining the concrete has to support the initial load of the wet concrete and finally the set concrete until it has gained sufficient strength to be self-supporting. It is essential that all joints in the formwork are constructed to prevent the escape of grout which could result in honeycombing and/or feather edging in the cast beam. The removal time for the formwork will vary with air temperature, humidity and consequent curing rate.

Typical Details ~

21mm thick plywood floor soffit formwork

15mm thick plywood edge beam formwork sides

edge beam

75 x 32 strut

cleat

21mm thick beam soffit

75 x 32 runner or stringer

100 x 75 crosshead or headtree

adjustable steel props

secondary beam formwork

150 x 50 soffit support joists at 600 c/c

margin support for beam formwork

Typical Formwork Striking Times ~

Beam Sides — 9 to 12 hours
Beam Soffits — 8 to 14 days (props left under) } Using OPC air temp
Beam Props — 15 to 21 days } 7 to 16°C

Column Formwork ~ this consists of a vertical mould of the desired shape and size which has to retain the wet concrete and resist the initial hydrostatic pressure caused by the wet concrete. To keep the thickness of the formwork material to a minimum horizontal clamps or yokes are used at equal centres for batch filling and at varying centres for complete filling in one pour. The head of the column formwork can be used to support the incoming beam formwork which gives good top lateral restraint but results in complex formwork. Alternatively the column can be cast to the underside of the beams and at a later stage a collar of formwork can be clamped around the cast column to complete casting and support the incoming beam formwork. Column forms are located at the bottom around a 75 to 100 mm high concrete plinth or kicker which has the dual function of location and preventing grout loss from the bottom of the column formwork.

Typical Details ~

21mm thick plywood column formwork sides

75 x 32 margin pieces forming support for incoming beam formwork

100 x 32 cleats at 600 °/c

100 x 50 soldiers or studs

noggins as required

clamps or yokes at spacings to suit anticipated pressures - for details see next page

lift out access piece to enable formwork to be cleaned out prior to casting

incoming beam formwork

raking struts if required

base located around kicker

Typical Striking Times 9 to 12 hours using OPC — air temperature 7 to 16°C

ALTERNATIVE SIDE FORMWORK CONSTRUCTION

Column Yokes ~ these are obtainable as a metal yoke or clamp or they can be purpose made from timber.

Typical Examples ~

steel wedge

column formwork

security chain or wire

steel blade or arm with 2 rows of 32 x 8mm slots

metal clamp - available in a range of sizes from 300 to 1400mm

100 x 32 cleats taken beyond width of panel to form rebate

yoke out of 100 x 75 timber

plate washer to both ends of bolt

hardwood wedges

16mm diameter bolt

SQUARE COLUMN

gangnail or plywood connecting plates to both faces

12mm min. gap

shaped timber yokes joined to form half yokes

hardboard or similar lining

25mm thick shaped staves

16mm diameter bolts

timber yokes out of 200 x 100

CIRCULAR COLUMN

Shaped Columns ~ the basic principles of rectangular or square columns are followed but purpose-made shaped yokes are sometimes required. Rebated columns can be formed with blocks or boxing thus —

column formwork

cleat

block or boxing

REBATED COLUMN

Wall Forms ~ conventionally made up of plywood sheeting that may be steel, plastic or wood faced for specific concrete finishes. Stability is provided by vertical studs and horizontal walings retained in place by adjustable props. Base location is by a kicker of 50 of 75mm height of width to suit the wall thickness. Spacing of wall forms is shown on the next page.

Wall formwork principles ~

Refs.: BS 6100-9: Building and civil engineering. Vocabulary. Work with concrete and plaster.
BS 8000-2.2: Workmanship on building sites. Code of practice for concrete work. Sitework with in-situ and precast concrete.
BRE Report 495: Concrete frame buildings, modular formwork.

*See next page and page 294.

Formwork sides to concrete walls of modest height and load can be positioned with long bolts or threaded dowel bars inserted through the walings on opposing sides. To keep the wall forms apart, tube spacers are placed over the bolts between the forms. For greater load applications, variations include purpose-made high tensile steel bolts or dowels. These too are sleeved with plastic tubes and have removable spacer cones inside the forms. Surface voids from the spacers can be made good with strong mortar. Some examples are shown below with the alternative coil tie system. Further applications are shown on pages 294 to 296.

Bolt

wall form — spacer tube

waling — strut

plate washer, nut and bolt or threaded steel dowel

Coil tie

plastic cone — two tie rods welded to coils (left in place)

washer

bolt threaded to match coils

Tie bolt

tube and cone spacers

waling plate washer

15 or 20mm standard diameter high tensile steel deformed screw threaded bar

wing nut

kicker, 50 to 75mm high x wall width

Precast Concrete Frames ~ these frames are suitable for single storey and low rise applications, the former usually in the form of portal frames which are normally studied separately. Precast concrete frames provide the skeleton for the building and can be clad externally and finished internally by all the traditional methods. The frames are usually produced as part of a manufacturer's standard range of designs and are therefore seldom purpose made due mainly to the high cost of the moulds.

Advantages:

1. Frames are produced under factory-controlled conditions resulting in a uniform product of both quality and accuracy.

2. Repetitive casting lowers the cost of individual members.

3. Off-site production releases site space for other activities.

4. Frames can be assembled in cold weather and generally by semi-skilled labour.

Disadvantages:

1. Although a wide choice of frames is available from various manufacturers these systems lack the design flexibility of cast in-situ purpose-made frames.

2. Site planning can be limited by manufacturer's delivery and unloading programmes and requirements.

3. Lifting plant of a type and size not normally required by traditional construction methods may be needed.

Typical Site Activities ~

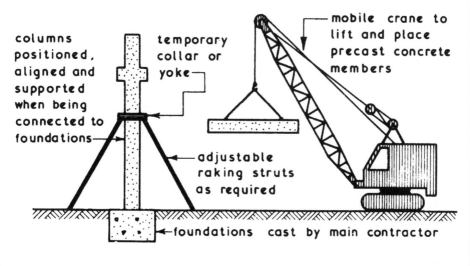

columns positioned, aligned and supported when being connected to foundations

temporary collar or yoke

mobile crane to lift and place precast concrete members

adjustable raking struts as required

foundations cast by main contractor

Precast Concrete Frames

Foundation Connections ~ the preferred method of connection is to set the column into a pocket cast into a reinforced concrete pad foundation and is suitable for light to medium loadings. Where heavy column loadings are encountered it may be necessary to use a steel base plate secured to the reinforced concrete pad foundation with holding down bolts.

Typical Details ~

Principles ~ the well known properties of concrete are that it has high compressive strength and low tensile strength. The basic concept of reinforced concrete is to include a designed amount of steel bars in a predetermined pattern to give the concrete a reasonable amount of tensile strength. In prestressed concrete a precompression is induced into the member to make full use of its own inherent compressive strength when loaded. The design aim is to achieve a balance of tensile and compressive forces so that the end result is a concrete member which is resisting only stresses which are compressive. In practice a small amount of tension may be present but providing this does not exceed the tensile strength of the concrete being used tensile failure will not occur.

Comparison of Reinforced and Prestressed Concrete ~

compression in upper fibres

load

stirrups at nominal spacings

anchor bars

close spaced stirrups giving resistance to diagonal tension or shear

main reinforcing bars providing tensile strength

tension in lower fibres

REINFORCED CONCRETE BEAM

tendon anchorage

load

slight initial tension in upper fibres - cancelled out by loading

tension cracks will not occur

stretched and anchored tendon - in trying to regain original length induces compression

hydraulic jack used to stress tendon

PRESTRESSED BEAM

tension
compression
tension

compression
tension

neutral axis

compression
compression

b
a
b - a =
c
c

PRESTRESS + DEAD LOAD = TRANSFER + LIVE LOAD = FINAL
STRESS   STRESS

STRESS DIAGRAMS

Materials ~ concrete will shrink whilst curing and it can also suffer sectional losses due to creep when subjected to pressure. The amount of shrinkage and creep likely to occur can be controlled by designing the strength and workability of the concrete, high strength and low workability giving the greatest reduction in both shrinkage and creep. Mild steel will suffer from relaxation losses which is where the stresses in steel under load decrease to a minimum value after a period of time and this can be overcome by increasing the initial stress in the steel. If mild steel is used for prestressing the summation of shrinkage, creep and relaxation losses will cancel out any induced compression, therefore special alloy steels must be used to form tendons for prestressed work.

Tendons – these can be of small diameter wires (2 to 7 mm) in a plain round, crimped or indented format; these wires may be individual or grouped to form cables. Another form of tendon is strand which consists of a straight core wire around which is helically wound further wires to give formats such as 7 wire (6 over 1) and 19 wire (9 over 9 over 1) and like wire tendons strand can be used individually or in groups to form cables. The two main advantages of strand are:

1. A large prestressing force can be provided over a restricted area.
2. Strand can be supplied in long flexible lengths capable of being stored on drums, thus saving site storage and site fabrication space.

Typical Tendon Formats ~

13 No. 15 mm diameter strands

12 No. 7 mm diameter wires

7 No. 15 mm diameter strands

wires stressed together

strands stressed singly

binding tape as required

plastic spacers at 3·000 c/c

strands stressed together

PARALLEL LAY CABLE

MONOSTRAND CABLE

MONOGROUP CABLE

Pre-tensioning ~ this method is used mainly in the factory production of precast concrete components such as lintels, floor units and small beams. Many of these units are formed by the long line method where precision steel moulds up to 120·000 long are used with spacer or dividing plates to form the various lengths required. In pre-tensioning the wires are stressed within the mould before the concrete is placed around them. Steam curing is often used to accelerate this process to achieve a 24-hour characteristic strength of 28 N/mm² with a typical 28-day cube strength of 40 N/mm². Stressing of the wires is carried out by using hydraulic jacks operating from one or both ends of the mould to achieve an initial 10% overstress to counteract expected looses. After curing the wires are released or cut and the bond between the stressed wires and the concrete prevents the tendons from regaining their original length, thus maintaining the precompression or prestress.

At the extreme ends of the members the bond between the stressed wires and concrete is not fully developed due to low frictional resistance. This results in a small contraction and swelling at the ends of the wire forming in effect a cone shape anchorage. The distance over which this contraction occurs is called the transfer length and is equal to 80 to 120 times the wire diameter. To achieve a greater total surface contact area it is common practice to use a larger number of small diameter wires rather than a smaller number of large diameter wires giving the same total cross sectional area.

Typical Pre-tensioning Arrangement ~

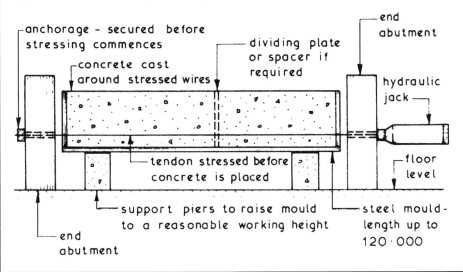

633

Post-tensioning ~ this method is usually employed where stressing is to be carried out on site after casting an in-situ component or where a series of precast concrete units are to be joined together to form the required member. It can also be used where curved tendons are to be used to overcome negative bending moments. In post-tensioning the concrete is cast around ducts or sheathing in which the tendons are to be housed. Stressing is carried out after the concrete has cured by means of hydraulic jacks operating from one or both ends of the member. The anchorages (see next page) which form part of the complete component prevent the stressed tendon from regaining its original length, thus maintaining the precompression or prestress. After stressing the annular space in the tendon ducts should be filled with grout to prevent corrosion of the tendons due to any entrapped moisture and to assist in stress distribution. Due to the high local stresses at the anchorage positions it is usual for a reinforcing spiral to be included in the design.

Curved Tendons for Negative Bending Moments ~

Typical Post-tensioning Arrangement ~

Anchorages ~ the formats for anchorages used in conjunction with post-tensioned prestressed concrete works depends mainly on whether the tendons are to be stressed individually or as a group, but most systems use a form of split cone wedges or jaws acting against a form of bearing or pressure plate.

Typical Anchorage Details ~

30 mm long spigot for duct connection

120 mm long × 120 diameter female cone

male cone driven into female cone

external flutes in concrete male cone to receive wires of parallel lay cable

grout hole

reinforced concrete female cone cast into end of concrete member

tensile steel spiral to hole

FREYSSINET ANCHORAGE

ribbed steel duct or sheath

grout hole

forge steel anchorage block

split cone wedge or jaws

socket for steel duct or sheath

fixing bolt holes

malleable cast iron anchorage and bearing plate cast into end of member

7 No. holes for strands and jaws

TYPICAL MONOSTRAND ANCHORAGE

Comparison with Reinforced Concrete ~ when comparing prestressed concrete with conventional reinforced concrete the main advantages and disadvantages can be enumerated but in the final analysis each structure and/or component must be decided on its own merit.

Main advantages:

1. Makes full use of the inherent compressive strength of concrete.
2. Makes full use of the special alloy steels used to form the prestressing tendons.
3. Eliminates tension cracks, thus reducing the risk of corrosion of steel components.
4. Reduces shear stresses.
5. For any given span and loading condition a component with a smaller cross section can be used, thus giving a reduction in weight.
6. Individual precast concrete units can be joined together to form a composite member.

Main Disadvantages:

1. High degree of control over materials, design and quality of workmanship is required.
2. Special alloy steels are dearer than most traditional steels used in reinforced concrete.
3. Extra cost of special equipment required to carry out the prestressing activities.
4. Cost of extra safety requirements needed whilst stressing tendons.

As a general comparison between the two structural options under consideration it is usually found that:

1. Up to 6·000 span traditional reinforced concrete is the most economic method.
2. Spans between 6·000 and 9·000 the two cost options are comparable.
3. Over 9·000 span prestressed concrete is more economical than reinforced concrete.

It should be noted that generally columns and walls do not need prestressing but in tall columns and high retaining walls where the bending stresses are high, prestressing techniques can sometimes be economically applied.

Ground Anchors ~ these are a particular application of post-tensioning prestressing techniques and can be used to form ground tie backs to cofferdams, retaining walls and basement walls. They can also be used as vertical tie downs to basement and similar slabs to prevent flotation during and after construction. Ground anchors can be of a solid bar format (rock anchors) or of a wire or cable format for granular and cohesive soils. A lined or unlined borehole must be drilled into the soil to the design depth and at the required angle to house the ground anchor. In clay soils the borehole needs to be underreamed over the anchorage length to provide adequate bond. The tail end of the anchor is pressure grouted to form a bond with the surrounding soil, the remaining length being unbonded so that it can be stressed and anchored at head, thus inducing the prestress. The void around the unbonded or elastic length is gravity grouted after completion of the stressing operation.

Typical Ground Anchor Details ~

GROUND ANCHOR FOR GRANULAR SOILS

GROUND ANCHOR FOR COHESIVE SOILS

Cold rolled steel sections are a lightweight alternative to the relatively heavy, hot rolled steel sections that have been traditionally used in sub-framing situations, e.g. purlins, joists and sheeting rails. Cold rolled sections are generally only a few millimetres in wall thickness, saving on material and handling costs and building dead load. They are also produced in a wide variety of section profiles, some of which are shown below.

Typical section profiles ~

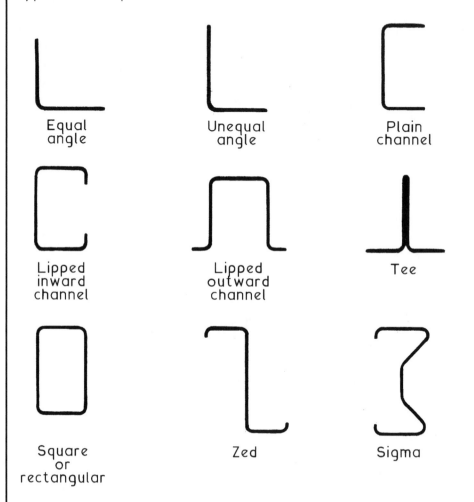

| Equal angle | Unequal angle | Plain channel |

| Lipped inward channel | Lipped outward channel | Tee |

| Square or rectangular | Zed | Sigma |

Dimensions vary considerably and many non-standard profiles are made for particular situations. A range of standard sections are produced to:

BS EN 10162: Cold rolled steel sections. Technical delivery conditions. Dimensional and cross sectional tolerances.

Structural Steelwork ~ standard section references:

BS 4-1: Structural steel sections. Specification for hot rolled sections.

BS EN 10056: Specification for structural steel equal and unequal angles.

BS EN 10210: Hot finished structural hollow sections of non-alloy and fine grain steels.

Typical Standard Steelwork Sections ~

UNIVERSAL BEAMS
127 x 76 x 13 kg/m to
914 x 419 x 388 kg/m

UNIVERSAL COLUMNS
152 x 152 x 23 kg/m to
356 x 406 x 634 kg/m

JOISTS
76 x 76 x 13 kg/m to
254 x 203 x 82 kg/m

CHANNELS
100 x 50 x 10 kg/m to
430 x 100 x 64 kg/m

HOLLOW SECTIONS
50 x 30 x 2.89 kg/m to
500 x 300 x 191 kg/m

EQUAL ANGLES
25 x 25 x 1.2 kg/m to
200 x 200 x 71.1 kg/m

UNEQUAL ANGLES
40 x 25 x 1.91 kg/m to
200 x 150 x 47.1 kg/m

HOLLOW SECTIONS
21.3 dia. x 1.43 kg/m to
508 dia. x 194 kg/m

NB. Sizes given are serial or nominal, for actual sizes see relevant BS.

Compound Sections — these are produced by welding together standard sections. Various profiles are possible, which can be designed specifically for extreme situations such as very high loads and long spans, where standard sections alone would be insufficient. Some popular combinations of standard sections include:

BEAM or COLUMN

steel plate welded to joists

standard joist, beam or column section

single   double   triple

CHANNEL

steel plate welded to channels

weld

standard channel

back to back

back to back with flange plates

toe to toe

GANTRY GIRDER

combination of standard channel, joist and plate sections welded together

Open Web Beams — these are particularly suited to long spans with light to moderate loading. The relative increase in depth will help resist deflection and voids in the web will reduce structural dead load.

Perforated Beam — a standard beam section with circular voids cut about the neutral axis.

Castellated Beam — a standard beam section web is profile cut into two by oxy-acetylene torch. The projections on each section are welded together to create a new beam 50% deeper than the original.

Litzka Beam — a standard beam cut as the castellated beam, but with overall depth increased further by using spacer plates welded to the projections. Minimal increase in weight.

NB. Voids at the end of open web beams should be filled with a welded steel plate, as this is the area of maximum shear stress in a beam.

Lattices – these are an alternative type of open web beam, using standard steel sections to fabricate high depth to weight ratio units capable of spans up to about 15m. The range of possible components is extensive and some examples are shown below:

PLATE GIRDER

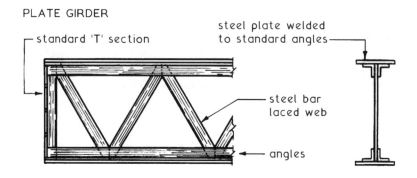

steel plate welded to standard angles

standard 'T' section

steel bar laced web

angles

TUBULAR LATTICE

end bearing plate

top and bottom tubular booms

D

tubular bracing

DOWELLED LATTICE

steel channels

timber insert for deck and ceiling fixing

steel dowel lacing

weld

NB. Span potential for lattice beams is approximately 24 × D.

Structural Steelwork Connections ~ these are either workshop or site connections according to where the fabrication takes place. Most site connections are bolted whereas workshop connections are very often carried out by welding. The design of structural steelwork members and their connections is the province of the structural engineer who selects the type and number of bolts or the size and length of weld to be used according to the connection strength to be achieved.

Typical Connection Examples ~

SIMPLE CONNECTION

SEMI-RIGID CONNECTION

RIGID CONNECTION

COLUMN TO FOUNDATION CONNECTION

633

Typical Connection Examples ~

'T' or similar section welded to beam as firring unless beam laid to fall

3mm clearance unless beam is continuous

universal column

universal beam site connected to cap plate

cap plate workshop fillet welded to column

universal column

TOP BEAM BEARING CONNECTIONS

upper column

web cleats to both sides workshop welded to cap plate

solid or laminated steel packing

site connections

fish plates workshop welded to lower column

upper column

lower column of equal size

lower column of unequal size

COLUMN TO COLUMN CONNECTIONS

depth of notch sufficient to clear flange thickness + root radius

notch length = distance from web face to flange edge + 10 mm to nearest 5mm

secondary beam

3mm clearance

site connections

main beam

secondary beam

web cleats to both sides welded to secondary beam in workshop

BEAM TO BEAM CONNECTION

NB. All holes for bolted connections must be made from backmarking the outer surface of the section(s) involved. For actual positions see structural steelwork manuals.

Types ~
Slab or bloom base.
Gusset base.
Steel grillage (see page 263).

The type selected will depend on the load carried by the column and the distribution area of the base plate. The cross sectional area of a UC concentrates the load into a relatively small part of the base plate. Therefore to resist bending and shear, the base must be designed to resist the column loads and transfer them onto the pad foundation below.

SLAB or BLOOM BASE   SLAB BASE WITH ANGLE CLEATS

GUSSET BASE   BOLT BOX

Bolt Box ~ a template used to accurately locate column holding down bolts into wet concrete. EPS or plastic tubes provide space around the bolts when the concrete has set. The bolts can then be moved slightly to aid alignment with the column base.

Welding is used to prefabricate the sub-assembly of steel frame components in the workshop, prior to delivery to site where the convenience of bolted joints will be preferred.

Oxygen and acetylene (oxy-acetylene) gas welding equipment may be used to fuse together light steel sections, but otherwise it is limited to cutting profiles of the type shown on page 631. The electric arc process is preferred as it is more effective and efficient. This technique applies an expendable steel electrode to fuse parts together by high amperage current. The current potential and electrode size can be easily changed to suit the thickness of metal.

Overlapping of sections permits the convenience of fillet welds, but if the overlap is obstructive or continuity and direct transfer of loads is necessary, a butt weld will be specified. To ensure adequate weld penetration with a butt weld, the edges of the parent metal should be ground to produce an edge chamfer. For very large sections, both sides of the material should be chamfered to allow for double welds.

BUTT WELD

NB. For greater thicknesses of parent metal, both sides are chamfered in preparation for a double weld.

FILLET WELD

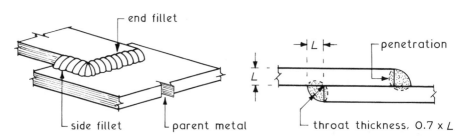

Ref. BS EN 1011-1 and 2: Welding. Recommendations for welding of metallic materials.

Bolts are the preferred method for site assembly of framed building components, although rivets have been popular in the past and will be found when working on existing buildings. Cold driven and 'pop' rivets may be used for factory assembly of light steel frames such as stud walling, but the traditional process of hot riveting structural steel both in the workshop and on site has largely been superseded for safety reasons and the convenience of other practices.

Types of Bolt:

1. Black Bolts ~ the least expensive and least precise type of bolt, produced by forging with only the bolt and nut threads machined. Clearance between the bolt shank and bolt hole is about 2 mm, a tolerance that provides for ease of assembly. However, this imprecision limits the application of these bolts to direct bearing of components onto support brackets or seating cleats.

2. Bright Bolts ~ also known as turned and fitted bolts. These are machined under the bolt head and along the shank to produce a close fit of 0.5 mm hole clearance. They are specified where accuracy is paramount.

3. High Strength Friction Grip Bolts ~ also known as torque bolts as they are tightened to a predetermined shank tension by a torque-controlled wrench. This procedure produces a clamping force that transfers the connection by friction between components and not by shear or bearing on the bolts. These bolts are manufactured from high-yield steel. The number of bolts used to make a connection is less than otherwise required.

Refs.:
BS 4190: ISO metric black hexagon bolts, screws and nuts. Specification.

BS 3692: ISO metric precision hexagon bolts, screws and nuts. Specification.

BS 4395 (2 parts): Specification for high strength friction grip bolts and associated nuts and washers for structural engineering.

BS EN 14399 (9 parts): High strength structural bolting assemblies for preloading.

Fire Resistance of Structural Steelwork ~ although steel is a non-combustible material with negligible surface spread of flame properties it does not behave very well under fire conditions. During the initial stages of a fire the steel will actually gain in strength but this reduces to normal at a steel temperature range of 250 to 400°C and continues to decrease until the steel temperature reaches 550°C when it has lost most of its strength. Since the temperature rise during a fire is rapid, most structural steelwork will need protection to give it a specific degree of fire resistance in terms of time. Part B of the Building Regulations sets out the minimum requirements related to building usage and size, BRE Report 128 'Guidelines for the construction of fire resisting structural elements' gives acceptable methods.

Typical Examples for 120 minutes' Fire Resistance ~

SOLID PROTECTION   HOLLOW PROTECTION

SOLID PROTECTION   HOLLOW PROTECTION

NB. For section factor calculations see next page.

Section Factors – these are criteria found in tabulated fire protection data such as the Loss Prevention Certification Board's Standards. These factors can be used to establish the minimum thickness or cover of protective material for structural sections. This interpretation is usually preferred by buildings insurance companies, as it often provides a standard in excess of the Building Regulations. Section factors are categorised: <90, 90–140 and >140. They can be calculated by the following formula:

Section Factor = Hp/A (m^{-1})

Hp = Perimeter of section exposed to fire (m)

A = Cross sectional area of steel (m^2) [see BS 4-1 or Structural Steel Tables]

Examples:

UB serial size, 305 × 127 × 42 kg/m

- section area of UB = 53.2 cm²

306.6 mm

- fully enclosed in concrete, 4 sides exposed

- web thickness = 8 mm

124.3 mm

Hp = (2 × 124·3) + (2 × 306·6) + 2(124·3 – 8) = 1·0944 m

A = 53·2 cm² or 0·00532 m²

Section Factor, Hp/A = 1·0944/0·00532 = 205

As beam above, but three sides only exposed

compartment concrete floor, f.r. = 120 minutes

fire protection

UB

Hp = 124·3 + (2 × 306·6) + 2(124·3 – 8) = 0·9701 m

A = 53·2 cm² or 0·00532 m²

Section Factor, Hp/A = 0·9701/0·00532 = 182

Refs.: BS 4-1: Structural steel sections. Specification for hot rolled
sections.

BS EN 1993-1: Design of steel structures.

Simple beam design (Bending)

Formula:

$$Z = \frac{M}{f}$$

where: Z = section or elastic modulus (BS 4-1)

M = moment of resistance > or = max. bending moment

f = fibre stress of the material (normally 165 N/mm² for
rolled steel sections)

In simple situations the bending moment can be calculated:

(a) Point loads

$$BM = \frac{WL}{4}$$

(b) Distributed loads

e.g.

$$BM = \frac{wL^2}{8} \quad or \quad \frac{WL}{8}$$
$$where \ W = w \times L$$

$$BM = \frac{wL^2}{8} = \frac{50 \times 4^2}{8} = 100 \text{kNm}$$

$$Z = \frac{M}{f} = \frac{100 \times 10^6}{165} = 606 \text{cm}^3$$

From structural design tables, e.g. BS 4-1, a Universal Beam
305 × 127 × 48 kg/m with section modulus (Z) of 612·4 cm³ about
the x-x axis, can be seen to satisfy the calculated 606 cm³.

NB. Total load in kN can be established by summating the weight
of materials — see pages 38 to 39: The total weight of materials
multiplied by gravity; i.e. kg × 9·81 = Newtons.

This must be added to any imposed loading:

People and furniture = 1·5 kN/m²

Snow on roofs < 30° pitch = 1·5 kN/m²

Snow on roofs > 30° pitch = 0·75 kN/m²

Simple beam design (shear)

From the previous example, the section profile is:

flange

y

serial size
305mm x 127mm x 48 kg/m

8·9mm

310·4mm

x— – – – —x

web sectional area
= 310·4mm x 8·9mm
= 2762·56mm²

y

125·2mm

Maximum shear force normally occurs at the support points, i.e. near the end of the beam. Calculation is made of the average stress value on the web sectional area.

Using the example of 200 kN load distributed over the beam, the maximum shear force at each end support will be 100 kN.

$$\text{Therefore, the average shear stress} = \frac{\text{shear force}}{\text{web sectional area}}$$

$$= \frac{100 \times 10^3}{2762 \cdot 56}$$

$$= 36 \cdot 20 \text{ N/mm}^2$$

Grade S275 steel has an allowable shear stress in the web of 110 N/mm². Therefore the example section of serial size: 305 mm × 127 mm × 48 kg/m with only 36·20 N/mm² calculated average shear stress is more than capable of resisting the applied forces.

Grade S275 steel has a characteristic yield stress of 275 N/mm² in sections up to 40 mm thickness. This grade is adequate for most applications, but the more expensive grade S355 steel is available for higher stress situations.

Ref. BS EN 10025: Hot rolled products of structural steels.

Simple beam design (deflection)

The deflection due to loading, other than the weight of the structure, should not exceed 1/360 of the span.

The formula to determine the extent of deflection varies, depending on:

(a) Point loading

$$\text{Deflection} = \frac{WL^3}{48EI}$$

(b) Uniformly distributed loading

$$\text{Deflection} = \frac{5WL^3}{384EI}$$

where: W = load in kN
    L = span in cm
    E = Young's modulus of elasticity (typically 21,000 kN/cm² for steel)
    I = 2nd moment of area about the x-x axis (see BS 4-1)

Using the example of 200 kN uniformly distributed over a 4 m span:

$$\text{Deflection} = \frac{5WL^3}{384EI} = \frac{5 \times 200 \times 4^3 \times 100^3}{384 \times 21000 \times 9504} = 0.835\,\text{cm}$$

Permissible deflection is 1/360 of 4 m = 11.1 mm or 1.11 cm.

Therefore actual deflection of 8.35 mm or 0.835 cm is acceptable.

Ref. BS EN 1993-1: Design of steel structures.

Summary of Properties Applicable to Loaded Beams ~

Beam type	Load type	Maximum shear	Maximum BM	Maximum deflection	Arrangement over span L
Simply supported	Central point load W	$\dfrac{W}{2}$	$\dfrac{WL}{4}$	$\dfrac{WL^3}{48EI}$	
Simply supported	UDL W	$\dfrac{W}{2}$	$\dfrac{WL}{8}$	$\dfrac{5WL^3}{384EI}$	
Ends fixed	Central point load W	$\dfrac{W}{2}$	$\dfrac{WL}{8}$ * $\dfrac{-WL}{8}$ •	$\dfrac{WL^3}{192EI}$	
Ends fixed	UDL W	$\dfrac{W}{2}$	$\dfrac{-WL}{12}$ * $\dfrac{WL}{24}$ •	$\dfrac{WL^3}{384EI}$	
Cantilever	Point load W at end	W	$-WL$	$\dfrac{WL^3}{3EI}$	
Cantilever	UDL W	W	$\dfrac{-WL}{2}$	$\dfrac{WL^3}{8EI}$	

     * At supports   • At mid-span

Note: Where a beam of constant properties, i.e. size, section modulus and 2nd. moment of area is used with the same type of end support to carry the same load:

• the bending moment will increase linearly with span, e.g. a doubling of the span doubles the bending moment.
• the deflection will increase by the span (L) cubed, e.g. doubling the span increases the deflection by eight times $(2)^3$.

Simple column design

Steel columns or stanchions have a tendency to buckle or bend under extreme loading. This can be attributed to:

(a) length
(b) cross sectional area
(c) method of end fixing, and
(d) the shape of section.

(b) and (d) are incorporated into a geometric property of section, known as the radius of gyration (r). It can be calculated:

$$r = \sqrt{\frac{I}{A}}$$

where: I = 2nd moment of area
A = cross-sectional area

Note: r, I and A are all listed in steel design tables, e.g. BS 4-1.

The radius of gyration about the y-y axis is used for calculation, as this is normally the weaker axis.

The length of a column will affect its slenderness ratio and potential to buckle. This length is calculated as an effective length relative to the method of fixing each end. Examples of position and direction fixing are shown on the next page, e.g. A Universal Column 203 mm × 203 mm × 46 kg/m, 10 m long, position and direction fixed both ends. Determine the maximum axial loading.

Effective length (l) = 0.7 × 10 m = 7 m
(r) from BS 4-1 = 51·1 mm

Slenderness ratio = $\frac{l}{r} = \frac{7 \times 10^3}{51.1} = 137$

From structural steel design tables the maximum allowable stress for grade S275 steel with slenderness ratio of 137 is 48 N/mm^2

Cross sectional area of stanchion (UC) = 5880 mm^2 (BS 4-1)

The total axial load = $\dfrac{48 \times 5880}{10^3}$ = 283 kN (approx. 28 tonnes)

The tendency for a column to buckle depends on its slenderness as determined by the ratio of its effective length to the radius of gyration about the weaker axis.

Effective lengths of columns and struts in compression ~

End conditions	Effective length relative to actual length
Restrained both ends in position and direction	0.70
Restrained both ends in position with one end in direction	0.85
Restrained both ends in position but not in direction	1.00
Restrained one end in position and direction. The other end restrained in direction only	1.50
Restrained one end in position and direction. The other end unrestrained	2.00

Position and direction fixed both ends

Position fixed both ends, direction fixed at one end

Position fixed both ends

Position and direction fixed at one end, direction only fixed at the other end

Position and direction fixed one end only

Position and direction fixed is location at specific points by beams or other means of retention. Position fixed only means hinged or pinned.

The effective lengths shown apply to the simplest of structures, for example, single storey buildings. Where variations occur such as cross braced support to columns, corrective factors should be applied to the effective length calculations. Guidance is available in BS EN 1993-1: Design of steel structures.

Portal Frames

Portal Frames ~ these can be defined as two-dimensional rigid frames which have the basic characteristic of a rigid joint between the column and the beam. The main objective of this form of design is to reduce the bending moment in the beam thus allowing the frame to act as one structural unit. The transfer of stresses from the beam to the column can result in a rotational movement at the foundation which can be overcome by the introduction of a pin or hinge joint. The pin or hinge will allow free rotation to take place at the point of fixity whilst transmitting both load and shear from one member to another. In practice a true 'pivot' is not always required but there must be enough movement to ensure that the rigidity at the point of connection is low enough to overcome the tendency of rotational movement.

Typical Single Storey Portal Frame Formats ~

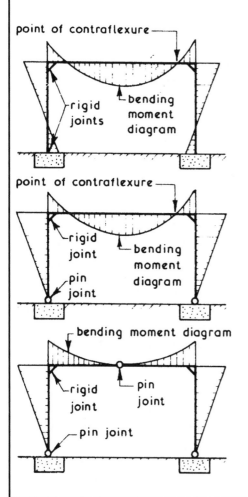

FIXED or RIGID PORTAL FRAME:

all joints or connections are rigid giving lower bending moments than other formats. Used for small to medium span frames where moments at foundations are not excessive.

TWO-PIN PORTAL FRAME:

pin joints or hinges used at foundation connections to eliminate tendency of base to rotate. Used where high base moments and weak ground are encountered.

THREE-PIN PORTAL FRAME:

pin joints or hinges used at foundation connections and at centre of beam which reduces bending moment in beam but increases deflection. Used as an alternative to a two-pin frame.

Typical Precast Concrete Portal Frame Details ~

300 × 200 spanning member or beam

600

beam

recess for purlin

rigid joint

2.400 × 600   up to 7.200

nut access hole

300 × 200 supporting member or column

20 mm dia. fixing bolts through dry splice joint

floor level

reinforced concrete pad foundation

9.000

TYPICAL SINGLE SPAN PORTAL FRAME
(frame spacing 4.500 to 6.000 ℅)

TYPICAL BEAM TO COLUMN JOINT

300 × 200 beam

valley gutter seating

300 × 200 beam

rigid joints

rigid joints

300 × 200 column

9.000

300 × 200 column

9.000

floor level

RC pad foundation

RC pad foundation

TYPICAL MULTI-SPAN PORTAL FRAME
(frame spacing 4.500 to 6.000 ℅)

25

1:2 cm/s grout

column wedge and grouted into pocket formed in foundation

2 × depth of beam

beam

600

dry splice joint

20 mm dia. fixing bolts

packing if required

TYPICAL SPLICE JOINT
(joint made at point of contraflexure)

reinforced concrete pad foundation to design

TYPICAL FOUNDATION DETAILS

647

Typical Precast Concrete Portal Frame Hinge Details ~

dowel bars forming pin

20

pitched spanning member or beam

reinforcement

joint filled with flexible rubber, bitumen compound, cork or similar material

3 No. leaves

reinforcement

2 No. leaves

steel hinge plate welded to ends of main bars and cast onto spanning member

steel pin

pitched spanning member or beam

TYPICAL APEX OR CROWN HINGE DETAILS

main bars

binders

supporting member or column

reinforcement

main bars

binders

cranked bars forming pin

joint filled with flexible rubber, bitumen compound, cork or similar material

steel hinge plate welded to ends of main bars and cast onto supporting member

20

holding down bolts

2 No. leaves

foundation

base plate

steel pin

TYPICAL FOUNDATION CONNECTION HINGE DETAILS

Typical Steel Portal Frame Details ~

site bolted ridge plates

UB section spanning member or beam

purlin cleat

haunch or knee gusset

gusset plate out of UB section

haunch gusset out of UB section welded to beam

site bolted fixing plate welded to beam

UB or UC section supporting member

floor level

reinforced concrete pad foundation

UB or UC section supporting member or column

TYPICAL SINGLE SPAN PORTAL FRAME
(frame spacing 4·500 to 6·000 °⁄c)

TYPICAL BEAM TO COLUMN JOINT

haunch or knee gusset

gusset plate out of UB section

UB section spanning member or beam

site bolted ridge plates welded to ends of beam

floor level

UB or UC section supporting member

RC pad foundation

RC pad foundation

TYPICAL MULTI–SPAN PORTAL FRAME
(frame spacing 4·500 to 6·000°⁄c)

supporting member or column

RC pad foundation

holding down bolts

base plate

butt jointed beams

web cleats if required

site bolted top and bottom fish plates

TYPICAL SPLICE JOINT
(joint made at point of contraflexure)

NB. pin joints can be formed using hinge plates as shown for PCC frames on previous page.

FOUNDATION DETAILS

649

Plywood Faced Lattice ~ framework of planed standard softwood sections with a plywood facing to both sides. A lightweight structure with high span to weight ratio. Spans to about 9m are possible with modest size timber members, providing economical construction for halls, community centres, etc. Based on the principle of a box beam comprising flanges or chords to resist bending, web stiffeners to control buckling and plywood facing to resist shear and bending as well as enhancing appearance.

plywood facing to both sides of softwood lattice beam

solid block apex butt jointed and bolted

typically 20°

stud

up to 6m depending on roof pitch and span

6 to 12mm plywood facing

stud/bracing/stiffener

planed sw chord

knee

leg or beam section

knee bracing

300 to 750mm depending on position in tapered frame and design span

support leg/column

stud

plywood face

steel fixing shoe bolted to foundation

reinforced concrete pad

Laminated Timber ~ sometimes called `Gluelam´ and is the process of building up beams, ribs, arches, portal frames and other structural units by gluing together layers of timber boards so that the direction of the grain of each board runs parallel with the longitudinal axis of the member being fabricated.

Laminates ~ these are the layers of board and may be jointed in width and length.

Joints ~

Width – joints in consecutive layers should lap twice the board thickness or one-quarter of its width whichever is the greater.

Length – scarf and finger joints can be used. Scarf joints should have a minimum slope of 1 in 12 but this can be steeper (say 1 in 6) in the compression edge of a beam:

T = laminate thickness

1 : 6 scarf joint

upper or compression edge of beam

min. 2 T

lower or tension edge of beam

a minimum of 24T between any joints in consecutive layers

1 : 12 scarf joint

Finger joints are more economical in the use of timber than the scarf joints

finger joint

laminated timber beam

Moisture Content ~ timber should have a moisture content equal to that which the member will reach in service and this is known as its equilibrium moisture content; for most buildings this will be between 11 and 15%. Generally at the time of gluing timber should not exceed 15 ± 3% in moisture content.

Laminated Timber

Vertical Laminations ~ not often used for structural laminated timber members and is unsatisfactory for curved members.

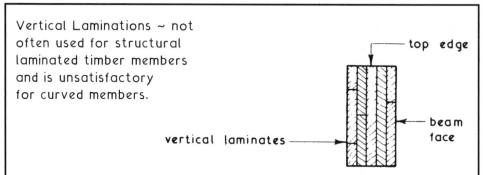

vertical laminates

top edge

beam face

Horizontal Laminations ~ most popular method for all types of laminated timber members. The stress diagrams below show that laminates near the upper edge are subject to a compressive stress whilst those near the lower edge to a tensile stress and those near the neutral axis are subject to shear stress.

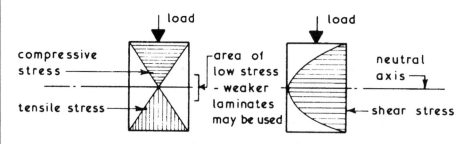

compressive stress

tensile stress

area of low stress - weaker laminates may be used

load

load

neutral axis

shear stress

Flat sawn timber shrinks twice as much as quarter sawn timber; therefore flat and quarter sawn timbers should not be mixed in the same member since the different shrinkage rates will cause unacceptable stresses to occur on the glue lines.

quarter sawn

flat sawn

not recommended

suitable if equilibrium moisture content is constant, otherwise the laminates tend to shrink away from one another

flat sawn reversed

satisfactory

quarter sawn

flat sawn

satisfactory but any shakes occurring here would weaken the beam

Planing ~ before gluing, laminates should be planed so that the depth of the planer cutter marks are not greater than 0·025mm.

Gluing ~ this should be carried out within 48 hours of the planing operation to reduce the risk of the planed surfaces becoming contaminated or case hardened (for suitable adhesives see next page). Just before gluing up the laminates they should be checked for 'cupping'. The amount of cupping allowed depends upon the thickness and width of the laminates and has a range of 0·75 mm to 1·5 mm.

Laminate Thickness ~ no laminate should be more than 50 mm thick since seasoning up to this thickness can be carried out economically and there is less chance of any individual laminate having excessive cross-grain strength.

Straight Members ~ laminate thickness is determined by the depth of the member, there must be enough layers to allow the end joints (i.e. scarf or finger joints – see page 651) to be properly staggered.

Curved Members ~ laminate thickness is determined by the radius to which the laminate is to be bent and the species together with the quality of the timber being used. Generally the maximum laminate thickness should be 1/150 of the sharpest curve radius although with some softwoods 1/100 may be used.

Typical Laminated Timber Curved Member ~

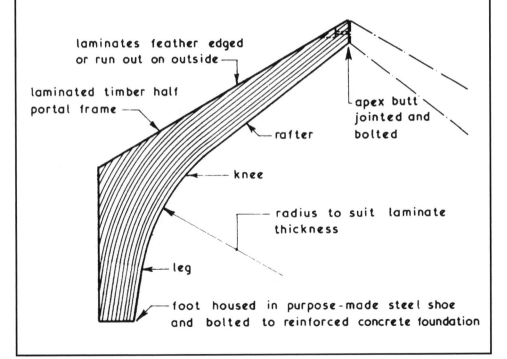

laminates feather edged or run out on outside

laminated timber half portal frame

apex butt jointed and bolted

rafter

knee

radius to suit laminate thickness

leg

foot housed in purpose-made steel shoe and bolted to reinforced concrete foundation

Adhesives ~ although timber laminates are carefully machined, the minimum of cupping permitted and efficient cramping methods employed mean it is not always possible to obtain really tight joints between the laminates. One of the important properties of the adhesive is therefore that it should be gap filling. The maximum permissible gap is 1.25 mm.

There are four adhesives suitable for laminated timber work which have the necessary gap filling property and they are:

1. Casein – the protein in milk, extracted by coagulation and precipitation. It is a cold setting adhesive in the form of a powder which is mixed with water, it has a tendency to stain timber and is only suitable for members used in dry conditions of service.
2. Urea Formaldehyde – this is a cold setting resin glue formulated to MR/GF (moisture resistant/gap filling). Although moisture resistant it is not suitable for prolonged exposure in wet conditions and there is a tendency for the glue to lose its strength in temperatures above 40°C such as when exposed to direct sunlight. The use of this adhesive is usually confined to members used in dry, unexposed conditions of service. This adhesive will set under temperatures down to 10°C.
3. Resorcinol Formaldehyde – this is a cold setting glue formulated to WBP/GF (weather and boilproof/gap filling). It is suitable for members used in external situations but is relatively expensive. This adhesive will set under temperatures down to 15°C and does not lose its strength at high temperatures.
4. Phenol Formaldehyde – this is a similar glue to resorcinol formaldehyde but is a warm setting adhesive requiring a temperature of above 86°C in order to set. Phenol/resorcinol formaldehyde is an alternative, having similar properties to but less expensive than resorcinol formaldehyde. PRF needs a setting temperature of at least 23°C.

Preservative Treatment – this can be employed if required, provided that the pressure impregnated preservative used is selected with regard to the adhesive being employed. See also page 545.

Ref. BS EN 301: Adhesives, phenolic and aminoplastic, for load-bearing timber structures. Classification and performance requirements.

Composite Beams ~ stock sizes of structural softwood have sectional limitations of about 225 mm and corresponding span potential in the region of 6 m. At this distance, even modest loadings could interpose with the maximum recommended deflection of 0·003 × span.

Fabricated softwood box, lattice and plywood beams are an economic consideration for medium spans. They are produced with adequate depth to resist deflection and with sufficient strength for spans into double figures. The high strength to weight ratio and simple construction provides advantages in many situations otherwise associated with steel or reinforced concrete, e.g. frames, trusses, beams and purlins in gymnasia, workshops, garages, churches, shops, etc. They are also appropriate as purlins in loft conversion.

SPANS <15 m
s/w flanges to resist bending

BOX BEAM

plywood web resists shear

s/w stiffeners control web buckling

LATTICE FRAME OR TRUSSED PURLIN

COR-PLY BEAM

corrugated plywood web

s/w flange

s/w flange

I SECTION BEAM

double or single plywood web

SPANS >15 m
BOARDED WEB GIRDER

web of diagonally opposed t&g boarding

steel plate core

FLITCH BEAM

standard s/w sections

bolts at 1m spacing

Parallel Strand Beam (PSB)

PSB ~ otherwise known as a parallam beam. Fabricated from long strands of softwood timber bonded with a phenol-formaldehyde adhesive along the length of the beam to produce a structural section of greater strength than natural timber of equivalent section. Used for beams, lintels, structural framing and trimmer sections around floor openings in spans up to 20 m. Can also be used vertically as columns.

Standard sizes ~ range from 200 × 45 mm up to 406 × 178 mm.

longitudinal strands of softwood timber adhesive coated and bonded under heat and pressure

Standard lengths 12, 15 and 18 m

Typical grade stresses [N/mm²] (compare with sw timber, page 142) ~

Bending parallel to grain	16.8
Tension parallel to grain	14.8
Compression parallel to grain	15.1
Compression perpendicular to grain	3.6
Shear parallel to grain	2.2
Modulus of elasticity (mean)	12750
Average density	740 kg/m³

Variation ~ for spans in excess of 20 m or for high loads, a flitch beam as shown on the previous page can be made by bolting a steel plate (typically 10 or 12 mm) between two PSBs.

Ref. BBA Agrément Certificate No. 92/2813.

Composite Joist ~ a type of lattice frame, constructed from a pair of parallel and opposing stress graded softwood timber flanges, separated and jointed with a web of V-shaped galvanised steel plate connectors. Manufacture is off site in a factory quality-controlled situation. Here, joists can be made in standard or specific lengths to order. Depending on loading, spans to about 8 m are possible at joist spacing up to 600 mm.

3mm dia. nails at 200mm c/c,
length 2.5 x board thickness

18 mm chipboard floor decking with joists at 450mm spacing (22mm @ 600mm) pva glued in the t & g and onto joists

typically 200, 225, 250 or 300

ex. 100 x 50 or 75 x 50

galv. steel web lacing

12.5mm plasterboard ceiling

3mm screws, 42mm long at 150mm c/c

voids for location of services

stress graded softwood top flange

steel web lacing

bottom flange

nail plate ends to galv. steel webs

solid timber ends to joist hanger

End bearing on inner leaf of cavity wall, silicone sealed to maintain airtightness. Alternatively lateral restraint-type joist hanger support or intermedite support from a steel beam.

Advantages over solid timber joists:

Large span to depth ratio.
High strength to weight ratio.
Alternative applications, including roof members, purlins, etc.
Generous space for services without holing or notching.
Minimal movement and shrinkage.
Wide flanges provide large bearing area for decking and ceiling board.

Otherwise known as tall, high rise or multi-storey buildings. Designed as an economic necessity where urban spread is prevented due to planning development constraints, e.g. green belt restrictions and as a response to high density living requirements in towns and cities. Tall buildings are also constructed to present an image of corporate status.

Building Types ~ residential apartments, hotels and office blocks.

Material Considerations ~ until the late 19th century when steel became commercially available, buildings of several storeys were constructed of brick masonry. By modern standards for height, with the exception of a modest rise to about four or five storeys, load-bearing masonry is uneconomic due to the necessary width of the lower walls to carry the superstructural loads. Therefore, framed structures of steel reinforced concrete or steel hot rolled sections are used, whereby the wall is infilling only, being relieved of any load bearing function except that of its own weight. The choice between reinforced concrete or steel for the framing is an economic decision dependent on the availability and cost of materials and appropriately qualified and experienced work force.

Design Constraints ~ the relationship between the superstructure, its foundations and the bearing capacity of the subsoil is the most important consideration. In particular, loading from vertical or gravitational forces in addition to exposure to horizontal or lateral wind forces and possibly ground movement from earthquakes.

Other Significant Design Factors ~

- Internal movement/circulation of occupants. Up to 20% of the floor area may be required to provide for vertical access in the form of stairs, lifts and escalators.
- Up to 15% of the volume of a building may be required to accommodate the services, i.e. plumbing, sanitation, drainage, ventilation, air conditioning, electrical cabling, etc. This is usually contained within suspended ceilings and raised floors.
- Occupancy type, building function and purpose will influence internal layout and structural floor load.
- External accessibility, often constrained in city and town centres. Movement must be factored in as this will affect the construction programme and subsequent efficient function of a building.

Traditional Rigid Frame ~ the structure is designed with rigidly connected welded and bolted joints between columns and beams. These joints sustain bending and provide resistance to lateral/ horizontal forces. Columns are positioned quite closely and internal columns may impose to some extent on the design of the interior layout.

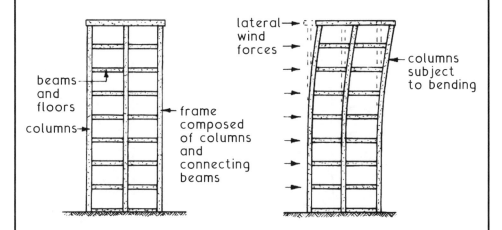

Core Structures ~ these are designed with a rigid structural core extending the full height of the building. The core is located centrally and the void within it is used to contain lifts and stairs. Lateral wind forces are transferred from the external wall cladding through the floor structure and into the core.

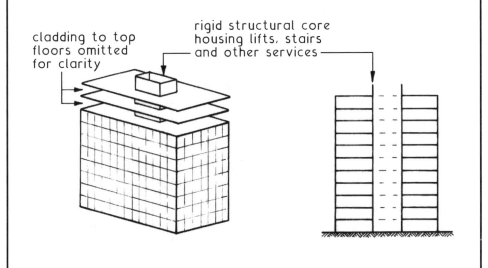

Hull or Tube Core ~ a variation of the central core structure shown on the preceding page, whereby the perimeter wall and its structural bracing contain all the floor area. The outer framing, bracing and cladding is known as the hull and it functions structurally with the internal core through the intermediary floors. The result is a rigid form of construction with a design potential for very tall buildings.

rigid structural core housing lifts, stairs etc.

alternative braced rigid framing

cladding to top floors omitted for clarity

rigid end shear wall

rigid internal shear wall

Shear Wall ~ lateral loading is resisted by rigid reinforced concrete external and internal walls. Floors act as diaphragms that transmit the lateral wind loads from façade cladding to shear walls. Long rectangular plan shaped buildings are suited to this design.

Diagonal Braced ~ a steel variation of the concrete shear wall. Structural walls are substituted with steel bracing which is in effect a series of vertical steel trusses. Columns are designed solely as compression members.

bracing

columns

Suspended, Propped and Cantilevered ~ variations on a design theme that reduce the ground space occupied by the structural components. This facilitates unimpeded and sheltered pedestrian and vehicular access.

Suspended ~ uses a central services structural core to resist lateral forces and to transmit vertical loads to the foundations. Floors are supported on beams secured to peripheral columns that hang from a roof level truss.

cross beams or trusses in both directions

internal core

hanger or suspended column

beams and floors span between columns and core

Section

Propped ~ a first floor cantilevered reinforced concrete slab or a steel structure that forms a base for peripheral columns. These columns carry the floor beams and structural floor slabs.

Cantilevered ~ each floor slab is cantilevered from a structural inner core.

Peripheral columns are not required and external cladding can be light weight infill panelling. The infilling must have sufficient structural resistance to lateral wind loads.

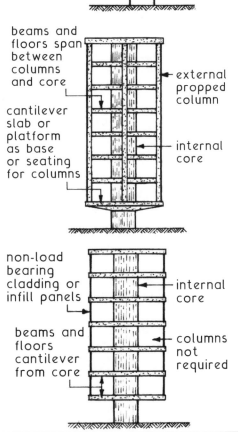

beams and floors span between columns and core

cantilever slab or platform as base or seating for columns

external propped column

internal core

non-load bearing cladding or infill panels

internal core

beams and floors cantilever from core

columns not required

Push-up ~ a steel frame construction method where the roof structure is assembled on the ground, then elevated by hydraulic jacking one floor at a time until the design height is achieved. At each floor lift, temporary supports are inserted whilst the space in between receives columns securely bolted to the preformed floor structure. The main advantage is a considerable reduction in the amount of heavy lifting plant and equipment needed by comparison with other construction methods. Also, with a roof covering applied, work at ground and upper floor levels can continue in all but extreme weather conditions.

Construction method ~

Roof construction at ground level

Roof structure elevated and temporarily supported

Ground floor constructed

hydraulic jacks located strategically

floors completed

Procedure repeated

Roof structure elevated above ground floor and temporarily supported

First floor constructed

first floor

ground floor

Steel Roof Trusses ~ these are triangulated plane frames which carry purlins to which the roof coverings can be fixed. Steel is stronger than timber and will not spread fire over its surface and for these reasons it is often preferred to timber for medium and long span roofs. The rafters are restrained from spreading by being connected securely at their feet by a tie member. Struts and ties are provided within the basic triangle to give adequate bracing. Angle sections are usually employed for steel truss members since they are economic and accept both tensile and compressive stresses. The members of a steel roof truss are connected together with bolts or by welding to shaped plates called gussets. Steel trusses are usually placed at 3·000 to 4·500 centres which gives an economic purlin size.

Typical Steel Roof Truss Formats ~

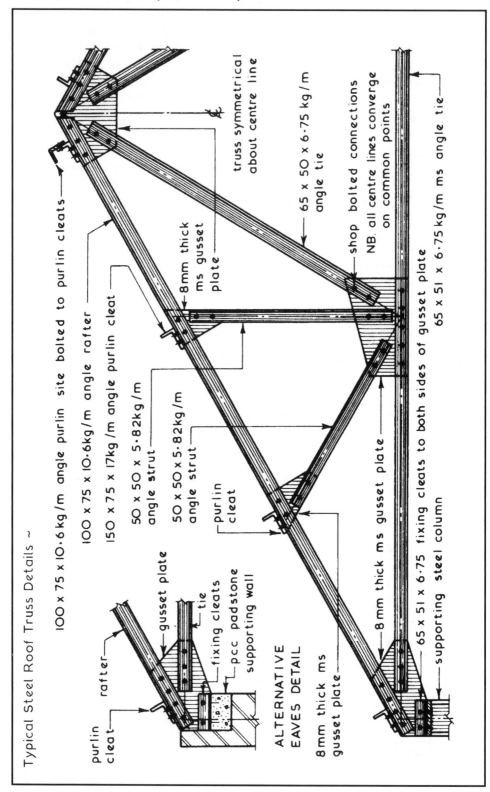

Typical Steel Roof Truss Details ~

100 x 75 x 10·6 kg/m angle purlin site bolted to purlin cleats

100 x 75 x 10·6 kg/m angle rafter

150 x 75 x 17 kg/m angle purlin cleat

50 x 50 x 5·82 kg/m angle strut

50 x 50 x 5·82 kg/m angle strut

purlin cleat

8 mm thick ms gusset plate

truss symmetrical about centre line

65 x 50 x 6·75 kg/m angle tie

shop bolted connections
NB. all centre lines converge on common points

65 x 51 x 6·75 kg/m ms angle tie

65 x 51 x 6·75 kg/m fixing cleats to both sides of gusset plate

8 mm thick ms gusset plate

supporting steel column

ALTERNATIVE
EAVES DETAIL

8 mm thick ms
gusset plate

purlin
cleat

rafter

gusset plate

tie

fixing cleats

pcc padstone
supporting wall

Sheet Coverings ~ the basic functions of sheet coverings used in conjunction with steel roof trusses are to:

1. Provide resistance to penetration by the elements.
2. Provide restraint to wind and snow loads.
3. Provide a degree of thermal insulation of not less than that set out in Part L of the Building Regulations.
4. Provide resistance to surface spread of flame as set out in Part B of the Building Regulations.
5. Provide any natural daylight required through the roof in accordance with the maximum permitted areas set out in Part L of the Building Regulations.
6. Be of low self-weight to give overall design economy.
7. Be durable to keep maintenance needs to a minimum.

Suitable Materials ~

Hot-dip galvanised corrugated steel sheets – BS 3083.

Aluminium profiled sheets – BS 4868.

Asbestos-free profiled sheets – various manufacturers whose products are usually based on a mixture of Portland cement, mineral fibres and density modifiers – BS EN 494.

Typical Profiles ~

CORRUGATED SHEETS

DEEP CORRUGATED SHEETS

TILE PROFILE SHEETS

Typical Purlin Fixing Details ~

STEEL ANGLE PURLIN

TIMBER PURLIN

ZED BEAM PURLIN

STEEL CHANNEL PURLIN

Typical Fittings ~

CLOSE FITTING RIDGE PIECE

BARGE BOARD

EAVES FILLER PIECE

EAVES CLOSURE PIECE

Typical Details ~

150 min.

50 min.

two-piece adjustable close fitting ridge

apex finishing piece

hook bolt

roof sheeting

insulation

lining sheet under insulation

cleat fixed to rafter

purlin fixed to cleat

rafter

rafter

gusset plate

tie

tie

APEX OR RIDGE DETAIL

stitch bolt

roof sheeting

eaves closure piece

eaves filler piece

stitch bolt

15

hook bolt

12

hook bolt

purlin

insulation

hook bolt

purlin

fascia

sheeting rail

flashing piece

external wall

wall sheeting

EAVES DETAIL USING CLOSURE PIECE

EAVES DETAIL USING FILLER PIECE

667

Double Skin, Energy Roof Systems ~ apply to industrial and commercial use buildings. In addition to new projects constructed to current thermal insulation standards, these systems can be specified to upgrade existing sheet profiled roofs with superimposed supplementary insulation and protective decking. Thermal performance with resin bonded mineral wool fibre of up to 250 mm overall depth may provide U-values as low as 0·13 W/m²K.

Typical Details ~

resin bonded mineral wool purlin with metal end caps
outer profiled metal sheeting
two layers of low density 'soft' insulation*
breather membrane
vapour control layer
inner profiled metal sheeting
Zed purlin

total depth* (mm)	approx. U-value
125	0·26
150	0·22
200	0·17
250	0·13

Alternative ~

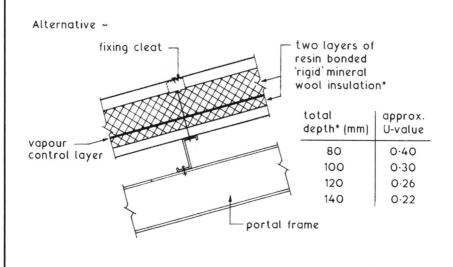

fixing cleat
two layers of resin bonded 'rigid' mineral wool insulation*
vapour control layer
portal frame

total depth* (mm)	approx. U-value
80	0·40
100	0·30
120	0·26
140	0·22

Further typical details using profiled galvanised steel or aluminium, colour coated if required ~

RIDGE

- cranked one-piece profiled ridge
- outer profiled sheeting
- ridge lining
- zed purlin

VALLEY GUTTER

- compressible profiled filler
- mineral fibre quilt insulation
- gutter lining
- thermal break 'plastic' spacer
- inner lining and gutter support

EAVES GUTTER

- galvanised steel or aluminium flashing
- radiused eaves piece
- zed purlin
- insulated trough gutter
- zed rail
- inner profiled sheeting, overlaps butyl or silicone sealed to provide vapour control layer – optional polythene vcl and breather membrane as shown on previous page

Long Span Roofs ~ these can be defined as those exceeding 12·000 in span. They can be fabricated in steel, aluminium alloy, timber, reinforced concrete and prestressed concrete. Long span roofs can be used for buildings such as factories, and large public halls and gymnasiums which require a large floor area free of roof support columns. The primary roof functions of providing weather protection, thermal insulation, sound insulation and restricting spread of fire over the roof surface are common to all roof types but these roofs may also have to provide strength sufficient to carry services lifting equipment and provide for natural daylight to the interior by means of rooflights.

Basic Roof Forms ~

Pitched Trusses - spaced at suitable centres to carry purlins to which the roof coverings are fixed. Good rainwater run off - reasonable daylight spread from rooflights - high roof volume due to the triangulated format - on long spans roof volume can be reduced by using a series of short span trusses.

Flat Top Girders - spaced at suitable centres to carry purlins to which the roof coverings are fixed. Low pitch to give acceptable rainwater run off - reasonable daylight spread from rooflights - can be designed for very long spans but depth and hence roof volume increases with span.

Northlight - spaced at suitable centres to carry purlins to which roof sheeting is fixed. Good rainwater run off - if correctly orientated solar glare is eliminated - long spans can be covered by a series of short span frames.

Monitor - girders or cranked beams at centres to suit low pitch decking used. Good even daylight spread from monitor lights which is not affected by orientation of building.

Pitched Trusses ~ these can be constructed with a symmetrical outline (as shown on pages 663 and 664) or with an asymmetrical outline (Northlight – see detail below). They are usually made from standard steel sections with shop welded or bolted connections. Alternatively they can be fabricated using timber members joined together with bolts and timber connectors or formed as a precast concrete portal frame.

Typical Multi-span Northlight Roof Details ~

NORTHLIGHT RIDGE DETAIL

NORTHLIGHT VALLEY DETAIL

Monitor Roofs ~ these are basically a flat roof with raised glazed portions called monitors which forms a roof having a uniform distribution of daylight with no solar glare problems irrespective of orientation and a roof with easy access for maintenance. These roofs can be constructed with light long span girders supporting the monitor frames, cranked welded beams following the profile of the roof or they can be of a precast concrete portal frame format.

Typical Monitor Roof Details ~

12 mm thick layer of stone chippings on 3 layers of built-up roofing felt

thermal insulation board

vcl

metal decking closure piece

1.75mm (Code 4) lead flashing

patent glazing

welded steel monitor frame fixed to top chords of girder

top chord of girder out of 2 No. mild steel angles

metal closure piece

struts and ties out of tee section bar

lattice girders spanning 15·000 at 4·500 ℀

perimeter support columns at 4·500 ℀

1.75mm (Code 4) lead flashing

patent glazing

roof decking and coverings as for monitor light roof

rainwater gutter

metal trim and closure

Flat Top Girders ~ attributed to Thomas Pratt an American engineer who with his father Caleb, patented their original truss design in 1844. Suitable for roof spans up to about 45 m. Effectively low pitched lattice beams used to carry purlins which support the roof coverings. One of the main advantages of this form of roof is the reduction in roof volume. The usual materials employed in the fabrication of flat top girders are timber and steel.

Typical Flat Top (Pratt Type) Girder Details ~

2 No. 250 × 75 top chords 75 mm apart

splice plates

corrugated or troughed roof sheeting

packing

225 × 75 purlins

steel fixing shoe

equal

200 × 75 'vertical' members

packing

splice plates

200 × 75 web members

2 No. 250 × 75 bottom chords 75 mm apart

steel fixing shoe

support column

Span - 20·000; Spacing - 3·000 ℅
Pitch - 5°; Material - SS graded softwood

purlin

bolt and timber connectors

'vertical' web

SECTION A-A

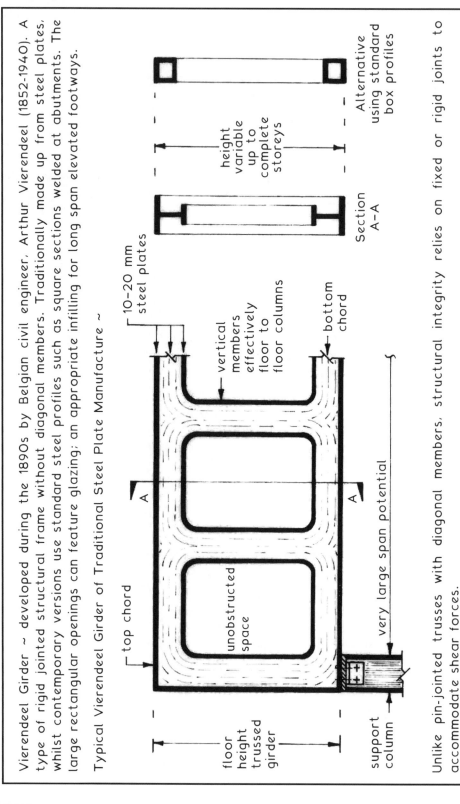

Vierendeel Girder ~ developed during the 1890s by Belgian civil engineer, Arthur Vierendeel (1852-1940). A type of rigid jointed structural frame without diagonal members. Traditionally made up from steel plates, whilst contemporary versions use standard steel profiles such as square sections welded at abutments. The large rectangular openings can feature glazing; an appropriate infilling for long span elevated footways.

Typical Vierendeel Girder of Traditional Steel Plate Manufacture ~

Unlike pin-jointed trusses with diagonal members, structural integrity relies on fixed or rigid joints to accommodate shear forces.

10-20 mm steel plates

vertical members effectively floor to floor columns

bottom chord

height variable up to complete storeys

Section A-A

Alternative using standard box profiles

top chord

unobstructed space

A

A

very large span potential

support column

floor height trussed girder

Bowstring Truss ~ a type of lattice truss formed with a curved upper edge. Bows and strings may be formed in pairs of laminated timber sections that are separated by solid web timber sections of struts and ties.

Spacing ~ 4.000 to 6.000 m apart depending on sizes of timber sections used and span.

Purlins ~ to coincide with web section meeting points and at about 1.000 m interim intervals.

Decking ~ sheet material suitably weathered or profiled metal sheeting. Thermally insulated relative to application.

Top bow radius ~ generally taken as between three-quarters of the span and the whole span.

Application ~ manufacturing assembly areas, factories, aircraft hangers, exhibition centres, sports arenas and other situations requiring a very large open span with featured timbers. Standard steel sections may also be used in this profile where appearance is less important, e.g. railway termini.

Variation ~ the Belfast truss that pre-dates the standard bowstring shown. It has much smaller interlaced struts and ties and is therefore more complicated in terms of assembly and for calculation of stress distribution. See next page.

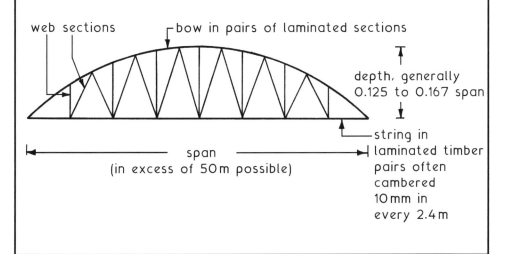

web sections — bow in pairs of laminated sections

depth, generally 0.125 to 0.167 span

string in laminated timber pairs often cambered 10 mm in every 2.4 m

span (in excess of 50 m possible)

Belfast Truss ~ established as one of the earliest forms of bowstring truss for achieving an efficient and economical roof construction over large spans. It was first used in the latter part of the 19th century and early part of the 20th century for industrial and agricultural buildings in response to the need for space uninterrupted by walls and columns within production, assembly and storage areas. A contribution to the name was a truss design devised by Messrs D. Anderson and Son, Ltd of Belfast, for supporting their patent roofing felt.

lattice location   alternative

45°

$\dfrac{\text{span}}{8}$

$\dfrac{\text{span}}{2}$

centre line radius (see calculation)

spans up to about 30.000m

A = purlins at about 1.000m spacing

Centre line radius = [(0.5 × span)² + (rise)²] ÷ (2 × rise)
E.g. A 16 m span with a rise of 0.125 × span.
Therefore, rise of truss = 0.125 × 16 = 2 m.
Centre line radius = [(0.5 × 16)² + (2)²] ÷ (2 × 2)
               = 68 ÷ 4 = 17 m.

Bowed Lattice Truss Details ~

Bowstring ~

steel or softwood fish plate (x2)

laminated bow (x2)

packing between bows

bracket or block

centre tie

strut

laminated tie (x2)

bolt and split ring connection

steel heel plate

bows

ties

Belfast ~

purlin

bows (2)

sheet decking

lattice bracing

strings (2)

plywood gusset

packing

steel angle

Typical softwood timber dimensions ~

Span (m)	6	12	18	24
Bow × 2 (mm)	38 × 20	63 × 25	75 × 32	75 × 50
String × 2 (mm)	125 × 20	200 × 25	250 × 32	300 × 50
Lattices (mm)	75 × 20	75 × 25	100 × 25	125 × 25

Connections ~ nails, screws and bolts have their limitations when used to join structural timber members. The low efficiency of joints made with a rigid bar such as a bolt is caused by the usual low shear strength of timber parallel to the grain and the non-uniform distribution of bearing stress along the shank of the bolt –

SHEARING EFFECT   STRESS DISTRIBUTION

Timber Connectors ~ these are designed to overcome the problems of structural timber connections outlined above by increasing the effective bearing area of the bolts.

Toothed Plate Connector – provides an efficient joint without special tools or equipment – suitable for all connections especially small sections – bolt holes are drilled 2 mm larger than the bolt diameter, the timbers forming the joint being held together whilst being drilled.

Split Ring Connector – very efficient and develops a high joint strength – suitable for all connections – split ring connectors are inserted into a precut groove formed with a special tool making the connector independent from the bolt.

Shear Plate Connector – counterpart of a split ring connector – housed flush into timber – used for temporary joints.

Space Deck ~ a roofing system based on a combination of repetitive inverted pyramidal units to give large clear spans of up to 22m for single span designs and up to 33m for two-way spans. Each unit consists of a square frame of steel angles connected with steel tubular bracing to a cast steel apex boss. The connecting boss has four threaded holes to receive horizontal high tensile steel tie bars. Threads are left and right handed at opposing ends of the tie bar to match corresponding threads in the boss. As the bar is rotated both ends tighten into a boss. Tie bars can be varied in length to alter the spacing of apex boss connectors. This will induce tension in the upper frame forming a camber for surface water drainage.

Assembly ~ usually transported to site as individual units for assembly into beams and complete space deck at ground level before crane hoisting into position onto the perimeter supports. A lightweight insulated structural roof deck system is appropriate in combination with rooflights mounted directly onto individual units if required.

Standard Unit Dimensions ~

1.2 m × 1.2 m on plan with depths of 750 mm or 1.2 m.

1.5 m × 1.5 m on plan with depths of 1.2 m or 1.5 m.

STANDARD UNIT   DECK ASSEMBLY

679

Space Deck Frame Support ~ can be on columns or a peripheral ring beam through purpose made bearing joints. These joints should be designed with adequate strength to resist and transmit vertical and horizontal loads that combine compressive and tensile forces.

Edge Treatment and Finishes ~ various possibilities; these include vertical fascias, mansard and cantilever.

Space Deck Edge Fixings and Finishes ~

FLAT FASCIA FINISH

MANSARD FINISH

COLUMN HEAD BRACKET

EDGE BRACKET

Space Frame ~ a concept based on a three-dimensional framework of structural members pinned at their ends, i.e. four joints or nodes that combine to produce a simple tetrahedron. As a roofing system it uses a series of connectors to join chords and bracing members. Single or double layer grids are possible, the former usually employed for assembling small domes or curved roofs. Space frames are similar in concept to space decks but they have greater flexibility in design and layout possibilities. Steel or aluminium alloy tubes have been the favoured material for space frames. Fibre reinforced composites are also viable.

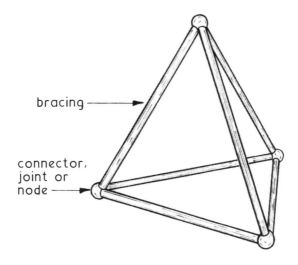

bracing

connector, joint or node

Origins ~ initially attributed to Alexander Bell (1847–1922), perhaps better known as the inventor of the telephone. During the early 1900s he experimented with octahedral and tetrahedral space truss structures. It was much later before the potential for space grid structures was recognised and produced commercially. One of the earliest being the German MERO system developed by Max Mengeringhausen (1903-1988) in the 1940s. Its name was devised from an abreviation of MEngeringhausen ROhrbauweise. In the 1960s and 1970s space frame technology moved into a new generation of super-systems capable of very long spans often exceeding 50 m. It is from the basis of the technological principles established during this era that contemporary applications are now designed.

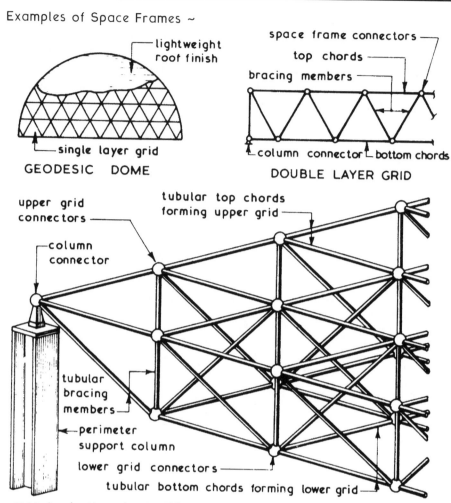

Examples of Space Frames ~

lightweight roof finish

single layer grid

GEODESIC DOME

space frame connectors

top chords

bracing members

column connector — bottom chords

DOUBLE LAYER GRID

upper grid connectors

column connector

tubular top chords forming upper grid

tubular bracing members

perimeter support column

lower grid connectors

tubular bottom chords forming lower grid

span to depth ratio 1 : 15 (corner supports) & 1 : 20 (edge supports)

TYPICAL DOUBLE LAYER GRID FORMAT

Development ~ during the 1960s and 1970s investment in public and private company research led to numerous systems of long span space frames being developed and introduced on a commercial scale. One of the better known is the 'Nodus' system created by British Steel Corporation (later Corus, now TATA). This concept formed the basis for later improvements and many contemporary systems use the principles of nodal jointing compatible with standard manufactured tubular metal sections. See next page for details.

Notes:

• All factory fabrication, leaving simple assembly processes for site.
• Node steel castings in two parts with machined grooves and drilled holes. Machined steel teeth connector welded to chord ends.

Space Frame Concept Based on the 'Nodus' System of Jointing ~

edge chord

standard joint bolted to column adaptor

top chord

60mm tubular top chord

standard joint

column adaptor

48 mm tubular bracing

48 mm tubular bracing

grid depth to span ratio 1:20 for edge support and 1:15 for corner support

standard joint

standard joint

60 mm tubular bottom chord

standard joint bolted to column adaptor

bottom chords

column adaptor

standard column support

standard column support

central high strength friction grip bolt

hexagonal bolt head recess

top casting with 45° lugs

chord

gasket clamped between castings

connector welded to chord

lower casting

chord

chords

lugs

forked connector welded to brace

nut washer

brace

split pin

clevis pin

brace

braces

forked connector welded to brace

brace

forked connector

chord

chord

top and bottom castings

chord

sealing gasket

683

Shell Roofs ~ these can be defined as a structural curved skin covering a given plan shape and area where the forces in the shell or membrane are compressive and in the restraining edge beams are tensile. The usual materials employed in shell roof construction are in-situ reinforced concrete and timber. Concrete shell roofs are constructed over formwork which in itself is very often a shell roof making this format expensive, since the principle of use and reuse of formwork cannot normally be applied. The main factors of shell roofs are:

1. The entire roof is primarily a structural element.
2. Basic strength of any particular shell is inherent in its geometrical shape and form.
3. Comparatively less material is required for shell roofs than for other forms of roof construction.

Domes ~ these are double curvature shells which can be rotationally formed by any curved geometrical plane figure rotating about a central vertical axis. Translation domes are formed by a curved line moving over another curved line whereas pendentive domes are formed by inscribing within the base circle a regular polygon and vertical planes through the true hemispherical dome.

Typical Examples ~

Barrel Vaults ~ these are single curvature shells which are essentially a cut cylinder which must be restrained at both ends to overcome the tendency to flatten. A barrel vault acts as a beam whose span is equal to the length of the roof. Long span barrel vaults are those whose span is longer than its width or chord length and conversely short barrel vaults are those whose span is shorter than its width or chord length. In every long span barrel vault thermal expansion joints will be required at 30·000 centres which will create a series of abutting barrel vault roofs weather sealed together (see next page).

Typical Single Barrel Vault Principles~

economic design ratios - width : span   1 : 2 to 1 : 5
rise : span 1 : 10 to 1 : 15

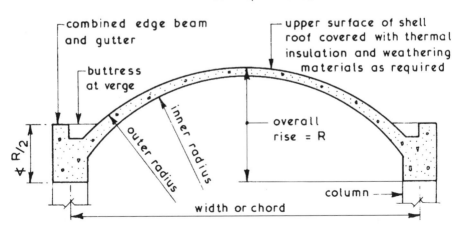

Typical Barrel Vault Expansion Joint Details ~

capping clips fixed to hardwood batten at required centres

40 x 25 h/w batten

copper or other suitable non-ferrous metal capping

100 mm high kerb

abutting barrel vault roofs

stiffening arch rib or diaphragm

filling material of cellular polythene, polyurethane or foam rubber

25 mm wide expansion joint

mastic or sealant

external face

abutting barrel vault support columns

compressible gap filling material

copper expansion strip

filling material of cellular polythene, polyurethane or foam rubber

25 mm wide expansion joint

Stiffening Beams ~ short barrel vaults often have large chords of over 12·000. In such cases stiffening beams should be placed at 3·000 to 6·000 centres to prevent buckling.

edge beam

barrel vault

upstand stiffening beams

barrel vault

stiffening diaphragm or downstand beams

edge beam

support column

NB. Ribs not connected to support columns will set up extra stresses within the shell roof; therefore extra reinforcement will be required at the stiffening rib or beam positions.

Other Forms of Barrel Vault ~ by cutting intersecting and placing at different levels the basic barrel vault roof can be formed into a groin or northlight barrel vault roof:

INTERSECTING BARREL VAULTS   STEPPED BARREL VAULTS

NORTHLIGHT BARREL VAULT

Conoids ~ these are double curvative shell roofs which can be considered as an alternative to barrel vaults. Spans up to 12·000 with chord lengths up to 24·000 are possible. Typical chord to span ratio 2:1.

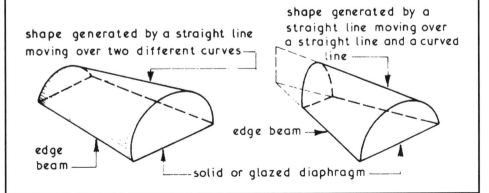

Hyperbolic Paraboloids ~ the true hyperbolic paraboloid shell roof shape is generated by moving a vertical parabola (the generator) over another vertical parabola (the directrix) set at right angles to the moving parabola. This forms a saddle shape where horizontal sections taken through the roof are hyperbolic in format and vertical sections are parabolic. The resultant shape is not very suitable for roofing purposes; therefore only part of the saddle shape is used and this is formed by joining the centre points thus:

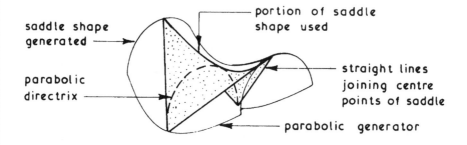

To obtain a more practical shape than the true saddle a straight line limited hyperbolic paraboloid is used. This is formed by raising or lowering one or more corners of a square forming a warped parallelogram thus:

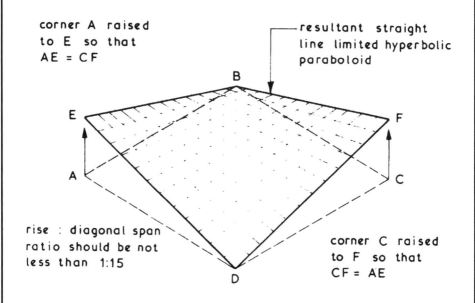

NB. For further examples see next page.

Typical Straight Line Limited Hyperbolic Paraboloid Formats ~

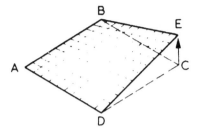

corner C raised to E

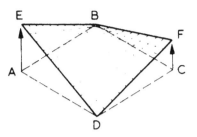

corner A raised to E and
corner C raised to F so that
AE ≠ CF

resultant hyperbolic
paraboloid

original
square

corner A lowered to E and
corner C raised to F so that
AE = CF

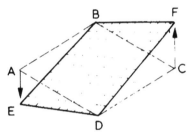

corner A lowered to E and
corner C raised to F so that
AE ≠ CF

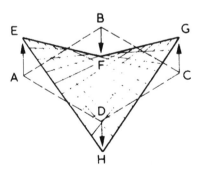

corners A & C raised to E & G
corners B & D lowered to F & H
so that AE = CG & BF = DH

Combination of Hyperbolic
Paraboloid Shell Roofs ~

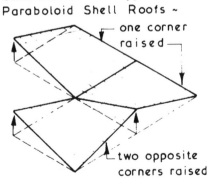

one corner
raised

two opposite
corners raised

NB. Any combination possible.

Concrete Hyperbolic Paraboloid Shell Roofs ~ these can be constructed in reinforced concrete (characteristic strength 25 or 30 N/mm²) with a minimum shell thickness of 50 mm with diagonal spans up to 35·000. These shells are cast over a timber form in the shape of the required hyperbolic paraboloid format. In practice therefore two roofs are constructed and it is one of the reasons for the popularity of timber versions of this form of shell roof.

Timber Hyperbolic Paraboloid Shell Roofs ~ these are usually constructed using laminated edge beams and layers of t & g boarding to form the shell membrane. For roofs with a plan size of up to 6·000 × 6·000 only two layers of boards are required and these are laid parallel to the diagonals with both layers running in opposite directions. Roofs with a plan size of over 6·000 × 6·000 require three layers of board as shown below. The weather protective cover can be of any suitable flexible material such as built-up roofing felt, copper and lead. During construction the relatively lightweight roof is tied down to a framework of scaffolding until the anchorages and wall infilling have been completed. This is to overcome any negative and positive wind pressures due to the open sides.

Typical Details ~

beam capping

roof finishes

top portion of laminated edge beam out of 8 No. 25 × 250 lamins

bolts at 600 °/c

bottom portion of laminated edge beam out of 8 No. 25 × 250 lamins

packing

mastic seal

infill panel

three layers of 20 mm thick t & g boards forming shell laid in the following manner:

1st layer - parallel to edge ||||||||||

2nd layer - diagonal ////

3rd layer - parallel to edge ≡≡≡

125 125

nails

75

The boards are nailed together and over a 2·000 to 2·400 wide zone parallel to the edge beams they are glued and nailed

690

Support Considerations ~ in timber hyperbolic paraboloid shell roofs only two supports are required:

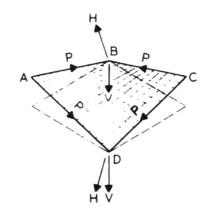

Edge beams are in compression forces P are transmitted to B and D resulting in a vertical force V and a horizontal force H at both positions; therefore support columns are required at B and D.

Vertical force V is transmitted directly down the columns to a suitable foundation. The outward or horizontal force H can be accommodated in one of two ways:

shell roof

edge beam

low corner

edge beam

low corner

buttress wall

shell roof

column

30 mm dia. high tensile steel tie bar

6 mm dia. wire ropes at 1·500 c/c

shell roof → wire ropes → tie bar to opposite corners

If shell roof is to be supported at high corners the edge beams will be in tension and horizontal force will be inwards. This can be resisted by a diagonal strut between the high corners.

Combination Roof Support Example ~

4 No. roof shells of equal loading joined together ⟶

Supports required at A; C; G and E. with ties between AC; CE; EG and GA. Forces at J cancel each other out; therefore no support required at J.

Folded Slab Roof Construction

A form of stressed skin reinforced concrete construction also known as folded plate construction. The concept is to profile a flat slab into folds so that the structure behaves as a series of beams spanning parallel with the profile.

Optimum depth to span ratio is between 1:10 to 1:15, or a depth to width of not less than 1:10, whichever is greater.

Roof format ~ pitched, monitor or multi-fold.

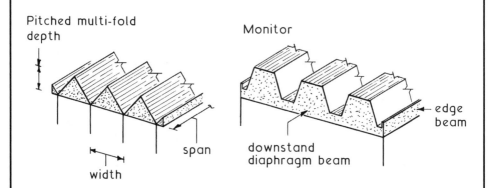

Pitched multi-fold
depth

Monitor

edge beam

span

downstand diaphragm beam

width

Several slabs of narrow thickness are usually preferred to a few wider slabs as this reduces the material dead loading. Numerous design variations are possible particularly where counter-folds are introduced and the geometry developed to include bowed or arched spans extending to the ground.

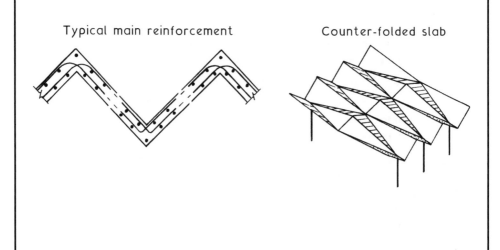

Typical main reinforcement

Counter-folded slab

Membrane Structure Principles ~ a form of tensioned cable structural support system with a covering of stretched fabric. In principle and origin, this compares to a tent with poles as compression members secured to the ground. The fabric membrane is attached to peripheral stressing cables suspended in a catenary between vertical support members.

Form ~ there are limitless three-dimensional possibilities. The following geometric shapes provide a basis for imagination and elegance in design:

- Hyperbolic paraboloid (Hypar)
- Barrel vault
- Conical or double conical

Hyperbolic paraboloid   Barrel vault   Conical

Double conical~

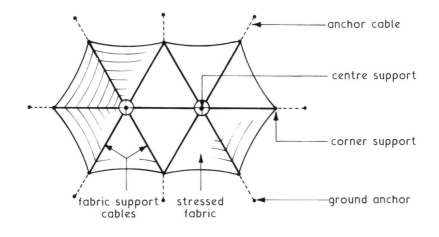

anchor cable

centre support

corner support

ground anchor

fabric support cables   stressed fabric

Membrane Roof Structures

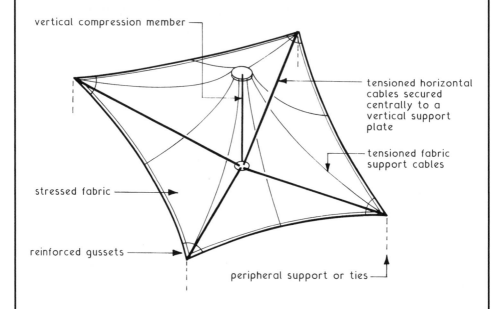

Simple support structure as viewed from the underside ~

vertical compression member

tensioned horizontal cables secured centrally to a vertical support plate

tensioned fabric support cables

stressed fabric

reinforced gussets

peripheral support or ties

Fabric ~ has the advantages of requiring minimal support, opportunity for architectural expression in colour and geometry and a translucent quality that provides an outside feel inside, whilst combining shaded cover from the sun and shelter from rain. Applications are generally attachments as a feature to entrances and function areas in prominent buildings, notably sports venues, airports and convention centres.

Materials ~ historically, animal hides were the first materials used for tensile fabric structures, but more recently woven fibres of hemp, flax or other natural yarns have evolved as canvas. Contemporary synthetic materials have a plastic coating on a fibrous base. These include polyvinyl chloride (PVC) on polyester fibres, silicone on glass fibres and polytetrafluorethylene (PTFE) on glass fibres. Design life is difficult to estimate, as it will depend very much on type of exposure. Previous use of these materials would indicate that at least 20 years is anticipated, with an excess of 30 years being likely. Jointing can be by fusion welding of plastics, bonding with silicone adhesives and stitching with glass threads.

Rooflights ~ the useful penetration of daylight through the windows in external walls of buildings is from 6·000 to 9·000 depending on the height and size of the window. In buildings with spans over 18·000 side wall daylighting needs to be supplemented by artificial lighting or in the case of top floors or single-storey buildings by rooflights. The total maximum area of wall window openings and rooflights for the various purpose groups is set out in the Building Regulations with allowances for increased areas if double or triple glazing is used. In pitched roofs such as northlight and monitor roofs the rooflights are usually in the form of patent glazing (see Long Span Roofs on pages 671 and 672). In flat roof construction natural daylighting can be provided by one or more of the following methods:

1. Lantern lights – see page 697.
2. Lens lights – see page 697.
3. Dome, pyramid and similar rooflights – see page 698.

Patent Glazing ~ these are systems of steel or aluminium alloy glazing bars which span the distance to be glazed whilst giving continuous edge support to the glass. They can be used in the roof forms noted above as well as in pitched roofs with profiled coverings where the patent glazing bars are fixed above and below the profiled sheets – see next page.

Typical Patent Glazing Bar Sections ~

ALUMINIUM ALLOY BAR   INVERTED BAR

STEEL BAR – LEAD SHEATHED   STEEL BAR – PVC SHEATHED

Typical Pitched Roof Patent Glazing Details ~

eaves closure piece

profiled roof sheeting

lead flashing dressed over glazing bars

bolt and clip

patent glazing bars at 600 ℅

insulation

single or double glazing

purlin

cleat

roof truss

shelf angle bearer and fixing shoe

glazing

TOP CONNECTION

patent glazing bar

fixing shoe and draught excluder

glass stop

shelf angle bearer

lead flashing

steel batten strip

bolt and clip

flashing piece

cleat

purlin

profiled roof sheeting and insulation

roof truss

BOTTOM CONNECTION

Lantern Lights ~ these are a form of rooflight used in conjuction with flat roofs. They consist of glazed vertical sides and fully glazed pitched roof which is usually hipped at both ends. Part of the glazed upstand sides is usually formed as an opening light or alternatively glazed with louvres to provide a degree of controllable ventilation. They can be constructed of timber, metal or a combination of these two materials. Lantern lights in the context of new buildings have been generally superseded by the various forms of dome light (see next page).

Typical Lantern Light Details ~

Lens Lights ~ these are small square or round blocks of translucent toughened glass especially designed for casting into concrete and are suitable for use in flat roofs and curved roofs such as barrel vaults. They can also be incorporated into precast concrete frames for inclusion in a cast in-situ roof.

Typical Details ~

Dome, Pyramid and Similar Rooflights ~ these are used in conjuction with flat roofs and may be framed or unframed. The glazing can be of glass or plastics such as polycarbonate, acrylic, PVC and glass fibre reinforced polyester resin (grp). The whole component is fixed to a kerb and may have a raising piece containing hit and miss ventilators, louvres or flaps for controllable ventilation purposes.

Typical Details ~

fixing clips ── kerb

600 to 1800

CIRCULAR PLAN

fixing clips ── flat, pyramid or segmental profiles

600 to 1800

kerb ──►

600 to 2400

RECTANGULAR PLAN

rubber seal ── double skin dome light

aluminium alloy framing

centre pivot aluminium alloy louvres ── opening control

single skin dome light

fixing clip and rubber seal

roof finish ──

roof finish ──

kerb and roof slab

kerb and roof slab

DOME AND RAISING PIECE

DIRECT FIXED DOME

Non-load-bearing Brick Panel Walls ~ these are used in conjunction with framed structures as an infill between the beams and columns. They are constructed in the same manner as ordinary brick walls with the openings being formed by traditional methods.

Basic requirements:

1. To be adequately supported by and tied to the structural frame.
2. Have sufficient strength to support own self-weight plus any attached finishes and imposed loads such as wind pressures.
3. Provide the necessary resistance to penetration by the natural elements.
4. Provide the required degree of thermal insulation, sound insulation and fire resistance.
5. Have sufficient durability to reduce maintenance costs to a minimum.
6. Provide for movements due to moisture and thermal expansion of the panel and for contraction of the frame.

Typical Details ~

Brickwork Cladding Support System

Note: Standard cavity wall insulated as required

reinforced concrete column

reinforced concrete perimeter beam

dovetail channel support rail set in concrete

6 mm steel angle bracket, min. ⅔ penetration into brickwork

brickwork movement joint

sliding brick anchor ~ (ties fit loosely over guide)

galvanised steel fish-tail tie

Application – multi-storey buildings, where a traditional brick façade is required.

Brickwork movement – to allow for climatic changes and differential movement between the cladding and main structure, a 'soft' joint (cellular polyethylene, cellular polyurethane, expanded rubber or sponge rubber with polysulphide or silicon pointing) should be located below the support angle. Vertical movement joints may also be required at a maximum of 12 m spacing.

Lateral restraint – provided by normal wall ties between inner and outer leaf of masonry, plus sliding brick anchors below the support angle.

Infill Panel Walls ~ these can be used between the framing members of a building to provide the cladding and division between the internal and external environments and are distinct from claddings and facing:

drained joint

structural frame

precast concrete storey height cladding panels attached to frame see pages 715 to 718

structural frame

rainscreen claddings attached to brick or block backing wall see pages 705 to 707

lightweight or solid infill panels between framing members see next two pages

CLADDING PANELS   PANEL & FACINGS   INFILL PANELS

Functional Requirements ~ all forms of infill panel should be designed and constructed to fulfil the following functional requirements:

1. Self-supporting between structural framing members.
2. Provide resistance to the penetration of the elements.
3. Provide resistance to positive and negative wind pressures.
4. Give the required degree of thermal insulation.
5. Give the required degree of sound insulation.
6. Give the required degree of fire resistance.
7. Have sufficient openings to provide the required amount of natural ventilation.
8. Have sufficient glazed area to fulfil the natural daylight and vision out requirements.
9. Be economical in the context of construction and maintenance.
10. Provide for any differential movements between panel and structural frame.

Brick Infill Panels ~ these can be constructed in a solid or cavity format, the latter usually having an inner skin of blockwork to increase the thermal insulation properties of the panel. All the fundamental construction processes and detail of solid and cavity walls (bonding, lintels over openings, wall ties, damp-proof courses, etc.) apply equally to infill panel walls. The infill panel walls can be tied to the columns by means of wall ties cast into the columns at 300 mm centres or located in cast-in dovetail anchor slots. The head of every infill panel should have a compressible joint to allow for any differential movements between the frame and panel.

Typical Details

Lightweight Infill Panels ~ these can be constructed from a wide variety or combination of materials such as timber, metals and plastics into which single or double glazing can be fitted. If solid panels are to be used below a transom they are usually of a composite or sandwich construction to provide the required sound insulation, thermal insulation and fire resistance properties.

Typical Example ~

face of column

face of column

reinforced concrete edge beam

reinforced concrete floor

aluminium alloy head section sealed with mastic and fixed at 600 ℅ to timber inserts

secondary beam

timber fixing inserts secured to beam at 600 ℅

aluminium alloy glazing bead

sealed double glazing units bedded in mastic and secured with beads

aluminium alloy box section transom fixed to haunches on jambs

composite or sandwich solid panel bedded in mastic and secured with beads

aluminium alloy fixing bead

aluminium alloy sill section bedded in mastic and fixed to kerb

reinforced concrete edge beam

reinforced concrete floor

aluminium alloy head section - jamb section similar

secondary beam

Lightweight Infill Panels ~ these can be fixed between the structural horizontal and vertical members of the frame or fixed to the face of either the columns or beams to give a grid, horizontal or vertical emphasis to the façade thus:

GRID OR FRAME EMPHASIS — panels fixed between columns and beams

HORIZONTAL EMPHASIS — panels fixed between beams and over columns

VERTICAL EMPHASIS — panels fixed between columns and over beams

Rainscreen Cladding ~ a surface finish produced by overcladding the external walls of new construction, or as a decorative façade and insulation enhancement to the external walls of existing construction. This concept provides an inexpensive *loose-fit* weather resistant layer. It is simple to replace to suit changes in occupancy, corporate image, client tastes, new material innovations and design changes in the appearance of buildings. Sustainability objectives are satisfied by re-use and refurbishment instead of demolition and rebuilding. Existing buildings can be seamlessly extended with uniformity of finish.

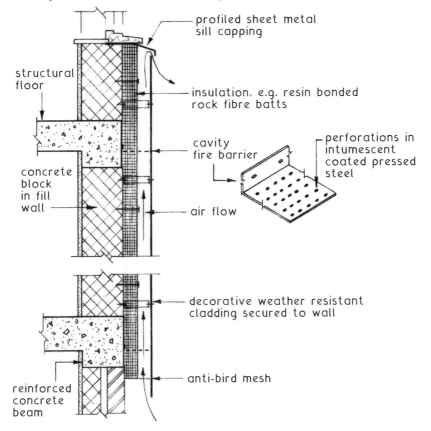

Principle Features ~

* Weather-proof outer layer includes plastic laminates, fibre-cement, ceramics, aluminium, enamelled steel and various stone effects.
* Decorative finish.
* Support frame attached to structural wall.
* Ventilated and drained cavity behind cladding.
* Facility for sound and thermal insulation.
* *Loose-fit* simple and economic for ease of replacement.

Standard sawn treated softwood sections of 38 mm minimum dimension.

50mm x 50mm vertical battens at 400mm to 600mm spacing

vapour permeable breather membrane

10mm to 15mm RSC overcladding

50mm

synthetic rubber weathering

infill or structural support wall

Vertical section

50mm screw fixing with plastic cap and washer

breather membrane

25mm

6mm max.

ventilated void

Plan sections

50mm x 50mm

support wall

100mm x 50mm

synthetic rubber seal

RSC

breather membrane

Plan sections at corners

3mm max.

synthetic rubber weathering

3mm space over synthetic rubber weathering

Note: Timber support battens to be pre-treated with waterproof preservative.

706

Aluminium alloy standard profile sections with extendable support brackets.

Vertical section

- profiled T or L carrier rail
- rigid insulation batt
- RSC panel secured with brackets bolted to wall at 400mm to 600mm spacing
- load bearing or infill wall
- aluminium weathering
- ventilation void

Plan sections

- self drill/tap screw
- EPDM* seal
- RSC
- wall bracket
- insulation
- bolted fixing

* Ethylene Propylene Diene Monomer synthetic rubber

Plan sections at corners

- vapour permeable membrane
- aluminium alloy L profile secured to cladding
- insulation retainer
- 3mm gap over L profile

Note: RSC materials should satisfy tests for fire propagation and surface spread of flame, ref. BS 476-6 and 7 respectively.

Glazed façades have been associated with hi-tech architecture since the 1970s. The increasing use of this type of cladding is largely due to developments in toughened glass and improved qualities of elastomeric silicone sealants. The properties of the latter must incorporate a resilience to varying atmospheric conditions as well as the facility to absorb structural movement without loss of adhesion.

Systems – two edge and four edge.

The two edge system relies on conventional glazing beads/fixings to the head and sill parts of a frame, with sides silicone bonded to mullions and styles.

The four edge system relies entirely on structural adhesion, using silicone bonding between glazing and support frame – see details.

upper edge or head of support frame

- polyethylene packing
- self-adhesive spacer tape
- aluminium or st/st support rail secured to structural frame

Structural glazing, as shown on this and the next page, is in principle a type of curtain walling. Due to its unique appearance it is usual to consider full glazing of the building façade as a separate design and construction concept.

BS EN 13830: Curtain walling. Product standard; defines curtain walling as an external vertical building enclosure produced by elements mainly of metal, timber or plastic. Glass as a primary material is excluded.

lower edge of support frame to sill

Note: Sides of frame as head.

- factory sealed double glazing
- structural sealant
- precured silicone spacer block
- silicone seal and pointing

Structural glazing is otherwise known as frameless glazing. It is a system of toughened glass cladding without the visual impact of surface fixings and supporting components. Unlike curtain walling, the self-weight of the glass and wind loads are carried by the glass itself and transferred to a subsidiary lightweight support structure behind the glazing.

Assembly Principles ~

ELEVATION

ASSEMBLY DETAIL   FIXING DETAIL

Curtain Walling

Curtain Walling ~ this is a form of lightweight non-load bearing external cladding which forms a complete envelope or sheath around the structural frame. In low rise structures the curtain wall framing could be of timber or patent glazing but in the usual high rise context, box or solid members of steel or aluminium alloy are normally employed.

Basic Requirements for Curtain Walls:

1. Provide the necessary resistance to penetration by the elements.
2. Have sufficient strength to carry own self-weight and provide resistance to both positive and negative wind pressures.
3. Provide required degree of fire resistance – glazed areas are classified in the Building Regulations as unprotected areas; therefore any required fire resistance must be obtained from the infill or undersill panels and any backing wall or beam.
4. Be easy to assemble, fix and maintain.
5. Provide the required degree of sound and thermal insulation.
6. Provide for thermal and structural movements.

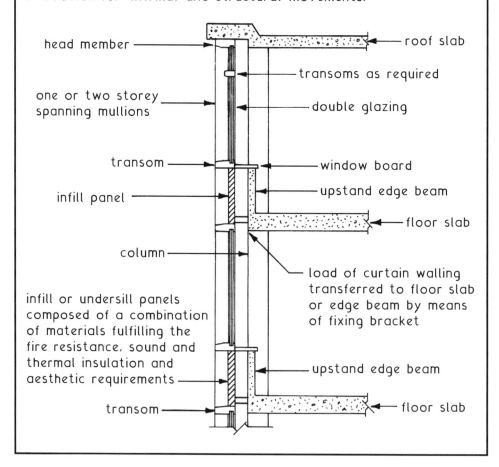

head member —

one or two storey spanning mullions —

transom —

infill panel —

column —

infill or undersill panels composed of a combination of materials fulfilling the fire resistance, sound and thermal insulation and aesthetic requirements —

transom —

roof slab

transoms as required

double glazing

window board

upstand edge beam

floor slab

load of curtain walling transferred to floor slab or edge beam by means of fixing bracket

upstand edge beam

floor slab

Typical Curtain Walling Details

Principles ~

extruded plastic cover plate and screws

neoprene gaskets

extruded aluminium alloy box mullion

double glazed fixed light

extruded aluminium alloy box transom

transom located on spigot fixed to box mullion – connection to be mastic sealed

mullion bolted to angle brackets through slotted holes – angle brackets secured to floor edge with bolts located in dovetail anchor slots to provide for thermal and/ or structural movement

infill or undersill panel

Fixing Curtain Walling to the Structure ~ in curtain walling systems it is the main vertical component or mullion which carries the loads and transfers them to the structural frame at every or alternate floor levels depending on the spanning ability of the mullion. At each fixing point the load must be transferred and an allowance made for thermal expansion and differential movement between the structural frame and curtain walling. The usual method employed is slotted bolt fixings.

712

Re-cladding existing framed buildings has become an economical alternative to complete demolition and rebuilding. This may be justified when a building has a change of use or it is in need of an image upgrade. Current energy conservation measures can also be achieved by the redressing of older buildings.

Typical section through an existing structural floor slab with a replacement system attached ~

Framing Detail

double glazed unit, outer pane tinted solar control glass

synthetic rubber gasket

extruded silicone sealing strip

hollow extruded polyester powder-coated aluminium transom or mullion

raised floor

skirting

transom (see detail)

mullion

existing r.c. floor slab

fire resisting silicone seal and neoprene isolating strip

mineral wool cavity barrier in support tray

mild steel fixing angles as framing support

bolts in expansion anchors

floor slab closer

suspended ceiling

VERTICAL SECTION

Load bearing Concrete Panels ~ this form of construction uses storey height load bearing precast reinforced concrete perimeter panels. The width and depth of the panels is governed by the load(s) to be carried, the height and exposure of the building. Panels can be plain or fenestrated providing the latter leaves sufficient concrete to transmit the load(s) around the opening. The cladding panels, being structural, eliminate the need for perimeter columns and beams and provide an internal surface ready to receive insulation, attached services and decorations. In the context of design these structures must be formed in such a manner that should a single member be removed by an internal explosion, wind pressure or similar force, progressive or structural collapse will not occur, the minimum requirements being set out in Part A of the Building Regulations. Load bearing concrete panel construction can be a cost effective method of building.

Typical Details ~

Concrete Cladding Panels ~ these are usually of reinforced precast concrete to an undersill or storey height format, the former being sometimes called apron panels. All precast concrete cladding panels should be designed and installed to fulfil the following functions:

1. Self-supporting between framing members.
2. Provide resistance to penetration by the natural elements.
3. Resist both positive and negative wind pressures.
4. Provide required degree of fire resistance.
5. Provide required degree of thermal insulation by having the insulating material incorporated within the body of the cladding or alternatively allow the cladding to act as the outer leaf of cavity wall panel.
6. Provide required degree of sound insulation.

Undersill or Apron Cladding Panels ~ these are designed to span from column to column and provide a seating for the windows located above. Levelling is usually carried out by wedging and packing from the lower edge before being fixed with grouted dowels.

Typical Details ~

PLAN ON COLUMN CONNECTION

VERTICAL SECTION

Concrete Cladding – Storey Height

Storey Height Cladding Panels ~ these are designed to span vertically from beam to beam and can be fenestrated if required. Levelling is usually carried out by wedging and packing from floor level before being fixed by bolts or grouted dowels.

Typical Details ~

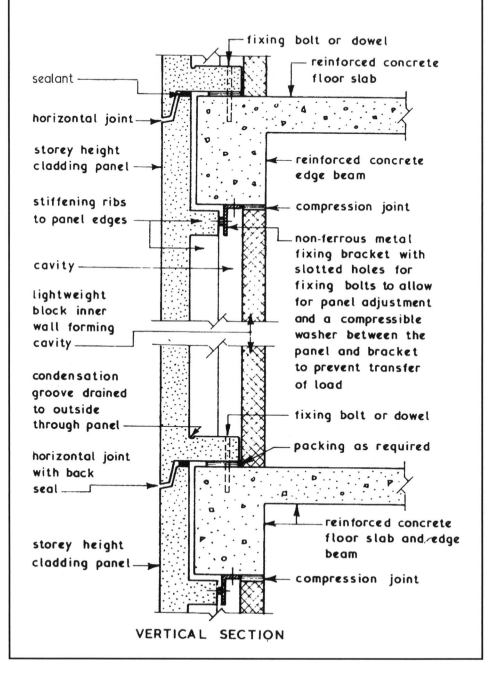

sealant

horizontal joint

storey height cladding panel

stiffening ribs to panel edges

cavity

lightweight block inner wall forming cavity

condensation groove drained to outside through panel

horizontal joint with back seal

storey height cladding panel

fixing bolt or dowel

reinforced concrete floor slab

reinforced concrete edge beam

compression joint

non-ferrous metal fixing bracket with slotted holes for fixing bolts to allow for panel adjustment and a compressible washer between the panel and bracket to prevent transfer of load

fixing bolt or dowel

packing as required

reinforced concrete floor slab and edge beam

compression joint

VERTICAL SECTION

Single Stage ~ the application of a compressible filling material and a weatherproofing sealant between adjacent cladding panels. This may be adequate for relatively small areas and where exposure to thermal or structural movement is limited. Elsewhere, in order to accommodate extremes of thermal movement between exposed claddings, the use of only a sealant and filler would require an over-frequency of joints or over-wide joints that could slump or fracture.

Two Stage ~ otherwise known as open drained joints. The preferred choice as there is a greater facility to absorb movement. Drained joints to cladding panels comprise a sealant to the inside or back of the joint and a baffle to the front, both separated by an air seal.

Comparison of single- and two-stage jointing principles ~

Plan views

Typical coefficients of linear thermal expansion (10^{-6}m/mK) ~
Dense concrete aggregate 14, lightweight concrete aggregate 10.

Ref. BS 6093: Design of joints and jointing in building construction.

Typical weathering detail ~

baffle

vertical dpc

stepped flashing

sealant

Where the horizontal lapped joint between upper and lower cladding panels coincides with the vertical open drained joint, a stepped apron flashing is required to weather the intersection. Lead is the natural choice for this, but reinforced synthetic rubber or reinforced plastic sheet may be preferred to avoid possible lead oxide staining over the panel surface.

Baffle material is traditionally of non-ferrous metal such as copper, but like lead this can cause staining to the surface. Neoprene, butyl rubber or PVC are alternatives.

Gasket ~ an alternative to using mastic or sealant to close the gap between two cladding panels. They are used specifically where movements or joint widths are greater than could be accommodated by sealants. For this purpose a gasket is defined in BS 6093 as 'flexible, generally elastic, preformed material that constitutes a seal when compressed'.

Location and Fit ~ as shown on the next page, a recess is provided in at least one of the two adjacent claddings. To be effective contact surfaces must be clean and free of imperfections for a gasket to exert pressure on adjacent surfaces and to maintain this during all conditions of exposure. To achieve this, greater dimensional accuracy in manufacture and assembly of components is necessary relative to other sealing systems.

Profile ~ solid or hollow extrusions in a variety of shapes. Generally non-structural but vulcanised polychloroprene rubber can be used if a structural specification is required.

Materials (non-structural) ~ synthetic rubber including neoprene, silicone, ethylene propylene diene monomer (EPDM) and thermo-plastic rubber (TPR). These materials are very durable with excellent resistance to compression, heat, water, ultra-violet light, ozone, ageing, abrasion and chemical cleaning agents such as formaldehyde. They also have exceptional elastic memory, i.e. will resume original shape after stressing. Polyvinyl chloride (PVC) and similar plastics can also be used but they will need protection from the effects of direct sunlight.

Refs.:

BS 4255-1: Rubber used in preformed gaskets for weather exclusion from buildings. Specification for non-cellular gaskets.

BS 6093: Design of joints and jointing in building construction. Guide.

Concrete Claddings – Gasket Joint Types

Non-structural gasket types (shown plan view) ~

HOLLOW/TUBULAR (cast into concrete during manufacture)

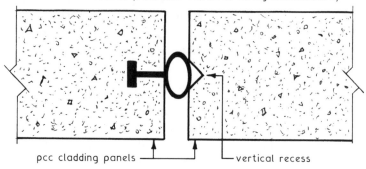

pcc cladding panels ———— vertical recess

SOLID DOUBLE SPLAY (fitted on site during assembly)

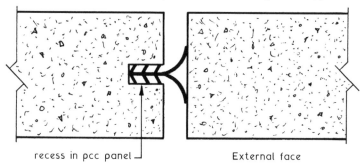

recess in pcc panel ⌐   External face

SOLID CRUCIFORM   ⌐ shoulder to tapered recess

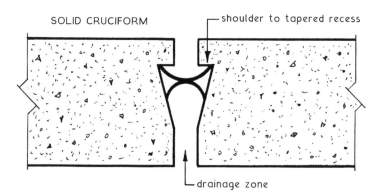

drainage zone

Gaskets have other applications to construction. See Double Glazing, Triple Glazing and Curtain Walling.

Concrete Surface Finishes ~ it is not easy to produce a concrete surface with a smooth finish of uniform colour direct from the mould or formwork since the colour of the concrete can be affected by the cement and fine aggregate used. The concrete surface texture can be affected by the aggregate grading, cement content, water content, degree of compaction, pin holes caused by entrapped air and rough patches caused by adhesion to parts of the formworks. Complete control over the above mentioned causes is difficult under ideal factory conditions and almost impossible under normal site conditions. The use of textured and applied finishes has therefore the primary function of improving the appearance of the concrete surface and in some cases it will help to restrict the amount of water which reaches a vertical joint.

Casting ~ concrete components can usually be cast in-situ or precast in moulds. Obtaining a surface finish to concrete cast in-situ is usually carried out against a vertical face, whereas precast concrete components can be cast horizontally and treated on either upper or lower mould face. Apart from a plain surface concrete the other main options are:

1. Textured and profiled surfaces.
2. Tooled finishes.
3. Cast-on finishes (see next page).
4. Exposed aggregate finishes (see next page).

Textured and Profiled Surfaces ~ these can be produced on the upper surface of a horizontal casting by rolling, tamping, brushing and sawing techniques but variations in colour are difficult to avoid. Textured and profiled surfaces can be produced on the lower face of a horizontal casting by using suitable mould linings.

Tooled Finishes ~ the surface of hardened concrete can be tooled by bush hammering, point tooling and grinding. Bush hammering and point tooling can be carried out by using an electric or pneumatic hammer on concrete which is at least three weeks old provided gravel aggregates have not been used, since these tend to shatter leaving surface pits. Tooling up to the arris could cause spalling; therefore a 10 mm wide edge margin should be left untooled. Grinding the hardened concrete consists of smoothing the surface with a rotary carborundum disc which may have an integral water feed. Grinding is a suitable treatment for concrete containing the softer aggregates such as limestone.

Cast-on Finishes ~ these finishes include split blocks, bricks, stone, tiles and mosaic. Cast-on finishes to the upper surface of a horizontal casting are not recommended although such finishes could be bedded onto the fresh concrete. Lower face treatment is by laying the materials with sealed or grouted joints onto the base of mould or alternatively the materials to be cast-on may be located in a sand bed spread over the base of the mould.

Exposed Aggregate Finishes ~ attractive effects can be obtained by removing the skin of hardened cement paste or surface matrix, which forms on the surface of concrete, to expose the aggregate. The methods which can be employed differ with the casting position.

Horizontal Casting – treatment to the upper face can consist of spraying with water and brushing some two hours after casting, trowelling aggregate into the fresh concrete surface or by using the felt-float method. This method consists of trowelling 10mm of dry mix fine concrete onto the fresh concrete surface and using the felt pad to pick up the cement and fine particles from the surface leaving a clean exposed aggregate finish.

Treatment to the lower face can consist of applying a retarder to the base of the mould so that the partially set surface matrix can be removed by water and/or brushing as soon as the castings are removed from the moulds. When special face aggregates are used the sand bed method could be employed.

Vertical Casting – exposed aggregate finishes to the vertical faces can be obtained by tooling the hardened concrete or they can be cast-on by the aggregate transfer process. This consists of sticking the selected aggregate onto the rough side of pegboard sheets with a mixture of water-soluble cellulose compounds and sand fillers. The cream-like mixture is spread evenly over the surface of the pegboard to a depth of one-third the aggregate size and the aggregate sprinkled or placed evenly over the surface before being lightly tamped into the adhesive. The prepared board is then set aside for 36 hours to set before being used as a liner to the formwork or mould. The liner is used in conjunction with a loose plywood or hardboard baffle placed against the face of the aggregate. The baffle board is removed as the concrete is being placed.

aggregate exposed by washing away adhesive

Special Effects ~ coloured cements and variations in aggregate content can be used with, or as a separate effect from, the surface treatments considered on the previous two pages. Two other special effect concretes that have been used extensively are:

• Granolithic
• Terrazzo (see next page)

Granolithic ~ a mix of cement, fine aggregate and granite or whinstone chippings in the ratio of 1:1:2 by volume. A dense, hard-wearing concrete characterised by the sparkle of granite. Specific applications include heavily pedestrianised floors particularly in public buildings, schools, entrance lobbies to apartment blocks and for floors in industrial production areas. Easy maintenance and durability are the main benefits, although it is notably cold to the touch and noisy under foot traffic.

Monolithic application to a standard concrete base is preferred. This should be within three hours of the substrate being placed. Otherwise a matured concrete base will need to be hacked to provide a key and then primed with a cement slurry to ensure adhesion. A PVA bonding agent may also be used as an alternative surface primer. The granolithic is effectively a screed of at least 20mm thickness as applied to a fresh concrete substrate, or at least 40mm thickness as applied to hardened concrete.

Base concrete thickness (mm)	Max. granolithic bay size (m^2)
150	30
100	15

Note: Bay joints abutted to coincide with base concrete joints.

Surface treatment is by steel trowelling at least three times at two- to three-hour intervals to produce a hard, uniform and abrasion resistant finish.

An economical alternative that may be adequate in less heavily used situations can be achieved by sprinkling the surface of newly laid wet concrete with a cement and granite mix in the ratio of 1:2. Finishing is with a wood float and steel trowel.

Terrazzo ~ an attractive concrete composed of coloured cement and fine aggregate in the ratio of 1:2 by volume, with irregular shaped fragments of marble bedded in randomly and close together.

Marble aggregate grades	Size (mm)
OO	1.5 to 2.5 (small panels)
O	2.5 to 3.0
1	3.0 to 6.0
2	6.0 to 10
3	10 to 12
4	12 to 20
5	20 to 25

Applied monolithically over a 15 to 25mm screed of cement and sand (1:3) with embedded non-ferrous metal or plastic dividing strips to produce maximum areas of 1m² over a standard concrete sub-base. Finishing is by light trowelling, coarse and then fine grinding with carborundum stone and water, followed by polishing. All this is a time consuming process extending over several days, thereby limiting the use of terrazzo to high budget projects.

Monolithic terrazzo floor construction

30 to 40mm terrazzo placed in areas of 1m² max. to control shrinkage

non-ferrous dividing strips

100mm min. structural concrete sub-base

15 to 25mm screed (1:3)

Synthetic polymer or resin-based binders are now quite common with thin-set terrazzo finishes of 6 to 10mm thickness. These are less susceptible to shrinkage cracking, but are limited to internal situations as they not as robust as traditional cement-based terrazzo.

Discoloration ~ manifests as a patchy surface finish. It is caused where there are differences in hydration or moisture loss during the concrete set, due to concentrations of cement or where aggregates become segregated. Both of these will produce moisture content differences at the surface. Areas with a darker surface indicate the greater loss of moisture, possibly caused by insufficient mixing and/or poorly sealed formwork producing differences in surface absorption.

Crazing ~ surface shrinkage cracks caused by a cement-rich surface skin or by too much water in the mix. Out-of-date cement can have the same effect as well as impairing the strength of the concrete.

Lime bloom ~ a chalky surface deposit produced when the calcium present in cement reacts to contamination from moisture in the atmosphere or rainwater during the hydration process. Generally resolved by dry brushing or with a 20:1 water/hydrochloric acid wash.

Scabbing ~ small areas or surface patches of concrete falling away as the formwork is struck. Caused by poor preparation of formwork, i.e. insufficient use of mould oil or by formwork having a surface texture that is too rough.

Blow holes ~ otherwise known as surface popping. Possible causes are use of formwork finishes with nil or low absorbency or by insufficient vibration of concrete during placement.

Rust staining ~ if not caused by inadequate concrete cover to reinforcement, this characteristic is quite common where iron-rich aggregates or pyrites are used. Rust-brown stains are a feature and there may also be some cracking where the iron reacts with the cement.

Dusting ~ caused by unnaturally rapid hardening of concrete and possibly where out-of-date cement is used. The surface of set concrete is dusty and friable.

Notes

726

7 INTERNAL CONSTRUCTION AND FINISHES

INTERNAL ELEMENTS
INTERNAL WALLS
CONSTRUCTION JOINTS
PARTITIONS AND TIMBER STRUT DESIGN
PLASTERS, PLASTERING AND PLASTERBOARD
DRY LINING TECHNIQUES
WALL TILING
DOMESTIC FLOORS AND FINISHES
LARGE CAST IN-SITU GROUND FLOORS
CONCRETE FLOOR SCREEDS
TIMBER SUSPENDED UPPER FLOORS
TIMBER BEAM DESIGN
REINFORCED CONCRETE SUSPENDED FLOORS
PRECAST CONCRETE FLOORS
RAISED ACCESS FLOORS
SOUND INSULATION
TIMBER, CONCRETE AND METAL STAIRS
INTERNAL DOORS
FIRE-RESISTING DOORS
PLASTERBOARD CEILINGS
SUSPENDED CEILINGS
PAINTS AND PAINTING
JOINERY PRODUCTION
COMPOSITE BOARDING
PLASTICS IN BUILDING

NB. roof coverings, roof insulation and guttering not shown.

trussed rafters
at 600 c/c

roof

non-load
bearing
partition

stairs - provides a means
of communication and
circulation between the
various floor levels
within a building

upper floor -
horizontal
division between
storeys - carries
floor loads to
walls

load bearing wall -
carries loads received
to the foundations

superstructure

insulated external
wall

floor screed

insulation

dpm

dpc

concrete
floor slab

foundations

hardcore

NB. All work below dpc level is classed as substructure.

728

Internal Walls ~ their primary function is to act as a vertical divider of floor space and in so doing form a storey-height enclosing element.

Other Possible Functions ~

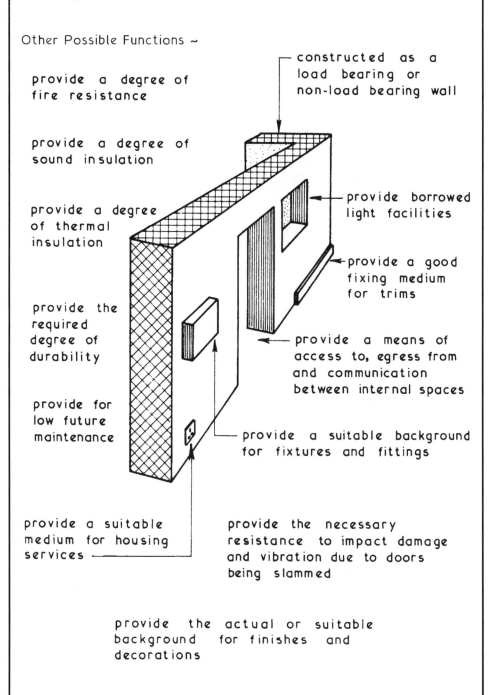

provide a degree of fire resistance

provide a degree of sound insulation

provide a degree of thermal insulation

provide the required degree of durability

provide for low future maintenance

constructed as a load bearing or non-load bearing wall

provide borrowed light facilities

provide a good fixing medium for trims

provide a means of access to, egress from and communication between internal spaces

provide a suitable background for fixtures and fittings

provide a suitable medium for housing services

provide the necessary resistance to impact damage and vibration due to doors being slammed

provide the actual or suitable background for finishes and decorations

Internal Walls ~ there are two basic design concepts for internal walls: those which accept and transmit structural loads to the foundations are called Load bearing Walls and those which support only their own self-weight and do not accept any structural loads are called Non-load bearing Walls or Partitions.

Typical Examples ~

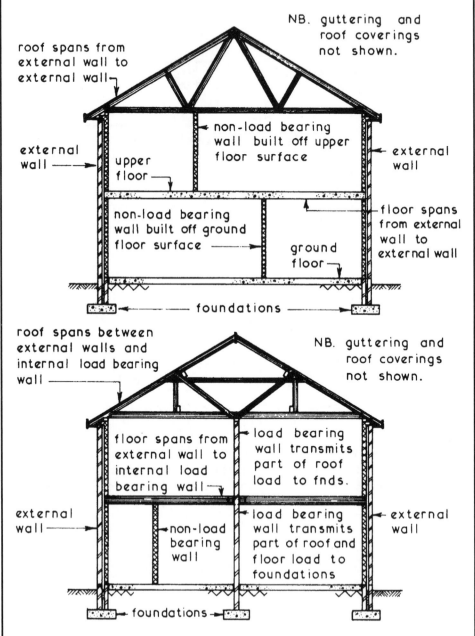

roof spans from external wall to external wall

NB. guttering and roof coverings not shown.

external wall

upper floor

non-load bearing wall built off upper floor surface

external wall

non-load bearing wall built off ground floor surface

ground floor

floor spans from external wall to external wall

foundations

roof spans between external walls and internal load bearing wall

NB. guttering and roof coverings not shown.

floor spans from external wall to internal load bearing wall

load bearing wall transmits part of roof load to fnds.

external wall

non-load bearing wall

load bearing wall transmits part of roof and floor load to foundations

external wall

foundations

Internal Brick Walls ~ these can be load bearing or non-load bearing (see previous page) and for most two-storey buildings are built in half brick thickness in stretcher bond.

Typical Details ~

roof struts transmit loads from purlin to wall

wall plate

ceiling joists transmit ceiling loads to wall

upper floor

lapped upper floor joists bearing on wall

wall transmits combined roof and floor loads to foundations

dpc and dpm to have continuity through wall

ground floor

foundations

LOAD-BEARING WALL

every alternate course bonded to external wall

external wall

internal wall

every alternate group of three brick courses block bonded to external wall

NB. only applicable where cold bridging is not a concern.

concrete lintel- size governed by opening span and loading - end bearing 100 mm minimum

JUNCTIONS AND OPENINGS

731

Internal Block Walls ~ these can be load bearing or non-load bearing (see page 730); the thickness and type of block to be used will depend upon the loadings it has to carry.

Typical Details ~

roof struts transmit loads from purlins to wall

ceiling joists transmit ceiling loads to wall

wall plate

block internal load bearing wall

floor boarding

lapped upper floor joists bearing on wall

wall transmits combined roof and wall loads to foundations

dpc and dpm to have continuity through wall

ground floor

dpc

dpm

foundations

LOAD-BEARING WALL

every alternate course block bonded to external wall

external wall

internal wall

expanded metal strip built into every bed joint of butt jointed internal wall

concrete lintel – size governed by opening span and loading – end bearing 100 mm min.

JUNCTIONS AND OPENINGS

Internal Walls ~ an alternative to brick and block bonding shown on the preceding two pages is application of wall profiles. These are quick and simple to install, provide adequate lateral stability, sufficient movement flexibility and will overcome the problem of thermal bridging where a brick partition would otherwise bond into a block inner leaf. They are also useful for attaching extension walls at right angles to existing masonry.

Application ~

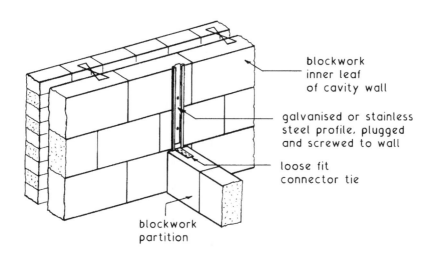

blockwork
inner leaf
of cavity wall

galvanised or stainless
steel profile, plugged
and screwed to wall

loose fit
connector tie

blockwork
partition

40 mm

8 mm

screw
slot

WALL
PROFILE ~ 2·4 m long

TIE ~ every block course and
every 3rd brick course

ribbed or
perforated surface

30 mm

100 mm

733

Movement or Construction Joints ~ provide an alternative to ties or mesh reinforcement in masonry bed joints. Even with reinforcement, lightweight concrete block walls are renowned for producing unsightly and possibly unstable shrinkage cracks. Galvanised or stainless steel formers and ties are built in at a maximum of 6m horizontal spacing and within 3m of corners to accommodate initial drying, shrinkage movement and structural settlement. One side of the former is fitted with profiled or perforated ties to bond into bed joints and the other has plastic sleeved ties. The sleeved tie maintains continuity, but restricts bonding to allow for controlled movement.

ties at 450 mm vertical spacing (1st tie at 225 mm)

former at 6 m spacing

lightweight concrete block partition

NB. former may incorporate an intumescent strip for fire-resisting walls.

mastic or sealant construction joint

plastic sleeved de-bonding tie

blockwork partition

PLAN

perforated or ribbed bonding tie

mastic or sealant

NB. Movement joints in clay brickwork should be provided at 12 m maximum spacing and 7.5 to 9 m for calcium silicate.
Refs.: BS EN 1996: Design of masonry structures.
PD 6697: Recommendations for the design of masonry structures.

Location ~ specifically in positions of high stress.
Reinforcement ~ expanded metal or wire mesh (see page 388).
Mortar Cover ~ 13 mm minimum thickness, 25 mm to external faces.

Openings ~

Concentrated Load ~

Suspended Floor~

Differential Movement ~ may occur where materials such as steel, brick, timber or dense concrete abut with or bear on lightweight concrete blocks. A smooth separating interface of two layers of non-compressible dpc or similar is suitable in this situation.

Typical Examples ~

Solid brickwork

T = thickness

	Fire resistance (minutes)		Material and application
T (mm)	120	240	
T (mm)	102.5	215	Clay bricks. Load bearing or non-load bearing wall.
T (mm)	102.5	215	Concrete or sand/lime bricks. Load bearing or non-load bearing wall.

NB. For practical reasons a standard one-brick dimension is given for 240 minutes' fire resistance. Theoretically a clay brick wall can be 170 mm and a concrete or sand/lime brick wall 200 mm, finishes excluded.

Solid concrete blocks of lightweight aggregate

T = thickness

	Fire resistance (minutes)			Material and application
	60	120	240	
T (mm)	100	130	200	Load bearing, 2.8–3.5 N/mm^2 compressive strength.
T (mm)	90	100	190	Load bearing, 4.0–10 N/mm^2 compressive strength.
T (mm)	75	100	140	Non-load-bearing, 2.8–3.5 N/mm^2 compressive strength.
T (mm)	75	75	100	Non-load bearing, 4.0–10 N/mm^2 compressive strength.

NB. Finishes excluded.

Party Wall ~ a wall separating different owners' buildings, i.e. a wall that stands astride the boundary line between property of different ownerships. It may also be solely on one owner's land but used to separate two buildings.

ct/s mortar or mineral wool fire stop between separating wall and underside of roof tiles

ridge

eaves

fire stopping in boxed eaves

upper floor

boundary line

party wall between dwellings functions as a separating wall for sound insulation and for fire compartmentation

ground floor

Where an internal separating wall forms a junction with an external cavity wall, the cavity must be fire stopped by using a barrier of fire-resisting material. Depending on the application, the material specification is of at least 30 minutes' fire resistance. Between terraced and semi-detached dwellings the location is usually limited by the separating elements. For other buildings additional fire stopping will be required in constructional cavities such as suspended ceilings, rainscreen cladding and raised floors. The spacing of these cavity barriers is generally not more than 20 m in any direction, subject to some variation as indicated in Volume 2 of Approved Document B.

Refs.:
Party Wall Act 1996.
Building Regulations, A.D. B, Volumes 1 and 2: Fire safety.
Building Regulations, A.D. E: Resistance to the passage of sound.

Requirements for fire- and sound-resisting construction ~

Typical masonry construction ~

vertical dpc ⌐

cavity stopped with a non-combustible
mineral wool closer unless cavity
is fully filled with mineral wool insulation

external cavity wall

plan
view

solid or cavity construction
of separating wall

Typical timber framed construction~

vertical dpc ⌐

cavity fire stopped as above

external cavity wall

insulation

one layer 12.5 mm plasterboard
lining, two layers where there
is a separating floor

plan
view

cavity construction
separating wall

Internal Partitions ~ these are vertical dividers which are used to separate the internal space of a building into rooms and circulation areas such as corridors. Partitions which give support to a floor or roof are classified as load bearing whereas those which give no such support are called non-load bearing.

Load Bearing Partitions ~ these walls can be constructed of bricks, blocks or in-situ concrete by traditional methods and have the design advantages of being capable of having good fire resistance and/or high sound insulation. Their main disadvantage is permanence giving rise to an inflexible internal layout.

Non-load Bearing Partitions ~ the wide variety of methods available makes it difficult to classify the form of partition but most can be placed into one of three groups:

1. Masonry partitions.
2. Stud partitions – see pages 740 to 743.
3. Demountable partitions – see pages 744 and 745.

Masonry Partitions ~ these are usually built with blocks of clay or lightweight concrete which are readily available and easy to construct thus making them popular. These masonry partitions should be adequately tied to the structure or load bearing walls to provide continuity as a sound barrier, provide edge restraint and to reduce the shrinkage cracking which inevitably occurs at abutments. Wherever possible openings for doors should be in the form of storey-height frames to provide extra stiffness at these positions.

Typical Details ~

masonry partition

dovetail anchors to alternate courses

RC column

cast-in wall ties to alternate courses

fish-tail cramps surfixed to alternate block courses or built-in wall ties

50 min.

masonry partition

block bonding

load bearing wall

Timber Stud Partitions

Timber Stud Partitions ~ these are non-load bearing internal dividing walls which are easy to construct, lightweight, adaptable and can be clad and infilled with various materials to give different finishes and properties. The timber studs should be of prepared or planed material to ensure that the wall is of constant thickness with parallel faces. Stud spacings will be governed by the size and spanning ability of the facing or cladding material.

Typical Details ~

Although generally non-load bearing, timber stud partitions may carry some of the load from the floor and roof structure. In these situations the vertical studs are considered struts.

Example ~ using the stud frame dimensions shown on the previous page, with each stud (strut) supporting a 5kN load.

Section   Elevation

Slenderness ratio (SR) of section = effective length ÷ breadth
On the partition face = 1250 ÷ 45 = 27.8
At right angles to the face = 2500 ÷ 95 = 26.3
Timber of strength classification C18 (see pages 141 and 142) has the following properties:

 Modulus of elasticity = 6000N/mm^2
 Grade stress in compression parallel to the grain = 7.1N/mm^2
 Grade stress ratio = 6000 ÷ 7.1 = 845

See table on page 194. By coordinating the SR of 27.8 (greater value) with a grade stress ratio of 845, a figure of 0.4 is obtained by interpolation.

Allowable applied stress is 7.1N/mm^2 × 0.4 = 2.84N/mm^2
Applied stress = axial load ÷ strut section area
      = 5000N ÷ (95mm × 45mm) = 1.17N/mm^2
1.17N/mm^2 is well within the allowable stress of 2.84N/mm^2; therefore 95mm × 45mm struts are adequate.

NB. See pages 192 to 194 for an application to dead shoring. Struts in trusses and lattice frames can also be designed using the same principles.

Metal Stud Partitions

Stud Partitions ~ these non-load bearing partitions consist of a framework of vertical studs to which the facing material can be attached. The void between the studs created by the two faces can be infilled to meet specific design needs. The traditional material for stud partitions is timber (see Timber Stud Partitions on page 740) but a similar arrangement can be constructed using metal studs faced on both sides with plasterboard.

Typical Metal Stud Partition Details ~

VERTICAL SECTION   HORIZONTAL SECTION

Plasterboard lining to stud-framed partition walls satisfies the Building Regulations, Approved Document B – Fire safety, as a material of 'limited combustibility' with a Class O rating for surface spread of flame (Class O is better than Classes 1 to 4 as determined by BS 476-7). The plasterboard dry walling should completely protect any combustible timber components such as sole plates. The following shows typical fire resistances as applied to a metal stud frame ~

30-minute fire resistance

75 mm

height limit 2.500

12.5 mm wallboard

metal channel stud frame

self-drilling/self-tapping screw fixings

60(90)-minute fire resistance

100 mm
(110)

height limit 3.400 (3.700)

2 No. 12.5 (15) mm wallboards

staggered screw fixings

120-minute fire resistance

110 mm

height limit 4.200

2 No. 15 mm firecheck plasterboards

metal box stud frame

NB. For plasterboard types see page 753.

Demountable Partitions

Partitions ~ these can be defined as vertical internal space dividers and are usually non-load bearing. They can be permanent, constructed of materials such as bricks or blocks or they can be demountable constructed using lightweight materials and capable of being taken down and moved to a new location incurring little or no damage to the structure or finishes. There is a wide range of demountable partitions available constructed from a variety of materials giving a range that will be suitable for most situations. Many of these partitions have a permanent finish which requires no decoration and only periodic cleaning in the context of planned maintenance.

Typical Example ~

glazed borrowed light

structural soffit

up to 3·000

extruded aluminium alloy head section

rubber sealing strips

1·200 wide modular partition panels

half module panel

ELEVATION

extruded aluminium alloy post

50mm thick partition panel out of 2 faces of 9·5mm plasterboard bonded to honeycomb core

phenolic resin skirting

floor jack giving 35mm adjustment

100

rubber sealing strips

abutment wall

structural floor

ABUTMENT DETAIL

VERTICAL SECTION

extruded aluminium alloy stud

extruded aluminium alloy post and door trim

door

HORIZONTAL SECTION

Demountable Partitions ~ it can be argued that all internal non-load bearing partitions are demountable and therefore the major problem is the amount of demountability required in the context of ease of moving and the possible frequency anticipated. The range of partitions available is very wide including stud partitions, framed panel partitions (see Demountable Partitions on page 744), panel to panel partitions and sliding/folding partitions which are similar in concept to industrial doors (see Industrial Doors on pages 467 to 469). The latter type is often used where movement of the partition is required frequently. The choice is therefore based on the above stated factors taking into account finish and glazing requirements together with any personal preference for a particular system but in all cases the same basic problems will have to be considered ~

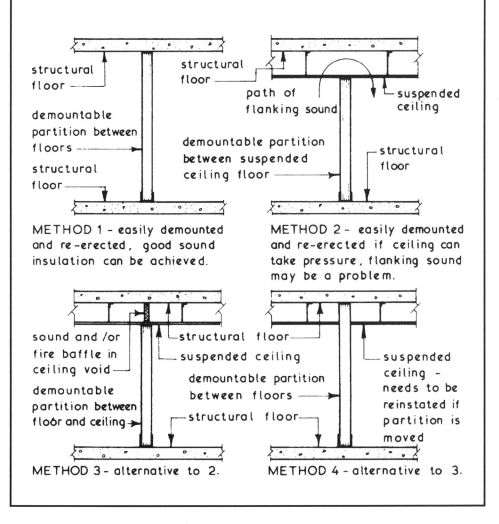

METHOD 1 - easily demounted and re-erected, good sound insulation can be achieved.

METHOD 2 - easily demounted and re-erected if ceiling can take pressure, flanking sound may be a problem.

METHOD 3 - alternative to 2.

METHOD 4 - alternative to 3.

Plaster ~ this is a wet mixed material applied to internal walls as a finish to fill in any irregularities in the wall surface and to provide a smooth continuous surface suitable for direct decoration. The plaster finish also needs to have a good resistance to impact damage. The material used to fulfil these requirements is gypsum plaster. Gypsum is a crystalline combination of calcium sulphate and water. The raw material is crushed, screened and heated to dehydrate the gypsum and this process together with various additives defines its type as set out in BS EN 13279-1: Gypsum binders and gypsum plasters. Definitions and requirement.

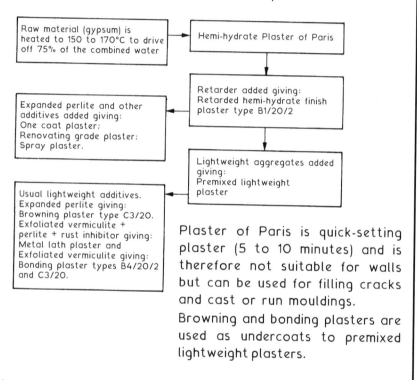

Plaster of Paris is quick-setting plaster (5 to 10 minutes) and is therefore not suitable for walls but can be used for filling cracks and cast or run mouldings.

Browning and bonding plasters are used as undercoats to premixed lightweight plasters.

All plaster should be stored in dry conditions since any absorption of moisture before mixing may shorten the normal setting time of about one and a half hours which can reduce the strength of the set plaster. Gypsum plasters are not suitable for use in temperatures exceeding 43°C and should not be applied to frozen backgrounds.

A good key to the background and between successive coats is essential for successful plastering. Generally brick and block walls provide the key whereas concrete unless cast against rough formwork will need to be treated to provide the key.

Internal Wall Finishes ~ these can be classified as wet or dry. The traditional wet finish is plaster which is mixed and applied to the wall in layers to achieve a smooth and durable finish suitable for decorative treatments such as paint and wallpaper.

Most plasters are supplied in 25kg paper sacks and require only the addition of clean water or sand and clean water according to the type of plaster being used.

Typical Method of Application ~

1. PREPARATION

surface well brushed with hard broom to remove loose material and dust

chases cut before plastering

wall surface to be dry

any metal fixings to be painted or galvanised to prevent staining

fixing plugs inserted before plaster is applied

2. UNDERCOATING

thin coats of undercoat plaster applied and built up to required thickness

floated undercoat brought to a true and level surface with a straight edge

fine wooden scratcher used to form key for finishing coat

3. FINISHING

finishing coat of plaster applied with steel trowel to give a smooth finish

trims and decorative finishes applied after plaster has set and cured

TYPICAL DATA FOR BRICK AND BLOCK BACKGROUNDS

textured surfaces can be obtained by using a sponge, hair brush, felt float or steel combs

Undercoat – 8 to 10mm thick
Finishing coat – 2mm thick
Setting times:
Undercoat – 2 hours
Finishing coat – 1 hour

Background ~ ideally level and of consistent material. If there are irregularities, three applications may be required; render (ct. and sand) 10-12mm, undercoat plaster 6-8mm and finish plaster 2mm.

Difficult backgrounds such as steel or glazed surfaces require a PVA bonding agent or a cement slurry brushed on to improve plaster adhesion. A wire mesh or expanded metal surface attachment may also be required with metal lathing plaster as the undercoat. This may be mixed with sand in the ratio of 1:1.5.

Soft backgrounds of cork, fibreboard or expanded plastics should have wire mesh or expanded metal stapled to the surface. An undercoat of lightweight bonding plaster with compatible finish is suitable.

Dense regular surfaces of low-medium suction such as plasterboard require only one finishing coat of specially formulated finishing plaster.

Corners ~ reinforced with glass-fibre scrim tape or fine wire mesh to prevent shrinkage cracking at the junction of plasterboard ceiling and wall. Alternatively a preformed gypsum plaster moulding can be nailed or attached with plaster adhesive (see page 844). Expanded metal angle beads are specifically produced for external corner reinforcement. These are attached with plaster dabs or galvanised nails before finishing just below the nosing.

galvanised steel
expanded metal

← nosing

Plastered walls   Plasterboard walls

External Corner Beads

Stucco is often used as a generalisation for plastered and rendered finishes to walls. This is very limited, as in the context of decoration and architecture it is a term that has acquired many interpretations and definitions that describe different styles of plastering and rendering to both interior and exterior walls. Some of these are used in the historical context and include elaborate ornamentation, particularly as applied to ancient buildings and classic styles of architecture. Stucco is also used as a material description of the mix composition, particularly with regard to its traditional lime base.

Architectural ~ often represented by carved, sculpted or moulded ornamental features as elaborate finish treatments to palaces, churches, mosques and other prominent buildings of religious and historical importance, not least those of the ancient Greek, Roman and Persian classical periods. Of particular architectural importance are the creative interpretations applied to the interior design and architectural features of Baroque (17th-century Italian) and Rococo (18th-century French) buildings.

Material (Traditional) ~ a mix of hydrated lime, fine sand and water used as a smooth, dense, hard covering to interior and exterior masonry walls. Animal or plant fibres may be added for strength with pigments and dyes for colour enhancement. Applied in two thin coats to masonry or three coats (scratch, brown and finish) to timber laths over timber framing.

Material (Contemporary) ~ typically composed of 3 parts hydrated lime to 10 parts fine sand with a nominal amount of cement to improve durability and sufficient water to make the mix workable. Glass fibres and synthetic acrylics may be added for strength. This mix can be used for repairs and renovation work to older buildings as it is less likely to crack or craze than cement and sand renders.

A high quality variation for interiors comprises fine gypsum plaster or hydrated lime mixed with marble dust and water to produce special feature finishes. There are many trade and commercial terms for this surface treatment, including polished plaster, marmorino and Venetian plaster.

Plasterboard ~ a board material comprising two outer layers of lining paper with gypsum plaster between – two edge profiles are generally available:

1. Tapered Edge – a flush seamless surface is obtained by filling the joint with a special filling plaster, applying a joint tape over the filling and finishing with a thin layer of joint filling plaster, the edge of which is feathered out using a slightly damp jointing sponge or steel trowel.
2. Square Edge – edges are close butted and finished with a cover fillet or the joint is covered with a glass-fibre scrim tape before being plastered.

Some jointing details are shown on page 755.

Typical Details ~

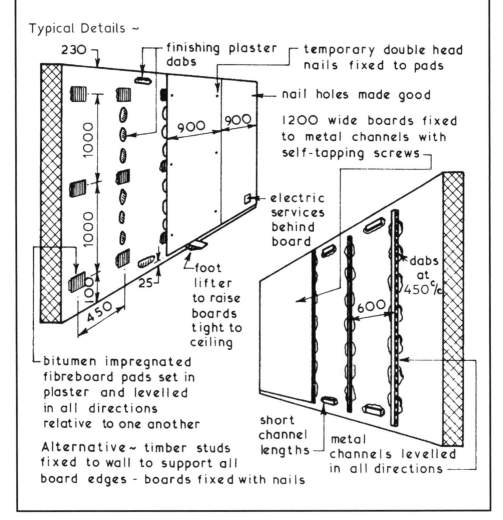

230 ⌐
finishing plaster dabs
temporary double head nails fixed to pads
nail holes made good
1000
900   900
1200 wide boards fixed to metal channels with self-tapping screws ⌐
1000
electric services behind board
100
25⌐
foot lifter to raise boards tight to ceiling
450
dabs at 450°/c
600
⌐bitumen impregnated fibreboard pads set in plaster and levelled in all directions relative to one another
short channel lengths⌐
metal channels levelled in all directions
Alternative~ timber studs fixed to wall to support all board edges - boards fixed with nails

Dry Linings ~ an alternative to wet finishing internal wall surfaces with render and plaster. Dry lining materials can be plasterboard, insulating fibre board, hardboard, timber boards and plywood, all of which can be supplied with a permanent finish or they can be supplied to accept an applied finish such as paint or wallpaper. For plasterboard a dry wall sealer should be applied before wallpapering to permit easier removal at a later date. The main purpose of lining an internal wall surface is to provide an acceptable but not necessarily an elegant or expensive wall finish. It is also very difficult and expensive to build a brick or block wall which has a fair face to both sides since this would involve the hand selection of bricks and blocks to ensure a constant thickness together with a high degree of skill to construct a satisfactory wall. The main advantage of dry lining walls is that the drying out period required with wet finishes is eliminated. By careful selection and fixing of some dry lining materials it is possible to improve the thermal insulation properties of a wall. Dry linings can be fixed direct to the backing by means of a recommended adhesive or they can be fixed to a suitable arrangement of wall battens.

Typical Example ~

strips of contact adhesive applied to wall and backs of boards as recommended by manufacturer so that strips on wall and boards match

wall to be sound, reasonably flat, dry and free of dust, dirt and grease

lining boards pressed firmly onto adhesive

backing wall

abutment joints can be moulded as a feature, covered with a fillet or if lining is to be decorated they can be filled or taped over

backing wall

holes for service outlets cut prior to fixing the boards

NB. For further examples see next page.

Typical Examples using Plywood or Similar Boarding ~

38 x 20 softwood head batten

cove moulding or butt joint with ceiling

38 x 19 softwood vertical battens at 400 ^{c}/c fixed to wall and packed as required to align with other battens

backing wall

butt, moulded or cover fillet to joint

38 x 19 noggins at 1·200 maximum centres

1·200 wide full height wallboards fixed with lost head nails or with adhesive

aluminium foil pinned to wall with battens if required*

38 x 20 bottom or skirting batten

skirting

cove moulding or butt joint with ceiling

38 x 19 softwood horizontal battens at 600 ^{c}/c fixed to wall and packed as required

backing wall

600mm wide full height boarding fixed with lost head nails or adhesive - for secret nailing rebated or t & g joints are an option

noggins at joints if required

aluminium foil lining if required*

skirting

holes for service outlets cut prior to fixing the boards

*alternatively use polythene sheet as a vapour check.

752

Plasterboard Types ~ to BS EN 520: Gypsum plasterboards. Definitions, requirements and test methods.

BS PLASTERBOARDS:

1. Wallboard – ivory faced for taping, jointing and direct decoration; grey faced for finishing plaster or wall adhesion with plaster dabs. General applications, i.e. internal walls, ceilings and partitions. Thicknesses: 9·5, 12·5 and 15 mm. Widths: 900 and 1200 mm. Lengths: vary between 1800 and 3000 mm. Edge profile square or tapered.

2. Baseboard – lining ceilings requiring direct plastering.
   Thickness: 9·5 mm. Width: 900 mm. Length: 1220 mm.
   Thickness: 12·5 mm. Width: 600 mm. Length: 1220 mm.
   Edge profile square.

3. Moisture Resistant – wallboard for bathrooms and kitchens. Pale green colour to face and back. Ideal base for ceramic tiling or plastering.
   Thicknesses: 12·5 mm and 15 mm. Width: 1200 mm.
   Lengths: 2400, 2700 and 3000 mm.
   Square and taper edges available.

4. Firecheck – wallboard of glass fibre reinforced vermiculite and gypsum for fire cladding. Pink face and grey back.
   Thicknesses: 12·5 and 15 mm. Widths: 900 and 1200 mm.
   Lengths: 1800, 2400, 2700 and 3000 mm.
   A 25 mm thickness is also produced, 600 mm wide × 3000 mm long.
   Plaster finished if required. Square or tapered edges.

5. Plank – used as fire protection for structural steel and timber, in addition to sound insulation in wall panels and floating floors.
   Thickness: 19 mm. Width: 600 mm.
   Lengths: 2350, 2400, 2700 and 3000 mm.
   Ivory face with grey back. Tapered edge.

NON-STANDARD PLASTERBOARDS:

1. Contour – only 6 mm in thickness to adapt to curved featurework. Width: 1200 mm. Lengths: 2400 mm and 3000 mm.

2. Vapourcheck – a metallized polyester wallboard lining to provide an integral water vapour control layer.
   Thicknesses: 9·5 and 12·5 mm. Widths: 900 and 1200 mm.
   Lengths: vary between 1800 and 3000 mm.

3. Thermalcheck – various expanded or foamed insulants are bonded to wallboard. Approximately 25–50 mm overall thickness in board sizes 1200 × 2400 mm.

Fixing ~ the detail below shows board fixing with nails or screws to timber battens. This is an alternative to using plaster dabs and pads shown on page 750.

Typical Fixing ~

batten spacing (c/c)

block or brickwork background

38 × 19mm softwood battens nailed or screwed to background at 450mm spacing

9.5mm tapered edge wallboard secured with 30 × 2mm galvanised nails or dry-wall screws at 150mm spacing

900mm

Guide to securing plasterboard to battens:

Board thickness (mm)	Board width (mm)	Batten spacing (mm)	Nail or dry-wall screw length (mm)
9.5	900	450	30
9.5	1200	400	30
12.5	600	600	40
12.5	900	450	40
19.0	600	600	60

Horizontal joints are avoided if possible with cross battens only required at the top and bottom to provide rigidity. Board fixing is with galvanised steel taper-head nails of 2mm diameter (2.6mm dia. for 19mm boards) or with dry-wall screws.

Jointing ~ boards should not directly abut, instead a gap of 3 to 5mm should be provided between adjacent boards for plaster filling and joint reinforcement tape. The illustrations show various applications.

screw or nail fixing
joint filler
50mm wide joint tape
joint filler
plaster skim finish

Standard Joint

gap filler
tapered edge board
finish tape
finish

Cut Edge

filler
finish
tape
finish

Internal Corner

filler
steel reinforced corner tape
filler
finish

External Corner

NB. Paper jointing tape is generally specified for dry lining tapered edge boards. External corners are reinforced and strengthened with a particular type of tape that has two strips of thin steel attached.

Glazed Wall Tiles ~ internal glazed wall tiles are usually made to the various specifications under BS EN 14411: Ceramic tiles. Definitions, classification, characteristics, evaluation of conformity and marking.

Internal Glazed Wall Tiles ~ the body of the tile can be made from ball-clay, china clay, china stone, flint and limestone. The material is usually mixed with water to the desired consistency, shaped and then fired in a tunnel oven at a high temperature (1150°C) for several days to form the unglazed biscuit tile. The glaze pattern and colour can now be imparted onto to the biscuit tile before the final firing process at a temperature slightly lower than that of the first firing (1050°C) for about two days.

Typical Internal Glazed Wall Tiles and Fittings:

Sizes – Modular   100 × 100 × 5mm thick and
                         200 × 100 × 6·5mm thick.

      Non-modular   152 × 152 × 5 to 8mm thick and
                         108 × 108 × 4 and 6·5mm thick.

Other sizes – 200 × 300, 250 × 330, 250 × 400, 300 × 450, 300 × 600 and 330 × 600mm.

Fittings – wide range available particularly in the non-modular format.

lugs to maintain joint spacing

SPACER TILES   ROUND EDGE   ROUND EDGE   ROUND EDGE
                              EXTERNAL   SQUARE HEAD
                              CORNER

ROUND EDGE AND   ATTACHED ANGLE TILE FITTINGS   BEAD
COVE FOOT   FITTINGS

Bedding of Internal Wall Tiles ~ generally glazed internal wall tiles are considered to be inert in the context of moisture and thermal movement, therefore if movement of the applied wall tile finish is to be avoided attention must be given to the background and the method of fixing the tiles.

Backgrounds ~ these are usually of a cement rendered or plastered surface and should be flat, dry, stable, firmly attached to the substrate and sufficiently established for any initial shrinkage to have taken place. The flatness of the background should be not more than 3mm in 2·000 for the thin bedding of tiles and not more than 6mm in 2·000 for thick bedded tiles.

Fixing Wall Tiles ~ two methods are in general use:

1. Thin Bedding – lightweight internal glazed wall tiles fixed dry using a recommended adhesive which is applied to the wall in small areas 1m² at a time with a notched trowel, the tile being pressed into the adhesive.
2. Thick Bedding – cement mortar within the mix range of 1:3 to 1:4 can be used or a proprietary adhesive, either by buttering the backs of the tiles which are then pressed into position or by rendering the wall surface to a thickness of approximately 10mm and then applying thin bedded tiles to the rendered wall surface within two hours.

Grouting ~ when the wall tiles have set, the joints can be grouted by rubbing into the joints a grout paste either using a sponge or brush. Most grouting materials are based on cement with inert fillers and are used neat.

Typical Example ~

REs or glazed square edge trimming tiles

REs (see Note)

REX (see Note)

spacer tiles with grout-filled joints

Note: The alternative treatment at edges is application of a radiused profile plastic trimming to standard spacer tiles.

Primary Functions:

1. Provide a level surface with sufficient strength to support the imposed loads of people and furniture.
2. Exclude the passage of water and water vapour to the interior of the building.
3. Provide resistance to unacceptable heat loss through the floor.
4. Provide the correct type of surface to receive the chosen finish.

Types ~

solid concrete bed laid over compacted hardcore – see pages 253 and 759

insulated screed to provide surface for floor finish

dpc

dpc

dpm

low heat loss

in domestic work on normal soils seldom any problems due to bearing capacity of subsoil

low maintenance

SOLID FLOOR ON LEVEL SITE

solid floor as above

original ground level

dpc

dpc

dpm

reduced level

if depth of fill exceeds 600 mm a suspended floor could be better due to the long term settlement of fill

low heat loss and maintenance

SOLID FLOOR ON SLOPING SITE

insulated suspended timber floor – for details see page 760

dpc

dpc

dpc

heat loss higher than above types

suspended floors have more resilience than solid floors and are therefore less tiring to users

maintenance higher than above types

SUSPENDED TIMBER FLOOR

This drawing should be read in conjunction with page 253 – Foundation Beds.

A domestic solid ground floor consists of three components:

1. Hardcore – a suitable filling material to make up the top soil removal and reduced level excavations. It should have a top surface which can be rolled out to ensure that cement grout is not lost from the concrete. It may be necessary to blind the top surface with a layer of sand especially if the damp-proof membrane is to be placed under the concrete bed.
2. Damp-proof Membrane – an impervious layer such as heavy duty polythene sheeting to prevent moisture from passing through the floor to the interior of the building.
3. Concrete Bed – the component providing the solid level surface to which screeds and finishes can be applied.

Typical Details ~

NB. a compromise to the above methods is to place the dpm in the middle of the concrete bed but this needs two concrete pouring operations.

Suspended Timber Ground Floors ~ these need to have a well-ventilated space beneath the floor construction to prevent the moisture content of the timber from rising above an unacceptable level (i.e. not more than 20%) which would create the conditions for possible fungal attack.

Typical Details ~

air bricks at 2·000 c/c in external walls with slate or similar trunking forming flue

board or similar flooring

dpc

75 min.

wall plate

sleeper wall in honeycomb bond

underfloor space to be clear of debris and cross ventilated

joists at 400 c/c fixed clear of external wall

insulation

dpc

150 min.

well compacted hardcore

15 N/mm² (1:3:6) concrete not less than 100 mm thick – top surface to have trowel or spade finish and to be no lower than highest adjoining ground level

125 × 50 joists at 400 c/c

insulation suspended on nylon netting

flooring

100 × 75 wall plate

dpc

half brick voids

mass concrete bed

hardcore

sleeper walls at 2·000 c/c

ELEVATION OF SLEEPER WALL

Precast Concrete Floors ~ these have been successfully adapted from commercial building practice (see pages 789 and 790), as an economic alternative construction technique for suspended timber and solid concrete domestic ground (and upper) floors. See also page 416 for special situations.

Typical Details ~

BEAMS PARALLEL WITH EXTERNAL WALL

POLYPROPYLENE VENTILATOR

cavity wall insulated as required

18 mm t&g chipboard over vapour control layer

insulation

cavity tray over vent

dpc

stepped ventilator

GL

coursing

beam and slip 150 mm min. block

dpc

organic material stripped; surface treated with weed killer: lower level than adjacent ground if free draining (not Scotland)

stepped telescopic sleeve

grill clips to sleeve; 1500 mm²/m run of wall OR 500 mm²/m² of floor area (take greater value)

lightweight concrete block, min. 7N/mm²

prestressed concrete beam min. 50N/mm²

60

100

60

130

TYPICAL BEAM/RIB AND BLOCK DETAIL

BEAMS BEARING ON EXTERNAL WALL

floor finish as above or screeded (reinforce in garage)

this block to wall strength

beam and block

dpc

vent

GL

dpc

if inner ground level is significantly lower, this area to be designed as a retaining wall

Domestic Suspended Concrete Ground Floor and Walls

Perspective ~

external brick and block
cavity wall insulated
as required

floor finish
as required
see previous
page

100 mm
lightweight
concrete block

prestressed
concrete beam

coursing slip

under floor
ventilator

deep strip
foundation

Internal Wall Support to Staggered Beams ~

prestressed
concrete beam

100 mm lightweight
concrete block

dpc

intermediate
support wall

762

Precast Reinforced Concrete Beam and Expanded Polystyrene (EPS) Block Floors ~ these have evolved from the principles of beam and block floor systems as shown on the preceding page. The lightweight and easy to cut properties of the blocks provide for speed and simplicity in construction. Exceptional thermal insulation is possible, with U-values as low as 0.2 W/m²K.

Typical Detail ~

structural screed ⌐

gas membrane (if required) ⌐

150
210

heel
toe

EPS infill block
1200 long, density
approx. 17 kg/m³,
cut to fit wall at periphery

inverted reinforced
concrete 'T' beams at 600 c/c

Cold Bridging ~ this is prevented by the EPS 'toe' projecting beneath the underside of the concrete beam.

Structural Floor Finish ~ 50 mm structural concrete (C30 grade) screed, reinforced with 10 mm steel Type A square mesh or with polypropylene fibres in the mix. A low-density polyethylene (LDPE) methane/radon gas membrane can be incorporated under the screed if local conditions require it.

Floating Floor Finish ~ subject to the system manufacturer's specification and accreditation, 18 mm flooring grade moisture-resistant chipboard can be used over a 1000 gauge polythene vapour control layer. All four tongued and grooved edges of the chipboard are glued for continuity.

Floor Finishes ~ these are usually applied to a structural base but may form part of the floor structure as in the case of floorboards. Most finishes are chosen to fulfil a particular function such as:

1. Appearance – chosen mainly for their aesthetic appeal or effect but should however have reasonable wearing properties. Examples are carpets, carpet tiles and wood blocks.
2. High Resistance – chosen mainly for their wearing and impact-resistance properties and for high usage areas such as kitchens. Examples are quarry tiles and granolithic pavings.
3. Hygiene – chosen to provide an impervious easy to clean surface with reasonable aesthetic appeal. Examples are quarry tiles and polyvinyl chloride (PVC) sheets and tiles.

Carpets and Carpet Tiles – made from animal hair, mineral fibres and man made fibres such as nylon and acrylic. They are also available in mixtures of the above. A wide range of patterns, sizes and colours are available. Carpets and carpet tiles can be laid loose, stuck with a suitable adhesive or in the case of carpets edge fixed using special grip strips.

PVC Tiles – made from a blended mix of thermoplastic binders; fillers and pigments in a wide variety of colours and patterns to the recommendations of BS EN 649: Resilient floor coverings. PVC tiles are usually 305 × 305 × 1·6 mm thick and are stuck to a suitable base with special adhesives as recommended by the manufacturer.

Quarry Tiles ~

65; 90; 113 & 137

16; 19; 21 & 28

Tongue and Groove Boarding ~ prepared from softwoods to the recommendations of BS 1297. Boards are laid at right angles to the joists and are fixed with 2 No. 65 mm long cut floor brads per joists. The ends of board lengths are butt jointed on the centre line of the supporting joist.

Maximum board spans are:
16 mm thick ~ 505 mm
19 mm thick ~ 600 mm
21 mm thick ~ 635 mm

75

22

secret nailing

Timber Strip Flooring ~ strip flooring is usually considered to be boards under 100 mm face width. In good class work hardwoods would be specified, the boards being individually laid and secret nailed. Strip flooring can be obtained treated with a spirit-based fungicide. Spacing of supports depends on type of timber used and applied loading. After laying the strip flooring it should be finely sanded and treated with a seal or wax. In common with all timber floorings a narrow perimeter gap should be left for moisture movement.

Chipboard ~ sometimes called Particle Board is made from particles of wood bonded with a synthetic resin and/or other organic binders to the recommendations of BS EN 319.

Standard floorboards are in lengths up to 2400mm, a width of 600mm × 18 or 22mm thickness with tongued and grooved joints to all edges. Laid at right angles to joists with all cross joints directly supported. May be specified as unfinished or water proof quality indicated with a dull green dye.

typical nominal size
225 x 75 x 25

tongue and groove joint

chamfered bottom edge

Wood Blocks ~ prepared from hardwoods and softwoods to the recommendations of BS 1187. Wood blocks can be laid to a variety of patterns, also different timbers can be used to create colour and grain effects. Laid blocks should be finely sanded and sealed or polished.

Large Cast-In-situ Ground Floors ~ these are floors designed to carry medium to heavy loadings such as those used in factories, warehouses, shops, garages and similar buildings. Their design and construction is similar to that used for small roads (see pages 165 and 166). Floors of this type are usually laid in alternate 4·500 wide strips running the length of the building or in line with the anticipated traffic flow where applicable. Transverse joints will be required to control the tensile stresses due to the thermal movement and contraction of the slab. The spacing of these joints will be determined by the design and the amount of reinforcement used. Such joints can either be formed by using a crack inducer or by sawing a 20 to 25 mm deep groove into the upper surface of the slab within 20 to 30 hours of casting.

Typical Layout ~

Surface Finishing ~ the surface of the concrete may be finished by power floating or trowelling which is carried out whilst the concrete is still plastic but with sufficient resistance to the weight of machine and operator whose footprint should not leave a depression of more than 3 mm. Power grinding of the surface is an alternative method which is carried out within a few days of the concrete hardening. The wet concrete having been surface finished with a skip float after the initial levelling with a tamping bar has been carried out. Power grinding removes 1 to 2 mm from the surface and is intended to improve surface texture and not to make good deficiencies in levels.

Vacuum Dewatering ~ if the specification calls for a power float surface finish vacuum dewatering could be used to shorten the time delay between tamping the concrete and power floating the surface. This method is suitable for slabs up to 300 mm thick. The vacuum should be applied for approximately three minutes for every 25 mm depth of concrete which will allow power floating to take place usually within 20 to 30 minutes of the tamping operation. The applied vacuum forces out the surplus water by compressing the slab and this causes a reduction in slab depth of approximately 2%; therefore packing strips should be placed on the side forms before tamping to allow for sufficient surcharge of concrete.

Typical Details ~

Concrete Floor Screeds ~ these are used to give a concrete floor a finish suitable to receive the floor finish or covering specified. It should be noted that it is not always necessary or desirable to apply a floor screed to receive a floor covering. Techniques are available to enable the concrete floor surface to be prepared at the time of casting to receive the coverings at a later stage.

Typical Screed Mixes ~

Screed Thickness	Cement	Dry Fine Aggregate <5 mm	Coarse Aggregate >5 mm <10 mm
up to 40 mm	I	3 to 4 1/2	-
40 to 75 mm	I	3 to 4 1/2	-
	I	1 1/2	3

Laying Floor Screeds ~ floor screeds should not be laid in bays since this can cause curling at the edges. Screeds can however be laid in 3·000 wide strips to receive thin coverings. Levelling of screeds is achieved by working to levelled timber screeding batten or alternatively a 75 mm wide band of levelled screed with square edges can be laid to the perimeter of the floor prior to the general screed-laying operation.

Screed Types ~

10 to 25mm thick screed

concrete floor slab

Monolithic Screeds –

screed laid directly on concrete floor slab within three hours of placing concrete – before any screed is placed all surface water should be removed – all screeding work should be carried out from scaffold board runways to avoid walking on the 'green' concrete slab.

Screed Types ⌄

40 mm thick screed

concrete floor slab

50 mm thick screed*

insulation

dpm

concrete floor slab

65 mm thick screed*

resilient quilt

concrete floor slab

abutment wall

*preferably wire mesh reinforced.

Separate Screeds –

screed is laid onto the concrete floor slab after it has cured. The floor surface must be clean and rough enough to ensure an adequate bond unless the floor surface is prepared by applying a suitable bonding agent or by brushing with a cement/water grout of a thick cream-like consistency just before laying the screed.

Unbonded Screeds –

screed is laid directly over a damp-proof membrane or over a damp-proof membrane and insulation. A rigid form of floor insulation is required where the concrete floor slab is in contact with the ground. Care must be taken during this operation to ensure that the damp-proof membrane is not damaged.

Floating Screeds –

a resilient quilt of 25 mm thickness is laid with butt joints and turned up at the edges against the abutment walls, the screed being laid directly over the resilient quilt. The main objective of this form of floor screed is to improve the sound insulation properties of the floor.

Latex Floor Screeds

Latex ~ a naturally occurring liquid from some plants, notably the rubber tree. Synthetic latexes are now produced from polymers and resins.

Latex Floor Screed ~ a modified screed, originally created by including particles of rubber or bitumen with cement and sand to achieve a hard-wearing, dust-free, impervious and easily maintained floor finish. Suitable in factories and public places such as schools. Contemporary latex screeds can include rubber and bitumen for industrial applications along with granite chippings for increased depth. Most latex screeds now have liquid resin or synthetic polymer additives to modify the cement and sand. These permit spreading in very thin layers and are ideal for levelling uneven and irregular surfaces of sound composition. The ease of use and workability has led to the term 'self-levelling screeds', which is not entirely correct, as they do require physical spreading and trowelling to a finish.

irregular existing tiled floor — thin levelling layer of latex screed prior to re-tiling

existing substrate, e.g. screed or power floated concrete

Availability ~ one or two part packs.

Single packs are dry based, premixed materials in 20 or 25 kg bags for the addition of water on site. Application is in 3 to 8 mm thickness. Some single packs are available with granite chippings for applications up to 25 mm in thickness.

Two part packs consist of a cement and sand based powder in 20 or 25 kg bags for use with a 5 kg container of liquid emulsion, usually of styrene-polymer composition. After mixing, up to a 12 mm thickness can be applied and up to 30 mm with a coarse sand aggregate.

Primary Functions:

1. Provide a level surface with sufficient strength to support the imposed loads of people and furniture plus the dead loads of flooring and ceiling.
2. Reduce heat loss from lower floor as required.
3. Provide required degree of sound insulation.
4. Provide required degree of fire resistance.

Basic Construction – a timber suspended upper floor consists of a series of beams or joists supported by load bearing walls sized and spaced to carry all the dead and imposed loads.

Joist Sizing – three methods can be used:

| 1. Building Regs. Approved Document A – Structure. Refs. *BS 6399-1: Code of practice for dead and imposed loads (min. 1.5 kN/m² distributed, 1.4 kN concentrated). *TRADA publication – Span Tables for Solid Timber Members in Dwellings. | 2. Calculation formula: $$BM = \frac{fbd^2}{6}$$ where BM = bending moment f = fibre stress b = breadth d = depth in mm must be assumed | 3. Empirical formula: $$D = \frac{\text{span in mm}}{24} + 50$$ where D = depth of joist in mm above assumes that joists have a breadth of 50 mm and are at 400 c/c spacing |

Support and Restraint ~

external wall — mortar joint recessed and air leakage sealed — joist — silicone mastic sealant

external wall — joist — galvanised steel joist hanger

90 mm min.

30 × 5 galvanised steel restraint straps at not more than 2·000 c/c

external supported wall —

packing —

38 mm min. thick support noggins at least half of joist depth

joists parallel to wall

400, 450 or 600 c/c

Timber Suspended Upper Floors

Strutting ~ used in timber suspended floors to restrict the movements due to twisting and vibration which could damage ceiling finishes. Strutting should be included if the span of the floor joists exceeds 2·5m and is positioned on the centre line of the span. Max. floor span ~ 6m measured centre to centre of bearing (inner leaf centre line in cavity wall).

Typical Details ~

external wall

38 × 50 sawn softwood herringbone strutting fixed side by side on centre line of joist span

folding wedges or suitable packing to each end of strutting

joists

50mm wide solid timber strutting giving high degree of restraint

joists

strutting fixed in line

strutting fixed either side of centre line - less restraint but easier to fix

joists

galvanised steel herringbone strutting fixed on centre line of joist span

Lateral Restraint ~ external, compartment (fire), separating (party) and internal load bearing walls must have horizontal support from adjacent floors, to restrict movement. Exceptions occur when the wall is less than 3 m long.

Methods:

1. 90 mm end bearing of floor joists, spaced not more than 1·2 m apart – see page 771.
2. Galvanised steel straps spaced at intervals not exceeding 2 m and fixed square to joists – see page 771.

600, 800, 900, 1000, 1200, 1500 or 1600 mm long

100 mm min.

Restraint strap, 30 × 5 mm cross sectional area

3. Joists carried by BS approved galvanised steel hangers.

BS restraint-type hanger

100 mm

150 or 200 mm

4. Adjacent floors at or about the same level, contacting with the wall at no more than 2 m intervals.

straps provide floor to wall contact at max. 2 m intervals

adjacent floors at or about the same level

Floor section

load bearing partition

intermediate floor level

Ref. BS EN 845-1: Specification for ancillary components for masonry. Wall ties, tension straps, hangers and brackets.

Wall Stability – at right angles to floor and ceiling joists this is achieved by building the joists into masonry support walls or locating them on approved joist hangers.

Walls parallel to joists are stabilised by lateral restraint straps. Buildings constructed before current stability requirements (see Bldg. Regs. A.D; A – Structure) often show signs of wall bulge due to the effects of eccentric loading and years of thermal movement.

Remedial Measures –

Retro-strap

Retro-stud

Through tie

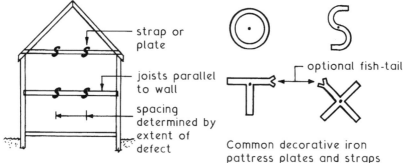

Location of straps and ties

Common decorative iron pattress plates and straps

Trimming Members ~ these are the edge members of an opening in a floor and are the same depth as common joists but are usually 25 mm wider.

Typical Details ~

TRIMMING TO STAIRWELL

TRIMMING AROUND FLUE

TRADITIONAL
TUSK TENON JOINT

TRADITIONAL
HOUSED JOINT

MODERN
JOIST HANGER

Timber Suspended Upper Floors – Joist Sizes

Typical spans and loading for floor joists of general structural (GS) grade:

Sawn size (mm × mm)	Dead weight of flooring and ceiling, excluding the self-weight of the joists (kg/m²)								
	< 25			25–50			50–125		
	Spacing of joists (mm c/c)								
	400	450	600	400	450	600	400	450	600
	Maximum clear span (m)								
38 × 75	1.22	1.09	0.83	1.14	1.03	0.79	0.98	0.89	0.70
38 × 100	1.91	1.78	1.38	1.80	1.64	1.28	1.49	1.36	1.09
38 × 125	2.54	2.45	2.01	2.43	2.30	1.83	2.01	1.85	1.50
38 × 150	3.05	2.93	2.56	2.91	2.76	2.40	2.50	2.35	1.93
38 × 175	3.55	3.40	2.96	3.37	3.19	2.77	2.89	2.73	2.36
38 × 200	4.04	3.85	3.35	3.82	3.61	3.13	3.27	3.09	2.68
38 × 225	4.53	4.29	3.73	4.25	4.02	3.50	3.65	3.44	2.99
50 × 75	1.45	1.37	1.08	1.39	1.30	1.01	1.22	1.11	0.88
50 × 100	2.18	2.06	1.76	2.06	1.95	1.62	1.82	1.67	1.35
50 × 125	2.79	2.68	2.44	2.67	2.56	2.28	2.40	2.24	1.84
50 × 150	3.33	3.21	2.92	3.19	3.07	2.75	2.86	2.70	2.33
50 × 175	3.88	3.73	3.38	3.71	3.57	3.17	3.30	3.12	2.71
50 × 200	4.42	4.25	3.82	4.23	4.07	3.58	3.74	3.53	3.07
50 × 225	4.88	4.74	4.26	4.72	4.57	3.99	4.16	3.94	3.42
63 × 100	2.41	2.29	2.01	2.28	2.17	1.90	2.01	1.91	1.60
63 × 125	3.00	2.89	2.63	2.88	2.77	2.52	2.59	2.49	2.16
63 × 150	3.59	3.46	3.15	3.44	3.31	3.01	3.10	2.98	2.63
63 × 175	4.17	4.02	3.66	4.00	3.85	3.51	3.61	3.47	3.03
63 × 200	4.73	4.58	4.18	4.56	4.39	4.00	4.11	3.95	3.43
63 × 225	5.15	5.01	4.68	4.99	4.85	4.46	4.62	4.40	3.83
75 × 125	3.18	3.06	2.79	3.04	2.93	2.67	2.74	2.64	2.40
75 × 150	3.79	3.66	3.33	3.64	3.50	3.19	3.28	3.16	2.86
75 × 175	4.41	4.25	3.88	4.23	4.07	3.71	3.82	3.68	3.30
75 × 200	4.92	4.79	4.42	4.77	4.64	4.23	4.35	4.19	3.74
75 × 225	5.36	5.22	4.88	5.20	5.06	4.72	4.82	4.69	4.16

Notes:
1. Where a bath is supported, the joists should be duplicated.
2. See pages 38 and 39 for material dead weights.
3. See pages 141 and 142 for softwood classification and grades.

Joist and Beam Sizing ~ design tables and formulae have limitations, therefore where loading, span and/or conventional joist spacings are exceeded, calculations are required. BS EN 1995-1-1: Design of timber structures and BS EN 338: Structural timber – strength classes are both useful resource material for detailed information on a variety of timber species. The following example serves to provide guidance on the design process for determining joist size, measurement of deflection, safe bearing and resistance to shear force:

joist data: span = 5 m
spacing = 0·4 m
fibre stress (f) = 7·5 N/mm²
compression perpendicular to grain = 2.4 N/mm²
shear parallel to grain (v) = 0.71 N/mm²
modulus of elasticity (E) = 10.800 N/mm²

Total load (W) per joist = 5 m × 0·4 m × 2·25 kN/m² = 4·5 kN

$$\text{or} : \frac{4\cdot5\ \text{kN}}{5\ \text{m span}} = 0\cdot9\ \text{kN/m}$$

Resistance to bending ~

4·5 kN (0·9 kN/m)

L = 5 m span

Bending moment formulae are shown on pages 640 and 643

$$BM = \frac{WL}{8} = \frac{fbd^2}{6}$$

Where: W = total load, 4·5 kN (4500 N)
L = span, 5 m (5000 mm)
f = fibre stress of timber, 7·5 N/mm²
b = breadth of joist, try 50 mm
d = depth of joist, unknown

Transposing:

$$\frac{WL}{8} = \frac{fbd^2}{6}$$

Becomes:

$$d = \sqrt{\frac{6WL}{8fb}} = \sqrt{\frac{6 \times 4500 \times 5000}{8 \times 7\cdot5 \times 50}} = 212\ \text{mm}$$

Nearest commercial size: 50 mm × 225 mm

Joist and Beam Sizing ~ calculating overall dimensions alone is insufficient. Checks should also be made to satisfy: resistance to deflection, adequate safe bearing and resistance to shear.

Deflection – should be minimal to prevent damage to plastered ceilings. An allowance of up to 0.003 × span is normally acceptable; for the preceding example this will be:

0.003 × 5000 mm = 15 mm

The formula for calculating deflection due to a uniformly distributed load (see pages 642 and 643) is:

$$\frac{5WL^3}{384EI} \quad \text{where} \quad I = \frac{bd^3}{12}$$

$$I = \frac{50 \times (225)^3}{12} = 4.75 \times (10)^7$$

$$\text{So, deflection} = \frac{5 \times 4500 \times (5000)^3}{384 \times 10800 \times 4.75 \times (10)^7} = 14.27 \text{ mm}$$

NB. This is only just within the calculated allowance of 15 mm, therefore it would be prudent to specify slightly wider or deeper joists to allow for unknown future use.

Safe Bearing ~

$$= \frac{\text{load at the joist end, W/2}}{\text{compression perpendicular to grain} \times \text{breadth}}$$

$$= \frac{4500/2}{2.4 \times 50} = 19 \text{ mm}$$

therefore full support from masonry (90 mm min.) or joist hangers will be more than adequate.

Shear Strength ~

$$V = \frac{2bdv}{3}$$

where: V = vertical loading at the joist end, W/2
     v = shear strength parallel to the grain, 0.71 N/mm²
Transposing:-

$$bd = \frac{3V}{2v} = \frac{3 \times 2250}{2 \times 0.71} = 4753 \text{ mm}^2 \text{ minimum}$$

Actual bd = 50 mm × 225 mm = 11,250 mm²

Resistance to shear is satisfied as actual is well above the minimum.

Typical Situations ~

It is necessary to ensure enough timber above and/or below a notch to resist horizontal shear or shear parallel to the grain.
To check whether a joist or beam has adequate horizontal shear strength:

$$v = (V3d) \div (2bh^2)$$

Using the data provided in the previous two pages as applied to the design of a timber joist of 225 × 50 mm cross section, in this instance with a 50 mm notch to leave 175 mm (h) clear:

$$v = (2250 \times 3 \times 225) \div (2 \times 50 \times 175 \times 175) = 0.496 \, N/mm^2$$

Shear strength parallel to the grain* is given as $0.710 \, N/mm^2$ so sufficient strength is still provided.
*see page 142.

Bressummer (or breastsummer) beam ~

bressummer
beam

A long, large section timber beam carrying joists directly or notched and housed (as shown). A dated form of construction for supporting a masonry wall and floor/ceiling joists in large openings. Often found during refurbishment work over shop windows. Steel or reinforced concrete now preferred.

Pipes and cables ~ should be routed discretely and out of sight, but accessible for maintenance and repair. Where timber joists are used, services running parallel can be conveniently attached to the sides. At right angles the timber will need to be holed or notched.

Holing ~ suitable for flexible cables and coiled soft copper micro-bore tubing. The preferred location in simply supported end-bearing floor joists is in the neutral axis. This is where compressive and tensile load distribution neutralises at the centre and where the material gets neither longer nor shorter when deflected.

Joist under load

*stress is represented by: loading ÷ cross sectional area
 strain is represented by: extension ÷ original length

NB. The relationship between stress and strain is most obvious with metals and plastics. When these are deformed by an applied force they return to their original size and shape after the force is removed. The two physical states of stress and strain are proportional within the elastic state just described. This is known as Hooke's Law and is described by the term elasticity measured in units of N/mm². Examples for softwood timber are given on page 142.

Hole limitations ~
  Diameter maximum: 0.25 x joist depth.
  Spacing minimum: 3 x diameter apart, measured centre to centre.
  Position in the neutral axis: between 0.25 and 0.40 x clear span, measured from the support.

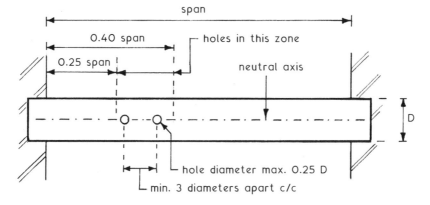

Notching ~ the only practical way of accommodating rigid pipes and conduits in joisted floors.
  Depth maximum: 0.125 x joist depth.
  Position between: 0.07 and 0.25 x clear span measured from the support.

Notching of a joist reduces the effective depth, thereby weakening the joist and reducing its design strength. To allow for this, joists should be oversized.

Timber Upper Floors – Fire Protection (1)

For fire protection, floors are categorised depending on their height relative to adjacent ground ~

Height of top floor above ground	Fire resistance (load bearing)
Less than 5 m	30 minutes
More than 5 m	60 minutes (30 min. for a three-storey dwelling)

Tests for fire resistance relate to load bearing capacity, integrity and insulation as determined by BS 476 – 21: Fire tests on building materials and structures. Methods for determination of the fire resistance of load bearing elements of construction.

Integrity ~ the ability of an element to resist fire penetration.

Insulation ~ ability to resist heat penetration so that fire is not spread by radiation and conduction.

Typical applications ~

30-MINUTE FIRE RESISTANCE

21 mm t & g wood board flooring

38 mm timber joists with noggins or struts to support board edges

12.5 mm plasterboard, joints taped, filled and plaster skimmed

40 mm galv. steel clout nails at 150 mm spacing

600 mm max. spacing

60-MINUTE FIRE RESISTANCE

21 mm t & g wood board flooring

50 mm timber joists with noggins or struts to support board edges

two layers of 15 mm plasterboard independently nailed with joints taped, filled and plaster skimmed

60 mm galv. steel clout nails at 150 mm spacing

600 mm max. spacing

Modified 30-minute fire resistance ~ a lower specification than the full 30-minute fire resistance shown on the preceding page. This is acceptable in certain situations such as some loft conversion floors in existing dwellings and in new-build dwellings of limited height. These situations are defined in Section 4.7 and Appendix A, Table A1 of Approved Document B1 to the Building Regulations.

Load bearing resistance to collapse — 30 minutes minimum.
Integrity — 15 minutes minimum.
Insulation — 15 minutes minimum.

MODIFIED 30-MINUTE FIRE RESISTANCE

21mm timber t&g floorboards or wood board decking

38mm min. width joists with noggins or struts to support edges of sheet board decking

9.5mm plasterboard joints taped, filled and plaster skimmed

30mm galv. steel clout nails at 150mm spacing

400mm spacing

Established floor construction ~ modified 30 minute fire resistant floor construction is often found during refurbishment of housing constructed during the latter part of the 20th century. Here, 9.5 mm plasterboard lath (rounded edge board 1200 mm long x 406 mm wide — now obsolete) was used with floor joists at 400 mm spacing. It is now the general practice to use a 12.5 mm plasterboard ceiling lining to dwelling house floors as this not only provides better fire resistance, but is more stable.

Note 1: Full 30-minute fire resistance must be used for floors over basements or garages.

Note 2: Where a floor provides support or stability to a wall or vice versa, the fire resistance of the supporting element must not be less than the fire resistance of the other element.

Ref. Building Regulations, AD B Fire safety, Volume 1 — Dwelling houses.

Reinforced Concrete Suspended Floors ~ a simple reinforced concrete flat slab cast to act as a suspended floor is not usually economical for spans over 5·000. To overcome this problem beams can be incorporated into the design to span in one or two directions. Such beams usually span between columns which transfers their loads to the foundations. The disadvantages of introducing beams are the greater overall depth of the floor construction and the increased complexity of the formwork and reinforcement. To reduce the overall depth of the floor construction flat slabs can be used where the beam is incorporated with the depth of the slab. This method usually results in a deeper slab with complex reinforcement especially at the column positions.

Typical Examples ~

150 to 350

slab

S = span ~ economic range 2·400 - 7·500

edge beam

beams

columns

ONE WAY SPANNING SLAB

150 to 300

slab

S = span economic range 4·000 to 8·000

beams

columns

TWO WAY SPANNING SLAB

strip of slab acting as a wide flat beam

225 to 400

slab

economic span range – centre to centre of beam strips ~ 6·000 to 9·000

column

TWO WAY SPANNING FLAT SLAB

Ribbed Floors ~ to reduce the overall depth of a traditional cast in-situ reinforced concrete beam and slab suspended floor a ribbed floor could be used. The basic concept is to replace the wide spaced deep beams with narrow spaced shallow beams or ribs which will carry only a small amount of slab loading. These floors can be designed as one or two way spanning floors. One way spanning ribbed floors are sometimes called troughed floors whereas the two way spanning ribbed floors are called coffered or waffle floors. Ribbed floors are usually cast against metal, glass-fibre or polypropylene preformed moulds which are temporarily supported on plywood decking, joists and props – see page 594.

Typical Examples ~

ONE WAY SPANNING RIBBED OR TROUGHED FLOOR

TWO WAY SPANNING COFFERED OR WAFFLE FLOOR

Ribbed Floors – these have greater span and load potential per unit weight than flat slab construction. This benefits a considerable reduction in dead load, to provide cost economies in other super-structural elements and foundations. The regular pattern of voids created with waffle moulds produces a honeycombed effect, which may be left exposed in utility buildings such as car parks. Elsewhere, such as shopping malls, a suspended ceiling would be appropriate. The trough finish is also suitable in various situations and has the advantage of creating a continuous void for accommodation of service cables and pipes. A suspended ceiling can add to this space where air conditioning ducting is required, also providing several options for finishing effect.

Typical mould profile –

steel, glass-fibre or polypropylene waffle mould

200, 250, 300 or 400mm

125mm

600, 800 or 900mm square

optional expanded polystyrene core

10° taper to sides

175, 250, 325 or 400mm

125mm

600mm centres

polypropylene trough mould lengths vary, may overlap or be cut

NB. After removing the temporary support structure, moulds are struck by flexing with a flat tool. A compressed air line is also effective.

Hollow Pot Floors ~ these are in essence a ribbed floor with permanent formwork in the form of hollow clay or concrete pots. The main advantage of this type of cast in-situ floor is that it has a flat soffit which is suitable for the direct application of a plaster finish or an attached dry lining. The voids in the pots can be utilised to house small diameter services within the overall depth of the slab. These floors can be designed as one or two way spanning slabs, the common format being the one way spanning floor.

Typical Example ~

ONE WAY SPANNING HOLLOW POT FLOOR

TYPICAL SECTION

Soffit and Beam Fixings ~ concrete suspended floors can be designed to carry loads other than the direct upper surface loadings. Services can be housed within the voids created by the beams or ribs and suspended or attached ceilings can be supported by the floor. Services which run at right angles to the beams or ribs are usually housed in cast-in holes. There are many types of fixings available for use in conjunction with floor slabs. Some are designed to be cast-in whilst others are fitted after the concrete has cured. All fixings must be positioned and installed so that they are not detrimental to the structural integrity of the floor.

Typical Examples ~

Precast Concrete Floors ~ these are available in several basic formats and provide an alternative form of floor construction to suspended timber floors and in-situ reinforced concrete suspended floors. The main advantages of precast concrete floors are:

1. Elimination of the need for formwork except for nominal propping which is required with some systems.
2. Curing time of concrete is eliminated, therefore the floor is available for use as a working platform at an earlier stage.
3. Superior quality control of product is possible with factory-produced components.

The main disadvantages of precast concrete floors when compared with in-situ reinforced concrete floors are:

1. Less flexible in design terms.
2. Formation of large openings in the floor for ducts, shafts and stairwells usually have to be formed by casting an in-situ reinforced concrete floor strip around the opening position.
3. Higher degree of site accuracy is required to ensure that the precast concrete floor units can be accommodated without any alterations or making good.

Typical Basic Formats ~

with imposed loading of 1·5 kN/m² spans up to 4·400 max.
SOLID AERATED CONCRETE – usual application roof slabs

cores formed with foamed plastic or inflatable formers
HOLLOW BOX SECTIONS – spans up to 10·000

Typical Basic Formats ~

structural concrete topping

450 to 800

floor finish

150 to 200

prestressed precast concrete inverted T beams

precast concrete or clay filler blocks or pots

ceiling finish

PCC BEAM AND POT COMPOSITE FLOOR - max. span 7·500

structural concrete topping

650

floor finish

150 to 250

prestressed pcc planks with lattice reinforcement

pcc or clay filler blocks or pots

ceiling finish

PCC PLANK AND POT COMPOSITE FLOOR - max. span 12·000

grouted joints

400 to 1200

screed and finish

100 to 250

dry cast precast concrete cored units

ceiling finish

PCC CORED UNITS — max. span 10·000

grouted joints

300 to 400

screed and finish

100 to 250

precast concrete channel units

attached ceiling if required

PCC CHANNEL UNITS - max. span 6·750

Bearing Considerations ~

75mm minimum

pcc unit

support

STEEL SUPPORT

75mm minimum

pcc unit

dry mortar or neoprene packing if required

support

CONCRETE SUPPORT

100mm min.

pcc unit

support

MASONRY SUPPORT

NB. spalling to end of pcc unit and/or edge of support will reduce effective bearing length.

Lateral Restraint and Structural Continuity Considerations ~

0·16 to 0·25 span

projecting reinforcement in top of grouted joint or in top of structural topping

edge support

0·16 to 0·25 span

0·16 to 0·25 span

pcc floor units

internal support

reinforcement placed in top of grouted joint or in structural topping

span

Opening Considerations ~

large opening formed in cast in-situ concrete panel or strip

small opening formed in body of pcc unit

cast in-situ RC floor strip and beams

pcc floor units

791

Steel fabricated beams can be used as an integral means of support for precast concrete floors. These are an overall depth and space-saving alternative compared to down-stand reinforced concrete beams or masonry walls. Only the lower steel flange of the steel beam is exposed.

To attain sufficient strength, a supplementary steel plate is welded to the bottom flange of standard UC sections. This produces a type of compound or plated section that is supported by the main structural frame.

Floor support

in-situ concrete filling

steel mesh reinforced structural topping

precast concrete floor units

Plated section

standard UC, serial sizes (mm): 152 × 152
203 × 203
254 × 254
305 × 305
356 × 368
356 × 406

100 mm

fillet weld

15 mm steel plate welded to lower flange

Note: For fillet weld details and other welding applications, see page 636.

A standard manufactured steel beam with similar applications to the plated UC shown on the previous page. This purpose-made alternative is used with lightweight flooring units, such as precast concrete hollow core slabs and metal section decking of the type shown on page 595.

Standard production serial size range ~

280 ASB   175-190

272-288   14-22

10-25

285-300

Dimensions in mm

300 ASB   190-203

310-342   24-40

27-40

300-313

Application ~

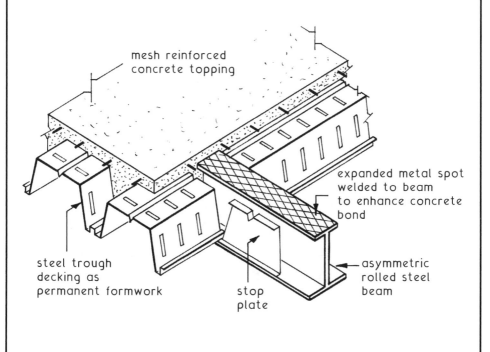

mesh reinforced concrete topping

expanded metal spot welded to beam to enhance concrete bond

steel trough decking as permanent formwork

stop plate

asymmetric rolled steel beam

Raised Flooring ~ developed in response to the high-tech boom of the 1970s. It has proved expedient in accommodating computer and communications cabling as well as numerous other established services. The system is a combination of adjustable floor pedestals, supporting a variety of decking materials. Pedestal height ranges from as little as 30 mm up to about 600 mm, although greater heights are possible at the expense of structural floor levels. Decking is usually in loose fit squares of 600 mm, but may be sheet plywood or particleboard screwed direct to closer spaced pedestal support plates on to joists bearing on pedestals.

Cavity fire stops are required between decking and structural floor at appropriate intervals (see Building Regulations, A D B, Volume 2, Section 9).

Application ~

PEDESTAL DETAIL

FLOOR SECTION

Sound Insulation ~ sound can be defined as vibrations of air which are registered by the human ear. All sounds are produced by a vibrating object which causes tiny particles of air around it to move in unison. These displaced air particles collide with adjacent air particles setting them in motion and in unison with the vibrating object. This continuous chain reaction creates a sound-wave which travels through the air until at some distance the air particle movement is so small that it is inaudible to the human ear. Sounds are defined as either impact or airborne sound, the definition being determined by the source producing the sound. Impact sounds are created when the fabric of structure is vibrated by direct contact whereas airborne sound only sets the structural fabric vibrating in unison when the emitted sound-wave reaches the enclosing structural fabric. The vibrations set up by the structural fabric can therefore transmit the sound to adjacent rooms which can cause annoyance, disturbance of sleep and of the ability to hold a normal conversation. The objective of sound insulation is to reduce transmitted sound to an acceptable level, the intensity of which is measured in units of decibels (dB).

The Building Regulations, Approved Document E: Resistance to the passage of sound, establishes sound insulation standards as follows:

E1: Between dwellings and between dwellings and other buildings.
E2: Within a dwelling, i.e. between rooms, particularly WCs and habitable rooms, and bedrooms and other rooms.
E3: Control of reverberation noise in common parts (stairwells and corridors) of buildings containing dwellings, i.e. flats.
E4: Specific applications to acoustic conditions in schools.
Note: E1 includes hotels, hostels, student accommodation, nurses' homes and homes for the elderly, but not hospitals and prisons.

Typical Sources and Transmission of Sound ~

795

Sound Insulation – Internal Walls and Floors (Dwellings)

The Approved Document to Building Regulation E2 provides for internal walls and floors located between a bedroom or a room containing a WC and other rooms to have a reasonable resistance to airborne sound. Impact sound can be improved by provision of a carpet.

Typical Details ~

75mm min. timber frame
45mm min. metal frame

2 layers of 12.5mm plasterboard each side, min. mass 10kg/m² each sheet

STUD PARTITION

1 layer of plasterboard as adjacent detail

25mm min. mineral wool min. density 10kg/m³

sw or woodboard (22mm) decking min. mass 15kg/m²

min. mass 120kg/m²

plaster finish or plasterboard each side

CONCRETE BLOCKWORK PARTITION

100mm min. mineral wood min. density 10kg/m³

12.5mm plasterboard ceiling, min. mass 10kg/m²

TRADITIONAL SUSPENDED TIMBER FLOOR

SUSPENDED CONCRETE FLOORS (See page 790)
Cored plank ~ min. mass 180 kg/m² with any top surface and ceiling finish.
Precast beam and filler block (pot) ~ min. mass 220 kg/m² with 40mm bonded screed and 12.5mm plasterboard ceiling on battens.

Separating Walls ~ types:

1. Solid masonry
2. Cavity masonry
3. Masonry between isolating panels
4. Timber frame

Type 1 – relies on mass

C = thickness
B = lightweight plaster or plasterboard
A = material
D = coursing

Material A	Density of A [kg/m³]	Finish B	Combined mass A + B (kg/m²)	Thickness C [mm]	Coursing D [mm]
Brickwork	1610	13 mm lwt. pl.	375	215	75
.. ..	.. ..	12·5 mm pl. brd.	.. ..	.. ..	.. ..
Concrete block	1840	13 mm lwt. pl	415	.. ..	110
.. ..	1840	12·5 mm pl. brd	.. ..	.. ..	150
In-situ concrete	2200	Optional	415	190	n/a

Type 2 – relies on mass and isolation

C = leaf thickness
A = material
B = lightweight plaster or plasterboard
butterfly type ties only
D = coursing
E = cavity width

Material A	Density of A [kg/m³]	Finish B	Mass A + B (kg/m²)	Thickness C [mm]	Coursing D [mm]	Cavity E [mm]
Bkwk.	1970	13 mm lwt. pl.	415	102	75	50
Concrete block	1990	..	..	100	225	..
Lwt. conc. block	1375	.. or 12.5 mm pl. brd.	300	100	225	75

Type 3 ~ relies on: (a) core material type and mass,
(b) isolation, and
(c) mass of isolated panels.

Core material A	Density of A [kg/m³]	Mass A (kg/m²)	Thickness C (mm)	Coursing D (mm)	Cavity (mm)
Brickwork	1290	300	215	75	n/a
Concrete block	2200	300	140	110	n/a
Lwt. conc. block	1400	150	200	225	n/a
Cavity bkwk. or block	any	any	2 × 100	to suit	50

Panel materials – B:

(a) Plasterboard with cellular core plus plaster finish, mass 18 kg/m². All joints taped. Fixed floor and ceiling only.

(b) 2 No. plasterboard sheets, 12·5 mm each, with joints staggered. Frame support or 30 mm overall thickness.

Type 4 — relies on mass, frame separation and absorption of sound.

Absorbent material – quilting of unfaced mineral fibre batts with a minimum density of 10 kg/m³, located in the cavity or frames.

Thickness (mm)	Location
25	Suspended in cavity
50	Fixed within one frame
2 × 25	Each quilt fixed within each frame

Separating Floors ~ types:

1. Concrete with soft covering
2. Concrete with floating layer
3. Timber with floating layer (see next page)

Type 1. Airborne resistance depends on mass of concrete and ceiling.
Impact resistance depends on softness of covering.

4.5mm uncompressed soft covering

screed

cast in-situ or precast concrete floor of mass including screed of 365kg/m², p.c.c. floor must have plasterboard fixed with resilient metal bars, and the void filled with mineral wool – 10kg/m³

plasterboard min. mass 9kg/m²

timber battens

Type 2. Airborne resistance depends mainly on concrete mass and partly on mass of floating layer and ceiling.
Impact resistance depends on resilient layer isolating floating layer from base and isolation of ceiling.

Bases: As type 1. but overall mass minimum 300 kg/m².

Floating layers:

18mm t & g timber (min. 12kg/m²) or wood-based boarding on 45 × 45mm battens

resilient layer

65mm screed (min. 80kg/m²)

mesh to protect resilient layer

concrete structural floor

plasterboard

timber battens

Resilient layers:

(a) 25 mm paper faced mineral fibre, density 36kg/m³.
Timber floor – paper faced underside.
Screeded floor – paper faced upper side to prevent screed from entering layer.

(b) Screeded floor only:
13 mm pre-compressed expanded polystyrene (EPS) board, or 5 mm extruded polyethylene foam of density 30–45 kg/m³, laid over a levelling screed for protection.

Ref. See BS EN 29052-1: Acoustics. Method for the determination of dynamic stiffness. Materials used under floating floors in dwellings.

799

Type 3. Airborne resistance varies depending on floor construction, absorbency of materials, extent of pugging and partly on the floating layer. Impact resistance depends mainly on the resilient layer separating floating from structure.

Platform Floor ~

floating layer
resilient layer
base
absorbent material
45mm min. width joist
plasterboard ceiling

NB. Minimum mass per unit area = 25kg/m².

Floating layer: 18 mm timber or wood-based board, t & g joints glued and spot bonded to a sub-strate of 19 mm plasterboard. Alternative sub-strate of cement bonded particle board in two 12 mm thicknesses, joints staggered, glued and screwed together.

Resilient layer: 25 mm mineral fibre, density 60–100 kg/m³.

Base: 12 mm timber boarding or wood-based board nailed to joists.

Absorbent material: 100 mm mineral fibre of minimum density 10 kg/m³.

Ceiling: 30 mm plasterboard in two layers, joints staggered.

Ribbed or battened floor ~

floating layer and 19 mm plasterboard on 45 x 45 mm battens
25 mm mineral fibre strip, density 80-140 kg/m³
100 mm mineral fibre quilt, density 10 kg/m³
30 mm plasterboard ceiling

NB. See next page for other examples of ribbed floors.

Type 3 (continued).

Alternative ribbed or battened floor ~

18 mm t&g boarding and 15 mm plasterboard
screwed to 45 x 45 mm battens

6 mm rubber tape

15 mm OSB

mineral fibre quilt

100 mm

two layers of
12.5 mm plasterboard

Ribbed or battened floor with dry sand pugging ~

Example 1

18 mm t&g timber or chipboard, joints glued

6 mm plywood
plus two layers
of 12.5 mm
plasterboard

25 mm mineral
fibre strip,
density
80-140 kg/m^3

50 mm dry sand
pugging 80 kg/m^3
min. not suitable
in damp situations,
e.g. kitchens and
bathrooms

Example 2
Alternative to Example 1

45 x 45 mm min. battens

45 mm min. width joist

polythene

NB. Plasterboard in two layers, joints staggered.
    OSB = Oriented strand board.

Sound Insulation — Improving Existing Construction

The intensity of unwanted sound that increases vibration of a separating wall or floor can be reduced to some extent by attaching a lining to the existing structure. Plasterboard or other dense material is suitable, but this will have only a limited effect as the lining will also vibrate and radiate sound. The most effective solution is to create another wall or ceiling next to the original, but separated from it.

Separating wall ~

timber stud frame

25mm mineral fibre insulation quilt minimum density 10 kg/m³

two layers of 12.5mm plasterboard

existing one-brick separating wall plastered both sides

cavity width at least 100mm

Separating floor ~

hardboard layer over plain edge floorboards

existing floor

independent ceiling

two layers of 12.5mm plasterboard

100m min. mineral wool density at least 10kg/m³

ceiling joists notched onto carbelled wall plate

Refs.: BS 8233: Sound insulation and noise reduction for buildings. Code of practice.
BRE Digest 293: Improving the sound insulation of separating walls and floors.

Primary Functions ~

1. Provide a means of circulation between floor levels.
2. Establish a safe means of travel between floor levels.
3. Provide an easy means of travel between floor levels.
4. Provide a means of conveying fittings and furniture between floor levels.

Constituent Parts ~

landing

upper newel post – notched over joist

handrail – spans between newel posts

wall string – fixed to wall

bottom newel post – rests on floor

tread – spans between strings

riser – infill between treads

margin piece

apron lining

balusters forming infill between string and handrail

outer string – spans between newel posts

string capping – provides seating for balusters

bottom step

STRAIGHT FLIGHT STAIRS

All dimensions quoted are the minimum required for domestic stairs exclusive to one dwelling as given in Approved Document K unless stated otherwise.

Terminology ~

pitch line - the line joining nosings

going

nosings

= going

aggregate of going + twice rise of a step to be 550 min. and 700 max.

tread

rise

riser

riser + tread = step

handrail - must provide adequate support and is required where total rise exceeds 600mm and to both sides if width exceeds 1·000

upper floor

pitch line

minimum headroom · 2·000

min. going 220mm

rise height max. 220 mm

900mm min. 1000mm max.

1100mm preferred

900mm min.

recommended floor to floor height 2·600

no openings which will allow a 100mm sphere to pass through

max. pitch 42°

* recommended min. width 800 mm

handrail →

width of string ignored

*A.D. K does not give a minimum dimension for stair width. See also page 808.

Step Formats ~

square nosing
tread
riser
butt joint

splayed nosing
tread
riser
rebate joint

rounded nosing
tread
riser
housing joint

NB. nosing types and joints are interchangeable between step formats.

string position

25 to 38 mm thick treads

glued triangulated brackets on centre line of stairs

triangular glue blocks

15mm deep housings

glued wedges

25 to 38 mm thick string

12 to 20mm thick risers

STAIR FLIGHT CONSTRUCTION

Bottom Step Arrangements ~

BULLNOSE STEP   SPLAYED STEP   `D´ STEP

Projecting bottom steps are usually included to enable the outer string to be securely jointed to the back face of the newel post and to provide an easy line of travel when ascending or descending at the foot of the stairs.

TYPICAL DETAIL AT BOTTOM NEWEL POST

806

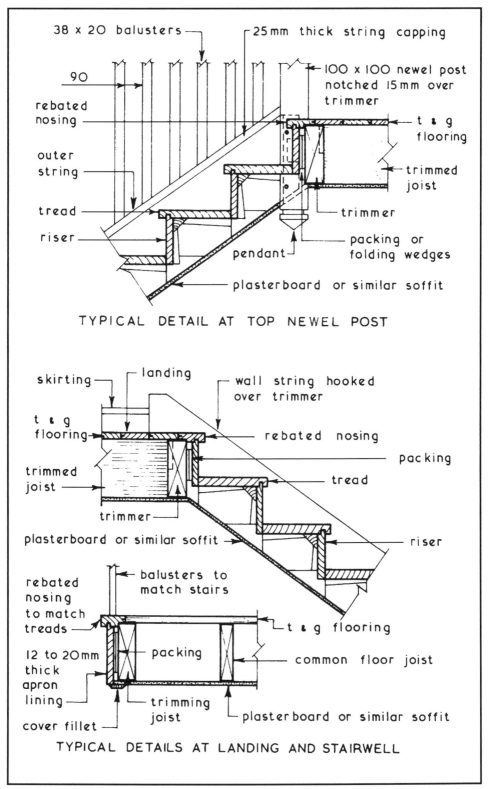

TYPICAL DETAIL AT TOP NEWEL POST

Top detail labels:
- 38 x 20 balusters
- 25mm thick string capping
- 90
- rebated nosing
- 100 x 100 newel post notched 15mm over trimmer
- t & g flooring
- outer string
- trimmed joist
- tread
- trimmer
- riser
- packing or folding wedges
- pendant
- plasterboard or similar soffit

TYPICAL DETAILS AT LANDING AND STAIRWELL

Landing detail labels:
- skirting
- landing
- wall string hooked over trimmer
- t & g flooring
- rebated nosing
- packing
- trimmed joist
- tread
- trimmer
- plasterboard or similar soffit
- riser
- rebated nosing to match treads
- balusters to match stairs
- t & g flooring
- 12 to 20mm thick apron lining
- packing
- common floor joist
- cover fillet
- trimming joist
- plasterboard or similar soffit

Timber Open Riser Stairs ~ these are timber stairs constructed to the same basic principles as standard timber stairs excluding the use of a riser. They have no real advantage over traditional stairs except for the generally accepted aesthetic appeal of elegance. Like the traditional timber stairs they must comply with the minimum requirements set out in Part K of the Building Regulations.

Typical Requirements for Stairs in a Small Residential Building ~

upper floor landing

wall string hooked over landing trimmer

minimum going 220 mm

minimum headroom 2.000

no opening which will allow a 100 mm diameter sphere to pass through

handrail

pitch line

minimum overlap 16 mm

balusters

treads housed into strings

newel post

900 mm min.

1000 mm max.

rise – 220 mm max.

no opening which will allow a 100 mm diameter sphere to pass through – see details on following page

outer string

maximum pitch 42°

floor level

Recommended clear width for all stairs is 800mm minimum, but 900 mm wall to wall or wall to centre of handrail is preferable. Clear width is defined in BS 585-1 as 'unobstructed width between handrail and face of newel', but see also page 804. A reduced clear width of 600mm is acceptable for access to limited use space such as a loft.

Aggregate of going plus twice the rise to be 550 mm minimum and 700mm maximum

Design and Construction ~ because of the legal requirement of not having a gap between any two consecutive treads through which a 100 mm diameter sphere can pass and the limitation relating to the going and rise, as shown on the previous page, it is generally not practicable to have a completely riserless stair for residential buildings since by using minimum dimensions a very low pitch of approximately 27½° would result and by choosing an acceptable pitch a very thick tread would have to be used to restrict the gap to 100 mm.

Possible Solutions ~

pendant newel post notched over landing trimmer

balusters

no openings which allow a 100 mm diameter sphere to pass through

outer string capping

pitch line

tread

wall string

upper floor landing

going

rise

outer string

< 100   Solution No.1 - nosing batten

< 100   Solution No.2 - tread batten

< 100

Solution No. 3 - intermediate batten

< 100

minimum overlap 16 mm

treads and battens housed and fixed into strings

Application – a straight flight for access to a domestic loft conversion only. This can provide one habitable room, plus a bathroom or WC. The WC must not be the only WC in the dwelling.

Practical Issues – an economic use of space, achieved by a very steep pitch of about 60° and opposing overlapping treads.

Safety – pitch and tread profile differ considerably from other stairs, but they are acceptable to Building Regulations by virtue of 'familiarity and regular use' by the building occupants.

Additional features are:

* a non-slip tread surface.
* handrails to both sides.
* minimum going 220 mm.
* maximum rise 220 mm.
* (2 + rise) + (going) between 550 and 700 mm.
* a stair used by children under 5 years old must have the tread voids barred to leave a gap not greater than 100 mm.

non-slip surface

paddle-shaped treads

going 220 mm min.

rise 220 mm max.

< 60°·30'

string

Plan

Ref. Building Regulations, Approved Document K1: Stairs, ladders and ramps: Section 1.29.

Timber Stairs ~ these must comply with the minimum requirements set out in Part K of the Building Regulations. Straight flight stairs are simple, easy to construct and install but by the introduction of intermediate landings stairs can be designed to change direction of travel and be more compact in plan than the straight flight stairs.

Landings ~ these are designed and constructed in the same manner as timber upper floors but due to the shorter spans they require smaller joist sections. Landings can be detailed for a 90° change of direction (quarter space landing) or a 180° change of direction (half space landing) and can be introduced at any position between the two floors being served by the stairs.

Typical Layouts ~

QUARTER SPACE LANDING STAIR

DOG LEG STAIR

OPEN NEWEL STAIRS

OPEN NEWEL STAIRS

half-pendant newel post
fixed to wall to receive
upper floor landing handrail

pendant
newel post
notched over
trimmer joist

handrail and
balusters

half space
landing

upper
floor

skirting

rebated nosing

wall string of
lower flight

treads and
risers forming
upper flight

riser

tread

string
capping

storey-height
newel post

handrail of lower flight abuts
to the underside of outer
string of upper string

bottom newel post

splayed bottom step

TYPICAL DOG LEG OR STRING OVER STRING STAIRS

For domestic situations a spiral stair of 800 mm clear width can provide an alternative compact, space-saving means of access to the upper floor of a private dwelling. With a clear width of only 600 mm this type of stair may also be used to access the space available in a roof void. Approved Document K to the Building Regulations refers the design and application of spiral stairs to guidance in BS 5395-2, as summarised on pages 831 and 832.

Typical timber spiral stair components

- upper newel post
- balusters
- landing
- steel tube or solid timber dowel central column
- tread
- annular spacer
- helical handrail
- Assembly
- lower newel post
- tapered treads
- floor pattress

NB. Clear width is measured between handrails or between central column and handrail. If strings are used, measurement is to or between strings. Take greater value.

In-situ Reinforced Concrete Stairs ~ a variety of stair types and arrangements are possible each having its own appearance and design characteristics. In all cases these stairs must comply with the minimum requirements set out in Part K of the Building Regulations in accordance with the purpose group of the building in which the stairs are situated.

Typical Examples ~

INCLINED SLAB STAIR

landings span from well edge to load bearing wall

stair flights span from floor to landing and from landing to floor

for detailed example see page 817

CRANKED SLAB STAIR

Stair flights span as a cranked slab from floor to landing edge beam and from landing edge beam to floor

If no structural support is given at landing levels stairs are called a continuous slab or scissor stair

Typical Examples ~

load bearing wall

structural frame

load bearing wall

panel wall

STRING BEAM STAIR

landings span from well edge beam to load bearing wall

string beams span from floor to landing and from landing to floor

stair flights span from string beam to load bearing wall or from string beam to string beam

landing

upper floor

floor

downstand string beam to well edge of flight

alternative – upstand string beam to well edge of flight

upper floor

spine wall

structural frame

lightweight cladding

2nd floor

landing

CANTILEVER STAIR

Landings cantilever on both sides of a stub beam which is a cantilever beam out of the rear edge of the spine wall

Stair flights are cantilever flights about the spine wall

1st floor

landing

ground floor

815

Spiral and Helical Stairs ~ these stairs constructed in in-situ reinforced concrete are considered to be aesthetically pleasing but are expensive to construct. They are therefore mainly confined to prestige buildings usually as accommodation stairs linking floors within the same compartment. Like all other forms of stair they must conform to the requirements of Part K of the Building Regulations and if used as a means of escape in case of fire with the requirements of Part B. Spiral stairs can be defined as those describing a helix around a central column whereas a helical stair has an open well. The open well of a helical stair is usually circular or elliptical in plan and the formwork is built up around a vertical timber core.

Typical Example of a Helical Stair ~

PLAN

SECTION THROUGH LANDING

In-situ RC Inclined Slab Stair — Typical Details ~

NB. in plan the risers in the upper flight are not in line with those in the lower flight. This is to ensure that the soffits of the two flights line through at their intersection with the soffit of the half space landing

KEY PLAN

For dimensional limitations see page 827.

Stair width subject to AD B: Fire safety, and AD M: Access to and use of buildings. Width measured as clear distance between walls or balustrade. Ignore string and handrail if projecting <100 mm (AD B, Volume 2).

In-situ Reinforced Concrete Stair Formwork ~ in specific detail the formwork will vary for the different types of reinforced concrete stair but the basic principles for each format will remain constant.

Typical RC Stair Formwork Details ~ (see previous page for Key Plan)

reversed cut string fixed to wall

outer cut string

riser board

margin piece

strut

string

soffit board

joist

carriage piece

SECTION - LOWER FLIGHT

margin piece

cleat

adjustable steel prop

carriage piece

NB. all formwork sizes to design.

joist

stair soffit board

wall board fixed to wall - alternative to reversed cut string

hanger

riser board

concrete outline

landing formwork as below

TYPICAL FORMWORK TO UPPER FLIGHT

outer cut strings to both edges

side form to landing

plywood riser boards with splayed bottom edge to enable complete trowelling of tread surface

struts

soffit board

cleats

props

margin piece

stair soffit board

carriage piece

strut

cleat

joist

sole plate

bracing as required

folding wedges

TYPICAL FORMWORK TO LOWER FLIGHT

Precast Concrete Stairs ~ these can be produced to most of the formats used for in-situ concrete stairs and like those must comply with the appropriate requirements set out in Part K of the Building Regulations. To be economical the total production run must be sufficient to justify the costs of the moulds and therefore the designer's choice may be limited to the stair types which are produced as a manufacturer's standard item.

Precast concrete stairs can have the following advantages:

1. Good quality control of finished product.
2. Saving in site space since formwork fabrication and storage will not be required.
3. The stairs can be installed at any time after the floors have been completed, thus giving full utilisation to the stair shaft as a lifting or hoisting space if required.
4. Hoisting, positioning and fixing can usually be carried out by semi-skilled labour.

Typical Example ~ Straight Flight Stairs

FLOOR JUNCTION DETAIL

Typical Example ~ Cranked Slab Stairs

upper return flight

in-situ RC rebated landing edge support beam

tread or going

rise

in-situ RC floor with rebated edge beam

waist

precast concrete stair flight and landings

lower return flight

upper return flight

in-situ landing edge support beam

10 mm wide joint with flexible filler

main bars

100 mm wide rebated bearing with packing if required

distribution bars

LANDING SUPPORT DETAIL

Typical Example ~ Spine Beam Stairs with Open Risers

double cantilever treads of precast concrete or a suitable hardwood timber

return flight

ends of spine beams housed in pockets cast into face of floor or landing beams

double cantilever precast concrete tread bolted to precast concrete spine with 2 No. fixing bolts

fixing bolts cast into spine beam

foot of spine beam housed in pocket cast into ground-floor slab

in-situ RC landing edge beam

waist

precast concrete spine beam

ground-floor slab

hardcore

damp-proof membrane

precast concrete double cantilever tread

reinforcement

fixing bolt slot made good

2 No. cast-in fixing bolts per tread

precast concrete spine beam

anchor bars

reinforcement to waist of spine beam

binders or stirrups

main bars

TYPICAL SECTION

821

Precast Concrete Spiral Stairs ~ this form of stair is usually constructed with an open riser format using tapered treads which have a keyhole plan shape. Each tread has a hollow cylinder at the narrow end equal to the rise which is fitted over a central steel column usually filled with in-situ concrete. The outer end of the tread has holes through which the balusters pass to be fixed on the underside of the tread below, a hollow spacer being used to maintain the distance between consecutive treads.

Typical Example ~

balustrade

edge beam under

upper floor

landing - cantilevered from floor

continuous handrail

tapered treads

150mm max. overlap of treads

concrete filled steel column

balustrade

PLAN

balustrade

upper-floor edge beam

landing slab

continuous handrail

column taken up to at least balustrade height and capped

balusters

treads

spacers between treads

lower or ground floor

SECTION THROUGH LANDING

Metal Stairs ~ these can be produced in cast iron, mild steel or aluminium alloy for use as escape stairs or for internal accommodation stairs. Most escape stairs are fabricated from cast iron or mild steel and must comply with the Building Regulation requirements for stairs in general and fire escape stairs in particular. Most metal stairs are purpose made and therefore tend to cost more than comparable concrete stairs. Their main advantage is the elimination of the need for formwork whilst the main disadvantage is the regular maintenance in the form of painting required for cast iron and mild steel stairs.

Typical Example ~ Straight Flight Steel External Escape Stair

door to open in direction of but clear of stairs

windows within 1·800 horizontally or vertically up or 9·000 down to be fixed and 1/2 hr. f.r.

minimum width as for internal stairs

steel plated landings on framed steel channels

landing width not less than stair width

continuous handrails 900 mm min. above pitch line

up

support column

universal beam at each floor level

support column

PLAN

perforated steel plates to landing

return flight

strings out of mild steel plate

perforated steel treads with 25 mm overlap of tread below

framed steel channels forming landing support

handrail omitted for clarity

LANDING JUNCTION DETAIL

Typical Examples ~ Steel Spiral Stairs

balustrade and handrail

40 × 20 convex polished metal handrail

25 × 25 landing newel

20 × 20 baluster

floor

12mm diameter pin

60 mm diameter tube

tread unit

tread units fitted over central tube

riser leg relieved for easy maintenance

balustrade and handrail

nut and washer to secure pin under lower tread unit

25 × 25 bottom newel

grip pattern

tread units

tube fixing plate

hole for central tube

pin holes

ELEVATION

ASSEMBLY DETAILS

square steel plate landing

square plan shape stairwell formed in structural floor with 75mm minimum clearance to edge of steel stairs

balustrade and handrail

NB. Treads can be left hand right hand with 12 or 16 riser per circle.

PLAN

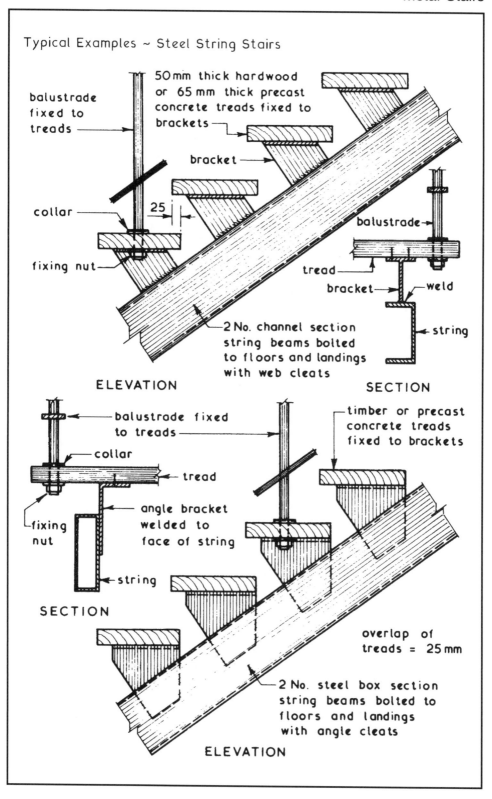

Typical Examples ~ Steel String Stairs

balustrade fixed to treads

50 mm thick hardwood or 65 mm thick precast concrete treads fixed to brackets

bracket

collar

25

fixing nut

balustrade

tread

bracket

weld

string

2 No. channel section string beams bolted to floors and landings with web cleats

ELEVATION

SECTION

balustrade fixed to treads

collar

tread

angle bracket welded to face of string

fixing nut

string

timber or precast concrete treads fixed to brackets

SECTION

overlap of treads = 25 mm

2 No. steel box section string beams bolted to floors and landings with angle cleats

ELEVATION

825

Balustrades and Handrails ~ these must comply in all respects with the requirements given in Part K of the Building Regulations and in the context of escape stairs are constructed of a non-combustible material with a handrail shaped to give a comfortable hand grip. The handrail may be covered or capped with a combustible material such as timber or plastic. Most balustrades are designed to be fixed after the stairs have been cast or installed by housing the balusters in a preformed pocket or by direct surface fixing.

Typical Details ~

removable snap on plastic handrail cover

metal top rail welded or screwed to standards

moulded and polished hardwood handrail screwed from lower face of metal rail

metal top rail welded or screwed to standards

standard or baluster

metal rails slotted to take standards fillet welded on underside

standard or baluster

cover plate if required

cover plate welded to standard

direct screw or bolt fixings

matching cement mortar filling

run lead or cement grout filling

ragged or deformed end of baluster or standard

pockets formed in concrete to receive ends of standards

Institutional and Assembly Stairs ~ serving a place where a substantial number of people will gather.

minimum going, 280 mm (may reduce to 250 mm if the building floor area <100 m²), maximum, 340 mm

rise 135 to 180 mm

The maximum pitch for gangways with seated spectators in assembly buildings is 35°.

Other Stairs ~ all other buildings.

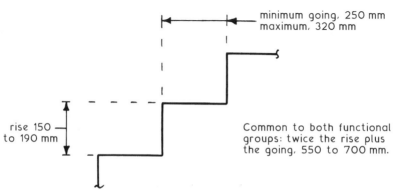

minimum going, 250 mm
maximum, 320 mm

rise 150 to 190 mm

Common to both functional groups: twice the rise plus the going, 550 to 700 mm.

Alternative guidance: BS 5395-1: Code of practice for the design of stairs with straight flights and winders.

The rise and going in both situations may be subject to the requirements of Approved Document M: Access to and use of buildings. AD M will take priority and the following will apply:

Going (external steps) ~ 280 mm minimum (300 mm min. preferred).
Going (stairs) ~ 250 mm minimum.
Rise ~ 170 mm maximum.

Other AD M requirements for stairs:

Avoid tapered treads.
Width at least 1200 mm between walls, strings or upstands.
Landing top and bottom, minimum length not less than stair width.
Handrails both sides; circular or oval preferred as shown on next page.
Door openings onto landings to be avoided.
Full risers, no gaps.
Nosings with prominent colour 55 mm wide on tread and riser.
Nosing projections avoided, maximum of 25 mm if necessary.
Maximum 12 risers; exceptionally in certain small premises 16.
Non-slip surface to treads and landing.

Measurement of the going (AD K) ~

going measured at centre of tread (see next page), minimum for private stairs 220 mm, other applications 250 mm

50 mm minimum tread width at newel (see additional recommendation, next page)

<1 m

For stair widths greater than 1 m, the going is measured at 270 mm from each side of the stair.

Additional requirements:

Going of tapered treads not less than the going of parallel treads in the same stair.
Curved landing lengths measured on the stair centre line.
Twice the rise plus the going, 550 to 700 mm.
Uniform going for consecutive tapered treads.
Other going and rise limitations as shown on the previous page and page 804.

Alternative guidance that provides reasonable safety for use in dwellings according to the requirements of Approved Document K is published in BS 585 – 1: Specification for stairs with closed risers for domestic use, including straight and winder flights and quarter or half landings.

Handrail profile ~

50 to 75 mm

32 to 50 mm diameter

50 mm

Round

50 mm wide x 39 mm deep

15 mm diameter min.

Oval

Basic requirements:

- Lines of all risers to meet at one point, i.e. the geometric centre.
- Centre going to be uniform and not less than the going of adjacent straight flights.
- Centre going ≥ going of adjacent parallel tread.
- Centre going ≤ 700 − (2 × rise) in mm.
- Going at newel post, not less than 75mm.
- Taper angle of treads to be uniform.
- Clear width at least 770mm.

Key:

Gc = centre going
Rc = radius of arc given by equation (see next page)
θ = angle subtended by each tread
W = clear width
E = risers meeting point to edge of clear width
V = nosing overhang

To check whether the design for winder flights will comply with recommended dimensions, measurements can be taken from scale drawings or calculations may be applied.

Calculations ~

$$Gc = 2Rc \, (\sin \, \theta \div 2)$$

where $Rc = \sqrt{([W \div 2] + E)^2 + (V)^2}$

E.g. W = 770 mm
    E = 150 mm
    V = 16 mm

$$Rc = \sqrt{([770 \div 2] + 150)^2 + (16)^2}$$

$$Rc = \sqrt{(385 + 150)^2 + 256}$$

$$Rc = \sqrt{(535)^2 + 256}$$

$$Rc = \sqrt{286225 + 256} = \sqrt{286481} = 535 \text{ mm}$$

$$Gc = 2 \times 535 \, (\sin 30° \div 2)$$

where $\sin 30° = 0.5$

$$Gc = 1070 \times (0.5 = 2) = 267 \text{ mm}$$

In most applications the winder flight will turn through a 90° angle on plan. Therefore, the angle θ subtended by each of three treads will be 30°, i.e. θ = turn angle ÷ N, where N = the number of winders.
For four winders, $\theta = 90° \div 4 = 22.5°$.
If the turn angle is other than 90° then $\theta = (180 - \text{turn angle}) \div N$.
E.g. Turn angle of 120° with two winders, $\theta = (180 - 120) \div 2 = 30°$.

Refs.: BS 585-1: Wood stairs. Specification for stairs with closed risers for domestic use, including straight and winder flights and quarter or half landings.
BS 5395-1: Code of practice for the design of stairs with straight flights and winders.

Summary recommendations of BS 5395-2:

Stair type[1]	Clear width[2]	Rise	Min. inner going[3]	Max. outer going[4]	Min. centre going[5]	2 × rise + going
A	600	170–220	120	350	145	480–800
B	800	170–220	120	350	190	480–800
C	800	170–220	150	350	230	480–800
D	900	150–190	150	450	250	480–800
E	1000	150–190	150	450	250	480–800

All dimensions in millimetres.
[1]See next page.
[2]Minimum clear width.
[3]270 mm horizontally from inner handrail or column face if no handrail.
[4]270 mm horizontally from outer handrail or string (take least value).
[5]Centre of clear width.

Clear headroom ~ measured from the pitch line (consecutive tread nosings at the geometric stair centre) vertically to any overhead obstruction. Normally 2.000 m, but acceptable at 1.900 m within 150 mm of the centre column.

Landing ~ minimum angle subtended at the stair centre is 60°. Intermediate landings, minimum angle is 45° or a plan area ≥ two treads (take greater area).

Loading guide ~ (No. of treads × 0.2) + (1.5 for the landing)
E.g. 14 treads:
$= (14 × 0.2) + (1.5) = 4.3 \text{ kN}$.

Refs.:
BS 5395-2: Stairs, ladders and walkways. Code of practice for the design of helical and spiral stairs.
Building Regulations, A.D. K: Protection from falling, collision and impact.

BS 5395-2, Stair types:

Category A ~
A small private stair for use by a limited number of people who are generally familiar with the stair. For example, an internal stair in a dwelling serving one room not being a living room or a kitchen. Also, an access stair to a small room or equipment room in an office, shop or factory not for public or general use. Subject to the provisions of A.D. B, possibly a fire escape for a small number of people. Typically, 1.300 to 1.800 m overall diameter.

Category B ~
Similar to category A, but providing the main access to the upper floor of a private dwelling. Typically, 1.800 to 2.250 m overall diameter.

Category C ~
A small semi-public stair for use by a limited number of people, some of whom may be unfamiliar with the stair. Examples include a stair in a factory, office or shop and a common stair serving more than one dwelling. Typically, 2.000 to 2.250 m overall diameter.

Category D ~
Similar to category C, but for use by larger numbers of people. Typically, 2.000 to 2.500 m overall diameter.

Category E ~
A public stair intended to be used by a large number of people at one time. For example, in a place of public assembly. Typically, 2.500 to 3.500 m overall diameter.

Note 1: With regard to means of escape in the event of a fire, minimum widths given may be insufficient. All applications to satisfy the requirements of Building Regulations, Approved Documents B1 and B2: Fire safety. This has particular reference to stair clear width relative to the number of persons likely to use the stair and protection of the stairwell.

Note 2: In addition to an outer handrail, an inner handrail should be provided for categories C, D and E.

Functions ~ the main functions of any door are to:

1. Provide a means of access and egress.
2. Maintain continuity of wall function when closed.
3. Provide a degree of privacy and security.

Choice of door type can be determined by:

1. Position – whether internal or external.
2. Properties required – fire resistant, glazed to provide for borrowed light or vision through, etc.
3. Appearance – flush or panelled, painted or polished, etc.

Door Schedules ~ these can be prepared in the same manner and for the same purpose as that given for windows on page 446.

Internal Doors ~ these are usually lightweight and can be fixed to a lining, if heavy doors are specified these can be hung to frames in a similar manner to external doors. An alternative method is to use doorsets which are usually storey height and supplied with prehung doors.

Typical door Lining Details ~

TYPICAL DOOR LINING   JAMB DETAIL

Internal Doors ~ these are similar in construction to the external doors but are usually thinner and therefore lighter in weight.

Typical Examples ~

common internal door size
1981 high x 762 mm wide

width range
305 to 838

height range from 1829 to 2032

facing materials:
hardboard
plywood
laminated
plastic

solid, skeleton frame or cellular core

edge lipping

FLUSH DOOR

glazed 450 x 450 mm observation panel

facing materials:
hardboard
plywood

edge lipping

GLAZED FLUSH DOOR

top rail

stile

lock rail

bottom rail

clear or obscure glazing in small panes

panels of narrow width louvres

LOUVRED DOOR

top rail

stile

glazing bars

bottom rail

GLAZED DOOR

Flush doors of lightweight construction are suitable to access many interior situations. If there is an additional requirement for resistance to fire, the construction will include supplementary lining as shown on pages 839 and 840. Fire resisting and non-fire resisting doors can be produced with identical flush finishes, but the fire doors must be purposely labelled as shown on page 838.

Examples of Non-fire Doors for Interior Use ~

SKELETON CORE   CELLULAR CORE

LATTICE CORE   SPIRAL CORE

Note 1: Overall thickness can vary between manufacturers. Typically 35 or 40 mm.

Note 2: Height and width dimension of 2032 mm × 813 mm also available from most joinery producers.

Internal Door Frames and Linings ~ these are similar in construction to external door frames but usually have planted door stops and do not have a sill. The frames are sized to be built in conjunction with various partition thicknesses and surface finishes. Linings with planted stops are usually employed for lightweight domestic doors.

Typical Examples ~

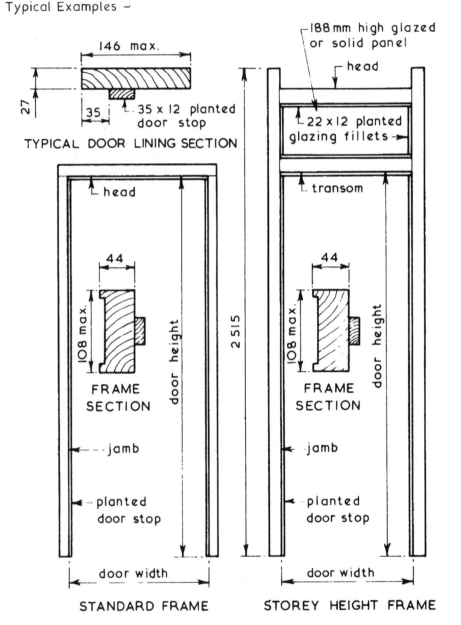

188 mm high glazed or solid panel

head

22 x 12 planted glazing fillets →

146 max.

27

35 x 12 planted door stop

35

TYPICAL DOOR LINING SECTION

head

transom

44

44

108 max.

108 max.

door height

2 515

door height

FRAME SECTION

FRAME SECTION

jamb

jamb

planted door stop

planted door stop

door width

door width

STANDARD FRAME

STOREY HEIGHT FRAME

Ref. BS 4787: Internal and external wood doorsets, door leaves and frames. Specification for dimensional requirements.

Doorsets ~ these are factory-produced fully assembled prehung doors which are supplied complete with frame, architraves and ironmongery except for door furniture. The doors may be hung to the frames using pin butts for easy door removal. Prehung door sets are available in standard and storey height versions and are suitable for all internal door applications with normal wall and partition thicknesses.

Typical Examples ~

packing as required to underside of preformed opening in wall

19 x 35 site-fixed architrave

57 x 43 framing

flush door

40

STANDARD HEIGHT DOORSET

doorsets fixed to wall or partition with 4 No. wood screws to each jamb

packing to underside of ceiling

ceiling

19 x 35 factory-fixed architrave

19 x 35 site-fixed architrave

20 x 13 site-fixed beads

door height 2040 widths 826, 726, 626, 526

hardwood threshold

hardwood threshold

19 x 35 factory-fixed architrave

57 x 43 framing

infill by contractor

factory-fixed bead

57 x 43 transom

flush door

40

maximum overall height 2400 head adjusts to give overall heights from 2230 to 2380

STOREY HEIGHT DOORSET

837

Fire Doorset ~ a 'complete unit consisting of a door frame and a door leaf or leaves, supplied with all essential parts from a single source'. The difference between a doorset and a fire doorset is that the latter is endorsed with a fire certificate for the complete unit. When supplied as a collection of parts for site assembly, this is known as a door kit.

Fire Door Assembly ~ a 'complete assembly as installed, including door frame and one or more leaves, together with its essential hardware [ironmongery] supplied from separate sources'. Provided the components to an assembly satisfy the Building Regulations – Approved Document B, fire safety requirements and standards for certification and compatibility, then a fire door assembly is an acceptable alternative to a doorset.

Fire doorsets are usually more expensive than fire door assemblies, but assemblies permit more flexibility in choice of components. Site fixing time will be longer for assemblies.

(Quotes from BS EN 12519: Windows and pedestrian doors. Terminology.)

Fire Door ~ a fire door is not just the door leaf. A fire door includes the frame, ironmongery, glazing, intumescent core and smoke seal. To comply with European market requirements, ironmongery should be CE marked (see page 75). A fire door should also be marked accordingly on the top or hinge side. The label type shown below, reproduced with kind permission of the British Woodworking Federation, is acceptable.

Ref. BS 8214: Code of practice for fire door assemblies.

30-minute Flush Fire Doors ~ these are usually based on the recommendations given in BS 8214. A wide variety of door constructions are available from various manufacturers but they all have to be fitted to a similar frame for testing as a doorset or assembly, including ironmongery.

A door's resistance to fire is measured by:

1. Insulation – resistance to thermal transmittance, see BS 476-20 & 22: Fire tests on building materials and structures.

2. Integrity – resistance in minutes to the penetration of flame and hot gases under simulated fire conditions.

Typical Details ~

838 or 914

83 x 38 framing

230

1·980

230

SECTIONAL ELEVATION
NB. intumescent strips in door edges provide an enhanced rating – see page 841.

83 x 34 door frame
25 x 35 planted stop screwed to frame
25
45
3mm maximum gap
DOOR FRAME DETAIL

— 45mm deep intermediate rail

— plasterboard lining 9·5mm thick to both faces

— third hinge optional

— 165mm deep lock or middle rail

— lipping to both edges

— 83 x 38 framing

— 3mm thick plywood facing

— steel or brass butt hinges

Glass panel – can be included if 6mm thick wired glass with a maximum size of 1·2 m^2 is used. Glass to be fixed with non-combustible beads with a melting point of ≮ 900°C. See also page 842.

60-minute Flush Fire Doors ~ like the 30-minute flush fire door shown on the previous page these doors are based on the recommendations given in BS 8214 which covers both door and frame. A wide variety of fire resistant door constructions are available from various manufacturers with most classified as having both insulation and integrity ratings of 60 minutes.

Typical Details ~

838 or 914

83 x 38 framing

230

1·980

230

92 x 59 solid door frame with 25mm deep rebate

25

54

3mm maximum gap
DOOR FRAME DETAIL

— 45mm deep intermediate rail

— plasterboard lining 9·5mm thick to both faces

— 1½ pairs of steel or brass butt hinges

— 165mm deep lock or middle rail

— lipping to both edges

— 5mm thick fire resistant board to both faces

— 3mm thick plywood facing to both sides

SECTIONAL ELEVATION
NB. intumescent strips in door edges and frame rebate would give above door an enhanced rating ~
see next page.

Glass panel ~ can be included if 6mm thick wired glass with a maximum size of 0·5 m^2 is used. Glass to be fixed with non-combustible beads with a melting point of ≮ 900° C. See also page 842.

Ref. BS 8214: Code of practice for fire door assemblies.

Fire and Smoke Resistance ~ doors can be assessed for both integrity and smoke resistance. They are coded accordingly, for example, FD30 or FD30s. FD indicates a fire door and 30 the integrity time in minutes. The letter 's' denotes that the door or frame contains a facility to resist the passage of smoke.

Manufacturers produce doors of standard ratings – 30, 60 and 90 minutes, with higher ratings available to order. A colour-coded plug inserted in the door edge corresponds to the fire rating. See BS 8214, Table 1 for details.

Intumescent Fire and Smoke Seals ~

intumescent seal with brush smoke barrier

pvc

25 mm minimum
solid rebate = FD60
planted rebate = FD30

45 mm (FD30)
54 mm (FD60)

3 mm maximum

83 × 59 s/w frame (FD30)
92 × 59 s/w frame (FD60)

pvc-coated intumescent seal glued into frame recess

The intumescent core may be fitted to the door edge or the frame. In practice, most joinery manufacturers leave a recess in the frame where the seal is secured with rubber-based or PVA adhesive. At temperatures of about 150°C, the core expands to create a seal around the door edge. This remains throughout the fire-resistance period whilst the door can still be opened for escape and access purposes. The smoke seal will also function as an effective draught seal.

Further refs.:

BS EN 1634-1: Fire resistance and smoke control tests for door, shutter and openable window assemblies and elements of building hardware.

BS EN 13501: Fire classification of construction products and building elements.

Apertures will reduce the potential fire resistance if not appropriately filled. Suitable material should have the same standard of fire performance as the door into which it is fitted.

Fire-rated glass types:

- Embedded Georgian wired glass
- Composite glass containing borosilicates and ceramics
- Tempered and toughened glass
- Glass laminated with reactive fire-resisting interlayers

Installation ~ hardwood beads and intumescent seals. Compatibility of glass type and sealing product is essential, therefore manufacturer's details must be consulted.

intumescent sealant

fire-rated safety glass

bead fixing

hardwood glazing bead

intumescent lining tape

door width and construction as shown on pages 839 to 841

Intumescent products:

- Sealants and mastics 'gun' applied
- Adhesive glazing strip or tape
- Preformed moulded channel

Note: Calcium silicate preformed channel is also available. Woven ceramic fire-glazing tape/ribbon is produced specifically for use in metal frames.

Building Regulations refs.:

A.D. M, Section 3.10, visibility zones/panels between 500 and 1500 mm above floor finish, and A.D. K, Section 10.
A.D. K, Section 5, aperture size (see page 458).

Typical Details ~

ex. 100 x 75 rectangular section
door frame head

ex. 100 x 50
door head

ex. 100 x 50
meeting stiles

edges of door
can be fitted
with draught
excluder with
or without an
intumescent
strip insert

pull
handle

ex. 100 x 75
door jamb
with curved
recess for
rounded edge
of door stile

clear or
wired glass

channel shoe
recessed
flush with
door face

ex. 100 x 50
door stile

ex. 200 x 50
bottom rail

skirting

double action floor spring
loose box sunk into floor

ELEVATION

glazing bead

meeting   stile radius

meeting
stiles

central pivot

glass

3mm max.

door stile

door jamb

SECTION

upper part of top
centre recessed
into head of
door frame

screw to raise
and lower pivot
pin

pivot

pivot pin

springs

lower part of
top centre recessed
into door head

DOUBLE ACTION FLOOR SPRING

TOP CENTRE

843

Plasterboard ~ a rigid board composed of gypsum sandwiched between durable lining paper outer facings. For ceiling applications, the following types can be used:

Baseboard -
1220 × 900 × 9.5mm thick for joist centres up to 400mm.
1220 × 600 × 12.5mm thick for joist centres up to 600mm.

Baseboard has square edges and can be plaster skim finished. Joints are reinforced with self-adhesive 50mm min. width glass fibre mesh scrim tape or the board manufacturer's recommended paper tape. These boards are also made with a metallised polyester foil backing for vapour check applications. The foil is to prevent any moisture produced in potentially damp situations such as a bathroom or in warm roof construction from affecting loft insulation and timber. Joints should be sealed with an adhesive metallised tape.

Wallboard -
9.5, 12.5 and 15mm thicknesses, 900 and 1200mm widths and lengths of 1800 and 2400mm. Longer boards are produced in the two greater thicknesses and a vapour check variation is available. Edges are either tapered for taped and filled joints for dry lining or square for skimmed plaster or textured finishes.

Plasterboards should be fixed breaking joint to the underside of floor or ceiling joists with zinc plated (galvanised) nails or dry-wall screws at 150mm max. spacing. The junction at ceiling to wall is reinforced with glass fibre mesh scrim tape or a preformed plaster moulding.

12.5mm plasterboard

joist →

1-2mm plaster skim finish

100 mm wide scrim tape under ceiling and wall plastered finishes

12.5mm plasterboard ceiling and skimmed plaster finish

cove moulding plaster bonded to background

two-coat plaster to wall

Alternative

Suspended Ceilings ~ these can be defined as ceilings which are fixed to a framework suspended from main structure, thus forming a void between the two components. The basic functional requirements of suspended ceilings are:

1. They should be easy to construct, repair, maintain and clean.
2. So designed that an adequate means of access is provided to the void space for the maintenance of the suspension system, concealed services and/or light fittings.
3. Provide any required sound and/or thermal insulation.
4. Provide any required acoustic control in terms of absorption and reverberation.
5. Provide if required structural fire protection to structural steel beams supporting a concrete floor and contain fire stop cavity barriers within the void at defined intervals.
6. Conform with the minimum requirements set out in the Building Regulations governing the restriction of spread of flame over surfaces of ceilings and the exemptions permitting the use of certain plastic materials.
7. Flexural design strength in varying humidity and temperature.
8. Resistance to impact.
9. Designed on a planning module, preferably a 300 mm dimensional coordinated system.

Typical Suspended Ceiling Grid Framework Layout ~

845

Classification of Suspended Ceiling ~ there is no standard method of classification since some are classified by their function such as illuminated and acoustic suspended ceilings, others are classified by the materials used and classification by method of construction is also very popular. The latter method is simple, since most suspended ceiling types can be placed in one of three groups:

1. Jointless suspended ceilings.
2. Panelled suspended ceilings – see next page.
3. Decorative and open suspended ceilings – see page 848.

Jointless Suspended Ceilings ~ these forms of suspended ceilings provide a continuous and jointless surface with the internal appearance of a conventional ceiling. They may be selected to fulfil fire resistance requirements or to provide a robust form of suspended ceiling. The two common ways of construction are a plasterboard or expanded metal lathing soffit with hand-applied plaster finish or a sprayed applied rendering with a cement base.

Typical Details ~

structural soffit

27 × 57 angle cleats

25 mm wide mild steel strap hangers at 1200 c/c

15 × 45 mild steel channels at 1200 c/c

slotted bolt fixings to provide levelling adjustment

one or two layers of of 900 mm wide × 12·5 mm thick plasterboard screwed to ceiling sections

perimeter channel

80 × 26 pressed steel ceiling sections at 450 c/c

ceiling finish

abutment wall

See also: BS EN 13964: Suspended ceilings. Requirements and test methods.

Panelled Suspended Ceilings ~ these are the most popular form of suspended ceiling consisting of a suspended grid framework to which the ceiling covering is attached. The covering can be of a tile, tray, board or strip format in a wide variety of materials with an exposed or concealed supporting framework. Services such as luminaries can usually be incorporated within the system. Generally panelled systems are easy to assemble and install using a water level or laser beam for initial and final levelling. Provision for maintenance access can be easily incorporated into most systems and layouts.

Typical Support Details ~

Typical Panelled Suspended Ceiling Details ~

847

Decorative and Open Suspended Ceilings ~ these ceilings usually consist of an openwork grid or suspended shapes onto which the lights fixed at, above or below ceiling level can be trained, thus creating a decorative and illuminated effect. Many of these ceilings are purpose designed and built as opposed to the proprietary systems associated with jointless and panelled suspended ceilings.

Typical Examples ~

Separating floor construction for sound insulation purposes. References: Robust Details, see page 67 and Building Regulations, Approved Document E: Resistance to the passage of sound.

- screed
- 6 mm synthetic rubber
- 150 mm min. in-situ or pcc floor, 365 kg/m^2
- self-adhesive rubber sealing strip
- hangers, channels and ceiling sections as shown on page 846
- mineral fibre thermal insulation quilt
- self-adhesive rubber sealing strip
- 12.5 mm plaster board

Alternative Finish with Floating Deck ~

- 18 mm min. moisture resistant chipboard
- 6 mm synthetic rubber
- screed over structural concrete

Further Building Regulations References ~

Approved Document B: Fire safety, Volumes 1 and 2 – Fire resisting cavity barriers in concealed spaces. Located at compartmented divisions within a building (see page 18), otherwise at a maximum spacing that will depend on the situation, building type and its function. Minimum fire resistance is 30 minutes but often more depending on the building use and purpose.

Approved Document L: Conservation of fuel and power – thermal insulation requirements.

Functions ~ the main functions of paint are to provide:

1. An economical method of surface protection to building materials and components.
2. An economical method of surface decoration to building materials and components.

Composition ~ the actual composition of any paint can be complex but the basic components are:

1. Binder ~ this is the liquid vehicle or medium which dries to form the surface film and can be composed of linseed oil, drying oils, synthetic resins or water. The first function of a paint medium is to provide a means of spreading the paint over the surface and at the same time acting as a binder to the pigment.
2. Pigment ~ this provides the body, colour, durability, opacity and corrosion protection properties of the paint. The general pigment used in paint is titanium dioxide which gives good obliteration of the undercoats. Other pigments include carbon black and iron oxide.
3. Solvents and Thinners ~ these are materials which can be added to a paint to alter its viscosity. This increases workability and penetration. Water is used for emulsion paint and white spirit or turpentine for oil paint.
4. Drier ~ accelerates drying by absorbing oxygen from the air and converting by oxidation to a solid. Soluble metals in linseed oil or white spirit.

Paint Types – there is a wide range available but for most general uses the following can be considered:

1. Oil-based Paints – these are available in priming, undercoat and finishing grades. The latter can be obtained in a wide range of colours and finishes such as matt, semi-matt, eggshell, satin, gloss and enamel. Polyurethane paints have a good hardness and resistance to water and cleaning. Oil-based paints are suitable for most applications if used in conjunction with correct primer and undercoat.
2. Water-based Paints – most of these are called emulsion paints, the various finishes available being obtained by adding to the water medium additives such as alkyd resin and polyvinyl acetate (PVA). Finishes include matt, eggshell, semi-gloss and gloss. Emulsion paints are easily applied, quick drying and can be obtained with a washable finish and are suitable for most applications.

Supply ~ paint is usually supplied in metal containers ranging from 250 millilitres to 5 litres capacity to the colour ranges recommended in BS 381C (colours for specific purposes) and BS 4800 (paint colours for building purposes).

Application ~ paint can be applied to almost any surface providing the surface preparation and sequence of paint coats are suitable. The manufacturer's specification and/or the recommendations of BS 6150 (painting of buildings) should be followed. Preparation of the surface to receive the paint is of the utmost importance, since poor preparation is one of the chief causes of paint failure. The preparation consists basically of removing all dirt, grease, dust and ensuring that the surface will provide an adequate key for the paint which is to be applied. In new work the basic buildup of paint coats consists of:

1. Priming Coats – these are used on unpainted surfaces to obtain the necessary adhesion and to inhibit corrosion of ferrous metals. New timber should have the knots treated with a solution of shellac or other alcohol-based resin called knotting prior to the application of the primer.
2. Undercoats – these are used on top of the primer after any defects have been made good with a suitable stopper or filler. The primary function of an undercoat is to give the opacity and buildup necessary for the application of the finishing coat(s).
3. Finish – applied directly over the undercoating in one or more coats to impart the required colour and finish.

Paint can applied by:

1. Brush – the correct type, size and quality of brush such as those recommended in BS 2992 (painters' and decorators' brushes) needs to be selected and used. To achieve a first class finish by means of brush application requires a high degree of skill.
2. Spray – as with brush application a high degree of skill is required to achieve a good finish. Generally compressed air sprays or airless sprays are used for building works.
3. Roller – simple and inexpensive method of quickly and cleanly applying a wide range of paints to flat and textured surfaces. Roller heads vary in size from 50 to 450 mm wide with various covers such as sheepskin, synthetic pile fibres, mohair and foamed polystyrene. All paint applicators must be thoroughly cleaned after use.

Painting ~ the main objectives of applying coats of paint to a surface are preservation, protection and decoration to give a finish which is easy to clean and maintain. To achieve these objectives the surface preparation and paint application must be adequate. The preparation of new and previously painted surfaces should ensure that prior to painting the surface is smooth, clean, dry and stable.

Basic Surface Preparation Techniques ~

Timber – to ensure a good adhesion of the paint film all timber should have a moisture content of less than 18%. The timber surface should be prepared using an abrasive paper to produce a smooth surface brushed and wiped free of dust and any grease removed with a suitable spirit. Careful treatment of knots is essential either by sealing with two coats of knotting or in extreme cases cutting out the knot and replacing with sound timber. The stopping and filling of cracks and fixing holes with putty or an appropriate filler should be carried out after the application of the priming coat. Each coat of paint must be allowed to dry hard and be rubbed down with a fine abrasive paper before applying the next coat. On previously painted surfaces if the paint is in a reasonable condition the surface will only require cleaning and rubbing down before repainting; when the paint is in a poor condition it will be necessary to remove completely the layers of paint and then prepare the surface as described above for new timber.

Building Boards – most of these boards require no special preparation except for the application of a sealer as specified by the manufacturer.

Iron and Steel – good preparation is the key to painting iron and steel successfully and this will include removing all rust, mill scale, oil, grease and wax. This can be achieved by wire brushing, using mechanical means such as shot blasting, flame cleaning and chemical processes and any of these processes are often carried out in the steel fabrication works prior to shop-applied priming.

Plaster – the essential requirement of the preparation is to ensure that the plaster surface is perfectly dry, smooth and free of defects before applying any coats of paint, especially when using gloss paints. Plaster which contains lime can be alkaline and such surfaces should be treated with an alkali-resistant primer when the surface is dry before applying the final coats of paint.

Paint Defects ~ these may be due to poor or incorrect preparation of the surface, poor application of the paint and/or chemical reactions. The general remedy is to remove all the affected paint and carry out the correct preparation of the surface before applying new coats of paint in the correct manner. Most paint defects are visual and therefore an accurate diagnosis of the cause must be established before any remedial treatment is undertaken.

Typical paint defects:

1. Bleeding – staining and disruption of the paint surface by chemical action, usually caused by applying an incorrect paint over another. Remedy is to remove affected paint surface and repaint with correct type of overcoat paint.

2. Blistering – usually caused by poor presentation allowing resin or moisture to be entrapped, the subsequent expansion causing the defect. Remedy is to remove all the coats of paint and ensure that the surface is dry before repainting.

3. Blooming – mistiness usually on high gloss or varnished surfaces due to the presence of moisture during application. It can be avoided by not painting under these conditions. Remedy is to remove affected paint and repaint.

4. Chalking – powdering of the paint surface due to natural ageing or the use of poor-quality paint. Remedy is to remove paint if necessary, prepare surface and repaint.

5. Cracking and Crazing – usually due to unequal elasticity of successive coats of paint. Remedy is to remove affected paint and repaint with compatible coats of paint.

6. Flaking and Peeling – can be due to poor adhesion, presence of moisture, painting over unclean areas or poor preparation. Remedy is to remove defective paint, prepare surface and repaint.

7. Grinning – due to poor opacity of paint film allowing paint coat below or background to show through, could be the result of poor application, incorrect thinning or the use of the wrong colour. Remedy is to apply further coats of paint to obtain a satisfactory surface.

8. Saponification – formation of soap from alkali present in or on surface painted. The paint is ultimately destroyed and a brown liquid appears on the surface. Remedy is to remove the paint films and seal the alkaline surface before repainting.

Joinery Production ~ this can vary from the flow production where one product such as flush doors is being made usually with the aid of purpose-designed and built machines, to batch production where a limited number of similar items are being made with the aid of conventional woodworking machines. Purpose-made joinery is very often largely handmade with a limited use of machines and is considered when special and/or high-class joinery components are required.

Woodworking Machines ~ except for the portable electric tools such as drills, routers, jigsaws and sanders most woodworking machines need to be fixed to a solid base and connected to an extractor system to extract and collect the sawdust and chippings produced by the machines.

Saws – basically three formats are available, namely the circular, cross-cut and band saws. Circular saws are general-purpose saws and usually have tungsten carbide tipped teeth with feed rates of up to 60·000 per minute. Cross-cut saws usually have a long bench to support the timber, the saw being mounted on a radial arm enabling the circular saw to be drawn across the timber to be cut. Band saws consist of an endless thin band or blade with saw teeth and a table on which to support the timber and are generally used for curved work.

Planers – most of these machines are combined planers and thicknessers, the timber being passed over the table surface for planing and the table or bed for thicknessing. The planer has a guide fence which can be tilted for angle planning and usually the rear bed can be lowered for rebating operations. The same rotating cutter block is used for all operations. Planing speeds are dependent upon the operator since it is a hand-fed operation whereas thicknessing is mechanically fed with a feed speed range of 6·000 to 20·000 per minute. Maximum planing depth is usually 10 mm per passing.

Morticing Machines – these are used to cut mortices up to 25 mm wide and can be either a chisel or chain morticer. The former consists of a hollow chisel containing a bit or auger whereas the latter has an endless chain cutter.

Tenoning Machines – these machines with their rotary cutter blocks can be set to form tenon and scribe. In most cases they can also be set for trenching, grooving and cross-cutting.

Spindle Moulder – this machine has a horizontally rotating cutter block into which standard or purpose-made cutters are fixed to reproduce a moulding on timber passed across the cutter.

Purpose-made Joinery ~ joinery items in the form of doors, windows, stairs and cupboard fitments can be purchased as stock items from manufacturers. There is also a need for purpose-made joinery to fulfil client/designer/user requirements to suit a specific need, to fit into a non-standard space, as a specific decor requirement or to complement a particular internal environment. These purpose-made joinery items can range from the simple to the complex which require high degrees of workshop and site skills.

Typical Purpose-made Counter Details ~

2·700

900

block board counter top with veneer, leather or similar finish

veneer band

timber band

veneer faced panels

kicking rail

ELEVATION

hardwood edging

920

counter top

hardwood edging

50

drawer with runners housed in sides

frame with projecting hardwood band

blockboard shelf

veneer faced blockboard front panels

swing or sliding doors could be fitted to cupboards

900

800

blockboard base

100

50

kicking rail with durable facing in a contrasting colour (e.g. black laminate)

SECTION

Typical Purpose-made Wall Panelling Details ~

ELEVATION

- cornice
- frieze
- capping
- stile
- flat panel
- framing rail
- dado rail
- raised dado panel
- skirting

3·300
2·100
300
900

20 mm thick softwood ground

20 mm thick softwood grounds

backing wall

20 mm thick softwood ground

40 mm thick soldiers

SECTION

- 75 × 75 cornice moulding
- 20 mm thick flat frieze
- 90 × 75 moulded capping
- 50 × 65 bolection moulding
- 12 mm thick flat panel
- 40 mm thick panel framing
- 35 × 75 moulded dado rail
- 40 mm thick raised and fielded dado panels

NB. all panelling to be in selected hardwoods.

- 40 mm thick moulded skirting
- 25 × 25 floor fillet

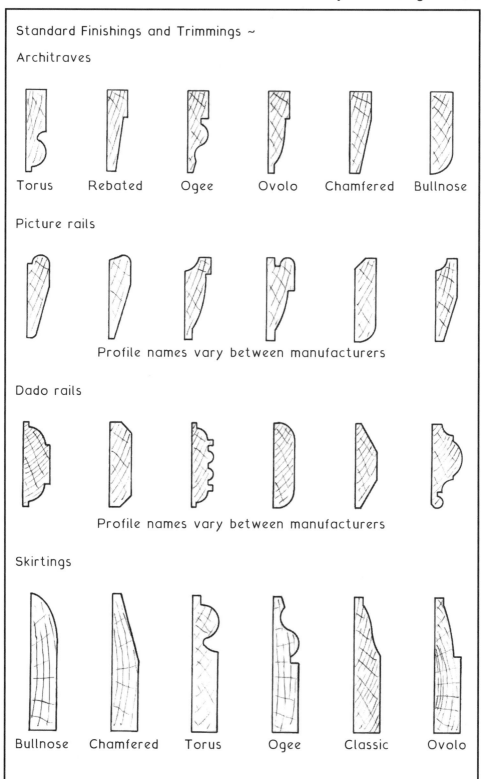

Standard Finishings and Trimmings ~

Architraves

Torus   Rebated   Ogee   Ovolo   Chamfered   Bullnose

Picture rails

Profile names vary between manufacturers

Dado rails

Profile names vary between manufacturers

Skirtings

Bullnose   Chamfered   Torus   Ogee   Classic   Ovolo

Joinery Timbers ~ both hardwoods and softwoods can be used for joinery works. Softwoods can be selected for their stability, durability and/or workability if the finish is to be paint but if it is left in its natural colour with a sealing coat the grain texture and appearance should be taken into consideration. Hardwoods are usually left in their natural colour and treated with a protective clear sealer or polish; therefore texture, colour and grain pattern are important when selecting hardwoods for high-class joinery work.

Typical softwoods suitable for joinery work:

1. Douglas Fir – sometimes referred to as Columbian Pine or Oregon Pine. It is available in long lengths and has a straight grain. Colour is reddish-brown to pink. Suitable for general and high-class joinery. Approximate density 530 kg/m^3.

2. Redwood – also known as Scots Pine. Red Pine, Red Deal and Yellow Deal. It is a widely used softwood for general joinery work having good durability, a straight grain and is reddish-brown to straw in colour. Approximate density 430 kg/m^3.

3. European Spruce – similar to redwood but with a lower durability. It is pale yellow to pinkish-white in colour and is used mainly for basic framing work and simple internal joinery. Approximate density 650 kg/m^3.

4. Sitka Spruce – originates from Alaska, Western Canada and Northwest USA. The long, white strong fibres provide a timber quality for use in board or plywood panels. Approximate density 450 kg/m^3.

5. Pitch Pine – durable softwood suitable for general joinery work. It is light red to reddish-yellow in colour and tends to have large knots which in some cases can be used as a decorative effect. Approximate density 650 kg/m^3.

6. Parana Pine – moderately durable straight grained timber available in a good range of sizes. Suitable for general joinery work especially timber stairs. Light to dark brown in colour with the occasional pink stripe. Approximate density 560 kg/m^3.

7. Western Hemlock – durable softwood suitable for interior joinery work such as panelling. Light yellow to reddish-brown in colour. Approximate density 500 kg/m^3.

8. Western Red Cedar – originates from British Columbia and Western USA. A straight grained timber suitable for flush doors and panel work. Approximate density 380kg/m^3.

Typical hardwoods suitable for joinery works:

1. Beech – hard close grained timber with some silver grain in the predominately reddish-yellow to light brown colour. Suitable for all internal joinery. Approximately density 700 kg/m^3.

2. Iroko – hard durable hardwood with a figured grain and is usually golden brown in colour. Suitable for all forms of high-class joinery. Approximate density 660 kg/m^3.

3. Mahogany (African) – interlocking grained hardwood with good durability. It has an attractive light brown to deep red colour and is suitable for panelling and all high-class joinery work. Approximate density 560 kg/m^3.

4. Mahogany (Honduras) – durable hardwood usually straight grained but can have a mottled or swirl pattern. It is light red to pale reddish-brown in colour and is suitable for all high-class joinery work. Approximate density 530 kg/m^3.

5. Mahogany (South American) – a well-figured, stable and durable hardwood with a deep-red or brown colour which is suitable for all high-class joinery particularly where a high polish is required. Approximate density 550 kg/m^3.

6. Oak (English) – very durable hardwood with a wide variety of grain patterns. It is usually a light yellow brown to a warm brown in colour and is suitable for all forms of joinery but should not be used in conjunction with ferrous metals due to the risk of staining caused by an interaction of the two materials. (The gallic acid in oak causes corrosion in ferrous metals.) Approximate density 720 kg/m^3.

7. Sapele – close texture timber of good durability, dark reddish-brown in colour with a varied grain pattern. It is suitable for most internal joinery work especially where a polished finish is required. Approximate density 640 kg/m^3.

8. Teak – very strong and durable timber but hard to work. It is light golden brown to dark golden yellow in colour which darkens with age and is suitable for high-class joinery work and laboratory fittings. Approximate density 650 kg/m^3.

9. Jarrah (Western Australia) – hard, dense, straight grained timber. Dull red colour, suited to floor and stair construction subjected to heavy wear. Approximate density 820 kg/m^3.

859

Composite Boards ~ factory-manufactured, performed sheets with a wide range of properties and applications. The most common size is 2440 × 1220 mm or 2400 × 1200 mm in thicknesses from 3 to 50 mm.

1. Plywood (BS EN 636) – produced in a range of laminated thicknesses from 3 to 25 mm, with the grain of each layer normally at right angles to that adjacent. 3,7,9 or 11 plies make up the overall thickness and inner layers may have lower strength and different dimensions to those in the outer layers. Adhesives vary considerably from natural vegetable and animal glues to synthetics such as urea, melamine, phenol and resorcinol formaldehydes. Quality of laminates and type of adhesive determine application. Surface finishes include plastics, decorative hardwood veneers, metals, rubber and mineral aggregates.

2. Block and Stripboards (BS EN 12871) – range from 12 to 43 mm thickness, made up from a solid core of glued softwood strips with a surface-enhancing veneer. Appropriate for dense panelling and doors.

   Battenboard – strips over 30 mm wide (unsuitable for joinery).
   Blockboard – strips up to 25 mm wide.
   Laminboard – strips up to 7 mm wide.

3. Compressed Strawboard (BS 4046) – produced by compacting straw under heat and pressure, and edge binding with paper. Used as panels with direct decoration or as partitioning with framed support. Also for insulated roof decking with 58 mm slabs spanning 600 mm joist spacing.

4. Particle Board

Chipboard (BS EN 319) – bonded waste wood or chip particles in thicknesses from 6 to 50 mm, popularly used for floors in 18 and 22 mm at 450 and 600 mm maximum joist spacing, respectively. Sheets are produced by heat pressing the particles in thermosetting resins.

Wood Cement Board – approximately 25% wood particles mixed with water and cement, to produce a heavy and dense board often preferred to plasterboard and fibre cement for fire cladding. Often three-layer boards, from 6 to 40 mm in thickness.

Oriented Strand Board (BS EN 300) – composed of wafer thin strands of wood, approximately 80 mm long × 25 m wide, resin bonded and directionally oriented before superimposed by further layers. Each layer is at right angles to adjacent layers, similar to the structure of plywood. A popular alternative for wall panels, floors and other chipboard and plywood applications, they are produced in a range of thicknesses from 6 to 25 mm.

5. Fibreboards (BS EN 622-4) – basically wood in composition, reduced to a pulp and pressed to achieve three categories:

Hardboard density at least 800 kg/m^3 in thicknesses from 3·2 to 8 mm. Provides an excellent base for coatings and laminated finishes.

Mediumboard (low density) 350 to 560 kg/m^3 for pinboards and wall linings in thicknesses of 6·4,9, and 12·7 mm.

Mediumboard (high density) 560 to 800 kg/m^3 for linings and partitions in thicknesses of 9 and 12 mm.

Softboard, otherwise known as insulating board with density usually below 250 kg/m^3. Thicknesses from 9 to 25 mm, often found impregnated with bitumen in existing flat roofing applications. Ideal as pinboard.

Medium Density Fibreboard, differs from other fibreboards with the addition of resin bonding agent. These boards have a very smooth surface, ideal for painting, and are available moulded for a variety of joinery applications. Density exceeds 600 kg/m^3 and common board thicknesses are 9, 12, 18 and 25 mm for internal and external applications.

6. Woodwool (BS EN 13168) – units of 600 mm width are available in 50, 75 and 100 mm thicknesses. They comprise long wood shavings coated with a cement slurry, compressed to leave a high proportion of voids. These voids provide good thermal insulation and sound absorption. The perforated surface is an ideal key for direct plastering and they are frequently specified as permanent formwork.

Plastics ~ the term plastic can be applied to any group of substances based on synthetic or modified natural polymers which during manufacture are moulded by heat and/or pressure into the required form. Plastics can be classified by their overall grouping such as polyvinyl chloride (PVC) or they can be classified as thermoplastic or thermosetting. The former soften on heating whereas the latter are formed into permanent non-softening materials. The range of plastics available give the designer and builder a group of materials which are strong, reasonably durable, easy to fit and maintain and since most are mass produced of relative low cost.

Typical Applications of Plastics in Buildings ~

Application	Plastics used
Rainwater goods	unplasticised PVC (uPVC or PVC–U).
Soil, waste, water and gas pipes and fittings	uPVC; polyethylene (PE); acrylonitrile butadiene styrene (ABS), polypropylene (PP).
Hot and cold water pipes	chlorinated PVC; ABS; polypropylene; polyethylene; PVC (not for hot water).
Bathroom and kitchen fittings	glass-fibre reinforced polyester (GRP); acrylic resins.
Cold water cisterns	polypropylene; polystyrene; polyethylene.
Rooflights and sheets	GRP; acrylic resins; uPVC.
DPCs and membranes, vapour control layers	low-density polyethylene (LDPE); PVC film; polypropylene.
Doors and windows	GRP; uPVC.
Electrical conduit and fittings	plasticised PVC; uPVC; phenolic resins.
Thermal insulation	generally cellular plastics such as expanded polystyrene bead and boards; expanded PVC; foamed polyurethane; foamed phenol formaldehyde; foamed urea formaldehyde.
Floor finishes	plasticised PVC tiles and sheets; resin-based floor paints; uPVC.
Wall claddings and internal linings	unplasticised PVC; polyvinyl fluoride film laminate; melamine resins; expanded polystyrene tiles and sheets.

Uses ~ to weather- and leak-proof junctions and abutments between separate elements and components that may be subject to differential movement. Also to gap fill where irregularities occur.

Properties:

• thermal movement to facilitate expansion and contraction
• strength to resist wind and other non-structural loading
• ability to accommodate tolerance variations
• stability without loss of shape
• colour fast and non-staining to adjacent finishes
• weather resistant

Maintenance ~ of limited life, perhaps 10 to 25 years depending on composition, application and use. Future accessibility is important for ease of removal and replacement.

Mastics ~ generally regarded as non-setting gap fillers applied in a plastic state. Characterised by a hard surface skin over a plastic core that remains pliable for several years. Based on a viscous material such as bitumen, polyisobutylene or butyl rubber. Applications include bitumen treatment to rigid road construction joints (page 167) and linseed oil putty glazing (page 449). In older construction, a putty-based joint may also be found between WC pan spigot outlet and cast iron socket. In this situation the putty was mixed with red lead pigments (oxides of lead), a material now considered a hazardous poison, therefore protective care must be taken when handling an old installation of this type. Modern push-fit plastic joints are much simpler, safer to use and easier to apply.

Sealants ~ applied in a plastic state by hand, knife, disposable cartridge gun, pouring or tape strip to convert by chemical reaction with the atmosphere (one part) or with a vulcanising additive (two part) into an elastomer or synthetic rubber. An elastomer is generally defined as a natural or synthetic material with a high strain capacity or elastic recovery, i.e. it can be stretched to twice its length before returning to its original length.

Formed of polysulphide rubber, polyurethane, silicone or some butyl rubbers.

Applications:
- Polysulphide ~ façades, glazing, fire protection, roads and paving joints. High modulus or hardness but not completely elastic.
- Polyurethane ~ general uses, façades and civil engineering. Highly elastic and resilient to abrasion and indentation, moderate resistance to ultraviolet light and chemicals.
- Silicone ~ general uses, façades, glazing, sanitary, fire protection and civil engineering. Mainly one part but set quickly relative to others in this category. Highly elastic and available as high (hard) or low (soft) modulus.

Two part ~ polysulphide- and polyurethane-based sealants are often used with a curing or vulcanising additive to form a synthetic rubber on setting. After the two parts are mixed the resulting sealant remains workable for up to about four hours. It remains plastic for a few days and during this time cannot take any significant loading. Thereafter it has exceptional resistance to compression and shear.

One part ~ otherwise known as room temperature vulcanising (RTV) types that are usually of a polysulphide, polyurethane or silicone base. Polysulphide and polyurethane cure slowly and convert to a synthetic rubber or elastomer sealant by chemical reaction with moisture in the atmosphere. Generally of less movement and loading resistance to two part sealants, but are frequently used in non-structural situations such as sealing around door and window frames, bathroom and kitchen fitments.

Other sealants:
- One part acrylic (water-based) RTV. Flexible but with limited elasticity. Internal uses such as sealing around door and window frames, fire protection and internal glazing.
- Silane modified polymer in one part RTV or two parts. Highly elastic and can be used for general applications as well as for façades and civil engineering situations.

Prior to 2003, several separate British Standards existed to provide use and application guidance for a range of sealant products. As independent publications these are now largely superseded, their content rationalised and incorporated into the current standard, BS EN ISO 11600: Building construction. Jointing products. Classification and requirements for sealants.

This International Standard covers materials application to jointing, classification of materials, quality grading and performance testing. This enables specific definition of a sealant's requirements in terms of end use without having to understand the chemical properties of the various sealant types. Typical criteria are movement potential, elasticity and hardness when related to particular substrate surfaces such as aluminium, glass or masonry.

Grading summary ~

BS EN ISO 11600 G, for use in glazing.
BS EN ISO 11600 F, for façade and similar applications such as movement joints.

Other suffixes or sub-classes ~

E = elastic sealant, i.e. high elastic recovery or elastomeric.
P = plastic sealant, i.e. low elastic recovery.
HM = high modulus, indicates hardness.*
LM = low modulus, indicates softness.*
*By definition HM and LM are high movement (20–25%) types of elastic sealants, therefore the suffix E is not shown with these.

Associated standards ~

BS EN ISO 6927: Buildings and civil engineering works. Sealants. Vocabulary.
BS 6213: Selection of construction sealants. Guide.
BS 6093: Design of joints and jointing in building construction. Guide.

Notes

8 DOMESTIC SERVICES

DRAINAGE EFFLUENTS

SUBSOIL DRAINAGE

SURFACE WATER REMOVAL

ROAD DRAINAGE

RAINWATER INSTALLATIONS

DRAINAGE SYSTEMS

DRAINAGE PIPE SIZES AND GRADIENTS

WATER SUPPLY

COLD WATER INSTALLATIONS

HOT WATER INSTALLATIONS

CISTERNS AND CYLINDERS

SANITARY FITTINGS

SINGLE AND VENTILATED STACK SYSTEMS

DOMESTIC HOT WATER HEATING SYSTEMS

ELECTRICAL SUPPLY AND INSTALLATION

GAS SUPPLY AND GAS FIRES

OPEN FIREPLACES AND FLUES

SERVICES – FIRE STOPS AND SEALS

TELEPHONE AND ELECTRONIC COMMUNICATIONS
INSTALLATIONS

Drainage Effluents

Effluent ~ can be defined as that which flows out. In building drainage terms there are three main forms of effluent:

1. Subsoil Water ~ water collected by means of special drains from the earth primarily to lower the water table level in the subsoil. It is considered to be clean and therefore requires no treatment and can be discharged direct into an approved water course.

2. Surface Water ~ effluent collected from surfaces such as roofs and paved areas and like subsoil water is considered to be clean and can be discharged direct into an approved water course or soakaway ~

3. Foul or Soil Water ~ effluent contaminated by domestic or trade waste and will require treatment to render it clean before it can be discharged into an approved water course.

Subsoil Drainage ~ Building Regulation C2 requires that subsoil drainage shall be provided if it is needed to avoid:

(a) the passage of ground moisture into the interior of the building or

(b) damage to the fabric of the building.

Subsoil drainage can also be used to improve the stability of the ground, lower the humidity of the site and enhance its horticultural properties. Subsoil drains consist of porous or perforated pipes laid dry jointed in a rubble-filled trench. Porous pipes allow the subsoil water to pass through the body of the pipe whereas perforated pipes which have a series of holes in the lower half allow the subsoil water to rise into the pipe. This form of ground water control is only economical up to a depth of 1·500. If the water table needs to be lowered to a greater depth other methods of ground water control should be considered (see pages 354 to 358).

The water collected by a subsoil drainage system has to be conveyed to a suitable outfall such as a river, lake or surface water drain or sewer. In all cases permission to discharge the subsoil water will be required from the authority or owner and in the case of streams, rivers and lakes, bank protection at the outfall may be required to prevent erosion (see next page).

Typical Subsoil Drain Details ~

Subsoil Drainage Systems ~ the layout of subsoil drains will depend on whether it is necessary to drain the whole site or if it is only the substructure of the building which needs to be protected. The latter is carried out by installing a cut off drain around the substructure to intercept the flow of water and divert it away from the site of the building. Junctions in a subsoil drainage system can be made using standard fittings or by placing the end of the branch drain onto the crown of the main drain.

Typical Examples ~

branch drains ─┐   branch drains ─┐   site boundary ─┐

HERRINGBONE   GRID IRON   MOAT or CUT-OFF

├─main drain   ├─main drain   │ to outfall

branch drains ─ spacing 6·000 to 10·000
                maximum length 30·000

TYPICAL OUTFALL DETAILS ~

dry jointed   retaining wall in   ─ river bank
subsoil   engineering bricks,
drain ─   min. 'severe' exposure   direction
                 to BS EN 771-1   of flow

direction   ─ concrete
of flow   last 3·000 to 5·000   slab
                 laid as surface water
                 drain to prevent marshlike
                 conditions at outfall

NB. Connections to surface water sewer can be made at inspection chamber or direct to the sewer using a saddle connector – it may be necessary to have a catchpit to trap any silt (see page 876).

General Principles ~ a roof must be designed with a suitable fall towards the surface water collection channel or gutter which in turn is connected to vertical rainwater pipes which convey the collected discharge to the drainage system. The fall of the roof will be determined by the chosen roof covering or the chosen pitch will limit the range of coverings which can be selected.

pitched roof

ridge

eaves gutter~ recommended minimum fall 1:360

fall

eaves

verge

roofing felt should extend into and below top of gutter to prevent water from being blown into eaves

rainwater pipe - can be fitted internally or externally, if internal it must have leak-proof joints

final discharge can be:

rainwater pipes and gullies must be arranged so as not to cause dampness or damage to any part of the building

Minimum Roof Pitches ~

Slates — depends on width from 25°

Handmade plain tiles — 45°

Machine made plain tiles — 35°

Single lap and interlocking tiles - depends on type from 12½°

Thatch — 45°

Timber shingles — 14°

1. Direct connection to a drain discharging into a soakaway

2. Direct connection to a drain discharging into a surface water sewer

3. Indirect connection to a drain by means of a trapped gully if drain discharges into a combined sewer

See page 879 for details.

flat roof

water check to verge

roof covering dressed into gutter

verge

eaves

fascia

fall

eaves gutter

rainwater pipe

Rainwater pipe final discharge **as given on** previous page

Minimum Recommended Falls for Various Finishes ~
Aluminium — 1:60   Lead — 1:120   Copper — 1:60
Built-up roofing felts — 1:60   Mastic asphalt — 1:80

pitched roof

minimum clear width 300mm to allow for cleaning

parapet

gutter laid to falls

rainwater head

alternative outlet

rainwater pipe

converging pitched roofs forming a valley

minimum clear width 300mm to allow for cleaning

gutter laid to falls

outlet

PARAPET GUTTER

gutter formed to discharge into internal rainwater pipes or to external rainwater pipes via outlets through the parapet

VALLEY GUTTER

gutter formed to discharge into internal rainwater pipes or to external rainwater pipes sited at the gable ends

paving drains away from building

paved area laid to falls of 1:60

yard gully — to be trapped with a 50mm minimum water seal if connected to a combined sewer

maximum paved area per gully = 400 m²

number and size of gullies governed by area being drained and/or shape of paved area

YARD GULLY COLLECTION

paving drains away from building

paved area laid to falls of 1:60

channel laid to falls of 1:120 and connected to drainage system with a trapped gully if it is a combined sewer outlet

maximum paved area per gully = 400 m²

number and size of channels governed by area being drained and/or shape of paved area

CHANNEL COLLECTION

could have grating cover

half-round glazed clayware open channel

continuous slot

precast concrete channel blocks

cast iron square mesh grating

precast or in-situ concrete box channel

Sustainable Drainage Systems (SuDS) otherwise known as Sustainable Urban Drainage Systems (SUDS) cover a variety of applications that are designed to regulate surface water run-off. Their purpose is to control the level of water in the ground during periods of intense rainfall, thereby reducing the risk of flooding.

Problem ~ growth in urbanisation, increase in population, density of development, extreme weather, global warming and climate change are some of the factors that contribute to a rise in ground water table levels and higher volumes of surface water run-off.

Solution ~ before developing land and undertaking major refurbishment projects, it is necessary to design a surface and ground water control system that relieves potential concentrations of rainwater. This should replicate or improve the natural site drainage that existed before groundworks (foundations, basements, etc.) disturb the subgrade.

Applications ~ installation systems that manage surface water by attenuation and filtration as required by the Flood Water Management Act. Measures may include site treatment, containment and rainwater harvesting (see Building Services Handbook) before surface water can be discharged into surface water sewers. SUDS controls such as swales and retention ponds are another option, but space for these is limited or non-existent in urban situations.

Objectives ~

• Improved amenity.
• Improved water resource quality.
• Reduced exposure to flooding.
• Minimised dispersal through foul water drainage systems.
• Regulated natural flow conditions.

Refs.:

• Flood Water Management Act ~ establishes a SuDS approval body (SAB) and amends the automatic right to connect surface water drains to a public surface water sewer, connection subject to conditional standards.
• Building Services Handbook, Part 8 — F. Hall and R. Greeno (Routledge).

Concrete Block Permeable Paving (CBPP) ~ unlike traditional impermeable surfaces that direct surface water to drainage channels and pipes, CBPP filters and removes pollutants before dispersal. Hydrocarbons are degraded and digested by naturally occurring microbes in the sub-base, therefore oil interceptors are not required. Silt traps are also not needed as the system retains silt. Block pavers filter and clean surface water before it is accommodated in the sub-base and slowly released into the ground. In less naturally draining subsoils the retained water percolates into perforated drainage pipes before flowing on to a drainage discharge system.

Permeable Block Paving Installations (see also page 168) ~

surface water filters through sand filled joints

level surface

upper permeable geotextile membrane

lower permeable geotextile membrane

Subgrades of good drainage medium

CBPP, Ref. BS EN 1338: Concrete paving blocks

consolidated hardcore permeable sub-base

perforated drainage pipe

Subgrades composed of material with limited drainage

50 to 75 mm bed of sharp sand

impervious flexible membrane/tanking

Subgrades of no capacity for infiltration

Highway Drainage ~ the stability of a highway or road relies on two factors:

1. Strength and durability of upper surface.
2. Strength and durability of subgrade which is the subsoil on which the highway construction is laid.

The above can be adversely affected by water; therefore it may be necessary to install two drainage systems. One system (subsoil drainage) to reduce the flow of subsoil water through the subgrade under the highway construction and a system of surface water drainage.

Typical Highway Subsoil Drainage Methods ~

Subsoil Drain - acts as a cut off drain and can be formed using perforated or porous drainpipes. If filled with rubble only it is usually called a French or rubble drain.

Open Ditch - acts as a cut off drain and could also be used to collect surface water discharged from a rural road where there is no raised kerb or surface water drains.

Surface Water Drainage Systems ~

Road Drainage ~ this consists of laying the paved area or road to a suitable crossfall or gradient to direct the run-off of surface water towards the drainage channel or gutter. This is usually bounded by a kerb which helps to convey the water to the road gullies which are connected to a surface water sewer. For drains or sewers under 900 mm internal diameter inspection chambers will be required as set out in the Building Regulations. The actual spacing of road gullies is usually determined by the local highway authority based upon the carriageway gradient and the area to be drained into one road gully. Alternatively the following formula could be used:

$$D = \frac{280\sqrt{S}}{W}$$

where D = gully spacing
S = carriageway gradient (per cent)
W = width of carriageway in metres

∴ If S = 1:60 = 1·66% and W = 4·500

$$D = \frac{280\sqrt{1\cdot66}}{4\cdot500} = \text{say } 80\cdot000$$

Typical Road Gully Detail ~

- carriageway paving
- cast iron road gully grating and frame
- footpath (see Roads – Footpaths on page 168)
- drainage channel (fall 1:200)
- 300 × 150 precast concrete kerb
- levelling brick course
- kerb foundation strip
- branch drain to surface water sewer
- stopper
- 85 min.
- sump
- 100 or 150 mm dia. outlet
- 150 mm thick mass concrete surround
- precast concrete or clayware road gully

Materials ~ the traditional material for domestic eaves gutters and rainwater pipes is cast iron but uPVC systems are very often specified today because of their simple installation and low maintenance costs. Other materials which could be considered are aluminium alloy, galvanised steel and stainless steel, but whatever material is chosen it must be of adequate size, strength and durability.

Typical Eaves Details ~

half round gutter - other profiles are ogee and box

stop end

gutter support bracket — outlet spigot

pitched roof covered with plain tiles

half round gutter

half round gutter

external wall

fascia fixing gutter brackets

rafter fixing gutter brackets

112° offset or swan neck

112° offset or swan neck

rainwater pipe

rainwater pipe

CLOSED EAVES

OPEN EAVES

For details of rainwater pipe connection to drainage see next page.

Note: Details show established construction with a block cavity closer course. New construction to have insulation continuity to prevent cold bridging. See page 507.

pipe clip, holderbat or spigot with projecting ears

rainwater pipe

sealed access cover

ground level

drain coupling

drain to surface water sewer or soakaway

mass concrete bed

external wall

ground floor

rainwater shoe

pipe clip, holderbat or spigot with projecting ears

rainwater pipe

sealed access cover to gully with 50mm minimum water seal

ground level

drain coupling

drain to combined sewer

mass concrete bed

external wall

ground floor

NB. For details of rainwater pipe connection to gutter see previous page.

Soakaways ~ provide a means for collecting and controlling the seepage of rainwater into surrounding granular subsoils. They are not suitable in clay subsoils. Siting is on land at least level and preferably lower than adjacent buildings and no closer than 5m to a building. Concentration of a large volume of water any closer could undermine the foundations. The simplest soakaway is a rubble-filled pit, which is normally adequate to serve a dwelling or other small building. Where several buildings share a soakaway, the pit should be lined with precast perforated concrete rings and surrounded in free-draining material.

BRE Digest 365 provides capacity calculations based on percolation tests. The following empirical formula will prove adequate for most situations:

$$C = \frac{AR}{3}$$

where: C = capacity (m³)
A = area on plan to be drained (m²)
R = rainfall (m/h)

e.g. roof plan area 60m² and rainfall of 50mm/h (0·05m/h)

$$C = \frac{60 \times 0·05}{3} = 1·0\,m^3 \text{ (below invert of discharge pipe)}$$

FILLED SOAKAWAY	HOLLOW SOAKAWAY

Depth (D) and diameter (d) approximately the same

Ref. BRE Digest 365: Soakaways.

Drains ~ these can be defined as a means of conveying surface water or foul water below ground level from one building only. Within the curtilage of that building they are the responsibility of the building owner.

Sewers ~ these have the same functions as drains but collect the discharge from a number of drains and convey it to the final outfall. Shared and public sewers are maintained by the local water and sewerage authority.

Basic Principles ~ to provide a drainage system which is simple, efficient and economical by laying the drains to a gradient which will render them self-cleansing and will convey the effluent to a sewer without danger to health or giving nuisance. To provide a drainage system which will comply with the minimum requirements given in Part H of the Building Regulations.

Typical Basic Requirements ~

All junctions should be oblique and in direction of flow

There must be an access point at a junction unless each run can be cleared from another access point.

Separate System ~ the most common drainage system in use where the surface water discharge is conveyed in separate drains and sewers to that of foul water discharges and therefore receives no treatment before the final outfall.

Typical Example ~

inspection chamber No. I

back inlet gully for sink waste at ground floor level

if subsoil is suitable the rainwater pipes may be allowed to be connected direct to soakaways

svp

HOUSE

IC No. 2

GARAGE

rwp

rwp

rwp

yard gully

access rw shoe

IC No.3

foul drain →

← surface water drain

foul water sewer

road gully

surface water sewer

road gully

Combined System ~ this is the simplest and least expensive system to design and install but since all forms of discharge are conveyed in the same sewer the whole effluent must be treated unless a sea outfall is used to discharge the untreated effluent.

Typical Example ~

inspection chamber No. 1

back inlet gully for sink waste at ground floor level

if subsoil is suitable the rainwater pipes may be allowed to be connected direct to soakaways

svp

HOUSE

GARAGE

IC No. 2

foul drain

rwp

rwp

rwp

yard gully

access gully

trapped gully

IC No. 3

combined drain

surface water drain

road gully

combined water sewer

road gully

Ref. BS EN 752: Drain and sewer systems outside buildings.

883

Partially Separate System ~ a compromise system – there are two drains, one to convey only surface water and a combined drain to convey the total foul discharge and a proportion of the surface water.

Typical Example ~

inspection chamber No.1

back inlet gully for sink waste at ground floor level

if subsoil is suitable the rainwater pipes may be allowed to be connected direct to soakaways

svp

HOUSE

GARAGE

IC No. 2

foul drain

rwp

rwp

rwp

yard gully

access rw shoe

trapped access gully

IC No.3

combined drain →

← surface water drain

road gully

combined water sewer

surface water sewer

road gully

Public Sewer ~ a sewer or drain that is owned or adopted by the local council or water authority/sewerage undertaker. Sewer pipes are at least 300mm nominal diameter, even when serving small housing sites. Surplus capacity will accommodate further connections for any later development without the expense of replacing the sewer.

Location ~ usually under public roads at a minimum depth of 1.2m, but may be within the boundary of a property where there has been later development or where it is proposed to further develop an established site. Old sewers, many of which were installed over 100 years ago, may not have documentation confirming their course. Others that were recorded are not necessarily accurate.

Damage Potential ~ some of the original sewers serving major cities were created as tunnels of brick construction and many are still functional. Whether tunnels or rigid clay pipes for tributary sewers, they will inevitably have suffered some deterioration from the effects of traffic vibration, superimposed loading, impact from new building work, road improvements and installation of other underground services in the vicinity. Cracking, fracture and even collapse can result, interrupting the drainage facility and possibly causing settlement damage to adjacent structures. Sewer repair on this scale will probably mean demolition of buildings or part of a building to effect access, or at least temporary structural support and underpinning.

Planning ~ initial consultation with the local planning authority to locate sewers. The building control department in conjunction with their highways department and possibly the local water authority/sewerage undertaking will determine from their records whether proposed building work is likely to be affected by sewer proximity.

Requirements where a sewer exists close by:

- New building work no closer than 3.0m to a sewer.
- Sewer diversion to satisfy the 3.0m dimension.
- Pipes of 150mm nominal diameter or less may be accepted within 3.0m distance if they are at a significant depth or protected by a reinforced concrete cover. This is more appropriate for drains, and guidance is available in Building Regulations Approved Document H, Section 2.

Ref. Water Industry Act.

Simple Drainage — Inspection Chambers

Inspection Chambers ~ these provide a means of access to drainage systems where the depth to invert level does not exceed 1·000.

Manholes ~ these are also a means of access to the drains and sewers, and are so called if the depth to invert level exceeds 1·000.

These means of access should be positioned in accordance with the requirements of part H of the Building Regulations. In domestic work inspection chambers can be of brick, precast concrete or preformed in plastic for use with patent drainage systems. The size of an inspection chamber depends on the depth to invert level, drain diameter and number of branch drains to be accommodated within the chamber. Ref. BS EN 752: Drain and sewer systems outside buildings.

Typical Details ~

Plastic Inspection Chambers ~ the raising piece can be sawn horizontally with a carpenter's saw to suit depth requirements with the cover and frame fitted at surface level. Bedding may be a 100 mm prepared shingle base or 150 mm wet concrete to ensure a uniform support.

The unit may need weighting to retain it in place in areas of high water table, until backfilled with granular material. Under roads a peripheral concrete collar is applied to the top of the chamber in addition to the 150 mm thickness of concrete surrounding the inspection chamber.

Typical Example ~

cast iron cover and frame

raising piece - one raising piece gives a chamber with a depth of 650 mm, two raising pieces gives a chamber with a depth of 1000 mm

drainpipes

base unit with 5 × 100 mm inlets and 1 × 100 mm outlet

pipe coupling

unused inlets left blanked off

Means Of Access - provision is required for maintenance and inspection of drainage systems. This should occur at:

* the head (highest part) or close to it
* a change in horizontal direction
* a change in vertical direction (gradient)
* a change in pipe diameter
* a junction, unless the junction can be rodded through from an access point
* long straight runs (see table)

Maximum spacing of drain access points (m)

To:	Small access fitting*	Large access fitting*	Junction	Inspection chamber	Manhole
From:					
Drain head	12	12		22	45
Rodding eye	22	22	22	45	45
Small access fitting			12	22	22
Large access fitting			22	45	45
Inspection chamber	22	45	22	45	45
Manhole				45	90

* Small access fitting is 150 mm dia. or 150 mm × 100 mm. Large access fitting is 225 mm × 100 mm.

Rodding Eyes and Shallow Access Chambers - these may be used at the higher parts of drainage systems where the volume of excavation and cost of an inspection chamber or manhole would be unnecessary. SACs have the advantage of providing access in both directions. Covers to all drain openings should be secured to deter unauthorised access.

Ref. Building Regulations, Approved Document H1: Foul Water Drainage.

Excavations ~ drains are laid in trenches which are set out, excavated and supported in a similar manner to foundation trenches except for the base of the trench which is cut to the required gradient or fall.

Typical Detail ~

sight rail

sight line parallel to trench base

level sight rail

painted white

sight rail

trench base cut to required gradient

traveller or boning rod

sight rails should be placed at not more than 15m ᶜ/c with 3 No. minimum per trench length

support post

LONGITUDINAL SECTION

CROSS SECTION

Joints ~ these must be watertight under all working and movement conditions and this can be achieved by using rigid and flexible joints in conjuntion with the appropriate bedding.

Typical Joint Details ~

cm/s 1:2

clay pipe

upvc pipe

polypropylene coupling

clay pipe

flow

flow

45°

tarred gaskin

rubber 'O' rings

RIGID JOINT

FLEXIBLE JOINTS

Typical Bedding Details ~

topsoil

150

rigid jointed pipe

150

mass concrete

topsoil

normal backfill

selected material - lightly tamped

selected material - hand tamped

granular material - well tamped

pipe dia. + 300mm min.

300 min.

100

flexible jointed pipe

Watertightness ~ must be ensured to prevent water seepage and erosion of the subsoil. Also, in the interests of public health, foul water should not escape untreated. The Building Regulaions, Approved Document H1: Section 2 specifies either an air or water test to determine soundness of installation.

AIR TEST ~ equipment: Manometer and accessories (see page 912)
                       two drain stoppers, one with tube attachment

Application ~

drain trench left open until test completed (retest after backfilling)

rubber tube   manometer

IC

hand bellows

expanding plug

expanding plug with tube attachment

Test ~ 100 mm water gauge to fall no more than 25 mm in five mins. Or, 50 mm w.g. to fall no more than 12 mm in five mins.

WATER TEST ~ equipment: Drain stopper
                          Test bend
                          Extension pipe

Application ~

extension pipe filled with water

open trench to observe any leakage

lower IC

1.5 m head

test bend

drain filled with water

expanding plug

Test ~ 1·5 m head of water to stand for two hours and then topped up. Leakage over the next 30 minutes should be minimal, i.e.:

100 mm pipe — 0·05 litres per metre, which equates to a drop of 6·4 mm/m in the extension pipe, and

150 mm pipe — 0·08 litres per metre, which equates to a drop of 4·5 mm/m in the extension pipe.

Drainage Pipes ~ sizes for normal domestic foul water applications:

<20 dwellings   = 100 mm nominal inside diameter
20–150 dwellings = 150 mm nominal inside diameter

Exceptions: 75 mm diameter for waste or rainwater only (no WCs)
            150 mm diameter minimum for a public sewer

Other situations can be assessed by summating the Discharge Units from appliances and converting these to an appropriate diameter stack and drain, see BS EN 12056-2 (stack) and BS EN 752 (drain). Gradient will also affect pipe capacity and when combined with discharge calculations, provides the basis for complex hydraulic theories.

The simplest correlation of pipe size and fall is represented in Maguire's rule:

4" (100 mm) pipe, minimum gradient 1 in 40
6" (150 mm) pipe, minimum gradient 1 in 60
9" (225 mm) pipe, minimum gradient 1 in 90

The Building Regulations, approved Document H1 provides more scope and relates to foul water drains running at 0.75 proportional depth. See Diagram 9 and Table 6 in Section 2 of the Approved Document.

Other situations outside of design tables and empirical practice can be calculated.

E.g. A 150 mm diameter pipe flowing 0.5 proportional depth.

150 mm (0·15m)
area of water flowing
0·5 proportional depth
wetted perimeter

Applying the Chezy formula for gradient calculations:

$v = c\sqrt{m \times i}$

where: v = velocity of flow (min for self-cleansing = 0.8 m/s)

     c = Chezy coefficient (58)

     m = hydraulic mean depth or;

$$\frac{\text{area of water flowing}}{\text{wetted perimeter}} \text{ for } 0.5 \text{ p.d.} = \text{diam}/4$$

     i = inclination or gradient as a fraction 1/x

Selecting a velocity of 1 m/s as a margin of safety over the minimum:

$1 = 58\sqrt{0.15/4 \times i}$

$i = 0.0079$ where $i = 1/x$

So, $x = 1/0.0079 = 126$, i.e. a minimum gradient of 1 in 126

Water Supply ~ an adequate supply of cold water of drinking quality should be provided to every residential building and a drinking water tap installed within the building. The installation should be designed to prevent waste, undue consumption, misuse, contamination of general supply, be protected against corrosion and frost damage and be accessible for maintenance activities. The intake of a cold water supply to a building is owned jointly by the water authority and the consumer who therefore have joint maintenance responsibilities.

Typical Water Supply Arrangement ~

site boundary

property of water authority

property of consumer ~ see next page

expansion loop or goose neck to relieve stress on connection due to pipe settlement

cast iron surface box (BS 5834-2)

750mm minimum ground for frost protection

150mm internal diameter stop valve guard in clayware (BS 5834-1)

screw-down cock

communication pipe at right angles to water authority main

mass concrete base to suit subsoil type

stop valve

water main - fully charged with water under pressure

property of water authority – see previous page

site boundary

property of consumer

750 mm minimum unless insulated against freezing

external wall

service pipe or rising main

to storage cistern and drinking water tap

drain-down valve

stop valve

service or supply pipe minimum internal diameter 15 mm

ground level

750 mm minimum

end of pipe sealed with plastic or mastic

to stop valve and main – see previous page

service pipe must not pass through a drainage inspection chamber

pipes passing under foundations should be encased in mass concrete

last 600 mm of service pipe to be insulated – protective pipe to be sealed with plastic or mastic

75 mm diameter drain pipes as protection for service pipe under building

Service Pipe Materials:

unprotected iron – not suitable
unprotected steel – not suitable
galvanised steel – may be acceptable
                          to water authority
lead – prohibited
copper – BS EN 1057
plastic – blue polyethylene BS EN 12201-2
              uPVC BS EN ISO 1452-2

General ~ when planning or designing any water installation the basic physical laws must be considered:

1. Water is subject to the force of gravity and will find its own level.
2. To overcome friction within the conveying pipes water which is stored prior to distribution will require to be under pressure and this is normally achieved by storing the water at a level above the level of the outlets. The vertical distance between these levels is usually called the head.
3. Water becomes less dense as its temperature is raised, therefore warm water will always displace colder water whether in a closed or open circuit.

Direct Cold Water Systems ~ the cold water is supplied to the outlets at mains pressure; the only storage requirement is a small capacity cistern to feed the hot water storage tank. These systems are suitable for districts which have high level reservoirs with a good supply and pressure. The main advantage is that drinking water is available from all cold water outlets, disadvantages include lack of reserve in case of supply cut off, risk of back syphonage due to negative mains pressure and a risk of reduced pressure during peak demand periods.

Typical Direct Cold Water System ~

NB. All pipe sizes given are outside diameters for copper tube.

Indirect Systems ~ Cold water is supplied to all outlets from a cold water storage cistern except for the cold water supply to the sink(s) where the drinking water tap is connected directly to incoming supply from the main. This system requires more pipework than the direct system but it reduces the risk of back syphonage and provides a reserve of water should the mains supply fail or be cut off. The local water authority will stipulate the system to be used in their area.

Typical Indirect Cold Water System ~

cold water storage cistern minimum capacity 230 litres if used as a feed cistern and storage or 115 litres for storage only

dust proof cover

22mm dia. overflow and warning pipe

22mm dia. cold water distribution pipe

isolating valves

WC cistern

overflow pipe

140 litre hot water storage cylinder

22mm dia. cold feed pipe

WC   BASIN   BATH

15mm dia.   15mm dia.   22mm dia.

15mm dia. cold water distribution pipe

15mm dia. service pipe or rising main

22mm dia. overflow pipe

drinking water outlet

SINK

BASIN   WC

drain valve

stop valve

drain off tap or valve

to water main

NB. All pipe sizes given are outside diameters for copper tube.

Direct System ~ this is the simplest and least expensive system of hot water installation. The water is heated in the boiler and the hot water rises by convection to the hot water storage tank or cylinder to be replaced by the cooler water from the bottom of the storage vessel. Hot water drawn from storage is replaced with cold water from the cold water storage cistern. Direct systems are suitable for soft water areas and for installations which are not supplying a central heating circuit.

Typical Direct Hot Water System ~

cold water storage cistern minimum capacity 230 litres

overflow

isolating valve

15 mm dia. service pipe or rising main

140 litre hot water storage cylinder

22 mm dia. cold feed pipe

22 mm dia. open vent or expansion pipe to release air and relieve pressure

450 min.

15 mm dia.

BASIN

BATH

22 mm dia. hot water supply pipe

28 mm dia. primary flow pipe

28 mm dia. primary return pipe

possible pumped secondary return pipe

in hard water areas primary circuit pipes could be 35 mm diameter

SINK

15 mm dia.

boiler

BASIN

15 mm dia. hot water supply pipe

drain valve

safety valve

NB. All pipe sizes given are outside diameters for copper tube.

Indirect System ~ this is a more complex system than the direct system but it does overcome the problem of furring which can occur in direct hot water systems. This method is therefore suitable for hard water areas and in all systems where a central heating circuit is to be part of the hot water installation. Basically the pipe layouts of the two systems are similar but in the indirect system a separate small capacity feed cistern is required to charge and top up the primary circuit. In this system the hot water storage tank or cylinder is in fact a heat exchanger – see page 903.

Typical Indirect Hot Water System ~

cold water storage cistern

overflows

36 litre feed and expansion cistern

isolating valves

15 mm dia. service pipe or rising main →

22 mm dia. vent or expansion pipes

15 mm dia. service pipe or rising main

22 mm dia. cold feed pipe →

140 litre indirect hot water storage cylinder →

22 mm dia.

gravity or pumped central heating circuit

BASIN BATH
15 mm dia.

drain valve

BASIN

22 mm dia. hot water supply pipe →

possible pumped secondary return pipe

15 mm dia. primary cold feed pipe

28 mm dia. primary flow pipe

15 mm dia. hot water supply pipe

BASIN

28 mm dia. primary return pipe

SINK

boiler →

safety valve

central heating circuit →

drain valve →

NB. All pipe sizes given are outside diameters for copper tube.

Mains Fed Indirect System ~ now widely used as an alternative to conventional systems. It eliminates the need for cold water storage and saves considerably on installation time. This system is established in Europe and the USA, but only acceptable in the UK at the local water authority's discretion. It complements electric heating systems, where a boiler is not required. An expansion vessel replaces the standard vent and expansion pipe and may be integrated with the hot water storage cylinder. It contains a neoprene diaphragm to separate water from air, the air providing a 'cushion' for the expansion of hot water. Air loss can be replenished by foot pump as required.

NB. p.r.v. = pressure relief (safety) valve.

Temperatures ~
Boiler flow and return, approximately 80°C and 70°C respectively.
Stored hot water, 60°C to 65°C (not less than 60°C).
Distributed hot water, not less than 55°C.
Supply to outlets, approximately 50°C.

Hot Water System Temperatures

High temperatures are necessary to prevent the development of waterborne pathogens such as legionella pneumophila. Known generally as legionnaires' disease, this deadly bacterial infection was named after numerous American military veterans attending a reunion at a hotel in Philadelphia in 1976 died from exposure to the contaminated water system. There have subsequently been many more outbreaks throughout the world with similar consequences. Organisms are most prevalent in aquatic environments maintained at temperatures between 25°C and 45°C. This includes undisinfected water in air conditioning systems, fountains, humidifiers, jacuzzis and any other situation producing suspended moisture droplets.

Ref. Water Supply (Water Fittings) Regulations.

Hot Water Outlet Temperature ~ at 50°C scalding is unlikely for most people, but there is a risk where appliances are used by young children, the elderly and those with loss of sensory perception.

Safe hot water outlet temperatures ~

    Bath   43°C

    Shower 40°C

    Wash basin 40°C

    Bidet   37°C

    Sink   48°C

Application ~ new-build and existing buildings that are subject to change of use, or alterations that involve installation of new bathroom facilities.

Installation ~ thermostatic mixing valves (similar to shower mixers) are required as close as possible to the hot water outlet to control water temperature. These can be manually set to blend the hot and cold water supplies at a fixed discharge temperature. These valves contain an automated fast shutdown facility in the event of a supply failure.

Typical Installation ~

blended hot water and cold water outlet 43°C

cold water outlet

appliance, e.g. bath

TMV within appliance enclosure as close as possible to outlets

hot water supply (50°C+)

cold water supply (<20°C)

Refs.: Building Regulations, Approved Document G3: Hot water supply and systems.
BS EN 1111: Sanitary tapware, thermostatic mixing valves (PN 10). General technical specification.
BS EN 1287: Sanitary tapware, low pressure thermostatic mixing valves. General technical specification.

Flow Controls ~ these are valves inserted into a water installation to control the water flow along the pipes or to isolate a branch circuit or to control the draw-off of water from the system.

Typical Examples ~

GATE VALVE
low pressure cistern supply

STOP VALVE
high pressure mains supply

PORTSMOUTH FLOATVALVE

DIAPHRAGM FLOATVALVE

BIB TAP
horizontal inlet - used over sinks and for hose-pipe outlets

PILLAR TAP
vertical inlet - used in conjunction with fittings

Cisterns ~ these are fixed containers used for storing water at atmospheric pressure. The inflow of water is controlled by a floatvalve which is adjusted to shut off the water supply when it has reached the designed level within the cistern. The capacity of the cistern depends on the draw-off demand and whether the cistern feeds both hot and cold water systems. Domestic cold water cisterns should be placed at least 750mm away from an external wall or roof surface and in such a position that it can be inspected, cleaned and maintained. A minimum clear space of 350mm is required over the cistern for floatvalve maintenance. An overflow or warning pipe of not less than 22mm diameter must be fitted to fall away to discharge in a conspicuous position. All draw-off pipes must be fitted with a gate valve positioned as near to the cistern as possible.

Cisterns are available in a variety of sizes and materials such as galvanised mild steel (BS 417-2), moulded plastic (BS 4213) and reinforced plastic (BS EN 13121 and 13280). If the cistern and its associated pipework are to be housed in a cold area such as a roof they should be insulated against freezing.

Indirect Hot Water Cylinders ~ these cylinders are a form of heat exchanger where the primary circuit of hot water from the boiler flows through a coil or annulus within the storage vessel and transfers the heat to the water stored within. An alternative hot water cylinder for small installations is the single feed or 'Primatic' cylinder which is self-venting and relies on two airlocks to separate the primary water from the secondary water. This form of cylinder is connected to pipework in the same manner as for a direct system (see page 896) and therefore gives savings in both pipework and fittings. Indirect cylinders usually conform to the recommendations of BS 417-2 (galvanised mild steel) or BS 1566-1 (copper). Primatic or single-feed cylinders to BS 1566-2 (copper).

Typical Examples ~

INDIRECT CYLINDER   'PRIMATIC' CYLINDER

Primatic Cylinders:

1. Cylinder is filled in the normal way and the primary system is filled via the heat exchanger, as the initial filling continues airlocks are formed in the upper and lower chambers of the heat exchanger and in the vent pipe.
2. The two airlocks in the heat exchanger are permanently maintained and are self-recuperating in operation. These airlocks isolate the primary water from the secondary water almost as effectively as a mechanical barrier.
3. The expansion volume of total primary water at a flow temperature of 82°C is approximately 1/25 and is accommodated in the upper expansion chamber by displacing air into the lower chamber; upon contraction reverse occurs.

Typical Examples ~

coupling nut

bead formed with swaging tool

copper tube

copper tube

coupling fitting

friction locking ring

MANIPULATIVE COMPRESSION JOINT

coupling nut

tapered compression ring

copper tube

coupling fitting

copper tube

NON-MANIPULATIVE COMPRESSION JOINT

coupling fitting

solder retaining groove

copper tube

copper tube

fine solder

SOLDERED CAPILLARY JOINT

screwed socket fitting

PTFE (polytetrafluoroethylene) tape or hemp and paste in thread

steel pipe

steel pipe

SCREWED JOINT

PVC coupling

solvent weld

PVC pipe

PVC pipe

SOLVENT WELD JOINT

copper coupling fitting

copper liner or sleeve

tapered compression ring

polythene pipe

polythene pipe

COMPRESSION JOINT

Typical Examples ~

weir overflow

outlet for 38mm diameter trap and pipe

BELFAST PATTERN SINK

tap holes

flutes

overflow

180 or 200mm deep bowl

SINGLE DRAINER STAINLESS STEEL SINK

Fireclay Sinks (BS 1206) - these are white glazed sinks and are available in a wide range of sizes from 460 × 380 × 200 deep up to 1220 × 610 × 305 deep and can be obtained with an integral drainer. They should be fixed at a height between 850 and 920 mm and supported by legs, cantilever brackets or dwarf brick walls.

Metal Sinks (BS EN 13310) - these can be made of enamelled pressed steel or stainless steel with single or double drainers in sizes ranging from 1070 × 460 to 1600 × 530 supported on cantilever brackets or sink cupboards.

Ceramic Wash Basins (BS 1188)

splash back

NB. sink could be supported on cantilever brackets.

fixing height 790 mm

overflow

bowl - depth 165 mm

plug and chain

plan size 457 x 653 mm

32 mm waste to BS EN 274

back nut and washer

pedestal support

38 or 78 mm seal trap

waste pipe

cleaning eye

Typical Examples ~

abutment wall

1675 to 1830

wall tiling

pillar taps

bath body

bath panel with toe recess

20mm dia. supply pipes

plug and chain

420 to 730

flexible overflow pipe

38mm trap

adjustable feet

LONGITUDINAL SECTION

700 to 870

abutment wall

wall tiling

adjustable feet

bath body

bath panel

CROSS SECTION

Baths ~ these are available in wide range of materials, sizes, designs and colours usually conforming to the recommendations of

BS 1189 - cast iron
BS 1390 - sheet steel
BS EN 198 - acrylic
BS EN 232 - connecting dimensions

adjustable height spray head

13 or 20 mm dia. supply pipe(s)

flexible tube

thermostatically controlled mixing valve

shower curtain or cubicle

abutment wall

wall tiling

600 x 600 up to 900 x 900

shower tray

180

38 mm trap

Shower tray ~ BS EN 251 - connecting dimensions

Showers ~ these can be freestanding with a curtain or cubicle enclosure or they can be an attachment to a bath mixer tap. Shower trays are usually made of glazed fireclay or acrylic plastic and occupy less space than a bath. To be efficient showers need a minimum head of water above the spray of 1·000.

906

Typical Examples ~

Wash-down Water Closet - BS EN 33 ~ common type which relies on flush of water to remove contents of bowl. Horizontal outlet now standard.

partition wall

flush pipe from high or low level cistern

governed by cistern type

one piece connector

BS1254 plastic wc seat

soil pipe with rigid or flexible joint

flushing rim

405

50mm minimum water seal

ceramic wc pan

Siphonic Water Closets ~ efficient and quiet in operation but higher risk of blockage if misused - can be single or double trap format.

partition wall

close-coupled low level cistern

after-flush chamber to reseal trap

710

plastic wc seat and cover

long leg of siphon

flushing rim

50mm minimum water seal

380

ceramic wc pan

soil pipe

float valve ┌ overflow

float valve ┌ overflow

pull chain

cast iron bell

piston and flap in piston chamber

siphon bend

flush pipe

flush pipe

HIGH LEVEL BELL-TYPE CISTERN
(obsolete, but many remain in use)

LOW LEVEL PISTON CISTERN
(6/4 litre dual flush to BS 1125)

Single Stack System ~ method developed by the Building Research Establishment to eliminate the need for ventilating pipework to maintain the water seals in traps to sanitary fittings. The slope and distance of the branch connections must be kept within the design limitations given below. This system is only possible when the sanitary appliances are closely grouped around the discharge stack.

Typical Details ~

perforated dome to top of pipe above roof level

100 mm dia. soil and vent pipe

6·000 max.

32 mm dia. waste pipe with 75 mm min. seal trap

wc with 50 mm min. water seal

maximum length 1·700
slope determined by length-
slope 20 to 120 mm /m

BASIN

BATH

WATER CLOSET

WC

3·000 max.
slope 18 to 90 mm/m

branch slope 9 mm /m
with 50 mm radius at
junction

40 mm dia. waste
pipe with 75 mm min.
seal trap

50 mm dia.
parallel branch

3·000 max.
slope 18 to
90 mm /m

wc branch

svp

SINK

200

*

50 mm
radius

40 mm dia.
waste pipe
with 75 mm
min. seal trap

large radius
bends

minimum vertical
distance from lowest
connection to drain
invert 450 mm

* no connection should
be made within the
shaded portion

Ventilated Stack Systems ~ where the layout of sanitary appliances is such that they do not conform to the requirements for the single stack system shown on the previous page ventilating pipes will be required to maintain the water seals in the traps. Three methods are available to overcome the problem, namely a fully ventilated system, a ventilated stack system and a modified single stack system which can be applied over any number of storeys.

Typical Examples ~

VENTILATED STACK SYSTEM used where grouping of appliances makes individual venting unnecessary – seals retained by cross venting to a separate ventilating stack

FULLY VENTILATED SYSTEM used where there are a large number of appliances which are widely dispersed or grouped in ranges

MODIFIED SINGLE STACK SYSTEM used to ventilate only those branch pipes exceeding length required for a single stack system

Minimum diameter for branch ventilating pipes = 25mm.

Air Admittance Valve

Air Admittance Valve (AAV) ~ also known as a Durgo valve. A pressure-sensitive device fitted at the top of a discharge stack.

Location ~ above the highest possible flood level of the uppermost appliance connected to the stack, usually the wash basin. For accessible maintenance and testing, an AAV is positioned within the ventilated roof space. Unsightly stack ventilation above a roof is eliminated, with savings in pipe installation time and weathering the stack to the roof covering.

Application ~ up to four dwellings of one-, two- or three-storey height, the fifth to be conventionally vented at the highest part of the drain serving all five dwellings. AAVs are not suitable for older installations where an interceptor trap is used on the drain to each dwelling and/or where the stack discharges to a cesspool or septic tank. For higher rise buildings the use of AAVs is also limited. For instance, they should not be used if periodic surcharging occurs or where more than one building is connected to a common drain. AAV manufacturers should be consulted for specific situations.

Refs.: Building Regulations A.D. H1: Foul water drainage.
BS EN 12056-2: Gravity drainage systems inside buildings.
BS EN 12380: AAVs for drainage systems.

Lead slate ~ so-named as originally designed to fit with the courses of slate-covered roofs. Sheet lead is sufficiently adaptable to be cut and welded into purpose-made flashings to suit various tile profiles, roof slopes and stack diameters. Overall size is determined by the type and size of the tile or sheet roof covering. E.g. where used with plain tiling and a 100mm nominal diameter stack, a width of about 400mm wide and depth of about 450mm is sufficient, with a 100mm upstand at the back.

upstand silicone sealed to stack

code 4 or 5 (1.75 or 2.00mm) lead

lead placed under tiles

upstand welded to 'slate'

lead dressed over tiles

Fabricated vent pipe flashing ~ an off-the-shelf, one-fits-all ventilating stack pipe weathering, otherwise known as a flashing boot. Factory manufactured from flexible aluminium sheet with a moulded rubber sleeve located into a central hole through which the pipe is fitted. The rubber is sufficiently flexible to adapt to various roof pitches and to maintain a watertight seal to the stack.

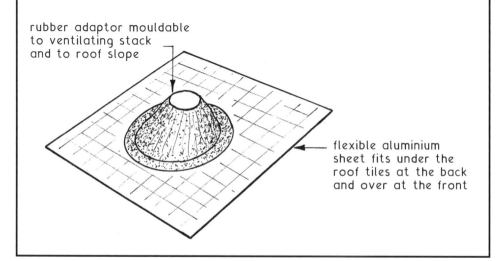

rubber adaptor mouldable to ventilating stack and to roof slope

flexible aluminium sheet fits under the roof tiles at the back and over at the front

Airtightness ~ must be ensured to satisfy public health legislation. The Building Regulations, Approved Document H1: Section 1, provides minimum standards for test procedures. An air or smoke test on the stack must produce a pressure at least equal to 38 mm water gauge for not less than three minutes.

Application ~

DISCHARGE STACK

MANOMETER

expanding plug

top of stack

all traps filled with water

expanding plug with tube attached

all traps to maintain at least 25 mm seal

control cock

rubber tube

hand bellows

access* plate

tube

protective metal or wooden box

W.G.

water level before displacement

glass tube

38 mm water gauge

manometer

to drain

* if access plate is not provided, top connection to first IC may be plugged and rubber tube inserted through wc pan seal.

NB. Smoke tests are rarely applied now as the equipment is quite bulky and unsuited for use with uPVC pipes. Smoke-producing pellets are ideal for leakage detection, but must not come into direct contact with plastic materials.

One Pipe System ~ the hot water is circulated around the system by means of a centrifugal pump, the flow pipe temperature being about 80°C and the return pipe temperature being about 60 to 70°C. The one pipe system is simple in concept and easy to install but has the main disadvantage that the hot water passing through each heat emitter flows onto the next heat emitter or radiator, therefore the average temperature of successive radiators is reduced unless the radiators are carefully balanced or the size of the radiators at the end of the circuit is increased to compensate for the temperature drop.

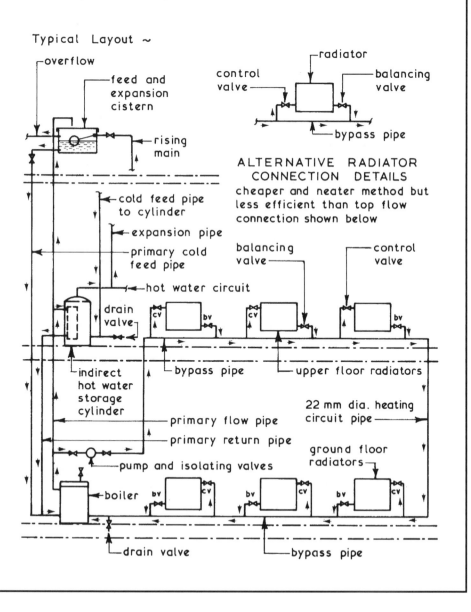

Typical Layout ~

ALTERNATIVE RADIATOR CONNECTION DETAILS
cheaper and neater method but less efficient than top flow connection shown below

Two Pipe System ~ this is a dearer but much more efficient system than the one pipe system shown on the previous page. It is easier to balance since each radiator or heat emitter receives hot water at approximately the same temperature because the hot water leaving the radiator is returned to the boiler via the return pipe without passing through another radiator.

Typical Layout ~

ALTERNATIVE RADIATOR
CONNECTION DETAILS
cheaper and neater method
but less efficient than top
flow connection shown below

Micro Bore System ~ this system uses 6 to 12mm diameter soft copper tubing with an individual flow and return pipe to each heat emitter or radiator from a 22mm diameter manifold. The flexible and unobstrusive pipework makes this system easy to install in awkward situations but it requires a more powerful pump than that used in the traditional small bore systems. The heat emitter or radiator valves can be as used for the one or two pipe small bore systems; alternatively a double entry valve can be used.

Typical Layout ~

holes through floor joist as required

manifold blanked off in centre to form two chambers

TYPICAL MANIFOLD DETAILS

Controls ~ the range of controls available to regulate the heat output and timing operations for a domestic hot water heating system is considerable, ranging from thermostatic radiator control valves to programmers and controllers.

Typical Example ~

Boiler - fitted with a thermostat to control the temperature of the hot water leaving the boiler.

Heat Emitters or Radiators - fitted with thermostatically controlled radiator valves to control flow of hot water to the radiators to keep room at desired temperature.

Programmer/Controller - this is basically a time switch which can usually be set for 24 hours at once-daily or twice-daily time periods and will generally give separate programme control for the hot water supply and central heating systems. The hot water cylinder and room thermostatic switches control the pump and motorised valve action.

for annotated details of hot water and heating circuits see pages 913 to 916

upper-floor radiators

control valve with thermostat

balancing valve

hot water circuit

indirect hot water storage cylinder fitted with thermostat

power supply to fused outlet

room thermostat fitted 1·200 to 1·500 above floor level

programmer / controller

ground floor radiators

pump

boiler

drain valve

motorised 3 port valve - hot water circuit only - heating circuit only - both circuits - no heat to either circuit boiler and pump turned off

Electrical Supply ~ in the UK electricity is generated mainly from gas, coal, nuclear and hydro-electricity power plants. Alternative energy generation such as wind and solar power is also viable and considered in Part 16 of the *Building Services Handbook*. Distribution is through regional companies. The electrical supply to a domestic installation is usually 230 volt single phase and is designed with the following safety objectives:

1. Proper circuit protection to earth to avoid shocks to occupant.
2. Prevention of current leakage.
3. Prevention of outbreak of fire.

Typical Electrical Supply Intake Details ~

external wall

consumer unit - sometimes housed in meter box

meter box containing sealing chamber, service fuse and neutral link, and meter - should be sited on an outside wall adjacent to an external door

10 mm^2 minimum equipotential bonding cable connected to metal services with bonding clamps

electricity supply company is responsible for cable up to and including the meter

ground level

300 to 450

mastic seal

to distribution main

incoming service cable

subcircuit wiring

mastic seal

100mm dia. protective duct

NB. For alternative arrangement of supply intake see following page.

Electrical Supply Intake ~ although the electrical supply intake can be terminated in a meter box situated within a dwelling, most supply companies prefer to use the external meter box to enable the meter to be read without the need to enter the premises.

Typical Electrical Supply Intake Details ~

subcircuit wiring

external wall

750 mm minimum clear space in front of meter box

consumer unit

cavity tray

external meter box containing sealing chamber, service fuse and neutral link, and meter - requires brick opening 400 mm wide × 600 mm high

10 mm^2 minimum equipotential bonding cable connected to metal services with bonding clamps

PVC or similar sheet as dpm behind meter box and cable

31

electricity supply company responsible for cable up to and including the meter

670 to 1070

ground level

300 to 450

to distribution main

incoming service cable

plastic protective duct with 350 mm minimum bending radius built into wall as work proceeds

NB. For alternative arrangement of supply intake see previous page.

Entry and Intake of Electrical Service ~ the local electricity supply company is responsible for providing electricity up to and including the meter, but the consumer is responsible for safety and protection of the company's equipment. The supplier will install the service cable up to the meter position where their termination equipment is installed. This equipment may be located internally or fixed externally on a wall, the latter being preferred since it gives easy access for reading the meter - see details on the previous page.

Meter Boxes - generally the supply company's meters and termination equipment are housed in a meter box. These are available in fibreglass and plastic, ranging in size from 450mm wide × 638mm high to 585m wide × 815mm high with an overall depth of 177mm.

Consumer Control Unit - this provides a uniform, compact and effective means of efficiently controlling and distributing electrical energy within a dwelling. The control unit contains a main double pole isolating switch controlling the line and neutral conductors, called bus bars. These connect to the fuses or miniature circuit breakers protecting the final subcircuits.

Typical Layout ~

1 - 45 amp shower circuit
2 & 3 - 32 amp ring circuits
4 - 32 amp cooker circuit
5 - 16 amp immersion heater
6 - 6 amp central heating
7 & 8 - 6 amp lighting circuits

Consumer's Power Supply Control Unit — this is conveniently abbreviated to consumer unit. As described on the previous page, it contains a supply isolator switch, live, neutral and earth bars, plus a range of individual circuit overload safety protection devices. By historical reference this unit is sometimes referred to as a fuse box, but modern variants are far more sophisticated. Overload protection is provided by miniature circuit breakers attached to the live or phase bar. Additional protection is provided by a split load residual current device (RCD) dedicated specifically to any circuits that could be used as a supply to equipment outdoors, e.g. power sockets on a ground floor ring final circuit.

RCD — a type of electromagnetic switch or solenoid which disconnects the electricity supply when a surge of current or earth fault occurs. See Part 11 of the *Building Services Handbook* for more details.

Typical Split Load Consumer Unit —

Note that with an overhead supply, the MAIN SWITCH is combined with a 100 mA RCD protecting all circuits.

Notes:

Circuits (1) to fixtures, i.e. lights, cooker, immersion heater and smoke alarms.

Circuits (2) to socket outlets that could supply portable equipment outdoors.

Electric Cables ~ these are made up of copper or aluminium wires called conductors surrounded by an insulating material such as PVC or rubber.

Typical Examples ~

rubber or PVC outer sheath
line - brown
cpc to earth - green and yellow
neutral - blue
rubber or PVC insulation
aluminium or copper conductors

SHEATHED CABLES

ductile seamless solid drawn copper sheath which acts as the circuit protective conductor (cpc) to earth

high conductivity copper conductors

densely packed pure magnesium oxide insulation

NB. magnesium oxide is hygroscopic; therefore ends of cable must be fitted with special sealing pots.

MINERAL INSULATED CABLE

Conduits ~ these are steel or plastic tubes which protect the cables. Steel conduits act as a cpc to earth whereas plastic conduits will require a separate cpc drawn in. Conduits enable a system to be rewired without damage or interference to the fabric of the building. The cables used within conduits are usually insulated only, whereas in non-rewirable systems the cables have a protective outer sheath.

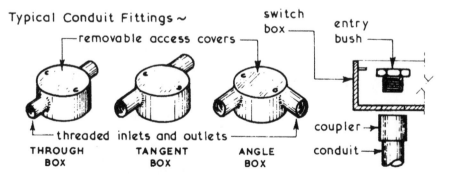

Typical Conduit Fittings ~

removable access covers

switch box

entry bush

threaded inlets and outlets

THROUGH BOX   TANGENT BOX   ANGLE BOX

coupler
conduit

Trunking - alternative to conduit and consists of a preformed cable carrier which is surface mounted and is fitted with a removable or 'snap-on' cover which can have the dual function of protection and trim or surface finish.

Wiring Systems ~ rewirable systems housed in horizontal conduits can be cast into the structural floor slab or sited within the depth of the floor screed. To ensure that such a system is rewirable, draw-in boxes must be incorporated at regular intervals and not more than two right angle boxes to be included between draw-in points. Vertical conduits can be surface mounted or housed in a chase cut into a wall provided the depth of the chase is not more than one-third of the wall thickness. A horizontal non-rewirable system can be housed within the depth of the timber joists to a suspended floor whereas vertical cables can be surface mounted or housed in a length of conduit as described for rewirable systems.

Typical Examples~

floor finish ─┐   ┌─ floor screed   ┌─ conduit and outlet box cast into floor slab

floor finish ─┐   ┌─ floor screed   ┌─ conduit fixed to floor slab before laying screed

└─ outlet box cast in or fixed in opening left in floor slab

┌─ external wall   floor finish ─┐   ┌─ notch not deeper than 0·125 D positioned not closer than 0·07 of span and not further away than 0·25 of span   ┌─ joist

D

conduit in upper edge of joist ─────   └─ ceiling finish   └─ holes for cables on neutral axis of joist - max. diameter 0·25 D - min. spacing 3 × dia. located within 0·25 & 0·4 of span

Cable Sizing ~ the size of a conductor wire can be calculated taking into account the maximum current the conductor will have to carry (which is limited by the heating effect caused by the resistance to the flow of electricity through the conductor) and the voltage drop which will occur when the current is carried. For domestic electrical installations the following minimum cable specifications are usually suitable:

Lighting Circuits -
neutral - as for line conductor

line conductor –
1·13 mm diameter
1 mm² cross section area

Lighting Circuits -
neutral - as for line conductor

line conductor –
1·38 mm diameter
1·5 mm² cross section area

Immersion Heater and Power Ring Circuits -
neutral - as for line conductor

line conductor –
1·78 mm diameter
2·5 mm² cross section area

32amp Cooker Circuit -
neutral - as for line conductor

line conductor –
7 No. 1·04 mm diameter wires
6 mm² total cross section area

All the above ratings are for the line and neutral conductors which will be supplemented with a circuit protective conductor as shown on page 921.

Electrical Accessories ~ for power circuits these include cooker control units and fused switch units for fixed appliances such as immersion heaters, water heaters and central heating controls.

Socket Outlets ~ these may be single or double outlets, switched or unswitched, surface or flush mounted and may be fitted with indicator lights. Recommended fixing heights are:

GENERAL — 150 min.

FOR THE ELDERLY — 825-900, 1200 if over work surface

door handle height 1040 with 300 min.

FOR THE DISABLED

Plugs ~
protective conductor to earth - green/ yellow cable
neutral - blue cable
cable grip
cap screw

BS 1363-1 plug
cartridge fuse —
up to 720 watt - 3 amp
up to 3000 watt - 13 amp
line - brown cable

Power Sockets ~ in new domestic electrical installations the ring final circuit is usually employed instead of the older obsolete radial system where socket outlets are on individual fused circuits with unfused round pin plugs. Ring circuits consist of a fuse or miniature circuit breaker protected subcircuit with a 32 amp rating for a line conductor, neutral conductor and a cpc to earth looped from socket outlet to socket outlet. Metal conduit systems do not require a cpc wire providing the conduit is electrically sound and earthed. The number of socket outlets on a ring final circuit is unlimited but a separate circuit must be provided for every 100 m² of floor area. To conserve wiring, spur outlets can be used as long as the total number of spur outlets does not exceed the total number of outlets connected to the ring and that there are not more than two outlets per spur.

Typical Ring Final Circuit Wiring Diagram ~

Lighting Circuits ~ these are usually wired by the loop-in method using a line, neutral and circuit protective conductor to earth cable with a 6 amp fuse or miniature circuit breaker protection. In calculating the rating of a lighting circuit an allowance of 100 watts per outlet should be used. More than one lighting circuit should be used for each installation so that in the event of a circuit failure some lighting will be in working order.

Typical Lighting Circuit Wiring Diagram ~

Electrical Accessories ~ for lighting circuits these consist mainly of switches and lamp holders, the latter can be wall mounted, ceiling mounted or pendant in format with one or more bulb or tube holders. Switches are usually rated at 5 amps and are available in a variety of types such as double or 2 gang, dimmer and pull or pendant switches. The latter must always be used in bathrooms.

Gas Supply — Basic Requirements

Gas Supply ~ potential consumers of mains gas may apply to their local utilities supplier for connection, e.g. British Gas and E.ON amongst several others. The cost is normally based on a fee per metre run. However, where the distance is considerable, the gas authority may absorb some of the cost if there is potential for more customers. The supply, appliances and installation must comply with the safety requirements made under the Gas Safety (Installation and Use) Regulations, 1998, and Part J of the Building Regulations.

Typical Gas Supply Arrangement ~

NB. For alternative gas supply arrangements see following page.

Gas Service Pipes:

1. Whenever possible the service pipe should enter the building on the side nearest to the main.
2. A service pipe must not pass under the foundations of a building.
3. No service pipe must be run within a cavity but it may pass through a cavity by the shortest route.
4. Service pipes passing through a wall or solid floor must be enclosed by a sleeve or duct which is end sealed with mastic.
5. No service pipe shall be housed in an unventilated void.
6. Suitable materials for service pipes are copper (BS EN 1057) and steel (BS EN 10255). Polyethylene (BS EN 1555) is normally used underground, but not above ground.

Typical Gas Supply Arrangement ~

LOW LEVEL ENTRY   HIGH LEVEL ENTRY

NB. For preferred method of entry see previous page.

Gas Fires

Gas Fires ~ for domestic use these generally have a low energy rating of less than 7 kW net input and must be installed in accordance with minimum requirements set out in Part J of the Building Regulations. Most gas fires connected to a flue are designed to provide radiant and convected heating whereas the room sealed balanced flue appliances are primarily convector heaters.

928

Gas Fire Flues ~ these can be defined as a passage for the discharge of the products of combustion to the outside air and can be formed by means of a chimney, special flue blocks or by using a flue pipe. In all cases the type and size of the flue as recommended in Approved Document J, BS EN 1806 and BS 5440 will meet the requirements of the Building Regulations.

Typical Single Gas Fire Flues ~

LINED CHIMNEY ON   FLUE PIPE ON   LINED CHIMNEY ON
EXTERNAL WALL   EXTERNAL WALL   INTERNAL WALL

Flue Size Requirements:

1. No dimension should be less than 63 mm.

2. Flue for a decorative appliance should have a minimum dimension measured across the axis of 175 mm.

3. Flues for gas fires – min. area = 12000 mm^2 if round, 16500 mm^2 if rectangular and having a minimum dimension of 90 mm.

4. Any other appliance should have a flue with a cross sectional area at least equal to the outlet size of the appliance.

Flue Blocks ~

90 × 183 (nom.) flue, minimum cross sectional area 16500 mm^2

Open Fireplaces ~ for domestic purposes these are a means of providing a heat source by consuming solid fuels with an output rating of under 50kW. Room heaters can be defined in a similar manner but these are an enclosed appliance as opposed to the open recessed fireplace.

Components ~ the complete construction required for a domestic open fireplace installation is composed of the hearth, fireplace recess, chimney, flue and terminal.

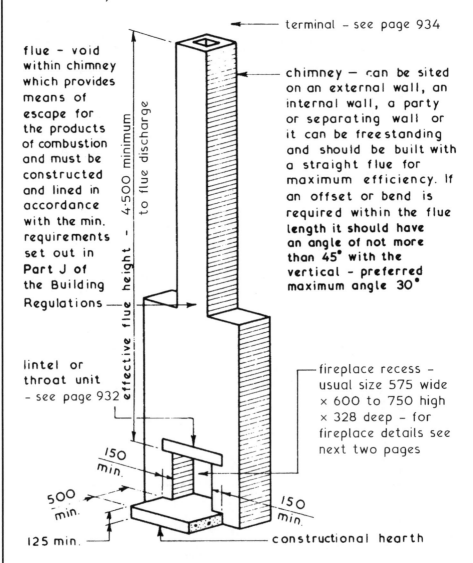

terminal – see page 934

flue – void within chimney which provides means of escape for the products of combustion and must be constructed and lined in accordance with the min. requirements set out in Part J of the Building Regulations

effective flue height – 4.500 minimum to flue discharge

chimney — can be sited on an external wall, an internal wall, a party or separating wall or it can be freestanding and should be built with a straight flue for maximum efficiency. If an offset or bend is required within the flue length it should have an angle of not more than 45° with the vertical – preferred maximum angle 30°

lintel or throat unit – see page 932

fireplace recess – usual size 575 wide × 600 to 750 high × 328 deep – for fireplace details see next two pages

150 min.

500 min.

150 min.

125 min.

constructional hearth

See also BS 5854: Code of practice for flues and flue structures in buildings.

Open Fireplace Recesses ~ these must have a constructional hearth and can be constructed of bricks or blocks of concrete or burnt clay or they can be of cast in-situ concrete. All fireplace recesses must have jambs on both sides of the opening and a backing wall of a minimum thickness in accordance with its position and such jambs and backing walls must extend to the full height of the fireplace recess.

Typical Examples ~

cavity wall with each leaf not less than 100mm thick

solid wall not less than 200mm thick

non-combustible cladding

solid external wall not less than 100mm thick

constructional hearth not less than 125mm thick

width of recess + 300mm min.

internal wall other than a separating wall minimum thickness 100mm

Traditional Fireplace Details ~

*200 mm min. if fireplace opening >500 mm × 550 mm

square lined flue of solid non-combustible blocks or bricks

rebated flue liners to BS EN 1457

external wall

175* min.

throat

flue gathering

100

fireplace surround to BS 1251 fixed to wall with screws through cast-in fixing lugs

BS 1251 fireback

25 mm wide non-combustible tape forming expansion joint

BS 1251 pcc lintel or hood unit — see detail below

1:2:4 lime: sand: broken brick filling

cm./sand screed

superimposed hearth

corrugated paper lining to form an expansion joint

ground floor

constructional hearth

dpc

ground level

rubble-filled void

half brick fender wall

mass concrete bed

compacted hardcore

NB. in solid floor construction the constructional hearth is an integral part of the oversite concrete bed.

225mm diameter hole for flue

1008mm long × 443mm wide × 65mm thick precast concrete raft lintel

precast concrete insert piece

760mm long × 335mm wide × 350mm high precast concrete throat gathering unit

TYPICAL PCC THROAT OR FIREPLACE HOOD UNIT

Open Fireplace Chimneys and Flues ~ the main functions of a chimney and flue are to:

1. Induce an adequate supply of air for the combustion of the fuel being used.
2. Remove the products of combustion.

In fulfilling the above functions a chimney will also encourage a flow of ventilating air promoting constant air changes within the room which will assist in the prevention of condensation.

Approved Document J recommends that all flues should be lined with approved materials so that the minimum size of the flue so formed will be 200mm diameter or a square section of equivalent area. Flues should also be terminated above the roof level as shown, with a significant increase where combustible roof coverings such as thatch or wood shingles are used.

Typical Examples ~

flue to terminate outside shaded area

flue to terminate at least 600mm above ridge and if within 600mm of ridge

rooflight

flue to terminate at least 1·000 above highest part of rooflight if within 2·300 of opening

2·300

ROOF WITH A PITCH OF OVER 10°

1·000 minimum

openable rooflight

over 2·300

within 2·300

1·000 minimum

ROOF WITH PITCH OF LESS THAN 10°

Typical Flue Liner and Chimney Pot Details ~

185 x 185 or
225mm dia.

300 to 900

20

clay rebated flue liner to BS EN 1457

clay chimney pot or flue terminal to BS EN 13502

150mm diameter

300 to 900

185 x 185 or
225mm dia.

Typical Outlet or Terminal Details ~

clay chimney pot or flue terminal

oversailing or offset brick courses forming capping

frost and thaw resistant or severe exposure quality bricks jointed in cement mortar 1:3

1:3 cement mortar weathering or flaunching

quarter brick offsets

high bond strength damp-proof course

clay flue liners jointed in cm.mt.

projecting clay flue liner as terminal

55mm overhang

moderate exposure quality clay bricks jointed in cement : lime : sand mortar

1:½:4 - 4½

precast concrete weathered coping

damp-proof course

clay flue liners jointed in cm.mt.

Refs.: BS EN 13502: Chimneys. Requirements and test methods for clay/ceramic flue terminals.

BS EN 1457: Chimneys. Clay/ceramic flue liners. Requirements and test methods.

BS EN 771-1: Specification for (clay) masonry units.

Typical Chimney and Roof Junction Details ~

flue liners

chimney stack

back gutter

stepped flashing

25mm turned into brick joint, wedged and pointed

70° angle

to be dressed over soakers

STEPPED FLASHING

25mm wide turn in

COVER FLASHING

roof coverings

25mm wide turn in

to be dressed over tiles

APRON FLASHING

soakers

apron flashing

to be dressed over fillet

BACK GUTTER

NB. All flashings, aprons and gutter linings to be formed out of 1.75mm lead or other durable material(s). Soakers out of 1.25mm lead.

flue liners

cover flashing

back gutter

chimney stack

damp-proof course

damp-proof tray

apron flashing

roof coverings

trimmed rafter

trimmed rafter

tilting fillet

25mm thick gutter boards

trimmer forming opening through roof

gutter blocks

trimmer min. 40mm from masonry

Ref. BS EN 1443: Chimneys. General Requirements.

Open Fireplaces and Flues

Chimney Construction –

chimney pot or flue terminal

flaunching cement-sand (1:3)

$\frac{1}{4}$ brick oversailing course

dpc

brick masonry
1.75mm lead
saddle flashing

dpc (optional)

dpc tray

Tray

Soaker

75mm

100mm

gauge + lap + 25mm

600mm min.
Max. 4·5 times least lateral dimension

highest point of intersection with the roof surface

Typical Chimney Outlet –

Clay bricks – Frost and thaw, severe exposure-resistant quality. Min. density 1500kg/m³.

Calcium silicate bricks – Min. compressive strength 20.5 N/mm² (27.5 N/mm² for cappings).

Precast concrete masonry units – Min. compressive strength 15 N/mm².

Mortar – A relatively strong mix of cement and sand 1:3. Cement to be specified as sulphate resisting because of the presence of soluble sulphates in the flue gas condensation.

Chimney pot – The pot should be firmly bedded in at least three courses of brickwork to prevent it from being dislodged in high winds.

Flashings and dpcs – Essential to prevent water which has permeated the chimney from penetrating the building. The minimum specification is 1.75mm lead, 1.25mm for soakers. This should be coated both sides with a solvent-based bituminous paint to prevent the risk of corrosion when in contact with cement. The lower dpc may be in the form of a tray with edges turned up 25mm, except where it coincides with bedded flashings such as the front apron upper level. Here weep holes in the perpends will encourage water to drain. The inside of the tray is taken through a flue lining joint and turned up 25mm.

Combustion Air ~ it is a Building Regulation requirement that in the case of open fireplaces provision must be made for the introduction of combustion air in sufficient quantity to ensure the efficient operation of the open fire. Traditionally such air is taken from the volume of the room in which the open fire is situated. This can create air movements resulting in draughts. An alternative method is to construct an ash pit below the hearth-level fret and introduce the air necessary for combustion via the ash by means of a duct.

Typical Established Details ~

*min. square or rectangular dimension, otherwise min. 200 mm dia. or equivalent area

external wall

throat

flue gathering

BS 1251 4-piece fireback

1:2:4 lime: sand broken brick filling

corrugated paper lining to form an expansion joint

dpc

flue

175* min.

100

rebated flue liners to BS EN 1457

internal wall finish

fireplace surround to BS 1251

heat-resisting tape

BS 1251 pcc lintel or hood unit - see page 932

open hearth fret

deepening bar

air flow control

superimposed hearth

NB. external ash box removal is permitted if opening is sealed with a non-combustible cover.

ash pit constructed of non-combustible material of not less than 50mm thickness

air flow valve

ash box - holds 3 to 4 days' ashes

125mm thick mass concrete floor

hardcore bed

100mm dia. smoke tight & non-combustible duct connected to the external air

Ref. BS 1251: Specification for open-fireplace components.

Lightweight Pumice Chimney Blocks ~ these are suitable as a flue system for solid fuels, gas and oil. The highly insulative properties provide low condensation risk, easy installation as a supplement to existing or ongoing construction and suitability for use with timber frame and thatched dwellings, where fire safety is of paramount importance. Also, the natural resistance of pumice to acid and sulphurous smoke corrosion requires no further treatment or special lining. A range of manufacturer's accessories allow for internal use with lintel support over an open fire or stove, or as an external structure supported on its own foundation. Whether internal or external, the units are not bonded in, but supported on purpose-made ties at a maximum of 2-metre intervals.

flue (mm)	plan size (mm)
150 dia.	390 × 390
200 dia.	440 × 440
230 dia.	470 × 470
260 square	500 × 500
260 × 150 oblong	500 × 390

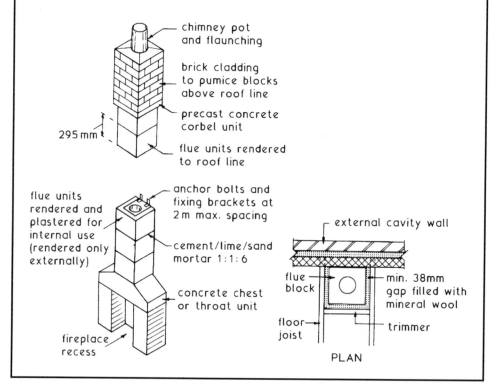

chimney pot and flaunching

brick cladding to pumice blocks above roof line

precast concrete corbel unit

flue units rendered to roof line

295 mm

flue units rendered and plastered for internal use (rendered only externally)

anchor bolts and fixing brackets at 2 m max. spacing

cement/lime/sand mortar 1:1:6

concrete chest or throat unit

fireplace recess

external cavity wall

flue block

min. 38mm gap filled with mineral wool

floor joist

trimmer

PLAN

Fire Protection of Services Openings ~ penetration of compartment walls and floors (zones of restricted fire spread, e.g. flats in one building) by service pipes and conduits is very difficult to avoid. An exception is where purpose-built service ducts can be accommodated. The Building Regulations, Approved Document B3: Sections 7 [Vol. 1] and 10 [Vol. 2] determines that where a pipe passes through a compartment interface, it must be provided with a proprietary seal. Seals are collars of intumescent material which expands rapidly when subjected to heat, to form a carbonaceous charring. The expansion is sufficient to compress warm plastic and successfully close a pipe void for up to four hours.

In some circumstances fire stopping around the pipe will be acceptable, provided the gap around the pipe and hole through the structure are filled with non-combustible material. Various materials are acceptable, including reinforced mineral fibre, cement and plasters, asbestos rope and intumescent mastics.

Pipes of low heat resistance, such as PVC, lead, aluminium alloys and fibre cement, may have a protective sleeve of non-combustible material extending at least 1m either side of the structure.

Telephone Installations ~ unlike other services such as water, gas and electricity, telephones cannot be connected to a common mains supply. Each telephone requires a pair of wires connecting it to the telephone exchange. The external supply service and connection to the lead-in socket is carried out by telecommunication engineers. Internal extensions can be installed by the site electrician.

Typical Supply Arrangements ~

extension telephone if required

underground supply cables must be installed when the building is constructed - they are hidden and therefore have little or no effect on the surrounding environment

lead-in socket

ground level

external wall

350 min.

underground supply cable in 50mm plastic duct

19mm internal diameter duct sealed at both ends

UNDERGROUND SUPPLY CABLE

overhead supply cable

lead-in socket

wall hook at or near eaves

19mm internal diameter duct sealed at both ends

extension telephone if required

socket

overhead supply cables are smaller and cheaper than underground supply cables — convenient but obtrusive

extension telephone if required

external wall

OVERHEAD SUPPLY CABLE

Electronic Installations – in addition to standard electrical and telecommunication supplies into buildings, there is a growing demand for cable TV, security cabling and broadband access to the Internet. Previous construction practice has not foreseen the need to accommodate these services from distribution networks into buildings, and retrospective installation through underground ducting is both costly and disruptive to the structure and surrounding area, particularly when repeated for each different service. Ideally there should be a common facility integral with new construction to permit simple installation of these communication services at any time. A typical installation will provide connection from a common external terminal chamber via underground ducting to a terminal distribution box within the building. Internal distribution is through service voids within the structure or attached trunking.

electronic communication ducts

alternative overhead access

trunking riser

lateral distribution duct

external terminal box

terminal chamber min. 300 × 300mm

450 mm min.

internal terminal and distribution box

lateral distribution terminal

incoming network services

incoming supply duct, 50mm min.

cable/pipe void

18mm plywood cover strip fixed to 50 × 50mm edging

screed

in-situ or pcc floor

Typical lateral distribution duct
(see also Part 15 – *Building Services Handbook*).

Notes

942

INDEX

Index

Index

curtain walling 708, 710–13; thermal performance 585
curved valley tiles 505, 512
cut-and-cover 339
cut-and-fill 319
cut tile cladding 487

dado rails 857
damp-proof courses (dpc) 408–14; bridging of 411–12; cavity walls 403; chemical 411–12; chimney stacks 936; insulating 414; openings 428, 429; *see also* cavity trays
damp-proof membranes (dpm) 408–14, 759
data management 81
datum 158
DC (Draft for public Comment) 73
DCLG (Department for Communities and Local Government) 34, 62, 71, 72, 76
DD (Draft for Development) 73
dead shoring 186, 187
death-watch beetle 544
decking, timber flat roofs 527
decorative suspended ceilings 848
decorative tiles 486
deep basement construction 309
deep strip foundations 251, 262
defects *see* construction defects; paint defects
demolition 195–9; rubble shutes 220; sustainable 199
demountable partitions 744–5
dense monolithic concrete 313
densities of materials 39, 551–2; concrete materials 328; stonework 371
dentil coursing 398
Department for Business Enterprise and Regulatory Reform (BERR) 76
Department for Communities and Local Government (DCLG) 34, 62, 71, 72, 76
deposit of plans 64, 68
DER (dwelling emission rate) 33, 567
designated mix (concrete) 330
designed mix (concrete) 330
dewatering 349
diagonal braced structure 660
diaphragm valve 901
diaphragm walls 406; deep basements 309–12; ground water control 356–7
diesel hammers 284
differential movement 735
dimensional changes in timber 148
dimensional coordination 53
dimensional grids 53
direct cold water systems 894
direct hot water systems 896
disability access *see* access for the disabled

discharge stacks, airtightness testing 912
discoloration of concrete 725
displacement piles 274–6, 354
display windows 585
ditches 876
documentation 20; coding systems 78–80, 82–3
dog leg stairs 811, 812
dog toothing 398
dome rooflights 698
dome structures 9
door frames: external 465; internal 836
door heads 465; thermal performance 580, 581
door jambs 465; thermal performance 580, 581
doors: draughtproofing 583; frames 465, 836; industrial 471–4; ironmongery 466; performance requirements 462; swings 41; thermal performance 560, 562, 585; types 463–4; *see also* external doors; internal doors
doorsets 837
door threshold 431
dormer windows 537–9
double acting hammers 284
double action floor spring 843
double conical membrane structures 693
double curvature shells 9
double glazing 435, 450; CO_2 reduction 568; sound insulation 450; thermal performance 561
double hung sliding sash 433, 439, 441
double lap tiles 505–6
double lap tiling 507–8, 512–13
double layer grid 682
double skin roof coverings 668
double swing doors 843
Douglas fir 858
dowelled lattice steel beams 632
downpipes 879
dpc *see* damp-proof courses (dpc)
dpm *see* damp-proof membranes (dpm)
Draft for Development (DD) 73
Draft for public Comment (DC) 73
draglines 212
drainage 868–91; access points 888; combined system 883, 884; foul water 868, 881; separate systems 882, 884; stack discharge systems 908–11; subsoil water 869–70; surface water 871–80; surveys 30
drainage pipes 891; storage on site 131
drained cavity system 317
drained joints 717–18

948

Index

Index

Index

Index